AN ANTI-FEDERALIST CONSTITUTION

AMERICAN POLITICAL THOUGHT

Wilson Carey McWilliams and Lance Banning
Founding Editors

AN ANTI-FEDERALIST CONSTITUTION

The Development of Dissent in the Ratification Debates

Michael J. Faber

University Press of Kansas

Published by the University Press of Kansas (Lawrence, Kansas 66045),
which was organized by the Kansas Board of Regents and is operated
and funded by Emporia State University, Fort Hays State University,
Kansas State University, Pittsburg State University, the University of
Kansas, and Wichita State University.

Library of Congress Cataloging-in-Publication Data
Names: Faber, Michael J., 1980– author.
Title: An anti-federalist constitution : the development of dissent in the
ratification debates / Michael J. Faber.
Description: Lawrence, Kansas : University Press of Kansas, 2019. |
Includes bibliographical references and index. | Series: American
political thought
Identifiers: LCCN 2018058852
ISBN 978-0-7006-2777-6 (hardback)
ISBN 978-0-7006-2778-3 (ebook)
Subjects: LCSH: Constitutional history—United States—18th century.
| United States—Politics and government—1783–1789. | BISAC:
POLITICAL SCIENCE / Constitutions. | LAW / Constitutional. |
POLITICAL SCIENCE / Political Process / Political Advocacy.
Classification: LCC KF4541 .F23 2019 | DDC 342.7302/9—dc23
LC record available at https://lccn.loc.gov/2018058852.

British Library Cataloguing-in-Publication Data is available.

Printed in the United States of America

10 9 8 7 6 5 4 3 2 1

The paper used in this publication is recycled and contains 30 percent
postconsumer waste. It is acid free and meets the minimum
requirements of the American National Standard for Permanence
of Paper for Printed Library Materials Z39.48-1992.

THIS BOOK IS DEDICATED TO MY WIFE, ANNE.

She does not share my love of early American history, but apparently she loves me enough to put up with it.

CONTENTS

PREFACE

The Constitution of the United States, even after more than two centuries, remains a mysterious document. We as a nation are engaged in a constant dialogue about what it means, and what was intended by those who wrote it. It has become commonplace to consult *The Federalist* for answers to these questions, but those essays represent one perspective (or perhaps three) on what the Constitution means. A fuller appreciation of the original meaning of the document, or rather the various meanings attached to clauses within it, requires a more complete analysis of the debates over ratification. It did not fall to the Federalists exclusively to decide what the Constitution did and did not allow the government to do, either. The opposition had a great deal to say about it, though their voices have generally been obscured over time, as they have been dismissed as mere obstructionists, or simply on the wrong side of history.

In order to understand the Constitution, it is essential to understand both the document and its origins. Much work has been done explaining the Constitution itself, and its writers and early defenders have been amply chronicled in both scholarly and popular literature. Its opponents, both at its creation and since, have not been so carefully examined. In this book I aim to tell a story about the ideas and people opposed to the ratification of the Constitution. Certainly this story has been told before, in different ways and by different people, but the examination has generally focused on people or events. Here I endeavor to tell a story about ideas, the development of the case for opposing ratification of the Constitution, which rapidly morphed into the case for substantial amendments to the document.

The Anti-Federalist opposition can best be understood as three related but distinct strands of political thought, at least at the outset. The first, which I have labeled Rights Anti-Federalism, was focused on the individual and the potential for governmental tyranny; this strand owed its existence rather directly to the ideals of the American Revolution, and it was centered in the south and, to a lesser extent, the west, places where suspicions of a far-off central government ran the highest. These Anti-Federalists wanted limits placed on the powers in the Constitution in order to protect the individual, generally in the form of a bill of rights. The second strand I have called Power Anti-Federalism. These individuals were less concerned about the people as individuals, and more concerned with the states as the defenders of the people. The ideas of Power Anti-Federalists were varied, but they all involved a more careful balancing of powers between the state and national governments; these were the truest federalists in the debate. Their strength was centered in the northeast, where the state governments were most entrenched in their power and most jealous of a national government that might strip it away. The third strand of Anti-Federalist thought, primarily focused in western and rural America, was Democratic Anti-Federalism. These radicals wanted to see a more positive and direct role for the people in any government, and were suspicious of anything that undermined popular sovereignty; to them the Constitution smacked of aristocracy. Some of the Democratic Anti-Federalists championed the states as the only governments able to truly reflect the voice of the people, while others wanted to see a simpler, more democratic structure in the national government.

These three strands did not remain separate, though; the first two often looked alike in their prescriptions for the Constitution, though they approached from different reasons, and they found much common ground during the course of the debate. As for the third group, some shifted to an emphasis on rights and representation, democratic themes that nonetheless fit with the more dominant strands, while the true radicals were marginalized in their opposition. Thus by the end of the ratification debates, there was a distinct and fairly consistent opposition position that favored a stronger federal system, a simpler and more transparent government, and an effective and extensive bill of rights. In short, there was a clear and coherent Anti-Federalist position, though we cannot see it unless we understand the development of that position over time from its three distinct forebears.

This book is essentially divided into three parts, vastly unequal in length. In the first two chapters I discuss the ideas of the Anti-Federalists in broad terms, and focus in particular on scholarly and popular perceptions of these losers of the ratification debates. I explain the three strands of Anti-Federalism in greater detail, and analyze three writers who should be familiar to any student of the ratification debates, each of which exemplifies one of the strands. This frames my argument in clearer terms, and clears the ground for a fresh look at the Anti-Federalist position. The next fifteen chapters tell the story of the resistance to the Constitution, focusing on ideas but following and explaining events and strategies. These chapters are not intended to be a thorough history of ratification; Pauline Maier's *Ratification* tells that story better than I can. Instead, I am telling one side of the story, in careful depth, with an eye on the development of ideas during the course of the debate. The final two chapters, which make up the third part of the book, return to broader arguments. The eighteenth chapter introduces a counterfactual Anti-Federalist Constitution that effectively sums up the opposition position in a convenient (albeit controversial) document. This version of the original Constitution has been substantially altered to account for the many and varied objections raised against it when it was being debated. It is heavily footnoted to justify the numerous changes that have been made, though of course it is only one version that might be made of the substantial body of Anti-Federalist objections to the Constitution. The nineteenth chapter discusses how such a Constitution may have worked in practice, and the legacy of the Anti-Federalists in early American history. When the dust from the ratification debates settled, the Anti-Federalists had done little to shape either the Constitution or American politics.

A few stylistic notes are appropriate here. First, the use of the term "Anti-Federalist," as well as its form, is somewhat controversial. Pauline Maier, in her impressive history of the ratification process, declines to use the term or any variation thereof except in direct quotations or where the opponents of the Constitution actually adopted the label. Though her reasoning is admirable, her decision takes away a degree of unity of purpose from the opposition. Although the Anti-Federalists did not like the name they had been assigned by the usurpers of their proper name, some name for the group is necessary to recognize the coherence and cohesion they developed during the course of the debates. Their preferred term, if they could not have "Federalist," was "Republican," but given that this term has been associated over time with more than one major political party, this would create too much confusion, so I have stayed with Anti-Federalist. This is more often rendered "Antifederalist," the version used by the *Documentary History of the Ratification of the Constitution*, but I have followed Herbert Storing and Saul Cornell in hyphenating the term. Antifederalist implies that the opponents of the Constitution opposed federalism, while Anti-Federalist makes clear that what they opposed were the Federalists. The fairest approach would be to dub the proponents of the Constitution "Nationalists" and its opponents "Federalists," but to strip the winning side of its chosen label would be exceedingly confusing. Thus I have settled on "Anti-Federalists" for those who fought against the proposed Constitution of 1787.

The process of ratification involved a lot of conventions, which can lead to some confusion when discussing what was said in those meetings. The most important, of course, was the Convention held in Philadelphia in the summer of 1787, at which the delegates wrote the Constitution. This was followed by seventeen conventions in fourteen states over the next four

years. To reduce confusion, and to highlight the importance of the Philadelphia Convention (sometimes referred to as the Constitutional or Federal
Convention), I capitalize all references to this Convention, using lowercase
for the state ratifying conventions except where the term appears next to the
name of the state. In quotations, I retain the capitalization in the original.

All quotations have been rendered here exactly as they appear in the
source from which I have cited them, with two exceptions: I have filled in
incomplete words and supplied missing words to prevent confusion (though
often I have just copied such from the source, if it was itself a reprint of the
original), and I have corrected obvious typographical errors. Capitalization,
punctuation, and spelling have been retained, though previous editors may
have changed these from the original manuscripts or newspapers. I have
generally cited from the most widely available source for the material, unless another source is more reliable and accurate. For essays, I have generally cited from *The Complete Anti-Federalist* (CAF) if the source in question
was included, and the *Documentary History of the Ratification of the Constitution* (DHRC) otherwise. Some do not appear in either of these sources
and have been cited from elsewhere. For the ratifying conventions I have
cited from the DHRC when available, and in other states I drew from Jonathan Elliot's *Debates in the Several State Conventions* (*Debates*), from other
published or unpublished notes of the debates, or directly from newspapers.

The quantity of published primary documents from the ratification debates is large and growing. The DHRC is the best source for those states for
which it has been published. For the states not yet covered, I have relied on
other published collections of documents, as well as several other sources. In
many cases I have relied on electronic versions of the original newspapers.
For these, the electronic archive at *America's Historical Newspapers* has
been irreplaceable. I also used the online collections of the Newspaper Digi-
talization Project of the North Carolina State Archives. The Maryland State
Archives offered invaluable notes from the state's ratifying convention; I
would like to thank in particular Maria Day, the Director of the Special Collections, who provided access to the online archive materials and helped me
find what I needed. Much of the early research for this book was conducted
during a two-year postdoctoral fellowship with the Program in American
Values and Institutions at Duke University; during that time I received the
generous support of the Jack Miller Center and the Thomas W. Smith Foundation. Michael Gillespie, Michael Munger, Russell Hanson, Darla Martin,
Aaron Keck, Danilo Petranovich, and Robi Ragan all either read drafts of
sections of the manuscript or helped me to develop the ideas. I presented
my Anti-Federalist Constitution in several places, and received a variety of

positive feedback that helped me to refine the project. Several anonymous reviewers provided helpful and detailed comments on the earlier drafts of this book, and their suggestions helped me to sharpen and refine my argument. It should go without saying, though, that I am solely responsible for any remaining errors in my argument.

This book has been in the works for so long that I have gone through several editors at the University Press of Kansas. I want to thank my current editor, David Congdon, for his assistance in the final stages of the publication process, and for seeing this through to print. Chuck Myers was very helpful in the middle stages as I revised earlier versions of the manuscript. The existence of this book, though, owes a great deal to my original editor. Fred Woodward began working with me very early in the project, back when the book was merely an idea in my head, and without his early guidance on how to structure the book, as well as some later comments on its development, it would never have been completed. Finally, my wife, Anne, has been very patient with me for the years it took for this project to mature from an idea into a rather long book; her support is important in all that I do, and it was indispensable in this venture.

1

The Anti-Federalists and the Development of Dissent

The Federal Constitution is now the subject of conversation from Newhampshire to Georgia. In some places there are persons who appear to be *raving mad*, both for and against the plan. It is but reasonable to observe, that if ever there was occasion for a people to deliberate with calmness, on as important a measure, as ever did, or ever will come under their consideration, now is the time.
—*Worcester Magazine*, November 8, 1787

THE DEBATE OVER ratification of the US Constitution was no calm deliberation; it was a knock-down, drag-out fight, "a cacophonous argument in which appeals to principle and common sense and close analyses of specific clauses accompanied wild predictions of the good and evil effects that ratification would bring."[1] It was perhaps the most contentious and divisive war of words in the history of the United States. And yet this virulent verbal combat receives little attention in popular perceptions of history. Most Americans recognize that the Revolution was long and bloody, but too many seem to think the Constitution was accepted without much dissent when handed to the people by George Washington. After all, how could anyone question something written by America's greatest patriots, the "Miracle at Philadelphia," so ably defended by Alexander Hamilton, James Madison, and John Jay in *The Federalist* (the only essays from the ratification debates at all widely read), and so central to American political culture as our chief sacred text? The dissenters must have been foolish men indeed, or enemies to the union.

Except, of course, that they were not. The Constitution was not written by our greatest patriots, it was written by *some* of them. Samuel Adams was not involved. Nor was Patrick Henry. George Clinton, though often forgotten in popular portrayals of the Revolution, was certainly among the most important colonial leaders. All three of these men could probably have secured a seat at the Convention in Philadelphia (and Henry was actually

offered one), but were not involved in the writing. Three of the individuals
who did serve in the Convention—Elbridge Gerry, a signer of the Declaration of Independence, George Mason, the author of the Virginia Declaration
of Rights, and Edmund Randolph, the governor of Virginia—refused to sign
the finished document. Several more left the Convention in protest of the
document that it was forming. All of these men opposed the Constitution
initially, and harbored doubts throughout the debate. So did lesser-known
leaders in the various states who had played important, though often forgotten, roles in the nation's independence. Rawlins Lowndes, Willie Jones,
Thomas Person, Richard Henry Lee, William Paca, George Bryan, Abraham
Clark, James Warren, John Lamb, and Nathaniel Peabody, among many
others, were individuals of distinction and accomplishment during the Revolution who fought against ratification. To assume that the Constitution
was the consensual work of the greatest patriots in the United States is to
dishonor these people who genuinely believed that the document was flawed
and dangerous.

And yet it is this ultrapatriotic and deifying view of the founding that
dominated studies of American history for the first century of the Constitution's history, and still captures the public imagination. Even as most of
the names even of the Federalists, those who favored ratification, have been
largely forgotten, their legacy, embodied in America's constitutional development, has been embraced in our politics and our collective views of history. The Anti-Federalists, those who opposed the Constitution in 1787 and
1788, have been given almost no credit. They are sometimes mentioned as
the driving force behind the Bill of Rights, but that is not quite accurate;
those first ten amendments were largely the result of efforts by Federalist
James Madison, and represented little more than a token effort to quell
opposition without yielding any substantive points or changes to the opposition.[2] Even scholars who discuss the Anti-Federalists often examine their
legacy in terms of the importance of opposition or conservatism.[3]

This book is an effort to rehabilitate the Anti-Federalists. It is an effort to
restore their thought to the respect it deserves, and to identify and explain
the Anti-Federalist ideology that emerged from the ratification debates.
Though the opposition began scattered and disjointed, during the course
of the debates it coalesced on a fairly consistent theory of government, at
least as consistent as that on which the Federalist position, as well as the
Constitution, was based. This ideology, which was more than a resistance
or conservatism, is deeply ingrained in American political thought, though
we are rarely aware of it, and even more rarely aware of who deserves the
credit for its influence.

THE DEVELOPMENT OF DISSENT

When the Philadelphia Convention released the result of its summer of deliberation in September 1787, the eventual opponents of the document were unprepared. Few of them had seats in the convention, and they had no document or even general governmental plan behind which they could rally. This presented two substantial problems for them: one of organization, and one of credibility. The organizational problem could be overcome with time, which was part of the reason that the Federalists were in a hurry to call state ratifying conventions. The credibility problem, though, was more serious. "By the neglect of the *objectors*, to offer *their system*," explained "An American," writing in the *Independent Chronicle* in Boston, "it is presumed, that either they have none, or it is such as they know will not be acceptable to the people,—or their design is to prevent and form of Federal Government.—Until the *objectors* explain themselves, by offering their own plan, to dispute with them is wasting time, and throwing arguments to the wind."[4] The Anti-Federalists, facing a concrete and comprehensive proposal for a new and stronger government, and unwilling to accept the change as proposed, had three basic options. They could find a way to reject it outright and return to the status quo, the Articles of Confederation; they could try to change the proposed system, either prior to ratification in the conventions or afterward through the mechanism outlined in Article V for amending the Constitution; or they could do what the American suggested and offer a concrete alternative. This latter option would have taken some time, as it probably would have required a second constitutional convention, something against which the Federalists fought vehemently.

Some Anti-Federalists did in fact offer alternatives. "Agrippa," for example, published the text of an article he wanted to see added to the Articles of Confederation to fix the main problems of that document, while "A Georgian" suggested alternative text for Article III of the Constitution to fix the dangers he foresaw in the proposed judiciary. Neither of these was really a new system; the former was a mere patch on a political system that even most Anti-Federalists acknowledged needed much more, and the latter suggested that only amendments were needed rather than an alternative constitution. In a sense, such efforts actually undermined the opposition. There were at least two examples of public efforts to offer a comprehensive alternative. In early 1788 the Political Club of Danville, Kentucky, a debating society consisting mostly of local lawyers and judges, formally debated the Constitution and began work on an amended document. They made it as far as the beginning of Article III, and then apparently gave up the effort. The changes the Club made included adding a bill of rights to the beginning of the document, cutting Senate terms in half to three years, removing the clauses granting Congress power over a national capital and guaranteeing the slave trade, and eliminating the Vice President.[5] The resulting partially amended Constitution was never published or distributed. Later that year a similar group in Pennsylvania styling itself "The Society of Western Gentlemen" published in the *Virginia Independent Chronicle* a fully revised version of the proposed Constitution with substantive changes. These changes reflect some of the prevailing Anti-Federalist sentiment, including adding a bill of rights, reducing the length of Senate terms, and removing the clauses concerning slavery; it also included some quirks peculiar to this particular group, such as an elimination of the ten-miles-square limitation on the size of the federal capital.[6] The publication elicited no response, but the enterprise undertaken by both of these groups is an interesting one. Although the Anti-Federalists did not collectively propose an alternative, the mere question of whether they could have, whether there was enough agreement for the opposition to speak with a unified voice, is a worthwhile one to explore. If the Anti-Federalists were united in a political vision (or at least could have been), if they were at least as philosophically coherent as the Federalists, if an Anti-Federalist constitution was even possible, we then have an alternative understanding of government by which we can better understand not only the founding era and subsequent American history, but the Constitution itself and its meaning. Unfortunately, this has never been adequately done, in large part because of how the Anti-Federalists were treated by the victorious Federalists, and even more so because of the nature of their treatment at the hands of historians.

THE SINISTER FOUNDERS

Beginning in 1787, the Federalists tried to portray their opponents as sinister and unpatriotic. "Monitor," for example, identified four types of Anti-Federalists: enemies of America, criminals, the greedy, and the ambitious.[7] This was of course a caricature in the context of a nasty prolonged political campaign, but the caricature lingered. The Federalists continued to abuse their opponents even after the Constitution and Bill of Rights were both ratified, and most of the Anti-Federalists saw at least setbacks in their future political careers as a result of their stance. When all of the dust was settled, historians continued the attack for the Federalists. It has been remarked that history is written by the winners, and that is especially true here. In reading many of these historical works, one gets the impression that the scholar feels threatened by the critique of the Constitution, and thus refuses to lend it any credence. Throughout the first century of American history, historians routinely portrayed the opposition as at best wrongheaded, if not downright selfish, or even evil. John Fiske was slightly more charitable, painting the opposition as mere obstacles to progress, and celebrating the label of Anti-Federalist: "It was fit that their name should have this merely negative significance, for their policy at this time was purely a policy of negation and obstruction."[8] Few scholars could engage in a thorough examination of Anti-Federalist thought, because the opposition writings were not widely available. Paul Leicester Ford was the first scholar to make a serious effort to compile and publish a broad range of materials from the ratification debates other than *The Federalist*, which was always widely read by scholars. Ford published his *Pamphlets on the Constitution* in 1888, and his *Essays on the Constitution* four years later. Both volumes contained Federalist as well as Anti-Federalist material, but Ford himself, like virtually all historians of his time, believed the Federalists right and their opponents fundamentally wrong.[9]

E. Wilder Spaulding, a biographer of George Clinton, offers a eulogy of the opposition worth repeating here, complete with its bitterness toward the general historical views of the American founding:

> Whether the United States were to become a nation or remain a federation, was the great issue of the 1780's. The controversy was to be settled by the triumph of the nationalists, but it must not be forgotten that there was at the time a large group of able and patriotic men who sincerely believed that a consolidated national government was not only unnecessary but was extremely dangerous to civil liberty. This group included such distinguished names as Patrick Henry, Richard Henry Lee, George Mason, James Monroe, Luther Martin, and Elbridge Gerry. Samuel Adams and Governors Hancock and Randolph also hesitated before crossing the Rubicon of consolidation. Historians may doubt the wisdom of such men, but they cannot doubt their sincerity and patriotism. They have, as a matter of fact, credited the nationalistic Federalists with a virtual monopoly of political wisdom and studiously overlooked the patriotism of the Antifederalist opposition. The latter our Federalist historians have not attempted to understand.[10]

By the time Spaulding published his biography, though, the treatment of the Anti-Federalists had already started to change. It would be another two decades before the ideas of the Anti-Federalists were seriously engaged by scholars, but the Progressive historians had already begun to revive interest in the opponents of the Constitution.

Charles Beard, who revolutionized scholarly perspectives on the American founding, saw in the Framers of the Constitution just the sort of aristocratic cabal that the Anti-Federalists were railing against all along.[11] This made the Federalists the sinister ones, and their opponents the defenders of liberty and justice. And Beard did indeed find the proponents of the Constitution to be underhanded and manipulative, willing to do whatever it took to get the document ratified. Since the leading Federalists were generally the best-educated and most politically experienced men in the states, they were able to set everything up to favor their cause. The Anti-Federalists were "beaten, outgeneralled, and outclassed in all the arts of political management."[12] The stakes were high for both sides, but the opposition did not have the resources to compete. The Federalists included the wealthy, holders of vast property and especially securities, while the Anti-Federalists were poor farmers and debtors. The battle over ratification was nothing less than class warfare, and as usual the wealthy had insuperable advantages.

This notion of class warfare was taken up by a number of other scholars in analyzing the ratification debates. Philip Crowl is typical, and perhaps exemplary, of this approach; "although these aspects of the fight were often obscured by the wordy legalism of pamphleteers and orators on both sides of the case," he wrote in the late 1940s, "thoughtful contemporaries did not shy away from recognition of the fact that here was a bona-fide class struggle."[13] While it is true that many Federalists decried the debtors and ignorant farmers that opposed ratification, while the more radical Anti-Federalists railed against the would-be aristocracy trying to cram the Constitution down the throats of the poor, such writers can hardly be included among the most "thoughtful" of Americans. The problem is that there is very little evidence to actually back up Beard's sweeping claims about the ratification debates as a class struggle. The evidence he did offer was carefully (and rather stridently) refuted by Robert Brown,[14] but the conclusion drawn by another critic, Forrest McDonald, is in many ways more valuable. "Economic interpretation renders intelligible many of the forces at work in the making of the Constitution," he concedes. "It is far from adequate to explain it in its entirety, however; this would require that countless noneconomic factors be taken into consideration."[15] Any single-factor explanation of the writing and ratification of the Constitution is going to be oversimplified and misleading. Beard's supporters shifted their emphasis in response to the criticism. Staughton Lynd, in his careful analysis of the politics of Dutchess County, New York, finds patterns that clash with many of the assumptions of Beard's critics, but he cannot conclude that Beard's assumption of self-interest by the wealthy was fundamentally correct in the county. "What was at stake was more than the realization of speculative windfalls in government securities, more even than a form of government," he explains. "It was the answer to the question, on which group in society would the political center of gravity come to rest."[16] This is in a certain sense more Beardian than Beard's own analysis. Still, the idea of class struggle is appealing, because it was so common in the debates themselves. Beard evidently believed that his conclusions were simply obvious: "No one can pore for weeks over the letters, newspapers, and pamphlets of the years 1787–1789 without coming to the conclusion that there was a deep-seated conflict between a popular party based on paper money and agrarian interests, and a conservative party centred in the towns and resting on financial, mercantile, and personal property interests generally."[17] Having personally pored for several years over this material (and thanks to more recent published collections of documents, as well as substantial electronic sources, undoubtedly examining more material than that to which Beard had access), I can say with confidence that this conclusion is not at all obvious. The participants in the great debate certainly discussed class, and the divisions were in part, though inconsistently, along economic lines, but the heart of the debate was a discussion about government, not about paper money or public debt.

As for the implication that the Federalists were smarter and better equipped to use underhanded means to win the fight, Beard's characterization does not ring true. In New Hampshire, the opposition was clearly overmatched, and the more skilled Federalists turned a minority into a majority against the parliamentary inadequacy of Joshua Atherton's leadership. The state's best opposition leader, Nathaniel Peabody, was not even elected as a delegate to the convention. In Massachusetts, it was targeted persuasion rather than parliamentary skill that won the day for the Federalists, though the proponents of ratification were better equipped for that close fight. Elsewhere, though, the issue was not one of skill or distinction. In three states no opposition showed up at all. In Pennsylvania and Connecticut, the Federalists won by brute force and taking the initiative to push a quick decision; in the former it was the minority that resorted to parliamentary tactics, including a legislative walkout to prevent a quorum and stop a convention (to which the Federalists responded by resorting to the help of a mob) and an effort to lodge an official protest in the convention minutes in order to score points in the public relations fight. In Maryland, the small minority managed to work a fivefold majority into admitting, more or less officially and on the record, that the Constitution was flawed and required amendment. In South Carolina, the opposition was up to the fight, but was defeated by long-standing malapportionment in favor of the coastal areas; the minority represented about half of the people of the state, perhaps more, yet had only a third of the convention seats.[18] In the North Carolina Convention, it was Anti-Federalist leader Willie Jones who ran the convention, skillfully putting the Federalists in the position of supplicants to whom he magnanimously granted the right to debate. In Rhode Island, the controlling country party held all the power and used every conceivable means to first prevent and then delay ratification; here it was the Federalists who were overmatched. In Virginia the fight was fairly even, and in New York it was the moderates, ultimately led by Melancton Smith, who outmaneuvered everyone else.

"MEN OF LITTLE FAITH" AND MEN OF LITTLE DISTINCTION

Beard's identification of the Anti-Federalists as the overmatched majority against the cabal of entrenched wealth and power represented a paradigm shift in the treatment of the Anti-Federalists, but it did not really do justice to the individuals involved or their arguments. They became simple-minded dupes incapable of resisting tyranny. Thus many of the patriots of the Revolution, men like George Clinton, Patrick Henry, George Mason, Elbridge Gerry, George Bryan, Samuel Chase, William Paca, and others, were reduced to the unenviable position of being on the wrong side of history, with no defenders. To be sure, several of the prominent Anti-Federalists did achieve success under the Constitution, but their historical reputations were still tarnished, even with Beard's rehabilitation.

Cecilia Kenyon explicitly critiqued Beard through a careful analysis of the Anti-Federalist position. Hers was the first serious attempt to analyze and evaluate the political thought of the opponents of ratification. They were not democrats, as Beard would have it, but republicans; they did not favor majoritarian principles and were not inclined to make the Constitution conform to such. In fact, as far as political principles, they were not far from the Federalists.

Advocates and opponents of ratification may have belonged to different economic classes and been motivated by different economic interests. But they shared a large body of political ideas and attitudes, together with a common heritage of political institutions. . . . The fundamental issue over which Federalists and Anti-Federalists split was the question whether republican government could be extended to embrace a nation, or whether it must be limited to the comparatively small political and geographical units which the separate American states then constituted. The Anti-Federalists took the latter view; and in a sense they were the conservatives of 1787, and their opponents the radicals.[19]

The Anti-Federalists were more democratic in their views on state and local government, because here their political philosophy permitted such an approach. But when it came to a national government stretched across thirteen states, with the potential to stretch across a continent, they balked. These "men of little faith" could not grasp the bold national vision presented by the Federalists, and hence could not share in that vision.

Here too we have Anti-Federalists relegated to a second-class position; it was not that they were scheming or misguided, but that the Federalists were more prescient and visionary. The concept was expanded by Robert Rutland, whose *Ordeal of the Constitution* tells the story of the ratification campaign through the eyes of the Anti-Federalists. He too concludes that the Anti-Federalists were leaderless, could not agree on a clear course of action, and most of all "never had an unlimited view of the Union." The most prominent Anti-Federalists "believed the strength of the republic rested in the powers possessed by each state as it struggled to meet its own problems," and that the people would not be well served by "a remote, impersonal government," a "distant Colossus where the emphasis would be on ceremonies and forms rather than a better life for the people."[20] The problem was not that their ideas were wrong, but that Federalist ideas were necessary to establish unity and national progress. The national government needed energy to be effective, and independent states were an obstacle.

Closely aligned with this vision is the notion advanced by Stanley Elkins and Eric McKitrick that the Federalists were younger and more dynamic, and the Anti-Federalists older and more set in their ways.[21] Certainly much of the Federalist leadership was comparatively young; Madison and Hamilton added a certain enthusiasm with their youth, and a number of rising stars like Fisher Ames of Massachusetts emerged out of the ratification debates. Leading the opposition, Patrick Henry, Richard Henry Lee, George Clinton, Elbridge Gerry, and Samuel Adams look rather old by contrast, and more than one significant Anti-Federalist emerged out of retirement to participate in the ratifying conventions. Then again Washington, Franklin, and Roger Sherman defended the Constitution, and plenty of young men, including future Presidents James Monroe and John Quincy Adams, the latter still a student, opposed the document. Jackson Turner Main dismissed this argument summarily, looking at the ages of delegates to the ratifying conventions: "All told, the Federalists were about two years younger than their antagonists. It is hard to see how this could have made any difference."[22]

Main is much more charitable to the Anti-Federalists in his analysis. He finds much to admire in the opposition, and at times he seems disappointed that they were not more successful. They certainly should have been: "Since the Federalists were a minority in at least six and probably seven states, they ought surely to have been defeated. Yet they came from behind to win."[23] This was due in part to superior organization by the Federalists, but it had a lot to do with the support of the two sides as well. Main, like Kenyon, was in large part responding to Beard; he contended that "[t]here was an embryonic class structure but it was potential only"; there were three classes, not two, and the "middling" class was not distinctly aligned with either side in the debates, and was not even all that clearly delineated from the other two. Main concedes that the division over the Constitution did break down largely upon class lines; wealthy men, and creditors in particular, generally supported ratification; debtors and poor farmers opposed it. This does not, however, fully explain the differences. The clearest indicator of the inadequacy of the Beardian class explanation is the general unanimity on the Constitution in urban areas. Towns throughout the country generally supported the Constitution; all classes within them tended to agree on this issue. Insofar as the division was economic, it was along the lines of the local economy. Towns were more engaged in commerce, and had more to gain from a more efficient commercial intercourse and better protection for property rights. Rural areas were more suspicious of central authority, but those farmers near the towns, who grew crops for trade rather than subsistence, were generally Federalists. The real split was not rich and poor, but mercantile and agricultural: "the struggle over the ratification of the Constitution was primarily a contest between the commercial and the non-commercial elements in the population. This is the most significant fact, to which all else is elaboration, amplification, or exception."[24] The distinguished and wealthy in the seaport and river towns supported the Constitution, while

the undistinguished and largely anonymous subsistence farmers and fron-
tiersmen were opposed.

In his analysis, Main offered a more careful and in-depth analysis than
the Anti-Federalists had received up until that point. He identifies two broad
strands of opposition thought: "those who emphasized the desirability of a
weak central government, and those who encouraged democratic control.
The democrats at this time accepted the doctrine of weak government, but
the advocates of weak government did not always believe in democracy."[25]
Thus there was a certain tension in their ideas, to be understood rather than
resolved. This in itself suggests a more complex picture of Anti-Federalism;
both Kenyon and Beard saw them as too homogenous, and thus missed
much of the argument. The democrats among the opposition were not an
insignificant group, though Main believed that it was "less than half" of the
Anti-Federalists, and these individuals were among "the more obscure and
the less well-to-do."[26] He is undoubtedly correct on these points, though
the proportion of Anti-Federalists who were truly democratic was probably
far, far less than half. Even so, Main is not incredibly concerned with the
distinctions; he still finds the distinction between the Anti-Federalists and
the Federalists as far more significant and interesting.

With the Beardian notion of the ratification struggle as class conflict severely weakened, if not quite refuted, other efforts have been made to understand the Federalist/Anti-Federalist divide. Gordon Wood is unequivocal
in drawing the line, in the process breathing new life into Beard's general
argument: the "quarrel" over the Constitution, Wood writes, "was fundamentally one between aristocracy and democracy." This was a social rather
than economic distinction, and in defending the claim Wood makes an effort to dissociate the more aristocratic Anti-Federalist leaders, like George
Mason and Richard Henry Lee, from the rank and file. This social divide
was also reflected in the self-selection of national versus state politicians,
and to a lesser extent in wealth, geography, and professional class. The Anti-
Federalists "were true champions of the most extreme kind of democratic
and egalitarian politics expressed in the Revolutionary era."[27] A social aristocracy is different from an economic one, but not by enough to prevent
Beard's defenders from embracing this position.

Wood revisited this interpretation two decades after essentially bolster-
ing Beard's analysis: "To rest something as monumental as the formation
of the Federal Constitution on such crude, narrow, and selfish motives was
Beard's mistake, and it should not be repeated."[28] Here he paints the Anti-
Federalists essentially as pluralists, advocating a clash of interests in policy-
making, with the caveat that only representatives that looked like the people

could really defend their interests. He still sees that as a divide between aristocracy and democracy, but the Anti-Federalists were pluralist democrats rather than simple majoritarian ones.

James Hutson disagrees on this issue. To put this in terms of simple aristocracy and democracy is as misleading as the distinctions of wealth and social class. The distinction was in the mindset of the individuals, but neither side entirely repudiated either natural aristocracy or popular rule. Instead, Hutson argues, we can understand the debate by drawing on the English concepts of court and country parties. The Anti-Federalists, in their concerns about corruption and general distrust of government, reflected a country position in opposition to the courtly nationalism of their antagonists.[29] Thomas Wren, in building on this concept through an analysis of the Virginia Ratifying Convention, finds that the fit is less than ideal, because both sides express elements of a country ideology; the conflict is essentially between country and court-country.[30]

ANTI-FEDERALIST THOUGHT REHABILITATED

This initial reconsideration of the Anti-Federalists, though it was generally not flattering in its portrayals, prompted more research and analysis, and defenders of these "forgotten founders" began to appear. Among the first, Steven Boyd insists that they did not lose the fight because they were outsmarted or outmaneuvered: "Rather than being unorganized, inept, and ineffectual, the Antifederalists proved an able, national political party. They had a concrete program and leaders to promote it; they campaigned effectively for seats in the state conventions; following ratification they persisted in their opposition in petition campaigns to repeal ratification and in state legislative elections; and through the conclusion of the first federal elections found support for their program and ideology."[31] Where Main and Rutland focused on the state ratifying conventions, Boyd was more concerned with the campaigns, the efforts to elect individuals to the conventions, the state legislatures, and the first Congress.[32] He does not deny that the Federalists outmaneuvered their opponents in the conventions, but this does not mean that the latter were unorganized, unsophisticated country rubes. The true legacy of the Anti-Federalists was to raise crucial objections and help establish a better and safer government. Their willingness to even debate the Constitution was a tacit acceptance of its legitimacy, should it be ratified. This is why the Anti-Federalist writings focus so extensively on the

Constitution, and why that document is the proper starting point for an alternative form of government.

What these later scholars do agree on is that the Anti-Federalists had something important to say. Their resistance was not merely self-interested or reactionary opposition to change. Still, the emphasis was consistently on what the Anti-Federalists were against: aristocracy, wealth and privilege, open commerce, hard money, consolidation, weakening of states, and so on. It was not until Herbert Storing's impressive (but incomplete) *Complete Anti-Federalist* that a serious attempt was made to explain what the Anti-Federalists were *for*. This latter phrase became the title of Storing's short monograph that served as an introduction to the collection of opposition writings. In it, he laments the treatment of the Anti-Federalists by historians, even recent ones, contending that they deserve to be counted among our nation's Founders.

> Champions of a negative and losing cause, they have found only a cramped place in the shadow of the great constitutional accomplishment of 1787. They have often been presented as narrow-minded local politicians, unwilling to face the utter inadequacy of the Articles of Confederation or incapable of seeing beyond the boundaries of their own states or localities. They have been described as men without principle, willing to use any argument to drag down the Constitution, yet willing, many of them, when the Constitution was adopted, to change their colors and become enthusiastic Federalists.[33]

All of these views ignore the substantial political ideas of the opposition. Storing aims to offer a "sustained, comprehensive attempt to examine the thought, the principles, the argument of the Anti-Federalists, as they were understood by the Anti-Federalists themselves and by other men of that time." He does not contend that the Anti-Federalists were ideologically monolithic, but he does observe that they were no more divided than the Federalists, many of whom actually had significant misgivings about the document they supported. Storing portrays the opposition as the defenders of the principles of the Revolution. "In the main, they saw in the Framers' easy thrusting aside of old forms and principles threats to four cherished values: to law, to political stability, to the principles of the Declaration of Independence, and to federalism." They had a vision of a virtuous republic, but the evidence at the time suggested that virtue was already crumbling, to be replaced as a driving social force by interest. The acceptance of this fact was why the opposition was so easily reconciled to the Constitution after the fact, and why few of them outright rejected the Constitution as a whole, instead of suggesting how it might best be amended. To try to uphold virtue in what was becoming an interest-based commercial republic was an impossible task, and this, rather than organizational or socioeconomic factors, was why the opposition could not win. "The Anti-Federalists lost the debate over the Constitution not merely because they were less clever arguers or less skillful politicians but because they had the weaker argument. They were, as Publius said, trying to reconcile contradictions."[34] Nonetheless, there was a unity and elegance to the political philosophy of the Anti-Federalists, and their argument was reasonable and sensible, if a bit too abstract and idealistic. It is an ideology worth understanding, because the opposition argument has reverberated through the ensuing centuries.[35]

Storing's emphasis on the unity and coherence of the Anti-Federalists, however qualified, became the dominant interpretation of the opposition. W. B. Allen and Gordon Lloyd are fairly typical on this point, in the introduction to their collection of Anti-Federalist writings:

> [R]especting the main points, the Antifederalists were not only in agreement but their position was coherent. They believed that republican liberty was best preserved in small units where the people had an active and continuous part to play in government. They thought that the Articles [of Confederation] secured this concept of republicanism. They argued that the Constitution placed republicanism in danger because it undermined the prop of small size. As a consequence, they argued that the system of representation under the new plan must be altered to secure what was formerly secured by small size. They believed that under the new plan the representatives would become independent from rather than dependent on the people. Lastly, they warned that unless restrictions were placed on the powers of the Congress, the Executive, and the Judiciary, the potentiality for the abuse of power would become a reality. These various approaches culminated in their insistence on a Bill of Rights which they saw satisfying the same function that small territory, representative dependency, and strict construction would perform for republicanism.[36]

This final point cannot be justified, though, at least not in reference to the Bill of Rights that was ultimately added to the Constitution. "Indeed, in one sense, the success of the Bill of Rights reflects the failure of the Anti-Federalists," writes Storing. "The whole emphasis on reservations of rights of individuals implied a fundamental acceptance of the 'consolidated' character of the new government. A truly federal government needs no bill of rights."[37] Some Anti-Federalists felt that an adequate bill of rights would make the Constitution safe, but most wanted to see structural changes in order to adequately protect individual rights, more properly check and balance the powers of government, or restore additional power to the people. Such structural changes would have better protected the rights of the people than mere parchment guarantees.

TYPES OF ANTI-FEDERALIST THOUGHT

The rehabilitation of the Anti-Federalists has led to a more careful examination of their writings. Few scholars, though, have carefully examined the ideas of the Anti-Federalists, or tried to examine the opposition position as a coherent political ideology.[38] Michael Lienesch stands out in this regard, establishing them as firm republicans, almost to a fault. His defense of Anti-Federalism against the frequent attacks of historians is based solidly on the idea that the opponents of the Constitution stood *for* something.[39] Efforts to understand and explain the diversity of the Anti-Federalists have been more common. The key element, though, is the surprising amount of consistency. Saul Cornell identifies nine issues raised repeatedly by the Anti-Federalists: consolidation, aristocracy, representation, separation of powers, judicial tyranny, the absence of a bill of rights, taxes, standing army, and the executive. Almost all writings against the Constitution explored several of these themes, and very few failed to include any.[40] These themes provide some hope for intellectual reconciliation of the different ideas. "Had Anti-Federalists ever met in convention," writes Jack Rakove, "they might well have been able to unite on a number of points that they generally shared."[41] The Anti-Federalists were advancing a philosophy of government, but they had not yet worked out an effective system of government; and, because of the nature of the ratification debates, they never would.

There was, however, distinct disagreement about the particular problems in the Constitution and how to fix them; these divisions would have made an Anti-Federalist convention a contentious event. Cornell identifies three strands of Anti-Federalism—elite, middling, and plebeian—and he argues that the third drove the other two to reconciliation with the Constitution and eventually a significant impact on the development of the government: "Recognizing the different visions of elites and middling Anti-Federalists makes it possible to appreciate the way in which plebeian radicalism actually forced Anti-Federalists into a more moderate stance toward the

Constitution. . . . Instead of developing an anti-constitutional tradition, elite and middling Anti-Federalists chose to work within the system created by the Constitution and create a loyal opposition."[42] Siemers generally agrees on this division, though he labels "plebeian" opposition with the much more colorful term "virulent Antifederalism."[43] Both scholars identify what Siemers calls a "contemporaneous canon" of writings that were widely available and widely read. This consisted essentially of a mixture of virulent and middling Anti-Federalism; the elite works were rarely reprinted, or saw more restricted distribution in pamphlet form. Both Cornell and Siemers saw elites struggling to present a message undistorted by the radicalism of the leveling elements in society. The Federalists, though, were more than happy to lump their opponents all together as a bunch of dangerous radicals.

This trichotomy of Anti-Federalists, though, is still caught up in the Beardian emphasis on social class. Not all plebeians were radicals, and not all elites were moderates. Some very conciliatory ideas came from obscure pens, and some radical ideas from political elites. Furthermore, in the absence of certain knowledge about the authorship of the vast majority of pseudonymous opposition writings, including several of the most elegant and insightful series, to use these labels tells us little. Certainly the virulent Anti-Federalists were virulent, but the relevant factor about many of them was that they were democratic, in some cases to the point of leveling. There was not always much difference between middling and elite objections; the variations within each group are more interesting than those between the two.

If we examine the Anti-Federalist writings in terms of ideas rather than author and style, we can draw some different and useful conclusions. There is little difference between elite and middling writings, but writers in both groups can be roughly divided into two main themes: Rights Anti-Federalism, which was fixated on the question of individual liberty, and Power Anti-Federalism, which was concerned with the balance of powers within the national government and between the national and state governments.[44] These are still broad groups, but they raise important issues in the development of opposition; it was the merging of these two groups that ultimately led to a coherent resistance and push for amendments. The letters of "Brutus" are exemplary of the latter strand of opposition thought. Though Brutus devoted an entire essay to the need for a bill of rights, he largely dropped the issue in the remainder of his essays. His concern was with the powers granted and how they might be limited, less to protect the individual than to ensure a smooth and effective operation of government at all levels. The "Federal Farmer," on the other hand, was an exemplar of Rights

Anti-Federalism. Every objection he raised against the powers granted by the Constitution came back to a question of how it might be used to oppress the people. In general, Power Anti-Federalists aimed to protect the states against the national government, and Rights Anti-Federalists aimed to protect individuals.

Most of the virulent Anti-Federalists were concerned with neither. (A few were, and can be properly classified in one of those two categories.) For most of them a constitution was not about empowering the government at all; it was about empowering the people. A properly established government did not need many safeguards, because its very structure would be a safeguard. The people cannot oppress themselves; a tyrannical government must be one in which the people do not rule. Thus "Centinel," the leading figure in this Democratic Anti-Federalism, could praise the simplicity of the powerful unicameral legislature of his state of Pennsylvania; in such a system, the people really do rule. The policies of such a government may not always be wise, or expedient, or even fair, but they reflect the popular will, and the popular will ought to be law. The middling and elite Anti-Federalists could not endorse such a Democratic position, of course; the Power and Rights Anti-Federalist positions implied very clearly that an elite, albeit one chosen by the people, ought to rule. Thus, as the ratification debates progressed, the latter two groups came together while keeping the radicals at arm's length.

The three strands of Anti-Federalist thought, not surprisingly, followed roughly along regional lines. The Rights position was centered in the south, the Power position in the northeast, and the Democratic in the west. There were examples of each everywhere, as individuals from New Hampshire to Georgia were reacting to the same proposed Constitution, but the political culture in each part of the country shaped the main contours of the debate in that region. The proslavery south seems at first to be an odd place for an argument based on individual rights, but it was a culture in which the economic ideal, as well as the source of political power, was individual plantation owners who exerted substantial power over their property. These large landowners wanted greater security for property, and assurances that the proposed new government would not interfere with their private affairs.

When we contrast this way of life with the politics of northeastern communities, centered on the famous town meetings that made such an impression on Alexis de Tocqueville as he traveled through the country a few decades later, the differences are striking. In the northeast, the primary concern of Anti-Federalists was not defending the property of individuals; it was protecting the autonomy of existing local political units. The national government threatened top-down policy edicts in the same way that the

state governments did, so Anti-Federalists in the northeast fought as vigorously against national control of states as they did against state control
of local government. They used the same methods, too: local control over
elections, and local representatives in government that could speak for their
neighbors in legislative deliberations. Representation, though, was a collective right; many northeastern Anti-Federalists were in favor of the practice
of instructing their representatives in how to vote on a given issue, and
those instructions were rooted in a clear understanding of majority rule and
community interests.

In western communities we also see localism, but of a different sort. In a
way the west combined the individualism and concern for property rights
of the south with the localism and emphasis on participation and representation of the northeast. Western Anti-Federalists were suspicious of any
distant government, whether state or national. In fact, even local government was often suspect, though not as often because it was closer. Proximity
mattered, and the only way to simulate proximity in a distant government
was through numerous and effective representation. The people should not
only elect their representatives; they should know their representatives intimately. Representatives should reflect the priorities of their constituents
as closely as possible, which meant that each representative should have as
few constituents as possible. Each individual, regardless of wealth or social
status, should have essentially direct access to government, and ordinary
people should be able to serve in the legislature and create the laws.

During the course of the ratification debates, these positions spread
throughout the United States, and Anti-Federalists everywhere started
adopting the best arguments regardless of their source. The radical position of the Democratic Anti-Federalists was generally seen by political elites
as too extreme and unworkable, but the Rights and Power Anti-Federalist
positions became increasingly entwined to the point that by the summer
of 1788 George Mason was making arguments in the Virginia Ratifying
Convention that looked remarkably similar to those made by Melancton
Smith in New York's Convention. Writers in Massachusetts and Rhode Island found common ground with writers in North and South Carolina.

READING AND EVALUATING
ANTI-FEDERALIST THOUGHT

The literature on the Anti-Federalists has expanded with the availability
of primary source materials. Jonathan Elliot's *Debates in the Several State*

Conventions was collected in the 1830s, and offered worthwhile material for several states, though other states were represented only by fragments, and some not at all. Paul Leicester Ford's two volumes of writings offered just a handful of examples of opposition writing, but they were the best that were available to many scholars for the first half of the twentieth century. Additional material was scattered in public libraries and private collections and required extensive efforts to obtain. In the 1960s, two collections of Anti-Federalist writings made the opposition more accessible to scholars than it had been in the past. Morton Borden's *The Antifederalist Papers* was carefully collected and edited into an effective, if overly contrived, essay-by-essay response to *The Federalist*. Cecilia Kenyon's *The Antifederalists* included a revised version of her earlier essay, as well as a fine selection of Anti-Federalist writings and speeches. Both of these works were valuable in opening up the possibility of wider consumption of the opposition arguments, but neither was extensive enough to allow for comprehensive scholarly analysis of Anti-Federalist ideas. It was Herbert Storing's *The Complete Anti-Federalist* that began to fill this void, providing five volumes of writings, including complete series (something neither Kenyon nor Borden offered for the more prolific writers) and covering the most critical states rather well.[45] This was only a start, though; as John Kaminski points out, this "complete" collection is far from complete, containing only about a sixth of the relevant available material, only one private letter, and virtually no material from the Anti-Federalist strongholds of North Carolina and Rhode Island.[46] A much more complete collection can be found, intermixed with Federalist materials, in *The Documentary History of the Ratification of the Constitution*, an enormous but incomplete project that, when finished, will offer the scholar a truly complete collection of the relevant materials. With this cornucopia of resources, it has become possible to appreciate and evaluate the entire scope of Anti-Federalist arguments, ideas, and political strategies. The opposition to the Constitution was extensive and complex, but certain patterns can be drawn from careful examination.

To understand the Anti-Federalist position and its development over time, there are at least three aspects of the ratification debates we must consider. First is the ideas themselves. There were substantial differences among the Anti-Federalists as to what a national government should look like, but all agreed that the Constitution was not the proper model. The disagreements fit within a broader understanding of republican government as government of the people; in fact, the primary debate among the opponents of the Constitution was how much agency the people ought to have in policy. Power Anti-Federalists believed that the people's representatives, who ought themselves to be close to and sympathetic with the people, should be able to enact policy within carefully circumscribed limits on their powers. Rights Anti-Federalists agreed to the notion of representation, but saw the people as more autonomous, engaged in their everyday lives and needing personal protections against government more than actively (but indirectly) shaping public policy. For Democratic Anti-Federalists, the people *were* the government; their representatives were not trustees of power called upon to exercise it judiciously, but merely convenient proxies for the voice of the people. They were to do what the people wanted. These three positions were conflicting only to a point; they shared a great deal of common ground as well, especially concerning the importance and mechanisms of representation. The ideas of the debate, though, were dynamic; each position changed as the political realities changed, and the first two groups adapted and combined while the third was largely left out (by their own choice, mostly) of any conciliatory process.

Second, we must consider the context of the debate, or rather debates. Kaminski, in his critique of Storing, writes that "the debate over the Constitution must be analyzed as thirteen separate debates conducted within each state with the internal politics of each state playing the predominant role."[47] This is true to an extent, but in reality there were not thirteen but *fourteen* debates (fifteen if the ratifying convention of Vermont in 1791 is included; there was more dissent and hence more of a debate there than in the first state, Delaware). The final debate, which Kaminski does not adequately recognize, is the national one; there was an ongoing argument about the Constitution that transcended state lines. In some ways, this debate was a continuation of the final discussions in the Philadelphia Convention, and the debates in Congress over what to do with the Convention's work clearly belong to it, as do the debates in the summer of 1788 over how to implement the new government. The major series of essays and many of the pamphlets were generally aimed at an audience broader than the state in which they were published. This is certainly true of *The Federalist* as well as the essays of the Federal Farmer, Centinel, and Brutus. These fifteen debates were overlapping, but they were not simultaneous. They occurred in a particular order, and the order mattered. M. E. Bradford is certainly correct when he suggests that the contest was decided in part by political pressure and a bandwagon effect. "Sequence," he contends, "not the power of persuasion or the force of political arguments, is the key to this narrative."[48] Part of this sequence, of course, is the speed with which the Constitution was considered; events happened very quickly, so it was difficult for the participants in the debate to really examine one event before the next one was upon them.

This was intentional on the part of the Federalists; giving the opposition too much time to organize may have been fatal to their designs. By keeping the sequence rapid, the Anti-Federalists were scrambling to catch up essentially the whole time, and they "somehow always managed to move too late and with too little."[49]

A third factor to recognize is the strategy involved, by both sides. The sequence and speed of the debates were part of the Federalist strategy, but there were other aspects to it as well, sometimes quite nuanced. On this point, several histories of the debate have been written. Both Rutland and Boyd present extensive accounts of the maneuvering and machinations of the Anti-Federalists during the ratification struggle, but the exemplary work here is Pauline Maier's *Ratification*, which traces the debates in more detail than any previous work. Maier occasionally loses sight of the big picture, but never for long; she presents a useful picture of each of the state debates in the general context of the national one.[50] I do not aim here to present a clear and impartial history of ratification, for I can add little to her book. Instead, I endeavor to examine the development of ideas rather than events, and examine how the events and strategies shaped and changed those ideas.

2

Three Strands of Anti-Federalism

THE ANTI-FEDERALIST RESISTANCE to the Constitution began on September 15, 1787, with Edmund Randolph. As the Philadelphia Convention was finishing the final touches on the proposed Constitution, Randolph proposed "that amendments to the plan might be offered by the State Conventions, which should be submitted to and finally decided on by another general Convention."[1] There are two reasons to use this motion as the starting point for the opposition to the Constitution. First, it is the earliest explicit opposition to the document as a whole, rather than some specific clause or part.[2] Most of the delegates, at some point during the Convention, opposed some aspect of the document that was ultimately approved, but such misgivings are not properly Anti-Federalist, because they do not reflect opposition to the Constitution or its ratification. Randolph's motion suggests at least discomfort, if not outright opposition, to the document, and implies that it ought not be approved and implemented as it stood. Second, Randolph's call for another convention, with outside input from the states, became a central talking point for the Anti-Federalists. Sometimes this took the form of criticizing the Philadelphia Convention for exceeding its authority, and sometimes it was presented in terms of properly representing the views of the people as a whole rather than a few dozen meeting in secret. Either way, the call for amendments became the primary goal for the Anti-Federalists, most of whom saw at least some good in the Constitution, as indeed Randolph did.[3] Immediately following Randolph's motion, both George Mason and Elbridge Gerry also voiced their objections to the document as a whole. The arguments made by these three, taken together, form much of the basis for subsequent objections to the Constitution.

Upon presenting his motion, Randolph did not elaborate on his reasons for objecting, beyond explaining that the powers given to Congress were "indefinite and dangerous." Two days later, he only elaborated so far as to express his concern that, without the possibility of amendment, the

Constitution would fail to be ratified, and "anarchy & civil convulsions" would ensue.[4] It was not until the tenth of October that he wrote out his objections in a letter to the Virginia House of Delegates. Randolph never sent the letter, but two months later it was printed as a pamphlet and became a significant early piece of Anti-Federalist literature. The primary objection raised by Randolph in this letter was the same one that he raised in convention, that amending before ratification was essential. He also offered a list of specific defects that he saw in the Constitution:

> I am sanguine in hoping, that . . . Virginia, will be seconded by a majority of the states. I hope, that she will be seconded 1. in causing all ambiguities of expression to be precisely explained: 2. in rendering the President ineligible after a given number of years: 3. in taking from him either the power of nominating to the judiciary offices, or of filling up vacancies which therein may happen during the recess of the senate, by granting commissions which shall expire at the end of their next session: 4. in taking from him the power of pardoning for treason, at least before conviction: 5. in drawing a line between the powers of Congress and individual states; and in defining the former; so as to leave no clashing of jurisdictions nor dangerous disputes: and to prevent the one from being swallowed up by the other, under the cover of general words, and implication: 6. in abridging the power of the Senate to make treaties the supreme laws of the land: 7. in providing a tribunal instead of the Senate for the impeachment of Senators: 8. in incapacitating the Congress to determine their own salaries: and 9. in limiting and defining the judicial power.[5]

Of these proposed changes, a third (numbers 1, 5, and 9) call for clarifications. Another third (numbers 4, 7, and 8) are relatively narrow issues. Only presidential term limits, changes in the nominating process for judges, and the treaty-making power of the Senate would be major changes, and all three played a substantial, though not really central, role in the emerging Anti-Federalist opposition.

George Mason, who seconded Randolph's motion, sounded what was to become a central theme in contending that the Constitution "would end either in monarchy, or a tyrannical aristocracy."[6] He agreed that another convention would be necessary, and that an all-or-nothing ratification ultimatum was counterproductive and improper. This argument was to be taken up by fellow Virginian Richard Henry Lee in Congress, but the Federalists were able to avoid such a call well into 1788, when the Massachusetts

Ratifying Convention became the first to propose amendments. By then, the idea of another convention had lost most of its momentum.

Of the three convention dissenters, Elbridge Gerry offered the least ambiguous reasons at the time. He listed eleven specific objections. His first eight objections included much that would become familiar in later debates:

> 1. the duration and re-eligibility of the Senate. 2. the power of the House of Representatives to conceal their journals. 3. the power of Congress over the places of election. 4. the unlimited power of Congress over their own compensations. 5. Massachusetts has not a due share of Representatives allotted to her. 6. 3/5 of the Blacks are to be represented as if they were freemen. 7. *Under* the power over commerce, monopolies may be established. 8. The vice president being made head of the Senate.[7]

He explained, though, that he could "get over all these" if only his three most significant objections were addressed, and these too were repeated throughout the ratification process. He cites the necessary and proper clause, the ability to raise armies and levy taxes, and the insecurity of trial by jury as the fatal flaws in the document.[8] These three, along with the absence of a bill of rights, would prove to be the central objections of the Anti-Federalists to the Constitution.[9] In a letter to the Massachusetts legislature shortly after the Convention, perhaps influenced by the objections of Mason, he added the influence of the President over the legislature and the absence of a bill of rights in listing its flaws.[10]

George Mason developed and listed his specific objections to the Constitution in the final days of the Convention, though it does not seem that he ever presented them in a speech before that body.[11] His objections follow Randolph's in some respects, and Gerry's in others, but the emphasis is decidedly different. First, he begins his objections with the absence of a bill of rights, suggesting that state bills of rights are useless because they are superseded by the Constitution, and the common law is no better because it is in no way protected by that document. Second, he suggests that the absence of a constitutional council for the President is a fatal flaw, and he offers a fairly detailed proposal for what shape such a council ought to take. Third, he focuses much of his critique on the Senate, which he believes will become the central power behind government, leading to an aristocracy or even a monarchy. Fourth, he raises the issue of commercial legislation, arguing, as many southerners did during the convention, that all such laws should require two-thirds votes in both houses of Congress. Finally, he briefly objects to the clause prohibiting Congress from interfering with the slave trade for twenty years, saying that this commerce "render[s] the United States weaker, more vulnerable, and less capable of defence."[12] In emphasizing these five broad objections, he proves to be less prescient than Gerry at anticipating the eventual Anti-Federalist position. Although the absence of a bill of rights and the powers of the Senate emerged as significant themes, the regulation of commerce did not receive a serious discussion outside of the Virginia Ratifying Convention, the constitutional council remained an idea confined to certain Anti-Federalists with a more elite and less democratic understanding of government, and the question of slavery, though discussed in many places, could not factor much into the opposition anyway because of sectional differences.

The objections of Mason, Gerry, and Randolph exemplify the first major problem faced by the Anti-Federalists: they had something to argue against, but no obvious coherent position from which to argue. Randolph's position that the Constitution had some flaws but not necessarily fatal ones runs in almost direct opposition to the positions of Gerry and Mason. The latter two, meanwhile, disagreed substantially on which flaws were the most critically in need of revision. There was no immediate coherence to the Anti-Federalist position, a point made quite effectively by Tench Coxe, writing as "Philanthropos," after the minority from the Pennsylvania Convention published its objections in December: "The objections severally made by the three honorable gentlemen and the Pennsylvania Minority are so *different*, and even *discordant* in their essential principles, that all hope of greater unanimity of opinion, either in *another convention*, or in *the people*, must be given up by those who know the human heart and mind, with their infinitely varying feelings and ideas."[13] The opposition became more unified as the debate wore on, but by that time the Federalists had largely succeeded in painting their opponents as parochial politicians with no serious theoretical understanding of government.

A close look at the development of the Anti-Federalist position, though, suggests that there were broad areas of agreement, and at least three distinct approaches among the Anti-Federalists. The first, and perhaps the most rationally developed and cogently argued, is the rights-based approach of Mason. These Rights Anti-Federalists emphasized the absence of a bill of rights and contended that the Constitution would end, intentionally or not, in tyrannical government. The second approach follows Gerry's objections. Such Power Anti-Federalists argued that the national government was too strong and the states too weak in the proposed Constitution, and that power was not well apportioned among the parts of the proposed federal government;

this position was more pragmatic and the effectiveness of its proponents varied widely. The third approach was not represented at the Convention, but it may have had the most adherents in the population at large. These individuals leaned on state sovereignty and popular participation; such Democratic Anti-Federalists suggested that if national government was needed at all, it should represent the people as directly as possible, and the people should retain control. The state legislatures at the time were generally far more democratic than the Congress described in the Constitution, and these opponents wanted to keep as much power as close to the people as possible. This meant a weak national government, though there was considerable variation in their ideas of just how weak such a government should be.

It is important to note that these three strands of thought were not contradictory or mutually exclusive; they differed more in emphasis than substance. Anti-Federalists of all three varieties generally favored a bill of rights, but only the Rights Anti-Federalists saw it as foundational rather than an added layer of protection. Most opponents of the Constitution believed that the people ought to rule through their representatives, but only the Democratic Anti-Federalists believed that this was the first (and perhaps only) principle of legitimate government. All Anti-Federalists were concerned about the powers granted by the Constitution, but only the Power Anti-Federalists saw their distribution as the primary flaw in the document, rather than its underlying ideology or philosophy of government.

Randolph can best be understood as a Power Anti-Federalist, but he was a lukewarm and reluctant one. He is emblematic of the significant group of moderates in the ratification debates. He would not fully endorse the Constitution, nor would he actively campaign against it or stand in the way of ratification. His position was not uncommon; many leading figures had objections and concerns, but saw union as the primary goal and would work toward it despite the flaws in the document that would ensure it.[14] Though Randolph called for a second convention early in the debates, he, like many others, would become convinced that changes had to be made after ratification, not before.

What followed these initial objections was a contentious and cacophonous battle that lasted about nine months, with echoes that lasted for years afterward. The debates cannot be effectively studied as a single point in time, because the terms of the debate changed as each state called a convention and made a decision on the Constitution. There is substantial value in examining the ratification debates as a narrative, because sequence was essential to the outcome. Had Anti-Federalist New York, for example, called a convention immediately, the opposition there might have rejected the

Constitution before the Federalists in Massachusetts secured their critical compromise; this might have strengthened the latter state's opposition to push harder for a second convention, and perhaps might have even succeeded. The fact that the first five conventions were overwhelmingly Federalist played no small part in creating momentum, and pushing skeptics like Samuel Adams and Edmund Randolph to seek a way to fix the Constitution without actually rejecting it. Nonetheless, a simple sequential retelling of the Anti-Federalist arguments in the order in which they were made tells us little without some groundwork establishing what we are looking for. In examining the narrative, we are looking for signs of what is happening within the opposition; we go from a great deal of diversity in objections in 1787 to a fairly united, and strikingly moderate, opposition in the summer of 1788. The story of why this happened is what this book aims to tell.

In order to do so, it is essential to say something more here about the three strands of Anti-Federalist thought. Dividing all of the Anti-Federalists into three camps is not necessary; the dividing lines are blurry, and become even more blurred later in the debate. Nonetheless, it is possible to find exemplars of the three arguments in the debate, and it is fortunate that the three most significant series of essays each represent one of the strands. A closer look at these three series will serve as a useful introduction to the broader narrative.

CENTINEL, DEMOCRATIC ANTI-FEDERALIST

Although the Democratic Anti-Federalists had no delegate at the Philadelphia Convention, they were well represented in the first wave of essays against the Constitution. Foremost among them was Pennsylvania's "Centinel," a prolific and particularly vitriolic writer who nonetheless saw fairly wide reprintings. Though his essays are not among the very best of the opposition writings, they were among the best of the radical wing of Anti-Federalism.

Starting in his first essay, Centinel developed a philosophy of government based on republican principles, suggesting that free government can only exist for a virtuous people with a fairly equal distribution of property. He proposes a simple government, praising the unicameral Pennsylvania legislature. Such a government remains responsible to the people because of short terms of office, rotation, and openness. Complexity in government is likely to render "the interposition of the people . . . imperfect or perhaps wholly abortive." The Constitution he found to be "a most daring attempt to establish a despotic aristocracy among freemen," for in virtually every contest the national government would prevail over the weaker states. Therefore the government the Constitution established would be wholly a national government, and such a government could not possibly take into account local concerns, and thus could not truly reflect the will of the people. He introduced the common Anti-Federalist idea that the President and Senate must eventually join forces and control government: "The President, who would be a mere pageant of state, unless he coincides with the views of the Senate, would either become the head of the aristocratic junto in that body, or its minion."[15] Centinel mentioned the need for a bill of rights, as well as some concerns about the judicial powers, but his central concern was representation, and in this he inaugurated the theory of Democratic Anti-Federalism. The basic idea was simple: the people ought to be as close to their representatives as possible, and the representatives ought to reflect the will of the people. This was not merely to suggest that all classes of people should be represented in Congress. Most Anti-Federalists believed that, in one way or another. Centinel wanted to see the people with a degree of control over their representatives. In the New England states, this was often accomplished through explicit instructions, but what Centinel encouraged was representatives who were keenly aware of what their constituents wanted, lest they be replaced in the next election cycle, which with annual elections was always just around the corner. Two-year terms, and a distant legislature, made this nearly impossible to achieve in the House of Representatives under the Constitution, and the Senate was far worse with its longer terms and indirect elections. The Senate, in fact, could only serve to reflect the wishes of the aristocracy, which he saw as fundamentally unnecessary since the aristocracy always had power and influence through wealth anyway.

These arguments by Centinel were reminiscent of the earlier radical writings of Thomas Paine. In *Common Sense*, Paine argued for a simple, popular democratic government, with annual elections. His national congress would consist of at least thirty delegates per state, elected out of regional districts. The president would be elected annually out of a randomly selected state's delegation. He leaves little room for scheming and intrigue. In *The Crisis*, Paine goes on to call for a stronger union, still built on basically democratic principles. Thus Centinel was tapping into a radical tradition that played a substantial role in the American Revolution, and this position was still popular, especially among farmers and rural Americans, who were distrustful of centralized power just as they had been distrustful of British rule.

Centinel immediately recognized the importance of prestige to the Federalist strategy. Writings in favor of the Constitution would often emphasize the gravitas and statesmanship of those who attended the Philadelphia Convention and signed the Constitution. Most of these individuals, though worthy of praise, were fundamentally local dignitaries, with little appeal outside of their respective states, but the document included signers from twelve states, as well as the illustrious George Washington and the venerable Benjamin Franklin, who both had powerful national appeal. Centinel took aim at Convention delegates, attempting to undercut this appeal to names. The signers from Pennsylvania were primary targets, especially Robert Morris and his "monopolising spirit," and James Wilson with his "superlative arrogance, ambition and rapacity," but Centinel also issued broad attacks on those "harpies of power," the Federalists, who were attempting "[s]o flagrant, so audacious a conspiracy against the liberties of a free people." It was not the prestige of Morris and Wilson that was most effectively carrying the Constitution, though, and Centinel did not hold back criticism even of Washington and Franklin, suggesting political naivety in the former and senility in the latter.[16] This was probably going a step too far, and undoubtedly cost him some sympathizers, but Centinel was not one to shy away from controversy. The Federalist appeal to great names had to be countered.

The specific arguments made by Centinel include many of the standard ones raised by the opposition everywhere, including the importance of jury trials, the jurisdiction of the courts, and the need for a bill of rights and especially protection for freedom of the press. He even moralizes, condemning the compromises over slavery, appealing to the moral sense of the Quaker population in Pennsylvania, and asking whether "the concurrence of the five southern states . . . [has] been purchased too dearly by the rest." His thematic emphasis is different from most of his colleagues, however, as he consistently praises popular participation and localism. The people, he insists, will not be won over by Federalist trickery; given time, they will rise up against the aristocratic conspiracy that is the Constitution, and it is best if they do so before ratification rather than having to overthrow the government afterward. The people ought to have a direct say not only in choosing representatives, but in writing laws, including the fundamental law. The Constitution, he suggests, ought to be presented for ratification not to the ratifying conventions, but directly to the people.[17]

All of this controversy was avoidable anyway, because the United States did not need a radical change in government. Centinel, like many of the more radically democratic opponents of the Constitution, saw no particular danger in the Articles of Confederation. The states were free to set their own policies; as much as the Federalists might complain about inconsistencies and even injustices, this arrangement was as it should be because most of the power of government rested close to the people. This federal system, he writes, is "the most perfect system of local government in the world." In fact, the best evidence of its good is that "from its first establishment, the ambitious and profligate have been united in a constant conspiracy to destroy it."[18] The Federalists might insist that failure to ratify the Constitution will lead to disunion or even anarchy, but this is simply not true. The idea that rejection of the Constitution would result in a division of the United States into separate confederacies had no basis in reality.

> This hobgoblin appears to have sprung from the deranged brain of *Publius*, a New-York writer, who mistaking sound for argument, has with Herculean labour accumulated myriads of unmeaning sentences, and *mechanically* endeavoured to force conviction by a torrent of misplaced words; he might have spared his readers the fatigue of wading through his long-winded disquisitions on the direful effects of the contentions of inimical states, as totally inapplicable to the subject he was *professedly* treating; this writer has devoted much time, and wasted more paper in combating chimeras of his own creation.[19]

Even if the concern was well founded, Centinel insists, the idea of civil war is preferable to despotism. Fortunately, the idea of the union breaking is at best unlikely, and probably not worth seriously considering.

Altogether, Centinel offers a coherent and consistent argument for simple government, close to the people. His preferred form of republicanism is highly democratic; representatives would be immediately chosen by the people at frequent intervals, and constantly reminded of where they came from and on whose behalf they were to speak. Most Anti-Federalists were not prepared to go this far; they saw the federal government as something entirely different from those of the states. For the United States to take its place among the nations of the world, something more than representatives who parroted their constituents would be necessary. Centinel, meanwhile, remained convinced that the only legitimate form of national government was localism writ large.

BRUTUS, POWER ANTI-FEDERALIST

Not all Anti-Federalists shared the radicalism of Centinel, but this does not mean that they were not combative. In fact, the most effective opposition pieces were those that were vehement in their arguments rather than vitriolic in their attacks. Perhaps the finest opposition writings to emerge from the debates were the essays of "Brutus" in New York. These essays responded rather directly to Federalist arguments, and were particularly aimed at countering the efforts of "Publius" in his *Federalist* essays.

Brutus presented a clear Power Anti-Federalist position. Like virtually all Anti-Federalists, Brutus wanted to see a bill of rights, but he was more concerned with the balance and distribution of powers than the rights of the people. In his second letter he suggests that "The principles, therefore, upon which the social compact is founded, ought to have been clearly and precisely stated, and the most express and full declaration of rights to have been made," but this was never made the centerpiece of (or even of particularly high importance in) his objections.[20] Even his claim that a bill of rights was even more necessary in a national government than the state governments was premised on an argument of governmental power: the Constitution will be a new social compact, superseding previous compacts, and thus previous protections must be put in place again.

The central concern of Brutus is consolidation. Everything in the Constitution pointed in this direction. He singles out the Necessary and Proper and Supremacy Clauses as evidence of consolidation, and proceeds to dismantle the idea of a consolidated national republican government; "a free republic," he writes, "cannot succeed over a country of such immense extent, containing such a number of inhabitants, and these encreasing in such rapid progression as that of the whole United States."[21] Because republican government must remain close and responsive to the people, the state governments are far more appropriate venues for republican principles than the nation as a whole. Though he agrees in principle with Centinel that representatives ought to be responsive, he does not see this in quite the same way. Simplicity in government is not given any special emphasis here; complexity is not a problem in itself—it only becomes a problem when the people cannot determine where the political power lies. Representatives, for Brutus, can be responsive without the people effectively dictating how they ought to vote; this is a substantially less democratic position than that taken by Centinel (though still substantially more democratic than the position of the Federalists, or the ideas in the Constitution itself).

Brutus begins his discussion of the specific parts of government with the House of Representatives, contending that the representation of slaves is unjust and a violation of republican principles. The Senate, on the other hand, in a consolidated government ought to be apportioned according to population as well. Because of the powers given to Congress, it is paramount that a proper degree of representation be achieved; this was not done in the

Constitution. Instead, he argues, "the representation is merely nominal—a mere burlesque." Collectively, the people of the states have two thousand representatives in their legislatures; this more extensive representation is a safer repository of power than sixty-five members of the House, or even ninety-one in both houses of Congress combined. Furthermore, he contends, it is not necessary to lodge this much power in a national legislature anyway; "one of the most capital errors in the system," Brutus argues, "is that of extending the powers of the foederal government to objects to which it is not adequate, which it cannot exercise without endangering public liberty, and which it is not necessary they should possess, in order to preserve the union and manage our national concerns."[22] In a certain sense, this sums up the Power Anti-Federalist position. Powers given to the national government should be few and defined, and only include those that are necessarily linked to national issues, and with which more distant (and implicitly less responsive) representatives can be trusted.

The power of taxation is the most grievous example of a power too extensive, which will lead to consolidation of all other powers. The states, left with no guaranteed power to raise revenue, will be unable to support themselves, and will become dependent on the national government or cease altogether to exist. The supreme executive and judicial branches of the national government will make it impossible for states to even attempt to resist federal encroachment. In addition, the vagueness of the phrases "common defence" and "general welfare" essentially permits Congress to raise taxes at pleasure, unchecked by any other institution. Even aside from the destruction of the states, Congress might levy oppressive taxes on any object of revenue they choose. It is the idea of excise taxes that especially disturbs Brutus, who discusses a variety of articles that might be targeted for revenue. Such taxes ought to be the exclusive province of the states, which "ought to have an uncontroulable power to raise a revenue, adequate to the exigencies of their governments."[23]

In the area of national security, too, the government is to be given too much power. Brutus takes on Publius directly on this point, particularly the latter's claim that the defense of the nation requires indeterminate powers in a national government. To counter this claim, Brutus observes that protection of the people is a joint responsibility, and thus the states too need a source of revenue. "The most important end of government," he writes, "is the proper direction of its internal police, and oeconomy," which is "the province of the state governments. . . . Is it not then preposterous, and in the highest degree absurd, when the state governments are vested with powers so essential to the peace and good order of society, to take from

them the means of their own preservation?" The preservation of state powers of taxation requires specific limits to the corresponding national power.
These limits, some Federalists (including Publius) claimed, are impossible
to reasonably set. Brutus disagrees, observing that all of the proposals to
strengthen Congress under the Articles of Confederation by expanding
taxing powers involved stipulated limits. No one had seriously proposed a
plenary power to tax Americans directly. Certainly some of the proposals
had been implausible, but they were all specific. There was already widespread agreement that Congress ought to have the power to levy imposts;
this would perhaps provide sufficient revenue immediately, and the revenue would increase over time as the nation became wealthier. Instead, the
Constitution gives to Congress not only unlimited taxing powers, but also
the power to borrow any amount of money. "I can scarcely contemplate a
greater calamity that could befal this country," he warns, "than to be loaded
with a debt exceeding their ability ever to discharge." Borrowing money
ought to be a last resort, only in times of war or crisis, and such borrowing
should not be from foreign governments or citizens if possible. Coupled
with military power, the Constitution thus gives the national government
"unlimitted authority and controul over all the wealth and all the force of
the union." With this being the case, no freedom is left to the states; they
will be mere dependents at the whim of Congress.[24]

The military, and especially a standing army, threatens tyranny as well.
Backed by the army, a Caesar or a Cromwell might arise to take control
of the nation; a Cincinnatus or a Washington will not always be in charge
of the military. He points out that this very nearly happened in the United
States in 1783. Had the circumstances surrounding the Newburgh Conspiracy been different, the United States may well not have been debating on a
new Constitution at all in 1788; rather a constitution might have been dictated to the country "at the point of a bayonet."[25] Fortunately, Washington
had been able to defuse the potential coup, largely through the force of his
personality and presence, rather than deciding to lead it and take charge of
his country.[26] If standing armies are a threat to liberty they should be prohibited: "No reason can be given, why rulers should be authorised to do,
what, if done, would oppose the principles and habits of the people, and
endanger the public safety, but there is every reason in the world, that they
should be prohibited from the exercise of such a power." Yet this is exactly
what the proposed Constitution fails to do, for the expressed reason that
we do not know what powers might be needed in the future. This is entirely
unacceptable to Brutus. It is important to allow for sufficient soldiers to be
maintained to garrison certain defensive positions and arsenals, but it would

be simple to permit Congress to do this without granting a general power to maintain a standing army. Brutus even suggests appropriate language that might have been used.[27] Such changes, though, must be made before the Constitution is ratified and implemented, because it is dangerous to give unchecked power and hope to limit it once granted.

It is the courts, though, that will really hold this government together and consolidate power. In particular, Brutus is concerned about the power of judges to determine the meaning of the Constitution. Because they may decide on cases "in Law and Equity," the Court will be authorized "to explain the constitution according to the reasoning spirit of it, without being confined to the words or letter."[28] The potential for abuse is nearly unlimited, as the Constitution will effectively say whatever the judges want it to say, and their word will be final. What Brutus anticipates is a tendency toward consolidation, and repeated rulings against the states. "Perhaps nothing could have been better conceived to facilitate the abolition of the state governments," he argues, "than the constitution of the judicial." The Supreme Court "will lean strongly in favour of the general government, and will give such an explanation to the constitution, as will favour an extension of its jurisdiction." There are three primary reasons for this. First, he relies on the idea that power corrupts, and even judges, once in power, will seek to expand their authority. The second, and even more convincing, reason is the Supremacy Clause; if congressional legislation takes precedence over that of the states, the courts will not be able to rule any other way in most cases. And any additional powers claimed for Congress through the judiciary will lead to an expansion of judicial power as well, as the Supreme Court's jurisdiction must be "commensurate" to all of the laws made by the national government, because "the supreme court should have authority to determine questions arising under the laws of the union." Brutus finds a third argument for consolidation in the Preamble: "the great end of the constitution, if it is to be collected from the preamble . . . is to constitute a government which is to extend to every case for which any government is instituted, whether external or internal." The idea of consolidation is the first goal listed: "to make a union of this kind perfect, it is necessary to abolish all inferior governments, and to give to the general one compleat legislative, executive and judicial powers to every purpose." Thus the courts, empowered to interpret the Constitution according to its spirit as well as its text, are very likely to find in this statement of principles ample reason to consolidate, "in Order to form a more perfect Union."[29]

Even beyond constitutional interpretation, the jurisdiction of the courts is much too broad. This jurisdiction covers every case except those between citizens of the same state, and Brutus predicts that will be absorbed as well. His claim that an individual could claim citizenship in another state simply to sue in federal courts seems a bit unlikely, but he points out that the English common law involves many less plausible fictions than this. Thus, he says, the jurisdiction of the national courts will extend to all cases. Even the appellate jurisdiction of the federal courts is dangerous. "I believe it is a new and unusual thing," he contends, "to allow appeals in criminal matters. It is contrary to the sense of our laws, and dangerous to the lives and liberties of the citizen." The Supreme Court, which will likely not include a jury, will have the power to examine the facts of the case as well as the law, and overrule a jury. In addition to this, the expense of appeals to the Supreme Court would be "endless and intolerable." Only the rich will be able to afford such appeals, leaving "the poor and middling class of people who in every government stand most in need of protection of the law" without a reasonable expectation of justice.[30]

These unnecessary powers are made even more dangerous by the nature of the position to be held by judges. The life terms, praised by the Federalists for making the judiciary independent of the executive and legislature, are a substantial part of the problem. In England, judges served for life because they needed to be independent of the crown. In a republican government, judges serving for life will be "independent of the people, of the legislature, and of every power under heaven. Men placed in this situation will generally soon feel themselves independent of heaven itself." They are rendered even more independent by the fact that no one in the national or state governments will have any power over them. Their salaries are fixed, or at least may not be lowered, and they may only be removed for "treason, bribery, or other high crimes and misdemeanors." They may not be removed for simple incompetence, and sinister motives are remarkably hard to prove as crimes. In short, the judges are far too independent, potentially thwarting the will of the people and certainly undermining basic republican principles. Brutus wonders "whether the world ever saw, in any period of it, a court of justice invested with such immense powers, and yet placed in a situation so little responsible."[31]

Brutus closed out his impressive series with a final letter on the Senate. He discusses the concept of separation of powers, conceding that "it is impracticable, perhaps, to maintain a perfect distinction between [the] several departments" because "it is difficult, if not impossible, to call to account the several officers in government, without in some degree mixing the legislative and judicial."[32] The people can directly check the legislature through elections, but the judiciary should not be elected because they need to be somewhat independent of public opinion and they must be learned in the law. The check on judges, then, as well as any other unelected officers of the government, must fall to some final arbiter, a court of impeachment. In the Constitution, of course, the trials for impeachment are to be held before the Senate. Unfortunately, Brutus argues, the Senate is improperly constructed, inadequately checked, and given far too much power.

The problem with the Senate is in the nature of the office of Senator. "Men long in office," he argues, "are very apt to feel themselves independent to form and pursue interests separate from those who appointed them. And this is more likely to be the case with the senate, as they will for the most part of the time be absent from the state they represent, and associate with such company as will possess very little of the feelings of the middling class of people." He concludes that the term of office ought to be shortened to four years, with individuals being ineligible for three years after serving in the Senate, and state legislatures retaining the right to recall their Senators. This position reflects a fairly moderate compromise on the proper terms for the Senate, one that does not undermine the role of the Senate in the federal system. Even then, though, he finds too much power in the Senate, a repository of legislative, executive, and judicial prerogatives; Brutus asserts that he "can scarcely imagine that any of the advocates of the system will pretend, that it was necessary to accumulate all these powers in the senate."[33] Several Federalists, of course, including Publius, make just this argument. Brutus promised more essays after this one, but unfortunately he did not deliver them. Nonetheless, his essays represent one of the most comprehensive arguments against the Constitution and against the philosophy of the Federalists.

Not all Power Anti-Federalists raised the same objections, of course, and not all agreed on every point. They did, however, all question the distribution of power in the Constitution, particularly the distribution between the branches of the federal government, and between that government and the states. They agreed that the Constitution could not be made truly safe without substantial structural changes, but at the very least the vague powers needed to be more sharply defined. They did not disagree with the underlying theory of the Constitution, though, as the Democratic Anti-Federalists did. Power Anti-Federalism was fundamentally republican in a manner similar to the republicanism of the Federalists, but they saw great danger in trusting republican principles to a powerful consolidated central government. The Constitution might be fixed to the satisfaction of these critics, but it would take a substantial overhaul. As ratification became inevitable, many of these Power Anti-Federalists scrambled to get what changes they could, including a more precise rendition of congressional powers, but in the end they had to settle for what became the Tenth Amendment, ensuring (in principle at least) that the states retained substantial prerogatives and powers.

THE FEDERAL FARMER, RIGHTS ANTI-FEDERALIST

Despite substantial opposition and friendly newspapers in both Boston and Philadelphia, New York was the effective center of the case against the Constitution. Though New York had its share of radicals, a number of significant moderate voices emerged in the state. Though Brutus offered the most effective direct response to Publius and other Federalist writers, the most elegant and compelling case against ratification was made by "The Federal Farmer." The Farmer's identity is even murkier than that of Brutus; writers from Massachusetts to Virginia have been suggested. As was intended with pseudonymous writings, though, what matters is not who wrote it, but what was written, and these letters offer a cogent and concise critique of the Constitution.[34]

The primary concern here is one of rights; the rights of the people, the Federal Farmer suggests, "should be made the basis of every constitution." Even the delegates to the Convention must have agreed to the importance of protecting rights, because they included Sections 9 and 10 of Article I, which amount to "no more nor less, than a partial bill of rights." Because some are listed, additional rights ought to be added if they are to be protected; without a proper bill of rights, the liberties of the people would be left to the whims of Congress. The reason they must be enumerated is simple: "men who govern, will, in doubtful cases, construe laws and constitutions most favourably for encreasing their own powers; all wise and prudent people, in forming constitutions, have drawn the line, and carefully described the powers parted with and the powers reserved."[35] This leaves the people two choices: protect their rights in their constitution, or watch those rights slowly erode until they are no longer protected at all. This is the central idea of the Rights Anti-Federalist position, that the people must protect their rights now or they will lose them later.

The Federal Farmer was also concerned with the extensive powers granted to the national government. The delegates to the Convention, in the Constitution, "propose to lodge in the general government very extensive powers—*powers* nearly, if not altogether, complete and unlimited, over the purse and the sword." These powers, he writes, must be lodged somewhere, but they must be lodged where they can best be monitored by the people. Thus representation must be extensive and robust for the liberty of the people to be defended against potential tyranny. The representation in the Constitution would not meet this standard: "[T]o suppose that this branch is sufficiently numerous to guard the rights of the people in the administration of the government, in which the purse and sword is placed," he writes, "seems to argue that we have forgot what the true meaning of representation is."[36] He convincingly argued that, on the basis of the size of the House alone, only men of wealth and fame will be elected, and thus the branch will not be very democratic. The people, properly speaking, will not be represented in the House, to say nothing of the Senate or the other parts of government. Furthermore, the ability of Congress to modify the time, place, and manner of elections creates at least the potential for even less adequate representation, although the Federal Farmer saw little chance of Congress exercising this power in a harmful way. Still, he suggests, that is part of the problem: too many of the powers given to the government present at least the potential for danger, and the success of republican government rests far too much on the chance of good political leaders. Relying on this puts the rights and liberties of the people forever in jeopardy, for one good Congress (or President) will not necessarily be followed by another. To rest the most consequential powers of government in an unrepresentative body is at least dangerous, if not outright folly, even if the Congress seems unlikely to exercise those powers.

Overall, the Federal Farmer believed that the Constitution would do too much too fast. Why not sharply limit the powers of Congress at first and grant more as needed? "Why not keep the power, and, when necessary, amend the constitution, and add to its other parts this power, and a proper increase of representation at the same time?"[37] He later seemed to contradict himself, suggesting that passing a constitution with known defects in hope of later amendments is dangerous:

> I am sensible, thousands of men in the United States, are disposed to adopt the proposed constitution, though they perceive it to be essentially defective, under an idea that amendments of it, may be obtained when necessary. This is a pernicious idea, it argues a servility of character totally unfit for the support of free government; it is very repugnant to that perpetual jealousy respecting liberty, so absolutely necessary in all free states.[38]

These two statements can, however, be reconciled. In fact, the Federal Farmer here echoed the language of the Federalists by suggesting that this is (or ought to be) an "experiment" in government. Unlike the Federalists, though, he would prefer to err on the side of too little power rather than too much. A government with too little power cannot force amendments on the people, but a government with too much can often prevent them. Thus he could consistently conclude that the government ought to be made weaker while it is within the easy power of the people to change, but that later changes might be necessary when a weak government calls for augmentation of its limited powers.

Although he does suggest that the national government will eventually swallow up the states, the Federal Farmer grounds his argument in the concept of liberty, and the importance of safeguards for the individual. Even his concerns about an extended republic were based on the idea that the individual will be lost in the multitude. This emphasis highlights the difference between Rights Anti-Federalism and Power Anti-Federalism.

The second series of essays by the Federal Farmer, like his first, was published and distributed primarily in pamphlet form. The second series is not as impressive or significant as the first, which has led these letters to be examined far less than the first pamphlet.[39] The Farmer's tone is still mostly conciliatory, suggesting that amendments are the proper course of action with respect to the proposed constitution. In the first letter of his second series, he concedes that the Constitution "affords, all circumstances considered, a better basis to build upon than the confederation." The reason for this is simple: union. Under the confederation the union is at risk, while the Constitution provided at least the potential to preserve it. "I feel an aversion to the disunion of the states, and to separate confederacies," he confesses, because "the states have fought and bled in a common cause, and great dangers too may attend these confederacies. I think the system proposed capable of very considerable degrees of perfection, if we pursue first principles."[40]

These first principles, for the Farmer, consist largely of the importance of individual liberties and rights. And the means of pursuing those principles are quite clearly prior amendments, because powers given to a national government are difficult to take back, and the people are unlikely to be sufficiently attentive to make any change after ratification. He wants to see prior amendments, because for as long as ratification is yet undecided, the people's attention will be focused on their government. Now is the time to secure rights, not later, and the unamended Constitution fails to do so. It is clear that the people "reserve all powers not expressly delegated to those who govern," but the people "like to be express and explicit about their essential rights, and not to be forced to claim them on the precarious and unascertained tenure of inferences and general principles."[41] This is why the demands for a bill of rights were so strong, and resonated so clearly, during ratification.

The Federal Farmer explains that there are two necessary conditions for a bill of rights to be superfluous: the rights reserved by the people must be indisputable, and the powers delegated to government must be carefully defined. The first condition may well be met, because of the strength of the common law tradition in America. We may be skeptical about the level of agreement, however, based on the variety of rights proposed in the various ratifying conventions if nothing else. Still, it is clear that the second condition is not met in the Constitution. The vague construction of several clauses, especially that granting Congress the power to pass laws "necessary and proper" for carrying out its other powers, make the grant of power at least somewhat open-ended. Furthermore, the few prohibitions on congressional power suggest a broader interpretation of the extent of that power. The Farmer suggests that denying Congress the right to bestow titles of nobility implies that otherwise that body would have such a power. The same goes for ex post facto laws. The inclusion of certain judicial rights, including habeas corpus and the right to trial by jury in criminal trials, suggests that others may well exist at the whim of Congress; if they too were to be protected, why not say so? If Congress has the power to raise and provision an army, why could it not quarter soldiers in private homes, even in times of peace? There are certainly ambiguities in the powers of Congress, and such ambiguities cry out for a bill of rights to protect the people.

The Farmer reminds us too of the educative function of a bill of rights: "We do not by declarations change the nature of things, or create new truths, but we give existence, or at least establish in the minds of the people truths and principles which they might never otherwise have thought of, or soon forgot." This is why the Magna Carta was so frequently confirmed and often read publicly in England; the rights of the people were kept always in the immediate view of the people themselves. The presence and even the publicization of a bill of rights, though, are not sufficient in this education; participation in juries and voting in elections "are the means by which the people are let into the knowledge of public affairs—are enabled to stand as the guardians of each others rights, and to restrain, by regular and legal measures, those who otherwise might infringe upon them." This notion of the importance of participation is an especially republican one, and when combined with his views on the militia, it gives a clear sense of the Farmer's sociopolitical principles. He praises the militia even as he critiques the idea of a standing army, suggesting that it is in widespread militia service that the safety of the republic is secured. In a republic, he argues, "it is essential that the whole body of the people always possess arms, and be taught alike, especially when young, how to use them."[42] This serves a double purpose: first, the militia is the ultimate line of defense against invasion; second, and perhaps more importantly, it serves as the final protection against tyranny. The people, after all, must retain the opportunity to resist government, should it become tyrannical.

In addition to his focus on rights, the Federal Farmer includes the prominent republican themes of representation and corruption. The Farmer insists that members of Congress under the Constitution are just as likely to be corrupted as any other group of men entrusted with power. The temptation to grant themselves special treatment, and the allure of political office, will affect them just as these affect other assemblies. Because of this, Congress will have incentive to maintain a standing army to enforce the laws, which demands higher taxes to pay these expenses. There is no reason to assume that they will find it agreeable to keep the people involved with government at all; the opposite is more likely. A gradual procession toward congressional tyranny is plausible, if not likely. It is in the democratic branch that the people's defense against this tyranny lies, provided such a branch is set up to establish proper representation. Such a branch of government needs the power of the purse, impeachment powers, and significant checks over a senate, aristocracy, or king. With a properly representative democratic branch of the legislature entrusted with appropriate powers, the Senate, President, and courts pose no real threat. Under such a government, he argues, the liberties of the people are best protected. The Constitution does not provide such a government. The problem, alarmingly, is that the House looks too much like the Senate; it will be filled with "the same kind of men—men having similar interests and views, feelings and connections—men of the same grade in society, and who associate on all occasions (probably, if there be any difference, the senators will be the most democratic.)"[43]

The Senate, meanwhile, cannot be expected to serve its proper purpose in the system, effectively representing the states. At the very least, states must have the power to recall their Senators. It would be preferable, however, to adhere to the same principles of good representation here. Six-year terms are too long to ensure that Senators answer to their constituents, the state legislatures; three or four years, he suggests, is plenty of time to provide the requisite stability in the branch while still ensuring that they remain close to their states. A rotation in office further ensures this representation of the state governments. He suggests two years ineligible for every four years served. "Even good men in office," he warns, "in time, imperceptibly lose

sight of the people, and gradually fall into measures prejudicial to them."[44]
Senators will gradually cease to represent the interests of the people of their
respective states, leaving the Senate unable to reflect state interests and preferences in legislation.

Representation in the House of Representatives follows similar principles
with different constituents. Proper representation in the House requires that
the people are able to elect representatives like them, not merely those from
a natural aristocracy or the wealthy upper class. The main impediment to
this in the Constitution is too few representatives; the House, he says, ought
to be at least doubled. Perhaps one representative per twelve thousand inhabitants would be a more appropriate ratio to obtain the advantages of a
smaller legislature that still enabled the people to be properly represented.

Republican principles, of course, demand more than simply representation. The executive power must be treated very carefully, for a monarch and
court are potentially every bit as dangerous to liberty as an aristocracy in
the legislature. The presidency established by the Constitution does nothing
to ease the Farmer's fears. Although the President is clearly not a king, his
potential to serve for life might make him indistinguishable from one. The
Federal Farmer approves a unitary executive, but he argues that eligibility
for reelection would encourage a President not only to focus exclusively on
his own reelection, but to try to position his children (or some other chosen
successors) for the office when he finally steps down. With a one-term limit,
the President would be motivated to make his mark on the office and the
country, because nothing he does can continue his time in office beyond
one term. This would prevent a President from aspiring to serve as king,
but it would not remove the temptation to create a royal court, if only for
a single term. The appointment power enables the President, with the help
of the Senate, to establish such a court, and the concept of a federal district
under the control of Congress would enable it. This district, he argues, will
be a "mere court" and "must soon be the great, the visible, and dazzling
centre, the mistress of fashions, and the fountain of politics."[45] A vain and
self-aggrandizing President will have ample opportunity to eschew republican simplicity for monarchical ostentation.

The idea of a federal district "must be founded in an apprehension of a
hostile disposition between the federal head and the state governments."
Even if no pseudoroyal court arises, the suggestion that Congress cannot be
beholden to state laws implies distrust of state governments, hardly a good
basis for a federal relationship. The absence of a clause guaranteeing to the
states powers not enumerated, as appeared in the Articles of Confederation,
further suggests that the states are to be conceded power only at the will of

Congress. The Supremacy Clause ensures that state constitutions will have no effect on federal laws, rendering the various bills of rights useless in such cases. In short, the state governments can do nothing to impede the national government, and provide no protection for the rights and liberties of citizens. The Farmer explains that "the state governments then we are told will stand between the arbitrary exercise of power and the people: true they may, but armless and helpless, perhaps, with the privilege of making a noise when hurt—this is no more than individuals may do."[46]

With the states effectively overpowered and undermined, then, the national government may govern directly over the entire country. Such government, the Farmer believes, is not possible in such a large country. It must act through either persuasion or force, and since it will be unable to persuade citizens at a great distance who will be rightfully skeptical of national legislation, force will be essential. Even if military force is unnecessary, the bureaucracy will be enough to undermine the prosperity of the country. "Military, and especially civil establishments," he explains, "are the necessary appendages of society; they are deductions from productive labor, and substantial wealth, in proportion to the number of men employed in them."[47] Such establishments threaten the liberty of the people as well as their prosperity; in any case the regular use of coercion spells the end of republican government.

In his penultimate letter, the Farmer explains what ought to be done with the Constitution. He emphasizes the importance of a federal republic, based on semisovereign states that serve "as the body or props, on which the federal head rests," such that the federal government cannot exist without them. The federal power, he argues, must operate through the states rather than bypassing them. The taxing power is a prime example: granting the national government the revenue from imposts is reasonable, but should the government need additional revenue through direct taxes, the states ought to become part of the collection. The Farmer suggests the preferred requisitions-first approach that would ultimately be embraced by almost all Anti-Federalists. He suggests that the national government should be given minimal powers, as an experiment; the powers of government can be expanded later as necessary, but powers already given are difficult to take back. There is no need to rush into anything; the Federalist contention that the situation is rapidly deteriorating is simply not true. "The defects of the confederation are extravagantly magnified," writes the Farmer, "and every species of pain we feel imputed to them."[48] This is an effort to mislead the people into a dangerous, rather than careful, innovation in government. The Farmer sees instead an opportunity for a carefully crafted confederate republic.

The Federal Farmer, like many Rights Anti-Federalists, addresses themes of consolidation, representation, and power, but continually returns to the liberty of the people. Could liberty be secured, he believed, the Constitution might be made acceptable. Here is where the Rights Anti-Federalists were the most open to compromise; a bill of rights, perhaps accompanied by some other small adjustments, would be suitable for them to support the Constitution. As such, it was this branch of the Anti-Federalists to which the Federalists turned for support when it became clear that they needed to convince at least some people to change their minds. It was this group that won a small victory with the first nine amendments to the Constitution, securing individual rights. It was these Rights Anti-Federalists who would ultimately hold the balance of power, especially in the crucial state of Virginia, and would pave the way for ratification over the objections of their colleagues.

3

First Impressions and Initial Objections

THE FIRST MAJOR battleground for the Constitution after the Convention was Congress. That body took up the debate over the proposed Constitution in late September, and already some of the strategies for both sides were taking shape. The debate was over what Congress should do with the Constitution. There was apparently no support for simply killing it by refusing to send it to the states, but several members, led by Richard Henry Lee, suggested amending it before it was sent for ratification. The Federalists wanted to see Congress approve the document and recommend it to the states. It was Abraham Clark of New Jersey, whose own sentiments on the matter were somewhat unclear, who suggested that Congress merely pass it on, without approval or even comment, with only the explanation that the Convention sent to Congress. Thus the Anti-Federalists were able to prevent official sanction of the document, while the Federalists saw it pass through Congress unscathed, and without the official objections that would likely have accompanied even an overall approval. Still, this was a Federalist victory, as Richard Henry Lee conceded: "They found it most eligible at last to transmit it merely, without approving or disapproving; provided nothing but the transmission should appear on the Journal. This compromise was settled and they took the opportunity of inserting the word 'unanimously,' which applied only to simple transmission, hoping to have it mistaken for an unanimous approbation of the thing."[1] Lee went a step further in a later letter, asserting that the opposition to the Constitution never had a chance against the Federalist majority in Congress. "It is sir most obvious," he wrote to Samuel Adams in late October, "that the Constitution proposed by the Convention could not have a dispassionate and impartial consideration in Congress. And indeed it had not." The Federalists were aggressive to the point of being pushy, and the Anti-Federalists simply did not have the votes to stop them. The claim of unanimity, misleading though it was, was seen by some as essential, because a divided Congress would weaken the chance of ratification. An enthusiastic endorsement was preferred, but the end result was better for the Federalists than any plausible alternative. As Edward Carrington of Virginia wrote to Madison before the debate began, "A lukewarmness in Congress will be made a ground of opposition by the unfriendly in the states."[2] It was unlikely for the Federalists to achieve the congressional endorsement they desired, though, because there was a small but dedicated opposition.

Nathan Dane raised the first objections, suggesting that the government established by the Constitution probably would not work unless it was supported by a standing army. It would thus advantage the few in power, and oppress everyone else. William Grayson was also vocal in opposition. It was Richard Henry Lee, though, that led the charge for the Anti-Federalists. He initially proposed that the Constitution be sent to the states with a statement that Congress is not authorized to act on it, because all thirteen states must agree to any alteration to the Articles of Confederation. When this failed, he suggested that Congress should examine and amend the proposed Constitution, or at least that the state conventions should be encouraged to do so. The need for amendments, and especially a bill of rights, was the primary thrust of his opposition; if Congress cannot alter the document, then surely the states should be allowed, and in fact encouraged, to propose amendments. After all, "To insist that it should go without amendments is like presenting a hungry man 50 dishes and insisting he should eat all or none."[3]

Lee offered to Congress a series of amendments, none of which gained any ground in the Federalist-dominated body. His goal was not to defeat the Constitution outright, but to improve it. He wanted to add a clause: "That standing Armies in times of peace are dangerous to liberty, and ought not to be permitted unless assented to by two thirds of the Members composing each House of the legislature under the new constitution."[4] This proposal would reappear in the amendments offered by several state conventions, and it became a central argument of the opposition. Similarly, Lee suggested some changes to the judicial system. He called for trial by jury for all cases, not just criminal cases, and he emphasized the importance of local trials. These proposals also became central to the Anti-Federalist position. Not all of Lee's proposals ended up in mainstream arguments, though. The concept of a privy council ultimately appeared in several places, including in an amendment proposed by the New York Ratifying Convention, but Lee's council would have had an unusual level of power. Although the eleven members would be selected by the President, Lee was willing to give to this council the power to approve all appointments, presumably including judges. Furthermore, the Vice President would be replaced as well, leaving the Senate to choose its own presiding officer. Such a council would give more power to the President, an idea that came to be quite distasteful to most Anti-Federalists. By the Virginia Ratifying Convention, when Patrick Henry railed against the Constitution for creating a presidential monarchy, few Anti-Federalists would have supported such a council as an arm of the presidency. Lee's final three proposals all pertained to the structure of Congress. His suggestion that the size of the House be increased became a very common one for the Anti-Federalists. His suggestion that the Senate be apportioned by population was far less popular, but certainly fit the emerging democratic principles of the opponents of the Constitution. His sincerity here, though, may be called into question when one considers his proposal to alter legislative voting. This ill-formed idea seemed to suggest that the House of Representatives ought to vote by state on laws, a peculiar idea that would have undermined the concept of popular representation in the House. It also would have made Lee's suggestion for expanding the House just so much needless expense, as the additional members would not have additional votes. This apparent inconsistency is emblematic of the entire set of proposals put forward by Lee; it was a haphazard agenda, hastily assembled in response to an initial reading of the Constitution. This reflected the Anti-Federalist position in September 1787: there was little time to organize, and even less to develop a coherent opposition theory of government. The Anti-Federalist position, as much as it was unified by the eventual ratification, developed organically from various unconnected and sometimes conflicting proposals.

At least one aspect of the Anti-Federalist position emerged clearly, though, from this first debate: an emphasis on the need for a bill of rights. Lee, in several letters in early October, stressed this point. "In this state of things," he wrote to George Mason, "the patriot voice is raised in vain for such changes and securities as reason and experience prove to be necessary against the encroachments of power upon the indispensable rights of human nature."[5] In a letter to William Shippen, Jr., he elaborated, articulating the beginnings of a theory of government that would underlie much Anti-Federalist thought. "If all men were wise and good there would be no necessity for government or law. But the folly and the vice of human nature renders government and laws necessary for the many, and restraints indispensable to prevent oppression from those who are entrusted with the administration of one and the dispensation of the other."[6] Of course, there was a distinct strand of opposition thinking that was more intensely democratic, trusting in human nature, but the most influential Anti-Federalists (and in fact most Federalists as well) tended to subscribe to this understanding of humanity.

PENNSYLVANIA CALLS A RATIFYING CONVENTION

Even before Congress officially submitted the Constitution to the states for their consideration, the Pennsylvania legislature had begun discussing the logistics of a ratifying convention. The Constitution, accompanied by a letter from the Pennsylvania delegates, was introduced to the legislature on September 17, the day the Convention adjourned. Benjamin Franklin, the state's chief executive, addressed the legislature the next day, advocating ratification and suggesting that Pennsylvania might offer to cede land to Congress for the nation's capital. During the next week and a half, a series of petitions were presented to the legislature, all calling for ratification. When delegate George Clymer proposed on September 28 that the legislature call a convention, Robert Whitehill, who would be a leading Anti-Federalist in the state's ratifying convention, suggested postponing the decision, but as the legislative session was about to expire he merely suggested waiting until the afternoon or the next day; the Anti-Federalists were unlikely to succeed in any more of a delay than that, unless they could convince enough delegates to wait for a decision by Congress on the Constitution. This, ultimately, was the argument and hope of the Anti-Federalists. They failed in this attempt, and on that morning, the same day Congress would decide to send the Constitution to the states, the Pennsylvania legislature voted to call a ratifying convention.

Even in their critique of the Constitution, the Anti-Federalists in the legislature were very mild. "Of the plan I believe there can be no doubt of its being wisely calculated for the purposes intended," said William Findley, who would also later be a key opposition voice in the state's convention, "but nothing is perfect, and this may be as well as could be expected, and I consider it as very deserving the commendation it received; but this can be no reason for hurrying on the measure with such precipitancy." Meanwhile, the Federalists responded with much stronger and more personal attacks, suggesting that the Constitution was too important "to be assassinated by the hand of intrigue and cabal." During these legislative debates the Federalists were forceful and confident while their opponents were hesitant and timid; clearly the opposition had not yet had an opportunity to plan and coordinate its efforts. This was essentially the Federalist plan, to act before opposition could be organized, or, in the words of Whitehill, "driving it down our throats."[7]

Whitehill's words proved to be prophetic. After the majority voted in the morning session of the twenty-eighth to call a convention, the afternoon session was short nineteen members, and thus failed to reach a quorum. The

Anti-Federalists, in order to halt business, had decided not to attend. When the sergeant-at-arms was sent to retrieve them, they refused. The next day, with the same members again failing to attend, the decision of Congress arrived from New York, and the sergeant-at-arms was again dispatched. Upon finding two of the absent members, just enough for a quorum, he showed them the resolution from Congress; the two, James McCalmont and Jacob Miley, still resisted. By this time a crowd, or perhaps more accurately a mob, had formed, and "broke into their lodgings, seized them, dragged them through the streets to the State House, and thrust them into the assembly room, with clothes torn and faces white with rage. The quorum was now complete."[8] McCalmont immediately requested that he be permitted to leave, but as he was necessary for a quorum, he was not granted that request.[9] Since the penalty for his absence was a fine of five shillings, McCalmont tried to pay it and leave, but was not permitted. He even attempted to walk out the door, but was apparently stopped, likely by members of the mob that dragged him there.[10] Forced to stay, McCalmont then proceeded to propose a number of alterations to the legislation for calling the convention, attempting to alter the place and time of meeting. He was of course unsuccessful, and the Federalists proceeded to set the details of the convention without Anti-Federalist input. The personal nature of the battle would continue throughout the ratification debates with ad hominem attacks and personal insults at times outnumbering the actual arguments. Such attacks occurred in most of the states, but in Pennsylvania they were particularly virulent.

After the legislative fight, the members who left the session published their reasons, explaining that it was the "constant practice" of the legislature to introduce legislation well in advance of any vote: "the rules were adhered so strictly that even the building of a bridge, or the laying out a road, could not be determined on without this form; but this the most important of all matters was to be done by surprise and, as we conceived, with design to preclude you from having it in your power to deliberate on the subject."[11] This explanation was the first Anti-Federalist writing in Pennsylvania to emphasize the importance of careful deliberation; in Pennsylvania of all states this advice was very pertinent, but essentially ignored, at least by the Federalist majority. The minority laid out a basic Anti-Federalist position. Although the document merely listed arguments without detailed explanation, it identified eight distinct flaws in the Constitution, which became significant objections for the Anti-Federalists.[12] It closed with a suggestion that the Articles should have been amended rather than discarded, and that the central government should have been given only the powers "to regulate commerce, equalize the impost, collect it throughout the United States, and have the entire jurisdiction over maritime affairs, leaving the exercise of internal taxation to the separate states."[13]

The first published critique of the Constitution in Pennsylvania came from an anonymous writer on September 26. It was not a harsh critique; in fact, the writer described the Constitution as "a well-wrought piece of stuff" likely to promote "the happiness and respectability of the United States."[14] The writer presented five objections: the proportion for representation ought to be fixed in a constitution, Congress should not have control over the times and places of elections, Congress should meet in a more convenient month than December, Congress should not have power to lay a capitation tax, and juries should proceed by majority rather than unanimity. The argument concerning juries in particular suggests the diversity of critique among the opponents of the Constitution, while the first two were fairly common objections.

This rather light critique touched off a particularly vituperative exchange in the newspapers. The four authors involved ultimately exchanged more insults than arguments. "Tar and Feathers" responded first, calling the original writer a "mock-patriot" and suggesting that he deserved public reprobation for his opposition. "Nestor" took the attack a step further, accusing the original writer of listing "imaginary defects" and "groundless conjectures" in order to poison the people's minds toward the Constitution. "Fair Play" responded with the assertion that an open discussion was needed. Such a discussion was unlikely, though, since the Anti-Federalists were nothing but "modern TORIES," according to Tar and Feathers. The Federalists, on the other hand, were, in Fair Play's words, "either *downright Tories, lukewarm Whigs*, or disaffected to the cause of America and the Revolution." Patriotic Whigs, it would seem, did not participate in the Tory-dominated discussion. The original writer, now writing as "Tullius," fired a few shots back at his interlocutors, effectively defending (but not really adding to) his original argument.[15]

Unfortunately, such attacks were not rare. The Federalists were notably more prolific in their insults early in the debate in Pennsylvania. The seceding members of the assembly were described in one newspaper as being "as the swine of old, possessed," "lying prophets," and "miscreants," and were even compared directly to Satan. They were accused of treating their constituents "like children who must be closely watched." Their report was described as "a strong sample of ingenious malignity and ill-nature—a master-piece of high coloring in the scare-crow way." One Federalist went so far as to suggest that the report must not have been written by any of the assemblymen, since they were "too illiterate to compose such an address." The Federalists also resorted to publishing essays falsely attributed to Anti-Federalists, portraying anyone who might oppose the Constitution as self-interested and anti-American. The Anti-Federalists, for their part, published personal attacks on Federalist leaders; Robert Morris and James Wilson were the most popular targets. Wilson was accused of inciting a mob to attack the residences of several key Anti-Federalists in Philadelphia on the night of the elections for the convention.[16] Even Benjamin Franklin and George Washington did not escape criticism; Centinel suggested that the concurrence of these two should in no way influence opinions on the Constitution:

> These characters [the Federalists] flatter themselves that they have lulled all distrust and jealousy of their new plan, by gaining the concurrence of the two men in whom America has the highest confidence, and now triumphantly exult in the completion of their long meditated schemes of power and aggrandisement. I would be very far from insinuating that the two illustrious personages alluded to, have not the welfare of their country at heart, but that the unsuspecting goodness and zeal of the one, has been imposed on, in a subject of which he must be necessarily inexperienced, from his other arduous engagements; and that the weakness and indecision attendant on old age, has been practiced on in the other.[17]

These were serious accusations, much bolder than most Anti-Federalists would dare. But it seems likely that many Anti-Federalist leaders, in Pennsylvania and elsewhere, concurred with the general sentiment Centinel presents. The essay by "John Humble" took a different approach, suggesting that the Constitution would establish an aristocracy, and that the Federalists wanted the "Lowborn" people to approve it without really considering it.[18] The Federalist strategy in the state certainly offers justification for this claim.

The Anti-Federalists, though, were hardly more virtuous. When the Pennsylvania assembly met in November to work out final details for the convention, including the payment of delegates, the Anti-Federalists once again attempted to obstruct the Federalist majority. Efforts were made to delay and even defeat the measure to pay delegates. The Anti-Federalists lost a significant battle to establish the quorum for the ratifying convention at two-thirds of members. After the Federalists saw their opponents prevent a quorum in the legislature by walking out, they wanted to prevent such obstructionist tactics in the convention, and set the quorum at a simple majority. The assembly elections that occurred on October 9, between the first and second legislative debates on the ratifying convention, suggest that the people of Pennsylvania had largely made up their minds, and that the legislators tended to match their constituents. Turnover was low, with the leaders of both sides generally reelected. The Anti-Federalists gained some seats, but the Federalists retained a majority. This, of course, did not make the debate any less contentious or partisan.

There were a few moderates in the state, however. One such individual, writing as "M. C.," suggested that a convention be called for drafting a bill of rights, without otherwise modifying the proposed Constitution. Such a bill of rights could be sent to the states for ratification along with the Constitution, preventing the danger of a second general convention while answering the concerns about the preservation of liberties.[19] This suggestion apparently won few converts despite wide reprintings, as the debate became increasingly polarized. The Rights Anti-Federalist position would dominate the opposition in Pennsylvania's ratifying convention, but the radical democrats were more active in the newspapers. M. C.'s idea may not have been practical, but it would likely have led to a more agreeable document with a wider base of support; the Anti-Federalists were not yet organized, though, so the Federalists were not in a conciliatory mood.

THE NATIONAL DEBATE BEGINS

By mid-November, when the Pennsylvania Convention met, the debate over the Constitution had begun in earnest in newspapers across the country. "Cato" was the first major Anti-Federalist to publish, and in his first letter he merely urges caution:

> Deliberate, therefore, on this new national government with coolness; analize it with criticism; and reflect on it with candour: if you find that the influence of a powerful few, or the exercise of a standing army, will always be directed and exerted for your welfare alone, and not to the agrandizement of themselves, and that it will secure to you and your posterity happiness at home, and national dignity and respect from abroad, adopt it—if it will not, reject it with indignation—better to be where you are, for the present, than insecure forever afterwards.[20]

This was typical of the early Anti-Federalist arguments, designed to counter the sometimes frantic push by the Federalists (most notably in Pennsylvania) to secure a quick ratification. It also served to counter the appeal to authority, especially to Franklin and Washington but also to the Convention more generally, on which many Federalist defenses of the Constitution relied.

About a week after Cato first appeared in New York, Centinel began publishing in Pennsylvania, adopting a more populist and strident tone. He too urged caution, chiding Pennsylvania Federalists for their "frenzy of enthusiasm" in trying to rush ratification, and insisting that the Constitution "ought to be dispassionately and deliberately examined," with "its own intrinsic merit the only criterion" for supporting it. His first essay, with its emphasis on the fullest possible representation and participation, was the first significant statement of the Democratic Anti-Federalist position.[21]

This position was not confined to Pennsylvania. In New England about two weeks after Centinel's first essay, "A Gentleman in a Neighbouring State" (Massachusetts, that is [the essay was published in Connecticut]) staked out a populist position, suggesting that "The form of government prescribed [by the Constitution] is too COMPLEX, couched in terms, in many instances *doubtful* as though there was some *art* used to cover the full extent of the powers delegated, to be easily understood, by all who ought to accept or reject the same."[22]

New England was not generally either radical or especially democratic, though. In early October, an anonymous writer in Massachusetts stated concisely the Power Anti-Federalist position, a position far more common in the northeast than the democratic one. This essay, widely reprinted, made the basic arguments of Power Anti-Federalism: the representatives in Congress are too few and too far removed to reflect the interests of their states, the regulation of commerce vested in Congress will extend to the internal commerce of the states, states will be unable to tax, the federal judiciary will take over a large part of state jurisdiction, and changes should be made before a system is adopted, because to do otherwise would make such changes far more difficult and less likely. About a week later in Virginia, no more a hotbed of democracy than Massachusetts, an essay published under the name "Cato Uticensis" also took up the cause of Power Anti-Federalism, suggesting that, although Congress under the Articles was too weak, the proposed Congress would be far too strong. He focused in particular on the question of taxation, suggesting that at the very least the tax collectors ought to be citizens of the state in which they collect. Instead, the Constitution sets up a competition between state and federal tax collectors, a contest that the states are sure to lose.[23]

In early November, the Federal Farmer joined the debate, laying out the importance of protecting rights in designing a national government, and effectively articulating the argument for a mixed form of government between confederation and consolidation.[24]

Shortly after the publication of the letters of the Federal Farmer, a letter from Richard Henry Lee to Edmund Randolph was printed in several newspapers. Lee made much the same argument that he made in Congress, including a list of amendments he proposed at that time, but his emphasis had shifted. He contended that the President and Senate jointly have most, and in some cases all, of the legislative power, as well as all of the executive power. The House of Representatives, by comparison, would be "a mere shread or rag of representation"; the power given to it "renders that house of little effect to promote good, or restrain bad government."[25] What power the House does have it shares with the Senate and President, and this legislative power covers almost any imaginable purpose, with no protection for the rights of individuals. Lee also suggests that commercial laws ought to require the votes of two-thirds of the members in both houses, to protect the southern states; this was to become a fairly common argument in Virginia and further south. In the text of the letter, he writes as a Power Anti-Federalist, but his proposed amendments are still grounded in the importance of a bill of rights. His position shifted somewhat in the first several weeks after the proposal of the Constitution; by this point he clearly would object to the Constitution even if a bill of rights were added, because the powers were simply too great. Still, Lee can best be understood as a preeminent Rights Anti-Federalist, because even his discussion of power was premised on the idea that rights are not adequately protected for individuals, but he was one of the earliest Anti-Federalists to begin to synthesize these two sets of objections.

It was in the New York newspapers, though, that the most significant debate occurred. The famous *Federalist* essays began with the publication of the first one on October 27, nine days after the publication of the first essay by Brutus; the two would go back and forth, responding almost directly to each other, and addressing similar questions.[26] Even in the absence of other writings these two series alone would have provided this state with the most substantial and high-minded debate in the country. This debate was about power; Brutus saw a dangerous ambiguity, possibly intentional, in the powers granted by the Constitution, and argued for a clear delineation of the distribution of power between state and national governments, and between branches of the national government.

In his third letter in late October, Cato, like Brutus, began to appear distinctly as a Power Anti-Federalist, explaining that republican government cannot exist in a large consolidated republic, and that the state republics will not survive the consolidation of the Constitution. Even several of the states were already too large for republican government. Thus to establish the kind of supreme powers in the national government that the Constitution confers is to undermine republican principles. Cato's fourth letter began a discussion of the specific powers of the government, and offered the earliest (and perhaps most extensive) substantial critique of the presidency. His position complemented that of Brutus, especially because the latter did not say much concerning the executive branch. Between Cato and Brutus, the opposition in New York was predominately within the paradigm of Power Anti-Federalism.

Although the debate in New York was dominated by big names (or perhaps big pseudonyms)—Publius, Brutus, Federal Farmer, and Cato—several less-known Anti-Federalists elaborated the opposition position in the state. In particular, there was also a distinct current of Democratic Anti-Federalism in the state. "Cincinnatus" takes up the issue of a bill of rights from a very democratic perspective. "A Son of Liberty" strikes a similarly democratic tone, going so far as to imply that a government under the Constitution will be akin to a return to British rule, complete with the implementation of "An odious and detestable *Stamp act*." "Brutus, Jr.," who evidently found the original Brutus inadequate, suggests that many of the delegates to the Philadelphia Convention were "possessed of high aristocratic ideas, and the most sovereign contempt of the common people." He also writes that the union is in no real danger, a common theme of the Democratic Anti-Federalists.[27] In fact, he writes, "If any tumults arise, they will be justly chargeable on those artful and ambitious men, who are determined to cram this government down the throats of the people, before they have time deliberately to examine it."[28]

In Massachusetts, too, there was a Democratic Anti-Federalist opposition, following the earlier essay by the Gentleman. Two notable writers stake out this position in series of essays. "John DeWitt" began with the common suggestion that America is in fact well situated, and not in any great danger, and thus he urged careful deliberation. He called the Constitution an "overturn of all individual Governments," a "new-fashioned set of ideas," and a "total dereliction of those sentiments which animated us in 1775." Because of this strong opposition position, he did not call for a bill of rights; in fact he explicitly declined to make that argument: "That the want of a Bill of Rights to accompany this proposed System, is a solid objection to it, provided there is nothing exceptionable in the System itself, I do not assert." He did not object to such a guarantee, though: "If," he continued, "there is at any time, a propriety in having one, it would not have been amiss here." However, such a guarantee was not strictly necessary, because for a Democratic Anti-Federalist, it was self-evident that "That which is not expressly granted, is of course retained." The reason for this is closely tied to the concept of popular sovereignty: "It will not be denied, that this people, of any under Heaven, have a right of living under a government of their own choosing."[29]

John DeWitt is predominantly concerned with the question of representation. He critiques the structure of the House of Representatives, suggesting that the individuals elected to that house "become strangers to the very people choosing them, they reside at a distance from you, you have no controul over them, you cannot observe their conduct, and they have to consult and finally be guided by twelve other States, whose interests are, in all material points, directly opposed to yours." Thus, he suggests, the House is limited in power, and each member of it is nearly powerless. By contrast, the Senate, which he described as "the only powerful branch" in the government, "totally fails in a fair, faithful, honest image of the people, and in equality of representation."[30] The people, he says, will not be heard; this simple fact makes the government proposed by the Constitution totally unacceptable and illegitimate. In the process of making this argument, John DeWitt effectively dismissed both Power and Rights Anti-Federalist positions.

> Place the Frame of Government proposed, in the most favorable point of view, magnify the priviledges held forth to the people to their fullest extent, and enlarge as much as you please, upon the great checks therein provided, notwithstanding all which, there cannot remain a doubt in the mind of any reflecting man, that it is a System purely Aristocratical, calculated to find employment for men of ambition, and to furnish means of sporting with the sacred principles of human nature.[31]

Even if the rights of the people are secured, and even if the checks and balances keep the exercise of power carefully controlled, the Constitution will still establish an aristocracy. Though Centinel may claim that there is not much variation among Anti-Federalists, DeWitt suggests that anything short of total opposition is a vote for aristocracy. Just as the possible fusion of Power and Rights Anti-Federalism is evident in Richard Henry Lee's shifting position, so is the incompatibility of radical Democratic Anti-Federalism with more temperate opposition.

"Vox Populi" presents a similar argument, though he does not cover as much ground. He objects in particular to the clause enabling Congress to set the time, place, and manner of elections, and he discusses the incompatibility of the national and state oaths of office. He also mentions the common Anti-Federalist objections on the issue of taxes and the absence of a bill of rights. Unlike John DeWitt, Vox Populi writes that a bill of rights is necessary in a government of "genuine civil liberty and *undefiled republicanism.*" His argument is grounded entirely in the notion of popular sovereignty. The constitution of Massachusetts, he argues, can only be changed by a vote of two-thirds of the people, so a majority of a convention has no authority to adopt a Constitution that would effectively alter the sovereign nature of the state. A Federalist writing as "Examiner" responded to the first essay of Vox Populi, accusing the latter of basing his arguments on jealousy and distrust.[32] Vox Populi accepts that characterization, pontificating on the origins of government:

> If I was not *jealous* that some person would injure me in some way, what could I have to induce me to give up my *natural* liberty, and part with part of my natural rights? If I did not *distrust* the rectitude of my fellow-creatures' future conduct towards me, what advantage could I ever expect to reap from a system of jurisprudence? Are not all the advantages which a person can expect to derive from entering into a state of civil government (or at least all he ought to expect) of a negative nature? Are they not all comprehended in this one general idea, *a prevention of injuries from others?*[33]

This theory of government is grounded in popular sovereignty, the primary emphasis of the Democratic Anti-Federalists. The very beginning of Vox Populi's essay lays out a very democratic position regarding the ratification debate: "I conceive it to be the *duty*, as well as the PRIVILEGE of each and every citizen of this commonwealth to investigate this matter fully, and ripen his mind for a suitable answer to the important question."[34] Clearly, this Anti-Federalist presents himself as a democrat.

Still, the dominant opposition position in the northeast was Power Anti-Federalism.[35] Elbridge Gerry predicted in a private letter that "the eastern States will soon rebel against it [the proposed Constitution], for it is not a Government adapted to their Genius, Habits, or aversion to arbitrary power." When William Widgery, in the legislature, suggested holding a popular vote on ratification, it was to alleviate the costs for towns sending delegates, not because of a desire for a more democratic process; his concerns were allayed by a decision to pay delegates out of the state treasury. The *Cumberland Gazette* of October 25 reported that several prominent (but unidentified) residents of Boston opposed the Constitution: "The length of time for which the President is to be chosen, and the extensive powers that are to be vested in the Judicial Court of the United States, are both objected to by those Gentlemen; who further say—that to adopt the Constitution in its present form, would be paving the way to an Aristocracy." "Hanno" objected to giving up the power to regulate commerce, going so far as to suggest that the people of Philadelphia voted to adopt the Constitution because they expected it to make that city "the center of all the trade of the continent." He suggested that powers over commerce should be very carefully considered. "That commercial regulations, particularly a navigation-act, will be beneficial, is agreed on all hands: but great attention is necessary to perfect a system of trade and revenue, which shall operate equally on all parts of the empire."[36]

There were variations in the Power Anti-Federalist position, and in particular some differences between opposition in New York and Massachusetts, but there was a great deal of consensus and consistency as well. "An Observor" summed up a fairly moderate form of this position, writing that "there should be a confederated national government, but . . . it should be one which would have a controul over national and external matters only, and not interfere with the internal regulations and police of the different states in the union." The emphasis here was on the balance of power, not the sovereignty of the people. William Symmes, in a letter to Peter Osgood, was typical of the northeastern Power Anti-Federalism in his description of the powers granted to Congress—"A more general dedition or surrender of all ye property in the United States to Congress could not perhaps have been framed"—and to the President—"was ever a commission so *brief,* so *general* as this of our President?" He particularly objected to the ambiguity, lamenting that "Too much is left perhaps for the future Congress to supply, which when supplied will be no part of the constitution."[37] Symmes contended that as much as can be explicitly written into the Constitution ought to be. The reliance on Congress to fill in the gaps on elections, on the extent of powers, on the jurisdiction of the courts, on the structure of government in the states, and on most other matters not fully enumerated in the Constitution was dangerous, if not downright foolish.

While the debate in Pennsylvania raged and the debates in New York and Massachusetts were warming up, the discussion was fairly muted south of Pennsylvania. In Maryland, former convention delegate Luther Martin published his objections as a pamphlet in January 1788, and the first significant Anti-Federalist essays (signed "A Farmer") did not appear until February. In the Carolinas, the debate did not really start until the South Carolina legislature began discussion in January about holding a ratifying convention, though a few opposition writings appeared, including that of a poet who asked his readers,

Ye, who have bled in Freedom's sacred cause,
Ah, why desert her maxims and her laws
When thirteen states are moulded into one,
Your rights are vanish'd and your honors gone.[38]

In Georgia, there was a little debate in November, but there was very little dissent in the state. It was in Virginia that the southern debate centered, and the Virginia Anti-Federalists tended to follow George Mason and Richard Henry Lee in emphasizing individual liberty and the absence of a bill of rights. William Grayson, who opposed the Constitution in Congress, emphasized the importance of a bill of rights in a letter to William Short: "In the first place I think liberty a thing of too much importance to be trusted on the ground of *implication*: it should rest on principles expressed in the clearest & most unequivocal manner."[39] He discussed the powers of the Constitution as well, but it was the people's liberty that primarily animated his opposition.

Although the Virginia opposition had many substantive objections, this was not a group as adamantly opposed to stronger central government (or even ratification of the proposed Constitution) as the more democratic ideologues in Pennsylvania, or even the Anti-Federalists of the northeast. The opposition in this state took a more moderate position; an anonymous correspondent in the *Virginia Independent Chronicle* was typical of this: "I have not only no objection to, but am extremely desirous of, a strong and general government, provided the fundamental principles of liberty be well secured." Even Richard Henry Lee, one of the most outspoken Anti-Federalists in all the states, believed that "the new Constitution (properly amended) as it contains many good regulations, may be admitted." He repeated this sentiment in a letter to Washington, expressing hope for amendments securing the rights of the people, added prior to ratification.[40]

The push for amendments, and especially amendments prior to ratification, was as strong here as it was anywhere. A writer in Virginia calling himself "A True Friend" and claiming to be a mediator of sorts between the two sides, suggested that the objections to the Constitution largely came down to the absence of a bill of rights, which ought to be added:

Let us then insert in the first page of this constitution, as a preamble to it, a declaration of our rights, or an enumeration of our prerogatives, as a sovereign people; that they may never hereafter be unknown, forgotten or contradicted by our representatives, our delegates, our servants in Congress: Let the recognition, and solemn ratification by Congress, of this declaration of rights, be made the *sine qua non* of the adoption of this new fœderal constitution, by each state. This precious, this comfortable page, will be the ensign, to which on any future contestation, time may induce between the governed and those intrusted with the powers of government, the asserters of liberty may rally, and constitutionally defend it.[41]

The idea that the addition of a bill of rights would answer Anti-Federalist objections carried some weight in Virginia, where Rights Anti-Federalism was the prominent opposition paradigm, but a similar suggestion in Pennsylvania, for example, did not resonate.[42] Still, the minority in the Pennsylvania Ratifying Convention would take up a distinctly Rights Anti-Federalist position, much less radical than the position of Centinel and the other radical opposition essayists in the state. As the Pennsylvania Convention was the first to be convened, all eyes were on Pennsylvania in late November for the first real test of the Federalists' strength.

4

Opposition in Pennsylvania

IN THE FINAL MONTHS of 1787, everyone was watching the state of Pennsylvania, where the first ratifying convention was to be convened. The writers in this state were more prolific, and the debates more intense, than anywhere else during this period. Much of this public conversation centered on a speech by James Wilson in the Pennsylvania state house on October 6 in defense of the Constitution, which became a lightning rod for Anti-Federalist attacks.[1] An impartial reader of the published text of the speech must acknowledge that it entails a serious attempt to answer the objections that had been raised against the Constitution. The main argument was intended to counter the increasingly frequent demands for a bill of rights to be added. Wilson argued that the national government established by the Constitution would be one of enumerated powers, in which anything not given is reserved by the states or the people; the state governments, by contrast, are governments of implied powers, so they possess any power that is not reserved. Thus a bill of rights would be at best superfluous, and at worst dangerous, as it would imply that the government had powers not expressly delegated. He then answered a series of specific objections: trial by jury will be preserved in the states, according to the varied local laws concerning juries; a small standing army is necessary, even in times of peace, to defend the borders of the United States; the Senate, far from establishing an aristocracy, cannot do anything without the concurrence of the House, the President, or both; the states will not be destroyed, because they are constituent parts of the system, and essential to the formation of the national government; and Congress will almost certainly rely on the impost, because direct taxes will face popular opposition, and will be unnecessary anyway. He suggested that the opposition to the Constitution has largely been driven by self-interested state politicians interested in protecting their own power.

Wilson's speech inspired a detailed refutation by "An Old Whig," who found Wilson's contention that all powers not given are reserved to be false and pernicious. The powers granted are vague and expansive, with no clause to limit Congress from interpreting its powers in the broadest possible manner. Between the Necessary and Proper and Supremacy clauses, "The Congress are therefore vested with the supreme legislative power, without controul." Furthermore, the guarantees of rights in the state constitutions cannot apply to the laws of Congress because of the Supremacy Clause. An Old Whig feared that the freedom of the press and trial by jury in civil cases were in danger, with the only safeguard being that Congress is unlikely to exercise its power, hardly any protection at all. He pointed out that the fact that Congress would be unlikely to ever infringe on rights is at least irrelevant to the question of whether to add a bill of rights, and probably dangerous. "Wise and prudent men," he suggests, in perhaps the best short statement of the necessity of a bill of rights, "always take care to guard against danger beforehand, and to make themselves safe whilst it is yet in their power to do it without inconvenience or risk.—[W]ho shall answer for the ebbings and flowings of opinion, or be able to say what will be the fashionable frenzy of the next generation?"[2] The amendment process described in the Constitution is certainly inconvenient; in fact, no amendments are ever likely to be made under that difficult system. By his fourth essay, an Old Whig stakes out a clear Rights Anti-Federalist position. Any legitimate government must rest on a bill of rights, because the people in forming the social compact do not give up all of their liberties. He discusses freedom of conscience at some length in his fifth letter, identifying it as the first and most important of the rights that ought to be protected. Such a right can be infringed solely through the use of enumerated powers, particularly the power over the militias and the power to tax. This is a direct refutation of Wilson's contention that a bill of rights is unnecessary because Congress will not have the power to interfere with the liberties of the people.

In his second letter, Centinel also responds to Wilson. Although he dismisses the speech as "the most flimsey sophistry," he proceeds to critique Wilson's major points. His critique adds little to an Old Whig's, but it is as lively as the rest of Centinel's arguments, though perhaps a bit less radical than his first, or at least less attack-oriented.[3] He still sees aristocracy at every turn, and he defends the unorthodox actions of the dissenting minority in the legislature. Centinel closes his second letter with a parting shot, of course, directed primarily at Wilson but also at the Federalists more generally; he insists that "such false detestable *patriots*" will lead the nation "into the jaws of *despotism* and *ruin*."[4]

An Old Whig, as a Rights Anti-Federalist, was not so hostile to antidemocratic components in a constitution. He critiques the presidency in much the way Centinel does, claiming that the holder of that office "is in reality to be a KING as much *a King as the King of Great-Britain*, and a King too of the worst kind;—an elective King."⁵ His solution, though, departs from that of Centinel; the office of the President, he argues, must be either substantially weakened or changed into a hereditary monarchy. In such a case there is no contest over who is to be king, and the "scene of horror and confusion" that the election of the President will present may be avoided. To set up such an office to which ambitious men may aspire is to endanger the republican nature of government; a stable hereditary monarch would be preferable, but a weaker presidency would be even better. The idea of reintroducing a monarch, anathema to Centinel, is merely distasteful to an Old Whig.

The Democratic Anti-Federalist position in Pennsylvania was not limited to Centinel. Two weeks before the convention, a new writer, signing his essays "Philadelphiensis," joined the debate with a position nearly as radical as Centinel's. He began, in the spirit of that author, with an attack on Federalist methods:

> When the advocates of a cause use their endeavours to stop a free and thorough investigation of the subject, we as naturally and as justly infer that the cause is a bad one, as that two and two make four. A good cause, like pure gold may be tried in the fire, and yet retain its full weight and value; or like the utensils of husbandry, grow brighter and fitter for use the more it is handled.⁶

He accuses the Federalists of answering "*reason* and *argument* with scurrility and personal invective," an accusation that, while not exactly unfair, could as easily be applied to the opponents of the Constitution. He also accuses the Federalists of trying to foster a one-sided debate by resorting to casting public aspersions upon the patriotism of those who oppose ratification. This, he claims, speaks volumes about how the proposed government would operate in practice.

Philadelphiensis continued to publish essays while the state convention met, with his fourth such essay appearing on the date of ratification. In that essay he begins by laying out his motives in writing against the Constitution:

> *My Fellow-Citizens,* I do not write to inflame your minds, but to inform them. I do not write with a view to excite jealousies, and exhibit imaginary evils, but to promote your peace: I have no intentions of encouraging you to oppose or alter your present free government; but on the contrary, I advise you, yea, I entreat you, not to change it for one that is worse: if you cannot procure a better, why, be doing [away?] with the old bad one.⁷

One must be quite generous to accept Philadelphiensis's contention that he does not aim to inflame, but he does predominately stick to arguments rather than invective and attack. He sets up the decision on ratification as one between freedom and slavery; even as he urges his fellow citizens to weigh carefully their alternatives, he makes it clear that there is only one acceptable outcome. To the freedom of the press he adds the freedom of conscience as the liberties destroyed by the Constitution, plus trial by jury and protection of property. He suggests that a standing army will be necessary to enforce the laws and keep the people in line. The expense of this standing army will keep taxes high, and will prevent Congress from raising an adequate navy, something that he contends that the states could do fairly easily under the Articles of Confederation. Such a circumstance, he suggests, is far preferable in terms of national defense to what the Constitution offers.

In attacking the Constitution, Philadelphiensis frequently looks back to the American Revolution for guidance on the issues of liberty and tyranny, suggesting that the Constitution would in fact be a reversal of the war for independence:

> Before we confirm this new constitution, let us ask ourselves this question—For what did we withdraw our allegiance from Great Britain; was it because the yoke of George the third was not sufficiently galling, that we cast it off, at the expence of so much blood and treasure, in order to accommodate ourselves with one of our own construction more intolerable? or, was it because the tyrant was three thousand miles off, that we revolted, in order to appoint one at home, who should correct us with scorpions instead of whips? If this were your design, I congratulate you on your success; hesitate not a moment then in the adoption of the new constitution: It is a perfect model, and answers your intentions completely.[8]

The Constitution is dangerous precisely because it would return the United States to tyranny, but of a more sinister and much closer kind. He has harsh words for those who participated in the Revolution, yet wrote this Constitution: "Unparalleled duplicity! that men should oppose tyranny under a pretence of patriotism, that they might themselves become the tyrants." He goes on to claim that the question of ratification is "an object of much greater concern" than even independence from Britain.[9] On this last point, it is clear that he was right, and in fact it seems clear from the debates that his contemporaries, on both sides of the question, agreed.

The essays of Philadelphiensis were not all attack. He does offer some constructive ideas on what government ought to do, and how it might best be set up:

> [W]e want an efficient federal government; we want an efficient federal government: this is the constant theme of the day. Well, my friends, I grant this. But what is the ultimate end of an efficient government: in what should it be efficient? I hope you anticipate my answer. The only thing in which a government should be efficient, is to protect the *liberties*, *lives*, and *property* of the people governed, from foreign and domestic violence. This, and this only is what every government should do effectually. For any government to do more than this is impossible, and every one that falls short of it is defective.[10]

This is not a simple call for a bill of rights; the very structure of a government must be such as to protect the freedom of the people. He does not follow Centinel in suggesting a simple unicameral system, except insofar as he supports the Articles. He does, however, endorse amending the Articles to make them more effective as a national governing document: "Were some additional powers for regulating commerce, and the *impost duties* for a limited time, granted to the present Congress; this would probably answer all our purposes."[11] He suggests in passing his hopes that a second convention will work on such amendments.

During the convention, an Old Whig took up the issue of amendments, asserting the right of the people, acting through the ratifying conventions, to alter the Constitution before approving it. They have a right, he says, to make any changes they collectively see fit, and he suggests a process by which amendments might be obtained. He proposes that each state's convention propose amendments to the Constitution. He argues that these amendments, like the objections already published by Anti-Federalists across the United States, are likely to "harmonize in a very great degree."[12] These amendments can then be submitted to Congress for another convention to be called. This second convention could then take into account these amendments and produce a modified document; the decision of this convention, he suggests, ought to be made binding. If such a convention cannot agree, or cannot be called, only then should the Constitution as written be presented to new state conventions, for a simple up-or-down vote without consideration of amendments.

Even with Centinel, an Old Whig, and Philadelphiensis dominating the debate, the Power Anti-Federalist position was not entirely absent from

Pennsylvania. In early December, "Many Customers" suggested several specific amendments to limit the powers of Congress and the courts. Specifically, they suggested removing from Congress the power to alter regulations concerning elections, and to lay direct taxes or excises. They advocated limiting the jurisdiction of the courts as well, and proposed that treaties must pass the House, by a majority vote of all members, as well as the Senate. The Customers mentioned that a bill of rights might be necessary, but claim that "if suitable amendments are made respecting the points enumerated, the necessity for going further on the present occasion, though not entirely done away, will be so far diminished as that it may be thought advisable to leave them to future consideration."[13]

In late October, a pamphlet appeared by a writer calling himself "A Federal Republican." Although he praised Centinel, he was clearly not a radical. His emphasis on the powers given to Congress distinguishes him from an Old Whig as well, making this pamphlet perhaps the best statement of the Power Anti-Federalist position to appear in the state of Pennsylvania. His argument is in some respects novel, but it does cover a great deal of familiar ground as well. He suggests that the House of Representatives ought to be apportioned equally among the states, just as the Senate was, because the natural superiority of large states gives them greater influence anyway without any advantages in representation; the latter advantage simply makes the small states insignificant. He is more concerned with the balance of power between states than most of his contemporaries. His main objection, though, is to the amount of power given to Congress. Article I, Section 8, he says, "bloats Congress with too much power, and leaves them without a guard to prevent the eruptions of human depravity."[14] On top of too much enumerated power, several vague expressions including "general welfare" and "necessary and proper" enable Congress to expand its reach almost indefinitely.

While the Federal Republican's suggestion for equal representation by states directly contradicts the Democratic Anti-Federalist position, he is almost dismissive of the Rights position. "A bill of rights," he admits, "should either be inserted, or a declaration made, that whatever is not decreed to Congress, is reserved to the several states for their own disposal." He holds up the second article of the Articles of Confederation as a proper example of such a declaration, though; the idea that a statement of this type is a suitable *replacement* for a bill of rights would be dismissed as dangerous by an Old Whig and the Federal Farmer. The emphasis here is clearly on power; the Federal Republican is clearly a republican (and a federalist) in the classic sense, implying that it is the structure of government and the distribution of powers that truly determine the freedom of the people. He even emphasizes civic virtue, warning his readers that "some degree of virtue must exist, or freedom cannot live."[15] This is not a position that is incompatible with the Democratic and Rights positions, but it is telling that the author makes no effort to find common ground even with his fellow Anti-Federalists. This essay underscores the diversity of the opposition at this stage in the debate.

Despite the dominance of radical democrats like Centinel and Philadelphiensis, and the presence of a few Power Anti-Federalists, it was the Rights position that would dominate the state's ratifying convention. A petition signed in Cumberland County requested that the convention include a bill of rights, and make several other changes to the Constitution to secure individual liberties.[16] In early November, "An Officer of the Late Continental Army," likely William Findley, published a list of objections that foreshadowed the arguments that would be made by Findley, Robert Whitehill, and John Smilie in the convention. He listed, without elaboration, twenty-three arguments against the Constitution, and closed with an exhortation to his fellow citizens to protect the rights and freedoms they possess by rejecting the proposed form of government:

> Let not a set of aspiring despots, *who make us* SLAVES and *tell us 'tis our* CHARTER, wrest from you those invaluable blessings, for which the most illustrious sons of America have bled and died; but exert yourselves, like men, like freemen and like Americans, to transmit unimpaired to your latest posterity those rights, those liberties, which have ever been so dear to you, and which it is yet in your power to preserve.[17]

There was a strong Rights Anti-Federalist tradition in Pennsylvania that was to dominate the ratifying convention. Findley himself ultimately led the charge. There is little in this piece, or in the convention debates, that fits well with the more radical democracy of Centinel.

THE PENNSYLVANIA CONVENTION

When the Pennsylvania delegates convened on the twentieth of November to discuss the Constitution, two-thirds of them already supported ratification. None of the delegates was to be swayed despite a lengthy debate; the convention was largely an academic exercise, a debating society rather than a real effort at persuasion. The minority, though, insisted on stating its case, and the majority, for all its efforts to hasten ratification, did not try to rush or silence those who spoke against the Constitution. The Federalists dominated the early procedural votes; the only three delegates to receive votes to serve as president of the convention were all Federalists, and four Federalists dominated the five-person committee to determine the rules. The Federalists prevented the convention from discussing the Constitution as a committee of the whole, which would have given the opposition greater freedom to discuss the document as a whole rather than clause by clause. They also defeated efforts to allow the minority to include their reasons for dissent in the official journals of the convention, as was generally allowed in the state legislature. None of this substantially limited the debate, but the proponents of the Constitution were clearly in control from the beginning.

Three members of the minority took up the burden of presenting the case against the Constitution. William Findley, John Smilie, and Robert Whitehill introduced an exhaustive list of objections to the Constitution. None of the three sounded as radically democratic as Centinel, but all three, representing western counties, did present some of the Democratic Anti-Federalist arguments that resonated with their constituents. Nonetheless, the opposition position here, at least in extant records of the debates, was predominately Rights Anti-Federalism.[18] Smilie attacked the Preamble to the Constitution for its failure to emphasize rights, in contradistinction to the Declaration of Independence and the Pennsylvania Constitution. Findley, too, put rights first: "The natural course of power is to make the many slaves to the few. This is verified by universal experience. . . . Powers *given*— powers reserved—ought to be *all* enumerated. Let us add a bill of rights to our other securities."[19] Out of forty-two Anti-Federalist speeches on the Constitution of significant length that appear in extant reports, twenty-nine make substantial reference to the absence of a bill of rights, or of a particular right, or discuss the general importance of liberty. The first eight amendments offered by Whitehill at the end of the convention essentially form a bill of rights, and the remaining seven in many cases implicitly reinforce individual liberty.[20]

The general contours of the debate make clear the development of the opposition, even within this short span of time. The objections became more radical and strident as the convention continued, while the defenders of the Constitution became more smug and confident. The early debates, particularly those concerning the procedural question of whether to discuss the Constitution in a committee of the whole, were really a continuation of the legislative debates over calling the convention, complete with the bitterness and bad blood. On November 24, as the debate was first getting underway,

John Smilie "observed that we were repeatedly told of the peculiar advantages which we enjoy in being able deliberately and peaceably to decide upon a government for ourselves and our posterity, but we find every measure that is proposed leads to defeat those advantages and to preclude all argument and deliberation in a case confessedly of the highest consequence to the happiness of a great portion of the globe." By December 5, it was clear to Findley that there would be no opportunity to amend the document before the inevitable ratification; the Federalist majority would not allow it. "It is the tyrant's plea: Take this or nothing."[21] And indeed, the opposition did not even truly have that choice, being badly outnumbered.

Throughout the debate, though, the three dissenters stuck to their argument for a bill of rights. They attacked the Federalist insistence that a bill of rights was unnecessary. If "the supreme authority naturally rests in the people," as both sides agreed, "does it follow that therefore a declaration of rights would be superfluous?" If there is no written statement of rights to which the people might look when government grows too powerful, Smilie explained, this supreme authority "is a mere sound without substance." At some point the government will violate individual liberties, because governments eventually push the limits of their powers. "In that event," Smilie contended, "the contest will arise between the people and the rulers. 'You have exceeded the powers of your office, you have oppressed us' will be the language of the suffering citizens. The answer of the government will be short: 'We have not exceeded our power; you have no test by which you can prove it.'" The solution to such a confrontation is an enumeration of rights in the Constitution. "We ought to know what rights we *surrender*," Smilie concluded, "and what we *retain*."[22]

Though the Anti-Federalists in the convention laid out a Rights Anti-Federalist position, it was a somewhat more radical version of that position than appeared elsewhere. Whitehill, for example, saw in the Constitution "a government which originates in mystery and must terminate in despotism" and Smilie predicted that the proposed government would create a "complete aristocracy," but the underlying democratic argument was absent. Even the most radical rhetoric generally invoked liberties. "If this Constitution is adopted," Smilie predicted shortly before the vote on ratification, "I look upon the liberties of America as gone, until they shall be recovered by arms."[23] This claim would not be out of place in the essays of Centinel, but here it was clearly a prediction rather than a call to arms.

The Federalist argument was presented here as forcefully as anywhere, with James Wilson and Thomas McKean proving to be able defenders and explainers of the Constitution, and the setting aided the cause. Even

the galleries joined in, as the mostly Federalist citizens of Philadelphia ap-
plauded some Federalist speeches and were not shy about intimidating those
who dared oppose ratification. On December 12, less than a week after
Delaware's vote made that state the first to approve, and after a rather extensive discussion, the convention voted to ratify the Constitution, 46–23.
The Anti-Federalists made a final effort to introduce amendments before the
vote, but the Federalists were firmly in control.

After the ratification vote, it quickly became clear that the Federalists
were determined to control the public perception of the vote. The opposition delegates were not permitted to record their reasons on the minutes, and
Whitehill's proposed amendments also did not appear in the record. When
Smilie attempted to insert them, Wilson resisted. Smilie, facing a strong and
cohesive majority, relented; the Anti-Federalists undoubtedly were already
determined to continue the fight in the newspapers. The Federalists' hopes
for conciliation, or at least acquiescence, were quickly dashed, when less
than a week later the *Pennsylvania Packet* published "The Address and Reasons of Dissent of the Minority of the Convention of Pennsylvania to Their
Constituents." The Anti-Federalists were not yet done with the discussion,
and were not about to concede the fight.

THE REPORT OF THE MINORITY AND THE
ONGOING DEBATE IN PENNSYLVANIA

There were two primary reasons that the Pennsylvania Federalists did not
attempt to compromise with their opponents. First, they did not need to;
with a strong majority in both the legislature and the convention they
could push through whatever they wanted without Anti-Federalist votes.
Second, and perhaps more important, they saw the opposition as radicals
with whom there was no feasible compromise. Reading Centinel and Philadelphiensis leaves one with the impression that the opposition would not
accept anything less than rejection of the Constitution, which suggests that
any Anti-Federalist effort to propose amendments would be nothing more
than an effort to derail ratification. The more moderate voices of Findley,
Smilie, and Whitehill in the convention did not penetrate the radicalism that
the Federalists saw in the opposition; the proponents of the Constitution
simply did not believe the overtures toward amendments.

After the convention, the reasonable efforts of the convention dissenters
were overshadowed by a renewed radicalism, courtesy of Samuel Bryan.[24]
The Dissent of the Minority was written not by any of the dissenting

delegates, but by Bryan, whose radicalism shows clearly in the argument. The fact that twenty-one of the twenty-three dissenters signed the Dissent gave this more radical Democratic Anti-Federalist position credibility as the "official" opposition position in the state. It is not clear why it was Bryan who wrote the dissent, but given its quick publication after the convention it is probable that he had already prepared a draft of a statement, perhaps even intended to be a Centinel essay, that could be quickly revised and circulated while the delegates were still attending the convention.

The Dissent lists three primary objections to the Constitution. First, republican government is not possible over an area as large as that of the United States. Such a country can only be free under a confederate republic, which would presumably resemble the Articles of Confederation, a loose collection of sovereign states. Second, "the powers vested in Congress by this constitution, must necessarily annihilate and absorb the legislative, executive, and judicial powers of the several states, and produce from their ruins one consolidated government, which from the nature of things will be *an iron handed despotism.*" Neither of these points differs substantially from the convention dissent, though on the second Bryan's rhetoric is somewhat harsher. These two points were fairly common across the opposition nationally, and neither suggests anything different or noteworthy about the Dissent. The third point, too, was common, but Bryan puts a distinctive spin on it. Even if it were feasible to create a republican national government, he contends, the Constitution would not do so, because it establishes a despotism. In explaining this, he briefly acknowledges the importance of rights, the central opposition argument in convention, in one short paragraph. Then he moves on to representation, at which point the essay takes a decidedly democratic turn. He writes that "the representation [in the legislature] ought to be fair, equal, and sufficiently numerous, to possess the same interests, feelings, opinions, and views, which the people themselves would possess, were they all assembled."[25] This goes much further than Whitehill's proposed amendment for the House to be "properly increased in number," and is a sentiment more democratic than the three dissenters expressed in convention. Bryan's suggestion that the Senate ought to be allocated by population rather than equally for states was something that the opposition in convention did not argue; Findley mentioned that the Senate was apportioned equally by state as something "rather to be lamented than avoided." James Wilson answered the point in a long speech near the end of the convention, but he did it offhandedly, as if it were a very minor issue.[26] Even if Bryan's version of the opposition was not directly contradictory to the convention resistance, it was notably different in emphasis—representation over rights—and it showed some noteworthy variation in specific arguments as well.

Again and again Bryan departs from the arguments from the convention. While the convention minority emphasized jury trials, Bryan focused on appeals. Where the minority were prepared to reserve broad taxing power to the states, Bryan clearly argues that all taxes are oppressive to varying degrees. Bryan and the minority were on the same page in certain areas, like separation of powers and standing armies, but they diverged just as often, with Bryan consistently more radical and more democratic.

Bryan is at his most democratic when he writes that the "strongest of all checks upon the conduct of administration, *responsibility to the people*, will not exist in this government."[27] At first glance, this seems consistent with the convention minority's position, but careful reading suggests that Bryan has departed considerably from them. Bryan wanted representatives who acted directly according to their constituents' wishes, while Findley, Smilie, and Whitehill were willing to accept legislators who acted according to their constituents' interests. If popular control is the best restraint on government, this calls for a simple government rather than a bill of rights. After all, why establish parchment barriers when one can put the people directly in control? A simple government with a unicameral legislature would have been easy to propose, as the dissenters were for the most part supporters of Pennsylvania's simple, unicameral constitution. The minority in the convention, however, explicitly accepted the idea of a bicameral legislature, and did not dispute the Federalist argument for it. "A single branch [of the legislature] I will concede," Findley said on December 3. "As the greatest part of the states have compound legislatures," Smilie said the next day, "I shall give up that point."[28] Centinel advocated a simple legislature, while the minority in convention did not. The convention dissenters aimed to prevent tyranny, while Bryan wanted to ensure that the people *were* the government. For Bryan, safeguards against abuse were not enough; what was needed was mechanisms to ensure popular participation. The Dissent took Bryan's view rather than the more conciliatory convention position.[29]

This shift in emphasis was important, because it shaped the tone of the opposition in Pennsylvania. In the absence of published convention debates, the Dissent *was* the voice of the Pennsylvania opposition; readers in other states might well conclude that Centinel's position was the primary opposition position there, when there was a substantial and reasonable Rights Anti-Federalism around which opponents of the Constitution might have rallied.

The response to the Dissent was significant, and portended a strong continued opposition in the state. John Armstrong, Jr., in a letter to Benjamin Franklin, found that "The tenor of the minority's Dissent . . . appears to have a wild and pernicious tendency!" A sympathetic reply published in the *Carlisle Gazette* in early January lends credence to this characterization; this essay was nothing short of a call to arms for the state's Anti-Federalists: "Discontent, indignation, and revenge already begins to be visible in every patriotic countenance; and civil discord already raises her sneaky head. And we are well convinced that nothing less than a total recantation and annihilation of the proposed aristocratic delusion will appease the insulted and enraged defenders of liberty." The *Independent Gazetteer* reported "that the present situation of public affairs is truly alarming," because the convention minority "are supported not only by their constituents but by a very considerable part of the whole body of the people of Pennsylvania."[30] Even the most devout Federalists must have been alarmed by the state of affairs.

The flames of opposition were once again stoked by the pen of Centinel. Samuel Bryan clearly had a busy month, publishing three more letters in his series in late December after the Dissent. In his first letter after Pennsylvania's ratification, he opened with strong rhetoric suggesting that the Constitution abandons the principles of the Revolution:

Incredible transition! the people who seven years ago, deemed every earthly good, every other consideration as worthless, when placed in competition with Liberty, that Heaven-born blessing, that zest of all others; the people, who, actuated by the noble ardor of patriotism, rose superior to every weakness of humanity, and shone with such dazzling lustre amidst the greatest difficulties; who, emulous of eclipsing each other in the glorious assertion of the dignity of human nature, courted every danger, and were ever ready, when necessary, to lay down their lives at the altar of liberty: I say the people, who exhibited so lately a spectacle, that commanded the admiration, and drew the plaudits of the most distant nations, are now revealing the picture, are now lost to every noble principle, are about to sacrifice that inestimable jewel, liberty, to the genius of despotism. A golden phantom held out to them, by the crafty and aspiring despots among themselves, is alluring them into the fangs of arbitrary power; and so great is their infatuation, that it seems, as if nothing short of the reality of misery necessarily attendant on slavery, will rouse them from their false confidence, or convince them of the direful deception; but then alas! it will be too late, the chains of despotism will be fast rivetted, and all escape precluded.[31]

The people, rather than acting to defend their liberty, "are weakly trusting their every concern to the discretionary disposal of their future rulers." This reflects a certain forgetfulness about the Revolution, and a blissful ignorance of how blessed America's situation truly is. In his appeals to the Revolution, and in his comments on the origins and purposes of government, he continues his very democratic themes, asserting that "the great end of civil government is to protect the weak from the oppression of the powerful, to put every man upon the level of equal liberty."[32]

Centinel believed that in the end the people would resist and rebuff this plan of government, even if it took another revolution. In the meantime, he explicitly suggests starting over on revising the Articles of Confederation: "as additional powers are necessary to Congress, the people will no doubt see the expediency of calling a convention for this purpose as soon as may be by applying to their representatives in assembly, at their next session, to appoint a suitable day for the election of such Convention."[33]

Centinel was not the only Anti-Federalist to call for a fresh start, revising the Articles rather than adopting the Constitution. The day after the state ratified the Constitution, "Alfred" suggested that the only reason that the Constitution has received as much approbation as it has is because of the failure of requisitions to supply money for the government; after all, he says, "*money* does every thing." Granting that, though, he asks, "cannot we regulate our finances, and lay the foundations for a permanent, certain revenue, without undoing all that we have done, without making an entire new government?" He writes that "the want *of public virtue, and the want of money*" are the primary problems under the Articles of Confederation, both of which can be fixed without destroying the existing political system.[34]

The most energetic rejection of the proceedings of the convention came from Philadelphiensis. The opening of his fifth letter makes the Dissent of the Minority seem fairly tame. "*My Fellow Citizens*," he began,

If the arbitrary proceedings of the convention of Pennsylvania do not rouse your attention to the rights of yourselves and your children, there is nothing that I can say will do it. If the contempt and obloquy with which that body (whose legality even may be questioned) has treated your petitions, can not bring you to think seriously, what then will? When a few Demagogues despising every sense of order and decency, have rejected the petitions of the people, and in the most

supercilious manner, triumphed over the freemen of America, as if
they were their slaves, and they themselves their lords and masters. I
say that if such barefaced presumption and arrogance, such tyrannical proceedings of the men, who, if acting constitutionally, were the
servants of the people, be not sufficient to awaken you to a sense of
your duty and interest, nothing less than the goad and the whip can
succeed: your condition must be like that of the careless and insecure
sinner, whom neither the admonitions nor entreaties of his friends, nor
even the threatnings of awaiting justice, could reclaim or convince of
his error; his reformation is neglected until it is too late, when he finds
himself in a state of unutterable and endless woe.[35]

The entire letter was a diatribe against the Federalists' attempts to impose
slavery on their fellow citizens. "If America is to be *great*," he contended in
his calmer sixth letter, "she must be *free*; freedom is her heart, her very life-
blood." This Constitution threatens that freedom, and thus robs the United
States of its potential greatness. "Neither *energy, strength* nor *respectability* can exist a moment in America after the adoption of this tyrannical
government." He reaffirms the Democratic Anti-Federalist contention that
the Constitution cannot be fixed without substantial structural changes; he
rejects the idea of a bill of rights as incompatible with the tendencies of the
Constitution, and thus such guarantees will not be agreed to by its supporters. Among frequent writers against the Constitution, only Centinel proved
to be as radical as Philadelphiensis. Centinel himself declared the author of
these letters to be deserving of "the thanks of every patriotic American" for
his contributions to the debate.[36] These two were not prepared to give up
the fight in Pennsylvania, or anywhere else.

5

Federalist Momentum

THE PENNSYLVANIA CONVENTION generated a lot of controversy, and the Report of the Minority played a central role in the national debate through early 1788, but it was not the only contest occurring in the final month of 1787. The states of Delaware, New Jersey, and Georgia all held ratifying conventions, with considerably less fanfare and bluster than the Keystone State. All of these states were expected to be good for the Federalists, and none of them disappointed; not a single delegate in any of the three states voted against ratification, giving the Federalists a total of four strong victories before the end of the year.

DELAWARE BECOMES
THE FIRST STATE

While Pennsylvania Anti-Federalists were struggling to slow down the champions of the Constitution, there was no such struggle in the neighboring state of Delaware. In early November, the legislature called for a ratifying convention. Despite hotly contested elections, complete with allegations of fraud and threats of violence, the Delaware Ratifying Convention met on December 3, and by December 7 they had ratified the Constitution unanimously. There was virtually no opposition, despite the highly contentious nature of the state's politics at the time. The *Delaware Gazette* reprinted a shorter version of Centinel's first essay on October 31, two weeks after printing the statement of the minority of the Pennsylvania legislature. Aside from these, and allegations that Pennsylvania's Anti-Federalists attempted to sway the convention by sending opposition materials, including the Centinel essays, to several delegates, there appears to have been no Anti-Federalist influence here at all. "Local conditions," as Robert Rutland puts it, "determined that antifederalism would not have the slightest hope in Delaware."[1]

NEW JERSEY'S UNANIMOUS RATIFICATION

The Anti-Federalist influence in New Jersey was hardly greater than in Delaware. Several Anti-Federalist essays from other states were reprinted there, but no true opposition emerged from within the state. By the end of October, the legislature of New Jersey had called a convention to meet in early December. The convention began its deliberations on Friday, December 14, and voted unanimously to ratify the Constitution on December 18, less than a week after neighboring Pennsylvania. The convention spent three days in debate; a number of objections were apparently raised, but those objections were effectively answered by David Brearley, who had been one of New Jersey's delegates to the Constitutional Convention.[2] In the end, none of the objections was apparently serious enough to lead to any real opposition to ratification.

Anti-Federalists were hard to find in the state. "A gentleman who lately travelled through New Jersey," reported the *Pennsylvania Gazette*, "assured us that among many hundred persons with whom he conversed about the federal government, he met but *one* man who was opposed to it, and he was a citizen of Pennsylvania." Congressman Abraham Clark was widely believed to have opposed ratification, but he made no public statements to that effect. He played a significant role in helping the Constitution through Congress with no endorsement or official opposition, but he seems to have done nothing to influence his state's ratification decision either way. Privately, in July 1788 after ratification was secured, he explained his feelings on the issue in a letter to Thomas Sinnickson: "I never liked the System in all its parts. I considered it from the first, more a Consolidated government than a federal, a government too expensive, and unnecessarily Oppressive in its Opperation; Creating a Judiciary undefined and unbounded." Nevertheless, he explained, he did not oppose ratification, instead hoping for eventual amendments.[3]

The closest thing to a New Jersey Anti-Federalist essay was one published by "A Farmer," in which the author proposed several amendments to the Constitution. Specifically, he advocated a sharper separation of powers and a three-person executive. The Farmer opened his essay, however, by explaining that the proposed Constitution "surpasses my most sanguine expectation," and anyone who opposes ratification "must evidently be actuated by sinister motives." This is not exactly serious opposition. The general consensus in the state was apparently legitimate, notwithstanding Beard's claim that the Federalists in the state "pushed through the ratification of the

Constitution without giving the agrarian party time to organize its forces."
Even if the opposition was disorganized, explains McCormick, it could have
contested legislative or convention elections, or circulated petitions after
ratification, as in neighboring Pennsylvania. The Federalists could not possibly have covered up all evidence of opposition down to the town level.[4] It is
far more plausible that the few opponents to ratification in the state simply
saw no reason to resist the overwhelming majority. Between the Farmer and
Abraham Clark, the Anti-Federalists had less of an impact in New Jersey
than in any other state save Delaware.

THE CONVENTION IN GEORGIA

In late October, without the benefit of much public debate on the Constitution, the Georgia legislature called a convention to meet in December. Little
time was devoted to discussing the convention, because the danger posed by
the Creek Nation was seen by virtually everyone as more pressing, as the
state prepared for war. The call for convention, though, included a significant provision that the Anti-Federalists everywhere would have liked to see:
the convention was instructed "to adopt or reject any part or the whole" of
the proposed Constitution. This language explicitly opened the door to the
possibility of amendments. Despite this, the delegates apparently never even
considered the possibility of rejecting certain clauses or articles, and the
Constitution was ratified unanimously after less than three days of debate.

   There was one substantial public debate in the newspapers, with a reluctant Anti-Federalist who signed his essays as "A Georgian" at the heart of it.
A Georgian suggested that the Constitution, while good in many ways, was
substantially flawed. He wrote that representation might be better secured,
that several powers given to Congress are improper or too broad, that the
President should be better restrained in the use of his powers, and that the
entire judiciary ought to be reconfigured. He goes so far as to suggest new
language for several parts, including all of Article III. He takes a Power
Anti-Federalist position, which stands out as unusual in the south, and his
position is certainly defensible. Two Federalists, writing as "Demosthenes
Minor" and "A Farmer," quickly attacked the Georgian, though only the
former made any real attempt to refute his critiques. "A Citizen" rose to the
Georgian's defense, asserting that "were I not afraid of Demosthenes and
the Farmer, I would venture to say that I think it might be a little amended."
The debate, largely unhelpful (outside of the Georgian's original letter),
was closed by "A Briton," who confessed his support for the Constitution

because he is owed debts for which, once the Constitution takes effect, he "shall no longer be defrauded by payments in paper money."[5]

Few private objections to the Constitution from the state are extant. One of note was raised in a letter written by Lachlan McIntosh to John Wereat, who would become the president of the state's ratifying convention. McIntosh suggested that the Constitution be ratified for a set term, perhaps several years, with another convention to be held at that time.[6] This is an idea that did not gain much momentum, though the opposition in Virginia and New York would later entertain similar proposals.

Ratification by the state of Georgia was never really in doubt. More than any other state, Georgia needed union. Beset by natives determined to hold the land they occupied, bordering on Spanish territory, and small in population, Georgia relied for its existence on help from its fellow states. The legislature in Georgia had clearly established that it favored stronger national government, voting to authorize amendments to the Articles of Confederation to give Congress expanded powers over commerce and taxation. As "A Georgia Backwoodman" put it in May, long after the state had decided to ratify, "All men saw no alternative" to ratification, because the state required federal protection. "Every one knew of no other remedy, and there was none but prefigured to himself those convulsive scenes which are too apt to afflict a government whose sinews were not sufficiently strengthened by the maturity of manhood." The state did not even propose amendments because the compact was so essential to the continued existence of the state, and amendments could wait.[7] The Georgia ratification closed out the year 1787, a year that found the Federalists impressively dominating the debate, and the Anti-Federalists still searching for common ground and an identity beyond simple opposition.

THE CARLISLE RIOT

While these states found a degree of consensus, the divide in Pennsylvania was growing. The radical Democratic Anti-Federalists in the western part of the state were seriously contemplating armed resistance, and the issue came to a head in Carlisle. On the twenty-sixth of December a celebration of the ratification of the Constitution was broken up by a riot. The Federalists hoped to break the opposition in this Anti-Federalist area, but instead managed to push them a little too far. Conflicting accounts emerged concerning the event, as both supporters and opponents of the Constitution attempted to spin the event into a repudiation of the other side, but some facts are clear. The Federalists had prepared a bonfire and brought a cannon to fire in celebration. A number of Anti-Federalists arrived armed with clubs and various weapons, and took the cannon by force and burned it, and in the process one brave or foolhardy Federalist, coincidentally named James Wilson, was beaten by the mob.[8] It is possible that his name contributed to the savagery of the attack, as James Wilson of Philadelphia was one of the most hated Federalists among their opponents. The other Federalists fled the scene, to regroup and return the next day armed with muskets. Then they had their bonfire, and read the ratification, and held their celebration. After a couple of hours of Federalist celebration, the Anti-Federalists returned to burn in effigy James Wilson (of Philadelphia) and Chief Justice Thomas McKean.

The public debate over the event underscored the remaining resistance to the Constitution, and a certain reluctance to accept the Federalist victory. "One of the People," writing to correct what he claimed was a Federalist misperception of the events, was probably about right in his estimate that celebrating ratification "was contrary to the minds of three-fourths of the inhabitants" of the county. Federalist John Montgomery found "a great Majoritty in opposition to the new Constitution" in Carlisle. Anti-Federalist John Jordan, a judge of the Cumberland County Court of Common Pleas and one of the arrested rioters, found in Carlisle "a great many cordial enemies" of the Constitution, asserting that he and his fellow dissenters "are determined here to do everything in our power to retain that liberty without which life is not worth the enjoying."[9]

The clearest statement in defense of the rioters and the riot itself appeared above the appropriate signature "The Scourge." This writer, almost certainly William Petrikin, was confident that he was writing on behalf of most of his fellow residents of Carlisle, and he happily celebrated the problems that the town caused for the supporters of the Constitution. "The various and repeated defeats which that party who arrogates to themselves the appellation of federalists has received from the friends of liberty in Carlisle," he writes, "has almost tortured their souls to distraction." The riots were apparently a great success. The Scourge goes on to criticize the Federalists for their characterization of the Anti-Federalists as a mob. "Candid public," he explains, "these are the men who endeavour by fraud and force, to cram down your throats a constitution which would immediately create them your rulers. . . . The most contemptuous and degrading epithets, is given to all such as are not of their faction; no better names than rabble, mob, chimney sweeps, ragamuffins, vile, contemptible, senseless, ignorant, suited only by nature to a state of insignificance and contempt, is conferred on such citizens as oppose the ambitious views of this imperious junto." In Philadelphia, he notes scathingly, the mob backed the Federalists, with no complaints by the "junto" then. In particular, it was a mob that dragged two legislators back into the session to make a quorum for calling a ratifying convention, and a mob in the galleries that heckled dissenters at that convention. "In a word were it not for the mob," he concludes, "the new constitution would not yet have been adopted in Pennsylvania."[10] It is not difficult to be sympathetic with this notion despite Petrikin's apparent endorsement of violence; in Pennsylvania the Federalists certainly deserved such verbal attacks.

In late February, twenty-one people were finally arrested for their participation in the riot, including the leading local Anti-Federalists. Seven of them refused to post bail and were held in prison for six nights. Their version of the story, published in the *Carlisle Gazette*, suggested that they were refused a fair hearing, denied habeas corpus and the opportunity to confront witnesses; the Federalists involved of course denied this. Within days, hundreds of local militiamen had assembled and marched on Carlisle, raising fears of the ratification debates turning violent. (Any doubt that the militia was Anti-Federalist in sentiment could easily be dismissed by the fact that its members were singing "The Federal Joy," a song that appeared at the end of the essay by the Scourge.) The entire issue was settled peacefully when the sheriff agreed to release the prisoners, and the prosecution was not pursued. Clearly the Anti-Federalists won the public relations battle, and had the full support of the local citizenry. This was not how the Federalists interpreted the events, of course; John Montgomery, in a private letter, wrote in March that the people, if "left to the dispassionate exercise of their own good sense," would support ratification, which is why the Anti-Federalists try "to keep the minds of the honest unsuspecting men in a continual state of inflammation, by the most impudent declamatory falsehoods." He suggests that the members of the militia, upon reflection, would realize that they had assembled and marched for "a trifling and unnecessary occasion" because they had been misled by a handful of "incendiaries."[11] This suggests not only a thorough disrespect for opposition, but an elitist dismissal of the ability of the people to make good collective decisions; one can easily imagine the consequences had Montgomery made these remarks publicly in Carlisle.[12]

Not every Anti-Federalist in Pennsylvania was a radical, though. "Hampden," in the *Pittsburgh Gazette*, suggested that the opposition in Pennsylvania merely wanted a more modest grant of power for the national government, rather than the open-ended one in the proposed Constitution.

"All the friends to our country have wished that the powers of regulating commerce and levying imposts should be vested in the general government. . . . All in this state who oppose the proposed system are willing to invest the general government with all the power that ever Congress asked for or declared to be necessary."[13] Though the author, probably William Findley, complimented the members of the convention, especially Washington, he suggested that there was not nearly so much unanimity as the Federalists had implied, not in the Philadelphia Convention and certainly not in Congress. The document deserved more careful scrutiny than the Federalists in the state were inclined to permit.

THE MAIL CONTROVERSY

The Carlisle Riot made both sides uneasy back in Philadelphia, but it did not generate much discussion in the public debates there. Instead, in early 1788 another controversy arose, instigated in large part by Centinel. His essays had been railing against the Federalists for their efforts to suppress opposition, especially by interfering with publication of the state's convention debates.[14] He further accused the post office of being part of the Federalist scheme to suppress dissent, failing to deliver Anti-Federalist newspapers, while "the devoted vehicles of despotism," the Federalist papers, "pass uninterrupted." This was probably a matter of bad timing rather than a sinister plot. Ebenezer Hazard, the postmaster general, had convinced Congress to change postal policies in order to reduce costs, by hiring post riders rather than stagecoach operators to deliver the mail. As part of the new policy, the previous practice of permitting newspapers to travel from printer to printer at no cost was changed to leave it to the discretion of the post riders. This was a particular problem north of Philadelphia, where stagecoaches were much more expensive and thus abandoned in favor of post riders. It is possible, and perhaps likely, that individual post riders tended to side with the Federalists and were in fact partial to Federalist newspapers and hostile to Anti-Federalist ones; after all, if nothing else, a stronger federal government likely meant more secure jobs for them. The idea of a grand conspiracy to shackle the free press was highly unlikely. There is no evidence that Hazard was especially partial, though his competence was certainly called into question over this controversy. Nonetheless, the Anti-Federalist narrative of an aristocratic junto conniving to force the Constitution on the unsuspecting people had plenty of room for a sinister postmaster general as a tool of the would-be aristocracy. Thus a series of comments on the situation, and the alleged conspiracy, showed up from New Hampshire to Virginia, but especially in Pennsylvania, where Centinel, as usual, could not resist turning the issue into a personal crusade for a free press. The "Officers of the Post Office" in New York and "M" in Philadelphia responded to his attacks with assertions that the accusations were false, but they had little they could say to prove it. Instead, they attacked Centinel's credibility, denouncing "the unmanly and cowardly assaults of such an unprincipled assassin," and insisting that "an anonimous political incendiary is below even contempt."[15]

The longest attack came from Eleazer Oswald, the stubborn, independent, Anti-Federalist editor of the *Independent Gazetteer*, the original home of the Centinel letters. He backed away from the latter author's claim that the post office was at fault; in fact, the Philadelphia post office he finds to be innocent in this matter, and generally exemplary. The blame for the whole controversy, Oswald writes, falls to Ebenezer Hazard and "the vile *edicts* of a despotic post-master." There is a certain degree of absurdity in the concept of a despotic postmaster, but Oswald writes it without irony. The problem, he says, is a concerted effort by Hazard to further the Federalist cause. In this claim he actually comes across more radical than Centinel, yet less partisan, as his primary concern is with the importance of a free press in a free society. Others took up this attack on Hazard as well; one critic, writing under the pseudonym Manco, refers to him as "this *little despot in office*."[16]

Hazard himself, writing to Jeremy Belknap in early March, denied any involvement in alleged efforts to prevent the circulation of Anti-Federalist materials. "The fact is," he wrote, "*the Office* has nothing to do with News Papers; it is a Matter merely between the Printers & the Riders who have the Carriage of them as a Perquisite. The two antifederal Printers in Phila. (Oswald & Bailey) & their Coadjutor, the brainless *Greenleaf* of New York, are the only ones who have published against the Office; & neither of them was a Printer before the War:—in short, the whole Noise appears to me to be an antifederal Manoeuvre." He later published a defense in late March, appearing first in the *New York Journal*, in which he denied that the post office had any responsibility to carry newspapers in the first place. He included a statement of facts concerning the legal status of newspapers in the mail. "A True Federalist" responded, referring to Hazard's list of facts as "low subterfuges and mean evasions." He, along with "Watchman" and "Algernon," relied on precedent to support their contention that the post office had a responsibility to distribute newspapers throughout the country. They were eventually joined in sentiment, albeit privately, by no less illustrious a personage than George Washington, who wrote to John Jay that "If the priviledge [of sending newspapers freely with the mail] was not from convention an original right, it had from prescription strong pretensions for continuance; especially at so interesting a period."[17] Hazard's defenders were few, and his tenure as postmaster general was to be ended shortly by President Washington.[18] In the general's state, the *Virginia Gazette* also published a series of criticisms of the post office and of Hazard. The printers of the paper, Matthias Bartgis and Nathaniel Willis, insisted that their conduct was based not on partisan motives, but on the principle that both sides ought to be heard; had the Anti-Federalists attempted to obstruct the flow of information, the *Gazette* would have exerted as much effort to expose that plot.

The controversy continued relatively unabated through May, by which time new essays on the Constitution were becoming much less common, and many older essays had managed to find wide circulation despite the failure to deliver newspapers. Still, the controversy demonstrates quite clearly a certain Anti-Federalist paranoia, not entirely unjustified, about Federalist plots to silence debate. The behavior of the partisans of ratification in Pennsylvania seemed ample evidence that the ratification process was not about fair debate and serious deliberation. The debate in Connecticut seemed to confirm this conclusion.

THE CONVENTION IN CONNECTICUT

In Connecticut, the Federalist fears that there was "a strong party forming against the Convention and much reason to fear" that the Constitution would not be ratified turned out to be unfounded. Despite the concern that "Democratics and Tories conspire against any change," the proposed Constitution moved quickly through the state legislature, which called a ratifying convention with little opposition. About four-fifths of the members of the assembly supported ratification. Those who did not faced public attacks in the newspapers, including accusations of financial interest in defeating the Constitution. The opponents, according to one newspaper, consisted primarily of men "who love themselves more than their country, and are in honorable or lucrative offices." In their attempts to influence the election of delegates, they were labeled "the *wrong heads* that are using their influence to embarrass public measures by their narrow politics." And those few Anti-Federalists who did win election as delegates were, to one Federalist newspaper, "Judases" who would likely have little impact on the final result.[19]

The opposition in Connecticut was sparse, and little Anti-Federalist writing is extant. In the state's newspapers, Federalist materials were dominant, with virtually no space devoted to opposition arguments. The Federalists controlled the papers, and aimed to prepare the public to accept the Constitution before it was even published. After its publication, Connecticut Federalists did what they could to keep Anti-Federalist materials out of the newspapers. Only five out-of-state pieces in opposition to the Constitution were reprinted, two of them specifically for the purpose of a Federalist refutation to be printed in the same newspaper. Several newspapers insisted that they never received any essays or letters against the Constitution. This cannot be verified of course, but the state's Anti-Federalists were evidently not very active in their cause. Some pamphlets and broadsides entered the state from New York, but it is not clear how much influence they may have had. It seems that the pamphlets sent by John Lamb had little effect; with the exception of some sent to James Wadsworth, they "were all secreted, burnt, and distributed amongst those for the new Constitution in order to torture, ridicule, and make shrewd remarks" about both the content and the authors. Hugh Ledlie added that he did not have the opportunity to see any of the material received by Wadsworth "until a few days before our Convention sat." It seems unlikely that many other Anti-Federalists in the state saw them either. This distribution of literature, by Lamb and others, was compared to the actions of loyalists during the Revolution, but it was a strategy dismissed in the *New York Daily Advertiser* as "useless" in the state, as most people had already taken a side.[20]

One Anti-Federalist newspaper essay, signed "The People," suggested that the Constitution was too vague, allowing for powers not sufficiently limited. In particular, he objected to the power of taxation given to Congress, the ability of representatives to vote for their own pay, the clause allowing Congress to alter regulations concerning elections, and the possibility of judicial appeals to federal courts that are likely to be far away from the original jurisdiction. "Let Congress have all the powers that is necessary for them," he concludes, "and let them be therewith content." Another, signed "An Old Soldier" and purporting to be the text of a speech given at a town meeting to elect delegates to the ratifying convention, took a more democratic turn, lamenting that the Constitution did not make the Senate and President directly elected by the people, and that it did not establish annual elections. This essay also notes, in passing, the absence of a bill of rights.[21]

The strongest extant critique of the Constitution in the state was from Benjamin Gale, a little-known doctor and businessman. Gale used rhetoric as strong as the opponents of the Constitution in any state, describing the document as "*dark, intricate, artful, crafty, and unintelligible [a]*

composition that I ever read or *see composed by man.*" He avowed that it
was illegal as well because it violated the Articles of Confederation, which
required unanimous approval by the state legislatures for any amendments
rather than ratification by nine states in conventions. He praised the resistance in Pennsylvania, suggesting that the heavy-handed tactics of the Federalists there tell a great deal about their motives. Gale's list of objections was
not especially original or consequential, but it was extensive. Gale himself
seems to have had virtually no impact on the ratification process in his state
or nationally; his town of Killingworth elected two delegates who voted for
ratification. Still, he stands out as a rare Anti-Federalist voice in a strongly
Federalist state. More common were slight misgivings, like that of William
Williams, who lamented that God was not mentioned in the Preamble. In
the same letter, though, he contended that the proposed Constitution, "with
this and some other faults of another kind, was yet too wise and too necessary to be rejected." This explains his vote for ratification, despite his
opposition during the debates in convention.[22]

There was, however, a clear undercurrent of uneasiness, if not outright
opposition; this probably emerged in the discussions of the Constitution
that took place in the various town meetings to elect delegates to the convention. The town of Preston stands out for its notable "instructions" for
its delegates. This remarkable document suggests both concerns about the
Constitution as it stands and a willingness to compromise. Recognizing that
the people must "give up such share of our rights as to enable government
to support, defend, and preserve the rest," the townsmen of Preston nevertheless insist that "Tis much easier to give more power into the hands
of government when more is necessary than to recover back where too
much is already given." Here we have a classic statement of Power Anti-
Federalism. The town further objects to the unlimited taxing power of Congress, the "long continuance of power in the senatorial body," and placing
so much power in the hands of judges with unlimited terms. There is also
a democratic element to these objections, as one might expect from a local
gathering accustomed to debating and deciding policy. Preston objected to
the amendment process in the fifth article, arguing that any changes in the
Constitution ought to require the approval of the people, as the state legislatures are "chosen for the purpose of making laws and not for the purpose
of altering the original compact of the people." This is a sophisticated and
nuanced understanding of constitutionalism, much more akin to the careful
federal balance of Power Anti-Federalism than to the radicalism of Centinel
and the Democratic wing of the opposition. This moderation is reinforced
by the town's request that the delegates "peruse these our sentiments with

deliberation," but ultimately "give your assent or dissent as you shall really think will terminate for the best good of the people of these states."[23] Here we have a constructive and compromising yet principled Anti-Federalism on the most local level, absent any of the intellectual leaders of the resistance to ratification. Preston's delegates, Jeremiah Halsey and Wheeler Coit, ultimately voted for ratification.

The actual ratification by the convention was never really in doubt. During the election of most of the convention delegates, Ezra Stiles counted 103 "Federal" men among the approximately 130 delegates elected by that point. Jeremiah Wadsworth predicted at least two-thirds of the delegates would be in favor of ratification, while Samuel Holden Parsons estimated the number of Federalists at 112 out of 175, with the remaining sixty-three being "doubtful."[24]

We have relatively little material from the debates in convention. Several Federalist speeches were recorded and published, but very little Anti-Federalist material is extant. In the only Anti-Federalist speech published in the newspapers, in full or in part, James Wadsworth, the acknowledged leader of the Anti-Federalists in the state,[25] contended that the powers of the purse and the sword would be given over wholly to the national government. He also argued that the power to tax would cover everything, and ultimately rest exclusively with Congress; he objected to the impost, suggesting that it would favor the southern states; and he suggested that the legislative power of Congress would eventually overwhelm any such power remaining with the states.[26] Ultimately, though, the Anti-Federalists never had much of a chance, and lost the ratification vote 128 to forty.

It is clear that the Anti-Federalists felt stigmatized and bullied by the majority, as in Pennsylvania. Ledlie, writing to Lamb, described the debates in and out of the convention in terms unflattering to the Federalists:

The late Convention, which met in this town the 3d instant and voted the new Constitution the 9th in the evening and finished the 10th, was carried on, by what I can learn, with a highhand against those that disapproved thereof. For, if I am not misinformed, when the latters were speaking, which by the bye were far from being the best orators (a few excepted), they were browbeaten by many of those Ciceroes, as they think themselves, and others of superior rank, as they call themselves, as also by the unthinking deluded multitude, who were previously convened as it is thought by many, for that purpose; which together with shuffling and stamping of feet, coughing, talking, spitting, and whispering, as well by some of the members as spectators, with other interruptions, etc., etc., too many to be here enumerated, which I am told is true, for I was not there myself, being at that time confined by a slight touch of the gout. All these menaces and stratagems were used by a junto who tries to carry all before them in this state, as well by writing as every other diabolical and evil pretense. And as the presses in this state are open to them, but evidently shut against all those that would dare and presume to write on the other side against the new Constitution, they have greatly the advantage and, by these means, stigmatize everyone they think acts or thinks to the contrary of what they say or do.[27]

Despite this treatment, the minority in the convention, unlike that of Pennsylvania, ultimately acquiesced in their defeat, earning the praise of several newspapers. The victorious Federalists, though, did not respond in kind, as the attacks on the opponents of the Constitution continued. Prominent Federalists sought to destroy the political careers of those who had opposed ratification. James Wadsworth became the target for most of the Federalist attacks, both before and after the state convention. Ledlie described him as "one of the many steeds that has behaved in character against the new Constitution and stood firm and intrepid, notwithstanding all the scoffs, flirts, browbeatings, flings, coughs, shuffles, threats, and menaces of the opposite faction in Convention."[28] Such attacks did not stop after ratification. Wadsworth was ultimately forced out of the state council by a concerted Federalist campaign and relentlessly attacked in public and private. William Williams and Eliphalet Dyer, meanwhile, were publicly excoriated for their opposition in convention despite their eventual votes in favor of ratification. Neither lost political positions as Wadsworth did, but they exemplify the mania with which the Federalists persisted in their relentless attacks in the state of Connecticut.

NEW YORK CALLS A CONVENTION

Just a few days after the decision by Connecticut, which itself took place on the same day that the Massachusetts Convention began, the legislature of New York was plotting tactics in its discussions on calling a ratifying convention. There was no substantive debate on the merits of the Constitution here, but the strategic maneuvers are suggestive of the type of fight to be made in New York. Governor Clinton, the unquestioned leader of the opposition in the state, remained publicly neutral in laying the reports of the Philadelphia Convention and Congress before the state assembly. "From the Nature of my Office," he explained in his speech opening the legislative session, "it would be improper for me to have any other Agency in this Business than that of laying the Papers respecting it before you for your Information."[29] No one in the room could have believed that the governor was neutral on the Constitution, but protocol required that he not get involved in this particular fight. He had ample support in both houses of the legislature, so his involvement was as unnecessary as it would have been impolitic.

The first salvo fired by the Anti-Federalists was an effort to change the state's oath of office, requiring officials to swear not to consent to anything "which had a *tendency* to destroy or *Alter* the present *constitution of the state*."[30] This would have put any official in an awkward position should he wish to support the proposed Constitution, which would certainly bring alterations. This ploy having failed, the Anti-Federalists next turned to the resolution calling for a ratifying convention. The debate and dispute were over the recital, or introduction, to the resolution. The Federalist position, ably defended by Egbert Benson, was to echo the language in the letter from Congress, passing the Constitution to the consideration of the people without any recommendatory language. Cornelius Schoonmaker made a motion to alter this to language effectively condemning the Philadelphia Convention for exceeding its legal bounds. This having failed, by just two votes, Samuel Jones tried to add the words "for their free investigation, discussion, and decision" to the end, but this attempt also fell short, to a slightly larger majority of five. In the end, the Federalists secured a modest victory similar to that achieved in Congress, securing a convention without an endorsement.

In the Senate, the opposition was even more determined to impede the progress of the Constitution, though their options were fewer. They were faced with a resolution from the Assembly, which they could either accept or reject but not amend. The Anti-Federalists, led by Abraham Yates, attempted to delay rather than defeat the resolution. There were some efforts to generate a substantive debate, and John Williams brought up, apparently in passing, the question of whether the convention might amend the Constitution before ratifying, but the discussion centered on the propriety of delay. Abraham Yates made clear his position by insisting that "there is not a step towards this business that I ever agreed to; nor is there a sentence in it that I ever will agree to." It is not entirely clear if he was discussing the resolution or the Constitution, but the words apply equally well to both. It seems likely he would have welcomed a fuller debate, if only to challenge James Duane's repeated insistence that he could adequately answer any objections his opponents might raise. Since Yates could do little but slow down the proceedings despite his professed opposition, Lewis Morris decided to poke some fun at him. In a speech before the Senate, "Mr. Morris thought it strange that a gentleman should want to postpone it who had declared his mind made up on the subject. For what does he want time?" The newspapers had some fun, too. "What shall we say," asked the *Pennsylvania Gazette*, "to the conduct of the Minority in the Assembly and Senate of New-York, who, after having four months to reflect upon the proposed constitution, yet desired to defer the submission of that important matter to the people."[31] In the end, the Senate confirmed the House resolution by a three-vote margin. The convention was on, though not until July, when most of the other states would have already made their decisions. This delay was apparently favored by both sides. The Federalists were concerned that a quick rejection by New York might sway other states, while momentum for ratification might make the difference in New York's decision. The Anti-Federalists, meanwhile, hoped that some other state, perhaps Virginia, might be the first to reject, taking the pressure and blame off of New York. Had the New York Anti-Federalists been prepared to take an early stand against the Constitution, the entire outcome might have been altered.

THE POWER OF NAMES

The Anti-Federalists of New York were content to wait in part because they saw signs that Massachusetts might oppose ratification and derail the entire process. A letter from Thomas Wait to George Thatcher in January suggested the power that the debates in Pennsylvania had in swinging public opinion. Wait confessed that he initially approved the Constitution, because of his esteem for George Washington and Benjamin Franklin. The treatment of the minority in Pennsylvania, though, made him sufficiently sympathetic to the opposition to read some of the Anti-Federalists essays. It did not take long for him to switch sides completely, and by early January he was writing with all the zeal of a convert. If the Constitution is adopted, he averred, it will be because too many of the people are willing to defer to Washington and Franklin rather than seriously considering the document's merits. He finds in a careful reading "a certain darkness, duplicity and studied ambiguity of expression running thro' the whole Constitution which renders a Bill of Rights peculiarly necessary." Wait was not the only convert to Anti-Federalism. An anonymous writer in the *Massachusetts Gazette* confessed to switching sides after reading the essays of the Federal Farmer, which he quotes at length. The idea that more people would oppose the Constitution if they simply read and understood it was a powerful argument. "A Farmer" in the state expressed doubts that many of his fellow citizens had carefully read the Constitution. "The hypothesis, that General Washington and Dr. Franklin made it," he worried, "is too strong an argument in the minds of too many, to suffer them to examine, like Freemen, for themselves."[32] It seems unlikely that anyone in Massachusetts was unfamiliar with the contents of the proposed Constitution by this point, but the influence of names was still substantial.

Names were important to the Anti-Federalists as well, though, and no names were more critical in the fight in this state, on both sides, than those of John Hancock and Samuel Adams. Hancock remained a mystery until he showed up midway through the ratifying convention. He had been at home for the first three weeks, complaining of his gout, though some suggested that it was a mighty convenient illness. As Rufus King puts in a letter during the convention, Hancock "is not yet able to attend the Convention, but I hope he will improve in his Health as soon as a majority shews itself on either side of the convention."[33] As for Adams, there is no doubt that he had concerns about the Constitution. He expressed those concerns privately to Richard Henry Lee in December; the Constitution he found to be national rather than federal, threatening the sovereignty of the states, which Adams saw as the protectors of individual liberty. There is no compelling evidence, however, that he participated in the public debates, either personally or under a pseudonym. Several essays were attributed to him, but none convincingly. Still, many Federalists believed that he was a staunch, if silent, Anti-Federalist. Christopher Gore wrote in December that "S. Adams is out full against it—there is ev'ry reason to conclude him the author of Helvidius Priscus."[34] He then proceeded in the same letter to tell of a dinner to be hosted by James Bowdoin at which he suspected Adams would attempt to uncover the Federalist strategy for the convention, in order to determine how he "might best counteract our intentions." This idea of Adams as a sort of Anti-Federalist spy (Gore insisted that he "shall not be entrapt by the craft of A[dams]") is far more amusing than it is credible.[35] Still, there is reason to believe that Adams was indeed very interested in the Federalist position and plans, but probably for the right reasons of determining his own position on ratification.

We know that in late December Samuel Adams asked Samuel Osgood for his opinion on the Constitution, a request with which Osgood was happy to comply. His formal opening suggests that this was an uncommon request by Adams. Osgood's answer begins with "you honor me, Sir, by requesting my sentiments. . . ." This would be rather out of place if the two routinely discussed political controversies. It is very unlikely that this was an isolated request, either, especially considering that others professed to have no knowledge of his position; the more likely explanation is that Adams was discretely obtaining various opinions on the Constitution in order to make his own judgment. He said as much in the convention, at least with regard to the debates there.[36] What, then, should we make of Gore's description of Adams's behavior at Bowdoin's dinner party?

> Mr Adams was open & decided ag[ains]t it—That such a Gov[ernmen]t coud not pervade the United States—that internal taxes ought not to be given to the Union—that the representation was inadequate—that a gov[ernmen]t might be formd from this—but this woud never answer and ought not to be adopted, but on condition of such amendments as woud totally destroy it—these objections were supported by such arguments & such only as appear in the pieces of Brutus & federal farmer—to close all he told me on our parting that people said they coud not find out the sentiments of Mr Adams—it was strange, for he had always been as explicit as he then was, and to Mr King he stated every objection then made—the next day when these observations came to be publickly mention'd—many appeard who declare that Mr A[dams] told them no one did or shoud know his sentiments on the subject.[37]

This is indeed strange behavior from someone who has not yet made up his mind. There are several explanations for this. It is highly unlikely that Gore was simply lying; he had no incentive to do so in a private letter. It is possible that Gore is exaggerating; perhaps the wine flowed a little too freely and his memory was a bit fuzzy. Or maybe it was Adams who had too much to drink and got carried away, exaggerating his own objections and looking for an argument. Given that we have no corroboration of the behavior of Adams at the party,[38] and because we have no other instance of his open opposition, it seems reasonable to conclude that Adams was not in fact "out full mouthed against the Constitution," as Rufus King put it, so much as expressing concerns and willing to be convinced. Though it was second-hand and written much later, Jeremy Belknap's account of the party is probably more accurate; he wrote that Adams suggested that the Constitution was flawed, but after the discussion said that "he was open to conviction."[39] The Federalists acted consistently with the idea that Adams could be convinced. Certainly the famed meeting of the tradesmen in the Green Dragon Tavern in December, led by none other than Paul Revere, was aimed at swaying Adams, though it could have been trying simply to silence his opposition.[40]

Whether outright opposition or cautious objections, his behavior was generally consistent with his earlier principles. The Federalist *American Herald*, just days before the compromise that would win ratification by the state, praised him, writing that "The Hon. Mr. A[dam]s, by persevering in his scepticism may possibly damn his well-deserved Fame, acquired in a long course of patriotism . . . [but] we cannot but admire the consistency of his character in adhering to his old principle of Republicanism."[41] Adams as an Anti-Federalist zealot makes little sense against such Federalist praise. For their part, the Federalists were ready to welcome Adams into their ranks, and Adams eventually came around to support the Constitution with recommended amendments.

The Anti-Federalists tried their best to attach their cause to other revered patriots as well. This is why Pennsylvania Anti-Federalists attempted to get Benjamin Franklin elected to the state convention, despite his signature on the Constitution. The Virginia Anti-Federalists attempted to claim Thomas Jefferson, then in France, so it seems appropriate that the opposition in Massachusetts alleged that John Adams, absent in England, was on their side. In the *American Herald*, "O" quotes at length (and very selectively) from Adams's *Defence of the Constitutions of the United States of America* to contend that Adams was opposed to the product of the Philadelphia Convention. Curiously, O asserts that the opposition of Adams, a man often accused of leaning too much toward aristocracy (natural or otherwise), rests on the danger that even the House of Representatives in the new government would be too aristocratic: the poor will have no say, because the rich will make the policies.[42] This runs counter to the inclinations of Adams himself, who supported the Constitution, albeit with misgivings.[43]

6

The Heart of the National Debate

ALTHOUGH THERE WAS much variety in Anti-Federalist arguments, there was less variation in opposition rhetoric. There is some legitimacy to a satirical recipe for an Anti-Federalist essay, first printed in Pennsylvania and reprinted in five other states:

> WELL-BORN, nine times—*Aristocracy*, eighteen times—*Liberty of the Press*, thirteen times repeated—*Liberty of Conscience*, once—*Negroe slavery*, once mentioned—*Trial by jury*, seven times—*Great Men*, six times repeated—Mr. WILSON, forty times—and lastly, GEORGE MASON'S *Right Hand in a Cutting-box*, nineteen times—put them altogether, and dish them up at pleasure. These *words* will bear boiling, roasting, or frying—and, what is remarkable of them, they will bear being served, after being once used, a dozen times to the same table and palate.[1]

During the first five ratifying conventions, the essays on the Constitution continued to appear, at an increasing rate. January and February 1788 represented the high point of the newspaper debates; many arguments against the Constitution were presented, but the different strands of Anti-Federalism had only begun to coalesce into a single opposition position.

POWER ANTI-FEDERALISM IN THE NORTHEAST

While the Pennsylvania Convention was in session, Brutus published two more essays in New York, continuing his assault on the powers given to the national government by the proposed Constitution. In particular, he attacks the open-ended congressional power to levy taxes. Cato, too, continued his essays in New York. Having addressed the presidency in his previous letter, he takes up the issue of representation in Congress. He covers familiar ground, emphasizing annual elections; he even advocates what he calls a "well-digested democracy" on the assumption that the people will become better informed and educated, and thus more qualified to make important decisions.[2] His discussion of representation is short, as he refers his readers to the letters of Brutus for a further exploration of the topic. Cato, like Brutus, takes up the issue of taxes, suggesting that heavy tax burdens are to be expected. Even if, as many Federalists had suggested, the national government opts to raise revenue solely through imposts, the cost will likely end up sufficiently high to stunt trade and stifle economic growth. The alternative, direct taxes, is no better, and may in fact be oppressive. Even in this latter case, he contends, taxes ought to be apportioned according to property, not number of inhabitants. Meanwhile, even as the House addresses the question of taxation, the Senate will be in a position to heavily influence if not outright corrupt it. And even if the House can resist the encroachments of the Senate, the latter body, with the President, can make law without the House, in the form of treaties. Cato finds this distribution of power alarming, and suggests that the Constitution simply grants too much to the national government.

In December, John Lansing and Robert Yates, two of New York's delegates to the Philadelphia Convention, wrote a joint letter to Governor George Clinton of New York explaining their departure from the Convention.[3] In the letter, they insisted that they left because they believed the Convention had exceeded the bounds of its authority and that the Constitution that was just beginning to take shape was too national, rather than federal, in its character. Their stature as political leaders and former delegates gave Lansing and Yates considerable credibility among opponents of the Constitution, and their arguments were distributed rather widely in early 1788. Their primary objection was to the consolidation of governmental power in a national government rather than its dispersion across the states. Yates and Lansing certainly had a sense of the political pulse of New York, perhaps the strongest bastion of Anti-Federalist thought and influence. When the two argue "that the leading feature of every amendment [to the Articles], ought to be the preservation of the individual states, in their uncontrouled constitutional rights," they certainly reflect the prevailing opinion of most of New York's political elite.[4] The sole New York delegate to sign the Constitution, Alexander Hamilton, was far from the mainstream opinion of his state, advocating instead a strong and energetic national government. The question of state sovereignty would be perhaps

the most central one in the contentious debates in New York over the proposed Constitution.

Several writers in the state took issue with very specific powers given to
the national government. One writer emphasized that only Congress may
propose amendments, because the states may not convene a convention
unless Congress shall formally call such a convention; this will make any
future limits to power unlikely to be added. "A Querist" took issue with
the clause stating that members of Congress shall be chosen "every second
year," suggesting that a variety of meanings could be attached to this phrase,
and Congress is effectively given sole power to interpret it. "A Republican"
contended that the clause guaranteeing the debts owed by the United States
implies that debts owed *to* the nation are no longer valid and may not be
collected. The prohibition of ex post facto laws, he explains, will prevent
such debts from being collected by the United States.[5]

In late November and early December, two distinct series of essays signed
"A Countryman" appeared in the *New York Journal*. The first to appear
was a radical in the mold of Centinel and Philadelphiensis. He suggested
that ratification would be the people's "*last sovereign act*, unless it should
be a violent resumption, by arms." He placed a special emphasis on liberty
with respect to slavery. The tacit endorsement of that institution, he argues,
reflects poorly on the delegates. He singles out Benjamin Franklin, who was
avowedly for the emancipation of slaves, as well as John Dickinson. This
objection is a radical one, because he was prepared to place the principle of
liberty above even the principle of union. Union is important, but not on
terms that undermine freedom. The delegates to the Philadelphia Convention must have understood this, but, the Countryman contends, they were
misled. Although most of them were well intentioned, nonetheless as a body
they were "insidiously drawn into the Measures of the more artful and designing Members, who have long envied the great Body of the People, in the
United States, the Liberties which they enjoy." These "artful and designing"
delegates evidently included Benjamin Franklin; the Countryman goes further than even Centinel in his attack on Franklin, calling into question the
Pennsylvanian's patriotism. He contends that Franklin "countenanced and
encouraged the Stamp Act," in part by threatening printers who attacked
the British government. Alexander Hamilton was also attacked for the sheer
audacity of his signing the Constitution on behalf of New York, as if he
alone might represent the state in the Convention.[6]

The Countryman presents a rather unusual reading of the Supremacy
Clause, claiming that other Anti-Federalists, including Centinel, have not
gone far enough in their denunciations of it. The issue here is that treaties

and laws made in pursuance of the Constitution need not be consistent with that document. There can be but one supreme, or highest, authority, yet treaties and laws, along with the Constitution, are to be supreme. Thus, he concludes, treaties and laws may add to and even alter the provisions of the Constitution. This reading is difficult to sustain under a reasonable interpretation of the words of the clause in question, but it is emblematic of the often willful misreading of the Constitution that pervaded the Democratic Anti-Federalist position. This Countryman proposes a list of amendments that must be made to the Constitution before adoption such that "we might become a happy and respectable people." These changes include a bill of rights, annual elections for the House, triennial elections for the Senate, restrictions on the powers of Congress over the army and militias, and removal of the clause permitting the slave trade. Interestingly, he omits the question of taxes, though he does imply that power should be sharply shifted back to the states.[7]

Another author, also signing his essays as "A Countryman," was more of a populist than his countryman, but nonetheless less radical and a Power Anti-Federalist. The president, he says, looks like a king, and the Senate like a House of Lords. He suggests that the House, if sufficiently large and virtuous, "might give the others a deal of trouble, and hinder them from doing much mischief for a good while."[8] Unfortunately, he predicts, the smallness of the House will prevent them from doing much good. Meanwhile, the states will have nothing they can do against the national government, due in large part to the Supremacy Clause. State officials, he observes, will be bound by an oath to uphold the federal Constitution, and fulfilling the terms of this oath may well require them to violate the terms of the oath they must take to uphold the state constitution. The states are ensured a republican form of government, but the national government will quickly depart from such a form and establish tyranny.

This Countryman, probably DeWitt Clinton, an ambitious nephew of Governor George Clinton of New York, wrote in a tone intended to convey the image of a common, if rather shrewd and politically minded, farmer discoursing on his understanding of the Constitution. Nonetheless, the ideas conveyed are well articulated and focused largely on the question of the powers of the national government. He briefly mentions trial by jury in his first essay, and mentions it again, along with rights of conscience and freedom of the press, in his final letter, but he spends far more time on the powers of Congress. His neighbor, the Countryman reports, warned that "we should be careful not to give a bit more power to our rulers than we could well help; for they would always find a way to get more fast enough, and they knew how to keep it when they once had it, so that we could never get any part of it back again."[9] He spends some time on the subject of taxes, making clear that duties and imposts are unlikely to present any hardship, but excise taxes and especially capitation taxes are likely to create a substantial burden. The New York state taxes, he complains, are already too high and difficult to pay. In his fifth letter in January, he puts together this taxation clause, particularly the part concerning the "general welfare" of the country, with the Necessary and Proper Clause, concluding that Congress can stretch its power as far as it likes.

The Countryman spends some time on the issue of slavery as well. He takes issue with the literal meaning of Article I, Section 9, that immigrants might have to pay ten dollars to the new government to enter the country. This serves only as a preface, though, for his attack on the Constitution's implicit acceptance of slavery. Claiming that a friend from Pennsylvania informed him that this clause concerned the slave trade, the Countryman proceeded into a vehement attack on the institution, which he called "an abomination to the Lord" destined to "bring down a heavy judgment upon our land." He invokes the Declaration of Independence and its claim that "all men were created equal; and that they were endowed by their creator with certain unalienable rights." Apparently slaves were not intended to be a part of this sweeping claim. Invoking God in such an insincere manner, he insists, is a bad idea, for "it is a terrible thing to mock the almighty." Surely divine vengeance is coming for such substantial national sins.[10] This is a stronger statement than almost any Anti-Federalist south of New York would make on slavery, but it does reflect a north-south division on the issue already brewing.

Perhaps the most distinctive part about the letters occurs in the third one, in which the Countryman and his neighbor visit the house of a local lawyer, who, along with several other lawyers present, is reluctant to comment on the breadth of implied powers, and instead suggests that the Constitution should be adopted first and fixed later. If the Constitution is not ratified, these lawyers explained to the two farmers, the country will fall into "anarchy (as they called it) and confusion." The Countryman's friend responded, apparently, by quoting "Mr. Beccaria and other great men (whose names I do not remember)."[11] Clearly this friend was a very well-read and learned farmer. Meanwhile, the Countryman proceeds to attack lawyers in general, and closes with another analogy, this time of moving from an old house to a new one.

> I should think it a very unwise thing to pull down an old house, in which I lived very comfortably for many years, and which had sheltered

me and my family, and move into a new house, just to gratify the pride and vanity of the children, because it was larger and appeared finer, on the outside, when I knew at the same time, that it was not well finished within, that the foundation was bad, the chimnies smoky, the roof leaky, and many of the posts rotten, so as to make it dangerous to go in it, and that it would cost me more than I was worth in the world to furnish and keep it in repair, and I am apt to believe if I got ruined by it, I should meet with few to pity me; and yet it is strange, we are told if we do not do something as foolish as this about the new government, we shall get a quarrelling; but let them quarrel that will, I am for continuing peaceably in the old house, and for mending it now and then, as it stands in need of it.[12]

The lawyers and merchants had a vested interest in making a radical change, even if it was not a good change for the country as a whole. The Federalists, this writer implies, include the self-interested (and even devious), as well as the well-meaning but clueless. His closing paragraph sums up this opinion of the defenders of the Constitution rather well. "Indeed," he writes, "take the new constitution all together, it is an odd jumbled kind of business, and yet some people say, they were very wise, honest men, who made it—though I have no doubt some of them might have been very honest, but I am widely mistaken, if the bulk of them were both honest and wise."[13]

New York's predominantly Power Anti-Federalist position was shared across the states of the northeast. The primary concern in the region was that "Power, without a check, in *any* hands, is tyranny; and such powers, in the hands of even *good men*, so infatuating is the nature of it, will probably be wantonly, if not tyrannically exercised." Samuel Adams was clearly in the mainstream of opposition thought in his objection to the distribution of power in the Constitution. "I confess," he wrote to Richard Henry Lee, "as I enter the Building I stumble at the Threshold. I meet with a National Government, instead of a fœderal Union of Sovereign States."[14] He questions whether a national legislature can govern a country of such varied climates and cultures. He implies that the liberties of the people would be better secured under a confederation, but the absence of a bill of rights is not a primary objection for Adams, as one might expect of the old patriot, or at least not in this letter.

In late November, an important series of essays appeared in Massachusetts under the pseudonym "Agrippa." These essays, though parochial and xenophobic[15] in their emphasis, were among the best-written objections to the Constitution. Agrippa, much like his New York colleagues Brutus and

Cato, takes a Power Anti-Federalist position. He is concerned with individual rights, but seemingly only commercial and property rights. As such, he
presents an understanding of government that emphasizes the importance
of protecting free markets and interfering only when necessary for the administration of justice and enforcement of contracts. His appreciation for
free market capitalism is unmistakable: "when business is unshackled," he
claims, "it will find out that channel which is most friendly to its course.
We ought, therefore, to be exceedingly cautious about diverting or restrain-
ing it." He finds in commercial enterprise "the great bond of union among
citizens." This is the case not in spite of the differences between states, but
because of those differences. "All the states have local advantages, and in
a considerable degree separate interests. They are, therefore, in a situation
to supply each other's wants." Union is brought about by general prosperity, which rests on industry, which requires freedom. Such freedom requires
government that is restrained in its power and cautious in its actions. And
what government power must exist ought to be predominately local. "It is
only by protecting local concerns, that the interest of the whole is preserved.
No man when he enters into society, does it from a view to promote the
good of others, but he does it for his own good."[16]

Agrippa raises many of the usual objections, emphasizing in particular
the conduct of the Federalists. He claims that the supporters of the Constitution have failed to provide an answer to any objection, except "such as have
acknowledged the truth of the objection while they insulted the objector."
He accuses the Federalists of trying to force the Constitution on the people.
The reason for such behavior, he suggests, is that the situation in America
is not bad; on the contrary, the laws are well administered, the people are
industrious and free, and no significant dangers threaten the union: "The attempt has been made to deprive us of such a beneficial system, and to substitute a rigid one in its stead, by criminally alarming our fears, exalting certain
characters on one side, and vilifying them on the other." Agrippa contrasts
this fear campaign with the reasoned arguments of the opposition; he finds
the Anti-Federalist position to be coherent and consistent across the United
States. "The same objections are made in all the states," he contends, "that
the civil government which they have adopted and which secures their rights
will be subverted" by the Constitution. The Articles, coupled with the state
constitutions, represent "the best calculated of any form [of government]
hitherto invented, to secure to us the rights of our persons and of our property." They form, "in the strictest sense of the terms, a federal republick."[17]

The Articles of Confederation could be fixed, Agrippa contends, by
giving to Congress the power to levy imposts and the power to regulate

commerce. This latter power, he clarifies, must be restricted to prevent any favoritism toward any state, part of a state, or particular corporation. In his tenth letter, in early January, Agrippa proposed a resolution to be adopted by the Massachusetts Ratifying Convention. The resolution begins with an unqualified rejection of the proposed Constitution, and proposes language for an amendment to the Articles:

XIV. The United States shall have power to regulate the intercou[r]se between these states and foreign dominions, under the following restrictions, viz. 1st. No treaty, ordinance, or law shall alienate the whole or part, of any state, without the consent of the legislature of such state. 2d. The United States shall not by treaty or otherwise give a preference to the ports of one state over those of another; nor, 3d. create any monopolies or exclusive companies; Nor, 4th, extend the privileges of citizenship to any foreigner. And for the more convenient exercise of the powers hereby, and by the former articles given, the United S[t]ates shall have authority to constitute judicatories, whether supreme or subordinate, with power to try all piracies and felonies done on the high seas, and also all civil causes in which a foreign state, or subject thereof actually resident in a foreign country and not be-ing British absentees, shall be one of the parties. They shall also have authority to try all causes in which ambassadours shall be concerned. All these trials shall be by jury and in some sea-port town. All imposts levied by Congress on trade shall be confined to foreign produce or foreign manufactures imported, and to foreign ships trading in our harbours, and all their absolute prohibitions shall be confined to the same articles. All imposts and confiscations shall be to the use of the state in which they shall accrue, excepting in such branches as shall be assigned by any state as a fund for defraying their proportion of the continental. And no powers shall be exercised by Congress but such as are expressly given by this and the former articles.[18]

By such an amendment, the people of Massachusetts (and, by extension, of the United States) "shall provide for all federal purposes, and shall at the same time secure our rights."[19]

Agrippa, called by one Federalist "the oracle of sedition" (and, added the writer, "sedition is the idol of Anti-Federalism"), published a second series of letters in early 1788. He continues his themes of private property and commerce, this time emphasizing the necessity of small, local government. He recognizes the importance of some type of national government, but advocates a "FEDERAL REPUBLICK." "By this kind of government each state reserves to itself the right of making and altering its laws for internal regulation, and the right of executing those laws without any external restraint, while the general concerns of the empire are committed to an assembly of delegates, each accountable to his own constituents. This is the happy form under which we live, and which seems to mark us out as a people chosen of God." To insist that local concerns be set aside in favor of national ones "is sapping the foundation of a free state." It is those local concerns, and especially selfish concerns over property, that form the very essence of freedom. The loss of property rights leads to a loss of freedom, which leads to a degradation of public virtue.[20]

Agrippa presents a compelling theory of enumerated versus implied powers in the legislature. Legislatures, he claims, have an inherent right to alter laws other than the constitution, so specific safeguards are essential in a proper constitution. This is why bills of rights are so important; all constitutions are essentially constitutions of implied powers. In this particular case, since the federal judicial power is to extend to cases concerning property between citizens, and since the jurisdiction of the courts must logically be coeval with the extent of legislative power, Congress will have the power "to legislate for all kinds of causes respecting property between citizens of different states." The Necessary and Proper and Supremacy Clauses only reinforce this implied power. The power to specifically regulate commerce, both external and internal, is even clearer. "They have indeed," he points out, "very nearly the same powers claimed formerly by the British parliament. Can we have so soon forgot our glorious struggle with that power, as to think a moment of surrendering it now?" Rather than give such full and extensive power to Congress, Agrippa suggests that limited powers be granted, potentially with additional powers as needed. He offers specific language for an amendment to the Articles of Confederation, which would extend congressional powers over commerce and create a judicial arm for the confederation. "Such a resolve explicitly limitting the powers granted," he suggests, "is the farthest we can proceed with safety. The scheme of accepting the report of the Convention, and amending it afterwards, is merely delusive." More power is necessary, but we ought not give too much. "I know it is a common complaint, that Congress want more power," Agrippa concedes, "But where is the limitted government that does not want it?" The power of Congress must be carefully extended to allow for better protection of property and local interests, without consolidation of political power. Agrippa considers this the very purpose of government. "In a republick," he writes, "we ought to guard, as much as possible, against the predominance of any particular interest. It is the object of government to protect them all. When commerce is left to take its own course, the advantages of every class will be nearly equal.—But when exclusive privileges are given to any class, it will operate to the weakening of some other class connected with them." Commerce is the primary feature of the United States, and the source of both its liberty and equality. Thus it ought to be the central concern of all who are involved in deciding the fate of the proposed Constitution.[21] Agrippa, though somewhat unusual among Anti-Federalists in his state as well as nationally, remains a distinct Power Anti-Federalist.

Another Power Anti-Federalist in Massachusetts, "Candidus," agreed in principle with Agrippa, arguing that "the States ought to confederate for the purposes of commerce and amity, rather than for those of legislation and taxation." He sums up what he deems to be the most common objections to the Constitution, almost all of which relate to the distribution of power therein. Candidus suggests that a new convention be held, and he, like Agrippa, proposes an alternative to ratifying the Constitution. This alternative, laid out in his second essay, is based on proposals previously made in Congress for modifying the existing government. He contends that this proposal answers all of the defects of the Articles of Confederation, while preserving a federal system. His proposal, though, was never seriously taken up, because there was no appropriate venue for it. The Massachusetts Ratifying Convention did not veer so far from the proposed Constitution as to suggest something entirely different, and Congress was not about to consider a different form of government while the Constitution was still under debate. The same could be said for the amendment to the Articles proposed by Agrippa. At the close of his first letter, Candidus struck a strongly republican tone, lamenting the lack of virtue in the population of the United States. "No government under heaven could have preserved a people from ruin, or kept their commerce from declining," he writes, "when they were exhausting their valuable resources in paying for superfluities, and running themselves in debt to *foreigners*, and to *each other* for articles of folly and dissipation:—While this is the case, we may contend about forms of government, but no establishment will enrich a people, who wantonly spend beyond their income."[22] The important message here, one that tends to get lost in the debate, is that peace, prosperity, and happiness are closely tied with the nature of the people. Government plays a role, of course, but it can only do so much to achieve such worthy goals.

In December, "Cornelius," apparently unfamiliar with the Anti-Federalist pieces published before his,[23] began with the common criticism that the

Constitution is not an amendment of the Articles of Confederation, and thus should be "justly considered as a perfidious violation of that fundamental and solemn compact, by which the United States hold an existence, and claim to be a people." He objects to the length of congressional terms, contending that such representatives, being so far removed from the people, will vote themselves sufficient salaries as to live luxurious lifestyles, to better compare to the wealthy citizens and foreigners with whom they are likely to associate. In addition, the powers to alter the manner of elections and to judge the qualifications of members will render both houses entirely independent of the will of the people. Cornelius departs from most of the Power Anti-Federalists in suggesting that to fix the Articles, Congress should be invested not just with the power to regulate commerce and establish imposts, but with a broader power to tax.[24] Still, he fits within that broad opposition tradition in his critique of the structure of government.

Although the opposition in Massachusetts consisted predominantly of Power Anti-Federalists, the Rights position was not entirely absent. An anonymous writer, who closed with "Guard your Rights, Americans!," suggests that the Constitution may be fixed simply by adding a statement of individual liberties. Another writer, signing as "C. O.," suggested that the passage of the Constitution would spell the end of freedom of the press, as the new government would aggressively prosecute anything it deemed libelous. "One of the Common People," writing in direct response to "One of the Middle-Interest," defended the importance of a bill of rights. "If we alienate a great part of the powers, at present contained in our state constitution, and vest them in congress," he asks, "why is it not as necessary that those alienated powers should be secured and limited by a declaration of rights, as that the remaining powers which are left in the hands of the state government should be thus guarded, especially if the greater half are alienated?" The problem is not that the grant of power to the national government is unlimited, but that it is left (necessarily) vague. The liberty of the press, for example, is not explicitly threatened, but Congress can make laws for the prosecution of libel, and the state bill of rights need not be considered. This author implies that the Constitution, with proper safeguards, may not be objectionable, but the absence of a bill of rights makes it unacceptable.[25]

Even the question of a bill of rights, though, was here subsumed by the Power Anti-Federalists. An anonymous writer in the *Cumberland Gazette* offered a distinctive twist on the question of a bill of rights, suggesting that such a bill in the federal Constitution ought to protect the states from national encroachment, just as the state bills protect the people from state interference. This is a different kind of bill of rights, because it would ensure rights for a different set of constituents.

In late December and early January, the first pair of essays by Helvidius Priscus appeared in the Boston *Independent Chronicle* attacking the Framers of the Constitution and their "*Heterogeneous Monster*." "It is well known," the author asserts, "that some of the late Convention were the professed advocates of the British system; that others stood suspended in equilibrio, uncertain on which side to declare, until the scale of fortune balanced in favour of America; that the political manoeuvres of some of them have always sunk in the vortex of private interest, and that the immense wealth of others has set them above all principle."[26] This collection of monarchists, reluctant patriots, schemers, and plutocrats is not to be trusted, because they have abandoned the principles of the Revolution. Helvidius Priscus calls for the youth of America to read the works of American patriots writing in the years 1763 through 1775, to recapture the spirit of that glorious time. The Constitution, contra revolutionary principles, consolidates power for the few rather than distributing it to the many. Helvidius Priscus was not a radical, though, except insofar as the old patriots of the Revolution could be considered radical in the more conservative climate of 1788. He offered little concrete argument, but he fit with the Power Anti-Federalist position common to Massachusetts.

Samuel Osgood, in a letter to Samuel Adams in early January, laid out a fairly comprehensive Power Anti-Federalist position that is typical of the state. The usual objections are there: the national government will have complete power of taxation; the federal courts will supersede the state judiciaries and ultimately eliminate them; the federal government will swallow up the states, reducing the several legislatures to little more than election boards; Congress ought not to have the power to regulate congressional elections; the ten miles square for the seat of the national government will be a haven for tyranny. There are a few unusual twists, including a rare argument that plaintiffs will resort to claiming citizenship in another state in order to sue in federal courts,[27] and that the capital city ought to have its own bill of rights, and deserves representation in Congress when it has a sufficient population. Osgood does depart from the typical Anti-Federalist position in several particulars, though. He agrees, for example, with James Wilson's contention that whatever powers are not given are reserved, but Osgood counters that "the great Question upon this is what is there of Consequence to the People that is not given." He also offers one of the best arguments to counter the Federalist hurry toward unconditional ratification of an unamended Constitution. "The all important Reason with many for adopting the Plan without Amendments," he writes, "is, that if we don't accept of the one proposed, we shall have none. This seems to allow that the Objections made against it, are good; the Plain Meaning of it, is then, that Despotism is better for us, than to remain as we are."[28] This is a powerful argument, and one for which the Federalists have no answer. Many Anti-Federalists suggested that the Federalists were in a hurry because the objections were valid, and that the Constitution's supporters were trying to trick the people into a hasty adoption. Osgood's logic is more sound; the Federalists were less afraid of a government too strong (perhaps not a despotism, but certainly a government that leaned in that direction) than the descent into anarchy they saw in the continuing Articles of Confederation.

In late December, "A Republican Federalist" began a significant series of essays arguing not only the imprudence but also the illegality of the proposed Constitution. Although his letters were addressed "To the Members of the Convention of Massachusetts," his primary audience was clearly the public. He divided opinions on the Constitution into three rather than two camps: those who wish to adopt, those who wish to reject, and those who seek amendments. He places himself in the third group. "We want a *free, efficient federal* government," he asserts, "and can only attain it, by a *candid, dispassionate*, discussion of the subject." Toward this end, he repeatedly calls for more time to consider the merits and defects of the proposed Constitution. "Surely it must appear that the plan, although *improperly before the State*, cannot with safety be rejected—that it cannot as it stands, be safely *accepted*—that the people will not be satisfied with a *ratification*, and the *delusive prospect of future alterations*—and that the only hope that remains of preserving the peace and happiness of this Commonwealth, is *from amending the plan in order to its adoption*." There is no danger in the delay necessary to identify the proper amendments to perfect this proposed system of government. "*Too much light cannot be thrown on the subject, neither can a short delay possibly injure us; but an hasty decision may irretrievably ruin us*."[29]

The Republican Federalist emphasized the legal issues surrounding ratification (hence his assertion that the Constitution was improperly before the state). Changing the constitution of Massachusetts (which would inevitably have to change to adapt to the proposed federal Constitution) required the support of two-thirds of the freemen of the state. Changing the current federal constitution, the Articles of Confederation, required the approval of every state legislature. The process for ratification ignored both of these, effectively undermining not only those constitutions, but the general principle of the inviolability of political compacts. From this argument, the

Republican Federalist confidently rewrites the preamble to reflect the true spirit of the Convention and its proper legal status:

> *We the people, do hereby publickly declare the violation of the faith which we have solemnly pledged to each other—do give the most unequivocal evidence, that we cannot ourselves, neither can any others, place the least confidence in our most solemn covenants, do effectually put an end in America, to governments founded in compact—do relinquish that security for life, liberty and property, which we had in the Constitutions of these States, and of the Union—do give up governments which we well understood, for a new system which we have no idea of—and we do, by this act of ratification and political suicide, destroy the new system itself, and prepare the way for a despotism, if agreeable to our rulers. All this we do, for the honour of having a system of consolidation formed by us the people.*[30]

His legal argument is sound; the Federalists are relying on their reputations and the quality of their arguments since they are circumventing legal channels for constitutional change. He takes care of the former argument succinctly. Names, he asserts, ought to have no bearing on the discussion; a good plan, he asserts, ought to be adopted even if written by "a *Caligula* or a *Nero*," while a bad one should be rejected even if written by individuals who "excel in wisdom and integrity *Lycurgus* or *Solon*."[31] As for the Federalist arguments, he astutely uses the Federalists' words against them. To James Wilson's denial that the Constitution aimed at consolidation, he answers with the words of the letter from the Philadelphia Convention referencing the necessity of "the consolidation of the union." He answers Thomas McKean's assertion that despotism, properly administered, may be good government with quotations from Montesquieu that despotism is based on fear rather than virtue.

It is not until his fifth letter that the Republican Federalist turns to specific objections to the content of the Constitution, and these objections, like most in Massachusetts, reflect a Power Anti-Federalist perspective. The representation in Congress is unclear; if southern slaves are included, it must be based on property, for representation based on population ought to count only freemen. The vague word "numbers" used in the clause concerning representation opens up either interpretation, and both represent violations of republican principles. Furthermore, Congress may reduce the representation, and alter the process of electing them, a power altogether unnecessary to restrain the states. When they have established their standing army and high taxes, the writer contends, this is exactly what they will do, to consolidate power in a baneful aristocracy. What is worse is that these very representatives may be foreigners, having lived in the country less than a decade.

"Massachusettensis" developed the argument of the irrelevance of the states under the Constitution more fully than others. He argues that there is no independent state authority recognized anywhere in the plan. Congress will have the power to direct state actions, including in the manner of elections of members of that body. Amendments must be approved by the states, but only after first being proposed by Congress. Even the ratification by state conventions is a means to bypass the established legal authorities of the several states, the legislatures. Each state is guaranteed a republican form of government, but not necessarily one of their choosing; Congress is implicitly given power over this as well. "Can this be uniting the American states?" he asks. "No—it amounts to beginning the American publick world anew."[32] This new beginning is not a federal system, but a consolidated one with subordinate, or perhaps even irrelevant, states as administrative units.

"Samuel" also takes a Power Anti-Federalist position, with a particular emphasis on representation. The number of seats assigned to each state in the first Congress, he observes, is imbalanced, in large part because Georgia is vastly overrepresented with three House members. He also finds the loose requirements for office troubling, warning that "a Pagan, a Mahometan, a Bankrupt, may fill the highest seat, and any and every seat" in the proposed government. The inclusion of a bankrupt in the list of undesirables places Samuel among the more elite Anti-Federalists, rather than the radical democrats, but the point is a valid one, especially in Massachusetts, where the ratifying convention would see more than a few Shaysites seated as delegates. Even more troubling than the lenient requirements for office and the imbalanced representation, though, is the oath of office. Samuel finds "something very singular" in an oath "to preserve, protect, defend and support this Constitution" rather than "to preserve, protect, defend and support the United States, or the people thereof, in their rights and privileges; it may from this no doubt be expected that Proclamations will conclude GOD SAVE THE CONSTITUTION!"[33] This is a rather novel argument, suggesting a subtle understanding of the importance of wording in even seemingly innocuous provisions. His suggestion that such an oath would prevent members of Congress from supporting amendments is somewhat absurd, but the general veneration of the Constitution is a point on which Samuel was prescient. That Constitution-worship might become a sort of replacement for religion is implied here; he is concerned that God has been written out of the Constitution. He suggests that religion is essential to the state, and that a refusal to so much as acknowledge God will doom American society to His wrath. So much for God saving the Constitution.

Nathaniel Barrell, writing to Federalist George Thatcher, also touched on themes of representation, without the religious overtones. He observed "that it is much easier to tell the objectors to turn their representatives out, than to do it—I cant but think you know how difficult it is to turn out a representative who behaves ill, even tho chosen but for one year—think you not 'twould be more difficult to remove one chosen for two years?" Six years, of course, is far too long, because the influence of Senators with such a long term will ensure continuance in office for life. As it stands, Barrell contends, the Constitution "intails wretchedness on my posterity—slavery on my children," yet he still sees the possibility that, with amendments, the proposed government might be made safe. Long terms combined with discretion over their own pay were simply too much; "A Farmer" in Massachusetts perceptively observed that members of Congress need not bear the same burdens they place on other citizens, because it is within their power to set their own salaries and thus ease the burdens accordingly. Thus we have Senators for life, well paid to offset any burdens they may place on the rest of the citizenry.[34]

What was even worse for many northerners was the implicit acceptance of slavery. In Massachusetts, for example, "Adelos" attacked the first clause of Article I, Section 9, preventing Congress from interfering with "that most cursed of all trades, the African slave-trade" for twenty years. He suggested that "the article ought to be expunged; or that we ought not to vote to give life to a constitution, which at its first breath will be branded with eternal infamy, by having a stamp of slavery and oppression upon it." The antislavery sentiment was not confined to the north, either. In early February, "A Virginian" tried to win the Quakers in the state over to the Anti-Federalist cause by suggesting that rather than allowing the slave trade to be reopened for two more decades, "it would better become us all as men and Christians, to endeavor to release those already under our care from the grievous burthens they are laboring under." In addition, the new government "will have it in their power to make war on any terms they please," and will no doubt conscript men to fight their wars, disregarding any conscientious objection.[35] These were the two most objectionable points for the Quakers, and the Virginian, like many practical Anti-Federalists, was willing to press any advantage he could get. Such arguments were much more common, and effective, further north, but slavery was at best an uncomfortable subject even in the Old Dominion.

Another anonymous writer in Massachusetts, in the *American Herald*, also articulated a Power position, with many typical objections and one interesting twist. The adoption of the Constitution, he argues, "is pregnant with consequences of the first magnitude, consequences of the most serious nature," because it would "subvert the most essential principles" of the state constitution as well as "set an unequivocal example of revolt from established constitutions" and "sanctify a revolt and overturning of governments."[36] Although many Anti-Federalists argued that, legally speaking, all thirteen state legislatures must approve any new constitution, few followed through to the logical consequence that the very permanence of *any* constitution would be undermined by the proposed ratification procedure.

In late January, "The Yeomanry of Massachusetts" weighed in on the debate, attacking the "aristocratick" party's efforts to win them over. The author of this piece calmly tears down the concept that the Constitution ought to be supported because of its attachments to great names. George Washington himself is the primary target. "We cannot think," Yeomanry writes, "the noble general, has the same ideas with ourselves, with regard to the rules of right and wrong." As a slaveholder, Washington cannot effectively stand for the liberty or equality of the people. Elbridge Gerry is instead offered by the Yeomanry as a man to be trusted and revered, not to be publicly mistreated as the Federalists have done. After all, Gerry "is much more consistent, than those who are for turning our republican government into a hateful aristocracy." The author suggests another convention to consider the objections raised. In creating a constitution for the state of Massachusetts, after all, "two trials were made before one would stick."[37] The second convention theme played well in Massachusetts, in large part because the state's constitution had required a second convention before it was approved.

"An American" also attacked George Washington, but on the subject of amendments. He criticized the general's imprudent and dangerous comments that the Constitution must be accepted without amendment, because it may be the last chance for effective government. Although the American does not "wish to put an uncandid construction" on Washington's words, he "cannot resist the conclusion, that the General has declared, that this Constitution shall be supported . . . by force." Why, he asks, can we not amend the Constitution before it takes effect, without bloodshed? Helvidius Priscus agreed; prior amendments were necessary for the Constitution, which was "calculated to involve [the people of Massachusetts] in a *servitude*, too complicated to be described, till its dreadful effects are experienced, when they may BE FORBIDDEN TO COMPLAIN." By falling into "the *gilded trap*," and ratifying unconditionally, the people would be reduced to the role of supplicants, dressed in sackcloth and begging for the government to voluntarily restore that liberty which has been lost. "A Bostonian" undoubtedly spoke for many when he insisted that "there are many alterations necessary to be made in the new Constitution before it will suit the people not only of Massachusetts but of New-England in general," but he also betrayed the localism of which the Anti-Federalists were so often accused.[38]

RIGHTS ANTI-FEDERALISM IN THE SOUTH AND WEST

While Power Anti-Federalism was dominant in the northeast, where the debate was centered in early 1788 due to the scheduled conventions in Connecticut, Massachusetts, and New Hampshire, Rights Anti-Federalists also continued to press their case. In Pennsylvania, an Old Whig made a return in early February after a long absence, publishing one final letter, which Storing describes as an "epilogue" to his earlier series. He lamented that the people of Pennsylvania have largely "quitted [the debate] with horror and disgust." The ratification question, he contends, "is too important for good men to suffer themselves to be diverted from giving it a full consideration by the bounding of squibs or the whizzing of political firebrands." He takes up in particular the question of prior amendments versus making changes after ratification. Since there is no guarantee that any amendments will be made after ratification, he reiterates that such changes ought to be obtained before the Constitution is approved. He closes with a call for a new convention. "A little prudence, a little patience, and a little serious reflection, would lead us to concur in calling a new convention, to revise the constitution proposed to us," he writes. "That convention, I have no doubt, if fully, freely, and deliberately chosen, would concur in some essential amendments; and we might yet be a united and a happy people."[39] Such amendments, based on the rest of the Old Whig's essay, would consist primarily in a bill of rights. It is worthwhile to note here that he calls for a convention to amend the proposed Constitution, not start over and change the articles. With five ratifications to this point, and most of the remaining states having already called conventions, the push to outright reject the Constitution and restore the Articles of Confederation was no longer viable. The ratification of Massachusetts, on the same day that the Old Whig's final essay appeared, confirmed this beyond doubt.

In Virginia, the objections of George Mason began to receive widespread circulation in the newspapers in late November, and they came under fire from various Federalists. "Philanthropos" wrote to defend Mason and attack the Constitution, which he saw as "calculated to produce despotism, thraldom and confusion" and "create convulsions to their utmost extremities." The problem stemmed from the powers given to the national government, but Philanthropos clearly belongs in the Rights Anti-Federalist tradition. "Our present constitution," he suggests, "with a few additional powers to Congress, seems better calculated to preserve the rights, and defend the liberties of our citizens, than the one proposed, without proper amendments." This sentiment was a common one in Virginia. The Rights position remained dominant in the state; George Lee Turberville, in a letter to James Madison in early December, identified the absence of a bill of rights as the "principal objection" of opponents of the Constitution. Thomas Jefferson, too, rested his objections to the Constitution on the absence of a bill of rights. Though in Paris at the time and thus not a direct participant in the debate, his views matched the views of the Virginia Anti-Federalists, especially those who found much to praise in the Constitution, but were hesitant to support ratification because of certain objections. He ultimately supported ratification despite his objections, like his fellow Virginian Edmund Randolph. In late December, Randolph's objections to the Constitution were made public. By this time, he was wavering in his opposition, as he feared the consequences of a rejection by Virginia. His wavering, though, led to public criticism by "A Plain Dealer," who took Randolph to task for suggesting that if amendments cannot be secured the Constitution ought to be ratified anyway. The governor had previously argued that the Constitution would lead to a monarchy or aristocracy; how can he suggest that such a thing is acceptable?[40] Clearly there was no room in the Anti-Federalist camp for wavering.

The call for a bill of rights was not the only Anti-Federalist cry in the state, though. A writer signing as "C. D.," quoting from the Articles of Confederation and Virginia's act sending delegates to the Philadelphia Convention, makes the simple but powerful argument that ratification by nine states acting through conventions has no legal basis for legitimacy whatsoever. Furthermore, if such acts be treated as legal, then the amendment process in the new Constitution will effectively be undermined, as nothing will stop future political actors from simply ignoring that process, as current ones ignored the process in the Articles.[41] Such an argument never gained much traction anywhere, as nearly all of the states called for conventions, thus implicitly endorsing the legitimacy of the ratification process.

Even in the western part of Virginia, in what would become the state of Kentucky, the Rights position was dominant. "I most heartily agree with you," William Fleming of Belmont wrote to Thomas Madison, cousin of

James Madison and brother-in-law of Patrick Henry, "that the Union of the American states ought to be consolidated. . . . [T]his would give us weight with foreign Nations . . . [while] an independant Sovereignty in each state, will . . . make us an easy prey to the first powerfull foreign invader, but can not the last inconvenience & the former advantage be obtained without depriving the Citizens of their priveleges? I think it may."[42]

Further west, on the other hand, Harry Innes of Kentucky raised Power objections against the Constitution, regarding the economic well-being of that area. He contended that "the adoption of that Constitution would be the destruction of our young & flourishing country." In particular, he had three objections. First, the eastern states, with superior numbers, will out-vote the western and southern on commercial regulations, and are likely to give up navigation of the Mississippi River. Second, an open trade policy would undermine markets for western products, and the states will have no means to prevent harmful imports. Third, citizens of Kentucky would probably need to travel far eastward to defend themselves in federal courts, as there would be no reason for anyone to sue them in Kentucky courts. Because of these reasons, Innes concluded that ratification will make the people of Kentucky "the mere vassals of the Congress and the consequences to me are horrible and dreadful."[43] A Kentucky group known as the "court party" produced a circular letter for distribution in which they argued that the Constitution was bad specifically for Kentucky. Their objections were also essentially Power Anti-Federalist concerns, assuming a Congress at best indifferent and at worst hostile to the western frontiers. They sum up the dangers of the Constitution for the western region:

> By the power to regulate commerce, we loose the Navigation of the Mississippi; population will cease, and Our lands become of little Value. By Uniform duties and imposts, and the prohibition of a tax or duty on Articles exported from any State, we Never shall be able to encourage Manufactaries and our wealth be carried to the Eastern & Southern States. The power Over the Militia, may leave us in a defenceless State and subject us to the ravages of the Merciless Savages; And Upon Our Separation being established, a Number of our Citizens will be draged by the power of the Fœdral Court Six or eight hundred Miles to contest their Legal Claims.[44]

This new government, they suggest, is no government for Kentucky.

The concerns about tyranny were not confined to the west, either. In January, in the *Virginia Independent Chronicle* in Richmond, "Tamony" argued against the power of the President. The Constitution, he writes, "does not secure a minority of the states, from local oppression, [and] is open to the encroachments of aristocracy, the ambition of an individual." That individual, "though not dignified with the magic name of King, . . . will possess more supreme power, than Great Britain allows her hereditary monarchs." He contends that force is the guiding principle of the Constitution, executed with the assistance of a standing army. Had the Constitution made a President ineligible for reelection, and provided for "a council answerable to the people" to advise, if not check, the President, the office of the chief executive might have been made safe. Further south, in South Carolina, an Anti-Federalist poet also lamented the monarchical-aristocratic leanings of the proposed Constitution. "In five short years of Freedom weary grown / We quit our plain republics for a throne; / *Congress* and *President* full proof shall bring, / A mere disguise for Parliament and King." The theme of consolidation was in the poem as well: "When *thirteen* states are moulded into *one* / Your rights are vanish'd and your honors gone."[45]

Virginians much further away than Kentucky were beginning to exert some influence as well. "I wish with all my soul," wrote Thomas Jefferson from Paris, where he was serving as an ambassador, "that the nine first Conventions may accept the new Constitution, because this will secure to us the good it contains, which I think great & important. but I equally wish that the four latest conventions, whichever they be, may refuse to accede to it till a declaration of rights be annexed." In such a bill of rights he hoped to see included "freedom of religion, freedom of the press, freedom of commerce against monopolies, trial by juries in all cases, no suspensions of the habeas corpus, no standing armies. these are the fetters against doing evil which no honest government should decline."[46]

Fellow Virginian William Short, also writing from Paris, was much less sanguine about America's prospects than Jefferson. He saw in the Constitution clear monarchical principles, but also saw no choice but to accept those principles. "[V]iolent as the dose is," he wrote to William Grayson, "the best thing we can do is to swallow it," for the choice comes down to "an acceptance of this constitution or a dissolution of the union."[47] His letter is among the most pessimistic assessments of America's future, regardless of the outcome of the ratification debates.

> You know among the learned there are two opinions respecting the human species relative to government. the one that they are capable of enjoying the purest degree of liberty, & that they were intended for it by the great author of all things—the other that nature never

intended them for any thing more than a partial degree of liberty &
that consequently the idea of a pure republic is a visionary idea.—Our
country, Sir, was the great standard to which these disputants always
refered.—consider what a victory the latter party has lately gained,
by America herself declaring that no government can exist without a
monarch; though he shall for a time be called a President.[48]

This was hardly a ringing endorsement of the Federalist position, but it
was an acceptance of their premise that rejection of the Constitution meant
disunion. James Madison, in February, saw no reason to compromise with
the opponents of the Constitution for this very reason. "I have for some
time been persuaded," he wrote to Edmund Pendleton on the twenty-first,
"that the question on which the proposed Constitution must turn, is the
simple one whether the Union shall or shall not be continued. There is in my
opinion no middle ground to be taken."[49] In the Virginia Ratifying Convention in June, Edmund Randolph, no longer wavering, would make the same
claim, and would come down firmly on the side of union, to the consterna-
tion of every Anti-Federalist delegate.[50]

In South Carolina, an individual writing as "Cato," presumably unconnected with New York's Cato or Virginia's Cato Uticensis, took a moderate view of the Constitution, praising most of the document and raising
essentially a single objection, concerning the reeligibility of the President
to that office. To allow for unlimited reelection is to open the door to monarchy or despotism. The idea that a good President ought to be kept by
the people carries little weight; after all, "America indeed would be poor,
if for every year in a century, she had not a different citizen deserving of
the presidentship." He praises the reduction of state sovereignty, suggesting
that the national government indeed ought to have power over the states. In
his second letter, he advances an argument concerning virtue in a republic
that suggests that his position is closer to that of the Federalists than other
Anti-Federalists. Virtue, he says, is not adequate to preserve the republic.
"I say that mankind are more actuated by the fear of punishment, than the
hope of reward; consequently that laws inflicting penalties, and providing
against exigencies, are more forcible, than sweet allurements to the general
good."[51] Such a sentiment could well have come from the pen of James
Madison, and it runs directly counter to the arguments of the more devoutly
republican Anti-Federalists, like the Federal Farmer and Candidus. Outside
of Cato, there was little Anti-Federalist writing in South Carolina, and Anti-
Federalist pieces from elsewhere, including Mason's objections, only began
to appear in the newspapers in December of that year.

The calls for a bill of rights were less insistent in the New England states than elsewhere, but in New Hampshire "A Farmer" found an enumeration of rights to be the most effective way to limit the excessive powers granted by the Constitution. Turning James Wilson's argument about reserved powers on its head, the Farmer suggests that the broad grant of powers implied by the Supremacy Clause, taken with the listing of congressional powers, makes this constitution an excellent example of the need for a bill of rights, even when powers not granted are reserved. Among the most important rights to be preserved are trial by jury and liberty of the press. The latter, he suggests, requires that no tax be placed upon newspapers; still, "if individuals will publish indecent pieces, leave them to the law of the land to abide the consequence." Liberty is not license. As for the former right, the Farmer suggests a national jury attached to the Supreme Court, chosen by lot from each state. These or similar measures are essential safeguards against tyranny. "Seize the happy moment," the Farmer implores his fellows, "Secure to yourselves and your posterity the jewel Liberty, which has cost you so much blood and treasure, by a well-regulated Bill of Rights, from the encroachments of men in power." He suggests that this may best be accomplished by instructing delegates to the New Hampshire Ratifying Convention to insist on a bill of rights as a condition of ratification.[52]

The Rights Anti-Federalist position was not absent in Massachusetts, either. "A Countryman" invoked the spirit of the Revolution, in which the countrymen of the state were called upon to provide for Boston while the British blockaded its port, all in the name of liberty. That liberty, the writer contends, is lost in the new Constitution. He does not oppose stronger national government; he undoubtedly speaks for many when he says that "We shall allow Congress the controul and regulation of trade, the revenue of all imposts and excises—with courts to carry their laws in execution, to try causes between State and State, public Ministers, &c. and the regulation of currency:—But we shall retain a trial by jury as our dearest privilege, as that democratic balance, which can never be corrupted by Government, or subverted by the chicane of Lawyers."[53]

DEMOCRATIC ANTI-FEDERALISM
AT THE MARGINS

It is easy to overlook the Democratic Anti-Federalist arguments, especially given that the best Power and Rights arguments were presented far more effectively. Nonetheless, this radical fringe of the opposition was significant, nowhere more so than in Pennsylvania. In January in that state, Centinel and Philadelphiensis, the most prolific radicals, were joined by another able defender of democracy, writing as "William Penn." Penn, it seems, found the others' attacks inadequate. He notes that he waited on joining the debate, "hoping that the subject would be taken up by some abler pen than mine," but that the existing objections, presumably including Centinel, Philadelphiensis, and the Old Whig, "have been mostly of the desultory kind." Like Centinel, Penn wrote to the common people of Pennsylvania, refraining from references to philosophical authorities because "truth needs nothing but itself to enforce conviction on unprejudiced minds." Unlike Centinel, Penn sticks to questions of principle and their practical applications, avoiding personal attack. He finds the purpose of governing to be the preservation of liberty, which he defines as *"the unlimited power of doing good."* Only in a democracy can liberty be preserved. It is protected, of course, by proper representation. Penn states as a maxim "that all power residing originally in the people, and being derived from them, they ought to be governed by themselves only, or by their immediate representatives." This, he suggests, is self-evident to the people of America. By power, he clearly means legislative power, and he advocates giving all legislative power to the legislature, insisting that it is dangerous to hand the executive a veto. Penn does not deny the importance of an executive, but he clearly prefers a weak one, with no share in legislation.[54]

Centinel's old ally Philadelphiensis also continued his argument, emphasizing once again in his seventh letter the dangers of a standing army and the importance of a navy. His eighth letter, though, published in late January, presents a different angle on the question. He calmly and deliberately tears into the Federalists once again for attempting to curtail the liberty of the press. Upon doing this, though, he makes the interesting argument that it is dangerous for an Anti-Federalist writer to allow his name to become known. To do so is "to expose his interest, his property, and perhaps his life, to the mercy of a revengeful, and probably a powerful party."[55] Given the experiences of many prominent opponents of the Constitution, especially in those states in which a strong majority favored ratification, the writer is probably correct on this point. Two months later, in March, the identity of Philadelphiensis himself was exposed by Federalist Francis Hopkinson, who suggested that the University of Pennsylvania ought to fire Benjamin Workman, an instructor of mathematics, for his authorship of the essays. Workman defended himself and his writings, and ultimately retained his position, but the concerns he expressed turned out to be prescient even in his own case.

His ninth essay, appearing on the same day as the Old Whig's final one, continues its author's flaming rhetoric and broad attacks on the "conspiracy against the freedom of America . . . by an infernal junto of demagogues." The President is to be a king, the Congress will hold absolute powers over the lives of the people, a standing army will be raised to support the decrees of both, and "[t]here is not a tincture of democracy in the proposed constitution" except for "nominal" elections to office. Still, Philadelphiensis, despite his radical rhetoric, calls for a second convention rather than an outright rejection, echoing the Old Whig. He offers with his support an ominous threat: "If the despots persist in pushing it on," he writes, "let them answer the consequences; they may fall a sacrifice to their own obstinacy; for liberty will triumph over every obstacle, even were a *standing army* opposed to it." This was close to endorsing armed rebellion; the accusation that Benjamin Workman, the author of these essays, was advocating sedition was not entirely without merit.[56]

As in Pennsylvania, the western parts of the northeastern states saw a more radical version of Anti-Federalism. Cincinnatus presented the most consistently democratic position in the state of New York, proclaiming the aristocratic nature of the Senate and praising the unicameral legislature in the Pennsylvania constitution. He tore into James Wilson's contention that the impost will be sufficient to pay for the national government, suggesting instead that the best way to pay the debts of the national government, as well as those of the states, is through the issuance of paper money. He closed his series on a very democratic note, contending that the power to control the manner of elections was "a fundamental right, in which the essence of liberty resides. It is in fact the root of all rights." Another New York Anti-Federalist turned to satire; writing as "One of the Nobility," he depicted the Federalists as aristocrats who thoroughly distrusted the common people as incapable of governing themselves.[57]

The more radical Anti-Federalists even went so far as to question the state's decision to hold a ratifying convention. John Williams of Poughkeepsie, in a letter published in the *Federal Herald* of Albany, proposed that the convention ought to pass the Constitution on to the people to decide by referendum. Williams's objections were typical ones: Congress might abuse its power to regulate elections, taxes will be too high (especially on "taverns and spirits," that most democratic potential source of revenue), Senators will serve for too long, and the equal representation in the Senate defies the principle of equality. In the *Country Journal*, a writer lampooned the Federalist concern for property rights. No expense or loss of liberty is too great, he wrote, "*to secure our property!*" And that is not the only benefit of the Constitution, he added after no fewer than seven repetitions of variations on that phrase; "we shall even have a standing army to *secure our persons.*"[58]

The Democratic Anti-Federalist position was rarer in Massachusetts than in New York, but it was represented. "A Federalist" took a radical populist stance that the people are "the grand inquest who have a RIGHT to judge of [the Constitution's] merits." In the long run, he suggests, the people will decide, and the Federalists cannot prevent such a decision. "At length the luminary of intelligence begins to beam its effulgent rays upon this important production; the deceptive mists cast before the eyes of the people by the delusive machinations of its INTERESTED advocates begins to dissipate, as darkness flies before the burning taper." The Federalist has some of the best prose, but little of substance to contribute. His assertion that he "had rather be a free citizen of the small republic of Massachusetts, than an oppressed subject of the great American empire" could have been a worthy Anti-Federalist rallying cry.[59]

In his final letter, published just days before the decisions in Delaware and Pennsylvania, John DeWitt wrote with less defiance and more outright anger than the Federalist. He tears into the proponents of the Constitution for their tactics in trying to stifle debate and engaging in personal attack. He insists that the Constitution will lead to a standing army, and Congress will decline to train or arm the militia, so no power could possibly resist its army. He adds that Congress will also employ a "swarm of revenue, excise, impost and stamp officers."[60] There is a great deal of frustration apparent in this letter, as John DeWitt was clearly not happy with the way the debate was going; there is a sense of desperation as well, that the people just do not understand the dangers associated with handing the national government the twin powers of the purse and the sword.

For the most part, the more radical opposition writers stopped short of actually advocating violence, but there were exceptions. Some writers in western Virginia were hinting at secession. "So much disappointed in their expectations are the people," wrote an anonymous correspondent near Holston, Virginia, "that they think it more eligible to revert to the tyranny of Britain, than bow the neck to domestic tyrants." The theme of tyranny via consolidation was a popular one here; William Russell, a Washington County planter and Revolutionary War veteran, concluded from the Necessary and Proper Clause in Article I, Section 8, "that no power is reserved or withheld from Congress. It seams to me," he continues, "if Congress, have a right to make all laws that may be necessary & proper, that no inferiour Legislature, can be more than a Mitiphysical nothing. It must be evident," he concludes, "that only force under the new constitution can dictate to Congress; which is a misery every good man wood wish to escape."[61]

Acceptance of the Constitution would not necessarily guarantee the preservation of the union. The Reverend James Madison, writing to his more famous cousin of the same name, expressed concern that "It's Execution, or it's Operation requires Sacrifices, w[hi]ch I suspect our State Legislatures, & that of Virg[ini]a in particular, will never be willing to make." Ultimately, it will need to be backed with force, because "no Gov[ernmen]t can be durable w[hi]ch is not perfectly conformable to ye Genius of ye People, unless it be supported by Force," and the reverend sees enough opposition to be concerned that the people, and especially their state assemblies, will not voluntarily submit. [62]

The danger of armed resistance was slight but real. On the other side of the debate, though, some Anti-Federalists were concerned that there was not more unarmed resistance. James Monroe, writing to Madison, lamented that no states seem inclined to reject ratification. If there were a few decidedly against the Constitution, he suggested, Virginia "might mediate between contending parties & lead the way to an union more palitable to all." The opposition to the Constitution in Virginia may have started out "very violent," but the Federalists perceived a calming of passions on the subject by early 1788. Tobias Lear reported in late January that "the people begin to reflect coolly upon the subject." This generalization, of course, did not apply to everyone; there was at least one dangerous and volatile firebrand in the state intent on heating up the opposition. The friends of the Constitution in the state were keeping a close eye on Patrick Henry, who all seemed to agree was their most dangerous opponent, notwithstanding the powerful objections of George Mason and the prestige of Governor Edmund Randolph. "Mr. Henry," wrote Edward Carrington, "is determined to amend & leave the fate of the measure to depend on all the other States conforming to the Will of Virginia. his language, is, that the other States cannot do without us, and therefore we can dictate to them what terms we please." His politics, according to Carrington, "have been so industriously propogated, that the people are much disposed to be his blind followers."[63]

What stands out most in the Anti-Federalist literature during the early months of 1788, though, is a certain bewilderment that the people are not more firmly on their side against the Constitution. There is a confidence that they have the better argument, and that a victory for the Constitution must be the result of fraud. After all, who could possibly dispute "the nervous reasonings of a Brutus, and the ingenious sentiments of a Candidus"? As "A

Farmer" in New Hampshire saw it, these writers (and presumably others as well),

> have opened the sore and probed it to the bottom; if any man, after reading their strictures upon the Constitution, can lay his hand upon his heart, and say it is best for us to adopt it, I shall in return pronounce, that he ought to be a slave forever, and will freely doom him to the cold and dreary regions of Nova-Scotia, there to wind up his days on clams and potatoes.[64]

There were undoubtedly many who embraced this view.

PROPOSING AMENDMENTS IN MASSACHUSETTS

Aside from more popular support, what was missing from the vast majority of these arguments against the Constitution was specific changes to be made to the Constitution, leaving it to convention delegates to propose detailed amendments. Those few who did offer even the language of suggested changes, though, provide an interesting focal point for a discussion of just what the opponents of the Constitution wanted. "Hampden," a moderate, presents one such set of proposals. Specifically, he suggests seven changes, with brief justifications for each. He proposes that these amendments be attached to the ratification of the state of Massachusetts with a requirement that the first Congress, the two houses acting jointly and voting by state, make any changes approved by seven of the states. Setting aside the question of the constitutionality of such a measure, since it requires a conditional ratification and a Congress elected under the Constitution they would be violating by amending, the idea is at least a practicable one, and one that perhaps more of the Anti-Federalists ought to have advocated. The amendments of Hampden answer many of the most prominent Power Anti-Federalist concerns in Massachusetts. It is interesting that his proposed amendments do not include a bill of rights, and nowhere does he imply that other amendments are needed for him to support the Constitution (though he does raise the possibility of other states proposing changes). This moderate Power position must have resonated among the moderates in the state and in the ratifying convention.

Agrippa too suggested amendments. In his closing letter he makes a final appeal for reason and compromise, suggesting fourteen specific amendments that ought to be made to the proposed Constitution. He writes that he would still prefer amending the Articles of Confederation to modifying the proposed Constitution, but he offers his amendments in the spirit of compromise. They suggest, he says, just how close those who want to amend the Constitution are to those who want to retain and modify the Articles. Every one of his fourteen proposals concerns the powers of the new government; despite his insistence on the importance of a bill of rights, only his thirteenth proposal, which upholds state bills of rights, discusses rights directly, and that suggestion is presented essentially as a modification of the Supremacy Clause. This is still a set of Power Anti-Federalist objections.

There were also proposals for securing rights in the Constitution, but they were less common. "Medium," for example, suggested conciliation: "Let those, therefore, who call themselves Fœderalists, lay aside a little of their arrogance, and . . . unite with their brethren in recommending a bill of rights, which is, in fact, the best security we can have against the encroachments of despotism." His efforts were answered by "A Citizen," who suggested that Medium was merely a Federalist pushing the same "stale and hackneyed reasons" common to all those advocating a swift ratification.[65] Medium's suggestion would become the Federalist strategy in Massachusetts and elsewhere, and it was a strategy aimed more at conciliation than deceit and trickery as the Citizen suggests.

Not all New England Anti-Federalists were prepared to accept an amended Constitution, though. An anonymous writer in the *Massachusetts Centinel* questioned whether the country might still be better served by fixing the Articles of Confederation. "A *real* Federalist," he begins,

> wishes to be informed, whether granting to Congress the Impost for twenty-five years; empowering them fully to regulate trade for the said term of time, and to equalize the representation of the States, together with giving them the sole right of coining and emitting money, would not render the Confederation as compleat as could reasonably be expected, and answer the most important purposes of the Federal Government, without subjecting us to the inconveniences, dangers, and the enormous expense that will inevitably attend our adoption of the new system of *national* government.[66]

This position was shared by "Ezra," who contended that the people of Massachusetts "are willing the federal Convention, should return to Philadelphia, and accomplish the business for which they were delegated, viz. to amend the Confederation.—They are willing to put power sufficient into the hands of the present Congress."[67] This includes giving Congress the power to regulate commerce and the ability to pay the country's debts. This does not require the sacrifice of liberties or the consolidation of power inherent in the Constitution.

7

Compromise in Massachusetts

THE STATE OF Massachusetts promised to be a difficult one for the Federalists. Samuel Bannister Harding sums up the problem well, observing that "by the close of 1787, we have in Massachusetts a democracy, incensed at what it considers the oppressions, actual and prospective, of the aristocracy, fairly united in its plans of political action, and abundantly confident of its power to decide all political matters whatsoever, unaided by the counsel or advice of the upper classes."[1] The western part of the state in particular would prove stubborn, but if the proponents of ratification could get over fears of aristocracy and consolidation ratification was certainly possible. The Federalist strategy here was a careful one, and ultimately brilliant, though aided by some unlikely allies.

Before a convention strategy could be put into an effect, an electoral strategy was necessary. The people of Massachusetts were unpredictable, and sentiments on the Constitution were uneven and largely unknown. Neither the Federalists nor the Anti-Federalists could reliably foresee what types of delegates the elections might return. Most of the leading Federalists, including all of those who signed the Constitution, were chosen as delegates. Francis Dana, who was elected to serve at Philadelphia but never attended, was also to be a delegate, and a zealous Federalist.[2] In Boston, John Hancock and Samuel Adams were both selected, because neither side dared oppose the two old patriots, despite uncertainty over where they stood on the question.[3] On the other hand, there were at least two potential leaders for the opposition who were not elected to the ratifying convention. Elbridge Gerry did not run for a seat, probably because he saw no chance of winning in his town of Cambridge. Nathan Dane, who worked closely with Richard Henry Lee in Congress to try to amend the Constitution before sending it to the states, was rejected by the voters of Beverly. Samuel Adams disappointed those Anti-Federalists who looked to him for leadership; he did not speak out against ratification, and his support was ultimately crucial to the deal that led to ratification with recommended amendments. As Jeremy Belknap, no friend to Adams, later put it, "A[dams] in ye Course of debate in Convent[io]n s[ai]d but little—what he s[ai]d was *rather in favor* of the Constitution." Although the *New York Journal* on January 7 asserted that the old patriots of Massachusetts, led by Adams, were lining up against the Constitution, this potential leadership never materialized. The actual leadership of the opposition in convention was left to relatively unknown delegates, who nonetheless put in an impressive performance. Unfortunately for them, they had to face a party led by three delegates to the Philadelphia Convention and a former governor, along with several prominent statesmen whose talents compared favorably to anything the Anti-Federalists could muster. The opposition tried to turn this against the Federalists. "An old saying, sir, is, that *a good thing don't need praising*," said Benjamin Randall, "but, sir, it takes the best men in the state to gloss this Constitution." This argument does not seem to have had an impact, or at least not one so large as the Federalist advantage in oratorical skills.[4]

Still, the opponents of the Constitution had numbers on their side. It appears that, had the convention held a vote on the Constitution immediately after convening, it would have failed. On January 22, delegate Samuel Nasson estimated that there were 192 delegates opposed to ratification, with only 144 in favor. Though this count may have been tilted too far against the Constitution, the Federalists also believed they had a deficit to make up, so they made sure to take things slowly and not attempt to browbeat the opposition into submission as in Pennsylvania and Connecticut. The goal here, after all, "was not just to win, but to win a victory worth having," writes Pauline Maier. "That was the hard lesson of Pennsylvania."[5] The Federalists insisted on a careful examination of the Constitution, buying time to cobble together a majority.

The battle lines were anything but clear, but in general the Federalists could count on eastern Massachusetts, while the western part of the state was at least skeptical if not outright hostile. The delegates from Maine were not enthusiastic about a stronger national government; Thomas Wait, writing in Portland, observed that "Five delegates in six" from Maine opposed ratification. And the western part of Massachusetts, with fresh memories of Shays's Rebellion, were conflicted over just how much power a national government ought to have to suppress rebellion. Many of these delegates were sympathetic to Shays, and some had even participated in the rebellion. Benjamin Lincoln notes that "[m]any of the insurgents are in Convention, (even some of Shay's Officers) a great proportion of those men are high in the opposition." Although the *Pennsylvania Mercury* counted sixty Shaysites among the Massachusetts delegates and Joseph Barrell found eighty,

Nathaniel Gorham's count of eighteen or twenty delegates who had been in Shays's army during the rebellion in 1786 is probably more accurate. As for those who were not Shaysites, the *Independent Gazetteer* wrote that "the old jealousy seems to prevail, viz. that the *Boston-folks* aim to rule and govern as they please, and are always setting themselves up as *patterns* for, and *dictators* to, the whole state."[6]

The meetings to elect the convention were so many little debates on the merits of the proposed Constitution.[7] The first and most important impression one receives from surviving documents is that this was not a debate with two sides. As Maier puts it, "The towns specialized in shades of gray: There were critical but subtle differences between votes to reject the Constitution, to reject it because no amendments were possible, to reject it 'as it now stands,' to accept it because with a few amendments it would be just fine, and to accept it without qualifications." These only further confounded any attempts to predict how the delegates would vote. If the town meetings were any indication, it was going to be close and it was going to be complicated. Those towns that stated objections tended to repeat the same objections that had appeared in the public debate, and these were sufficient to convince some towns to demand a vote against ratification from their delegates, but not many were unequivocally against the Constitution. "In fact," Maier writes, "at least ten towns passed resolutions or adopted formal instructions against ratification of the Constitution 'as it now stands,' which again suggested that with some changes the Constitution might be acceptable." The people of the town of Paxton indicated in instructions to their delegate, Abraham Smith, that they might be willing to support the Constitution if amendments could be made prior to ratification, but since Smith was "appointed for the Sole purpose of acting on One Single Question, Viz a Ratification or Rejection of the whole," he should vote against it. The town of Harvard formally stated that amending the Articles of Confederation would have been preferable to proposing a new frame of government.[8]

It was Northampton that really set the tone for the debate in the convention. The people of this town, electing delegates jointly with Easthampton, provided a short treatise on the role of a delegate rather than a set of instructions on how to vote. The document, which served as a model for other towns, points out that the towns' delegates, Benjamin Sheldon and Caleb Strong, would have access to "the collected wisdom of the state" in order to properly decide how to vote. The towns express "the fullest confidence" in the "political wisdom, integrity and patriotism" of their delegates, and "submit the all-important question" to their judgment.[9] The delegates, in short, were to listen and deliberate. It is likely that Caleb Strong, also a delegate to the Philadelphia Convention, had a hand in this statement, and hoped that Anti-Federalist towns might adopt it. His influence in convention would be important, but this set of instructions, which undoubtedly influenced at least half a dozen other towns directly and an indeterminate number of delegates indirectly, might well have had a decisive impact. It certainly set the tone for a deliberative discussion, and for the substantial number of delegates who seem to have made up their mind while sitting in convention.

The outcome was, to say the least, unknown. Many of the predictions were simply partisan propaganda. "Ezra," for example, predicted that the Constitution would fail in the convention, because "It can hardly be supposed possible, that a people like this, after having undergone so much loss of blood and treasure, for the purpose of securing their liberties, should now vote them all away." On the other side, some of the more rabid Federalists saw things as the printer of the *Massachusetts Gazette* did, expecting the "quibbling, scribbling opposition—mercy! how diminutive!" to "bark till they're blind" and "rail till their mouths froth," only to be defeated by the superior arguments and eloquence of the Federalists in convention. Most of the Constitution's supporters were not so sanguine. Theophilus Parsons offered a much better assessment of the state of the delegates at the beginning of the convention, colored only slightly by his Federalist leanings. "The weight of abilities, properties and probity," he wrote, "is decided in favor of the Constitution, but I fear the balance of numbers is against it. Great numbers come determined, and upon them reason or argument will make no impression." All was not lost, however, for "among the opposers there are men of integrity and candor who declare they come not decided, but are ready and desirous of being informed. The effect of argument upon these will determine the fate of the Constitution and I have therefore some faint hopes." In short, there were moderates who might swing to whichever side was more persuasive, or at least made the better offer. This was crucial to a Federalist victory.[10]

Nathaniel Freeman, Jr., had his doubts. In a letter to John Quincy Adams in early January, he worried that the opposition would be stubborn, and that the convention would not be a good venue for winning converts. "As the great subject of the federal Constitution is advancing to a decision," he wrote,

> the anxiety of suspense in both parties is wrought to the highest pitch. That it ever will be adopted in this Commonwealth without

amendments I have not an idea. We have every appearance of a violent
opposition. Men are inflamed. In the heat and animosity of party, arguments will not be able on either side to stem the torrent of prejudice.
Passion will usurp controul over dethroned reason, and, perhaps, the
deliberations of our Convention end in such a tumultuous rage as to
disgrace the boasted intelligence of man. There will be near four hundred delegates. An unwieldy assembly. Too much so for dispassionate,
cool investigation."[11]

Not all Federalists were as pessimistic as Freeman, or as optimistic as Parsons; there was a great variety of assessments and expectations. No one
really knew what to expect out of the several hundred delegates from across
the state, from as far away as Maine, many of whom were political un-
knowns and hence unpredictable.

On the other hand, neither side really believed that there would be a great
deal of persuasion going on. As one scholar puts it, "The business of that
assembly was, to be sure, not so much disinterested deliberation as it was
to hear what everyone knew would be a vigorous case put against the Constitution and then to see what kind of circumstantial argument might issue
from its friends and champions."[12] Each side was entrenched, and neither
knew for sure its own strength; but there were at least some undecided moderates to win over, and they would hold the balance of power. Some might
be converted by argument, and here the Federalists had a distinct advantage since they counted among them most of the finest orators and political
leaders in the state. Others, however, might need to be convinced in other
ways. John Hancock, absent from the convention at the beginning due to an
attack of his gout, loomed large in his absence. His election as convention
president underscores his importance to both sides, but his position was
unclear. Even when he appeared to be decided on the issue, it might well be
risky for either side to rely on him; as Rufus King put it diplomatically in a
letter to James Madison, "his character is not entirely free from a portion
of caprice."[13] To Federalists, the Governor was something of an enigma;
certainly a supporter of strong union, but also a proponent of democracy.
To the Anti-Federalists he was the governor who was lenient toward Shays's
rebels, restoring order to the state without breaking the backs of the western
farmers; he was a man of the people, a champion of Massachusetts, and a
supporter of democracy. Perhaps most importantly, he was a pragmatist
open to a deal. Mere persuasion was not likely to carry the day with Hancock, and he had enough supporters to make a difference among those few
who were undecided.

COMPROMISE IN CONVENTION

There were three crucial events in the Massachusetts Convention that altered the Anti-Federalist resistance in the state, and all three served to undermine the opposition. The first, and a harbinger of things to come, was the treatment of Elbridge Gerry. Gerry, one of the state's delegates to Philadelphia, was not a delegate to the ratifying convention because his constituents were strongly Federalist. As one of the few dissenting delegates in Philadelphia, and the only member of the Massachusetts delegation not elected to this convention, he was a person of interest not only to Anti-Federalists but also to moderates. William Widgery, a strong opponent of the Constitution, first proposed that Gerry be invited to sit in on the convention, a proposal to which the Federalists ultimately acquiesced. It certainly helped the opposition cause that it was Samuel Adams who seconded Widgery's initial motion; Adams represented a crucial undecided moderate bloc. Gerry accepted the invitation, but shortly thereafter the Federalists decided it was best to try to get rid of him, because his "known opinion and high personal character gave a confidence to the opponents of the constitution, which it would be difficult to destroy." Their strategy was "to keep him silent or make him lose his temper." They accomplished the former, for a while, by limiting Gerry's participation to answering questions, and even then the convention decided that questions must be asked and answered in writing. This arrangement did not sit well with Gerry, who "sat biting the head of his Cane," obviously itching to dive into the heart of the debates. His attempt to do so, on the subject of apportionment of the Senate, led to an altercation with Francis Dana, in which Gerry did indeed lose his temper and the two almost came to blows. After this incident, Gerry refused to return to the convention. Dana too left the convention for a time, but he managed to convey the impression that he was standing on principle, fighting for the proper conduct of an elected assembly. Gerry on the other hand, in part because of the Federalist control of much of the press, appeared petulant and childish. His rather unsuccessful appearance and apparently sulking departure harmed the opposition more than it helped, and what little he managed to write to the convention did little to further the argument against ratification.[14]

The behavior of Samuel Adams was the second key point in the convention, and it seriously undercut the credibility of the Anti-Federalists. His position on the Constitution was something of a mystery at the beginning, though almost everyone assumed he would speak against ratification. This assumption was wrong. He did not speak much at all early in the convention, commenting only on procedural issues and asking questions of the Federalists. Two weeks into the convention he delivered a short speech in which he claimed to be undecided, and that he was there to listen to the arguments and make up his mind. All of his actions early in the convention support this contention. He seconded the initial motion to invite Gerry, to hear another dissenting voice. He insisted on more than one occasion that the members of the convention remain in order, and address the clause under consideration without straying to more general concerns or other parts of the document. His willingness to be persuaded was made especially clear by an event on the fifteenth of January. Caleb Strong, Fisher Ames, and others spoke on that day in answer to a question asked by Adams concerning why annual elections were made biennial. During Ames's speech Adams cut in to explain that "he only made the inquiry for information, and that he had heard sufficient to satisfy himself of its propriety."[15] This must have been a dramatic moment; here was one of the alleged leaders of the Anti-Federalists in the state of Massachusetts insisting that the Federalists need say no more, for he had been convinced of the propriety of one of the more controversial clauses in the entire Constitution.[16] John Fiske's version of this event underscores the importance of the moment. Upon hearing the explanation for the change in the term of office, "[Adams] replied, 'I am satisfied.' 'Will Mr. Adams kindly say that again?' asked one of the members. 'I am satisfied,' he repeated; and not another word was said on the subject in all those weeks. So profound was the faith of this intelligent and skeptical and independent people of the sound judgment and unswerving integrity of the Father of the Revolution!" It is not quite true that nothing else was said on the subject, but biennial elections rather suddenly ceased to be a major point of objection in the discussion.[17] It was his speech on January 24 explaining his ambivalence, though, that was to be most crucial to the Federalist cause. Several Anti-Federalists were trying to open up discussion to the Constitution in general, instead of the focus on individual clauses. Adams rather dramatically rejected this idea, arguing that "We ought not . . . to be stingy of our time, or the publick money, when so important an object demanded them: and the publick expect that we will not."[18] The motion died without even a formal vote, and the Federalists continued their slow onslaught against the doubts of the moderate delegates.

As the tide began to turn and the Anti-Federalists began to worry that the Constitution might be ratified, John Hancock showed up on the scene with a set of proposals for amendments, to accompany an unconditional ratification. Here was the third crucial moment in the convention, and the point at which a Federalist victory became all but assured, though the margin was bound to be thin. Up until January 30 Hancock had been sitting at home in ill health, laid up with what one biographer called "a timely attack of gout." He no doubt received reports on what was happening in convention, and his illness was mighty convenient as it meant he did not need to say anything in public about the Constitution. "Hancock is still confined," Rufus King wrote to George Thatcher on January 20, "or rather he has not yet taken his Seat; as soon as the majority is exhibited on either side I think his Health will suffer him to be abroad." His eventual arrival was both dramatic and decisive. He was carried into the Long Lane Church on a litter, wrapped in flannels, and the morning after his initial arrival he explained that he had a conciliatory plan to offer to the convention. After a recess to build suspense, he suggested an unconditional ratification attached to a proposed list of amendments.[19]

By this time, it was already clear that Samuel Adams was not a reliable Anti-Federalist, but his backing of Hancock's proposal removed all doubts as to his position. His support of Hancock in the convention was undoubtedly something of a surprise to many delegates, as the two had been political adversaries for most of the time since the end of the Revolution. The traditional interpretation of Adams's decision to back Hancock's amendments puts Adams as a hanger-on, trying to back the winning side and borrow some of the governor's glory, or as a weak old man who had been browbeat and blackmailed by the Federalists into submission. Jürgen Heideking suggests that the pressure put on Adams by the meeting at the Green Dragon Tavern was sufficient to keep him quiet in the convention. Maier, on the other hand, suggests that Adams must have been involved in drafting the Hancock amendments, because his active support of them "is otherwise inexplicable, since he had nothing to gain but the satisfaction of his constituents." A more plausible explanation of Adams's involvement is offered by Michael Gillespie. He suggests that Adams truly was undecided, or rather conflicted, about the Constitution. Early in the ratifying convention he remained deliberately neutral, because he did not want to either facilitate or hinder ratification. His question concerning annual elections was in fact a clarification; even more, it was an invitation to the Federalists to explain a controversial aspect of the Constitution in plain, practical terms rather than abstract and theoretical ones that were not likely to sway the skeptics. His effort to defend the procedure of the convention to consider the Constitution by paragraphs was an authentic effort to bolster democratic deliberation. His attempt at additional amendments, far from grasping for some share of Hancock's glory, was a simple effort to unite as many of the Anti-Federalists behind the Constitution as possible. When the idea proved to be divisive, Adams did not merely let the issue drop; instead, since some members persisted even when he tried to withdraw his suggestion, he actively fought against the proposal as a threat to political unity and ratification. Adams did believe that a stronger national government was needed, and although he was concerned about securing the rights of the people, the decidedly republican nature of the ratification process must have allayed those fears somewhat. It must have appeared to him likely that some amendments would be successfully made after ratification in order to safeguard the people against the dangerous ambiguities in the Constitution.[20]

Adams was clearly a convert, but it was not so clear with Hancock. Harlow Giles Unger suggests that Hancock "leaned slightly against ratification" initially, though he was careful not to take a public position. M. E. Bradford suggests that Hancock had no position at all on the Constitution, and was simply bought off with promises of electoral support and the tantalizing possibility that he might be elected the first President, should Virginia (and George Washington) remain outside the union. He may be drawing on the accusations of Stephen Higginson, writing in 1789 above the signature "Laco," who contended that Hancock opposed the Constitution until it appeared that it might have enough support to pass, and then demanded a payoff from the Federalists in exchange for his support; in this account, Hancock "never was consulted about" the conciliatory proposal he read in the convention, "nor knew its contents." He merely read the words that had been handed to him, without so much as copying them into his own handwriting. Josiah Quincy was slightly more generous to Hancock, alleging merely that the latter switched sides because "the idea that the Constitution might be carried in opposition to his opinion was dreadful."[21]

Gillespie finds all of these interpretations unconvincing, pointing out that Hancock showed signs of supporting the Constitution before the alleged bargain would have been struck. Biographers Thomas Amory and Herbert Allen agree. James Sullivan, a close confidant of the governor, asserted that Hancock had prepared his amendments *before* the convention met, and decided to support ratification; though this is almost certainly false, the idea of amendments probably occurred to the governor early on, and he may well have had some general ideas as to the shape those proposals ought to take. Belknap's allegation that "Hancock is the ostensible Puppet in proposing amendments" is undoubtedly nothing more than partisan bluster. In the words of Amory, "[Hancock's] popularity was beyond [the Federalists'] power to subvert, and such an overture was neither consistent with his character nor theirs." John Hancock was nobody's puppet. As Thomas

O'Connor and Alan Rogers put it, "it was Hancock's patriotism and the specter of what might happen to the new nation if the Constitution were rejected" that convinced him to take the stance that he eventually did. [22] He saw an opportunity to play the role of conciliator, and incidentally add to his personal fame, and he bided his time for the proper opportunity, when he was most likely to have a decisive impact. That time came after Adams made up his mind to support ratification.[23] The idea of recommended amendments, however, was already being discussed by Hancock and his circle before the convention began.[24] The idea gained some traction when it was presented publicly by Hampden, probably James Sullivan, a moderate Anti-Federalist and close associate of the Governor. Hampden's argument, well received by the public, planted the seed in the Federalists' minds that here was a plan of concession that did not threaten the ultimate success of ratification. The fact that the essay was believed to have been written by a close friend of Hancock, a critical figure for the Constitution's success, made it even more palatable, because its success was more probable. In fact, it was most likely moderate Anti-Federalists, including Sullivan, perhaps James Warren, and probably Samuel Adams and Charles Jarvis, who authored and advocated recommended amendments;[25] Samuel West, who switched to the Federalist side during the convention debates, was allegedly the first to approach Hancock about conciliatory amendments.[26] Although some have contended that the Federalists recruited and sent Reverend West to convince Hancock, it is likely that Hancock approached the Federalists and not the other way around. With Adams on board as well as Hancock, it must have seemed almost a sure thing to the Federalist leaders in the state.[27] In many respects, Adams was more important to the Federalists than Hancock. Both were old patriots, but the latter was better known as a practical politician, while the former was much more persistent in his political principles. Plus, no one really knew where Hancock stood on the Constitution, while Adams was widely assumed (and rightly so) to have serious reservations, even if he was not outright opposed. It is impossible to tell just how many votes each swung for ratification, but one or the other would probably not have been sufficient for the Federalist victory.

Hancock and Adams were praised by the Federalists for their support of ratification. The former was generally given most of the credit for ratification; Henry Jackson wrote to Henry Knox that "Governour Hancock has gained himself immortal Honor, in his conduct upon this occasion—it is certain if he had not taken an active—indeed a very active part in favor of the adoption, we never should have gained a vote in favor of it." Adams, on the other hand, who at the beginning of the debate was described

by one writer as "an arch Devil," was after the convention generally mentioned with astonishment as a key ally. Undoubtedly more than a few Anti-
Federalists excoriated the two Bostonians as turncoats, if only in private.
They were certainly accused of abandoning their principles, giving in to
"political pressures and public promises of the Federalists." But both men
were clearly Anti-Federalists in principle. "Adams and Hancock," according to Gillespie, "had an explicit vision of the good regime, and within the
limits of their political circumstances, they sought to bring it into reality. . . .
They envisioned America as a close-knit federation of sovereign republics
in which the states would be independent and sovereign in realizing their
own visions of the good life." It is clear that most of the Anti-Federalists
shared some version of this vision, while the most ardent Federalists clearly
did not. This was a politically moderate position, allowing for a stronger
national government, but the basic principle is shared with even the most
radical of the Anti-Federalists. Thus Adams and Hancock belong among the
Anti-Federalists in spirit and vision, even though their eventual votes did not
align with the opposition.[28]

The particular amendments offered by Hancock must have been disheart-
ening to the leadership of the opposition. There was nothing there that had
not already been insisted on or conceded by the Federalists during the public
debates until this point. The amendments, the first to be formally proposed
by a ratifying convention, are worth reprinting here in full:

> And as it is the opinion of this Convention that certain amendments
> & alterations in the said Constitution would remove the fears & quiet
> the apprehensions of many of the good people of this commonwealth
> & more effectually guard against an undue administration of the Fed-
> eral Government, The Convention do therefore recommend that the
> following alterations & provisions be introduced into the said Con-
> stitution.
>
> *First*, That it be explicitly declared that all Powers not expressly del-
> egated by the aforesaid Constitution are reserved to the several States
> to be by them exercised.
>
> *Secondly*, That there shall be one representative to every thirty
> thousand persons, according to the Census mentioned in the Consti-
> tution until the whole number of the Representatives amounts to Two
> hundred.
>
> *Thirdly*, That Congress do not exercise the powers vested in them
> by the fourth Section of the first article, but in cases when a State shall
> neglect or refuse to make the regulations therein mentioned or shall

make regulations subversive of the rights of the People to a free & equal representation in Congress agreeably to the Constitution.

Fourthly, That Congress do not lay direct Taxes but when the Monies arising from the Impost & Excise are insufficient for the Publick exigencies nor then until Congress shall have first made a requisition upon the States to assess levy & pay their respective proportions of such Requisition agreeably to the Census fixed in the said Constitution, in such way & manner as the Legislature of the States shall think best, & in such case if any State shall neglect or refuse to pay its proportion pursuant to such requisition then Congress may assess & levy such State's proportion together with interest thereon at the rate of Six per cent per annum from the time of payment prescribed in such requisition

Fifthly, That Congress erect no Company of Merchants with exclusive advantages of Commerce.

Sixthly, That no person shall be tried for any Crime by which he may incur an infamous punishment or loss of life until he be first indicted by a Grand Jury, except in such cases as may arise in the Government & regulation of the Land & Naval forces

Seventhly, The Supreme Judicial Federal Court shall have no jurisdiction of Causes between Citizens of different States unless the matter in dispute whether it concerns the realty or personalty be of the value of Three thousand dollars at the least nor shall the Federal Judicial Powers extend to any actions between Citizens of different States where the matter in dispute whether it concerns the Realty or Personalty is not of the value of Fifteen hundred dollars at the least.

Eighthly, In civil actions between Citizens of different States every issue of fact arising in Actions at common law shall be tried by a Jury if the parties or either of them request it.

Ninthly, Congress shall at no time consent that any Person holding an office of trust or profit under the United States shall accept of a title of Nobility or any other title or office from any King, Prince or Foreign State.

And the Convention do in the name & in behalf of the People of this Commonwealth enjoin it upon their Representatives in Congress at all times until the alterations & provisions aforesaid have been considered agreeably to the Fifth article of the said Constitution to exert all their influence & use all reasonable & legal methods to obtain a ratification of the said alterations & provisions in such manner as is provided in the said Article.[29]

The first suggested amendment was a change that the Federalists had been insisting was unnecessary, because redundant, ever since James Wilson's state house speech explaining the Constitution as one of enumerated powers. The second, sixth, and eighth could easily be done by legislation in the first Congress, and were probably not necessary as amendments since none was especially controversial. The third matches with the predominant Federalist explanation of Article I, Section 4, anyway; no one was seriously arguing that Congress should modify state regulations concerning where and how to hold elections. The same could be said for the fourth proposal; no prominent Federalist suggested that Congress ought to levy direct taxes, when the impost and perhaps excises would probably be sufficient to cover the expenses and debts of the government, at least at first. The scheme for requisitions backed by force was one that the Federalists may well have been willing to try anyway if the financial situation required more revenue, and it could have been done by Congress under the Constitution as written. The fifth and ninth simply demanded inaction from Congress, and neither seemed terribly likely actions for Congress to take; certainly neither was a major point of contention in the debates. Only the seventh proposal really required a constitutional amendment, and was a serious point of contention. Even the form of recommended amendments undermined the real effectiveness of the proposal to do more than assuage fears; as one delegate put it, "I think that if the want of these amendments were sufficient for me to vote against the Constitution, the addition, in the manner proposed by your Excellency, will not be sufficient for me to vote for it, as it appears to me very uncertain whether they ever are a part of the Constitution." Prior amendments were essential, because "to grant a power . . . in hopes to recover it again by humble petitions, is an absurdity." Other delegates expressed concerns that the amendments would never be adopted, and perhaps would never be seriously considered. The set of amendments, taken together, represented little more than a hollow compromise designed to placate certain skittish moderates and win over just enough votes. Hancock proposed the amendments, according to Edmund Randolph, "not in the form of objections, but *to remove fears,* and I do not conceive that Mass[achuset]ts may be yet said to be fairly inlisted." Still, Randolph expressed satisfaction, because the opposition in the state was largely dominated by Shaysites and "gentlemen of bad fame." He was already beginning to shift back to the Federalist side of the debate, like his moderate brethren in Massachusetts. James Madison, meanwhile, saw the amendments as "a blemish, but . . . in the least offensive form."[30]

Hancock's amendments do not fully reflect the objections raised by Anti-Federalists during the state convention. Those arguments were actually fairly typical of the public debate, so little needs to be said of them here. The basic theme of the opposition here was a clear Power Anti-Federalism. Charles Turner perhaps summed it up best: "Relinquishing an *hair's breadth* in a constitution is a great deal; for by small degrees has liberty in all nations, been wrested from the hands of the people. I know great powers are necessary to be given to Congress, but I wish they may be well guarded." William Widgery made much the same argument later, in more colorful terms: "I cannot see," he said, "why we need swallow a *great* bone for the sake of a *little* meat, which if it should happen to stick in our throats, can never be got out." As far as substance, taxation was the big issue. The power of taxation granted by the eighth section of Article I effectively meant giving up all forms of property, at least theoretically. One delegate claimed that "in giving this power we give up everything," while another lamented that "no more power could be given to a despot, than to give up the purse-strings of the people." Several delegates insisted that the taxing power was intended to result in poll taxes, a certain price per person, and thus burden the poor far more than the rich. The supporters of the Constitution fired back with the contention that the Anti-Federalists were objecting based on implausible interpretations that would never be endorsed by the representatives of the people, to which William Symmes offered a scathing reply. "The Congress *shall* have power—it does not say that they shall *exercise* it," he acknowledged, "but our necessities say, they *must* and the experience of ages says, that they *will*, and finally, when the expenses of the nation, by their ambition are grown enormous, that they will oppress and subject." Samuel Thompson taunted the Reverend Samuel West on religious grounds for making the argument that America's legislators would be good. "This," Thompson insisted, "is quite contrary to the common language of the clergy, who are continually representing mankind as reprobate and deceitful, and that we really grow worse and worse day after day." If the legislators were to be potential tyrants, though, the tax collectors were to be monsters: "a standing army of ravenous collectors; harpies perhaps from another State, but who, however, were never known to have bowels for any purpose, but to fatten on the life-blood of the people." If anyone had suggested a power like this for the federal government a decade earlier, "he would have been called a tory." In addition to taxes, objections were raised to the powers granted to Congress to regulate elections, the protection of slavery, the federal city, and the size of the legislature. Delegates objected to the terms of Congress, the absence of rotation and recall, and the ability of members to set their own pay and decide when to suppress their journals. Several delegates wanted to see religious tests for holding office, because non-Christians could not be trusted with the powers of government. The absence of religion was even noted at the very beginning, when Charles Turner suggested that a reference to God ought to have been included in the Preamble. The dangers of a standing army, a common theme in Anti-Federalist objections, were made vivid by Samuel Nasson, who evoked the memory of the Boston Massacre, blaming it on the presence of a standing army in Boston at the time.[31]

Some typical Rights Anti-Federalist objections appeared as well. The absence of a guarantee for trial by jury was noted, though uneventfully save Abraham Holmes's remarkable statement that Congress would have the power to "institute judicatories, little less inauspicious than a certain tribunal in Spain, . . . that diabolical institution the INQUISITION." Holmes also predicted "that RACKS and GIBBETS, may be amongst the most mild instruments" of the legislated punishments for crimes established by Congress. The Federalists did not bother to answer this point, except to observe that the Anti-Federalists continued to find the worst possible abuse, no matter how implausible, and judge the Constitution thereby. The clause guaranteeing habeas corpus was objected to upon Power grounds; Congress ought not to be able to suspend that right indefinitely. The necessity of a bill of rights was discussed only a handful of times; Charles Taylor suggested that such a bill could be written "in a few hours" if one started with the Massachusetts version. The issue did play a noteworthy role in briefly disrupting the very end of the convention, when Samuel Adams proposed that several guarantees of rights be added to Hancock's proposed amendments. This short list of rights "*gave an alarm to both Parties*—the Antifeds supposed [that] so great a Politician would not offer these amendts unless he tho't there was danger on these Points—[the] Feds were afraid [that] new Converts would desert." John C. Miller describes this motion as an attempt to push back against the Federalists who had forced him into submission on the Constitution, but the known facts contradict this. Adams almost immediately tried to withdraw his proposal "lest it scuttle the compromise he supported," but ended up having to vote against it when the Anti-Federalists pressed the issue.[32]

Though the Federalists clearly outmaneuvered their opponents, and the opposition may well have been undone by the clever machinations of a moderate junta hell-bent on compromise, the Anti-Federalists did try a few things to derail ratification. Their early efforts to discuss the Constitution as a whole, rather than by clause, were stymied largely by the efforts of Adams. After Hancock proposed his amendments, they tried to have the convention adjourn, on the entirely plausible rationale that the delegates ought to consult their constituents about those amendments before making a decision on them. This too failed, and by a margin of nearly a hundred votes. The next

day the opponents of ratification watched two of their most capable advocates, Charles Turner and William Symmes, publicly defect; each announced
his support for ratification and Hancock's proposed amendments. This came
a day after Nathaniel Barrell gave a speech listing the defects he saw in the
Constitution and pleading for the opportunity to discuss the issue with his
constituents before voting, before concluding that "I am almost tempted to
risque their displeasure and adopt it without their consent."[33] By this point
the opposition had lost, but considering the deck was stacked against them,
the Anti-Federalist performance in this convention was heroic. The vote was
close despite the influence of Adams and Hancock, and the talents defending
the Constitution. Even to the end no one could be quite certain of the outcome; though the galleries were packed, "you might have heard a Copper
fall on the Gallery floor, their was Such a profound Silence" while the roll
was being called.[34] The vote was 186 to 167; the Constitution was ratified
by a margin of only nineteen votes. Ten delegates switching to vote against
ratification rather than in favor would have reversed the outcome, and the
Federalists had certainly swayed more than that with their arguments and
Hancock's proposal.

The Federalist tactics in Massachusetts paid off even after the ratification vote, in a way that was to be even more troubling to the opposition.
The minority was permitted to speak its mind, raise its objections, and
engage in a full and fair discussion of the Constitution. "Throughout the
session," Harding explains, "the opponents of the Constitution seem in the
main to have been treated with delicacy and consideration. Their objections were respectfully listened to; their arguments patiently answered over
and over again."[35] With the exception of the ugly incident with Elbridge
Gerry, the majority was very careful in its treatment of a minority that did
not in fact begin as a minority at all.[36] The Federalists were out not to *defeat* the minority so much as to *convince* it: "[F]ar from thinking or acting
as an arrogant, disdainful elite, the Federalists who served as delegates in
the Massachusetts Ratifying Convention firmly believed in the reasonable-
ness, 'the genius' of the people." They clearly wanted the people to back
the Constitution, not have it forced upon them, and this meant winning
over the opposition (and wavering) delegates. What happened after the
ratification vote reflected this good will. Delegate after delegate who voted
against ratification stood up to acknowledge their defeat and pledge to support the convention's outcome. One promised to "use his utmost exertions
to induce his constituents to live in peace under, and chearfully submit to"
the Constitution, while another said he would "endeavour to convince his
constituents of the propriety of its adoption." William Widgery, one of

the leaders of the opposition in convention, volunteered "to sow the seeds of union and peace" among his constituents. In all, no fewer than eight Anti-Federalists, and probably more, expressed a willingness to accept the outcome without further protest. This was to pay off handsomely in the public relations battle to follow the convention, as the close state of Massachusetts was firmly in the Federalist column, unlike the still tumultuous state of Pennsylvania.[37]

It is perhaps not surprising that Massachusetts was the first state to recommend amendments; as Harding points out, the people of Massachusetts were accustomed to calling for alteration of documents presented for their approval, including the Articles of Confederation and the state constitution of 1780. In approving these documents, "the right [of the towns] to reject specific sections and to propose amendments was expressly recognized and was freely exercised." This is reflected in the fact "that the prime element in the opposition was the distrust with which men brought up in the democratic atmosphere of the New England town-meeting viewed all delegated power; and their inordinate desire to maintain a constant and efficient check upon all persons to whom it was found necessary to intrust a portion of their authority."[38] The Constitution certainly did not offer a strong check over the magistrates by the people; the proposed amendments would have moved the document in that direction, if only slightly.

RESPONSE TO MASSACHUSETTS

Edward Carrington was probably not far from the truth when he wrote, in a letter to Henry Knox on March 13, that "[t]he decision of Massachusetts is perhaps the most important event that ever took place in America, as upon her in all probability depended the fate of the Constitution."[39] Certainly a rejection by the state would have reverberated in New Hampshire and New York, and probably Virginia, and it may have emboldened Rhode Island to more forcefully and finally reject ratification. Here was the turning point in the ratification debates, and it marked a shift for the Anti-Federalists. Here was another option for those who were skeptical about the proposed document: they could voice their objections and demand amendments without resorting to defeating the document outright and being left with only the Articles of Confederation on which to fall back for national government. More than a few Anti-Federalists must have reexamined the Constitution to find that which was truly objectionable, and prepared to swallow their minor complaints.

Not all Anti-Federalists turned to compromise, however. In late February, Centinel, in his fifteenth letter, weighed in on the outcome of the Massachusetts Convention, suggesting that the close vote, qualified by a request for amendments, "cannot afford the conspirators much cause for triumph," in part because the circumstances of the state, especially Shays's Rebellion, ought to have made the people favorable to a stronger central government to provide for law and order. He writes that this nineteen-vote majority suggests not the strength of the Federalists, but their weakness. Centinel thought he smelled blood in the water, and was prepared to ramp up his campaign for outright rejection. In a later letter, published in April, he would add that the outcome may have been different had the post office not prevented the dissemination of newspapers from Pennsylvania. In particular, had the Massachusetts delegates been able to read the "unanswerable" Dissent of the Pennsylvania Minority[40] before the convention voted to ratify, "it would in all probability have enabled patriotism to triumph," and presumably led to a vote against ratification. Philadelphiensis too found hope for the Anti-Federalist cause in the ratification of Massachusetts. He suggests that "the freemen of New-England, the best soldiers on the continent, have had their eyes opened, and begin to see through the conspiracy." The margin of victory was only nineteen out of nearly four hundred, which he considers as "little better than a rejection." The methods of the Federalists to win this small majority, of course, were reprehensible, and the amendments proposed by Hancock were a mere power play by one "who hopes to be appointed the *little king* if not the *big one*"; they would not answer any of the most serious objections to the proposed system of government.[41]

Hancock's proposal did, however, force the Anti-Federalists to change their approach, even as much of the rhetoric remained the same. They could not very well argue against amendments, but they could not acquiesce in the unconditional ratification attached to the compromise. This put them in an awkward procedural position; they were advocating *prior* amendments, insisting that any ratification be conditional. As "A Farmer and Planter" in Maryland implored his fellow citizens, "You, who have an opportunity of getting the news-papers, no doubt have seen the farce and parade at Boston!—they adopted the federal government, and afterwards proposed amendments—let us be wiser—let us not adopt it until it is amended."[42] This was of course a perfectly logical and sensible position, but one that was difficult to articulate to a mass audience. They were gradually losing the public debate even before Massachusetts, and now their argument looked more technical and legalistic, while the Federalists appeared as moderates willing to compromise. "Amendments are amendments," one can easily imagine a wavering farmer or mechanic saying to himself, "what does it matter if they come before or after ratification?" The form of ratification may have even led some to believe that the amendments were already accepted as part of that decision.

Still, the opposition in Massachusetts was not yet done. There was no formal report by the minority, as there was in Pennsylvania and would be in Maryland, but three delegates did publish a brief explanation of their votes against ratification. None of these delegates, Consider Arms, Malichi Maynard, and Samuel Field, played a significant role in the debates in the convention, but the three established in their essay a clear Anti-Federalist position adjusted for the Hancock compromise. Though they insist in closing that they would not rebel against the Constitution if it were eventually adopted, their essay as a whole is anything but conciliatory. The three emphasize at some length the extent to which the Federalists seem to be relying on good rulers, an assumption that Arms, Maynard, and Field do not share. A government must be designed to protect against bad rulers; otherwise, in the essay's most eloquent phrase, the arguments in favor of such a government are "founded altogether upon a slippery *perhaps*." The three go on to ask their readers, "why should we voluntarily choose to trust our all upon so precarious a tenure as this?"[43]

The essay covers much of the ground of opposition in the convention, but the authors save their most vehement attacks for slavery, objecting to the three-fifths clause and insisting that the Constitution ought to have abolished the slave trade for good. The people of Massachusetts, they contend, may well be called upon to assist in the defense of the southern states, and implicitly to defend slavery, a wicked institution in which they want no part, with their fortunes and their lives. The authors go so far as to imply that America will face God's wrath for this mortal sin. "Phileleutheros," concurring with the delegates, put it starkly: "If we cannot connect with the southern states without giving countenance to blood and carnage, and all kinds of fraud and injustice," he wrote, "I say let them go." Arms, Maynard, and Field close on a combative note: "We cannot slip this opportunity of manifesting our disgust at the unfair methods which were taken in order to obtain a vote in this state, which perhaps was the means of producing the *small* majority of *nineteen*, out of nearly three hundred and sixty members. What those methods were is well known." It was not just Pennsylvania radicals accusing the Federalists of unprincipled tactics; the fight was clearly still on here, despite the apparent acquiescence of the opposition at the end of the convention.[44]

Arms, Maynard, and Field were not the only dissenting convention delegates prepared to continue the fight. Samuel Thompson apparently headed to New Hampshire to fight against ratification by that state. He was reported to be "roaring about like the old Dragon to devour the *Child now it is born* and breathes forth fire, arrows, and Death," and acting "as if the Devil had possessed him," but apparently he made few converts. "A Hint" attacked the clergy for backing the Constitution, "introducing *Politics* into their Sermons, instead of adhering strictly to the Gospel." In mid-March, six weeks after the state's ratification, the *Massachusetts Centinel* found the opposition still "attempting to disseminate the seeds of anarchy and confusion."[45]

This opposition most significantly manifested itself in the state legislature. The House of Representatives refused to appropriate the funds to print and disseminate a planned address on behalf of the convention, explaining the proceedings and outcome, perhaps because the address "was supposed to be an attempt to reconcile the People of this Commonwealth to the *Tory* proceedings of their late Delegates." Later, when Hancock gave a speech explaining the ratification, several Anti-Federalists attempted to insert a scathing official reply. The form of the state's ratification, according to Phanuel Bishop's suggested language, "does not seem well calculated" to preserve the "safety and welfare" of the people of Massachusetts. The suggested amendments "neither comport with the dignity or safety of this Commonwealth." The proposed reply disputed the legitimacy of both the state convention and that which wrote the Constitution. Though the more moderate Anti-Federalists ultimately prevented such language from passing, they could only manage to do so by preventing any reply at all to the governor's speech. Such a reply would have accomplished little, except to cause confusion among the people trying to decide which set of representatives had final authority on the issue. The results, according to George Minot, would have been "dreadful," but the moderates managed to win out again. The legislature might well have gone much further; at least one Anti-Federalist tentatively suggested (privately) that it might nullify the convention's decision to ratify. This suggestion was wisely discarded, for if there were not enough support for a negative reply to Hancock's speech, any further attempts would make the opposition appear dangerous and desperate.[46]

There were enough moderate Anti-Federalists in the House to thwart the most radical opposition, and most such moderates were now helping to legitimize the Constitution in the state, or at least remaining out of the way. The number of converts was growing, and the number of opponents continued to shrink. The *Hampshire Gazette* carried a signed proclamation

in April from Belchertown, previously Anti-Federalist, in which the inhabitants "declare that we acquiesce in the ratification of the federal constitution," and that they would offer no further resistance. The *Massachusetts
Centinel* asserted in May that "above four-fifths of the inhabitants of this
large State" now support the Constitution. Even Elbridge Gerry did not
seem inclined to push the opposition further. Just a week after ratification
in Massachusetts the *Hampshire Chronicle* reported that Gerry believed it
his duty to support the will of the majority. He had never entirely opposed
the Constitution anyway; he merely found it to be riddled with dangerous
flaws. In the words of his biographer James Austin, Gerry "inclined to accept it conditionally, and seems to have thought that while the people had
'the power to amend they were not under the necessity of rejecting it.'"
Gerry's acquiescence was not complete, though. He still maintained a degree
of bitterness, if only in private letters to fellow Anti-Federalists, against the
Federalists, those "vigilant enemies of free government" who continue "to
hunt down all who remain attached to revolution principles," exhibiting an
"insufferable arrogance" and unjustified elitism. He also expressed hope
in a letter to James Warren that Virginia and New York would make their
ratifications conditional upon prior amendments. He tried, to no avail, to
remain out of politics as much as possible, though he was drafted against
his wishes as a candidate for governor in 1788, and later as a candidate for
Congress. His position at this point can perhaps be best expressed as John
Quincy Adams expressed his: "I am now converted," he wrote in his diary,
"though not convinced." Still, the unconvinced converts who insisted they
would accede to the majority were as good as their word, even to the point
of suppressing an official dissent as had been published in Pennsylvania and
would appear in Maryland. By contrast, in the words of Silas Lee, "Many
who have been much opposed to the Constitution are become warm advocates for it."[47]

That the compromise of Massachusetts marked the beginning of the
end for the Anti-Federalist cause was not lost on the more astute Anti-
Federalists. There were, of course, seven states remaining, and three more
ratifications necessary, but some of the more pessimistic opponents of ratification already saw the writing on the wall. Among this group was Mercy
Otis Warren. Her pamphlet, signed "A Columbian Patriot," suggests that
revolutions often generate "the most mortifying instances of human weakness," which explains "the extraordinary appearance of a few names, once
distinguished in the honourable walks of patriotism, but now found on the
list of the Massachusetts assent to the ratification of a Constitution, which
. . . must soon terminate in the most *uncontrouled despotism*." Surely she

had in mind Hancock, Bowdoin, and other Revolutionary patriots, but her foremost target was clearly Samuel Adams, who could well have become the unquestioned leader of the Anti-Federalists had he stuck to his principles. Perhaps he was convinced by reasoned arguments, but more likely he and others simply succumbed to the immense pressure placed on any who dared speak against the proposed government: "[W]hen patriotism is discountenanced and public virtue becomes the ridicule of the sycophant—when every man of liberality, firmness, and penetration, who cannot lick the hand stretched out to oppress, is deemed an enemy to the State—then is the gulph of despotism set open, and the grades to slavery, though rapid, are scarce perceptible." Warren does not explicitly condone the tactics of her fellow Anti-Federalists, but she is absolutely convinced that the opposition ideas (and ideals) are the correct ones, and those of the Constitution the corrupt ones. The Federalists "are endeavouring by all the arts of insinuation, and influence, to betray the people of the United States."[48]

The Columbian Patriot is not all doom and gloom rhetoric; the pamphlet includes a fairly standard array of arguments against the Constitution. She writes about representation, asserting that "the best political writers have supported the principles of annual elections with a precision, that cannot be confuted, though they may be darkned, by the sophistical arguments that have been thrown out with design, to undermine all the barriers of freedom." She writes of a standing army that "freedom revolts at the idea." Concerning the absence of a bill of rights, she emphasizes the importance of protecting freedom of conscience and of the press, suggesting that "The rights of individuals ought to be the primary object of all government, and cannot be too securely guarded by the most explicit declarations in their favor." She finds both Congress and the courts too powerful, the Electoral College undemocratic, and representation inadequate, especially given the long terms of office and the absence of a provision for rotation. Perhaps most significantly, she reflects on the general illegality of the entire proceeding; not only did the Philadelphia Convention exceed its powers, but the process of ratification, by requiring the approval of only nine states, is dangerous to the principles of law and constitutions. She fears that "we shall soon see this country rushing into the extremes of confusion and violence, in consequence of the proceedings of a set of gentlemen, who disregarding the purposes of their appointment, have assumed powers unauthorised by any commission, have unnecessarily rejected the confederation of the United States, and annihilated the sovereignty and independence of the individual governments." In short, the Constitution is both illegal and dangerous, and the Federalists have exacerbated the problem by trying to push it through ratification quickly. "The mode in which this constitution is recommended to the people," she argues, "to judge without either the advice of Congress, or the legislatures of the several states, is very reprehensible—it is an attempt to force it upon them before it could be thoroughly understood." Here she comes very close to questioning the abilities of the freemen of Massachusetts to make reasoned judgments on the Constitution; this pamphlet is no radical democratic piece. It fits more clearly, like most writings in the state, with the Power Anti-Federalist paradigm, with its concern for an overbearing government that is not properly checked or balanced.[49]

Warren closes on a note that manages to be poetic, pessimistic, and extraordinarily arrogant all at once: "let the sublimer characters," she writes, "the philosophic lovers of freedom who have wept over her exit, retire to the calm shades of contemplation, there they may look down with pity on the inconsistency of human nature, the revolutions of states, the rise of kingdoms, and the fall of empires."[50]

8

Setbacks in the Northeast

IN LATE FEBRUARY, Postmaster General Ebenezer Hazard, undoubtedly still smarting from Anti-Federalist allegations of corruption in the post office, gloated about the ratification of Massachusetts in a letter to Mathew Carey. "The Antifederalists appear to me to be almost tired of Opposition:—even their Golia[t]h, the Centinel, flags. Their Conduct has been very extraordinary & improper, & has only served to render them contemptible." While it is true that the rate of new publications against ratification (and for it as well) was slowing down, the Anti-Federalists had certainly not given up the fight. To the contrary, they were just beginning to coalesce into an organized and coherent opposition, though they would prove to be more organized in some places than in others.[1]

In Centinel's state of Pennsylvania the opposition continued strong, though Centinel's hostility had largely given way to his energetic kindred spirit Philadelphiensis, who continued to stir up trouble for the supporters of the Constitution. He charged the Federalists with "stupid irony, falsehood, scurrility, and abusive language," and defiantly insisted that he would not stop his attacks on the Constitution. He asks again why a good constitution would inspire its supporters to try to silence debate and opposition. It is because the Constitution is a dangerous one that the Federalists must resort to unsavory methods to force ratification on the people before the document can be fully understood and discussed. "The *President-general*, who is to be our *king* after this government is established," Philadelphiensis insists, "is vested with powers exceeding those of the most *despotic monarch* we know of in modern times." America, he claims, has lost its best chance to establish a true democracy, which he considers the freest system of government. Instead, "under the proposed one, composed of an *elective king* and a standing army, officered by his sycophants, the starvelings of the Cincinnati, and an aristocratical Congress of the *well-born*, an iota of happiness, freedom or national strength cannot exist." He finds encouragement in the closeness of the Massachusetts vote, though, and suggests that the people are beginning to really examine the Constitution and develop serious doubts despite the prestige of the delegates to the Philadelphia Convention.[2]

In his eleventh letter, Philadelphiensis professes shock that there is not more of an outcry against the Constitution. "Who is so dimsighted," he asks, "as to suppose that a constitution so essentially differing from the principles of the revolution, and from freedom, and opposed by so respectable a body of freemen, could be established in America; or if it were possible by force or surprise to put it in motion, could it exist any space of time? Nay, the idea is futile, and common sense spurns at it." Philadelphiensis, ever the optimistic democrat, firmly believed that the people were behind him, fighting the good fight against an aristocratic cabal that hated the principles of the American Revolution. Among his specific objections, he argues here that Pennsylvania, because it has consistently paid its debts, will be forced to pay off the debts of other states as well. Furthermore, the taxes levied by Congress will be "as oppressive as tyranny can make them," because there will always be an excuse for such a complicated government to spend a little more. And as bad as Congress might be with its unlimited power to tax, the President, or rather elected King, will be far worse, more likely a tyrant than any hereditary monarch. The solution to these problems is amendments, before ratification, preferably proposed by a second constitutional convention. After all, "it is admitted almost universally that it wants amendments." "Let another Convention be immediately called, and let a system of government fitted to the pure principles of the Revolution, be framed," he suggests in closing, that the United States of America might "become the seat of liberty, peace, friendship and happiness; and her government have ample *energy* and *respectability* among the nations of the earth; yea, she will thereby be rendered the great arbiter of the world." Perhaps no other writer put quite so much faith in the prospects of a second convention.[3]

The radicals played well in the western counties in Pennsylvania, which were up in arms, mostly figuratively so far, over what they saw as a conspiracy by some rich Philadelphians to threaten their liberties and their livelihoods. The resistance was again gaining momentum. "Every hour the new Constitution loses ground in this part of the state," reported "a gentleman of veracity" in Franklin County. "In the counties this side the Susquehanna, we are pretty well in unison, determined to oppose the chains forged for us by the Wellborn." The problem was simple: the western part of the state was "enraged" by the circumstances of the ratifying convention. This was not merely a figure of speech; Richard Bard warned in a letter to John Nicholson that certain leading Federalists in Philadelphia, "if they should have any occassion to travel toward the Westenen [*sic*] end of this state I think that it would be prudent in them to make their Wills before they leve Home." The threat of violence was not idle either; by one report, no fewer than eight people were killed in a fight over the Constitution in far western Washington County. Benjamin Blyth, Sr., who would later be involved in organizing the Harrisburg Convention, undoubtedly spoke for many of his countrymen when he described the Federalists as a "zealious & Powerfull party of Citizens who wish to Goveren the Rest, ever restless for Power uncontrowled."[4]

In early April, Centinel drew to a conclusion his eighteen-part attack on the Federalists and their Constitution. The tactics of the Federalists he describes as "so repugnant to truth, honor, and the well-being of society, as would disgrace any cause." The issue here is one of deception; he contends that the proponents of the Constitution, willing to do whatever it takes to secure ratification, have prevented the flow of information and even outright lied to the people. He tears into the Federalists for "persuading the people of one place, that the people everywhere else are nearly unanimous in favor of the new system," and thus attempting to convince them that the opposition is weak and isolated. Such tactics were, for Centinel, not only unforgivable, but also indicative of dangerous motives and a threat to the liberty of the people. The Federalists, he believed, were out to subvert the will of the people and destroy the democratic elements of the nascent nation.[5]

This notion of a Federalist conspiracy was the theme of a brief but clever piece, published in April, signed "None of the Well-Born Conspirators." The author made an effective attack on the term "federalist" as applied to the supporters of the Constitution. They cannot be federal in the most common use of the term, because they "evidently aim at nothing but the elevation and aggrandizement of a few over the many." The term "federal," however, deriving from the Latin *Foedas*, may also denote a covenant against the liberties of the people, a conspiracy. "Perhaps the consciences of the conspirators in the *dark conclave*," the author suggests, "urged them to assume a name which might be in some measure a key to disclose their perfidy. . . . Take the word Federalism directly or indirectly," he concludes, "and it amounts neither to more nor less in its modern acceptation than a conspiracy of the *Well-born few*, against the sacred rights and privileges of their fellow citizens."[6]

The idea of an aristocratic plot to overthrow the liberties of the people was also taken up by "Aristocrotis." In this effective satire, the author claims that the Constitution establishes an aristocratic government, aside from a few "dangerous concessions made to the plebians." Fortunately, the power of Congress to alter state regulations of House elections will nullify any hopes of the people to be represented in the national government, and the abolition of annual elections will render their complaints less frequent. Since Congress may also alter the time of elections, they might gradually extend the terms into election for life. If any problems should arise, the national government will have a standing army and control over the militia "to quell insurrections that may arise in any part of the empire on account of pretensions to support liberty, redress grievances, and the like." When prosecuting such liberty-seeking rebels, there will be no need for juries, an absurd institution that places decisions of law in the hands of the ignorant. Religion, too, is to be stamped out, along with the rights of the people; "such an energetic government as the new constitution" has no need for the former to keep the citizens in line, preferring law and punishment instead, and it cannot tolerate the latter. Because of the dangerous rights of the people, especially the odious freedom of the press, great care must be taken in securing ratification of the Constitution. Those who dare to oppose ratification "with barefaced arguments, obstinate reason and stubborn truth," he writes, "must be branded as enemies to their country and to the union of the states."[7]

The radical Democratic Anti-Federalists were not the only resistance in the state. "A Farmer," who wrote more like a lawyer, set out in April to educate the masses in Pennsylvania about the theory and nature of government, presenting a fairly clear and sophisticated Power Anti-Federalism. He explains that constitutions exist to restrain the legislative authority, though "[s]carcely hath the wisdom of man, matured by the experience of ages, been able with all the checks, negatives and balances either of ancient or modern invention to prevent abuses of this high sovereign authority." The main purpose of the Farmer's essay is to explain the difference between a federal republic and a consolidated government, and show how the Constitution creates the latter rather than the former. He lays out a clear definition of a federal republic, in which sovereign states surrender part of their sovereignty to a federal government. The states retain authority over internal affairs, ceding to the federal body powers over external and interstate affairs. "The perfection of a federal republic," he explains, "consists in drawing the proper line between those objects of sovereignty which are of a general nature, and which ought to be vested in the federal government, and those which are of a more local nature and ought to remain with the particular governments." It is very difficult to lay down an adequate rule for this separation, but when once done the rules can be adjusted as contingency dictates. The Constitution is not properly federal; the states will be reduced to "mere electors or boards of appointment," having some ministerial power but not a trace of sovereignty.[8] The Farmer closes on an ominous note, highly appropriate to the ongoing debate in Pennsylvania:

> Whilst posts are prevented from carrying intelligence, whilst newspapers are made the vehicles of deception, and dark intrigue employs the avaricious office-hunters, who long to riot on the spoils of their country, the great body of the people are coolly watching the course of the times, and determining to preserve their liberties, and to judge for themselves by the principles of reason and common sense, and not by the weight of names.[9]

Though he disagreed with the Farmer in emphasis and philosophy, the Centinel must have been pleased with such a passage.

Despite this continued resistance in Pennsylvania, the ratification debate was going well for the Federalists. The Constitution had not received quite as positive a reception as they had hoped, but it was doing better than they could reasonably have expected. Congress had not endorsed the document, but had endorsed the method of ratification. Six straight states had ratified, three of them unanimously and two with large majorities. The only close state had presented a roadmap for how to win over the undecided without altering the document or making major concessions. The process was about to get difficult, though. Anyone who expected New Hampshire to follow the lead of Massachusetts was about to be disappointed, and anyone who expected Rhode Island to fall into line without resistance was just plain delusional.

A ROADBLOCK IN NEW HAMPSHIRE

A week after the ratification by Massachusetts, the convention in New Hampshire was set to convene. There was not much of a public debate in the state prior to the convention, but what was published was fairly civil and clearly aimed at persuasion. In February, "A Friend to the Rights of the People" produced an essay that included nine "remarks" on the flaws of the Constitution for the people of New Hampshire. In the same newspaper, "A Friend of the Republic" offered some brief comments addressed to the convention delegates. The two likely came from the same pen, and certainly carry the same general message: a distrust of national government and a defense of republican localism.[10] The author raised some of the usual objections as well as a few less common themes among the remarks. The author's critique of luxury—"European fashions have been transplanted into America," after all, and the capital erected by Congress will no doubt be a lavish and decadent place to rival the capitals of Europe—suggests a rustic republican simplicity entirely appropriate to the political culture of late eighteenth-century New Hampshire, which was more democratic in its inclinations than most of its sister states. He also argues that appointed officers, even judges, make "suitable tools for the purposes of tyranny and oppression"; any magistrates with substantial power, he implies, ought to be elected. The clause regarding the admission of new states, he asserts, will prevent Vermont from joining the union without New York's consent, and the latter state is more likely to call on the federal military to subdue the former by force than consent to recognize its separate statehood. He also includes an impressive, if brief, defense of the importance of religion in republican government, critiquing the prohibition on religious tests for office. He contends that "no man is fit to be a ruler of protestants, without he can honestly profess to be of the protestant religion." To prevent such religious tests, he argues, is to undermine religion, and to threaten an important support of civil society and the state. In the end he suggests that the powers to be given under the Constitution threaten the liberties of the people, and that a new plan ought to be developed to "better secure the liberties of the subjects." In the essay addressed to the delegates, the Friend suggests that the Constitution would mean nothing less than surrendering the liberties of the people of New Hampshire to Congress. "Let Congress have, what they have hitherto asked for," he suggests to the delegates, "to regulate *Trade and Commerce*. They have told you that was sufficient, why will you give them more?" He suggests that any national constitution ought to include a bill of rights. He wishes the delegates divine inspiration: "May the God who governs the universe," he writes, "direct your steps." Finally he closes by exhorting the delegates to "Be as zealous to ward off *public evil, as others are to bring it on*; and you have a fair chance to prevent it for ages yet to come." Whether the Friend had much influence on the delegates is hard to say, but the state would prove to be a trickier one than Massachusetts.[11]

The New Hampshire Ratifying Convention was a caricature of the weakness of the opposition throughout the nation. Nationally the Federalists had superior talents; in New Hampshire they included virtually every major political leader in the state. Everywhere the opposition was accused of simply parroting arguments made by others; here Joshua Atherton, practically alone in vocal opposition in convention, was accused, apparently justly, of recounting often conflicting opposition arguments from the newspapers.

The newspapers themselves tended to lean Federalist throughout the states, but nowhere were they more decidedly in favor of the Constitution than New Hampshire, where there were roughly twelve Federalist essays printed for each one in opposition to the Constitution.[12] Throughout the various states the Federalists had the advantage in political strategy; in New Hampshire the proponents of the Constitution swiped a majority right out from under the Anti-Federalists. The opposition in New Hampshire, with some effective leadership, may have been able to hand the Constitution its first defeat, perhaps very quickly in the convention, as they had a clear majority at the beginning, but they were outdone in every possible way.

Because of all of their advantages, the Federalists in the state were optimistic about the Constitution's prospects, but there was a persistent mistrust of national government among the populace. The people of the state were not about to be pushed into ratification. "The towns of New Hampshire," explains Albert Batchellor, "were active, alert, and intelligent organizations, intensely independent, intensely self-reliant, and intensely democratic." They were not blindly sending delegates, but examining the Constitution and deciding how they felt about its provisions. At least thirty towns sent instructions to Exeter along with their delegates, and most of these instructed their bearers to vote against ratification. This had been an issue in Massachusetts, albeit a minor one; in New Hampshire probably a quarter of the convention was bound to vote against ratification no matter what they thought of the Federalist arguments in the convention. The instructions from the towns, though, do not reflect either stubbornness or ignorance; instead, they should be seen collectively as "evidence of deliberation." In the town meetings to elect delegates, the Constitution was read and discussed, and select committees were often appointed to draft objections as well as instructions. "The Constitution itself was carefully studied by a good many people," writes Nancy Oliver, "conscious that the issue was of enormous significance to themselves and to posterity. In most of the towns the Constitution was read and discussed before delegates were chosen." The people of New Hampshire did not act precipitously in their elections, nor were they uninformed on the issues.[13]

Even if the Anti-Federalists had the numbers, though, the leadership gap was obvious early in the convention. The Anti-Federalists had Joshua Atherton of Amherst, who was indefatigable in his opposition,[14] but no one else stepped up for them. Perhaps the most effective Anti-Federalist leader in the state, Nathaniel Peabody, was selected to represent the towns of Atkinson and Plastow, but declined a seat in the convention.[15] There was no opposition delegate sufficiently distinguished to be a qualified candidate to serve as president of the convention, so this position fell, without controversy, to Federalist John Sullivan. The Federalists also positioned themselves to write the rules of the convention, including two key points: that a motion to adjourn would take precedence over other motions, and that the yeas and nays may only be recorded on the ratification question. It is likely that the Federalist leaders foresaw the strategy they would need to employ, and were prepared to adjourn in order to have more time to overcome objections, and especially to get town instructions reversed.

The opposition, on the other hand, seems to have done little to prepare for the convention; they were apparently relying on numbers to win the day. In every convention most of the delegates were quiet, but this tendency was even more pronounced here.[16] Most of the heavy lifting in debates was done by Atherton, whose preparation seems to have consisted primarily of reading newspaper essays and accounts of the other conventions. The *New Hampshire Spy*, rather than reporting his arguments, simply noted that he largely repeated the ones made in Massachusetts. Concerns about elections, monarchy, tyranny, and the evils of slavery were highlighted. There was an extended debate about the clause in Article VI prohibiting religious tests for office; Deacon Matthias Stone saw such tests as essential, the means by which religious freedom might best be preserved. His position was strikingly close to advocating ecclesiastical Christian government.

The judiciary received a more extensive discussion here than in many other states; this discussion suggested what was unique about the state's opposition. In particular, Atherton was concerned about the appellate jurisdiction of the federal courts. He insisted that he could "never consent . . . that a citizen of New Hampshire should be dragged from his peaceful home—from his neighbors, friends, and his family, to *Head Quarters*, to his utter ruin, where perhaps the cause in dispute is very trifling," nor "that an officer of revenue, rapacious and unfeeling, as they are universally known to be, shall have it in his power in any dispute with a citizen of this state, to carry this dispute before judges interested to increase the revenues of the continent, and who therefore will always decide in favour of an unprincipled collector of excise."[17] Here we see the familiar argument, made most forcefully by Brutus, that the courts will be interested in reinforcing federal power at the expense of the states, but Atherton's rhetoric has a distinct parochialism that is absent from Brutus. The complaint here was not that the national government would be too powerful, but that the people of New Hampshire would be directly harmed by the exercise of national power. The complaint was not even one of rights, at least not in the typical sense. The Anti-Federalists were clearly, and probably quite honestly, concerned with the danger faced by the small farmer when a big government is indifferent to his livelihood and his personal expenses. The problem is not abuse of power so much as its indifferent use, and the distance of New Hampshire from any plausible capital city only exacerbated the problem.

The overall tone of the Anti-Federalist opposition in New Hampshire was distinctive, and does not fit neatly into any category of Anti-Federalism. It partook of the Rights position, with its emphasis on religious liberty and procedural judicial rights. It had a democratic element in its focus on the individual and his role in government. It certainly had its share of radical rhetoric, with Atherton promising *"tyranny* in the extreme and *despotism with a vengeance!"* should the Constitution be ratified. Benjamin Stone suggested that "our situation would not be much happier by changing one set of tyrants for another—British for American tyrants."[18] Still, the character of the opposition, like much of the Anti-Federalism of the northeast, was based in questions of power. It was a different perspective on political power, certainly—the power of the righteous and industrious individual exercised against the power of the overbearing and indifferent national government—but the two portions of the debates for which we have the most extant material raise questions about the jurisdiction of the courts and suggest that Congress will have the power to limit religious practice, whether enumerated or not. New Hampshire's Power Anti-Federalism was not eloquent or especially philosophical, the state contributing far less to the debate than it did to the overall outcome, being the ninth state to ratify and the first in which the Federalists would overcome a clear opposition majority.

This feat was accomplished by the tactical maneuver of an adjournment. Upon completing their discussion of the Constitution by clause, Federalist John Langdon moved for the convention to adjourn to a future day. This motion elicited some confusion among the Anti-Federalists, who were apparently unprepared for it. Atherton's best response was yet another general tirade against the Constitution, but ultimately the Federalists had the votes to secure adjournment. The reason for this tactic was the delegates bound by constituent instructions to oppose ratification. A report in the *Massachusetts Centinel* in late February explained the situation succinctly: "In order to give time to those Delegates in the Convention of New-Hampshire, who were instructed to vote against the Constitution, to return home, and get their instructions taken off, that hon[orable] body, on Friday last, adjourned, to meet at Concord, in that State, on the third Wednesday in June next. No other question was taken."[19] The reactions seem to have been mixed, from Federalist panic (and Anti-Federalist gloating) to cautious optimism by the proponents of ratification.[20] The *New York Morning Post* reported that "there was little hopes it would have a greater number of friends in June than it now has," which the paper reckoned at little more than a third of the delegates, while a correspondent in the *New York Journal* expressed "no doubt the ratification will take place" in June. After all, says the latter writer, the problem in the convention was the result of "the intrigues of a few notoriously vile characters" who misled many New Hampshire towns "to fetter their delegates with positive instructions to vote in all events against the constitution." In convention, he claims the Federalists won over many of these delegates, who were now "desirous to consult their constituents" and get their instructions changed. John Langdon, who was in a good position to assess the Constitution's prospects as one of the state's leading Federalists, explains in a letter to Rufus King of Massachusetts that "after spending ten days in the arguments a number of opponents came to me, and said, they were convinced and should be very unhappy to Vote against the Constitution, which they (however absurd) must do, in case the question was called for," because they had been instructed to do so by their constituents. Langdon "therefore moved for the adjournment which was carried though much opposed by the other side. This question determined a majority in favor of the Constitution had it not been for their Instructions. This shews the fatality of the times." Langdon expected that, by the time the convention reconvened, the Federalists would have a clear majority, unfettered by unfavorable orders from constituents. Meanwhile, the Federalist newspapers were generally optimistic in their published comments, "pretending that the Constitution had suffered no serious setback and the bandwagon was still rolling."[21]

Still, there was some unease that the adjournment would appear at least a symbolic defeat of the Constitution; this was especially likely with the misinformation and speculation circulating. About the same time as the adjournment Atherton received several pamphlets from John Lamb in New York, and began circulating them in the state, in an effort to reinforce Anti-Federalist sentiment and win over some wavering Federalists. One Federalist expressed concern about the vote to adjourn, fearing that "it will have a bad effect. The publick mind has been fluctuating, with regard to the system proposed—at least in considerable districts of the community. . . . I am quite unable to say, what effect this unexpected conduct in Newhampshire may have."[22] No one else knew, either, but both sides were forced to move on, and return to the question of New Hampshire in the summer. The philosophical debate over the Constitution was not impacted, but the strategic situation was suddenly more precarious for both sides.

RESISTANCE IN RHODE ISLAND

In Rhode Island, the people had other things on their minds than the Constitution. Many of the readers of the *Providence Gazette* on March 29 no doubt were more interested in reading the lead essay, signed "Bread and Beer," "on the Nature and Use of raising BARLEY," than they were in reading the substantial coverage of the Constitution in the same issue. Bread and Beer himself poked fun at the constitutional material in the papers in introducing his lighter fare.[23] Still, the Constitution was vigorously debated here as elsewhere, though with a stronger opposition and weaker defense.

The rest of the country exhibited a low opinion of Rhode Island, and of its politics.[24] During the Constitutional Convention, rumors swirled that the delegates had "resolved that Rhode-Island should be considered as having virtually withdrawn herself from the union," and that if the state should fail to pay her debts, then the United States would resort to force. This was of course not true, but undoubtedly many people hoped it might be. Francis Dana, in a letter to Elbridge Gerry just before that convention completed its business, expressed apparently sincere hope that the state would refuse to send delegates to Congress, as it had refused to attend the Convention, and thus give grounds to be eliminated from the union. At this point, Rhode Island might be split up between Massachusetts and Connecticut; Dana even proposed a dividing line. This was for the good of the people of Rhode Island, of course: "they never can be secure under the present form of government, but will always labor under the greatest mischief any people can suffer, that of being ruled by the most ignorant and unprincipled of their fellow citizens." Even William Ellery, a prominent citizen of Rhode Island, expected the state to be divided if it did not agree to the Constitution. On July 28, 1788, just before learning of New York's ratification, he wrote, "This State will stand out as long [as] it can;—but if New york accedes,—it will, it must soon come in.—If it should continue to be obstinate to the last;—it is not invincible. It may be annihilated, and divided between Massachusetts and [Connecticut]."[25] "Rogue Island" was a source of embarrassment for respectable Americans everywhere; as it was the only state to fail to send delegates to the Philadelphia Convention, it was hard to say how interested it might be in actually participating in the ratifying process.[26]

This perception of the state was driven by its partisan politics, which were in turn shaped by the most democratic political system anywhere in the states, and probably anywhere in the world. This invited divisive partisanship, so in Rhode Island there was a clear two-party divide, and the two parties were far apart in policies and philosophy. The merchant interest in the seaport towns was represented by the mercantile party, which consisted of many of the state's most prominent citizens but was held in suspicion by most of the poor inland farmers. The economic downturn in the mid-1780s led to a stunning victory in 1786 by the country party, which represented rural interests and advocated a radical democratic ideal very different from the elitism of the mercantile party. Running on the slogan and platform "To Relieve the Distressed," the party's accession to power led to a wave of paper money and prodebtor policies. Here creditors were required to accept payment of debts in the state's paper money, or forfeit all rights to collect the debt at all. The country party became overwhelmingly Anti-Federalist in the debate over ratification, though there were some exceptions, most notably Governor John Collins, who, though an advocate for paper money, supported the Constitution. Despite Collins's position, the Federalists in the state were quick to relate the country leaders to Anti-Federalism, and to place both firmly on the issue of paper money. The opposition to the Constitution thus became associated with a desire to avoid paying debts and a willingness to violate property rights, and its leaders became self-interested politicians grasping to hold their power and offices. "The Majority in this State wear long faces," wrote William Ellery in October. "The prospect of an abridgment of their power to do mischief, is extremely painful to them." Another Federalist lamented that "the Great Majority of our Rulers are Compos'd of the Common People in the Country who are uninfluenc'd by the Principles of reputation and Justice." The elitism was readily apparent; the country leaders were nothing but base ruffians. "A viler and more abandoned sett of beings," wrote yet another Federalist, "never disgraced any Legislative, Judicial or Executive Authorities since the Fall of Adam." The mere opposition of Rhode Island was even used by some Federalists to suggest how sound the Constitution must be. A Federalist in Philadelphia went so far as to suggest that the Federalists throughout the country cannot "have a stronger proof of the goodness of their cause than [Rhode Island's opposition]." Another added that "the best reasons yet given by the wisest politicians, in favour of the new constitution, do not amount to a greater proof of its excellence, than the disapprobation of these people."[27] A writer in Massachusetts took the attack a step further, expressing a desire that Rhode Island might outright reject the document.

> It is ardently to be wished . . . that the little nest of villains, who inhabit the petty territory of R. I. may not have the grace to accept of the CONSTITUTION that boon from heaven, offered to an half-ruined

country, in order to restore it to a state of happiness and splendor—
May they be divided in their councils, and at length scattered, as a
people, among the other States, and all political power, which they
have forfeited as a State, taken from the sinful hands of those who
have uniformly abused it, ever since they have been known as a government; and who are at length become a *"hissing and a byword
among the nations."*[28]

None of this fazed the Anti-Federalists in Rhode Island; they seemed to care
little about the opinions of the people of the other states.

All across America, the Federalists were critical of Rhode Island's ruling country party, but no state produced criticism quite as virulent as that
of Rhode Island itself. John Francis observed with some degree of shock
that "Tories were never detested with half the Zeal, that Antifederalists are
now—And there needs no greater confirmation of a Villain than an Opposition to the Favorite Government." The *Newport Herald*, a newspaper
as strongly Federalist as any in the union, began dropping hints early that
any state considering rejecting the Constitution was hostile to American
union and good government. "Should any state reject this salutary system,"
the paper printed in late September, "unbiassed posterity will consign their
names to an infamous immortality." A month later it added that "This is
the seed time of union—the State that should be now unfederal will plunge
herself into merited disgrace, if not annihilation."[29] As the debate wore on,
the paper turned specifically against the country party. In January one of the
more poetic Federalists put his feelings about the Anti-Federalists in verse,
in a poem that ends with the following lines:

Thus you may see the antifederal's way,
They love to borrow, but they hate to pay;
And I aver, by sacred reason's rules,
That antifederal men are knaves and fools.[30]

By February the paper printed that

The enemies of the New Constitution, says a Correspondent, consist
of jealous, and uninformed characters, who oppose it for conscience
sake. Ambitious men, who aspire after unbounded popularity.—And
last of all, The indolent, the abandoned and the offscouring of the
earth, who have no prospects but in a state of anarchy, where maraud-
ers, freebooters and knaves are licensed and encouraged.[31]

The "correspondent" was likely the printer himself, or may as well have been, so close was this to the general editorial sentiment of the newspaper. The paper engaged in satire as well; in June, "A Friend to Paper Money" mockingly attacked the Federalist press, calling it "the nuisance of society" and a "malicious machine of ingratitude" for "thundering defamation against [Rhode Island's] leading characters." He concluded by calling for "banishing the *printer*, and *burning the press*" for daring to oppose the state's paper money scheme. Henry Channing wrote of the *Herald* that "The majority call it the scourge—It indeed makes them bleed and groan."[32] A writer in the more balanced (but still generally pro-Constitution) *United States Chronicle* fired back:

> It is disagreeable (says a Correspondent) to observe the scurrilous Pieces, which weekly appear in *Mr. Edes' Newport Herald*, against this State, and indeed against all who do not agree in political Opinion with a certain *Junto* in that Town. It is an old Adage that—*It is a* bad Bird *that bewrayeth* its own nest—These Folks therefore must be *bad Birds*, not to say *factious and seditious Citizens*.[33]

The Anti-Federalists fired back their own insults and epithets, holding their own against the most creative Federalists. "Lycurgus" alone offered enough derogatory names to answer virtually all of the ones thrown at the country leaders; he identified the Federalists in Rhode Island as "speculators, extortioners, usurers, jugglers, and false friends," and "whining, canting, office-hunting, aristocratic blockheads."[34] This was not the rhetoric of a party that would back down. The fight was on.

After the ratifications by Connecticut and Massachusetts, there was some hope for the Federalists in Rhode Island. George Washington, ever the optimist, wrote to John Jay in early March that "there can be little doubt of Rhode Island following the example of her Eastern brethren." What is not clear is why Washington, normally an astute political observer, believed the state would follow its neighbors this time, when it had taken its own course so many times before. Perhaps early spring simply brings hope in Virginia. Even in the press not all writers were critical. A correspondent in the *Freeman's Journal* in Philadelphia offered a rare defense of "Rogue Island" against the attacks, citing its strong record during the Revolution and its efforts to both stop the slave trade and free its slaves. But this was indeed unusual everywhere in the other twelve states.[35]

At the heart of Rhode Island's reputation were the country party's paper money policies, which are worth a few more words here. Frank Green Bates, writing in the late nineteenth century, excoriates the policy. "Conceived in ignorance, and supported by folly and dishonesty, it had brought discord, repudiation, and misery," concludes Bates. Later scholars have been less harsh. Irwin Polishook points out that six other states issued paper money in the 1780s, but "Rhode Island bore the brunt of interstate attacks on these emissions, even from those other states that printed paper money," because only Rhode Island demanded that a creditor accept the paper or forfeit the right to collect the debt. This was a crucial difference. Maier, drawing on Polishook, puts a more positive spin on the state's paper money policies, noting that they "would allow Rhode Island to redeem its public debts without widening the gap in wealth between a few speculators and everyone else," as well as "end the state's need to make massive annual interest payments, reduce its tax burden, and put it back on a reasonably sound fiscal basis."[36] The reason that the policies were so popular was not a disregard for property or the creditor class, or even a general knavery, as the mercantile party leaders suggested; the policies were popular because they were perceived to be helping put the state on a more firm economic foundation, and ease the burdens of the recession. There were ramifications, of course; when the merchants held power in the state, Rhode Island had been reliable at paying its requisitions and performing its duties to the Confederation. The more localistic country party was far less reliable, and saw no problems with weakening federal ties. Polishook, who is sympathetic to Rhode Island's policies in the 1780s, suggests that the state, by refusing to send delegates to the Philadelphia Convention, and then withdrawing its delegation from Congress and neglecting to send a new one, was "choosing to repudiate the Union rather than join its sister states in the new federal system." The country leadership saw no problems with this; other states could just mind their own business.[37]

Not all of the country policies were widely condemned, however. On the last day in October 1787, in the same session that first considered (and rejected) calling a ratifying convention, the Rhode Island legislature outlawed the slave trade in the state. This was to play a significant role in American political development, but only a small role in the debates over ratification. The abolitionists in the state, led by Moses Brown, were highly disappointed that the Constitution not only protected the slave trade for the next twenty years, but also made it impossible for any state to grant asylum and freedom to slaves who escaped to its borders. Still, the abolitionists tended to support the Constitution and stronger national government. Samuel Hopkins wrote to Levi Hart in late January 1788 that he was concerned that if the Constitution were not adopted, the result might well be civil war. The issue of slavery, though, might lead to such a war even after ratification. This was not a point on which to fight ratification.[38]

More salient to the suspicious Rhode Islanders was the idea of an over-arching, powerful central government. "The Thing that the Sons of Liberty greatly feared," wrote one Anti-Federalist in early January 1788, "the conventioneers are trying to bring upon them." "I conceive Sir," another writer contended, "that a Constitution ought to be so founded if possible, that the worst of men, entrusted with power, could not use it to the destruction of the liberties of the people." The emphasis on liberty was stronger here than elsewhere in New England, and the Anti-Federalists were particularly vehement about the freedom of the press. They resisted efforts to stifle voices in opposition to the Constitution, most prominently in neighboring Massachusetts. One such writer, in his request for the *Providence Gazette* to reprint the essays of Cincinnatus, wrote that "The proposed new Constitution was confessedly sent abroad for examination, and every attempt to obstruct *free enquiry* is a sure indication of a *little mind*, as well as a *bad cause*. 'FAIR PLAY IS A JEWEL.'—shame then on those men of narrow souls—those pedling politicians—those little aspiring despots and office-hunters—who by their illiberal censure would aim to influence the press, that sure and best preservative of the rights of freemen." "Argus" asked in early November, "Why, if the proposed Constitution is a good one are its Supporters afraid to have any Thing said against it? Why are they for hurrying it down our Throats, before we have opened our Mouths? . . . But pray, my good Friends, give us a Chance to read it once or twice over before we say whether we like it or not." Freedom of the press became a persistent theme here. A writer in the *United States Chronicle* offered perhaps the strongest argument regarding the danger to the freedom of the press presented anywhere in the thirteen states. If the national government should prosecute a critical printer for libel, it would be a federal case, as the government itself would be a party; this case could be tried (at least on appeal) without a jury, before judges appointed by the prosecuting party. Similarly (though less plausibly), Congress could pass a law establishing "licensers" responsible for preapproving any pieces to be printed about the national government, and the Supremacy Clause would ensure that the states could do nothing to dispute them.[39]

Underlying the discussion of rights, though, was a strong current of Power Anti-Federalism. For country leaders in Rhode Island, the central (and perhaps only) problem with the Constitution was that it stripped the state of its prerogatives. This represented the greatest part of their appeal to the people of the state, and it was highly beneficial to the Anti-Federalist cause. Polishook contends that the Anti-Federalist advantage in the state derived from two main factors. First, the opposition message "rested on a bedrock of local control and states' rights to which the freemen were firmly attached." Second, they held the key political offices in the state, thanks in part to the popularity of the paper money policies of the country party. This party leadership was probably the more significant factor of the two in the state's decisions about ratification. "The Antifederalists were better organized, propaganda in the newspapers was readily discounted by the average citizen, and the country party leadership was every bit a match for the most astute men in the Federalist camp."[40] By effective mobilization and campaigning, the Anti-Federalists marshaled impressive public support.

Much of the opposition message, here as elsewhere, was one of defense. The people were unimpressed by great names, and were little influenced by philosophical arguments. Here was a politics of interest. "Vir" aggressively attacked the idea that the Constitution ought to be favored because George Washington supported it. The argument, not the prestige of its author, is what ought to matter. "The *free* genius of America is not to be thus *bullied* into the sinister views of the *designing* part of the community, by the glare of *titles*, the shining string of *dignified names*, and the *pompous* parade of *illustrious patriots*." On the other hand, the Anti-Federalists were not prepared to let go of their own sympathetic authority figures. "Philelaetheros" defended the three nonsigners at the Philadelphia Convention, relating a parable about the advisers of King James I. Only one among all the king's advisers dared to dispute the king's word, according to the story; this one stood against the majority and exhibited greater wisdom in doing so. Phile-laetheros closes by asking "whether it is not as probable that the *three* dissenters mentioned are as likely to be honest men, as King James' *one*?—and whether MAJORITY is *surely* and *always* right?"[41]

THE RHODE ISLAND REFERENDUM

It took a while for the state to take significant action on the Constitution. In October 1787, the legislature received via Governor Collins the reports of the Philadelphia Convention and of Congress concerning the proposed Constitution. By this time, the country party leaders had already decided that settling the state debts using paper money would take precedence over any reorganization of the federal system; inaction was to be the state's initial response to any proposal from Philadelphia. Still, the Federalists would make an effort. Henry Marchant of Newport proposed that the state print and distribute copies of the Constitution, and that the towns elect delegates to a ratifying convention. The majority in the legislature was willing to do the first, "to preserve the appearance of *federalism*" in the sarcastic comment of the *Herald*, but no more. The motion aroused "warm opposition" despite Marchant's plea that the assemblymen "consider it with coolness and deliberation." The debate was not just on the question of calling a convention, but on the merits of the proposed Constitution. Marchant's motion failed by a large majority, and the legislature instead passed a resolution to have the Constitution printed and distributed. The Federalists immediately accused their opponents of acting solely to protect their paper money scheme, with the *Herald* insisting that the Country leaders would not even consider "any plan which does not quadrate with their darling privileges of making *paper money*," but they could do little to prompt any action at all on the Constitution. Just for good measure, the legislature at the same session sent Congress an apologetic letter for their failure to send delegates to that body, promising to send representatives to the next session. When Abraham Whipple insisted that the legislature should immediately make provisions for fulfilling that promise, he was ignored. Also ignored was a motion to provide for Rhode Island's payment of requisitions to Congress.[42]

The Federalists took their case to the public. One wrote in early November that the state legislators "have *no Right* to refuse calling a Convention of the People, to consider of the proposed Federal Constitution,—as the People at large have a *Right* to judge of the Propriety or Impropriety of adopting it, however the present Members may be opposed to it." This was a ground on which the Federalists could hope for a slim chance of success, but the opposition would turn it back on them by going a step further and calling for a referendum instead. After allowing the Federalists to again move for a convention, a motion that was defeated by a nearly three-to-one margin in the assembly, the Country leaders instead proposed that the freemen vote directly in their respective towns. Holding a referendum, Maier explains, "was consistent with the policies of the Country Party, which had a partiality for referenda. It would also deny Federalists, centered in the commercial towns of Newport and Providence, an opportunity to talk other delegates into supporting the Constitution (or to 'decoy' them, in the words of a Rhode Island assemblyman), as they had done with some success in Massachusetts and New Hampshire." This was the proper strategic move for a party that was firmly in control, and it made perfect sense in the context of state politics. Rhode Island was fundamentally a federal system, with the towns holding the bulk of the political power, and the assembly answering quite directly to their constituents. The collective opinion of the towns was unequivocal, despite some pockets of dissent. As the legislature's next session approached, a writer from Providence wrote that the leaders of the state assembly "intend PROTESTING against the TREASONABLE ATTEMPTS made by their *Sister States* to *expunge* the *Old Constitution* by *adopting* the *New*!!!" Here again we see a willingness to cast aside union altogether if necessary to secure local prerogatives.[43]

The idea of a statewide referendum was effectively advanced by the country party leadership as a reasonable (and more appropriate) alternative to a state ratifying convention. "The majority members argued that, since the new federal system would deprive the freemen of many of their former privileges, they should be offered the opportunity of judging the Constitution directly without the intercession of a ratifying convention," writes Polishook. The Federalists objected, insisting that such a method was irregular and would not be binding regardless of the outcome; at any rate, they argued, it would not reflect the will of the people but "the decision of the willful men who bossed the town meetings."[44] The Anti-Federalists, firmly in control, ignored the objections and voted for a referendum by a significant majority, and furthermore rejected a proposed amendment that the people might instead instruct their representatives to call for a ratifying convention, so the Federalists again took their argument to the public. "If the freemen of the State, on the fourth Monday of March, should *unanimously* vote for the Constitution, it cannot be considered as a valid ratification; for the Constitution itself provides only for a ratification by *State Conventions*," explained "A Freeman." Because of this, he urged his fellow citizens to refrain from voting. "In a State Convention all the light and information which may be collected from every part of the State will be afforded, and this body, when convened, will not be confined to a single day to deliberate and decide." The towns, instead of voting on the Constitution, ought to instruct their assemblymen to call a ratifying convention. It is not clear why "artful and designing men" were likely to influence the town meetings, but not a state convention, as "A Freeman" (probably a different one, publishing in the *Newport Herald* rather than the *Providence Gazette*) suggested; perhaps it would be the wrong kind of artful men, of the wrong political persuasions. "An astonishing revolution is taking place all around us," adds "A Rhode Island Landholder" in another Federalist appeal, "in the peaceable erection of a new Confederacy, in which we are invited to join, and shall THE PEOPLE not be allowed an opportunity of publicly and unitedly deliberating and consulting together in a Convention, whether it be best to join therein or not?" He too called for a boycott of the referendum and instructions for the legislature to call a convention.[45]

The referendum took place on March 24, and the Federalist boycott was highly successful, at least at suppressing the Federalist vote. Only 237 people voted for ratification, versus 2,714 votes against the Constitution. In Newport, among the most Federalist towns in the state, the vote was ten opposed and only one in favor, out of several hundred eligible voters. Federalist Providence, with about five hundred freemen eligible to vote, made the boycott even more obvious, with a single voter casting a vote against ratification, and nary a Federalist showing up at the polls. Only two towns voted in favor of ratification. The Federalist boycott, though, clearly did not cost them a chance at victory; contemporary estimates placed the potential number of additional Federalist votes at up to about twelve hundred, which would have still given the Anti-Federalists nearly a two-to-one victory, even if no more Anti-Federalists turned out.[46] The referendum was clearly a foregone conclusion,[47] and this is exactly the message that the Federalists emphasized in its aftermath. One writer estimated that seven-ninths of the people in the state opposed ratification and supported the country party leadership.[48] As they were driven by "PRIVATE INTEREST, RUDE LICENTIOUSNESS, and UNBRIDLED PASSION!" there was little hope of reasonable debate or persuasion. Even so, other Federalists wrote, the vote did not reflect the well-meaning people who nonetheless opposed the Constitution because they wanted to see changes first made. "Amendment" submitted to the *Providence Gazette* a list of eleven amendments that were allegedly proposed at a town meeting discussing the Constitution. The document, Amendment writes, "may tend to shew, that the minds of all the freemen could not have been taken on said day *by yea or nay only*."[49] This too was a general theme, that a convention was necessary for deliberation and possible amendment; the Federalists here had to concede the need for changes essentially from the beginning.

Examining the results of every town would be tedious and unenlightening, especially since most towns recorded nothing of substance except the votes. Six towns (other than Providence) unanimously rejected the Constitution, and a dozen produced majorities of at least a hundred votes against it. It is not clear how many towns had debates, but given that only seven towns had at least ten votes on each side (only four had twenty, and only Federalist towns Little Compton and Bristol had anything resembling parity in numbers), such debates would have been rather lopsided. A glimpse into the mind of the Anti-Federalists is offered by the vote of one John Rice in Coventry (which voted 180–0 against ratification). Rice, according to the town record, voted "nay until Large Amendments and alterations are made and a Constitution planed that the Common People can understand and that cannot be Construed two or three ways plain & Expressing the Rights of the Several States and the Rights of Congress in Feoderial Union." In the count, of course, this merely went down as "nay." The town of Bristol, 26–23, produced a petition to the legislature calling for a ratifying convention. Providence too produced such a petition; this extended statement about the importance of deciding on the Constitution in a ratifying convention is significant for its nuanced discussion of the philosophical origins of democratic society. The signers suggested that a gathering of all the people would be appropriate if feasible, but in this case, "where is the spot commodious for assembling all the freemen of this State?—And where is the man who could be heard to advantage by such a numerous assembly?" The mode provided for by the legislature is described as "inexpedient and improper," and the petition explains eight points in some detail to support its request for a convention. The petition is respectful and well reasoned, which is more than can be said for the instructions drawn up by Newport for its representatives, which called the referendum "unconstitutional, unprecedented, inefficacious, and inconsistent." Despite the belligerent tone, these instructions present a four-point argument that is similar to that of Providence. At the meeting itself, with Henry Marchant presiding, the idea of voting by referendum was reportedly "reprobated in the most unqualified terms.—It was said that this deviation from the mode exhibited a determined obstinacy in unfederalism." The town of Westerly also instructed its representatives to push for a convention, but the specific instructions are not extant; very likely they resembled the calm respect of Providence rather than the rash hostility of Newport.[50]

The Anti-Federalists were not listening to any of these pleas. They decided that their referendum was conclusive. With 2,952 votes, fewer than half of the eligible freemen had voted (contemporary estimates placed the total at approximately seven thousand), but the numbers were overwhelmingly one-sided. As much as the Federalists might insist that was a result of their boycott, it is highly probable that many Anti-Federalists stayed home too since there was no chance of losing the vote. When the legislature reconvened on the last day of March, Marchant again moved to call a ratifying convention, and it was again rejected by a large majority. Anti-Federalist John Sayles then suggested "That the House should proceed to appoint a committee of our BEST MEN to frame a Constitution for the United States, and transmit the same to Congress." The *Newport Herald*, in reporting this motion, ridiculed it, but it is likely that it was itself a sardonic reply to the repeated Federalist efforts to call a convention. The majority in the legislature then had a letter to Congress drafted, to be sent by Governor Collins. This letter defended the decision of the state to hold a referendum, based "upon pure Republican Principles," rather than call a convention. It insisted that the people of Rhode Island desired continued union and recognized the defects of the Articles of Confederation, and even that they saw some good in the Constitution. There is a hint of separatism in the closing sentence: "it will ever be our Disposition," the letter reads, "to endeavor to promote whatever appears to us to be of public Utility, and to harmonize as much as possible." In other words, Rhode Island would not remain in the union except on its own terms, but was interested in remaining. This must have infuriated the Federalist minority.[51]

A month after the referendum, Rhode Island held its annual elections. This year those elections offered voters a clear choice between the mercantile party and a ratifying convention on one hand, and the country party and continued opposition to the Constitution on the other. Both parties were content to make the election about the Constitution. That the country party won in a landslide speaks volumes about the priorities of the state, for good or ill.

9

Summer Convention Elections

THE VIRGINIA FEDERALISTS scarcely noticed the Rhode Island referendum. In late April Washington wrote to Lafayette, without irony, that "The Convention[s] of Six States only have as yet accepted the new Constitution. No one has rejected it." By June it had been ratified "by eight States without a negative." Apparently a rejection would only count for Washington if done in convention, but the people of Rhode Island had clearly and unequivocally rejected the Constitution.[1]

Perhaps the debate in Virginia was too intense for anyone to pay much notice to the small northern state. In late February, "The Impartial Examiner" published one of the best Virginia essays against the Constitution. He suggests that the American people, in their consideration of the Constitution, appear as "a restless and dissatisfied people . . . who perpetually seeking after new things throw away one blessing in pursuit of another." There is no reason, he says, to erect a new government "before we have sufficiently tried the virtues of the old." This is not to say that the Framers of the Constitution had any sinister motives, only that the people ought to carefully read and consider rather than simply deferring to the influence of great names. A careful look at the Constitution, he contends, ought to convince the people of Virginia not to ratify. The grant of power to Congress, he argues, is excessive to the point of dangerous. The confederation had too few powers, but this Constitution grants too many; "can any one think," he asks, "that there is no medium between want of power, and the possession of it in an unlimited degree?" It is a maxim in politics, he continues, "that a free people ought to intrust no set of men with powers, that may be abused without controul." He lists some specific objections to the powers granted, including the excise tax, which "has justly become an object of general derision," and standing armies, which, "[b]esides being useless, as having no object of employment, . . . are inconvenient and expensive." The federal judiciary, he writes along with many of his colleagues, "wears the aspect of imperial jurisdiction, clad in a dread array, and spreading its wide domain into all parts of the continent."[2]

   The real issue here, though, is one of rights. The Impartial Examiner articulates the Rights Anti-Federalist position as well as anyone in the thirteen states. He explains that "a social community cannot take too much precaution when they are about to establish the plan of their government." The reason for this is simple: "the liberty of a nation depends, not on planning the frame of government, which consists merely in fixing and delineating the powers thereof; but on prescribing due limits to those powers, and establishing them upon just principles." The proposed Constitution has no such limits, or at least insufficient limits. The states will offer no protection because the Supremacy Clause renders them no danger to the federal government. The Examiner puts a new twist on this common opposition argument, though; he finds danger in the clause because it threatens state bills of rights. The Constitution, he claims, not only "expunges" those rights guaranteed by the state constitutions, "but is proposed without any kind of stipulation for any of those natural rights, the security whereof ought to be the end of all governments." "If this constitution should be adopted," he writes, "here the sovereignty of America is ascertained and fixed in the fœderal body at the same time that it abolishes the present independent sovereignty of each state."[3] Thus he conflates the argument against consolidation with the one in favor of a bill of rights, all while expressing concern over the powers granted to Congress. This blending of Rights and Power arguments was a prelude to the opposition argument in the Virginia Convention.
   Increasingly the Virginia Anti-Federalists, like their counterparts in New York, seemed to recognize that compromise was not only possible, but essential. Richard Henry Lee, who had largely retired from the public debate by January, had not relented in his demands for amendments. In a letter to Federalist James Gordon, Jr., he answered several objections to his insistence on the need for changes prior to ratification. Expecting amendments after ratifications is foolish: "how absurd would it be," he asked Gordon, "for the people to agree to a constitutional evil to-day and to-morrow call for a legislative redress of that evil!" Lee acknowledged the importance of union, but insisted that it must be a union upon proper principles, namely, a guarantee of individual rights. "To trust to future events for remedy of evils that we have ourselves once created, is like choosing to be sick, because a doctor may possibly cure us!"[4] By this time Lee had accepted the idea of ratification, or rather expected it would happen, and aimed to help shape the terms.
   There was a democratic opposition to ratification in Virginia as well, and this portion of the opposition was less reconciled to any compromise on political principles. John Leland, an outspoken proponent for religious freedom, gave a democratic twist to the Rights position. Though his main

argument was for a bill of rights, and particularly a guarantee of religious freedom, he echoed Centinel's call for simple government: "I utterly oppose any Division in Legislative Body," he wrote, "the more Houses, the more parties,—the more they are Divided; the more the Wisdom is Scattered." "Republicus" too took up the call for simplicity. He began with a very democratic understanding of both liberty and equality. Liberty, he says, involves doing what we please, under the guidance of reason, and equality stems from respecting the liberty of others. Protecting this liberty is the purpose of government, and we enter into society as political equals. Thus a proper constitution should provide for equal representation, with representatives elected for short terms. Those legislators must have constitutional power to make such laws as their constituents desire, limited only by the constitution and not by any other countervailing power in or outside of society. In order to fulfill this democratic impulse, a simple legislature is best; for a simpler system is "less liable to disorder," and allows for clear, visible responsibility in government. There is no need for a Senate to represent an aristocratic, moneyed, or any other interest in society, because society has but one common good. To discredit bicameralism, he asks his readers, "is a minority in one house, properly entitled to rule over a majority in the other? Are they not as likely to check a good bill as a bad one? and has it not in fact often happened?" Even if bicameralism were a good idea, the Senate established by the Constitution would violate the principle of equality in representation, serve for far too long, and possess far too much power. Republicus considers the proposed Senate "as a servile and ill-judg'd imitation of the house of lords in the British parliament."[5]

He also offers one of the strongest objections to the Electoral College, again from a democratic perspective. The President, he contends, is far too important and powerful to be elected by "Electors, of electors, and those again electors of other electors." There is no need for such a powerful executive, but any individual invested with substantial political power ought to be elected by the people, and answerable to them. As it stands, he expects the President to consolidate power in order to continue himself in office and become a king. He even takes a shot at the Constitution's support for slavery; the prohibition on Congress interfering with the slave trade until 1808 he describes as an "excellent clause . . . in an Algerian constitution: but not so well calculated (I hope) for the latitude of America."[6] Republicus is prepared to extend his principle of equality to Africans, arguing that to enslave them is to destroy their liberty, and indirectly to degrade ours. Republicus's conclusion effectively sums up the Democratic Anti-Federalist position so predominant on the western frontier:

To conclude, I can think of but one source of right to government, or any branch of it; and *that is the people*. They, and only they, have a right to determine whether they will make laws, or execute them, or do both in a collective body, or by a delegated authority. Delegation is a positive actual investiture. Therefore if any people are subjected to an authority which they have not thus actually chosen; even though they have tamely submitted to it, yet it is not their legitimate government: they are wholly passive, and as far as they are so, are in a state of slavery.[7]

Most Virginia Anti-Federalists, and in fact most politically prominent Virginians, could never accept such a formulation, but political ideas were different in the frontier of Kentucky.

There were still plenty of Virginians who had not yet decided whether to support the Constitution. George Lee Turberville, writing to Madison, was candid about his objections to the Constitution. He expressed concern about Section 4 of the first article, suggesting that Congress ought not to intervene in elections unless a state should fail to establish suitable regulations. In this he was far from alone. He did raise a very practical suggestion that was rarely addressed, however, in pointing out the clear problem with requiring only nine states for the Constitution to take effect. "Suppose . . . that 2, 3 or 4 States shou'd reject the constitution—are they to form a separate confederation?—or are the nine to exercise coercion to bring them in?—or are they to be declared out of the Confederation?—This is by far the most exceptionable part of the Whole piece." William Nelson, Jr., objected to the reeligibility of the President, who he believed would become a king for life, and his sons after him. If the President were made ineligible to serve a second term, he wrote to William Short, "I think the necessity of an union w[oul]d induce me to assent to it without hesitation." Edmund Randolph's fears were not assuaged by the end of February, despite the best efforts of Virginia Federalists to win him over: "pray answer me," he wrote to Madison, "what is to become of our debit for the old cont[inenta]l money? Shall we not be obliged to compensate the Indiana company for our legislative violence? Does not the exception as to a religious test imply, that the congress by the general words had power over religion?" Still, he seems to have expected success for the Constitution in Virginia. He predicted "a coalition between the high and low fœderalists[.] Nothing less can save the fœderal gov[ernmen]t."[8]

Not all of the Virginia Anti-Federalists were on the fence, or even standing next to it. Caleb Wallace, joining the debate late because of the death of his son early in 1788, laid out a series of objections in a letter in early May, insisting that "our American sages have erred." Wallace finds many dangerous powers given to the proposed government, and he writes that the omission of a bill of rights "almost induces me to suspect the virtue of their intentions." The capital will be a profligate court city, and the President will have adequate offices to bestow to create a class of courtesans for that city. Meanwhile, the western lands, without the protection of tariffs to limit foreign competition, will never prosper; only the state governments are in a position to encourage nascent industries through careful regulation of trade, but the Constitution strips away these powers. Finally, the power of taxation is much too broad, and dangerous. Wallace suggests another constitutional convention, "to which I can see no impediment but obstinacy." Even if there were no other reason to call a new convention, it should be done simply because the previous convention's delegates "exceeded their Commission," and to let that stand sets a dangerous precedent. In late May, George Mason, who was growing increasingly hostile to ratification, wrote to Thomas Jefferson for the first time since the Philadelphia Convention. Apparently knowing that his reader was sympathetic to adding a bill of rights, Mason explained that he was discouraged from insisting on such clauses in the Constitution "by the precipitate, & intemperate, not to say indecent Manner, in which the Business was conducted, during the last week of the Convention." He sent with his letter a copy of his published objections, mentioning a few more in passing, relating largely to state powers and rights, before noting that "it would be tedious to enumerate all the Objections," adding that he is "sure they cannot escape Mr. Jefferson's Observation."[9]

The emphasis on rights was prevalent in the public debates in Virginia. "Every intelligent person must know," wrote "A Virginia Planter," "that all the world is now groaning in a Hell of Slavery (America and Switzerland excepted)." The Constitution, if hastily adopted, might well place America in such a state alongside Europe. The Planter suggests that the ratification process ought to be slowed down, so that amendments may be considered, particularly to limit the expansive and vague powers of Congress. "What cannot Congress do," he asks, "with an army at their heels, the revenue in their pockets and with the full and absolute disposal of the militia? How do other nations fare in that predicament?"[10] There is no suggestion here that the Constitution be rejected outright, only that it be carefully considered first, and amended to protect the liberties of the people. This is a far more moderate position than those taken further north.

The most convincing oracle of both moderation and Rights Anti-Federalism in Virginia, though, was "Senex," who wrote in part to defend

Richard Henry Lee against the frequent attacks published against him. In this obscure essay, printed only in the *Virginia Independent Chronicle*, Senex extols the free press, that "faithful guardian" of the people, "bringing to light the silent advances of ambition—by informing the community at large of the good or evil that may flow from any proposition. The present crisis confirms it beyond the reach of scepticism," because in the absence of a vigorous debate the Constitution would have been precipitously adopted without serious consideration. Instead, Senex writes, "Reason reassumes her scales, proclaiming with awful energy from north to south, that the rights retained by the people do not counter-balance the powers conveyed away,—that the evils of a relaxed government have been great, but contrary extremes may be greater."[11] Once again, the argument is for not rejection, but amendment; if the rights of the people may be adequately protected then the powers of the Constitution might be made safe.

"Brutus" also wrote in defense of Lee, and advocated a bill of rights, but he spent more words discussing the importance of separation of powers. Although Brutus still fits better with Rights Anti-Federalism, some Virginians took a more power-oriented stance. "A Federal Republican," for example, makes a simple and effective argument against the tax power in the proposed Constitution. Congress, he suggests, ought to assign the money owed by each state, for the states to collect themselves, as under the Articles of Confederation. The Articles themselves were adequate to take the United States through a war, and no defects were noticed until peacetime. The proposed Constitution, on the other hand, is based on different principles: rather than legislators rotated in office and subject to recall, constituents will have no control whatsoever over their representative other than waiting for the next election. To give to such a small and independent body "the very important power of taking money out of our pockets" is an invitation to tyranny, and there is no real redress should the federal tax collector abuse his power. And should the people resist, "the power vested in Congress of sending troops for suppressing insurrections, will always enable them to stifle the first struggles of freedom."[12]

"A Ploughman" took up the cause of Democratic Anti-Federalism in aristocratic Virginia, asserting that "the People at large" are "the source of majesty, power and dominion, for all authority and constitutional right of government originates with, and proceeds from, the People." The people, unfortunately, seemed about to "rivet the chains of perpetual slavery" on themselves by adopting the proposed Constitution, by accepting a standing army capable of enforcing any policy Congress should choose to make, and by agreeing to pay the costs of this oppression through onerous taxes. The army, in fact, in due time may overthrow Congress and establish a military dictatorship, and in the end every American will be left a slave.[13]

Despite these arguments and all the opposition rhetoric, George Washington seemed to think that nothing more was needed to win over the Anti-Federalists than a simple explanation of the proposed Constitution: "nothing is wanting to render the people so favourably disposed towards it as to put the decision beyond a doubt," he wrote to Benjamin Lincoln, "but a proper representation of, and information upon the subject."[14] The Federalists would have such an opportunity in the elections for the state ratifying convention, and they would find that, by and large, informing the people did not move them into the Federalist column.

UNCERTAINTY IN THE VIRGINIA ELECTIONS

The contests of March were both exciting and uncertain. The elections were, by all accounts, highly deliberative, as the people of Virginia seem to have understood the crucial importance of their state. As an advertisement for a meeting in Frederick County to discuss the proposed document put it, "the fate of an empire may depend on the vote of a day!"[15] Several prominent Anti-Federalists lived in counties in which they would face tough election battles. Fortunately for them, the legislature had decided that delegates need not be residents of the county from which they were elected; several Anti-Federalists took advantage of this opportunity.

George Mason lived in Fairfax County, near George Washington. The latter, of course, could have had a seat in convention had he wanted one, but despite rumors he resisted every effort to draft him into appearing. As for Mason, he had the misfortune of living in a strongly Federalist county, so he ultimately decided to seek election (successfully) elsewhere, in Stafford County.[16] Mason aggressively campaigned against the Constitution, "exerting every nerve to crush the system in its bud." The Federalists were appalled by his behavior. "That gentleman has descended to lower artifice & management upon the occasion," wrote John Blair Smith to Madison, "than I thought him capable of." "I think he might have been satisfied," complained David Stuart about Mason, "with the publication of his objections, without taking the pains to lodge them at every house."[17] "Impartiality," attacking Mason for his rhetoric, quotes the latter's election day speech as an example of the kind of campaigning that was so distressing to the Constitution's friends: "My Fellow-Citizens," Mason is alleged to have

said, "you have been often told of the wisdom and virtue of the federal
convention, but I will now inform you of their true character—the deputies
to that body from the states to the southward of us were *Coxcombs*; the
deputies from Virginia you know pretty well; the majority of the deputies
from the middle states were intriguing office-hunters; and those from the
eastern states fools and knaves."[18] Tobias Lear offered John Langdon a very
similar account of Mason's speech in a letter to John Langdon a day before
Impartiality appeared. Mason was not pulling punches, and he was apparently gaining converts. According to one account, John Pope and Richard
Chichester were campaigning heavily in Fairfax County; the latter "had his
pockets full of Mason's objections; which he leaves wherever he calls." It is
not clear how much impact this had, but it certainly did not help the Federalist cause.[19]

Other Anti-Federalists faced an easier battle. Patrick Henry was firmly
in control in Prince Edward County, where he had, according to Edward
Carrington, "pretty well prepared the people for being his blind followers—his demagogues are loud in their clamours against the Constitution,
professing a determination to reject unless amendments can be had even at
a hazard of standing alone." Madison was especially alarmed by Henry,
and "could think of no dastardly act" that the man would not make to
win the day, including breaking up the union itself. William Grayson took
up this theme. In an election day speech, according to Hugh Williamson,
Grayson showed his constituents a very small snuff box. "Perhaps said he
you may think it of Consequence that some other States have accepted of
the new Constitution, what are they? when compared to Virginia they are
no more than this snuff Box is to the Size of a Man." This kind of radical
rhetoric was apparently fairly common; another Anti-Federalist, William
Graham of Rockbridge, "sounded the Bell of Sedition & raised an uncommon Commotion."[20]

The Anti-Federalists were not shy about openly attacking their opponents in the press. In Warwick County, "A Freeholder of Warwick" took
delegate Cole Digges to task for his "duplicity of character," publishing
short paragraphs by several individuals revealing that Digges represented
his position on the Constitution differently to different people, alternately
advocating ratification, calling for amendments, and outright opposing the
Constitution.[21] Apparently the duplicity worked; Digges was elected by his
constituents.

James Monroe, the future President who was to be a key moderate voice
in convention, was elected handily from Spotsylvania. His constituents sent
him and his colleague John Dawson to Richmond with a fascinating set of

instructions. They wrote that they "presume not to decide on the various parts and combinations of the proposed system," yet they apparently felt compelled to include a list of objections.[22] Still, the voters of Spotsylvania "mean not thereby to break the Union," so they directed their delegates to vote for ratification if nine states should have already ratified by the time of the vote.[23] Although nine states would have ratified by Virginia's vote, the convention would only know about eight of them; Monroe and Dawson both voted against ratification.

The Anti-Federalists were not alone in their occasional struggles against a hostile majority of voters. Edmund Randolph, by now a lukewarm supporter of the Constitution rather than a tentative objector, expressed concerns about his prospects. "Nothing but a small degree of favor, acquired by me, independently of the constitution, could send me," he wrote, "my politicks not being sufficiently strenuous against the const[itutio]n. [John] Marshall is in danger; but [convention candidate William Foushee] is not popular enough on other scores to be elected, altho he is perfectly a Henryite." By early March Randolph's election, along with that of Marshall, seemed to him all but assured, "as there seems to be little or no opposition," yet in the end Marshall polled just eleven votes ahead of Foushee. Randolph finished first by a wide margin. Both would play crucial roles for the Federalists.[24]

James Madison's home county, Orange, showed signs of opposing the Constitution, or at least demanding amendments. At least half a dozen people in Virginia, including his father, wrote to Madison insisting that he return home from New York, where he was serving in Congress, to run for the state convention in person. Madison did not wish to be a delegate to that convention at all, in part because he saw the idea of the authors of that document taking part in the decision to ratify as inappropriate, but mostly because the convention would entail "very laborious and irksome discussions" in which he would have to publicly oppose personal friends on matters of principle. Still, in order to secure the adoption of the Constitution, he reluctantly consented, and arrived home just before the election, with just enough time to save the Federalist cause in the county. Much was at stake here, for should Madison have failed to win election, the symbolism would have been a powerful weapon for the Anti-Federalists, even aside from the loss of a crucial voice for the defenders of the Constitution. Henry Lee went so far as to suggest that if Madison should lose election in Orange County, "several countys in Kentucky would on application by let[te]r elect you." This expedient turned out to be unnecessary, as Madison arrived home in time to give an extensive speech to the voters of Orange, in which he apparently "turn[ed] the sinners of Orange from their wicked ways," according to Edward Carrington, and won enough converts for ratification, to ensure his election along with fellow Federalist James Gordon, Jr. "It is very probable," Madison wrote after the election, "that a very different event would have taken place as to myself if the efforts of my friends had not been seconded by my presence."[25] The state ratifying convention would have been a different event indeed without the Father of the Constitution; Mason and Henry would have welcomed such an event.[26]

In the elections, writes Norman Risjord, "each side went to great pains to field its first team. Every prominent man in the state, except Washington and Richard Henry Lee, secured a seat." Washington was trying to stay out of the partisan fray, knowing that his position would be amply represented by James Madison. Lee too was absent by choice; he did not stand for election from his home county of Westmoreland, the voters of which elected two Federalists. Lee's brother Arthur tried to persuade him to change his mind, noting that George Mason "laments very much" that Lee would not be a delegate, and that he could win election from Fauquier County if the people of Westmoreland were too Federalist in their sentiments. There were plenty of rumors swirling as to why Lee had ceased to campaign against the Constitution, including that he was displeased with the character of the rest of the opposition, and that his family was against him. The latter was simply not true; only his cousin Henry Lee was a publicly avowed Federalist among the prominent Lees, and two of his sons would run for seats in the first Congress, one as a Federalist and the other as an Anti-Federalist. Lee's own reason for declining to run for a seat was health, but his claim that he "could not be in Richmond and be in health" seems but a poor excuse to stop participating in the public effort to secure amendments. Privately, though, he had not changed his mind at all.[27]

In April and May Lee wrote three significant letters that demonstrated his revised position on the Constitution. The first, a mild rebuke to Samuel Adams for his support of ratification with recommended amendments, emphasized the consolidated nature of the proposed government, and defended the traditional notion of the small republic. "If it were permitted an individual to question so enlightened an assembly," he asks, "why submit to a system requiring such amendments, and trust to creatures of our own creation, for the correcting of evils in it that threaten the destruction of those ends for which the system was formed?" Indeed, if changes were needed to the Articles of Confederation, "why, for that reason, exterminate the present plan [the Articles], and establish on its ruins another, so replete with power, danger, and hydra-headed mischief?" Lee's second and third letters were more strategic in nature. To George Mason he emphasized that the states that had not yet decided on the Constitution would be watching Virginia, and he urged moderation. He suggested that Virginia should ratify and recommend amendments, on the condition that if satisfactory changes were not made within the first two years under the new government the state would withdraw from the union. This would enable the Federalists to avoid a second convention, while also ensuring that they would earnestly seek conciliatory amendments rather than sweep the whole idea under the rug. Although he expressed some reservations about the Massachusetts amendments, he wrote that if those amendments were coupled to his own earlier recommendations, "the most essential good consequences would be the result." Such a combination would have united the basic points of the Power and Rights opposition positions. Writing to Federalist Edmund Pendleton, Lee emphasizes that virtually everyone wants amendments, but there is great disagreement as to how to obtain them. He notes the importance of explicit protection of rights; "since the violation of these cannot be necessary to *good* government, but will always be extremely convenient for bad." Most significantly, he repeats from his letter to Mason his call for circumspection, using much the same language, because four other states will be watching Virginia, and he suggests exactly the same plan for proposing amendments. Pendleton did not take his suggestion, and Lee's plan was not seriously discussed in convention. It is clear that Lee had not given up the fight; he was still critical of the Federalists, and not in mild terms. He insisted "that a consolidated, and not a federal government, was the design of *some*, who formed this new project. . . . The dazzling ideas of glory, wealth, and power uncontrolled, unfettered by popular opinions, are powerful to captivate the ambitious and the avaricious." He was not above the political accusations that characterized so much of the debate.[28]

Not all of the campaigning was nasty, bitter, and partisan, though. Henry Tazewell, who had objections to the Constitution, resided in the Federalist county of York, yet was sufficiently popular that he may well have secured election anyway. The reason he gave for not becoming a candidate was that he did not want to have to publicly debate against his closest friends, who supported ratification. The warmth and kindness of the York election did not end there, either. According to Tazewell's son, writing several decades later, "an old man by the name of Charles Lewis" stepped forward on election day and gave a remarkable speech in which he announced that he would not support any of the candidates, all of whom had come out for or against the Constitution. Instead, "he had made up his mind, to vote in favor of persons who so far as he knew had formed no opinion as yet, who were still open to conviction, and . . . prepared to examine [the Constitution] impartially" in convention. He suggested George Wythe and John Blair, two revered old patriots. The Federalist candidates almost immediately endorsed the suggestion, and insisted that voters who supported them ought to vote for Wythe and Blair instead. The latter two were elected unanimously.[29] If this story were true, it would be remarkable that no one challenged the nonsense of this old man; his "impartial" candidates were both delegates to the Philadelphia Convention, and Blair had signed the final document. Wythe had left the Convention early to return to his wife, who was seriously ill, but he was known (or at least suspected) to support the Constitution. The whole thing seems like a Federalist setup to undermine any opposition that might have formed. It clearly worked.

The idea of voting for delegates "open to conviction" was not a popular one; the people of Virginia so consistently voted for like-minded candidates that, in Pauline Maier's words, the election was "something akin to a referendum on ratification." Seen in this light, the vote was too close to call. Though many delegate lists predicting votes on ratification were created, and some speculation was published concerning who held a majority of seats, there was enough disagreement to cast them all in doubt. "The results," Maier explains, "were reassuring to nobody."[30]

ANTI-FEDERALIST DOMINANCE IN NORTH CAROLINA

Meanwhile, south of the border in North Carolina the convention elections went differently. Here the Federalists were badly outnumbered, and the opposition dominated. Still, the elections in the state were contentious and hard-fought by both sides. In Hertford County, a Baptist preacher named Lemuel Burkitt, an Anti-Federalist seeking election to the state convention, used his pulpit to attack the Constitution and win the votes of his flock. Elkanah Watson, appalled at this partisan sermon, interrupted and created something close to a riot. Another fight took place in the county on election day, which resulted in the candles at the polling place being extinguished. Out of the darkness, Burkitt emerged victorious, though the majority of the delegation was Federalist.[31] In the western part of the state the elections were similarly chaotic, though the Anti-Federalists had more success. The Federalists put up a fight, though. According to John Brown Cutting, in one western county the operation of . . . intrigues . . . probably induced a majority of the voters to bestow their suffrages on men extremely obscure and unfit from excessive ignorance—as is alleged—to discuss or decide upon so great a question. In consequence of this conception the election was interrupted by those who wished men more enlighten'd—or as the phrase is—more *fœderal*. And by force of club-law their antagonists were defeated.[32]

Cutting is probably referring to the elections in far western Sumner County, the only county west of the mountains that returned any Federalist delegates to the convention. Everywhere else in that region the opposition to ratification won out.[33]

The elections turned violent in Dobbs County. The Federalist slate for the convention was headed by seven-time former governor Richard Caswell, and included several other prominent state officeholders. The Anti-Federalist ticket consisted of five men who had collectively served exactly one term in the state legislature; it was headed by another Baptist preacher, Abraham Baker. The voting was orderly, but the counting was not. The Anti-Federalists consistently outpaced the Federalists in the voting, to the chagrin of the Federalists. "It scarcely seemed possible to them that Richard Caswell could be defeated by Preacher Baker; they decried the character and ability of their successful opponents and cursed the folly of the people." According to a newspaper account, one of the Federalist candidates, Colonel Benjamin Shepherd, "with sundry others, cast out many aspersions and very degrading and abusive language to the other candidates, or any person on their part, with so much as one provoking word." Their opponents no doubt replied in kind. At this point, Shepherd reportedly threatened to beat one of the election inspectors, and then proceeded to lead an angry and violent mob to carry out the threat. The votes were being counted at night by candlelight, so the mob first extinguished the candles, and then proceeded to attack with clubs anyone in their way. Isaac Croom, one of the Anti-Federalist candidates, was among the victims, along with the county sheriff.[34] Another election was reluctantly called, and the Anti-Federalists boycotted in protest. Neither slate of delegates was ultimately seated in the convention.[35] A week after the initial election, Shepherd engaged in a heated (and ultimately violent) argument over the Constitution with a Mr. William Barfield. According to one newspaper report, Shepherd attacked Barfield with a whip, at which time an apprentice of Barfield's attacked the colonel with an axe, with which he "cut off a side of his face, and broke his collar bone." Shepherd's

nephew took a few shots at the apprentice with his uncle's rifle; the resulting injuries cost the apprentice his arm.[36] Although the *Maryland Chronicle* reported that Shepherd died from his injuries, he apparently showed
up to try to claim a seat at the ratifying convention, and was a member of
the state legislature later that year. Another account, in the *State Gazette
of South Carolina*, made Shepherd the victim rather than the instigator
of violence. This version identified Shepherd as "a man of considerable
property and great influence in Dobbs County," kindly visiting an elderly
neighbor "with whom he had lived in the greatest friendship and harmony." A discussion about the Constitution descended into insults tossed
at Shepherd, who replied, "Your language is too abusive to be submitted
to. Nothing but your age now protects you from that punishment which
you should receive." At this point, the Anti-Federalist, not given a name
in this version of events, left to round up his followers and find some axes.
Shepherd, not knowing that they would return for him, left for home,
and on the way was attacked until he was "on the ground, almost void of
speech, and insensible, the blood running from his nose, mouth and ears
in considerable quantities." Several Federalist friends intervened. The rifle
now belonged to the Anti-Federalists, and it was Shepherd's kinsman who
lost an arm.[37] It is difficult to tell which version is closer to the truth; the
latter was correct about Shepherd surviving the attack, but given Shepherd's poor behavior at the elections it seems reasonably likely that it was
he who initiated the violence.

The Federalists who were not driven to violence were still exasperated.
Archibald Maclaine wrote that "we have a set of fools and knaves in every
part of the State, who seem to act as by concert; and are uniformly against
any man of abilities and virtue." The Federalists saw their opponents as
willfully ignorant, resisting the wisdom and integrity of the Federalist
leaders of the state. The state was to be a difficult one for the Federalists,
though. The opposition was strong, and its focus was clearly on rights.
"The majority of the delegates who were elected, in almost every county
from which we have been able to obtain a return," reported the *Maryland
Journal* in late April, "have promised that the preservation of the civil and
religious rights and liberties of their fellow-citizens, declared and secured
under our *present* government, would be the ruling principle of their conduct."[38] The state convention would ultimately refuse to ratify until a bill
of rights was adopted; a second convention then relented and approved
the document after such a bill had been drawn up in Congress and looked
likely to be added.

THE FEDERALISTS OVERWHELMED
IN NEW YORK

In late April, New York, like Virginia and North Carolina, saw heavily contested elections with both sides well organized.[39] The Anti-Federalists were prepared to "use every art, & strain every nerve to gain their points." In the words of one rather poetic Federalist, by "conjuring up immaginary phantoms, to delude those people, who have neither sense or direction," the Anti-Federalists were "like the witches in Macbeth, dancing round the chaldron of sedition, each throwing in his proportion of spells, for the confusion of his country."[40] The Federalists, meanwhile, were "useing every Effort in their power to prevent all kind of information from going to the people, thereby to delude and Mislead them." The people of New York were advised to "knock off the shackles of those *ambitious men, who owe their own power, to their talents of deceiving the people.*" These words were in the context of an essay in favor of the Constitution in Federalist Kings County, but they could have served as the slogan for either side anywhere in the state.[41]

In the aftermath of the Massachusetts compromise, the debate in New York continued as it had been, with scarcely any change. While Massachusetts wrapped up its convention compromise and New Hampshire tried to work out its own, Brutus began his extensive critique of the powers of the judiciary. He saw in the powers of the courts the potential for consolidation, and the demise of the states. His was not the only attack on the judiciary, but it had relatively little company on that subject.

Abraham Yates, Jr., believed by some to have been Brutus, was certainly the author of the much less convincing, though perhaps more learned and certainly more footnoted, essays signed "Sidney."[42] In these essays he draws on almost every writer cited by the Anti-Federalists in a comprehensive, though tedious, philosophical discussion of republican government. He emphasizes the importance of mixed government, steering clear of both monarchy and democracy, and implies that the Constitution is much too close to the former. He argues that political power has been abused under the Confederation, in which Congress has little power. How much more abuse must we expect, he asks, if we grant Congress with extensive powers? In the process of this discussion, he takes several shots at the Federalists: his most effective is the observation that "we have got into a habit of doing business either in secret or in haste." He also offers a memorable analogy; he compares the Federalists to a "horse-hunter," who finds and tames a wild horse, breaking its spirit and forcing it into bondage and servitude. This, Sidney suggests, is what the Federalist leaders aim to do to the American people. Ratification is not about liberty or self-government, but rather about taming, ruling, and breaking the spirit of the people.[43]

Some New York Anti-Federalists, apparently displeased with the dour intellectual tones of Brutus and Sidney, turned to satire and irony to make their points and to add some levity to the very serious debate. "Expositor" lampooned the common Federalist argument that the Constitution needs no bill of rights, because it is itself a bill of rights. This is obvious, the author writes, when one examines the Preamble; the convention delegates clearly intended to secure rights for themselves and their posterity, never mind the rest of the people. How, he asks, could the Anti-Federalists be so blind as to demand a separate bill of rights? He sees in the Constitution an effort to establish a ruling class. Those elected to the House, to continue themselves in office, will be reelected every two years at first. These biennial elections, though, "no doubt, will be improved to triennial and septennial, in time; as the constitution admits of improvement, you know." Senators, meanwhile, will obtain sufficient control over state legislatures to continue themselves and their families in that body. Should someone other than the privileged ruling class manage to get elected, of course, there is a clause to take care of it: two-thirds of members in each house can vote to expel a member. "*Not for disorderly behaviour*, you will please to observe, sir, though it may appear so, at first view, but absolutely." That the ruling elite intends to remain in office indefinitely is made clear by the requirements for office. These requirements, he observes, will allow the people "to prefer age and folly to youth and understanding." He later asks, regarding the Senate qualifications, "Are not several of the effects of old age as incompatible with the office or duty of a good legislator as some of the levities or follies of youth?" The Expositor goes on a tirade against the three-fifths clause, during which he suggests that northern livestock ought to be as entitled to representation as southern slaves; he concludes this aside with his opinion that the three-fifths clause is "*a most daring insult* offered to the free men and freeholders" of New York, and Hamilton's acceptance of the clause in the Philadelphia Convention was "an *unparalleled departure* from his duty to this state, as well as to the United States." In the middle of this vaguely antislavery rant, Expositor presents a rather interesting and unique argument about direct taxes. The idea that Congress might levy a head tax, he contends, will discourage marriage and procreation in the north, while the southern states will continue to add slaves and thus representation. He even goes so far as to imply that women will perform abortions rather than have children, in order to avoid potentially ruinous taxes. The argument is clever, but not terribly effective; it is hard to imagine many northerners making decisions on marriage and children solely to avoid taxes.[44]

Another irreverent satirist, signing as "Suilbup" ("Publius" spelled backward), attacked the aristocratic tone of the Federalists, satirically mocking the opponents of the Constitution for their resistance. "Insolent plebian dogs—dare they say the New Constitution is not good, when their betters say it is?" Those betters, he continues, will establish a noble aristocracy: "we must have princes and noblemen; but for the present we will give them other names—you know it is no matter what names they have, if they have the power—we must have an army too—it will be easy to get money then: for if the people won't pay, it is only sending the army to collect it."[45]

Despite the levity and satire, New York saw the most intellectually rigorous debate over the merits of the proposed Constitution. Among the best arguments is the pamphlet by "A Plebeian," probably Melancton Smith, in April. This essay aims to persuade the people of New York to insist on amendments prior to ratification of the Constitution. The Plebeian observes that the leading Federalists have accepted that amendments must be made, but now insist that they must be made after the proposed government goes into effect. The mere acknowledgment that changes are needed, he suggests, "afford[s] strong evidence, that the opposers of the constitution have reason on their side, and that they have not been influenced, in the part they have taken, by the mean and unworthy motives of selfish and private interests with which they have been illiberally charged." This is a remarkable statement; it suggests that the debate has changed significantly in the months since the Massachusetts ratification, and that the Anti-Federalists (or at least some of them) are prepared to acquiesce in the Constitution if properly changed, and put behind them the ugliness of the earlier debates. Of course, the question about how it should be changed, or rather when, was an open one. The Plebeian contends that there is no hurry to implement the new government, that there is plenty of time to work out the details and make the appropriate changes, because the United States is not facing any serious threats, military or economic. Furthermore, the author argues, there is broad agreement on what needs to be changed. The major points of objection, according to the Plebeian, are that the Constitution consolidates the states into a general government, that the representation is too small, that the tax power granted is too broad, that the jurisdiction of the courts is too wide and jury trials are not secure, that the Congress may alter the regulations on elections established by the states, that the Senate involves a dangerous mixture of powers, and that a standing army might be established by Congress. It is telling that the Plebeian does not include a bill of rights among the objections to which the opposition generally agrees; New York was firmly in the Power Anti-Federalist camp, and the question of rights was secondary, when it came up at all. The idea of interstate coordination on amendments was still little more than an idea, and the Rights and Power Anti-Federalists had still not yet joined forces.[46]

The Plebeian acknowledges the importance of giving the federal government authority to regulate trade, but he denies that this will have a substantial impact on the general prosperity. "The truth is, this country buys more than it sells: It imports more than it exports. There are too many merchants in proportion to the farmers and manufacturers. Until these defects are remedied, no government can relieve us." A strong central government will not produce prosperity; only "frugality and industry" can do that. "Earn much and spend little, and you will be enabled to pay your debts, and have money in your pockets; and if you do not follow this advice, no government that can be framed, will relieve you." The Plebeian closes his pamphlet with an appeal to the voters of New York to elect "such men as have been uniform in their opposition to the proposed system in its present form, or without proper alterations." Such men, he says, can be trusted, while anyone insisting on ratification before amendment is unreliable and dangerous.[47]

There were Rights Anti-Federalist appeals in New York as well. "If you wish the establishment of a national government with powers to usurp and destroy your constitutional rights and liberties," wrote "A Tenant," "then go and give your votes for the establishment of this new constitution." He suggests that the voters select delegates who will insist on amendments, presumably a bill of rights, prior to adoption. If the voters fail to do so, explained Abraham Bancker, they "will give too great a scope to a Domineering Party and tend to overturn those Liberties for which many of their Friends have bled and Died."[48]

The New York Anti-Federalists were the best-organized opposition in the nation, and they entered the elections well prepared. The resistance was centered in New York City, where John Lamb chaired the Federal Republican Society, which aimed to serve as a central clearinghouse of information for the opposition nationwide. Even here, though, it took a while to get organized. Lamb, along with committee secretary Charles Tillinghast, worked diligently to distribute out-of-state pamphlets throughout New York.[49] These two, on behalf of the Committee, also circulated New York pamphlets to the other states. In May Lamb sent out a series of letters to Anti-Federalists in six states to try to arrange for cooperation in securing amendments. His letters to Maryland and South Carolina were too late, and those to Pennsylvania were of course not intended to sway the convention there, long since over. His main concerns were New Hampshire, North Carolina, and Virginia, all of which had yet to decide on the Constitution. Lamb hoped to establish a coordinated resistance, to insist on amendments prior to ratification. By early June the Committee had apparently settled on amending rather than defeating the Constitution; one can only imagine how events might have been different if the whole effort had begun a little sooner. In the hands of Paca and Chase, the proposal for coordination might have won over more delegates in Maryland, and the opposition in South Carolina may have had more success in proposing amendments. Perhaps Samuel Adams in Massachusetts would have backed such a plan, and John Hancock could have taken the lead (and the president's chair) in a convention called to resolve the differences among the recommended state amendments. By the time that Lamb's coordination efforts seriously began, of course, the Constitution's momentum was hard to stop; eight ratifications without conditions had made at least one more a near certainty. Rawlins Lowndes of South Carolina acknowledged as much in his reply to Lamb, after the state had accepted the Constitution.

> Had your Plan been proposed in time I doubt not it might have produced very good Effect in this Country: A Strong Systematic Opposition wherein the Opinions and Sentiments of the different States were Concenter'd, and directed to the same specific Objects, would have had a Weight, which the Advocates for the Constitution must have submitted to, and have removed the force of an Objection, strongly insisted upon, arrising from the seeming diversity & dissimilarity of the several amendm[en]ts contended for.[50]

Lowndes's fellow South Carolinian Aedanus Burke admitted a lack of organization in the state. "In the first place, we in the Opposition, had not, previous to our Meeting, either wrote, or spoke, hardly a word against it, nor took any one step in the matter. We had no principle of concert or union, while its friends and abettors left no expedient untried to push it forward." For Joshua Atherton in New Hampshire and Samuel Chase in Maryland, too, the idea of coordination came too late. Even with circumstances as they were, Lamb's network had potential. The fundamental problem with the Federal Republican Society was simple, though: on a national level, it was poorly organized and ineffective. Linda Grant DePauw describes the Society as a "small and incompetent group" that had far less impact than historians typically assume, and the available evidence supports this description.[51]

In Albany, meanwhile, the Albany Antifederal Committee embraced the label placed upon them by the Constitution supporters, and served as a more effective, though more local, organizing body for resistance to ratification. Unfortunately for them, the printers were not inclined to help; by March there were three Federalist-leaning papers in Albany, and the Committee decided that this was a situation that required correction. In a rare instance of Anti-Federalist pressure on a Federalist printer, the members of the Committee sent letters to Melancton Smith and Abraham Yates seeking assistance, and offered substantial financial support for anyone who wanted to set up a newspaper to take up the opposition cause. These two must have involved Lamb, who apparently made some efforts to set up a printer in Albany. The idea of another competitor must have convinced printer Charles Webster, who published one paper in the city and copublished another, to relent to Anti-Federalist pressure, because the Albany Antifederal Committee wrote to Lamb at the end of the month that further assistance was not needed.[52]

In April, just before the New York Convention elections, the Albany Antifederal Committee issued a statement opposing the Constitution and endorsing a slate of candidates for Albany County. In this statement they included a list of thirty-four objections. Eighteen involved powers granted to the national government by that document, and eleven more involved the separation of powers or federal structure. Only five involved rights not adequately protected. They concluded that the Constitution must be materially amended before it is adopted, or rejected outright. The Federal Committee published a point-by point response, to which the Anti-Federalists delivered a scathing reply. A second Antifederalist Committee response suggested that the Federalist refutations "consist chiefly of positive assertions, without any arguments to support them—unmeaning denials, or reluctant admissions of points which have been stated by us, and which the force of truth ought and will, sooner or later, carry home to the bosom of every man who is in the least degree disposed to a dispassionate enquiry."[53]

This resistance in Albany was led in part by the town's mayor, John Lansing, Jr., who had served as a New York delegate to the Philadelphia Convention. In that capacity he came under fire in the newspapers from "A Citizen," George Metcalf, who insisted that he, along with fellow delegate Robert Yates, acted "in the paltry views of party spirit" in their opposition to the Constitution and their early departure. Lansing was not prepared to let this attack go unanswered; he revealed that Metcalf was the author and that he had lived in Canada during the Revolution, and then closed by threatening to prosecute him for the publication. Metcalf defended himself a few days later, reaffirming his patriotism (and New York citizenship), and again portraying Lansing as partisan and petty. The mayor would perhaps have been well advised to leave this one alone, but the Anti-Federalists of New York were not prepared to sit back and permit these kinds of attacks by Federalists. "A Lover of Truth and Decency" wrote that the Federalists, "destitute of character, take a malevolent pleasure in destroying the reputation of others. . . . The vicious are at enmity with the good. The advocates of tyranny hate the staunch friends of liberty."[54]

Not content to defend the reputation of their leaders, the Anti-Federalists tore into the proponents of the Constitution. Y. W. suggested that the Constitution was designed to protect those who intended to default on their debts to the United States, drawing from a series of motions made in the Philadelphia Convention concerning qualifications for office holding. Because of such ulterior motives, the Federalists were trying to push ratification by deceiving the people. "Will a Majority of the great Body of the People of the United States contentedly consent to support a Government founded in Usurpation & Fraud," asked Hugh Hughes in April, "when they once become fully sensible of the Advantages which have been taken of their Confidence & Credulity?" William Smith was even more critical, suggesting that the Federalists are endeavoring to "Get into the Aristocratical Saddle they may ride With pleasure for there is provision made for Whips Spurs and every other Apparatus Nessassary for a Comfortable Journey." In this he echoed a metaphor that Luther Martin attributed to Elbridge Gerry.[55]

The most significant event in New York in April, though, had nothing to do with ratification: the Doctors' Riot. Some medical students had been digging up corpses for dissection, which when known resulted in a mob rising up against them. A number of the most prominent residents of New York, including Governor Clinton as well as Federalists Alexander Hamilton and John Jay, worked together to quell the mob and restore order, and both Clinton and Jay, among others, were injured during the riots. Though the riots had nothing to do with the ratification debates, several writers suggested privately that they might convince some Anti-Federalists of the need for stronger government.[56] It is unlikely that the riots made much of an impact, but with the ratification vote in the state as close as it was, if two delegates were swayed the effect was decisive.

As the convention elections approached, both sides were prepared for the campaign. Suffolk County suffered "an inundation of Pamphlets both for and against the Proposed Constitution," but the campaigning by the opposition ticket, led by Thomas Tredwell "paint[ing] the dreadful consiquences that will follow this adoption of the Constitution in as high coulers as the Prophet Daniel did the distress of the Babilonians previous to their destruction," seems to have made the difference as the Anti-Federalists won a close contest. In Columbia County the Anti-Federalists were "circulating with amazing assiduity the reasons of dissent of the minority of Pennsylvania." In Washington County a Federalist insisted that material in support of the Constitution must arrive soon or "I fear the federalists will be overpowered." In each of these three counties the opposition was successful. In Westchester County, the Anti-Federalists were "indefatigable in their exertions to prejudice the minds of the people against the Constitution," but failed to secure the convention seats. The opposition put serious effort into Federalist Richmond County as well. Here they were accused of "much Policy and Chicanery" and "low and subtile Craftiness"; one Federalist even suggested that "some Evil Enemy" was interfering with his mail. In the end the Federalists won a close vote, but the opposition declared it a moral victory. "R," responding to "Q" in the *New York Journal*, who declared that the delegates for that county were Federalists, wrote "that only one of the members for convention from Richmond county is federal, and even that one declares himself open to conviction, which by the buy is not the character of a fed." Both delegates would ultimately support ratification.[57]

The Anti-Federalists knew they probably would not be able to claim any kind of victory, real or moral, in New York City; still they put up a public fight. "There are men in the federal ticket," wrote an Anti-Federalist in the *New York Journal* in mid-April, "who will make fortunes by speculating in your state debts, and will insult your credulous ears with the sound of your own chink speculators; and men, noted for their avarice, would disgrace the dignity of legislation, and make a mock of your confidence." The legislature, he continued, would become as "the temple of Jerusalem," complete with money changers, "a DEN *of* PUBLIC T——s." Better to be "represented by antifederal disinterestedness than federal roguery and avarice." An opposition ticket as suggested by that author was not going to win, though. Instead, some Anti-Federalists in the city made efforts to obtain election for Governor George Clinton, in order to win one opposition seat from a heavily Federalist county. They went so far as to place Clinton atop proposed Federalist tickets in the hopes of splitting the votes. Others suggested compromise tickets, putting Alexander Hamilton and James Duane with John Lamb and Melancton Smith. They were even accused of handing out counterfeit election tickets "with the Governor at the head, but so folded down as not to be perceived." In the end, though, the opposition party in the city was aptly described by "A Citizen" as "drowning men . . . catching at straws." The final vote tally favored the Federalist candidates by a twenty-to-one margin over Clinton, the leading Anti-Federalist. Fortunately for the opposition, its leaders made certain to secure election to the convention from other counties.[58]

New York City was never a crucial battleground for the Anti-Federalists, though. The counties of Ulster, Dutchess, and Albany, sending a combined twenty delegates to the state convention, represented the core of Anti-Federalist strength. The county of Ulster was perhaps the most decidedly Anti-Federalist part of the state. The Federalists here were left to resort to tactics akin to those used by the opposition in New York City, nominating alternative opposition tickets in hopes of dividing the votes. There were several public appeals to unity, including a lengthy essay by "A Dutchess County Anti-Federalist" that emphasized the importance of defeating ratification over any disagreement over the best delegates. The only significant question was whether to run the Governor as a candidate here where he was ensured of election or elsewhere in the hopes of taking an otherwise Federalist seat. The safer course was adopted, with Clinton becoming part of the delegation from Ulster. In Dutchess County too the voters managed "to refuse the gilded pill proffered in this newly fangled constitution" by electing an Anti-Federalist delegation led in effect by New Yorker Melancton Smith. Smith raised some controversy among Anti-Federalists because of his residence in New York City, making Federalists salivate over the prospects of a split opposition vote, but the Anti-Federalist leadership managed to convince its rank-and-file voters that Smith's presence in the city, in the words of "Cassius," "has given him an opportunity of prying into the designs, and seeing through the schemes of the advocates of despotism." The Federalists saw positives in the Dutchess County loss, noting that "at the beginning of the year it was the better opinion that there were hardly one twentieth of the Electors inclined to the federal side," while the end result was merely a two-to-one margin. This was a hollow moral victory, of course, but the Federalists could claim little success in the state in general.[59]

The county of Albany may well have been the most critical battleground in the state. Alexander Hamilton claimed in a letter to Madison that "All depends upon Albany where both sides claim the victory."[60] In that county, the Federalists were on the defensive from the beginning, insisting that their slate of candidates was

> fully impressed with that Spirit of Amity and Conciliation, which has lately been evinced by the Conduct of our Sister State of Massachusetts, on the great NATIONAL QUESTION; and it is our general Wish and Expectation, that the New Constitution be adopted as nearly as possible upon the same Principles—that is, by Ratifying and Confirming

the Constitution in its present Form, and strongly recommending the Amendments proposed by that State, as well as any others which may, on a full Investigation of this Important Business, be found requisite.[61]

This is a full reversal from Pennsylvania, and a far cry even from Massachusetts, in which the idea of amendments was a concession eventually agreed to out of necessity. The necessity was obvious here from the very beginning of the convention elections. Meanwhile, the Anti-Federalists of Albany County were aggressive from the beginning; they were willing to compromise, but only if the compromise involved amending before adopting. The debate in the county largely took the form of dueling circulars by the two committees, with objections raised and answered and then renewed, and disagreements over who believed what about the Constitution (including a surprisingly lively debate about how Scotsmen in New York City felt about the document).[62] There was also a great deal of personal campaigning; the Federalists tried to explain to the crowds the advantages of the Constitution, but they were undermined by the Anti-Federalists, who tended to follow them and address the same crowds afterward. In the end, notwithstanding Hamilton's assertion that both sides claimed victory, the Anti-Federalists returned an impressive two-thousand-vote margin out of a little over seven thousand votes cast, an outcome "as successful as the most sanguine expected."[63]

New York law required that the votes not be counted for several weeks after balloting, and both sides were apprehensive. A small majority was frequently predicted, but in the end the Anti-Federalists took two-thirds of the convention seats, and secured election for all of their most significant leaders. Henry Knox was clearly partisan in his claim that "[t]he weight of abilities and personal character will be greatly on the side of the Feds"; certainly the Federalists had effective leadership in Alexander Hamilton and John Jay, but the abilities of Melancton Smith, George Clinton, Abraham Yates, and the other opposition leaders were not trifling. It would be an impressive gathering of talent on both sides.[64]

10

Missed Opportunities in Maryland

WITH SIX STATES having ratified, and the Federalists still dominating the public debate, time was running out for the Anti-Federalists by spring 1788. The small victories in New Hampshire and Rhode Island did little for the opposition cause. They needed a substantial win, and such a win would require both a coherent message and effective organization. The message was developing coherency, with the Power and Rights positions beginning to converge, but in the next two states to hold conventions the organization fell short. In South Carolina legislative malapportionment mattered more than poor planning, but in Maryland the Anti-Federalists simply missed a significant opportunity.

THE DEBATE IN MARYLAND BEGINS

The state of Maryland was slow to enter the debate over the Constitution. Despite the contentious and partisan conflict north in Pennsylvania, the developing discussion in Virginia to the south, and eastern Delaware's quick ratification, very little of substance appeared in Maryland until January 1788. Several out-of-state pieces were reprinted, and the Federalists set out to vilify their opponents as "evil and designing men, fraudulent debtors, Anti-Federalists, insurgents, &c." Only one noteworthy exchange originating in the state appeared in the newspapers in 1787. In the *Maryland Journal*, "Caution" began with an attack on the haste with which the Federalists were attempting to secure ratification. "An attempt to *surprise* you into any *public* measure," he wrote, "ought to meet your indignation and contempt. When violence or cunning is substituted for argument and reason, suspicion should take the alarm, and prudence should dictate the propriety of deliberation." The Constitution, he writes, deserves "the most mature and deliberate consideration, and a free and full examination." His primary complaint is a circulating petition stating that the legislature ought to call a convention, and that the Constitution ought to be ratified *"without any amendment or alteration."* Such a petition is not about requesting deliberation in convention, but about unqualified consent before such deliberation. Caution offers six reasons for delay, primarily centering on the idea that the people do not yet have ample information because opponents of the document have not yet had a chance to plead their case. He closes with an implication that the Federalists are engaged in a sinister plot to obtain ratification without due consideration. "A Friend to the Constitution" replied in the next issue, accusing Samuel Chase as the author of Caution, and suggesting that, since the Philadelphia Convention recommended that state conventions be called to "assent and ratify" the Constitution, the legislature ought to use those words. This argument leads the Friend to the peculiar conclusion that calling the convention *"involves the legislature in a complete approbation of the Constitution."* Thus Caution is merely trying to defeat the Constitution, which was probably true.[1]

After "Caution," the first significant Anti-Federalist pieces published in Maryland were several essays and letters by Luther Martin, including his "Genuine Information," a partial account of the Convention adapted from a speech he delivered to the state legislature in November. The debates in the state, such as they were, have an isolated quality to them, as if Maryland was completely set apart from the other states. Certainly several out-of-state pieces were republished, including the objections of Yates and Lansing as well as those of Edmund Randolph, but writings from Maryland seem to have had little impact elsewhere. Luther Martin, the key Anti-Federalist figure here, evoked little response in Massachusetts and New York. Even his fight with the Connecticut "Landholder," probably Oliver Ellsworth, led to an apparently in-state imposter answering Martin under Ellsworth's pseudonym, rather than an interstate response from Connecticut. This is not to say that there were no good writings in Maryland; in addition to the impressive (if tedious) "Genuine Information," Maryland's "Farmer" (never reprinted outside of the state) is a worthwhile read. But the debate in the state stands apart from the national one, and warrants a separate treatment.

Luther Martin, probably the most verbose delegate at the Constitutional Convention,[2] delivered his sentiments to the Maryland legislature in a speech on November 29. Although all five delegates to the Philadelphia Convention were invited to speak, it was Martin who stole the show (and said the most). An edited and expanded version of this speech appeared in twelve lengthy installments in the *Maryland Gazette*, and was later published as a pamphlet. It is an exaggeration to describe the pamphlet as "the ablest argument extant against the fundamental principles of the proposed government," or worse, "*the* Anti-Federalist Paper," as some of his defenders do. It was, however, an impressive and exhaustive piece of work; Martin is straightforward and honest in a debate full of strategic misinformation.[3]

It does not take Martin long to express exactly where he stands. "Could there possibly be a greater indignity and insult offered to the majesty of the free States, and the free citizens of America," he asks in an introductory open letter, "than for the very men who were entrusted with powers for the preservation and security of their rights, and for the establishment of a permanent system to promote their happiness, to make use of that power to destroy both the one and the other?" He portrays the convention as a secret conclave up to nefarious schemes. The rule of secrecy, for Martin, proves that the delegates knowingly colluded for their own purposes; as for Martin, he "had no idea, that all the wisdom, integrity, and virtue of this State, or of the others, were centered in the convention." In particular, those purposes seem to have been the enslavement of the small states by the large ones, specifically Virginia, Pennsylvania, and Massachusetts, which would together have the votes to control legislation. This was all laid out in the Virginia plan, which Martin included in full in his pamphlet. Even the last-minute change to representation, allowing one representative for every thirty thousand people instead of every forty thousand, comes under Martin's fire; this is clearly a ploy by the states with the most land (specifically Virginia, North Carolina, and Georgia) to ensure more representatives in the future, as their western fronts become populated.[4]

Martin identified three parties in the Philadelphia Convention. The first was monarchists, some of whom openly avowed the position while others secretly harbored it. The second group consisted of those who were merely looking for the best deal for their home states, mostly the largest states but also the southern ones. The third party, in Martin's eyes the good guys, was "truly federal and republican," and its delegates fought for the preservation of the federal system and the state governments. This third group wished for amendments to the Articles of Confederation rather than a new constitution, and recognized that when new defects might be found in the future another such convention may be called. The equality of votes among states was the crucial point here for Martin, and initially for his allies as well. The states, Martin explained, were as individuals in a state of nature with respect to any national constitution, and as such were entitled to an equal voice regardless of population, area, or wealth. This is the proper principle of equality in a federal system, not proportional representation by population. "So if one State pays more to the federal government," he wrote in explanation, "it is because as a State, she enjoys greater blessing from it; she has more wealth protected by it, or a greater number of inhabitants, whose rights are secured, and who share its advantages." This insistence on state sovereignty earned Martin and others the enmity of the nationalists. He contends that the advocates of consolidation threatened him and his like-minded brethren that they would not have another opportunity to meet and discuss these issues in convention. Upon reflection, Martin accepted this as true, because when the states "discovered the part *this* convention had acted, and how much its members were *abusing the trust* reposed in them, the States would never trust *another* convention."[5]

The states, according to Martin, expected the Convention to respect and protect their sovereignty. In this sense the Great Compromise, securing equal representation in one house and proportional in the other, was the central betrayal of trust. For the small states to agree to this would be "consenting, after [the large states] had struggled to put *both their feet on our necks*, to take *one of them off*, provided we would consent to let them *keep the other on*, when they knew at the same time, that they could not put *one foot* on *our necks*, unless *we would consent to it*, and that by being permitted to keep on that one foot, they should *afterwards be able to place the other foot on whenever they pleased.*" Yet agree to it they did, to the chagrin of Martin, but it was not without a fight. "It has been observed," Martin wrote, "that the debate respecting the mode of representation, was productive of considerable warmth, this observation is true; but, Sir, it is equally true, that if we could have *tamely* and *servilely* consented to be *bound in chains*, and *meanly condescended* to *assist* in *rivetting them fast*, we might have avoided all that warmth, and have proceeded with as much calmness and coolness as any stoick could have wished." Martin was not one to lie down and give up the fight, and his resistance did not end with his departure from Philadelphia.[6]

Martin raises many familiar objections to the power and structure of the proposed government. His central objection, though, is that the Convention chose to abandon a federal system in favor of a consolidated one. There was no reason offered at the Convention for creating a consolidated government, or for rejecting federal forms, beyond the fact that the *existing* federal system was flawed.[7] The desire for consolidated government was driven by issues not of principle, but of interest. There was no need for a bicameral legislature, for example, in a truly federal system. He suggested that the states ought to be permitted to issue paper money and bills of credit, even if only with the permission of Congress. Even the extension of the confederation was an important point: the western territories, he believed, ought to be able to free themselves from the eastern states that claim them, and establish themselves as separate and independent states. The eastern states, he insisted, have no intention of consenting to such a separation.

The structure of the proposed national government was also problematic. Like many Anti-Federalists, Martin took issue with the Senate. Six years, he argued, would be too long a term: "[F]or *six years* the *senators* are rendered totally and absolutely *independent of their States*, of *whom* they ought to be the *representatives*, without any *bond* or *tie* between them." Instead of such a system, Senators ought to serve for a single year, be paid by the states, and be subject to recall. Such a long term in the nation's capital will remove any prospects for a political career in the state at the conclusion of that term; thus the Senator will remain with the national government and "he is *lost* to his *own State*." Thus far his objections were typical. He also saw problems with the powers of the Senate, but Martin was the only Anti-Federalist of any significance to suggest that the proposed Senate was too *weak*. The Constitution, he argued, by giving to the House the sole authority to introduce revenue acts, would make the Senate little more than observers, waiting for the House to take action. Since almost any piece of legislation affects revenues and expenditures in some way, almost every act will be construed as a revenue bill, and the Senate, presumably superior in abilities and wisdom, will play second fiddle to the more raucous democratic House of Representatives.[8]

Just as the House would overshadow the Senate, the President would have power over both. Because of his unlimited reeligibility for office, Martin predicts that he will effectively be an elected monarch, and his ability to pardon anyone who should break the law on his behalf will likely make him a corrupt and dangerous king indeed. The legislature will be under the control of the President, who decides whom to appoint to the presumably many and lucrative positions in the government. A kingly President is entirely out of place in a proper federal system.[9]

Martin's objections to the courts were typical of the opposition. The federal jurisdiction is too extensive; jury trials are in danger, at least upon appeal; a defendant must trek all the way to the capital to defend himself upon appeal to the Supreme Court in civil cases. His solution, though, was atypical. He suggests that the state courts would have worked well as a court of first resort, with the federal courts having only limited appellate jurisdiction. This would have saved money as well as recognizing the primary importance of the states in the system.

Martin's language was particularly colorful, and he was not inclined to pull punches. For example, he described the power to levy excise taxes as "a power very odious in its nature, since it authorises officers to go into your *houses*, your *kitchens*, your *cellars*, and to examine into your *private concerns*." Excises, of course, are only the beginning; they will be followed by direct taxes and other forms of taxation, "to *sluice* [the people] at *every vein* as long as they have a *drop* of blood, without any controul, limitation, or restraint." Such taxes will no doubt be collected by citizens of other states, so they will not be restrained by compassion for their neighbors. Martin had some choice words about slavery as well. He pointed out wryly that in their efforts to avoid using the word "slaves," the delegates unintentionally inserted a clause in Article I, Section 9, that would allow Congress to tax immigrants as well as imported slaves. At this point, though, his objections turned deadly serious. To allow the states to continue the slave trade, he insisted, "ought to be considered as a *solemn mockery of*, and *insult to*, *that God* whose protection we had then implored [in the Declaration of Independence], and could not fail to hold us up in *detestation*, and render us *contemptible* to every *true friend* of liberty in the world." Instead, Martin suggested, "we ought *rather to prohibit expressly* in our *constitution*, the *further importation* of *slaves*; and to *authorise* the general government from time to time, to make such regulations as should be thought most advantageous for the *gradual abolition* of *slavery*, and the *emancipation* of the *slaves* which are already in the States." He predicts that if Congress may not interfere with the slave trade until 1808, it will never interfere with that practice, or with the institution more generally. This is abolitionism, pure and simple, from a delegate who represented a slave state. Martin was treading dangerous ground, given the setting, and pressing a position that would have driven the southern states out of the union, but these objections would certainly resonate in New England. On the other hand, suggesting that Congress have the power to regulate slavery runs counter to Martin's federalism, and he offers no explanation for why this ought to be a national rather than state issue.[10]

In the end, Martin espouses an unusual Anti-Federalist position. His emphasis on states and a decentralized federal system was much stronger than almost any other Anti-Federalist, and it was unusual in that it was a truly national federalism rather than a localistic endorsement of his own state. Thus far he is pressing a Power Anti-Federalist position. Still, the question comes down to one of the people's liberty, threatened substantially by the proposed government. The Constitution, he said, "instead of *guarding against* a *standing army*, that *engine* of *arbitrary power*, which has so *often* and so *successfully* been used for the *subversion* of *freedom*, has in *its formation*, given it an *express* and *constitutional sanction*, and hath *provided for its introduction.*" This sets up the despotism; what remains is for the people to be stripped of their means of defense. Here is Martin as a Rights Anti-Federalist. By adopting the Constitution, he writes, "we give the general government every provision it could wish for, and even *invite* it to *subvert* the *liberties* of the *States* and *their citizens*, since we give them the right to encrease and keep up a standing army as numerous as *it* would wish, and by placing the militia under *its* power, enable it to leave the militia *totally unorganized, undisciplined,* and *even to disarm them.*"[11] This combination of Rights and Power Anti-Federalism suggests that a synthesis was possible between the two, and Martin was the first significant figure to really fuse them.

Despite these often harsh and unyielding criticisms, Martin insisted that he held no personal animosity toward his distinguished fellow delegates. He suggests instead that many of them were the misled victims of a few designing men with antirepublican aims. He points this out to remind his readers that "it is our duty not to suffer our eyes to be so far dazzled by the splendor of names, as to run blindfolded into what may be our destruction." He insisted that the largest mistake into which the delegates were led was the mode of ratification. The Constitution, Martin explained, ought to be subject to the approval of Congress and the state legislatures, rather than ratifying conventions. This was consistent with his contention that the federal government was a matter of the states, acting as individuals, joining together under a federal head. To follow the course proposed in Article VII "has a tendency to set the *State governments* and their *subjects* at *variance* with each other—to *lessen* the *obligations* of *government*—to *weaken* the *bands* of *society*—to introduce *anarchy* and *confusion*—And to *light* the *torch* of *discord* and *civil war* throughout this continent." In the end, he closed on a dramatic note, insisting that he would give up all present and future offices and all property, and "reduce myself to indigence and poverty, . . . if on *those terms only* I could procure my country to reject those chains which are forged for it."[12]

Martin published several other letters in defense of Elbridge Gerry against attacks by "Landholder."[13] In them he offered more details of the debate in convention, including a very fitting metaphor, which he attributed to Gerry:

The conduct of the advocates and framers of this system, towards the *thirteen states*, in pretending it was designed for their advantage, and gradually obtaining power after power to the general government, which could not but end in *their* slavery, he compared to the conduct of a number of *jockeys*, who had thirteen *young colts* to break—they begin with the appearance of kindness, giving them a lock of hay, or a handful of oats, and stroaking them while they eat, until being rendered sufficiently gentle, they suffer a halter to be put round their necks—obtaining a further degree of their confidence, the jockeys slip, a curb bridle on their heads, and the bit into their mouths, after which the saddle follows of course, and well booted and spurred, with good whips in their hands, they mount and ride them at their pleasure, and although they may kick and flounce a little at first, not being able to get clear of their *riders*, they soon become as *tame* and *passive* as their *masters* could wish them.[14]

This was an apt metaphor for both the Constitution itself and the manner in which the Federalists pursued ratification. Gerry, according to Martin, believed, in the convention, "that the government, if adopted, would *terminate* in the *destruction* of the *states*, and in the *introduction* of a *kingly* government." Martin went on to defend Gerry in several addresses, insisting that in many instances the two delegates "perfectly harmonized in opinion," while in others they were at least sympathetic to each other's objections.[15] He also defended himself against a variety of accusations raised by a Maryland "Landholder" concerning his behavior in convention. In this defense, he largely repeated the points made in his Genuine Information, but these letters testify to Martin's consistency and integrity; it is worth remembering that Martin was the only significant Anti-Federalist in the nation who was willing not only to publish his sentiments signed with his own name, but also to publicly defend them against accusations, even those he deemed ridiculous.

Martin won over some fans among the Anti-Federalists; Centinel was most perhaps the most profuse in his praise. "He has laid open the conclave," Centinel writes of Martin, "exposed the dark scene within, developed the mystery of the proceedings, and illustrated the machinations of ambition." This "illustrious patriot," Centinel observes, has the Federalists "exerting for his destruction, the mint of calumny is assiduously engaged in coining scandal to blacken his character, and thereby invalidate his testimony," but Martin, "undaunted by the threats of his and his country's enemies, is nobly persevering in the cause of liberty and mankind." Centinel was not alone in his opinion of Martin, but no other Anti-Federalist went to such rhetorical lengths to designate him an oracle of truth and justice.[16] Still, Martin was an easy target for the Federalists. He had a fondness for excessive quantities of words, matched only by his reputed fondness for drink. He was portrayed as a drunken windbag, accused of lying about the proceedings of the Philadelphia Convention to inflate his own importance, and generally attacked on a largely personal level. The Federalists, it seems, did everything but engage his arguments. Those arguments seem to have had little impact north of Maryland, Centinel's encomiums notwithstanding, and they received less attention in the south than other, less worthy writings. Thus his synthesis of two broad tracks of Anti-Federalist thought had little direct impact.

Overshadowed by Martin's rather loud voice was one of the most intellectual series of essays in the ratification debates. Signed "A Farmer," it unfortunately was not reprinted outside of the state. The Farmer, who Storing suggests was probably Constitutional Convention delegate John Francis Mercer, insisted that he was not out simply to inflame the people; "it is not my intention to ring an alarm bell," he writes, explaining that he "would rather conciliate than divide." There are parts of the essays that are decidedly inflammatory rather than conciliatory, but overall the argument is sound and mostly consistent. He does not reject the Constitution entirely, for he sees serious flaws in the Articles of Confederation, but he argues that the Constitution, rather than threatening dissolution of the union, goes too far in the other direction toward tyranny. The primary defect was the absence of a bill of rights. This absence was the most significant failure of the Philadelphia Convention. Surely the delegates could have assembled an adequate bill of rights; the Farmer could not fathom "that the late convention were incompetent to a task that has never been undertaken in the separate States without success."[17]

In advocating a bill of rights, the Farmer attacks the Federalist argument that the Constitution is one of enumerated powers. Congress is not explicitly granted the power to establish jury trials in civil cases, he argues, yet the Federalists, on the defensive against claims that trial by jury is at risk, insist that Congress may do so. What is this, the Farmer asks, but an implied power? "If we imply this power," he pushes further, "may we not imply any other?" And if additional powers are implied, who but Congress can decide which ones are necessary and proper? The danger here is not simply unscrupulous congressmen; even well-meaning legislators can slip into dangerous territory. "There is no public *abuse* that does not spring from the necessary *use* of power," he writes, "it is that insensible progress from the *use* to the *abuse*, that has led mankind through scenes of calamity and woe, that make us now shrink back with horror, from the history of our species." The Farmer saw it as obvious that "we must never give an assembly the power of giving itself power." The legislature, invested with power, will always thirst for more; those emoluments available honestly will not be enough, so corruption will creep in. Representatives, he contends, can always enrich themselves through such corruption. A rotation in office "only encreases the evil by rendering them more rapacious." The solution to the problem of legislative corruption is a strong, independent executive. For the executive, though, rotation is even worse; either he will fail to do his job, or, if he is effective in office, he can expect to be hounded by his enemies once he leaves office and again takes his place as a private citizen. Combining the Senate with the executive, especially one with a short term in office, will inevitably destroy the liberty and ruin the prosperity of America. Proper representative government, the Farmer suggests, requires an executive and a senate who serve for life. The Vice President can serve as a useful office for smoothing over succession and preventing hereditary monarchy, as he can ascend to the presidency. This, obviously, is not a politically feasible solution in the United States, but the Farmer finds it preferable to the tyranny he expects under the Constitution.[18]

The prospects for republican government are grim in the Farmer's eyes. "Alas!" he laments, "I see nothing in my fellow-citizens, that will permit my still fostering the delusion, that they are now capable of sustaining the weight of SELF-GOVERNMENT: A burthen to which Greek and Roman shoulders proved unequal."[19] Democracy, on the other hand, showed some promise here.[20] He writes that the people of America "are more fit for self-government, than they are at present for any of the safe and solid governments, founded on representation." He suggests that laws could be presented directly to town meetings for discussion and voting; this he finds preferable to representative democracy for America.[21] The distinction is an important one; to let the people choose directly on political questions is less dangerous than to let them choose representatives. This stems from the Farmer's insightful analysis of socioeconomic class in America. Class, for him, comes down to wealth. "Where *wealth* is hereditary, *power* is hereditary, for *wealth* is *power*—Titles are of very little, or no consequence—The *rich* are *nobility*, and the *poor plebeans* in all countries—And on this distinction alone, the true definition of aristocracy depends." After drawing this distinction, he identifies what sets apart democratic and aristocratic government. "An *aristocracy*," he writes, "is that influence of power, which property may have in government; a *democracy* is the power or influence of the people or numbers, as contradistinguished from property." Thus America will have an aristocracy regardless of its form of government, which guarantees political conflict along class lines. "Between these *two* powers, the aristocracy and democracy, that is the *rich* and *poor*," he warns, "there is a constant warfare." The Constitution, and in fact representative government, simply grants advantages to the rich. After all, he argues, "let the smallest appearance of commotion peep out again in any part of the Continent, and there is not a rich man in the United States, who will think himself or his property safe, until *both* are surrounded with standing troops." Why set up a government that will enable the rich to defend themselves in such a way, at the cost of liberty? A standing army is not needed in a proper democracy. "Let the body of the people be interested in the defence of a *good* government," he writes, "and my countrymen need not fear being surprized by all the slaves and brutes that the despots of the old and new world can arm against them.—There will then need no distinction of a threatened war, and our establishment may at all times be limited to the purposes just mentioned." To have a standing army is to resort to force, which is to disarm the citizenry, undermine the legitimacy of government, and threaten (if not destroy) liberty. "There are but *two* modes of governing mankind, by just and equal law, enforced impartially on all ranks of society, or by the sword:—If such laws cannot be obtained, or the obtainment is attended with too much difficulty, the sword will supply their place." The rich, who will have influence over representatives, are quite comfortable granting those representatives the sword; the people ought not to accept any such policy. Many of the state constitutions prohibit a standing army in peacetime, so the national constitution ought to include a similar clause.[22]

Ultimately, a national government will give way to clashing interests and disputes, until it inevitably degenerates into the rule by a single individual, despotism. The people should not accept any government in which they cannot prevent such an outcome. This calls for a simple, democratic system. "Thirteen complicated forms all under one form of government, still more complicated," the Farmer warns the people, "seem to bid defiance to all *responsibility*, (the only test of good government) as it can never be discovered where the fault lies."[23] Despite the democratic implications of his notion of simple government and his assessment of class warfare, the Farmer is best understood as a Rights Anti-Federalist: a bill of rights is the first line of defense, necessary before any other changes are even worth making. Nonetheless, his argument suggests that the Rights position was not incompatible with Democratic Anti-Federalism. Both the Farmer and Martin demonstrate that the distinction between Rights and Power Anti-Federalism is a blurry one, for the rights of the people might best be defended by adjusting the powers of the government, which is what both of these writers aim to do. Here we see the first significant blending of the various strands of Anti-Federalism, but few outside of Maryland seem to have noticed the argument.

As the state ratifying convention approached, both Martin and the Farmer increasingly emphasized the absence of a bill of rights. Martin especially emphasized the importance of getting such protections added to the Constitution before ratification; the difficulty of making changes, he writes, "will be increased an hundred fold after this system is adopted."[24] As usual, Martin is more colorful than most in his analogies:

> Let me ask you, my fellow-citizens, what you would think of a Physician, who, because you were slightly indisposed, should bring you a dose, which properly corrected with other ingredients might be a salutary remedy, but, of itself was a deadly poison, and with great appearance of friendship and zeal, should advise you to swallow it immediately, and trust to accident for those requisites necessary to qualify its malignity, and prevent its destructive effects?—Would not you reject the advice, in however a friendly a manner it might appear to be given, with indignation, and insist that he should first procure, and properly attemper, the necessary ingredients, since after the *fatal draught* was once received into your bowels, it would be too late, should the antidote prove unattainable, and death must ensue?—With the same indignation ought you, my fellow-citizens, to reject the advice of those *political quacks*, who, under pretence of healing the disorders of our present government, would urge you *rashly to gulp down* a constitution, which, in its present form, unaltered and unamended, would be as certain death to your liberty, as *arsenick* could be to your bodies.[25]

Martin goes on to defend the conduct of the Anti-Federalists against charges that they are merely inflammatory, and not to be relied upon. "Those who would wish to excite and keep awake your jealousy and distrust," he insists, "are your truest friends." The people must question the Constitution, he says, and they must either obtain satisfactory changes or reject it outright in favor of the imperfect, but safe, Articles of Confederation. To make this point, Martin retells one of Aesop's fables, in which a nation of frogs asked Jupiter for a king. Jupiter sent them a log, which would have made a fine monarch had the frogs simply pursued their interests and not questioned the efficacy of a government of so little splendor. Instead, upon the insistence of some frogs that the log was not adequate, they requested of Jupiter a more splendid government that is "energetic and efficient," upon which request they received a crane, who proceeded to appropriate his subjects for dinner. The Articles of Confederation, Martin tells his less astute readers, is the log, and the Constitution is the crane. "I think the *harmless, inoffensive,* though *contemptible Log*," Martin concludes, "infinitely to be preferred to the *powerful*, the *efficient*, but *all-devouring* Crane."[26]

The Anti-Federalist resistance in Maryland was not particularly democratic, though, despite Luther Martin's often radical rhetoric. The contest in this state was, in the words of Philip Crowl, "an internecine war waged within a single, small and wealthy ruling class."[27] In the state, "most concern over the Constitution centered on the absence of a bill of rights and not on the need for 'a more perfect union.'" There were, of course, Power Anti-Federalist objections; early in 1788, "Caveto" warned of the dangers of arbitrary power, and in March "Neckar" suggested that the prohibition of ex post facto laws would prevent the US Congress from establishing provisions for collecting on the debt owed to the nation, including state arrears, and that taxes would be unevenly levied throughout the nation.[28] Still, the primary writings against the Constitution here dealt with rights.

In April, the Maryland Farmer published several more essays. His sixth essay lists the primary objections to the Constitution that prompted him to publish further essays, staking out a clear Rights position:

> the omission of a declaration to ascertain the *rights* of the several *States*, and the *rights of individuals*, the primary object of every good and free government, particularly the trial by jury on suit against a *federal* officer for abuse of authority;—the want of proper checks to prevent the abuse, or annihilation of those rights;—the manifest danger to public liberty from a standing army, without limitation of number, in time of peace.[29]

The Farmer was among the most philosophical writers in the debate, and his seventh letter, in five parts,[30] offers an extended discussion of the theory and history of governments. He closes with the claim that the condition of the United States is better than that of most of the world. The state constitutions are not perfect, or close to it, but they are not likely to descend into tyranny. The proposed national Constitution, on the other hand, poses just such a danger, though the danger may well have been too abstract and hypothetical to make much impact on the Farmer's audience.

FAILURE TO ORGANIZE

In practical terms, of course, what mattered was not the public debate, but the state ratifying convention. The echoes of the Pennsylvania Convention were reverberating in Maryland as that convention approached. The *Maryland Journal* took both sides to task for their behavior in the Pennsylvania Convention, charging both Federalists and Anti-Federalists with "accusing each other of want of reason and argument, and expressing the most perfect contempt for each other's abilities and persons." The convention, in short, represented "the very summit of party spirit," which many in Maryland were hoping (in vain) to avoid.[31] In fact, the outcome in Maryland was ultimately to be more similar to Pennsylvania than any other state. As in that state, the opponents of ratification were badly outnumbered in convention, so they would turn to the newspapers to have their arguments heard.

There was one substantial difference, though: the outcome here was highly uncertain to outside (and even inside) observers. This seems unusual in retrospect, as the eventual vote was overwhelming, but Maryland's politics were something of an enigma. "What appeared certain on the surface," writes Gregory Stiverson, "could crumble under a barrage of argument and secret deals when the delegates actually met." The state had, after all, held up the Articles of Confederation for several years demanding amendments; there was no reason to assume that such would not be the case with the Constitution.[32]

The public debate in the state was sparse; according to Pauline Maier, "the electorate in Maryland was, by all accounts, surprisingly uninterested in the contest over the Constitution."[33] Maryland was not known for raucous democratic politics, but the level of participation and conflict was remarkably low even by the standards of the state. Three-quarters of the convention delegates were chosen with no recorded opposition. The makeup of the convention was a reversal of almost every other state; the Federalists had a strong majority (of the seventy-six delegates chosen, sixty-four were Federalists), but the opposition boasted superior leadership. With the fiery Samuel Chase and former governor William Paca, "the intellect behind Chase's rhetoric," leading the opposition, ably assisted by dissenting Philadelphia Convention delegates Luther Martin and John Francis Mercer, the possibility that they might successfully sway a majority of the Convention, at least to the cause of conditional ratification with amendments, could not be discounted.[34]

In some areas, the Anti-Federalists ran an aggressive campaign. Jeremiah Chase and John Francis Mercer distributed a handbill in Anne Arundel County, and perhaps beyond, listing the changes that ought to be made to the Constitution before ratification. Its text was rather simple:

BILL of RIGHTS.
LIBERTY of CONSCIENCE.

TRIAL by JURY.
NO EXCISE.
NO POLL TAX.
No Standing Army in Peace, without limitation.
No whipping militia, nor marching them out of the state, without
consent of the General Assembly.
NO DIRECT TAXATION, WITHOUT PREVIOUS REQUISITION.[35]

This is a simple and direct Rights Anti-Federalist appeal, complete with implications of impending tyranny. Mercer fleshed out those implications as they distributed the handbills; he "spoke darkly of plots linking the Constitution to the machinations of Robert Morris and 'a Juncto with a French Interest.'"[36]

"A Farmer and Planter" struck a similar tone, writing just before the convention elections. He describes the Constitution as an aristocratic plot, "the most artful plan that ever was formed to entrap a free people."[37] His descriptions are vivid; he has excise collectors entering houses and destroying possessions in order to search for goods on which the tax may not have been paid, as well as soldiers from other states descending on those who refuse to pay their taxes, bringing ruin to all. The author implores his fellow citizens to be careful whom they elect. "Be wise, be virtuous, and catch the precious moment as it passes, to refuse this new-fangled federal government," he writes, "and extricate yourselves and posterity from tyranny, oppression, aristocratical or monarchical government."[38] His warning seems to have fallen on deaf ears.

There were few hotly contested elections in the state, and many that were unopposed. The Anti-Federalists won convention seats in only three counties. In Anne Arundel County, Chase and Mercer "conducted a whirlwind campaign in the four days preceding the election," including the aforementioned handbills, to defeat a potential delegation led by Charles Carroll of Carrollton and replace it with one led by Samuel Chase, all by a margin of fewer than fifty votes.[39] Upon their victory, the *Maryland Journal* declared that this was merely the result of the people becoming informed about the dangers posed by the Constitution to the rights of the people. "With Information," the paper read, "the People in every County would act in the same Manner, and reject a Government that, unless considerably altered, will, most probably, enslave them and their Posterity." In Baltimore County, the Anti-Federalists won handily in one set of returns, though there was a rival count that placed the Federalists ahead. The Federalists did not contest the declared Anti-Federalist victory because it was clear that they had an

overwhelming majority in favor of the Constitution in the convention even
without these seats. In Harford County, three Anti-Federalists who were
not residents of Harford, including Luther Martin and William Paca, were
elected in violation of the legislative stipulation that delegates must be residents of the counties that elected them. The Anti-Federalists almost pulled
off a sneaky victory in the town of Baltimore, where initially there were
only two candidates for two convention seats. Those two candidates, Samuel Sterrett and David McMechen, both entertained private doubts about
the Constitution, but said nothing publicly. The Anti-Federalists were quietly pushing the idea that the voters should choose delegates who could exercise free judgment on the Constitution, rather than those who had already
made up their mind, and should certainly not elect any Philadelphia Convention delegate. "Freeman" disputed these arguments and called for more
clearly Federalist candidates. When questioned on their beliefs, Sterrett and
McMechen played coy, and were convincingly defeated by a couple of Federalist candidates, John Coulter and Philadelphia delegate James McHenry.
Overall, this was a remarkably poor showing; Stiverson observes that "if
Paca and Chase had not left their home counties to run as delegates in other
areas where they were personally popular and politically well-connected, it
is probable that the antifederalist delegation in Maryland's ratification convention would have consisted of only the four Baltimore County delegates
led by Captain Charles Ridgely of Hampton." On the other hand, had the
Anti-Federalists been better organized and more effectively led, they may
have been able to tap into latent support among otherwise apathetic voters:
"antifederalists were too disorganized," explains James Haw, "to permit us
to assess accurately their true potential strength."[40] There is no reason to
believe that the Anti-Federalists would have been able to muster a majority
in any case, but a stronger minority would likely have secured at least recommended amendments, and perhaps even won conditions for ratification.

MARYLAND FEDERALISTS IN CONTROL

The convention began business on April 21. The Federalist delegates, sensing their strength in numbers as they met in caucus, made an unusual but
very practical decision; the Maryland Ratifying Convention was the only
one with any opposition not to examine the Constitution by clause, opting
instead for a general discussion. In this manner the possibility of amendments, or of votes on particular clauses, was ruled out immediately. Similarly unusual was the Federalist side of the debate. Even in Pennsylvania,

where an inflexible majority refused even to permit the minority to enter objections on the convention record, the Federalists dutifully addressed objections to the Constitution, speaking at length in defense of the proposed form of government. In Maryland, the debate was entirely one-sided; the Federalists, "although repeatedly called on, and earnestly requested, to answer the objections, if not just, remained inflexibly silent." The proponents of ratification were determined to wrap up the business of the convention as quickly as possible, before their opponents could delay or defer the vote, and they saw no advantage in answering objections. Rumors were flying that the minority would push for an adjournment, as in New Hampshire, and wait for Virginia to act first. This fear of delay is clear in Alexander Contee Hanson's explanation for the Federalist silence, that "no valuable purpose could be answered by protracting the mere formality of a ratification." Even apart from delaying tactics, the majority may well have been concerned about losing their own votes to the opposition; the Anti-Federalists' "most effective weapon," suggests Gregory Stiverson, was "the ability of Paca and Chase to present a compelling case when permitted to engage in a free-wheeling debate," which they could not do without an opponent. The Federalists did not even bother to challenge the election of Chase, Paca, and Martin, three Anti-Federalist leaders who were inappropriately elected by counties in which they did not live, because the majority was sufficiently large and did not want to invite any reason for prolonged argument.[41]

The Federalists were prepared to let the opposition say as much as it wanted against ratification, since the Federalist leaders knew they had votes to spare. The Anti-Federalists kept them waiting; the three most significant opposition leaders failed to arrive on the first several days of the convention. Samuel Chase arrived on the morning of the fourth day, and immediately launched into his objections to the Constitution. Chase's speech, of which the only extant records are his own notes and a few short notes by other delegates,[42] consisted of "familiar antifederalist rhetoric . . . delivered with Chase's typical hyperbole and bombast."[43] The proposed government, he argued, has a duality to it: it is a federal government insofar as it rules over states, and a national government as it governs "We the People." In both cases, it is clearly supreme, swallowing the states and all local distinctions into the vortex of national policy. Chase argues that a country as large as the United States can be governed "on democratical principles only by a Confederation of small republics exercising all the powers of *internal* government, but united by league as to their *external* foreign concerns."[44] In this he refers to Montesquieu, as well as fellow Anti-Federalists Brutus and Cato. He goes on to discuss the dangers of a reelected President and courts with overly broad jurisdiction, and suggests that the tax power should be exercised through mandatory requisitions on the states. He devotes a considerable amount of effort to representation. "To form a proper and true representation each order [of society] ought to have an opportunity of choosing from each a person as their representative," his notes read; "this is impossible from the smallness of the number—65." The people chosen will be from among the elite, and will represent only that elite:

> Can six men be found in Maryland who understand the interests of the several orders of men in this state and are acquainted with their situation, wants and would act with a proper sense and zeal to promote their prosperity—If such could be found will they be chosen by the people? No—but few of the Merchants and those only of the opulent and ambitious will stand any chance. The great body of farmers and planters cannot expect any of their order—the station is too elevated for them to aspire to—the distance between the people and their representatives will be so very great that there is no probability of a farmer or planter being chosen.—Mechanics of every branch will be excluded by a general voice from a seat—only the *gentry*, the *rich* and well born will be elected. . . . The station is too high and elevated to be filled but by the *first men* in the state in point of fortune and influence.[45]

It is telling that this section of Chase's notes is the most elaborate, and the closest to a prepared speech rather than an outline. Clearly he saw this as central to his argument against the Constitution, but it is certainly not the whole argument. His notes include an extensive list of rights that ought to be protected in the new Constitution, as well as listing nearly three-dozen specific objections to that document. It is not clear how many of these points were actually made in his speech, but he probably covered much, if not most, of his material during the course of the convention.

Chase spoke for two and a half hours before declaring himself exhausted, and the Federalists said nothing. No Anti-Federalist rose to take up Chase's argument either, so the convention delegates merely waited for a while, then adjourned for dinner. The plan, according to Hanson, was to vote on the Constitution in the afternoon, because "altho' it might be proper to give each member an opportunity of declaring his sentiments, it could not be expected, that the whole body should await the pleasure of a few individuals." William Paca, a former governor of the state and, like Chase, a signer of the Declaration of Independence, changed the Federalists' plans by arriving after the dinner recess. Upon his arrival, he announced that he had some amendments to suggest, and requested another night to finalize his proposals. This request "succeeded in breaching the majority's hitherto monolithic unity," as Thomas Johnson, a former state governor and a Federalist who was more than a little uneasy with the unamended Constitution, spoke in defense of Paca's request. The convention acquiesced in an adjournment (without, as Hanson emphasized, officially acquiescing in amendments or their necessity).[46]

The next morning Paca rose to present his amendments, only to face coordinated hostility: thirteen Federalist members, one from each Federalist county and town, interrupted Paca to announce *"that they were elected and* INSTRUCTED *by the people they represented, to ratify the proposed constitution, and that as speedily as possible, and to do no other act; that after the ratification their power ceased, and they did not consider themselves as authorised by their constituents to consider any amendments."*[47] When Paca attempted to read his proposals anyway, his right to do so was challenged and he was ruled out of order. The amendments were not entered in the convention record, and they were not officially discussed. The Anti-Federalists, though, were going to have their say. The plan for the opposition had been to focus debate on the amendments, but it never got off the ground because Paca was not permitted to introduce them. The discussion became unfocused, starting with another speech by Chase. He was again melodramatic in his objections, suggesting that the Philadelphia delegates were "guilty of treason if they attempted to make a new Government without authority." He discussed the rights of Marylanders that would be lost, the inadequacy of representation, and the dangers of a powerful Senate. He contended that the President ought not to be eligible for continual reelection, that the courts would have too wide a jurisdiction, and that even the small guarantee of a jury trial in criminal cases would be made nugatory by appeal in fact as well as law. Chase closed with a brief discussion of the status of the Constitution in the other states, acknowledging that he was willing to "take it thro' necessity, if Virginia did," and that "[i]f the majority adopt the government, I shall acquiesce." Paca added to these comments, emphasizing the importance of trial by jury. The next day Mercer took the floor to discuss the process by which the Constitution was written in Philadelphia, suggesting that the final document was "not the result of Mature deliberations," but that "capital alterations" were made just before the close of the convention. He spent a great deal of time discussing the earlier versions of the Constitution, which he supported, and attacking the rash and precipitate changes made in the final days, when he was absent. The convention, after all, was "not *orderly*" while he attended, so it was likely chaotic in the end. By that point the delegates were "too much fatigued" to make proper decisions. Because of his failure to attend the final days of that convention, this was little more than speculation and bombast from Mercer. Like Chase, he closed with a discussion of rights, and lamented that no bill of rights was included in the proposed plan of government. Incidentally, the absence of a bill of rights may well have been the result of fatigue from a long summer, as it was suggested by Mason in the closing days of the Convention, but Mercer missed those days. Next up was Jeremiah Townley Chase, who largely repeated his cousin's arguments. He did add some discussion about the extent of the power potentially contained in the general welfare clause of Article I, Section 8, and he emphasized once again the necessity of a bill of rights. Samuel Chase then again rose, to attack the undemocratic election of the President, and to point out that the Constitution contains a partial bill of rights, though one certainly inadequate. Then it was Mercer again, contending that the Senate had too much executive power, the President ought to have a council, and the two together, through the power to make treaties, will destroy the republic.[48]

The Federalists said nothing. They steadfastly refused to be drawn into a debate. The *Maryland Journal* wrote that "The Minority were heard with a candid and profound Attention.—Their Talents and Abilities were amply displayed; and, but from the clearest Impressions of the best of Causes, they might have been more successful."[49] There was nothing else to be done but to vote, for the Federalists had the votes and did not need the discussion. When the Anti-Federalists had finished speaking their piece, the Constitution was ratified unconditionally by a vote of sixty-three to eleven.

Paca's vote was among those in favor of ratification. He may have made a deal with the Federalists, exchanging his vote for the opportunity to have his amendments considered, but it seems likely that he genuinely preferred a flawed Constitution with the hope of amendments to rejecting the document outright.[50] Immediately following the vote he rose again, explaining that "he had only given his assent to the government under the firm persuasion, and in full confidence, that such amendments would be peaceably obtained, as to enable the people to live happy under the government." The Federalists, briefly in a conciliatory mood, permitted him to introduce his amendments at this point, "and a general murmur of approbation seemed to arise from all parts of the house, expressive of a desire to consider amendments."[51]

The amendments were then referred to a committee of thirteen, including four Anti-Federalists, which apparently met in a cordial and conciliatory mood. No fewer than thirteen recommended amendments "were separately agreed to by the committee, most of them by an *unanimous* vote, and all of them by a *great majority*." The mood seemed to extend beyond the committee and even the convention. After the ratification vote but while the committee on amendments deliberated, the *Maryland Journal* expressed hope "that the great and essential Rights of the People will be declared and secured." Everyone seemed to be in favor of amendments securing certain rights and liberties. The conciliation was not total, however; fifteen other amendments were rejected by a majority of the committee. The minority then attempted to get three of those discussed before the entire convention along with those that received general approbation, but they were outvoted. At this point something strange happened: the committee majority decided not to report any amendments out of committee. The documentary record does not make it clear why this happened, but it put an end to Anti-Federalist hopes for recommended amendments. The minority insisted that the Federalists were not negotiating in good faith, and had already decided they would not give the opposition any official voice. Hanson contends that it was the minority that destroyed any prospect of conciliation, by refusing an address of explanation that was to accompany the proposals, and by insisting that others be brought to debate on the floor of the convention, despite their rejection by the committee. Paul Leicester Ford, in his interpretation of the event, is too generous to the majority in Maryland, suggesting that the Federalists intended to acquiesce in suggesting amendments, "and only refused to carry out this compromise, when an ulterior motive was discovered."[52] John Thomas Scharf, in his *History of Maryland*, tells a different story. After a committee was appointed to consider amendments, and while the committee met, the convention voted to consider only amendments reported out of that committee. The Federalist majority on the committee then voted "that they would make no report of any amendments whatever, not even of those which they had almost unanimously agreed to," thus derailing any hopes for formally recommended amendments.[53] Scharf quotes a newspaper correspondent, who claims to have heard the reason for this from a member of the committee. To propose an amendment was to admit a defect in the Constitution, and "by agreeing to a *number* of amendments they would give an advantage to the *opponents* of the government, who would represent that it's friends admitted, that it was greatly defective," and thus support the Anti-Federalist case for changes prior to ratification. This is largely consistent with Hanson's account, though the latter suggests that it was the Anti-Federalists who walked away from the concessions (quite literally, as "the chairman [Paca] arose, declared, he would return to the convention; and thus was the committee broken up").[54] Whether Paca had an "ulterior motive" is at best doubtful; Ford tends to almost reflexively vilify the

Anti-Federalists in his work, always assuming sinister designs. Paca did, after all, vote for unconditional ratification, disappointing his fellows in the opposition, because he believed that the convention would call for the changes he saw as necessary. This would hardly make sense for a man who intended to fight ratification at all costs. Further evidence of the bad faith of Hanson and the Federalists is the fact that the address to be attached to the amendments made clear that the amendments were those of the minority, and that the majority was not really in favor of any changes; given this, re-fusing to allow most of the minority's amendments is quite illogical.

Still, had the Anti-Federalists on the committee not pushed for additional amendments, thirteen would have been debated on the floor of the con-vention, and perhaps formally recommended along with the ratification. The initial committee approval of these proposals was "a stunning victory" because the Anti-Federalists "convinced their adversaries that the proposed Constitution was flawed—in at least thirteen respects." Mercer and Chase at least found this compromise insufficient, however. The latter insisted in committee on his right to bring up other proposed amendments in conven-tion, regardless of the committee report. Mercer, meanwhile, had worked out a deal with Federalists William Tilghman and Richard Potts that re-sulted in the thirteenth of the approved amendments, promising in exchange that he would seek no more. He almost immediately reneged on the deal, suggesting others and supporting Chase's efforts to bring up his ideas in convention. This was too much for the Federalists, and gave Hanson the opportunity to convince his Federalist colleagues to accept nothing at all. In the end, the Anti-Federalists, "with a stunning success within their grasp . . . lost everything by insisting on pushing for still more amendments."[55]

The amendments themselves were primarily limits on governmental power in order to protect the rights of the people against potential en-croachment by government. Many of them safeguarded basic rights and liberties. Collectively, they fall firmly within the Rights Anti-Federalist para-digm. The amendments that were initially approved would have guaranteed jury trials and limited the jurisdiction of the federal courts, maintaining that of the state courts. They would also have placed certain limits on the treatment of soldiers and the militia, and protected individual property and the press. The lynchpin to the whole set, though, was the first one, which de-clared simply "That Congress shall exercise no power but what is expressly delegated by this constitution." How well such language could have been enforced is anyone's guess, but it was a crucial statement of principle, de-manding carefully limited government. The amendments that did not receive approval from the committee, but that the Anti-Federalists were prepared to set aside, would have further restricted standing armies, added a council to advise the President, protected religious liberty and conscientious objection to military service, declared congressmen to be the servants of the people, protected the right to petition the government, and required two-thirds of Congress to approve commercial legislation. These are not minor issues; certainly the opposition believed that they were conceding a great deal by not bringing these up on the floor of the convention. They wanted to focus instead on three that were rejected by the committee: that the militia may not be marched out of its home state without approval from that state, that Congress may not make or alter electoral regulations unless a state is unable or unwilling to do so, and that Congress must give states a chance to raise their own taxes to pay their quotas before Congress may levy direct taxes within the state.[56] Here is the crux of the argument; Paca and his colleagues wanted to prevent the national government from intervening directly within a state unless it was absolutely necessary. A bill of rights was important, of course, but the majority was prepared to concede certain essential rights like freedom of the press and trial by jury. The fight was over just how far the national government would be able to interfere with the functioning of the states. And this the majority could not accept, for it suggested a fundamental flaw in the federal structure of the proposed Constitution. That the flaw was there is difficult to dispute with the benefit of hindsight, but the Federalists would not admit to its existence. They chose instead to give up on the hope of conciliation and consensus to preserve the illusion of perfection in the Constitution. Fifteen Federalists would ultimately line up with the minority in voting against adjournment, presumably because of a desire to consider recommending amendments, but the majority could easily spare the votes.

Upon the dissolution of the committee, Paca reported back to the convention that the committee had failed to agree on an official report. Jeremiah Chase suggested that the convention might make its own decisions on the proposals, but the Federalist majority had already ruled out that possibility. His cousin Samuel then gave one final speech to the convention. He insisted that the people ought to have the opportunity to pass judgment on the proposed amendments, and added an ominous warning that the "Conduct [of the convention] shall go forth to the World." He stated the three amendments he wanted added to the committee's list, and explained both the concessions made by the minority and the conditions insisted upon by the majority. The convention, by suppressing even the largely consensual amendments, "shut out light . . . least Virginia should be influenced." The blatant disregard for the voice of the people on the question of amendments was understandable, of course; after all, "High & mighty people have no feeling for poor." The speech by Chase was lengthy and bombastic, but once again failed to make an impression on the majority.[57] Neither Mercer nor the Chases nor even the widely respected Paca could make any headway against the sheer numbers of the Constitution's supporters. As for Luther Martin, who did serve as a delegate in the state ratifying convention, the recorded debates suggest that he was uncharacteristically quiet. One of his few biographers sums up the denouement of his part in the ratification debates succinctly: "He fought unto the last ditch, then he fell silent. In a grim irony, Luther Martin was unable to address the Maryland ratifying convention of April 1788. He was beset by laryngitis, the common cold of the loquacious, which, as a sardonic observer noted, 'saved a great deal of time & money to the state.'"[58] Despite Martin's best efforts, Maryland too lined up in the Federalist column. But the minority in the convention would not remain silent for long in the public debate.

Much of the public account of the state ratifying convention was presented to the people in the form of a dissent published by the convention minority, similar to that produced in Pennsylvania. Like their Pennsylvania colleagues, the Maryland minority used their newspaper essay to complain about their treatment in convention and to disseminate their proposed amendments that were not allowed into the official record. Unlike the Pennsylvanians, though, the Marylanders were not combative; their dissent, absent the scathing pen of Samuel Bryan (it may well have been written by the moderate William Paca), was conciliatory, expressing genuine concern for the welfare of the country and a call for compromise and unity. "We consider the proposed form of national government as very defective," they wrote, "and that the liberty and happiness of the people will be endangered if the system be not greatly changed and altered."[59] The amendments were simply submitted to the public and explained; the delegates trusted to the people to demand necessary changes.

The surest indication that the Maryland dissent had little impact was the fact that the Federalists saw no need to issue a public response. Alexander Contee Hanson prepared a thorough defense of the convention majority, but it was not published, though it may have circulated in Virginia.[60] This was likely because the dissent itself was not widely reprinted or distributed. "A widely circulated address or an agent at the assembly door in Richmond might have given Patrick Henry the ammunition he needed," concludes Norman Risjord. "But the Marylanders never made the effort. It was their ultimate failure."[61]

11

Futility in South Carolina

THE DEBATE OVER RATIFICATION in South Carolina, as in Maryland, has a detached feel to it; it is as if the people there were having an entirely separate discussion, independent of the national conversation. Unlike in Maryland, though, it is very clear why South Carolina was such an outlier. In the state, there was really only one issue, and every other issue came back to it: slavery. The Anti-Federalists saw in the Constitution an existential threat to this essential aspect of their economic well-being. The Federalists insisted that the document protected the institution of slavery from outside interference from the northern states. All else was subordinate in the debate. The most significant contribution to the national debate came early, from Rawlins Lowndes, in his positive defense of both the institution of slavery and the Articles of Confederation.

RAWLINS LOWNDES AND THE LEGISLATIVE DEBATE

A week after Connecticut's ratification vote, before the news of that vote had spread to the deep south, the South Carolina legislature took up the question of calling a ratifying convention. Unlike similar debates in other state legislatures, though, here there was a substantial debate on the merits of the proposed Constitution. Rawlins Lowndes, representing Charleston in the legislature and knowing that his Federalist constituents would not elect him to the ratifying convention once called, decided to make his opinions known in this venue. The Federalists in the legislature certainly took notice; on three separate occasions it took no fewer than five of the Constitution's supporters to answer him and his arguments, though he stood alone in opposition until the final day of the debate.

Lowndes's primary argument was that the present government under the Articles of Confederation was not bad. It had faults that needed to be corrected, but that was no reason to throw it out altogether. "We are now governed by a most excellent constitution," he says,

> one which had stood the test of time, and carried us through difficulties supposed to be insurmountable—one that had raised us high in the eyes of all men, and given to us the enviable blessings of liberty & independence—a constitution sent us like a blessing from heaven, yet were we impatient to trample it under foot; and for what? why, to make way for another that give power for a small number of men to pull down the fabric which we have spent our blood to raise. Charters are sacred things.[1]

The argument for amending the Articles rather than starting over was a simple one. Lowndes asked his fellow legislators "whether a man should be looked on as wise, who possessing a magnificent fabric, upon discovering a flaw, instead of repairing the injury should pull it down and build another." Instead of repairs, the Federalists wanted to embark upon an experiment in government, veering from time-tested political forms into uncharted waters. "[A]n experiment!" exclaimed Lowndes, "[W]hat risque the loss of our political existence on experiment! No; Sir, if we are to make experiments let them be such as may do good, but which cannot possibly do any injury to our own liberties, or those of our posterity." This particular experiment meant a consolidation of government, the potential for aristocracy or tyranny, and the loss of the sovereignty, and even usefulness, of the state governments. This was a dangerous change when the United States already had a working government, even if that government certainly could work better than it did.[2]

His "glowing eulogy on the old constitution" was accompanied by substantial arguments against the content of the proposed Constitution. He argued that the northern states would predominate in the House, and that the south would be powerless against northern influence. After all, southerners needed to buy northern goods and sell their goods in northern markets, and they relied on New England shipping. On this latter point, Lowndes doubted that "it was in the power of the eastern states to furnish a sufficient number of ships to carry our produce." Whether they could produce a navy sufficient for national defense was also questionable, but even if they did that would not bode well for the south. He contends that "if gentlemen adverted where this navy, so necessary, must come from, not from the southern states, but the northern ones, they would easily perceive to whom this country would belong."[3]

Lowndes found substantial problems in the powers of Congress, especially that of taxation. He compared the Constitution's power of taxation, unfavorably, with that of England before the Revolution. The colonies then could raise revenue as they preferred, so long as they paid what was owed. "In this new constitution," on the other hand, "every thing is transferred, not so much power being left us as lord North offered to guarantee to us in his conciliatory plan."[4] The idea that representatives would be paid out of the federal treasury he compared to England paying the royal governors and judges. Even more power would be taken from South Carolina, in the loss of its impost duties and the ban on paper money. The state impost, he noted, previously paid state expenses. As for paper money, South Carolina had responsibly and effectively managed it when emergencies required it. He also questioned the safety of jury trials in civil cases, and especially emphasized the importance of local juries. The powers of the presidency were no less alarming. He objected to the broad powers given to the President, and particularly to his ability to convene Congress when and where he chose.

> On the whole this was the best preparatory plan for a monarchical government that he had read. . . . How easy the transition, no difficulty occurred in finding a king; the president was the man proper for this appointment. The senate hail him king, constituted, according to Mr. Adams's description, from the *well-born*, will naturally say to one another, "You see how we are situated, certainly it is for our country's benefit that we shall be all lords,["] and lords they are.[5]

He suggested that it was unlikely ever to see a President from South Carolina or Georgia; they would likely all come from the northern states, or the largest ones.

Lowndes vehemently defended slavery and the slave trade, suggesting that the state's delegates at Philadelphia did not win enough concessions on this issue. It was the clause preventing Congress from interfering with the slave trade for twenty years that particularly irked Lowndes, because it implied that thereafter Congress might do what it wished about slavery. He defended the institution, insisting that the slave trade "could be justified on the principles of religion, humanity, and justice; for certainly to translate a set of human beings from a bad country to a better, was fulfilling every part of these principles." In making this argument, he was foreshadowing the arguments that would be made decades later against the abolition movement. The people of the northern states, Lowndes concluded, "don't like our slaves, because they have none themselves, and therefore want to exclude us from this great advantage."[6] He objected to the potential tax on the importation of slaves, noting that the northerners will pay no such taxes. An impost will have to be paid, of course, but the price will be passed on to the consumer, which ultimately meant that the south would bear the burden.

Overall, Lowndes presented a fairly comprehensive critique of the Constitution, and called for a second convention for amendments. His Power Anti-Federalism stood out as an anomaly in South Carolina, but the theme of liberty did arise frequently, as in most Anti-Federalist arguments. His stance against the Constitution ultimately had little impact on the national debate, but it was an admirable stand for what he perceived as the interests of South Carolina. Harriott Ravenel sums up the whole legislative fight succinctly. "The great peculiarity of this debate was that it was fought by one man against ten or more, and those ten the ablest men in the State," she writes. "The attitude of Mr. Lowndes in this great controversy is like nothing so much as that of the boy who, setting his back to a tree, dares the whole school to come on. Of course the boy loses the fight, *we* know beforehand that it must be so, but he hopes, trusting to his strong right arm, and we praise his pluck and prowess."[7]

Not everyone was enamored of Lowndes's "pluck and prowess," however. David Ramsay, one of the most influential Federalists in the state and a member of both the legislature and the ratifying convention, complained about Lowndes to Benjamin Rush. "He has not one continental or foederal idea in his head," Ramsay wrote, "nor one of larger extent than that of a rice barrel." The opposition, according to Ramsay, consisted of self-interested farmers concerned about shipping rates and driven by "a narrow illiberal jealousy of New England." "He appears to me rather as a set, obstinate, almost superannuated character," wrote another observer, "and am told he always does oppose new things, & raise up bugbears & scarecrows." This hostility notwithstanding, Lowndes boldly stood against some of the most distinguished leaders in the state to expose the dangers inherent in the Constitution, "dangers that were so evident, that when he ceased to exist, he wished for no other epitaph than to have inscribed on his tomb, Here lies the man that opposed the constitution, because it was ruinous to the liberty of America."[8]

Lowndes was not quite alone in his objections in the legislature. Henry Pendleton raised objections to the impeachment and treaty powers, and several legislators rose to question the powers of Congress over religion. Only one of Lowndes's colleagues, though, rose to give a substantial speech against the Constitution, and only after Lowndes's solo act had inspired

some courage to stand against the Federalists. James Lincoln "solemnly declared, that the more he heard the more he was persuaded of [the Constitution's] evil tendency. What does this proposed constitution do?" he asked.
"[I]t changes, totally changes the form of your present government from
a well-digested, well-formed democratic—you are at once rushing into an
aristocratic government." Ratification will put an end to liberty, for the
power of government will be given "into the hands of a set of men who live
one thousand miles distant from you. Let the people but once trust their
liberties out of their own hands, and what will be the consequence? first, an
haughty imperious aristocracy; and ultimately a tyrannic monarchy." The
President will hold office for life. The liberty of the press, which "must have
been purposely omitted," will be in danger. Finally, he asked, "Why was
not this constitution ushered in with a bill of rights? are the people to have
no rights? Perhaps this same president and senate would by and by declare
them, he much feared they would." Lincoln then "concluded, by returning
his hearty thanks to the gentleman who had so ably opposed this constitution—it was supporting the cause of the people, and if ever any one deserved
the title of *Man of the People*, he on this occasion most certainly did."[9]

By this point there was little left to be said by the opposition; the decision
on the Constitution, after all, would be made by another body of delegates
elected for that purpose. The legislature unanimously approved the idea of
a convention. An effort by the backcountry legislators to locate the convention somewhere other than Charleston fell by one vote; the legislature
chose Charleston as the convention location by a vote of 76–75. Lowndes
himself, voting for Charleston as the location, was effectively the deciding vote, although a convention anywhere other than strongly Federalist
Charleston would have likely favored the Anti-Federalists. Had a majority
been opposed to the convention in Charleston, though, the legislature may
well have deadlocked, which may in turn have prevented or at least delayed
a convention. Lowndes, however, was not willing to resort to such tactics,
having already had his say on the Constitution, and he was equally unwilling to support any step that might lead to a western relocation of the capital
from Charleston.

None of this debate was of much use to Anti-Federalists elsewhere. The
Newport Herald, a Rhode Island newspaper that favored ratification, noted
upon receiving reports of Lowndes's arguments that they "must operate
strongly with these northern States to immediately ratify it," and it is difficult to disagree with that sentiment.[10] The concerns about slavery would not
have resonated in the north, and they would have been received with some
distaste even in North Carolina and Virginia.

Rawlins Lowndes was correct in his expectation that he would not be elected by his constituents to be a delegate to the convention. As he explained it in a letter to John Lamb in June, "I had not the Hon[o]r to be of our Convention: an open and explicit avowal of my Sentiments in the Assembly when the Subject was Agitated there, which were irreconcilable to the Constitution, as well in mode as Substance, did not meet with the Concurance and approbation of my Constituants in Charleston, and I was therefore rejected in their Choice of Delegates for the Convention." He was, however, elected as a delegate by St. Bartholomew's Parish, where he owned several large plantations and which he had represented in several assemblies before the Revolution. He refused to serve, perhaps because he did not wish to represent anyone other than his constituents in Charleston, as his letter to Lamb implies. If they did not want him as a delegate, he would not be a delegate. Alternately, he may have simply seen his service there as futile, with ratification a foregone conclusion. One biographer suggests that the reason he fought so hard in the legislative debate was because he assumed he would not be a delegate; to have later attended the convention "he doubtless regarded as tantamount to a violation of his word." Whatever his reason for declining, he had already made clear his position, and the Anti-Federalists who did serve in the convention would push those arguments in his absence, fighting for a losing cause.[11]

SOUTH CAROLINA GIVES ITS ASSENT

In early May the state's convention met to pass judgment on the Constitution. The Federalists had a clear majority,[12] but they made no attempt to stifle the minority. This may have been in part in recognition that the majority was artificial. "The delegates opposed to the Constitution," Nadelhaft writes, "probably represented a majority of the state population, and Antifederalism was stronger in the state at large than the ratification vote indicated."[13] Charleston and the coastal areas, heavily Federalist, were overrepresented by severe malapportionment in the legislature, and this was reflected in the constituencies for the convention as well. The Federalists, though they could easily win in convention, had to tread carefully to avoid a western uprising against the Constitution in the state, potentially worse than that occurring in Pennsylvania. They were prepared for a free and open debate, ready to answer questions and objections from the opposition. Early on, the proponents of ratification, bordering on arrogant, were even prepared to ask the questions for them. David Ramsay commenced the condescension with an opening question about why the proposed Congress would be bicameral. "He did not ask this for information on his own account, believing himself pretty well acquainted with the subject," according to the *City Gazette*, "but for the satisfaction of other gentlemen who had not been able to satisfy themselves on the propriety of so material an alteration in the government."[14] The Anti-Federalists really did not need the help, and Charles Cotesworth Pinckney,[15] who answered Ramsay's question, did not really need the opening. Dr. Peter Fayssoux demonstrated fine skill at grilling General Pinckney, and the two had a rather extensive debate on representation. Fayssoux contended that the large states would be able to impose their will on the small states, pointing out that the Federalists in Pennsylvania and Massachusetts insisted, to win over doubters, that the Constitution gave those states a degree of preeminence in the national legislature. He did not doubt that the apportionment was a reasonable compromise; the South Carolina delegates to Philadelphia "made the most of a bad bargain" to get the state the best possible share of governmental power. If the alternative to the proposed government were none at all, that would be acceptable, but there was already a government of the United States and "he could not consent to receive [a government] that might rend the bond of union in pieces." The minority did not shy away from the idea of keeping the Articles of Confederation. At one point John Rutledge complained that his opponents found it "very easy to find fault," so he asked, "why don't gentlemen who are so ready in this, bring forward some plans of their own?" John Bowman gave a clear and rather poetic answer: "If it was the ragged old coat which had made us like a blackguard throughout Europe, let us try to make it better."[16] This could have been a rallying cry for the Anti-Federalists nationally, if only anyone outside of the state heard it. The debates were not reprinted in other newspapers.

The theme of the opposition here was tyranny, and subsequent loss of liberty. David Ramsay was not entirely correct in his expectation that those "objections that operate elsewhere do not operate here," and "that the objections of our antifederalists are almost peculiar to the State." Indeed, despite a somewhat different emphasis many of the same objections arose. Though much of the discussion centered on the powers of government, it was Rights Anti-Federalism that predominated. Aedanus Burke raised the specter of despotism, contending that even dissolution of the union may well be preferable to tyranny: "anarchy was not so dangerous as despotism, for a war must be succeeded by peace, but despotism was a monster very difficult to be got rid of." The danger of a tyrant was centered, for Burke, in the presidency and the Senate. In fact, the Senate might be the more dangerous branch; Burke hinted that it might well run the government without meaningful oversight from the people. He explained that "in this general government, it ought to be remembered that the senate are in fact the executive body, and as they are under influence of the prince or president, and distant from us 900 miles, it was probable that we might be in the dark as to their conduct for six years." It took four Federalists to answer the argument, and none denied the executive nature of the Senate. Much was made of the Senate's power to try impeachments; in this, it could effectively shield the President from the wrath of the people. The President, according to Burke, would be "a prince under a republican cloak," and Burke "wondered it was not possible to find other judges to try him for crimes, than his accomplices." As for the House, Fayssoux contended that it would be too corrupt to effectively serve the people. He objected to the power of Congress to pay itself, coupled with continual eligibility for reelection. This combination caused the delegate to wonder "whether the liberty of the country was safely lodged." The problem was not that Congress might set excessive pay; it was that pay might be so low that "none would accept of a share in the government but such as had other interests to answer."[17]

The Anti-Federalists raised other objections as well, including the prospect of a distant capital and the absence of religious tests for office. The latter must have made an impression on the Federalists, as it was included among the four proposed amendments adopted by the convention. In all, the delegates spent two days debating Congress and another on the presidency. Apparently the judiciary did not prompt much debate, though, as the convention spent only a single day on the five final articles of the Constitution. The most significant topic of debate on this day seems to have been the clause concerning the oath of office, which outlawed religious tests; this was the only part of these five articles to be addressed in the proposed amendments adopted by the convention.

The Anti-Federalists in convention lost the ratification vote for a number of reasons, of which the superior eloquence and numbers of the Federalist majority were the most significant. The delegates of the South Carolina convention were also heavily influenced by the earlier state conventions, and this worked consistently against the opposition. The circular letter from John Hancock explaining the Massachusetts ratification was read before either the Constitution or the state legislation authorizing a ratifying convention, which set the Federalists up to ratify with proposed amendments, and gave the opposition little argument for opposing such a scheme. When news of ratification by Maryland arrived, Peter Fayssoux, up to then the most vocal critic of the Constitution in convention, stated that he would "desist from a line of conduct in opposition, which as it would only tend to irritate and inflame men's minds, would be criminal."[18] Thereafter, the opposition was left to others; the Anti-Federalists had lost their most able convention spokesman. Still they fought, rhetorically and procedurally. On May 21, General Thomas Sumter moved for an adjournment "in order that time may be given for further consideration on a subject of such vast magnitude." Since the rules of debate gave precedence to a motion to adjourn, this occupied the convention for a good deal of time and resulted in a "most animated debate," but the Anti-Federalists simply did not have the votes.[19] Before a vote on the Constitution, the result of which was a foregone conclusion, the majority turned to the question of amendments. The reason for this, according to Pauline Maier, was "to reconcile an opposition to the ratification of the Constitution that was more powerful outside than inside the convention, thanks to the severe underrepresentation of inland districts."[20] This also explains why the proposed amendments are so few, and do not really reflect flaws in the documents so much as concerns about how powers might be used. There was a powerful and numerous opposition here, not fully represented by the debates in either the legislature or the convention.

The views of this silent majority were ably reflected, though, by Patrick Dollard of Prince Frederick's Parish. In an impassioned speech in opposition to ratification, he attacked the Federalists and defended democratic principles. Dollard insisted that nearly every one of his constituents opposed the Constitution because it contained no bill of rights. These people, he said, "are by no means against vesting Congress with ample and sufficient powers; but to make over to them, or any set of men, their birthright, comprised in Magna Charta, which this new Constitution absolutely does, they can never agree to." This is not all, of course; a failure to secure rights would not be especially dangerous in setting up a weak government. Unfortunately, this proposed government "is big with political mischiefs, and pregnant with a greater variety of impending woes to the good people of the Southern States, especially South Carolina, than all the plagues supposed to issue from the poisonous box of Pandora." Dollard predicted trouble for the eastern elite should they ratify over these upcountry objections. "They say they will resist against it," he warned, "that they will not accept of it unless compelled by force of arms, which this new Constitution plainly threatens; and then, they say, your standing army, like Turkish janizaries enforcing despotic laws, must ram it down their throats with the points of bayonets." He concludes on a strikingly democratic note, insisting that "the general voice of the people is the voice of God." Alexander Tweed, of the same parish, followed Dollard[21] with a less fiery but more powerful speech, insisting that although he attended the convention with an open mind and would not simply vote the uninformed will of his constituents, he saw serious flaws in the document. The state and nation have an opportunity to engage in a much-needed reform of government, and the delegates have a moral responsibility to take their time on the question. "We are not acting for ourselves alone," Tweed reminded his colleagues, "but to all appearances for generations yet unborn." Tweed would vote for ratification, but in this speech he was highly critical of the scare tactics of the Federalists.[22]

Even in the face of such opposition, though, the Federalists were not prepared to give much ground. The amendments proposed by the committee, which were eventually approved by the convention, are telling on this point. None of the four proposed amendments was a significant alteration in the power of the government, nor were they significant safeguards of liberty. Congress was called upon to not exercise its power to interfere in election procedures, unless a state shall fail to provide for elections, and to avoid levying direct taxes until all other routes, including requisitions, have been tried. Both of these were avowed Federalist positions; they reflect how the Constitution's supporters claimed the respective powers would be used anyway. Neither of these required an actual change to the Constitution, either; the only proposal brought forth by the committee that would require a change was that the clause concerning the oath of office should be changed to read "no other religious test," affirming that an oath is inherently religious. This amendment seems to have been the response to an especially impassioned speech by the Reverend Francis Cummins, who was alarmed by the secular nature of the document and would have preferred to see the Constitution say that "no religious denomination shall ever have preference to another in matters of state, and all religious societies shall have equal liberty and protection." Inserting "other" was his second choice.[23] The only change of the four that carries much weight is one that, for the Federalists, merely stated a fact: "That the states respectively, do retain every power not expressly delegated by this constitution to the general government of the union." This was little more than a restatement of James Wilson's argument against a bill of rights, because the Constitution was one of enumerated powers. Clearly these proposals were nothing but a (largely empty) conciliatory gesture to the opposition, who probably numbered in the majority in the state.

The convention minority were not buying it, however. Like the Maryland minority, they wanted more concessions. Unlike the Marylanders, though, they managed to take their argument directly to the floor. Aedanus Burke led the charge, moving that the President be limited to a single term in office.

This proposal, after debate, elicited a roll call vote, and lost 68–139. Next up was a proposal to prevent officeholders from accepting any gift from foreign nations, removing the ability of Congress to grant exemptions; this also failed, by voice vote. The Anti-Federalists made one more unsuccessful try to change the powers of Congress, to deny the federal government the right to march a state militia out of the state without permission from the governor. After these three failed, the report of the committee was read, at which point John Bowman made one last effort, this time to establish a new committee to draw up a bill of rights to propose. When the Federalists would not agree even to this, the opposition knew its cause was lost, and relented. The Constitution and the committee's unamended report passed 149–73.

After the vote, a number of Anti-Federalists, echoing their brethren in Massachusetts, promised to "exert themselves to the utmost of their abilities to induce the people quietly to receive, and peaceably to live under the new government."[24] The minority members making such a promise included Aedanus Burke and Peter Fayssoux, the two most vocal critics of the Constitution in convention.

The Federalists still expected the worst, and seemed a little surprised when there was no violence or serious resistance. "Notwithstanding the threats of some every thing is peaceable & quiet in this country," David Ramsey wrote to John Kean in late June. "The new constitution becomes daily more acceptable & it is now the general wish that it may have a speedy operation." "People here give themselves little or no Concern about Politicks," William Spotswood reported in early July. "[T]hey are not at all Events so violent as in Pennsylvania."[25] The comparison with Pennsylvania was obvious, and shows up repeatedly in private correspondence, but the bottom line in South Carolina is that the same kind of radical opposition did not develop.

This is not to say there was not continued opposition; it was merely expressed in words rather than through violence. In private, Burke affirmed his Anti-Federalism in a letter to John Lamb. He explains the reasons for the Federalist victory in the state. "In the first place," he wrote, "we in the Opposition, had not, previous to our Meeting, either wrote, or spoke, hardly a word against it, nor took any one step in the matter. We had no principle of concert or union, while its friends and abettors left no expedient untried to push it forward." As a result, the Federalists managed to secure ratification "notwithstanding 4/5 of the people do, from their Souls detest" the Constitution. "In the interiour Country," he warns, "all is disgust, sorrow, and vindictive reproaches against the System, and those who voted for it. . . . You may rely upon it if a fair Opportunity offers itself to our back Country men they will join heart and hand to bring Ruin on the new Plan unless it be materially altered." If Burke is to be believed, there was potential for the South Carolina upcountry to join western Pennsylvania in resistance, but such resistance never materialized. The debate in the state was over, and the opposition leaders would play very small roles in the remainder of the national debate.[26]

12

The Virginia Convention

IN EARLY JUNE, with eight states having ratified, all eyes were turned south toward Virginia. Very few people outside of New England were paying much attention, if any, to New Hampshire, about to reconvene its adjourned (and closely split) convention. New York was generating interest, but the strong Anti-Federalist majority elected to the state's convention reduced the suspense considerably. At any rate, with New York commencing debate two weeks after Virginia, its outcome looked dependent on the largest state in the union. The convention in Richmond, with a close Federalist/Anti-Federalist split and a significant number of delegates of unknown sentiments, was the center of the political drama in the summer of 1788.[1] The Virginians themselves believed that everyone else was waiting to see what they would do. Richard Henry Lee argued that all four other states that had not yet decided would await Virginia's decision, and presumably mimic it. George Washington suggested in late April that "the opposition *here* ascribe [New Hampshire's adjournment] wholly to complaisance towards Virginia," and urged his correspondent James McHenry to see that a similar result was not obtained in Maryland. Edward Carrington expected New Hampshire to ratify before Virginia decided, but was concerned that a rejection by Virginia "would, in one moment, give additional life to the Minority in Pensylvania, whose opposition has taken a stubborn stand, & the appeal may, in that quarter, be to the sword."[2]

The Federalists had plenty of reason for optimism, though. The state boasted perhaps the two most important Federalist leaders in the nation, James Madison and George Washington. The latter would not serve in the convention, leaving the former to do most of the heavy lifting. Although he was described by Washington's personal secretary Tobias Lear as "the only man in this State who can effectually combat the influence of Mason and Henery," Madison had ample support in convention. One factor that substantially helped the Federalists was the common sentiment that the Constitution, though flawed, was preferable to the alternative of disunion.

Edmund Randolph eventually came to this point, framing his vote for ratification as a vote for union over disunion.[3] Paul Carrington, the state's chief
justice, arrived at the same sentiment; "he dislikes the Constitution," his
brother wrote to Madison, "but dreads the consequences of a disunion so
much, that he is determined to place us in no situation which shall in the
least degree hazard such an event." On the other hand, there were at least
a few Virginians who initially supported the Constitution, but later developed doubts. One such (anonymous) individual explained his feelings on the
Constitution "which I am candid to own at first met with my approbation,
but which, I am, on an investigation, convinced will endanger those liberties for which America gloriously contended, during an eight years war."
Surely there were more than a few people who fell into this category, but
most of the converts tended to lean the other way. They were moderate
Anti-Federalists, or reluctant Federalists, and Governor Randolph was the
leading example.[4]

The side ultimately taken by the moderates was determined in large part
by how they saw the options. Some, like Randolph, chose between the Constitution and disunion; this choice was simple for most. Others saw the
choice as federalism versus consolidation, and favored state sovereignty.
The *Virginia Gazette* of April 23 summed up the question in Virginia in a remarkably nonpartisan way, observing that Federalists and Anti-Federalists
saw that question differently:

> The great political question now is, observes a Federalist, whether
> America shall or shall not have a government that will make of thir-
> teen states a united people, happy amongst themselves, and respected
> by other nations. To effect the former, the adoption of the federal gov-
> ernment, is the only alternative.
>
> An Anti-federal says, the great political question now is, whether
> the states of America, united by their solemn faith and common in-
> terests, shall continue to be a federal republic, so constructed in its
> forms, and vested with such complete and extensive general powers,
> as will embrace every federal object, and render the general govern-
> ment great, energetic and respectable; and preserve to the states their
> independence in the full and free exercise of their internal sovereignty,
> and consequently the people free, intelligent, prosperous and happy:
> or, whether they shall adopt a consolidated government, of such a
> nature, and so extensive, as never did, nor never can, in the nature of
> things, preserve confidence in government, or happiness and political
> freedom to the people.

> *Thus different interests create different views, and until the important question is decided, a union of sentiment cannot be expected.*[5]

The final statement is the crucial one: the two sides would not be reconciled. Instead, one side was going to have to lose, and then acquiesce. It was not yet clear which side it would be.

The *Gazette* was stuck in its perception that there were only two sides of the question, though. Several Virginians saw at least three.[6] On the eve of the convention, William Short identified the parties as "federalists, tho[s]e who desire the constitution but with amendments, antifederalists." He was undoubtedly correct to observe that "It is the middle body w[hi]ch will probably decide the question." Short was six months behind James Madison, who drew the same divisions in a letter to Jefferson. The goal for the Federalists was not to win over the opponents of the Constitution, but to not lose those who favored an amended Constitution.[7]

The concept of "Federalists who are for amendments" is amply illustrated by "Denatus," who wrote during the early part of the convention. "I object to the said constitution," he explained to his readers, "but, wish that may it be adopted, and if possible, with amendments.—This appears strange. Be pleased to suspend your opinions, until you hear my reasons." His objections were not strange at all, and in fact they place him among mainstream Anti-Federalists. First, the Philadelphia Convention was authorized only to amend, not to propose a new government; thus the document itself is illegal. Even if this were not the case, though, the Constitution "appears incomprehensible and indefinite. . . . The constitution of a wise and free people, ought to be as evident to simple reason, as the letters of our alphabet.—This constitution I think is calculated for men of high monarchical principles, and to swallow up the constitutions of the different states." Also, Denatus insists, such a frame of government must be built upon a bill of rights, which should defend state prerogatives as well as individual liberty against federal encroachment. He does make one unusual suggestion, that the Constitution should require the establishment of educational institutions to instill moral virtues, but overall he held a moderate Rights Anti-Federalist position, except, of course, that he favored ratification. This was clearly the situation of many moderates throughout the country, but in Virginia the position was especially pronounced. Denatus wanted to see the Constitution "amended, and then adopted—It certainly has a great many excellent qualities, and as many bad ones. . . . If we adopt it without amendments, the seeds of our ruin are sown. If we reject it, disunion, the highest injustice, perhaps anarchy, and thousands of calamities will be the consequence." Perhaps, then, what was needed was a compromise between those who wanted prior amendments and those who favored the document as it stood.[8]

These "Federalists for amendments" held the balance of power in the convention. Edmund Randolph had gone fully to the Federalist side, but others favored ratification with amendments, and were willing to consider making those changes after ratification. One such individual wrote a two-part essay near the end of the convention, signed "A Delegate Who Has Catched Cold," in which he advocated amendments, whenever they might be secured. Those who demanded prior amendments could not claim that their proposals would ensure a flawless government, and the opponents of amendments could not guarantee the safety of the people against certain dubious clauses. Thus, wrote the Delegate, the only sensible course of action was a trial run: ratify the Constitution for a limited period of several years, making changes as necessary, and start over at the end of that time should the Constitution proves dangerous. He suggested that the primary change that was needed was the addition of a bill of rights.[9] The Delegate's preferred method of ratification never received much attention in the Virginia Convention, but it was proposed (unsuccessfully) by the New York Anti-Federalists.

The public debate on the merits of the Constitution continued, even as most Virginians were making up their minds and choosing sides. The Impartial Examiner wrote four more letters in May and June, though none so long or impressive as his first. He begins with a discussion of despotism, explaining that arbitrary power *is* despotism and leads to tyranny. The Constitution would be a step down this path, despite its deceptive appearance; "it is framed in the *republican stile*; and, although fraught with the seeds of *despotism*, the apparent lovliness of its outward garb hides all the *deformity* of its inward corruptions." In evaluating the Constitution, the Examiner suggests that it was the responsibility of the people "diligently to enquire, *first*, whether this system was coincident with their *standing maxims of liberty*; and, if so—whether conducive to *good policy*. If found derogatory to the former—any consideration respecting the latter should be unnecessary."[10] One cannot make a clearer statement of the Rights Anti-Federalism so dominant in the state. Nonetheless, he continues, the Federalists have ignored the crucial first question and built their case on the argument that the Constitution would be good policy. Liberty, he suggests, rests on representation, and this is inadequate in the Constitution. The House offers inadequate representation, while the Senate, elected by the state legislatures rather than the people, offers none at all. The President will be even further removed from representative principles, yet he has a substantial share in the legislative power through the veto. The Impartial Examiner closes by returning to rights; the rights of the people are secure under the Articles of Confederation and the constitution of Virginia, but are at risk under the proposed Federal Constitution. The Articles require revisions, to be sure, but there is no reason to replace a government too weak with one far too strong. He asks, why not simply fix those parts that are broken? Powers to regulate commerce and raise revenue would serve the purpose.

The discussion of how to make the Constitution safe for liberty, or how to make the Articles sufficiently strong, was happening in private conversations and letters as well as public essays and convention debates. "Public addresses were made at every gathering of the people," Hugh Blair Grigsby notes. "The court green, the race-course, and the muster-field, resounded with disputations. The pulpit as well as the rostrum uttered its voice, and the saint and the sinner mingled in the fierce *melee*." The proper balance between governmental power and personal liberty was the running theme. Theodorick Bland mixed metaphors in a colorful letter to Arthur Lee in mid-June, while the convention deliberated. "On the one hand," he wrote, "I see my Country on the point of embarking and launching into a troubled Ocean without Chart or Compass to direct them, one half the Crew hoisting sail for the land of *Energy*—and the other looking with a longing aspect on the Shore of Liberty." He offered a reasonable assessment of the state of the convention: "I really at this time think there is a decided majority for anterior amendments that is, who do not think it prudent to mount a fiery high-blooded Steed without a bridle."[11]

As the convention opened, both sides believed that they were close to a majority, but there was also broad agreement that about eight to twelve delegates were still undecided. The consensus seemed to be that the Federalists had an advantage, but there was disagreement over the magnitude of this lead. At the end of March, Arthur Lee counted a "5 or 6 Majority for the Constitution" in the state.[12] Others suggested that the lead was three or four times this size. On April 28 David Henley sent a list of delegates elected, with their likely positions on the Constitution, to his father. The exact origin of the list is unknown, but it was apparently distributed among at least a few Federalists. The list identified eighty-five delegates as "Federal," three as "Doubtful," and sixty-six as "Antifed." It left off the delegates from eight western counties, not having information on those elections. Henley's list serves as a reminder that the vast majority of delegates came to Richmond with their minds made up. Seventy-nine of Henley's eighty-five "Federals" ultimately voted for ratification, and sixty-four of his sixty-six "Antifeds" voted against. This does not mean, though, that the result was a foregone conclusion. To demonstrate this, we need to take a closer look at the numbers. Two of the Federalists listed actually lost their election to a pair of Anti-Federalists, and five voted differently from the predictions. If we remove the two nonelected Federalists and add in the Anti-Federalists who actually won, move those five who switched sides to "undecided" (where we will also place the "doubtful"), and remove the one Federalist, Thomas Pierce, who did not record a vote in the final tally, the actual numbers are seventy-nine Federalists, sixty-six Anti-Federalists, and eight undecided. This leaves fifteen other delegates present for the vote on ratification, those from the western counties for which Henley's list did not have returns. Eighty-five delegates would be the minimum number necessary for a majority, so the Federalists needed at least six votes from the eight undecided (three voted in favor) and the fifteen unknown (seven). The Kentucky delegates may have been the least set in their voting preferences, and hence the most susceptible to persuasion. The oratory of Patrick Henry might well have been just the thing to make up their minds for them.

THE VIRGINIA CONVENTION BATTLE

The opening of the convention clearly generated a great deal of excitement and suspense. Grigsby makes much of Patrick Henry and Edmund Pendleton as the nominal leaders of the two primary factions in the convention. He paints a vivid picture of their arrival at Richmond on the same day, and the excitement they generated among observers. "Public expectation was at its height when it was known that Patrick Henry and Edmund Pendleton, who, for a quarter of a century, had been at the head of the two great parties of that day, were about to engage in another fierce conflict in the councils of their country."[13] Pendleton's leadership of the Federalists was largely symbolic. His leadership of the convention, on the other hand, was official, as he was unanimously elected its president. On Monday, June 2, Pendleton addressed the delegates to thank them and to implore them to have an open and reasonable debate.

> The Trust is *Sacred & important*, and requires our most Serious *Attention*. Let us calmly reason With each other, as Friends, having all the same end in *view*, the real happiness of our *Constituents*, avoiding all *heats, Intemperance & Personal Altercations*, which always *impede*, but never *Assist Fair* Investigation. Let us Probe the Plan to the

Bottom, but let us do it *with Candor, temper* & mutual *Forbearance*: & finally decide as our Judgment shall direct.[14]

Patrick Henry was to participate in heat, intemperance, *and* personal altercations, and the Federalists were anything but innocent on these points, but nowhere else did the Constitution receive a fuller discussion. George Mason helped see to that by moving, successfully, that the Constitution be debated by clause, and that no decisions be made until every clause had been discussed.[15] The debate was a remarkable one; James Breckinridge, observing the debate, was impressed with both sides: the delegates, he wrote to his brother John, "have been elaborate, elegant, eloquent, & consequently entertaining and instructive."[16]

One might add tense and dramatic; Patrick Henry made sure of that. When he requested that the resolutions calling for the Philadelphia Convention be read, the Federalists tried to steer the discussion away from whether that convention exceeded its powers by proposing a new constitution rather than amending the old. The issue was irrelevant, suggested Pendleton, because Congress had called for the states to hold ratifying conventions, and the people of Virginia had elected them to debate the merits of the Constitution. Henry relented in his demand for the resolutions to be read, because his point had been made.[17] Instead, the Preamble and first two sections of the Constitution were read, and the great orator bided his time as George Nicholas expounded, at great length, upon the concept of representation in the proposed Congress. This orderly performance, addressing the clauses under consideration, was to be for naught, for it was followed by Henry's first wide-ranging diatribe against tyranny and the Constitution, and the idea of a clause-by-clause debate was essentially tossed aside. It would be ten days before the next clause of the Constitution was read and officially considered.

Henry's broad harangues against the Constitution left no doubt where he stood on the question: "I look on that paper as the most fatal plan, that could possibly be conceived to enslave a free people.—If such be your rage for novelty, take it and welcome, but you never shall have my consent."[18] Henry's wide-ranging approach to debate is instructive, however, as it helps to make clear the opposition position in broad strokes of principle rather than specific objections to clauses.[19] In fact, what we see in the Virginia Convention, particularly in the arguments of Henry and Mason, is a comprehensive statement of what really amounts to *the* national Anti-Federalist position. Henry, in his diatribes against monarchy and consolidation, primarily argues from a Power position, with generous nods toward the Rights

objections, while Mason does just the opposite. The two positions are almost seamlessly merged here; both Henry and Mason had closely followed
earlier debates, and had clearly conferred on their approach. The result was
a coherent opposition built from objections from all quarters.

For Mason, the goal was to secure the union without threatening the
rights of the people. Rights, he suggested, could be protected better by the
states than by a distant national government. "Whether the Constitution
be good or bad," Mason argued, the broad power of taxation "clearly
discovers, that it is a National Government, and no longer a confederation." This change, he insists, "is totally subversive of every principle
which has hitherto governed us. This power is calculated to annihilate totally the State Governments." Any form of national government is going
to be flawed. "To a Government, which, in the nature of things, cannot
but be defective," he said, "no powers ought to be given, but such as are
absolutely necessary."[20] Here we have an argument about power, for the
purpose of securing rights.

Henry too saw a dangerous consolidation of power. "Among other
deformities," he claimed, "it has an awful squinting; it squints towards
monarchy: And does not this raise indignation in the breast of every true
American?" This "squinting" would ultimately come to far more. "Away
with your President, we shall have a King," he thundered. "The army will
salute him Monarch; your militia will leave you and assist in making him
King, and fight against you: And what have you to oppose this force?
What will then become of you and your rights? Will not absolute despotism ensue?" Liberty was Henry's main theme, not consolidation. "Guard
with jealous attention the public liberty," he implored his fellow delegates.
"Suspect every one who approaches that jewel. Unfortunately, nothing will
preserve it, but downright force: Whenever you give up that force, you
are inevitably ruined." Securing liberty did not simply mean adding a bill
of rights; it required a properly designed government that could not become tyrannical. Such a government would remain in its place, and permit
the country to grow and prosper peacefully. To this end Henry mocked
the grand imperial aspirations of many of the Federalists. "If we admit
this Consolidated Government," he said sardonically, "it will be because
we like a great splendid one. Some way or other we must be a great and
mighty empire; we must have an army, and a navy, and a number of things;
When the American spirit was in its youth," he continued, "the language of
America was different: Liberty, Sir, was then the primary object."[21] Henry,
of course, was one of the prime movers in that movement, and he invoked
it effectively.

I am fearful I have lived long enough to become an old fashioned fellow: Perhaps an invincible attachment to the dearest rights of man, may, in these refined enlightened days, be deemed *old fashioned*: If so, I am contented to be so: I say, the time has been, when every pulse of my heart beat for American liberty, and which, I believe, had a counterpart in the breast of every true American: But suspicions have gone forth—suspicions of my integrity—publicly reported that my professions are not real—23 years ago was I supposed a traitor to my country: I was then said to be a bane of sedition, because I supported the rights of my country: I may be thought suspicious when I say our privileges and rights are in danger. But, sir, a number of the people of this country are weak enough to think these things are too true.[22]

The danger here was precisely that this Constitution could so effectively crush revolution, regardless of the justness of the cause. We cannot trust our rulers not to abuse power, so we must retain the power to overthrow them if necessary. "This, Sir, is my great objection to the Constitution, that there is no true responsibility—and that the preservation of our liberty depends on the single chance of men being virtuous enough to make laws to punish themselves." Earlier in the speech, Henry insisted that his "great objection" was "that it does not leave us the means of defending our rights; or, of waging war against tyrants." For Patrick Henry, these two were statements of the same objection. The only way to secure true responsibility was to ensure that the people have options against oppressive government.[23]

The issue is not one of union or disunion, as the Federalists claimed. For William Grayson, the key question was one of human nature. "There are two opinions prevailing in the world," he explains. "The one, that mankind can only be governed by force: The other, that they are capable of freedom and a good Government." If the latter is true, the Articles of Confederation should be amended, and the sovereign states should provide the appropriate republican form of government. Sufficient powers could in that case be added to Congress. But if people must be governed by force, says Grayson, "then be as gentle as possible." Establish a President and Senate for life, and a House of Representatives elected every three years, with powers similar to those of the British House of Commons. Thus the people can have some voice, but there will be rulers to make sure that the government is stable and effective.[24]

The Anti-Federalists, of course, were not advocating such a system; they believed that the people could be trusted to govern themselves. Grayson too seemed to believe this. His optimism about human nature extended to the delegates to the Philadelphia Convention; Grayson, unlike Henry, be-lieved they acted in good faith and did the best they could. Unfortunately, the product of that illustrous body was deeply flawed and dangerous. The powers granted were too strong, and in need of correction. Henry insisted that such a correction must come before ratification: "At present we have our liberties and privileges in our own hands. Let us not relinquish them. Let us not adopt this system till we see them secured." A bill of rights ought to be attached to the frame of government, and "every implication should be done away." But this must be done *before* the Constitution is ratified; to do otherwise is lunacy. "When it is confessed to be replete with defects, is it not offering to insult your understandings, to attempt to rea-son you out of the propriety of rejecting it, till it be amended? Does it not insult your judgments to tell you—adopt first, and then amend?" What makes the problem more pressing is the amendment process itself. Henry argued that there would never be any amendments to the Constitution, because three-quarters of the states would not agree. "A trifling minority may reject the most salutary amendments. Is this an easy mode of securing the public liberty?" He was equally doubtful that two-thirds of Congress would ever acquiesce in any limitations on government. William Grayson concurred: "The consent of so many States are necessary to introduce amendments, that I fear they will with great difficulty be obtained." Hav-ing a few states refuse to ratify the Constitution might create just enough leverage to obtain the necessary changes. If amendments cannot be se-cured before nine states have ratified, then Virginia ought to remain inde-pendent until those states have agreed to the necessary changes, especially a bill of rights but also limitations on the broad powers to be granted to the federal government.[25]

When it came to the powers of the proposed government, there were two issues that overshadowed all others: taxation and the military. "Congress by the power of taxation—by that of raising an army, and by their controul over the militia, have the sword in one hand, and the purse in the other," said Henry, asking "Shall we be safe without either?"[26]

Henry tore into the Federalist argument for a broad federal tax power. "The power of direct taxation was called by the Honorable Gentleman [Ed-mund Randolph] the soul of the Government: Another Gentleman [Francis Corbin], called it the lungs of the Government. . . . If money be the vitals of Congress, is it not precious for those individuals from whom it is to be taken? Must I give my soul—my lungs, to Congress?" He expounded on po-litical economy, insisting that "no nation ever paid its debts by a change of Government, without the aid of industry. You never will pay your debts but by a radical change of domestic œconomy. At present you buy too much, and make too little to pay. Will this new system promote manufactures, industry and frugality?" The tax power ought to be kept as close to the people as possible, so that those who could exercise that power could be closely watched. Grayson reiterated this point, noting that by surrendering the power to tax, the people "give up every thing, as it is the highest act of sovereignty: Surrender up this inestimable jewel, and you throw a pearl away richer than all your tribe." The powers of government follow the power to tax, and that will be vested in the Congress. Worse, it will be vested in the *majority* of Congress, which will not end well.[27]

The other power that should be guarded with as much jealousy as the tax power is the military. The militia was an especially troubling point of contention; Congress was not only to organize and train them, but to arm them as well. "Are we at last brought to such a humiliating and debasing degradation," Henry asked, "that we cannot be trusted with arms for our own defence?" The army will thus take the place of an armed citizenry, and, in the words of Mason, "when once a standing army is established, in any country, the people lose their liberty. When against a regular and disciplined army, yeomanry are the only defence—yeomanry unskilled and unarmed, what chance is there of preserving freedom?"[28] Henry backed up Mason on this point.

> The argument of my honorable friend [George Mason], was, that rulers *might* tyrannize. The answer he received, was, that they *will not*. In saying that they *would not*, he [James Madison] admitted that they *might*. In this great, this essential part of the Constitution, if you are safe, it is not from the Constitution, but from the virtues of the men in Government. If Gentlemen are willing to trust themselves and posterity to so slender and improbable a chance, they have greater strength of nerves than I have.[29]

The solution was to be more careful about giving power; the people, Henry insisted, ought to be eternally suspicious of their government. "Too much suspicion may be corrected. If you give too little power to-day, you may give more to-morrow. But the reverse of the proposition will not hold. If you give too much power to-day, you cannot retake it to-morrow: For to-morrow will never come for *that* purpose."[30]

In response to these concerns about both taxing and military power, Madison offered a curious and telling defense of the proposed national government and critique of the opposition position. "Does it mean that the sword and purse ought not to be trusted in the hands of the same Government?" he asked. "This cannot be the meaning. For there never was, and I can say there never will be, an efficient Government, in which both are not vested. The only rational meaning, is, that the sword and purse are not to be given to the same member." Thus, he argued, the purse was given to Congress, and the sword to the President, with ample checks on both. This prompted Henry to pounce; Madison could not win this point. "It is now confessed that this is a national Government," Henry noted. "There is not a single federal feature in it. . . . The Honorable Member [James Madison] was pleased to say, that the sword and purse included every thing of consequence. And shall we trust them out of our hands without checks and barriers?" For Henry, the government of Virginia was the people's government, and the national government was something else. "Where are the purse and sword of Virginia? They must go to Congress. What is to become of your country? The Virginian Government is but a name. It clearly results from this last argument that we are to be consolidated. We should be thought unwise indeed to keep 200 Legislators in Virginia, when the Government is in fact gone to Philadelphia or New-York. We are as a State to form no part of the Government."[31]

Both Madison and Henry fundamentally (and perhaps willfully) misunderstood the Federalist/Anti-Federalist divide, and both missed the nuance that sat at the middle of this debate. For the opposition, "government" meant the federal system, encompassing state and national governments. For the Federalists it meant the national government, with the state governments as subordinate parts. For the supporters of the Constitution to claim that the powers of the purse and sword are in different hands, they needed only to show that they had been placed in different branches of the national government. For an Anti-Federalist, to put the purse and sword in different hands was to place one with the states, and one with the national government. For the opposition, the national government *was a single set of hands, a single part of government.* The other parts were the states. Legislative, executive, and judicial mean little when one examines government from a federal perspective; the powers are shared across branches anyway. To place a power in a set of hands other than Congress, for the Anti-Federalists, it *must* be placed in the hands of the states, because there is no other place where Congress cannot make at least partial use of it. Without some powers going to the federal government, this would not be a federal system. Without the military powers specifically being placed in national hands, it is hard to envision the United States as a nation in any meaningful way. A nation must have some claim to sovereignty in order to engage in diplomacy and war. However, from the perspective of the Anti-Federalists, the people must retain the power of the purse *as closely as possible to themselves*, in the hands of their closest representatives. The most perspicuous of the Anti-Federalists, like James Monroe, recognized the need for this balance, and actually advocated a true Federal Republic, rather than the mere confederation of Henry and Grayson.

The Anti-Federalists trusted the future magistrates least where their power was greatest. The clause granting Congress unlimited jurisdiction over a federal district prompted specific objections from several delegates, culminating in a general statement of the principle of limited government from Henry: "I know the absolute necessity of an energetic Government. But is it consistent with any principle of prudence or good policy, to grant unlimited, unbounded authority, which is so totally unnecessary, that Gentlemen say it will never be exercised? But Gentlemen say, that we must make experiments. A wonderful and unheard of experiment it will be, to give unlimited power unnecessarily!"[32] There was little Madison could say to that, except to repeat that Henry was imagining dangers that were simply not plausible.

Despite how little Madison and Henry found to agree upon, there was a plausible middle ground in the debate. James Monroe, in a speech on the tenth of June, was singularly candid about the choice between the Confederation and the Constitution, and conciliatory about finding middle ground. "What are the powers which the Federal Government ought to have?" he asks.

> I will draw the line between the powers necessary to be given to the Federal, and those which ought to be left to the State Governments. To the former I would give controul over the national affairs: To the latter I would leave the care of local interests. Neither the Confederation, nor this Constitution, answers this discrimination. To make the first a proper Federal Government, I would add to it one great power—I would give it an absolute controul over commerce. To render the system under consideration safe and proper, I would take from it one power only—I mean that of direct taxation. I conceive its other powers are sufficient without this.[33]

He suggested that the Constitution clearly consolidated power in the national government, because that government holds complete power over the resources of the nation, especially the revenues. He expressed fear "that it will ultimately end in the establishment of a Monarchical Government."[34]

What the opposition ultimately wanted to see was a better federal balance. Henry in particular saw in the Constitution an overbearing federal government that would emasculate the states. "Abolish the State Legislatures at once," suggested Henry. "What purposes should they be continued for? Our Legislature will indeed be a ludicrous spectacle—180 men marching in solemn farcical procession, exhibiting a mournful proof of the lost liberty of their country—without the power of restoring it." Instead, the state will have to rely on "the chosen ten," who are bound to disappoint the high hopes and expectations of the people of the state, as the delegates to the Philadelphia Convention did by exceeding their commission. "Will the ten men you are to send to Congress, be more worthy than those seven were? If power grew so rapidly in their hands, what may it not do in the hands of others?" After all, Virginia's congressional delegates would almost certainly be a less impressive group than the state's Philadelphia delegates.[35]

A proper federal system, according to Henry, is built on a balance between state and national governments, and effective checks by which one might restrain the other. Paper assurances are no good; only real power left in the hands of the states and the people will work. Unfortunately, in the Constitution "there are only ideal balances. Till I am convinced that there are actual efficient checks, I will not give my assent to its establishment." That there was no efficient state check over the President and the courts was bad enough, but even in the legislature, with one house to represent the people and one to represent the states, there was no real opportunity for control. "The only semblance of a check is the negative power of not re-electing them. This, Sir, is but a feeble barrier when their personal interest, their ambition and avarice come to be put in contrast with the happiness of the people." Even the weak check of being able to vote out the corrupt is made even weaker by the power given to Congress to control the publication of its journals. "The liberties of a people never were nor ever will be secure, when the transactions of their rulers may be concealed from them. The most iniquitous plots may be carried on against their liberty and happiness. . . . I appeal to this Convention if it would not be better for America to take off the veil of secrecy."[36]

What stands out about these Power Anti-Federalist arguments, though, is the extent to which they were premised on concern for the liberties of the people. Monroe grounded his objections to the tax power in the need for a bill of rights. "I am a decided and warm friend to a *Bill of Rights*—the polar star, and great support of American liberty," he insisted, "and I am clearly of opinion, that the general powers conceded by that plan, such as the impost, &c. should be guarded and checked by a Bill of Rights."[37] Monroe was a Power Anti-Federalist, suggesting that a change in tax power would be sufficient to make the Constitution safe, but he made the argument from a clear Rights position.

Mason made the case for a bill of rights early in the convention, noting that the people of Virginia, in forming their state government, "would not trust their own citizens, who had a similarity of interest with themselves, and who had frequent and intimate communication with them," to have power over their sacred rights and liberties.[38] Why then is there no bill of rights attached to this Constitution? "Where is the barrier drawn between the Government and the rights of the citizens, as secured in our own State Government?" The rights are protected only at the whim of our representatives, and that is no security at all. In a proper representation there would be some hope that the people might defend themselves, but not under the representation described in the Constitution. "Instead of 160 [representatives for Virginia], there are but 10—chosen, if not wholly, yet mostly from the higher order of the people—from the great—the wealthy—the *well-born*. The *well-born*— Mr. Chairman, that Aristocratic idol—that flattering idea—that *exotic* plant which has been lately imported from the ports of Great-Britain, and planted in the luxuriant soil of this country."[39] A proper representation would reinforce written protections of the rights of the people, because no bill of rights will fully protect the people from so-called representatives intent on doing harm to the public for personal gain. And if corruption is widespread in the British House of Commons with its 550 members, we should expect much greater danger of corruption in a House with merely sixty-five.[40]

"The necessity of a Bill of Rights appears to me to be greater in this Government," Henry observed, "than ever it was in any Government before."[41] Virginia's present government, argued Henry, secured the rights of the people through its bill of rights.

> She is called upon now to abandon them, and dissolve that compact which secured them to her. She is called upon to accede to another compact which most infallibly supercedes and annihilates her present one. Will she do it?—This is the question. If you intend to reserve your unalienable rights, you must have the most express stipulation. For if implication be allowed, you are ousted of those rights. If the people do not think it necessary to reserve them, they will be supposed to be given up.[42]

The Federalist argument that the rights of the people were safe because Congress has no enumerated power to infringe them was rejected sharply.

Certain rights are in fact protected, despite this claim about enumerated powers. Henry said "that there is a Bill of Rights in that Government. There are express restrictions which are in the shape of a Bill of Rights: But they bear the name of the ninth section [of Article I]. . . . The restraints in this Congressional Bill of Rights, are so feeble and few, that it would have been infinitely better to have said nothing about it. The fair implication is, that they can do every thing they are not forbidden to do." The rights of the people, he says, "are guarded in no other part but this ninth section." There is no reason not to list the necessary rights. "A Bill of Rights may be summed up in a few words. What do they tell us?—That our rights are reserved.— Why not say so? Is it because it will consume too much paper?" Henry concluded with confidence that the convention would rectify this omission. "I trust that Gentlemen, on this occasion, will see the great objects of religion, liberty of the press, trial by jury, interdiction of cruel punishments, and every other sacred right secured, before they agree to that paper." Securing the rights of the people serves as a check on governmental power, just as carefully controlling power helps secure the rights of the people.[43]

The Federalist response on this point was comparatively feeble. George Nicholas offered the rather weak argument that a bill of rights "is but a paper check," and will not actually restrain government. "Had there been an exception, or express infringement of those rights, he might object," adds Governor Randolph. "But I conceive every fair reasoner will agree, that there is no just cause to suspect that they will be violated."[44] Once again, the proponents of the Constitution, instead of answering the charge that the powers were too broad and vague, insisted that we need not fear our leaders. This was the Virginia Federalist refrain, and it was the weakest point against Henry and his allies.

The Federalists tried to parry the attacks of Henry, often without much success. Henry Lee, answering Patrick Henry's long speech on June 9, observed that "the Honorable Gentleman seems to have discarded in a great measure, solid argument and strong reasoning, and has established a new system of throwing those bolts, which he has so peculiar a dexterity at discharging."[45] He accused Henry, of all people, of undue admiration for the British monarchy. Madison could match Henry on particular points and clauses, but not in rhetoric or imagery. Throughout the convention, the Federalist response to Henry was generally delivered by Edmund Randolph, who, while not quite a rhetorical match for Henry, nonetheless came closer than anyone else advocating the Constitution. Meanwhile, Henry was not the least bit deterred by the lineup against him. He seemed to gain energy from the rebuttals that generally appeared weak and defensive against his rhetoric, while Randolph appeared increasingly worn down by the pressures of the debates.

RANDOLPH'S SWITCH

Henry was not the central figure in the convention, though. It was not Madison either, despite his tireless explanation of clause after clause. In terms of the ratification decision, the key figure was Randolph, and the key event was his conversion (or apostasy, depending on one's point of view). His position, somewhat a mystery to everyone before the convention opened, was revealed in his first major speech. Following Henry's opening salvo, in which the old patriot boldly accused the Philadelphia Convention delegates of usurpation by speaking as "We the People" without the authority to do so, Randolph rose and declared almost defiantly his support for ratification. He insisted that he had always favored "a firm energetic government" despite his reservations on the Constitution, and that he "never will assent to any scheme that will operate a dissolution of the Union, or any measure which may lead to it":

> As with me the only question has ever been, between previous, and subsequent amendments, so I will express my apprehensions, that the postponement of this Convention, to so late a day, has extinguished the probability of the former without inevitable ruin to the Union, and the Union is the anchor of our political salvation; and I will assent to the lopping of this limb (meaning his arm) before I assent to the dissolution of the Union.[46]

The implications of this speech were immediately clear: Randolph had declared himself for unconditional ratification. Randolph's rather complete reversal is explained by his repeated insistence that ratification was the only way to preserve the union. Like Samuel Adams before him and Melancton Smith after, the Governor saw the decision as between union and disunion, and he was not willing to risk the latter.[47]

The Governor apparently took everyone by surprise; both sides expected him to remain quiet in the convention, at least until he had made up his mind, presumably late in convention. Instead he quickly took up the cause of the Federalists, and became one of its most effective articulators. This move was a pleasant surprise for James Madison, who wrote triumphantly about it to Rufus King and George Washington. Theodorick Bland suggested that

Randolph was "reprobated by the honest on both sides" for his switch in position. There is little evidence of ill treatment beyond a few insinuations by Henry in convention speeches, and clearly both sides still courted the Governor because he "is too precious a morsel to be *spued* out." Washington was sure that Randolph's switch would "have considerable effect with those who had hitherto been wavering." William Grayson was worried about such conversions; by his count the number of delegates on each side was "as nearly equal as possible" to open the convention, but Randolph's change of heart, coupled with the news of South Carolina's ratification arriving the same day, would probably shift the balance. The idea that rejecting the Constitution meant disunion could win over wavering delegates, and Randolph made this case forcefully and repeatedly.[48]

Patrick Henry was not impressed by Randolph's argument that Virginia ought to ratify because most of the other states had done so. "It is said eight States have adopted this plan," he declaimed. "I declare that if twelve States and an half had adopted it, I would with manly firmness, and in spite of an erring world, reject it." At any rate, Randolph's contention that the choice for Virginia was union or separation was nothing more than a "bugbear." "The fact is that the eight adopting States can hardly stand on their own legs." The states that had already adopted, and those that may have adopted, had no reason to try to rush or force Virginia into the union. Instead, he insisted, Virginia may take some time to carefully consider the new government, and need not decide right away. He was not advocating secession, he explained; it was on the *terms* of union that he disagreed with his fellows. "I see great jeopardy in this new Government," he asserted. "I see none from our present one." In fact, the Articles of Confederation deserve "the highest encomium."[49]

Henry relentlessly went after Randolph, praising the Governor's refusal to sign the Constitution at the end of the Philadelphia Convention and questioning his change of heart. Randolph's "enlightened mind, knowing that system to be defective, magnanimously and nobly refused its approbation. He was not led by the illumined—the illustrious few. He was actuated by the dictates of his own judgment; and a better judgment than I can form." Of course, somewhere between Philadelphia and Richmond, Randolph lost his way. George Mason made much the same claim. Randolph, he said, "seems to raise phantoms, and to shew a singular skill in exorcisms, to terrify and compel us to take the new Government with all its sins and dangers. I know that he once saw as great danger in it as I do." The implication was that the Governor was at least inconsistent, and at worst unprincipled.[50]

Throughout the convention Henry listened like a hawk. When Randolph made a poor choice of words, Henry was ready to pounce. "The Honorable Gentleman has anticipated what we are to be reduced to, by degradingly assimilating our citizens to a herd," he noted. The Governor insisted that he used the word "herd" "merely to convey an idea of a multitude," but Henry managed to make the Federalists appear hostile to the kind of democracy favored by western Virginians. And Henry would not let go of this powerful word, using it again to attack his opponents as undemocratic.

> Sir, I ask you, and every other Gentleman who hears me, if he can retain his indignation, at a system, which takes from the State Legislatures the care and preservation of the interests of the people; 180 Representatives, the choice of the people of Virginia cannot be trusted with their interests. They are a mobbish suspected *herd*. This country has not virtue enough to manage its own internal interests. These must be referred to the chosen ten [Virginia Representatives in the House]. If we cannot be trusted with the private contracts of the citizens, we must be depraved indeed.[51]

The people, Henry believed, were opposed to the Constitution. This was why the Federalists dismissed them as a herd; they would not quietly accept this Constitution being forced upon them. "It is said, the people wish to change the Government," he said. "Should the people wish to change it, we should be innocent of the dangers. It is a fact, that the people do not wish to change their Government. . . . I am persuaded that four-fifths of the people of Virginia must have amendments to the new plan, to reconcile them to a change of their Government."[52]

Randolph did not take kindly to Henry's criticism. "I find myself attacked," he declared, "in the most illiberal manner, by the Honorable Gentleman, (Mr. *Henry*) I disdain his aspersions, and his insinuations. His asperity is warranted by no principle of Parliamentary decency, nor compatible with the least shadow of friendship; and if our friendship must fall—*Let it fall like Lucifer, never to rise again*." Randolph defended his patriotism and integrity in the face of Henry's assault. Henry rose to insist that he did not mean to offend, but Randolph was not yet done. He replied that he was pleased with Henry's apology, and "that were it not for the concession of the Gentleman, he would have made some men's hair stand on end, by the disclosure of certain facts." When Henry insisted that Randolph say whatever it was he had to say, the Governor backed off, but it is still remarkable that the confrontation did not end up in a duel, or apparently go beyond the floor of the convention.[53]

Randolph was certainly a believer in the Federalist doomsday scenarios of disunion and internal strife, but others were not convinced. The Anti-Federalists engaged these predictions with a combination of reasoning and sarcasm. Though the Federalists won over Randolph with the union argument, they were not so convincing to Randolph's fellow nonsigner in the Philadelphia Convention. George Mason teased George Nicholas for the latter delegate's statement that if he had not already convinced the doubters that he would give up. "I am one of those unhappy men who cannot be amused with assertions," says Mason. "A man from the dead might frighten me, but I am sure that he could not convince me without using better arguments than I have yet heard." His humor was not appreciated by the Federalists.[54]

William Grayson followed with more caustic sarcasm. Randolph had warned of the danger of war and invasion; Grayson was less than convinced:

> We are now told by the Honorable Gentleman (Governor *Randolph*) that we shall have wars and rumours of wars; that every calamity is to attend us, and that we shall be ruined and disunited forever, unless we adopt this Constitution. Pennsylvania and Maryland are to fall upon us from the North, like the Goths and Vandals of old—The Algerines, whose flat sided vessels never came farther than Madeira, are to fill the Chesapeake with mighty fleets, and to attack us on our front. The Indians are to invade us with numerous armies on our rear, in order to convert our cleared lands into hunting grounds—And the Carolinians from the south, mounted on alligators, I presume, are to come and destroy our corn fields, and eat up our little children! These, Sir, are the mighty dangers which await us if we reject. Dangers which are merely imaginary, and ludicrous in the extreme! Are we to be destroyed by Maryland and Pennsylvania? What will Democratic States make war for, and how long since have they imbibed a hostile spirit?[55]

Grayson may have been better received, or perhaps merely wittier, than Mason; Grigsby writes that "his sally was received with roars of laughter from both sides of the house."[56] Disunion, he continued more seriously, was nothing more than a figment of overactive Federalist imaginations. Grayson was blunt: "Disunion is impossible."[57] The people of the various states are united not by the Confederation, but by mutual ties of affection and patriotism.

Even if the union were secure either way, though, it is not clear what relation an independent Virginia might have with the other states under the Constitution. Henry was not worried, though. He insisted that there was no hurry to ratify, because the other states would not attempt to exclude Virginia. "If disunion will really result from Virginia's proposing amendments, will they not wish the re-establishment of the Union, and admit us, if not on such terms as we prescribe, yet on advantageous terms? Is not Union as essential to their happiness, as to ours?" The danger of disunion was at best overstated, and probably entirely illusory. There was in fact no real danger, internal or external. "You are told there is no peace, although you fondly flatter yourselves that all is peace—No peace—a general cry and alarm in the country—Commerce, riches, and wealth vanished—Citizens going to seek comforts in other parts of the world—Laws insulted—Many instances of tyrannical legislation. These things," Henry insisted, "are new to me." As for the great powers of the Old World, Henry pointed out that "Europe is too much engaged about objects of greater importance to attend to us. On that great theatre of the world, the little American matters vanish." The mere fact that the Federalists insisted on such dangers, though, says a great deal about the proposed government. "When Gentlemen are thus driven to produce imaginary dangers, to induce this Convention to assent to this change," he opined, "I am sure it will not be uncandid to say, that the change itself is really dangerous." On the other hand, the Constitution might damage our peaceful relations with Europe. Henry suggested that with the creation of a new government old treaties will be made invalid, and European powers will be wary to make new ones with a country so eager to create a grand and glorious imperial government. Such countries will no doubt have "serious reflections" on the "schemes of popular ambition" implied in the proposed Constitution.[58]

The more Randolph heard the less convincing he became; arguing with Henry wore him down. As the convention progressed, he became increasingly agitated about the prospect that the state might fail to ratify the Constitution. On June 16, he explained "that he had some objections to the clause [granting Congress the power to tax for the 'general welfare']. He was persuaded, that the construction put upon it by the Gentlemen, on both sides, was erroneous;—but he thought any construction better than to go into anarchy."[59] The next day he went further in expressing his fears, admitting that the Necessary and Proper Clause

is ambiguous, and that that ambiguity may injure the States. My fear is, that it will by gradual accessions gather to a dangerous length. . . .

But, Sir, are we to reject it, because it is ambiguous in some particular instances? I cast my eyes to the actual situation of America; I see the dreadful tempest, to which the present calm is a prelude, if disunion takes place. I see the anarchy which must happen if no energetic Government be established. In this situation, I would take the Constitution were it more objectionable than it is.[60]

His transformation from reluctant Anti-Federalist to terrified Federalist was complete.

THE ISSUE OF KENTUCKY

Randolph was not the only delegate caught between the two sides. His influence was substantial, but he still only had one vote. The delegates from Kentucky, whose positions were unclear, had fourteen votes; these were likely enough to swing the convention vote on ratification either way. These votes were so critical, in fact, that on June 13 the convention temporarily gave up all pretense of discussing the Constitution by clause in order to engage in an extended discussion of the navigation of the Mississippi River. The object for both sides was to convince the delegates from Kentucky.

It may have been William Grayson who prompted this with a speech on the eleventh in which he argued that the Constitution would likely result in substantial conflict between regional factions in the new government. "I hope that my fears are groundless," he said, "but I believe it as I do my creed, that this Government will operate as a faction of seven States to oppress the rest of the Union." The next day, Grayson reprised this argument. "The greatest defect," he insisted, "is the opposition of the component parts to the interests of the whole." There will be state and regional interests that run counter to the national interest, and in any case the national interest will come down merely to the interest of the majority. The main issue at stake is taxation; any taxes issued by Congress "cannot be uniform throughout the States without being oppressive to some." Yet Congress will be given this power, thus removing the states' power to defend themselves, for "the State which gives up the power of taxation has nothing more to give." The other major issue, though, is regional: commerce. The commerce and resources of the western territories, potential future states, were at risk, for Congress had no incentive to act in their best interests. Here the focal point was navigation of the Mississippi River. If the north could prevent shipping via that river, Grayson argued, they might severely slow the emigration to the west, thus preserving their majority representation in the House of Representatives, as well as preventing the new states that might be formed on the frontier, which would change the balance in the Senate. Thus rather than simply having no reason to fight to protect western economic interests, the northern states would have a perverse incentive to actually harm those interests.[61]

The Anti-Federalist appeal to the delegates from Kentucky was clear: "the interest of the Western Country would not be as secure under the proposed Constitution, as under the Confederation," insisted James Monroe, "because under the latter system, the Mississippi could not be relinquished without the consent of nine States, whereas by the former, he said, a majority, or seven states, could yield it." Randolph decried the "wrong inducements offered, to influence the delegation from Kentucky." He recurred to the law of nations to defend Kentucky's right to navigate the Mississippi. It is clear from the proceedings, though, and from the eventual votes of Kentucky, that the opposition won this round. Henry, as usual, was more eloquent, and his arguments were irresistible. "It is said that we are scuffling for Kentucky votes, and attending to local circumstances," said Henry. "But if you consider the interest of this country, you will find that the interest of Virginia and Kentucky are most intimately and vitally connected."[62] The Federalists were left to rely on arguments that the Senators and President could be trusted, or Madison's ill-conceived suggestion that the House of Representatives might intervene. Henry jumped on that claim to issue a sweeping denunciation of the Constitution. "Will the Honorable Gentleman say, that the House of Representatives will break through their balances and checks, and break into the business of treaties?—He is obliged to support this opinion of his, by supposing, that the checks and balances of this Constitution are to be an impenetrable wall for some purposes, and a mere cobweb for some other purposes. What kind of Constitution then can this be?"[63] Either the checks are real and treaties (among other things) are beyond the reach of the people's representatives, or the checks are merely illusory and the Congress may dictate its own powers. Either way, the Constitution is dangerous.

The afternoon of the thirteenth brought a sort of intermission to the proceedings, as the convention adjourned early because of "a very Heavy storm of Hail, wind & rain, which blew open the Windows, & renderd the House too wet & uncomfortable to proceed." James Madison took advantage of the time to write several letters, in which he assessed the Constitution's chances. He concluded that "the event is as ticklish as can be conceived." He believed that "the vote of Kentucky will turn the scale, and there is perhaps more to fear than to hope from that quarter." James Breckinridge concurred about the Kentucky delegates: "Madison[']s plain, ingenious, & elegant reasoning," he wrote on the same day, "is entirely thrown away and lost among such men." This was especially frustrating because the Federalists believed that the arguments made by the opposition about the Mississippi River were specious. The Anti-Federalists, though, were no more pleased about Kentucky than Madison. William Grayson too described the situation as "ticklish," writing to Nathan Dane a few days later that "ten out of 13. of the Kentucki members" were opposed to ratification, "but we wanted the whole." In fact, the western opposition in general seemed to be slipping ever so slightly, and the Anti-Federalists could not afford to lose the votes. Grayson went so far as to suggest that the Federalists had recently brought up the question of Kentucky statehood in Congress in order to win over a few votes in the Virginia Convention. For both sides, the day, with its extra time out of convention, was "wholly occupied in endeavouring to gain over the members from the Kentuckey district."[64]

DEBATING THE DETAILS

The day after the extended discussion of navigation rights on the Mississippi River, the convention finally moved on with its clause-by-clause discussion of the Constitution, reading the third section of Article I and working its way into the powers of Congress in the eighth section. During this discussion, Madison was fully in his element, answering each specific objection with a detailed clause-by-clause defense. The powers of Congress, here as elsewhere, were highly contentious. Aside from the taxing and military powers discussed above, three objections are worth noting here.

The discussion on slavery is especially striking, in the state that held the most slaves in the union. The conversation focused on the prohibition of Congress interfering in the slave trade until 1808. Mason, the owner of a substantial number of slaves, lamented that the slave trade was to be resumed, but still defended slavery as it existed in Virginia. Although the "infamous traffic" in slaves was to be allowed, he said, "we have no security for the property of that kind which we have already. There is no clause in this Constitution to secure it; for they may lay such a tax as will amount to manumission." Patrick Henry seconded the idea, asking, "why it was omitted to secure us that property in slaves, which we held now? He feared its omission was done with design." The discretion given to Congress over the publication of its journals and receipts also raised Mason's ire; he said that he "did not conceive that the receipts and expenditures of the public money ought ever to be concealed. The people, he affirmed, had a right to know the expenditures of their money. But this expression was so loose, it might be concealed forever from them, and might afford opportunities of misapplying the public money, and sheltering those who did it."[65] Here too the notion of a national government far removed from Virginia, driven by its lust for power, was raised against the proposed Constitution.

There was a brief but pointed discussion about the continental debt that presaged the later debate over Hamilton's plan to pay off that debt. Henry and Mason insisted that under the Constitution the United States, and the state of Virginia, will have to pay off all of the paper money and other obligations from the Revolution at face value rather than their depreciated market value. "The amount," insisted Mason, "will surpass the value of the property of the United States." Madison made the claim that the government is no more obligated to pay the debt at face value under the Constitution than under the Articles of Confederation. Henry rejected this, crying injustice over paying speculators face value when they purchased the notes "at one for a thousand."[66]

As the convention finished discussing Article I, the debate became faster paced yet less edifying. It was not that the opposition let up in its arguments, or that the defenders of the Constitution became less effective. On the contrary, George Mason became more insistent and James Madison became stauncher in debate. By this point, though, the main arguments were already made, and the two sides contended over details. The process for electing the president was "perfectly dissatisfactory," largely because of the outsize influence of small states and the potential for foreign influence. The only people who would have virtually no influence on the selection would be the citizens at large; Mason insisted that this means of electing the President is "a mere deception—a mere *ignus fatuus* [delusive hope] on the people of America." The people would have no representation in the chief executive, and with no limitation that executive should be expected to serve for life.[67]

The powers of the President also received substantial critique. George Mason worried about the danger of a President leading the army in person, as well as the absence of an executive council to hold the President in check. The pardoning power would merely enable the President to protect those who do his (perhaps illegal) bidding. The President could govern through treaties, as long as he had enough allies in states near the capital; the vote could be taken with a minimal quorum before Senators from further states could even arrive. These treaties could go so far as to cede territory to a foreign power; thus could a President undermine the unity and stability of the union itself. The Vice-President, too, was deemed dangerous; the position was described as "not only an unnecessary but a dangerous officer."[68]

Monroe, Grayson, and Henry all critiqued the impeachment process as well. Grayson asked his fellow delegates, "How will you punish him if he abuse his power? Will you call him before the Senate? They are his counsellors and partners in crimes." Henry called the impeachment process "a mere sham—a mere farce. When they do anything derogatory to the honor or interest of their country, they are to try themselves!" This is no defense against potential tyranny. The only protection here is the assumption that America's rulers will not overstep their clearly stated powers into the realm of implication. Mason urged caution and deliberation: "We have it in our power to secure our liberties and happiness on the most unshaken, firm, and permanent basis.—We can establish what Government we please.—But by that paper we are consolidating the United States into one great Government, and trusting to constructive security."[69] This is protecting rights through limiting powers, a clear synthesis of the two primary opposition arguments.

The federal courts were to be even more dangerous than the President. Each of the Anti-Federalist leaders took some shots at this article. Mason led off, asking, "what is there left to the State Courts? Will Gentlemen be pleased, candidly, fairly, and without sophistry, to shew us what remains? There is no limitation. It goes to every thing." Patrick Henry continued his crusade against tyranny: "I have already expressed painful sensations at the surrender of our great rights, and I am again driven to the mournful recollection," he opined. "The purse is gone—The sword is gone—and here is the only thing of any importance which is to remain with us." He called this section "a more fatal defect than any we have yet considered. . . . In what a situation will your Judges be in," he asked, "when they are sworn to preserve the Constitution of the State, and of the General Government? If there be a concurrent dispute between them, which will prevail? They cannot serve two masters struggling for the same object." The Supremacy Clause demanded that the judges obey the federal Constitution when there is a conflict. "The Judiciary are the sole protection against a tyrannical execution of laws. But if by this system we lose our Judiciary, and they cannot help us, we must sit down quietly, and be oppressed." The Supreme Court, Grayson argued, "has more power than any Court under Heaven."[70]

The attacks also extended to the issue of jury trials. Grayson worried that if there were juries in federal trials, they may be drawn from anywhere in the state; they might be strangers rather than neighbors. For the Anti-Federalists, juries were not enough; they must be juries from the vicinage, with trials held as locally as possible, otherwise the right to a jury was effectively gone. As usual, for Henry this turns into a first step to tyranny: "When Congress, in all the plenitude of their arrogance, magnificence, and power, can take it [the right to a trial by jury] from you, will you be satisfied?—Are we to go so far as to concede every thing to the virtue of Congress? Throw yourselves at once on their mercy—Be no longer free, then their virtue will predominate."[71] If his fellow Virginians are prepared to give up their judicial rights along with the powers of the purse and the sword, they will have nothing left to give.

While the Federalists, most memorably Edmund Pendleton and John Marshall, defended the judiciary with lawyerly arguments and precise legal definitions of terms, Patrick Henry, never one to quibble over legal precision, fell back on decidedly populist rhetoric. "Poor people do not understand technical terms—Their rights ought to be secured in language of which they know the meaning," insisted Henry. "A Constitution," he added later, "ought to be like a beacon, held up to the public eye so as to be understood by every man." Grayson too lamented the imprecise and uncertain language of the document, despite the Federalist lawyers' explanations, noting that "he did not believe there existed a social compact upon the face of the earth, so vague, and so indefinite, as the one now on the table." Even Edmund Randolph criticized the extent of the Court's jurisdiction, lamenting that it was not made more specific, and that appeals may be made on fact as well as law. The Federalists were not impressed. "The Gentleman, Sir, means to frighten us by his bugbears and hobgoblings—his sale of lands to pay taxes—Indian purchases, and other horrors," said Adam Stephen of Berkeley County, in response to Henry. "If the Gentleman does not like this Government," he suggested, "let him go and live among the Indians." Stephen even offered to teach Henry the language of the natives. Henry did not take him up on the offer.[72]

13

Anti-Federalists of New York

As Virginia's convention turned to Article II, with the outcome still in doubt, the convention in New York began. As in most of the other states, a prominent political leader was chosen as president of the convention; what was different here from every prior convention is that it was an Anti-Federalist, Governor George Clinton, who was selected. The Anti-Federalists held a clear advantage in numbers in the convention, and they were at least equal to the Federalists in the caliber of their leadership. Despite these disadvantages, though, John Jay was hopeful. "There is much Reason to believe that the Majority of the Convention of this State will be composed of anti fœderal Characters," he wrote to Washington, "but it is doubtful whether the Leaders will be able to govern the Party." Jay found hope in the idea that many of the Anti-Federalists were moderates who would likely accept an amended Constitution, and who might be convinced to ratify with recommended amendments. In Virginia, there were Federalists who were for amendments; in New York, there were Anti-Federalists who were for ratification. "The greater Number" of the opposition, Jay explained to Washington near the end of June, were "averse to a vote of Rejection—some would be content with recommendatory amendments—others wish for explanatory ones to settle Constructions which they think doubtful—others would not be satisfied with less than absolute and previous amendments; and I am mistaken if there be not a few Who prefer a Separation from the Union to any national Government whatever." The Federalists merely needed to win over the first two groups to frustrate the hopes of the latter two.[1]

Initially, the heterogeneity of the opposition presented no problem. Early in the convention, James Hughes fully expected victory. "Unanimity and Harmony reigns among the Anties," he wrote to John Lamb, "the Promptitude with which they assembled—their Concurrence in Sentiment and their Determination to bend their Force to the same Point are the highest Evidences thereof—and shut out the Shadow of Hope, in the Federalists, of creating Divisions."[2] There was clearly some ideological cohesion among the opposition, and the Anti-Federalists in New York were organized to an extent not seen elsewhere. They had a clear leader in Clinton, and the Governor delegated to John Lamb the responsibility of coordinating with other states, and to Melancton Smith the important role of getting New York's opposition into line. These efforts really showed in the smashing victory in the convention elections. Further organization efforts were needed, though; apparently the opposition did not develop a clear plan for what to do with the Constitution. It appears that they never intended to simply reject it outright, but no one knew for sure exactly how amendments would be handled.

The private letters of the Federalists showed decidedly mixed assessments of their opponents, and many were inclined to praise them. In public, though, nothing but disdain was admitted. "A Friend to Order and Peace" accused the opposition of "unworthy principles":

> They are aware that their dignity, importance and emoluments may be sunk by it: And they bawl out against aristocracy, and get the poor unthinking multitude to join them in the cry, only because they now form the aristocracy themselves, and are unwilling to risk a fall from their warm and well feathered nests; which, rather than lose, they would dissolve the confederacy of the states, make us a rope of sand, render us incapable of any exertions for our own preservation and safety, and expose us to civil dissentions and wars, and render us a ready prey to every foreign invader.[3]

This was a typical (and typically inflammatory) critique. The opposition, motivated by such principles, was expected either to see reason, changing their mind after hearing Federalist arguments, or to move out of the way. Abraham Bancker complained of the intransigence of the "stiffnecked and refractory" Anti-Federalists, writing that they "have come here, not to hear at leisure and with deliberation a fair and ample discussion of the Constitution . . . but they have come here for the express purpose, and with a manifest Intention, either to reject the proposed Constitution, or what is the same in effect, not to embrace it, but upon their own Conditions."[4] This is a typical example of Federalist arrogance and hypocrisy; the proponents of the Constitution, of course, being on the *correct* side of the issue, had no need to listen to argument or consider changing their positions. The Federalists could scarcely fathom such unwillingness to compromise. Contrary to this description, however, the New York opposition was in fact as flexible as that of any state, with many members reversing position to accept unconditional ratification with proposed amendments. The eventual conduct of the state convention makes this very clear. Still, many leading Federalists wanted conversion, not compromise.

The Federalists were prepared to fight. Alexander Hamilton spearheaded an impressive and determined Federalist minority, after penning most of the most erudite, comprehensive, and clear defense of the Constitution. George Clinton paid Hamilton a backhanded compliment on his debate performance, which echoed his writings on the Constitution; Clinton referred to the former as "a second Edition of Publius, well delivered." In a later letter to John Lamb, he mockingly refers to Hamilton as "the little Great Man," who is "employed in repeating over Parts of Publius to us." Still Clinton never denied Hamilton's effectiveness. Hamilton did not single-handedly win the debate, or convince wavering Anti-Federalists to support ratification, but he did present the strongest and most cogent arguments for ratification in the convention.[5]

Outside of the convention, the people of New York, like those of Pennsylvania, were passionate and divided to the point of violence. There was an air of danger surrounding the state's debates. The *New York Morning Post* on June 17 reported that "the rage of party, relating to the new Constitution, has rose to an alarming height, in some of the counties in this state; that several bloody affrays had taken place in consequence thereof, in one of which, it is said, a Col. Hartshorn, of Fishkill, lost his life."[6] A Fourth of July celebration in Albany turned into a riot, with Federalists and Anti-Federalists fighting over the Constitution, resulting in injuries on both sides. Abraham Lansing, while not denying Anti-Federalist culpability for the riot, insisted in a letter "that the quarrel . . . was unintentional on our side—and would not have happened had our Friends and their antagonists not been heated with Liquor." The violence was nonetheless alarming, though; "what madness! what strange infatuation!" wrote John Henry Livingston, "what will be the end!" Not every Fourth of July celebration ended in such a way, though. In Dutchess County the Anti-Federalists were firmly in control. A gathering in Fredericksburgh drank thirteen toasts, including to Governor Clinton along with General Washington, as well as the Federal Farmer and the Plebian. The toasts also celebrated annual elections, and that the Constitution "be so amended as to secure freedom to the citizens of the United States, and give sufficient energy to government." Such peaceful protests were far more common, despite the supercharged political atmosphere.[7]

There was talk of sedition and secession as well. Rumors were rampant that the city of New York would split off and join New Jersey in the union while the rest of the state fended for itself. Others believed that the city, or part of it, might well join Connecticut instead or form a new state entirely. Even before the Constitution approached its requisite adoption by nine states, when the idea of separate confederacies looked like a real possibility, one newspaper contended that "Staten-Island, from its fœderalism and contiguity to New-Jersey, will abandon New-York, and cling to the confederacy, whether great or small, to which New-Jersey belongs." Another writer believed that the seceding area would include "Long Island, Staten-Island, York-Island, and Westchester county," a section that "pays about one half the taxes of the whole State." These were all just speculation, though; Theophilus Parsons points out that "no evidence has been uncovered by either the Clintonians or modern historians to prove that the Federalists ever engaged in a separatist plot." Linda Grant DePauw observes that "If there was a serious secession movement in New York City it was a remarkably quiet one." The idea was nonetheless discussed by prominent Federalists, though only in vague terms, as "something [they] believed was threatening, but which [they], personally, had no part in." Furthermore, not a single Anti-Federalist seems to have mentioned it as an issue, suggesting it must not have been an especially serious concern, though it was at least plausible.[8]

Peaceful compromise looked more likely than secession. Earlier in the summer, the opposition was publicly contemplating amending rather than rejecting the Constitution. "Indeed no sincere friend to this country can ever wish to see it organized and executed without amendments," wrote "A Spectator," "for in that case it may justly be expected, that in less than twenty years it would be equally as arbitrary and despotick as that of the republic of Venice. . . . The four states, who will and ought to reject the constitution as it now stands, together with the powerful minority of some of these states who have adopted it, will compel the new Congress" to make amendments, or risk armed resistance from disgruntled Anti-Federalists. The question was whether those amendments should be conditions attached to ratification, or whether New York would follow the model of Massachusetts. Alexander Hamilton was sufficiently confident that the opposition was prepared to accept the latter that he suggested as much to Anti-Federalist leader Abraham Yates in May. Yates replied that they would not "be guilty of such an absurdity." An alternative to conditional ratification was brewing in the state, however, hinted at by a "Gentleman from New York," in the *Independent Gazetteer*. "Why in the name of common sense," he asked, "did not those seven states [that already ratified the Constitution] prescribe limits, by fixing a period to its duration?" This was to become the prevailing plan of the state's opposition.[9]

The stakes were high as the convention approached, and the outcome was uncertain despite the Anti-Federalist advantage in delegates. The *Hudson Weekly Gazette* insisted that the decision was reducible to two questions, First, Is a national government necessary at all, or, is not the state of New-York able by itself to remain a separate state, distinct from and unconnected with the other state in the union? Secondly, If union is necessary, upon what terms and by what form of government is that union to be preserved? Is the one offered adapted to that purpose or what better can be devised?

The opposition, of course, stood by the idea that the Constitution was inadequate, but the alternatives were not really clear. The *Gazette* expected the Anti-Federalists to unveil such an alternative course. "If the constitution is so distorted and deformed as they pretend, let them . . . instead of mending, make a new one." With no such plan forthcoming, the *Gazette* insisted that the question "is now reduced to this single point—whether we shall unite with the other states in adopting this new form of government, or separate ourselves entirely from them?"[10]

THE FEDERALIST MINORITY

The beginning of the convention saw the Federalists in a difficult position. Had the Anti-Federalists then called for an immediate vote, Governor Clinton could probably have mustered the majority required to reject the Constitution outright. But this was not the goal of the opposition, who saw continental support for the proposed government; they knew that the more prudent course was to insist on changes. This required a full discussion, and the suggestion of amendments along the way. The Federalists too favored a full debate, believing that their only chance was to hear favorable news from New Hampshire and Virginia before the New York Convention made its decision. When Chancellor Livingston rose on the first day of debate to give an hour-long speech about the necessity of adopting the new frame of government, it is doubtful that many delegates were swayed at all, but when he closed with a proposal that the convention discuss the Constitution by clause and not vote on anything until the discussion was completed there was no resistance. Both sides saw such a procedure as necessary.

The opposition in New York, despite its big majority, was also in a tough spot. It was clear by the start of the convention that the Constitution would be ratified by nine states and go into effect, so the real question was whether New York would rejoin the union on these terms, try to set its own, or strike out on its own as an independent nation. For all intents and purposes, the Articles of Confederation were dead, despite John Lansing's rather glowing endorsement and his assertion that the existing Congress "could be vested with a power to raise men and money," and that that would make it a viable national government.[11]

The problem, of course, was that the terms of the Constitution were unacceptable. Too much power was to be shifted to the national government, and there would be insufficient safeguards for individual rights. Melancton Smith undoubtedly spoke for many of his colleagues in saying that "he was disposed to make every reasonable concession, and indeed to sacrifice every thing for a Union, except the liberties of his country, than which he could contemplate no greater misfortune. But he hoped we were not reduced to the necessity of sacrificing or even endangering our liberties to preserve the Union. If that was the case, the alternative was dreadful." The government was simply too ambitious; "the superstructure," Smith explained, "is infinitly too large for the foundation."[12]

Governor Clinton made the argument for small government close to the people as effectively as anyone in the convention, noting that in such governments, "mal-administration is easily corrected, and designs unfavorable to liberty frustrated and punished." In larger republics, such small infractions tend to go unnoticed. Clinton spoke in a decidedly conciliatory manner, like Smith. "I am open to conviction," he said, "and if my objections can be removed, I shall be ready frankly to acknowledge their weakness." He was immediately attacked by Hamilton as hostile to national government, to which he replied that Hamilton "may wish for a consolidated—I wish for a federal republic. The object of both of us is a firm energetic government: and we may both have the good of our country in view; though we disagree as to the means of procuring it. It is not fair reasoning," he continued, "to infer that a man wants no government at all, because he attempts to qualify it so as to make it safe and easy."[13]

The Constitution, as the opposition saw it, was consolidated rather than federal, undermining the very idea of popular local control over magistrates. Smith noted that Livingston had essentially admitted that the Constitution was a plan of consolidation. "He hoped the gentleman would be complaisant enough to exchange names with those who disliked the Constitution," Smith observed wryly, "as it appeared from his own concession that they were Federalists, and those who advocated it Anti-Federalists."[14] A proper sense of federalism was not the only thing missing, either; Smith found the Constitution deficient in republican principles.

The issue was, in a word, aristocracy, and that nascent aristocracy was to be centered in the Senate. The Senators, suggested Gilbert Livingston, would become rather comfortable in the federal capital, far from the prying eyes of their constituents. "In this Eden, will they reside, with their families, distant from the observation of the people," he explained. "In such a situation, men are apt to forget their dependence—lose their sympathy, and contract selfish habits. . . . The senators will associate only with men of their own class; and thus become strangers to the condition of the common people." Melancton Smith repeatedly emphasized this theme. Representatives, he argued, ought to be primarily members of the middling classes, the yeomanry, who are more likely to show restraint and economy when making laws and spending money. Such men are likely to be much better acquainted with the particular situations of their countrymen, an especially important consideration when considering what types of taxes to levy. The wealthy, on the other hand, who form a natural aristocracy, will lack the proper sympathy, and will be freer with the public funds. The goal ought to be to establish government built on republican principles, something that the Federalists have rejected "as chimerical and such as ought to be expelled from society," according to Smith. "Who would have thought ten years ago, that the very men who risqued their lives and fortunes in support of republican principles, would now treat them as the fictions of fancy?" Republicanism requires that power be given slowly and carefully, because generally the people "cannot take Power back" once it is given.[15]

On the twenty-third of June, Robert Livingston fired back against Smith. "The honorable gentleman from Dutchess," he said sardonically, "who has so copiously declaimed against all declamation, has pointed his artillery against the rich and the great." If the wealthy and educated are not to be elected representatives, he asks, "who, in the name of common sense, will he have to represent us? Not the rich; for they are sheer aristocrats. Not the learned, the wise, the virtuous, for they are all aristocrats. Who then? Why, those who are not virtuous; those who are not wise; those who are not learned: These are the men, to whom alone we can trust our liberties." Although several observers claimed that Livingston got the best of Smith in this exchange, it is hard to draw that conclusion from the printed debates. Smith was quick to counterattack: "I have heard nothing to day, which has not been suggested before," he said, on a day on which Livingston had so far dominated the debate, "except the polite reprimand I have received for my declamation." Livingston's attacks, he said, mean little, because "[w]hen he attempts to explain my ideas, he explains them away to nothing; and instead of answering, he distorts, and then sports with them." No doubt Livingston was the more impressive orator, but he comes across as an immature bully while Smith seems reasonable and conciliatory; justice is clearly on Smith's side when he claims that his position has been "grossly misrepresented."

Smith was drawing a fine distinction between two concepts that we would today identify as plutocracy and meritocracy; as Saul Cornell explains, "Antifederalists like Smith were most concerned about the dangers of an aristocracy of wealth, power, and privilege. The problem of an aristocracy of talent was hardly an issue."[16]

Livingston probably did not much help the Federalist cause by his hostile rhetoric, but John Jay's more reasonable approach may have undone the damage. In responding to Smith, Jay actually called on Smith in the convention to correct him if he had misinterpreted Smith's point. When Smith offered an explanation, Jay amended his argument to address what Smith said. He closed his speech with the assertion that "I argue from plain facts—Here is no sophistry; no construction; no false glosses, but simple inferences from the obvious operation of things. We did not come here to carry points."[17]

Jay was even more important to the Federalists in private discussions than he was in the public debate. The Federalists were doing what they could to sway the more moderate Anti-Federalists, and here Jay's diplomatic touch was undoubtedly effective. Charles Tillinghast reported to John Lamb on June 21 that "[Hamilton], the Chancellor [Livingston], & Mr. Jay are continually singling out the Members in Opposition (when out of Convention) and conversing with them on the subject. The latter's manners and mode of address would probably do much mischeif, were the members not as firm as they are." In order to prevent such influence, writes DePauw, the Anti-Federalists took "defensive measures," which "consisted chiefly in segregating themselves strictly from the Federalist members of the convention."[18]

Tillinghast's confidence was not warranted; the majority in opposition to the Constitution was already eroding, largely thanks to Jay's efforts. Jay was probably the crucial figure for the Federalist side, not Hamilton; his conciliatory efforts in and out of the convention helped establish a safe moderate position for ratification with recommended amendments.

CONSIDERING AMENDMENTS

Until circumstances forced their hand, however, the opposition was not prepared to take the conciliatory option of ratification with recommended amendments. The Anti-Federalists' first choice was to set the terms under which New York would ratify, and for most of them this meant conditional amendments. The convention discussed a long list of possible changes. To achieve more effective representation in the House of Representatives, Smith proposed doubling its size, so each member could have fewer constituents and the body as a whole could be less susceptible to corruption. Samuel Jones suggested that Congress not be permitted to exercise its power in Article I, Section 4, to regulate elections unless a state should prove unable or unwilling to establish such regulations. Smith wanted to add a clause stating that each state shall be divided into districts for electing members of the House, with a majority of votes determining the winner in each such district.[19] Lansing also proposed that members of Congress be ineligible to any appointed office during their term.

The Senate, too, saw its share of debate. Gilbert Livingston proposed that Senators be ineligible for immediate reelection and be subject to recall by the state legislatures. The latter idea was defended by Lansing, who argued that "if it was the design of the plan to make the senate a kind of bulwark to the independence of the states; and a check to the encroachments of the general government; certainly the members of this body ought to be peculiarly under the controul, and in strict subordination to the state who delegated them." Lansing attributed the absence of corruption in the Confederation to the threat of recall, which kept delegates in Congress from overstepping their authority. Melancton Smith also supported this change. "When a state sends an agent commissioned to transact any business, or perform any service," he said the next day, "it certainly ought to have a power to recall him." This would provide an added protection to the states without significantly undermining the stability or effectiveness of the Senate.[20]

This point became a significant argument for the Anti-Federalists, as it was an opportunity to paint the Federalists as antidemocratic. The Senate was designed to protect the states, but this proposal to better protect them was decried by the Federalists as an invitation to mob rule. The inconsistency here suggested that the defenders of the Constitution were merely paying lip service to the states and the people. The true intention was to marginalize the states, and centralize power far from the people. The proliferation of appointed offices and the extreme independence of the Senators made the Constitution truly undemocratic and dangerous as written. This was the general theme of the opposition here, that the powers given to the proposed government would permit the growth of an aristocracy of the rich and powerful. But the problem was not wealth; it was wealth connected to political power. The wealthy could not dominate the poor except through the power of a strong central government, and the Constitution would give them this. Here was the point on which the Federalists, even when Chancellor Livingston was not implicitly reaffirming it in his haughty speeches, simply could not convince the opposition. It would not be the arguments of the Federalists but the circumstances of ratification that would swing enough opposition votes to secure ratification in New York.

It was the powers of Congress that saw the most debate. Article I, Section 8, inspired many amendments from the opposition here, starting with the tax power. "The command of the revenues of a state," John Williams contended, "gives the command of every thing in it. He that hath the purse, will have the sword; and they that have both, have every thing." To curb this excessive power, he proposed an amendment barring Congress from taxing any domestic manufactures, levying direct taxes unless the impost and excise are insufficient, or assessing direct taxes before attempting requisitions. This would have added limitations to a power overly broad. Melancton Smith insisted that the powers of Congress must be "precisely defined" and that power must be balanced to "preserve harmony" among the various parts of the system, meaning the states and the national government. An unlimited power to tax, even apart from the other powers, upsets this balance; "all governments," he insisted, "find a use for as much money as they can raise." The fact that the system of requisitions under the Articles did not work perfectly (though Smith insisted that it worked reasonably well) does not justify granting such an extremely open-ended power as the Constitution would give Congress. Even worse, it was not clear whether the states would be left any ability to levy taxes. The Federalists never convinced their opponents to accept their interpretation that the power was concurrent, or that such concurrent powers were wise. "Concurrent Jurisdictions are dangerous," George Clinton argued; "they ought as far as possible to be avoided— they may and in all probability will endanger the peace and harmony of the union. They involve the political absurdity of imperium in imperio, so destructive to every idea of good gov[ernmen]t." Instead, the opposition wanted to see most revenue sources left exclusively to the states, with some given exclusively to the national government. As Melancton Smith quipped, "the state governments ought to hold the purse, to keep people's hands out of it."[21]

The tax power was only the beginning of the objections to the powers of Congress. Lansing proposed that a two-thirds vote be required to borrow money, with Smith insisting that such a change would be to "restrain [Congress] from running you in Debt or running you into War & devastation." Lansing also wanted a two-thirds requirement for keeping a standing army in times of peace. Jones proposed that Congress may not establish highways or post roads in any state without the state's consent. Smith advocated that the states retain more control over the militia, including the right to refuse to permit the militia to be marched out of the state. He also suggested removing the clause giving Congress exclusive jurisdiction over a capital, but he did not formally propose an amendment. Thomas Tredwell opposed any power to lay a capitation tax. Finally, Lansing proposed a change to the Necessary and Proper Clause: "Provided, that no power shall be exercised by Congress, but such as is expressly given by this constitution; and all other powers, not expressly given, shall be reserved to the respective states, to be by them exercised." The last several sections of Article I saw a few revisions as well: the prohibition of ex post facto laws was not to apply to efforts to recover debts owed to the United States, Congress was to report receipts and expenditures to the public at least annually, and Congress was to approve of no titles of nobility for anyone holding office under the United States.[22]

The primary problem with the powers of Congress was their open-ended nature. "The legislature is the highest power in a government," explained John Williams; "whatever they judge necessary for the proper administration of the powers lodged in them, they may execute without any check or impediment." If this was not clear in principle, then the final clause of Section 8 left no doubt. Such an indeterminate grant of power left open the possibility of all kinds of abuses. "Ingenious men may assign ingenious reasons for opposite constructions of the same clause," he continued. "They may heap refinement upon refinement and subtilty upon subtilty, until they construe away every republican principle, every right sacred and dear to man." Therefore, "[n]o . . . important point should be left to doubt and construction."[23]

If Congress could claim broad powers by implication, it left little power to the states. This was a significant problem because the Anti-Federalists saw the states as an integral part of a federal republic rather than as subordinate administrative units. The idea was to effectively divide and enumerate powers, to prevent friction between the two levels of government. Robert Livingston's contention that the state and national governments are "both supreme," the former over "internal and domestic objects" and the latter over "national objects," was rejected out of hand as absurd.[24] This is perhaps the way the Constitution *should* be, but the vague language and emphasis on concurrent jurisdictions undermined it.

Article II saw fewer proposed amendments than Article I, all coming from Melancton Smith. He proposed that the President serve for seven years, and be ineligible for reelection, as was originally agreed to in the Philadelphia Convention. He also advocated that the President not command the military in person, and not be permitted to pardon treason. He proposed an amendment creating a council to advise the President, and to approve the appointment of officers. Finally, Smith suggested that all commissions be in the name of the United States, rather than the President.

Samuel Jones took the lead on Article III, offering nearly a dozen resolutions to change the judiciary. He wanted Congress to create only appellate courts, with exceptions for enforcing admiralty laws and punishing piracy. The national and state governments, he explained, "should be made to harmonize with & support each other—therefore Jurisdiction in the first Instance should be committed to the State Courts." Otherwise, the two judiciaries will engage in "Continual Squabbles . . . until one Court swallows the other." His other amendments mostly dealt with jurisdiction, protecting the states, as well as citizens in many cases, from being sued in federal courts; the jurisdiction of the courts was not to be "increased, enlarged, or extended by any fiction, collusion, or mere suggestion." Perhaps the most interesting proposal was to allow an effective appeal from decisions of the Supreme Court: when an individual harmed by the decision should request it, the President may establish a commission to investigate, empowered with the right to overturn all or part of the Supreme Court's decision. This commission was to be appointed by the President, with the consent of the Senate. Jones insisted that it was dangerous to have no means of overturning a bad decision by the Supreme Court.[25]

Articles IV and V escaped censure, but Lansing wanted to change the Supremacy Clause in Article VI. He proposed that no treaty should supersede the constitution of any state, or contradict a law of the United States. Smith followed up with a modification to the oath of office, requiring that magistrates agree not to infringe upon the state constitutions. After the entire Constitution had been read, a few miscellaneous amendments were introduced. Tredwell wanted a two-thirds vote to declare war. Smith offered a detailed amendment preventing Congress from establishing special privileges, such as immunity from taxes or prosecution, for the residents of the federal district. He also suggested that Congress be prevented from granting monopolies. Finally, to close out the proposed amendments, Lansing formally proposed a bill of rights to be inserted before Article I. This proposal seems almost an afterthought in the context of the convention, as most of the opposition was of the Power Anti-Federalist variety, but it was a nod to national unity and incorporating the objections of the other states. The Rights and Power Anti-Federalist positions were not as effectively merged here as in Virginia, but both factored into discussions of how to fix the Constitution.

14

The Constitution Ratified

WHILE THE VIRGINIA DELEGATES were discussing the presidency and the convention in New York was settling its rules of debate, in New Hampshire the ratifying convention reconvened after four months of political maneuvering. In Pennsylvania the opposition had been ambushed; in Connecticut they were bullied; in Massachusetts they fell victim to persuasion as well as the defection of Samuel Adams, a man who they believed to be staunchly in their camp. In New Hampshire they were simply outmaneuvered, and the Federalists managed to pull victory from the jaws of defeat. Lynn Warren Turner observes that the records from the two state conventions suggest that "the leaders on both sides were more skilled in parliamentary tactics than in constitutional theory," but the Federalists seem to have had the advantage in both. In February the votes were there to defeat the Constitution, and several members who were wavering were bound by instructions from their constituents to oppose ratification. Although the Anti-Federalists put in some effort to maintain their majority into June, their efforts were not enough, in part because the Federalists were far busier. "They had a product to sell," explains Lawrence Straus, "and used all the means at their disposal to save the Constitution."[1] The media campaign was intense, but one-sided; the Federalists controlled all of the newspapers. Straus describes the campaign:

> Letter after letter promised Federalist victories in North and South Carolina, Virginia, and New York to be won by America's " . . . heroes, philosophers, and patriots . . . her best blood," over " . . . a few hypocrites and old tories . . . ," whose influence extended " . . . especially in the backcounties where the people are very illiterate and have little or no information on the subject."[2]

In the words of Forrest McDonald, the Federalists "sought to persuade not through reason but through ignorance, through influence and rumor and fear." There was little the Anti-Federalists could do against the onslaught except hold their ground. In this they were largely successful, primarily through personal and direct campaigning among the people, though the Federalists managed to chip away just enough at the support for the opposition.[3]

To begin with, the Federalists managed to get one town, Hopkinton, to rescind its instructions for its delegate to oppose ratification. They also managed to get several new Federalist delegates elected from towns previously unrepresented, and others who missed the first session to attend the second.[4] The proponents of ratification were only able to obtain marginal improvements, however; the vast majority of Anti-Federalist delegates and towns were intransigent. "It is evident," writes Albert Stillman Batchellor, "that four months of discussion, agitation, and review of all the arguments for and against the constitution made few changes in the status of the towns on this great question." The apparent refusal of many towns to rescind instructions (since more than one delegate must have requested such a change) reflects "a fixedness of conviction that is worthy of admiration and respect." The Federalists certainly did not see it this way, but they did manage to add to their numbers. They also apparently managed to subtract from their opponents' numbers, as several Anti-Federalist delegates were absent when the convention reconvened. The proponents of the Constitution were able to further their cause on the first day of the second session, as each contested election that came before the convention was decided in favor of the Federalist candidate, including one that replaced a hostile delegate to the first session, Aaron Allen of Walpole, with Federalist Benjamin Bellows. A few votes were all the Federalists really needed; they dared not hope for an overwhelming victory, just a victory. Delegate Pierce Long reported that the Federalists were "determined to take the question—when we saw a probability of obtaining it—if by a majority of one only." That majority was not quite there initially, but they knew they were close.[5]

Facing these changes favoring the Federalist cause, Joshua Atherton made one final push against the Constitution. On June 19, he attempted to reopen the entire debate, stating (perhaps threatening?) that "he only considered his former observations as an introduction to what he had yet to offer." Despite Federalist efforts to move directly to the discussion of proposed amendments, the convention relented and allowed Atherton to make his case again. He then launched into an extensive list of objections, only a few of which were included in the *New Hampshire Spy*'s account, because "the whole of them would nearly fill this paper."[6] This speech drew only brief Federalist responses before the convention turned to amendments. Atherton was not finished yet, though. When the proposed amendments were reported by the committee assigned to write them, he moved for a conditional ratification of both Constitution and amendments. When the Federalists managed to postpone the consideration of the motion (indefinitely, as it turned out), Atherton tried for adjournment, ostensibly so that the people of New Hampshire might have the opportunity to look at the amendments. This gambit also failed, as he undoubtedly knew it would. The Anti-Federalists were simply overmatched, but Atherton left no option untried.

In the end, the vote was more firmly for ratification than either side probably expected,[7] and the opposition, as in Massachusetts, "expressed their determination to return home and use their endeavours to induce the people to live quietly under the new government." Atherton was not persuaded; instead, writing to John Lamb shortly after the vote, he lashed out at the Federalists, minimizing the importance of their victory and attacking their tactics. Their small, ten-vote majority, he said, "gave them but little Cause of Triumph," especially since the most prestigious leaders of the state were virtually all in favor of ratification. "I believe it will be conceded by all," he continued, "that they did not carry their Point by Force of Argument and Discussion; but by other Means, which were it not for the Depravity of the humane Heart, would be viewed with the warmest Sentiments of Disapprobation."[8] Nonetheless, it was a crucial victory for the Federalists, no matter how close the vote.

VIRGINIA BECOMES
THE TENTH PILLAR

With New Hampshire's ratification, the Constitution had its necessary nine states, though it would have been an odd union indeed without Virginia, North Carolina, and New York; it would have existed in three unconnected parts with substantial gaps. In Virginia, the delegates were unaware that New Hampshire had acted so quickly upon reconvening; they made their own decision on ratification without knowing that they would be the tenth state rather than the ninth. And the final outcome was not yet known, even the day before the crucial votes. The "undecided delegates continued to plague the vote-counters until the very end." "The final question is likely to be decided by a very small majority," wrote Madison on June 24. "I do not know that either party despairs absolutely." The Anti-Federalists were still fighting, in the press as well as the convention. On June 19, "Independent" observed that the state convention was evenly divided, but insisted that "a great majority of this Commonwealth is in the opposition," and if the Constitution should be ratified, it will "be consigned to those bitter reflections which are the certain harbingers of misery and despair. What can you promise to yourselves," he asked the delegates, "from precipitating your country into a *step* that at present can answer no valuable purposes, but may, on the other hand, be attended with the depravation of that darling liberty, in support of which such a host of heroes have *bled* and died?" The writer concluded with a cogent question: "Can that mode of government be good," he asked, "which so much divides the free and independent citizens of this Republic?"[9]

Meanwhile, in the convention, Patrick Henry was far from finished. He spoke with the assurance of a man who knew his cause was both just and popular, and with the conviction of a man who would take the same stand even if he stood alone. Still, he sensed a convention majority lining up against him, despite what the people of Virginia might think, and he fell back on the principles of the Revolution: "Old as I am, it is probable I may yet have the appellation of rebel," he proudly proclaimed on June 20. "I trust that I shall see Congressional oppressions crushed in embryo. As this Government stands, I despise and abhor it."[10] Clearly he meant to stand by his earlier statement that he would oppose ratification even if twelve and a half states had already adopted.

The Federalists intended to finish the Virginia Convention on the Massachusetts model of recommendatory amendments. On June 24, George Wythe offered such a proposal, including a prefatory statement defending the rights of the people. "No right," it read, "can be cancelled, abridged, restrained or modified" by any part of the new government; it specifically included "liberty of conscience and of the press," but although it suggested the importance of protecting rights it did not offer a specific bill of rights. Henry objected to this form of ratification because "it admits that the new system is defective, and most capitally."[11] To call for immediate amendments suggests as much, and to accept such a flawed frame of government is foolish. The danger the proposed government presented to Virginia was very real; the property of Virginia, and especially that in slaves, was threatened. Members of Congress

> will search that paper, and see if they have power of manumission.—
> And have they not, Sir?—Have they not power to provide for the general defence and welfare?—May they not think that these call for the abolition of slavery?—May they not pronounce all slaves free, and will they not be warranted by that power? . . . As much as I deplore slavery, I see that prudence forbids its abolition. . . . In this situation,

I see a great deal of the property of the people of Virginia in jeopardy, and their peace and tranquillity gone away. . . . This is a local matter, and I can see no propriety in subjecting it to Congress.[12]

Henry's alternative proposal was conditional ratification with prior amendments. If nothing else, Virginia should insist on a bill of rights. "If you will in the language of freemen, stipulate, that there are rights which no man under Heaven can take from you," Henry told the delegates, "you shall have me going along with you:—Not otherwise. . . . The Government unaltered may be terrible to America; but can never be loved, till it be amended." The Federalists insisted that it was arrogant for Virginia to insist that her sister states agree to amendments, but Henry was unmoved. "Have we not a right to say, *hear our propositions?*" he asked. "Why, Sir, your slaves have a right to make their humble requests. Those who are in the meanest occupations of human life, have a right to complain." He suggested that amendments be approved and sent to the other states for their approval prior to Virginia's ratification.[13]

Edmund Randolph made his position on prior amendments very clear: "nothing but the fear of inevitable destruction, would lead me to vote for the Constitution in spite of the objections I have to it." But this fear of disunion was not the primary motivating factor for most of those who voted for unconditional ratification. The Federalist position in the Virginia Convention is best summed up in a remarkable letter written by convention president Edmund Pendleton to absent Anti-Federalist Richard Henry Lee in the middle of the convention. Lee had expressed hope in an earlier letter that Pendleton would side with the opposition and vote for prior amendments to the Constitution. Pendleton disappointed those hopes. The amendments he wanted to see would "eradicate the *seeds* of future *mischief,*" rather than remove immediate dangers. On the other hand, "certain ruin" will follow dissolution of union, and "Union is only to be preserved by a *Fœdral Energetic* Government, and . . . the Articles of Confederation Possess not an Atom of such a Government." It is hard to imagine a clearer statement of the moderate position taken by Pendleton and Randolph, and undoubtedly by many other delegates. The danger of disunion was more imminent than the danger of abuse of power under the Constitution. Furthermore, insisting on amendments would not be conducive to union: to the states that did not request amendments, Pendleton claimed, Virginia "shall appear w[i]th *Hostile* Countenances, unfavorable to a cordial reception." Pendleton was not overly concerned about rights; he wrote that "I esteem the great *Barriers* of liberty not *violated* in the Plan, tho' I may not think them sufficiently *Secured*." He rejected the idea of a bill of rights, pointing out that there may be a danger in enumerating some rights, because such a list could be interpreted to exclude those rights not listed. Instead, a clause reserving to the states powers not enumerated would be sufficient: "Declare the *Principle*—as more Safe than the *Enumeration*." Further protections can be written into the laws, "thereby admitting of being varied more easily as experience shall require."[14]

Moderates like Pendleton were convinced, and others like Randolph were driven to acquiesce by fear, but most Anti-Federalists were not persuaded. As the vote neared, John Dawson, a little-known delegate from Fredericksburg who was embarking upon what would be an impressive political career, gave a moving speech that summed up much of the opposition feeling in the assembly. He praised the delegates to Philadelphia, and claimed that he was inclined to support their work until he read it; at this point, he "was convinced of this important, though melancholy truth, 'that the greatest men may err,' and that their errors are sometimes of the greatest magnitude." Dawson expressed concern over consolidation, saying that "I shall lament exceedingly, when a confederation of independent States shall be converted into a consolidated Government; for when that event shall happen, I shall consider the history of American liberty as short as it has been brilliant, and we shall afford one more proof to the favorite maxim of tyrants, 'that mankind cannot govern themselves.'" This document would secure neither American liberty nor the principles on which the nation was founded. He invoked the Revolution effectively, contending that "in my humble opinion, had the paper now on your table, and which is so ably supported, been presented to our view ten years ago (when the *American spirit* shone forth in the meridian of glory, and rendered us the wonder of an admiring world) it would have been considered as containing principles incompatible with republican liberty, and therefore doomed to infamy." In the end, Dawson rejected recommended amendments, because without at least a bill of rights prior to ratification the Constitution was simply too dangerous. "I am persuaded, that by adopting it, and then proposing amendments, that unfortunate traveller liberty is more endangered than the Union of the States will be by first proposing these amendments." There were time and opportunity to fix the document before approving it.[15]

William Grayson followed Dawson. He too argued for prior amendments, dismissing the idea that the ratifying states will outright reject Virginia's petitions. "Six or seven states have agreed to it. As it is not their interest to stand by themselves, will they not with open arms receive us?" The union, he implies, is held together primarily by commercial ties: "Tobacco will always make our peace with them." Too many Virginians were prepared to take this precipitous and dangerous step of ratification before amendments; Grayson suspected that this had a great deal to do with the influence of George Washington. He ruminated on the symbolic importance of the general in the debate over the Constitution: "I think that were it not for one great character in America, so many men would not be for this Government. We have one ray of hope—We do not fear while he lives: But we can only expect his *fame* to be immortal. We wish to know, who besides him, can concentrate the confidence and affections of all America?"[16] It is difficult to contest this assertion that Washington's calming presence convinced at least a few people to give the Constitution a try, to undertake the experiment, who otherwise would have opposed ratification. Just a few votes in the state convention, though, would have reversed the tide.

Madison pushed hard for unconditional ratification with recommended amendments. Rather than reiterating the argument that the other states would not acquiesce, he turned to the diversity of Anti-Federalist proposals. "Can it be presumed then, Sir, that Gentlemen in this State, who admit the necessity of changing, should ever be able to unite in sentiments with those who are totally averse to any change?" asks Madison. There are too many competing proposals for the states to agree on any prior amendments. This was a tactical error, and Henry was ready to pounce. When it came to reaching agreement among the states, he suggested, there was no difference between prior and subsequent amendments. "His arguments, great as the Gentleman's abilities are, tend to prove that amendments cannot be obtained after adoption." At least the rights of the people must be secured before the Constitution can be seriously considered.[17]

Henry was prepared to close out the Anti-Federalist opposition in dramatic fashion, making dire predictions about the future of America under the Constitution. Responding to Madison's arguments, he gathered his thoughts for a final dramatic statement that was to be assisted by the weather:

> He tells you of the important blessings which he imagines will result to us and mankind in general, from the adoption of this system—I see the awful immensity of the dangers with which it is pregnant.—I see it—I feel it.—I see *beings* of a higher order anxious concerning our decision. When I see beyond the horrison that binds human eyes, and look at the final consummation of all human things, and see those intelligent beings which inhabit the æthereal mansions, reviewing the political decisions and revolutions which in the progress of time will

happen in America, and the consequent happiness or misery of mankind—I am led to believe that much of the account on one side or the other, will depend on what we now decide. Our own happiness alone is not affected by the event—All nations are interested in the determination. We have it in our power to secure the happiness of one half of the human race. Its adoption may involve the misery of the other hemispheres.[18]

This was an intense conclusion to a powerful performance by a great orator. But the words alone do not convey the scene. The published debates are succinct on this point, perhaps to downplay the drama since the reporter was a known Federalist; immediately following the paragraph above, they read simply "Here a violent storm arose, which put the House in such disorder, that Mr. *Henry* was obliged to conclude." According to a later reminiscence, as Henry invoked the celestial beings,

> a storm, at that instant arose, which shook the whole building, and the spirits whom he had called, seemed to have come at his bidding. Nor did his eloquence, or the storm, immediately cease—but, availing himself of the incident, with a master's art, he seemed to mix in the fight of his ætherial auxiliaries, and "rising on the wings of the tempest, to seize upon the artillery of Heaven, and direct its fiercest thunders against the heads of his adversaries." The scene became insupportable; and the house rose, without the formality of adjournment, the members rushing from their seats with precipitation and confusion.[19]

Since the debates continue with a brief discussion of whether to formally vote on ratification the next day, and then a motion to adjourn, this recollection cannot be entirely accurate. Grigsby fills in some additional details, stating that as the members were about to leave in confusion, "a gleam of sunshine penetrated the hall, and in a few moments every vestige of the tempest was lost in a glorious noon-day of June." With the calmer weather, he says, the delegates resumed their business. The account is surely somewhat exaggerated, but this must have been a dramatic moment, in which it seemed that Henry "had indeed the faculty of calling up spirits from the vasty deep."[20] It was a fitting final push for rejecting the Constitution and insisting on amendments, even though the effort was to fall short.

On June 25, the day of the vote, "the opponents of the Constitution were in a dangerous mood." There were rumors that the Federalists intended to renege on their willingness to support subsequent amendments, just as soon as ratification was secured. There were whispers that the Anti-Federalists might walk out rather than submit to a ratified Constitution. Such an opposition faction would almost certainly have prevented Virginia from taking part in the new government, and may well have triggered civil war. In the aftermath of Henry's dramatic thunderstorm speech, George Nicholas insisted that further debate "will answer no end but to serve the cause of those who wish to destroy the Constitution," and requested a vote on George Wythe's proposal for ratification. John Tyler immediately requested that Henry's alternative proposal be discussed and voted on as well. Benjamin Harrison then took up Henry's cause, calling Wythe's proposal "unwarrantably precipitate, and dangerously impolitic." He pointed out that the small states demanded substantial concessions before agreeing to the Articles of Confederation, so they ought to at least hear and consider the concerns of Virginia now. James Monroe added that "[h]e could not conceive that a conditional ratification would in the most remote degree endanger the Union, for that it was as clearly the interest of the adopting States to be United with Virginia, as it could be her interest to be in Union with them."[21] Again there was this recourse to interests; no state was going to do anything rash just because Virginia had doubts.

John Tyler then unleashed a "fierce and uncompromising assault" against the kinds of amendments the Federalists expressed a willingness to support. Such amendments, he said, "will not alter one dangerous part of it. It contains many dangerous articles. No Gentleman here can give such a construction of it, as will give general satisfaction." Tyler immediately took his argument a step further to defend the status quo: "By our present Government every man is secure in his person, and the enjoyment of his property. There is no man who is not liable to be punished for misdeeds. I ask what is it that disturbs men when liberty is in the highest zenith? Human nature will ever be the same. Men never were, nor ever will be satisfied with their happiness." The proposed Constitution "contains a variety of powers too dangerous to be vested in any set of men whatsoever. . . . Instead of unanimity, it has produced a general diversity of opinions, which may terminate in the most unhappy consequences." The Anti-Federalists, Tyler insisted, were willing to accept the general system contained in the document, but first they wished "to do away ambiguities, and establish our rights on clear and explicit terms. If this be done, we shall be all like one man—we shall unite and be happy."[22]

Henry offered yet another final plea for prior amendments. "The great and direct end of Government is liberty," he said. "Secure our liberties and privileges, and the end of Government is answered. If this be not effectually done, Government is an evil." Certain changes were needed in the structure of the proposed government, but a bill of rights was the most essential need. By this point, Henry had recognized that the tide had turned against him. "If I shall be in the minority," he concluded his final speech, "I shall have those painful sensations, which arise from a conviction of being overpowered in a good cause. Yet I will be a peaceable citizen!—My head, my hand, and my heart shall be at liberty to retrieve the loss of liberty, and remove the defects of that system—in a constitutional way." The Federalists must have been relieved to hear this, as public opposition from the great orator would have been a threat to stability and public safety.[23]

After Henry's speech, and a final plea by Edmund Randolph for history to be kind concerning his motives, all that remained was the votes, and the amendments. Henry's proposal for prior amendments failed by a vote of eighty-eight to eighty. The Constitution was then ratified unconditionally by a vote of eighty-nine to seventy-nine. William Heth reported that "the scene was truly awful & solemn" when the vote was taken. Another observer estimated "upwards of a thousand spectators, with minds agitated by contending and opposite opinions," witnessing "the most grand and solemn [scene] I ever beheld." Above all, the vote was dignified and free of tumult or celebration.[24]

A committee was then appointed to draft amendments; this committee used a draft of amendments prepared by George Mason and others, and advocated by Patrick Henry, as the basis for its proposed amendments. Substantial modifications were made; the resulting amendments contained a full bill of rights and notable changes in the structure of the proposed government. Since the Federalists had a majority on the committee, they could have more sharply limited the proposed amendments if they were all of one mind. Clearly they were not. Some among them must have supported the extensive changes sought by the Anti-Federalist minority, and probably most saw it as a political necessity to recommend sweeping amendments in order to avoid an opposition revolt as happened in several other states. At least two influential Federalist committee members, Edmund Randolph and Paul Carrington, had opposed the Constitution initially.

The bill of rights, included first in the official ratification, was fairly straightforward. Though it was more a statement of principle than a list of potential amendments, half of the twenty statements made it into the eventual Bill of Rights in some form. There was nothing here that was especially controversial, but there was also nothing that represented a substantial limitation of the government established by the Constitution. The twenty amendments, though, were different, in that they represented significant changes to the power and structure of the proposed federal government. Of these, only the first, "That each state in the Union shall respectively retain every power, jurisdiction, and right, which is not by this Constitution delegated to the Congress of the United States, or to the departments of the federal government," would in substance become part of the first ten amendments. Two others, concerning the apportionment of House seats and the compensation of Congressmen, were embodied in the first two formally proposed amendments, which were not ratified at the time. The other seventeen aimed to clarify and limit the powers of Congress and of the government more generally. The most important change was the third amendment on the list:

> When the Congress shall lay direct taxes or excises, they shall immediately inform the Executive power of each State, of the quota of such State according to the census herein directed, which is proposed to be thereby raised; and if the Legislature of any State shall pass a law which shall be effectual for raising such quota at the time required by Congress, the taxes and excises laid by Congress shall not be collected in such State.[25]

The taxing power was widely seen as the most significant power given to Congress, so limiting that power and ensuring state control over the collection of revenue were a high priority for the Anti-Federalists. Apparently it was important to the moderates in convention as well. The Federalists made an effort to strike this amendment from the list, but they could muster only sixty-five votes to do so, with eighty-five delegates voting against the change. This twenty-vote margin was twice the size of the vote to ratify, indicative of the strong agreement among Anti-Federalists and moderates that such a change was warranted.[26] The list of amendments also included requirements of a two-thirds supermajority to pass commercial laws or maintain a standing army in peacetime, that states retain control of their militias and soldiers not be enlisted for more than four years except during war, that the President be limited to two terms before having to spend eight years out of office, that Congress not interfere in state electoral regulations unless the state shall fail to act, and several other comparatively minor changes.[27] These changes combine the Rights and Power Anti-Federalist positions; the bill of rights was extensive and came first, while the amendments included significant structural changes. The Federalists were ultimately forced to concede all of these amendments, because the moderates in the convention wanted to see changes made, and were prepared to side with the Anti-Federalists on those changes now that ratification had been secured. Since all of these amendments were merely recommendatory, though, the price was not more than the Federalists were willing to pay. They were prepared to fight most of these amendments, but for now they would relent because ratification was the first and most important goal.

After the vote to ratify, Stephen Austin expressed a hope that the convention minority might behave as the Massachusetts and South Carolina minorities did, and "shew some disposition to acquiess in what they have so fairly lost." This seems to have been the case. Patrick Henry had already promised peaceful efforts to pursue amendments in the mode prescribed by the Constitution, and the opposition delegates had decided not to continue their public opposition after the convention. The leading Anti-Federalists did in fact acquiesce. There would be no uprising, no effort to disrupt the new Constitution except through the amendment process described therein. James Monroe put a decidedly positive Anti-Federalist spin on his state's ratification, in a letter to Jefferson in Paris. The form of ratification, he contended, "must be consider'd, so far as a reservation of certain rights go, as conditional, with the recommendation of subsequent amendments." The amendments themselves seem to have pleased many of the Anti-Federalists. In early July, William Nelson wrote a lengthy letter to William Short, ruminating on Virginia's proposed amendments. If these amendments are adopted, he wrote, "the mode of trying the president may be esteemed almost the only defect remaining in it." The key question, of course, was whether they would ever be adopted. Not all Anti-Federalists were so content, however. The *Virginia Gazette and Independent Chronicle* on June 28 published an obituary for "Constitutional Liberty." The essay included a stirring account of how the deceased was killed through treachery in the Virginia Convention. The essay closed with the epitaph: "Here lies the blessed body of our CONSTITUTIONAL LIBERTY in hopes of a glorious resurrection."[28]

The Anti-Federalists would have won in Virginia with a change of six votes. Thus it is worthwhile to examine where such votes might have come from; several delegates with serious reservations on the Constitution clearly switched sides either before or during the convention. Edmund Randolph was of course the most prominent, and he has been discussed at some length above. Paul Carrington, also mentioned above, set aside his objections to support ratification, for reasons similar to Randolph's. A newspaper report drawn from a private letter suggested that a delegate named Zephaniah Jackson, "a man of great influence in the back-Counties & esteemed Antifœderal, has warmly joined the fœderal party." The only problem is that there was no delegate by that name in the Virginia Convention. The letter probably mistakenly identified Zachariah Johnston, who voted for ratification.[29] Humphrey Marshall of Fayette County may have disobeyed specific instructions when he voted for ratification; at any rate, he favored amendments when he was elected as a delegate, but he "'became perfectly convinced that *previous amendments*' were unattainable." These represent four votes that the Anti-Federalists lost; two other delegates from Kentucky, who voted for ratification along with Marshall, would have given the opposition a majority. Two elected delegates failed to attend the convention, but these two, according to James Madison, were "known to be divided on the subject" of ratification. There were undoubtedly others, though, who looked at the question as Randolph did, and the potential Anti-Federalist votes were many.[30]

NEW YORK ANTI-FEDERALISTS CONCEDE DEFEAT

Virginia's ratification would finally break the will of the New York Anti-Federalists. The news from New Hampshire, received on the twenty-fourth of June while the New York Convention was still debating the early sections of Article I, had virtually no effect, despite the Federalist insistence that it changed the entire question. "The confederation," insisted Livingston, "was now *dissolved*. The question before the committee, was now a question of policy and expediency." Melancton Smith was not buying this, at least not yet. He replied to Livingston that the news "had not altered his feelings or wishes on the subject. He had long been convinced that nine states would receive the constitution." John Lansing was similarly unaffected. "We acknowledge that our dissent cannot prevent the operation of the government," he said after Smith. "Since nine states have acceded to it, let them make the experiment." One can imagine the Federalists tearing out their hair over this attitude. The convention then resumed its discussion as if none of the states had ratified. The Federalists, frustrated by the nonimpact of New Hampshire, found themselves persistently arguing that the nine states already on board were relevant to New York's decision. Finding few arguments against one of the suggested amendments, James Duane asked, "how do we know the proposal will be agreeable to the other states?" Smith quickly pointed out that such an objection "would go against proposing any amendment at all."[31] Clearly the Federalists were grasping here, unable to swing the debate in their favor. They were left waiting for news from Virginia.

A little over a week later, on July 2, the news came. Now not only had the Constitution been ratified by the requisite number of states, but the largest and most influential state had accepted the Constitution with only recommended amendments. With the news came an even more vehement flurry of amendments by the Anti-Federalists, as well as a change in Federalist strategy. Before the news, the Federalists "disputed every inch of ground," reported Nathanial Lawrence to John Lamb, but after the news from Virginia they "quietly suffered us to propose our amendments without a word in opposition to them." The Federalists were done debating; the issue, as they saw it, was decided. Even some Anti-Federalists must have agreed that the debate had gone on long enough; two days earlier, during the discussion of Article I, Section 8, George Clinton suggested moving on rather than rehashing old arguments about the powers of Congress. Perhaps some delegates were anxious to return home, and others may have been wavering in light of Federalist arguments. Clinton was rebuked not by the fiery Livingston or the insistent Hamilton, but by John Jay. Why hurry, Jay asked, "to get home to cut our Grass"?[32] After Virginia was known to have ratified, cutting the grass must have had a stronger appeal. And by this time it was clear that at least some Anti-Federalists were prepared to support the Constitution to preserve the union.

Still the Anti-Federalists insisted that they were "united as one man." The opposition party "took no more notice of [the news of Virginia's ratification] than if the most trifling occurrence had been mentioned." A few Anti-Federalists were starting to shift their position, including Melancton Smith, but not yet enough to affect the outcome. On July 2, just before news of Virginia's ratification arrived in Poughkeepsie, Hamilton wrote to Madison about the prospects for ratification in New York. "Our arguments confound," he wrote, "but do not convince—Some of the leaders however appear to me to be convinced *by circumstances* and to be desirous of a retreat. This does not apply to the Chief, who wishes to establish CLINTONISM on the basis of *Antifœderalism.*"[33] It is not clear exactly why Hamilton believed his arguments confounded his opponents, as the opposition in convention ably countered virtually every point raised in defense of the Constitution. Fortunately for Hamilton and his allies, though, the Chief's hold on his forces was slipping.

When the clause-by-clause discussion of the Constitution ended, the real debate began. The Anti-Federalists still faced three choices. Outright rejection of the Constitution was virtually unthinkable with ten states, including Virginia, having ratified. Unconditional ratification, with or without recommended amendments, was unacceptable to most of the opposition, since they saw the Constitution as fundamentally and dangerously flawed. This left some sort of conditional ratification, under which New York might set the terms of its acceptance. Tied up in this question was the long list of amendments that had been proposed during the course of the convention. A committee was appointed to sort through these and propose a list along with a form of ratification. The committee organized the amendments into three groups: explanatory, conditional, and recommendatory. The conditional amendments generated the most controversy, because in the proposal they were attached to an ultimatum that, if they were not accepted, New York might withdraw its ratification. There were only four amendments in this group: that Congress may not raise a peacetime standing army except by a two-thirds vote; that Congress levy no direct taxes or excises on domestic manufactures; that the state militia not be ordered out of its home state without the approval of the governor, or kept out longer than six weeks without consent of the legislature; and that Congress not alter regulations concerning elections unless a state shall refuse or neglect to establish such regulations.

The committee was far from unanimous. Jay insisted that the word "conditional" be removed; otherwise there was no sense in even discussing the merits of the amendments. The Federalists would admit of no conditions. Jay also accused the Anti-Federalists of acting in bad faith, introducing a full proposal for acceptance by the committee rather than coming prepared to discuss and compromise. The committee discussions, such as they were, did reveal significant hope for the Federalists, though; according to one Federalist writer, Melancton Smith and Samuel Jones "discovered a disposition somewhat moderate" even as the other Anti-Federalists "were quite violent."[34]

Since the Anti-Federalists held a majority on the committee as well as in the convention, the Federalists could do nothing to force the committee's hand. The form of ratification proposed by the committee was conditional, which set off the final chaotic battle in the convention. For about a week, the delegates discussed several proposals for the form of ratification, with little order and few actual votes. Jay began the fight, moving on July 11 that the Constitution be ratified unconditionally. This prompted a rather heated, but civil, discussion between Jay and Smith, with Smith insisting that the convention not ratify before it had decided how to propose amendments. An outright adoption was unacceptable. At this point Smith was advocating a second national convention to settle amendments, with delegates chosen in a more representative fashion. George Clinton made another push for prior amendment, or even outright rejection, arguing that the Constitution violated basic principles of confederation. The states, he insisted, are the "creative principle," the component parts that ought to be represented, equally, and ought to control their chosen magistrates in the national government. The proposed Constitution failed on all of these counts. The objects of the government, stated in the Preamble, "include every object for which government was established amongst men, and in every dispute about the power granted, it is fair to infer that the means are commensurate with the end." In short, the government was complete, consolidated, and antifederal in the true meaning of the term; it would inevitably lead to the destruction of the states.[35]

Proposals for forms of ratification were tossed out left and right. Smith proposed that the state ratify unconditionally with the stipulation that New York might choose to withdraw after several years if satisfactory changes were not made to the Constitution; this idea, soon abandoned by Smith, was reintroduced later by Lansing in an effort to close the Anti-Federalist ranks against unconditional ratification. Hamilton offered a ratification modeled on Virginia's, but did not formally introduce it (though Duane did a few days later). Federalist John Sloss Hobart proposed an adjournment until September so that delegates might consult their constituents, who might have changed their minds. Since there was no reason for those who supported the Constitution to change their minds upon hearing that the ninth and tenth states had ratified, this was clearly an effort to put pressure on Anti-Federalist delegates; it was soundly rejected, 22–40.

Meanwhile, Melancton Smith was working on a new proposal, one he hoped might unite the delegates in the center. This was an act of political courage, breaking with his colleagues in proposing the middle ground that many claimed they were seeking. This new version was more comprehensive, encompassing most of the amendments proposed during the course of the state convention, but ultimately ratifying, if not quite unconditionally, at least nearly so. Its expression was less forceful; the ratification would be made "with a firm reliance and on the express condition that the rights aforesaid, will not and shall not be lost, abridged, or violated, and that the said Constitution shall, in the cases above particularised, receive the construction herein before expressed, . . . and in the confidence that whatever imperfections may exist in the Constitution, will as soon as possible be submitted to the consideration of a General Convention."[36] The reviews were mixed. For the Federalists, this still looked suspect, since it contained the word "condition" in connection with certain statements and a call for a second convention. For the Anti-Federalists, this was betrayal, creating the clear break in their ranks that the leaders of the opposition feared. "I suspect it will not please either side of the house," Smith explained, but he insisted that he "propose[d] it from the sincerest desire to accommodate." Smith's new proposal was followed by a discussion of his old one, reintroduced by Lansing. This clause-by-clause discussion took three days and involved a number of changes; the Anti-Federalists voted cohesively enough to carry virtually every point.[37]

After the string of amendments, the last question to be decided was whether the ratification by the state would be conditional on amendments or not. This was, however, a complex question, because the nature of the potential conditions was varied. Isaac Roosevelt identified four distinct groups within the convention at this point: "one of which for an Adoption with Conditions[;] one for a given time in order to withdraw if a General Convention is not obtained in that time; one for an adjournment[;] and one for an absolute Ratification." These four did not divide neatly into Federalist and Anti-Federalist; the situation was perhaps even more muddled here than in Virginia. Melancton Smith may well have belonged to a fifth group, for recommendatory amendments. In order to achieve this, though, he had to remove the conditions attached to his proposal. He managed to soften the language in the introduction, removing one use of the term "condition," in a bipartisan 40–19 vote that momentarily united Clinton, Lansing, Yates, Hamilton, Jay, and Livingston, but this was a minor point and Smith was proposing more eloquent language. The real battle was moments later, when Samuel Jones moved to change the words "upon condition" in the clause insisting on another convention to "in full confidence." This would turn the condition of ratification into a mere request, though certainly a forceful one. Smith immediately arose and insisted that he still believed the Constitution defective, but he believed that union was too important to risk. Amendments, he said, would not be obtained prior to the Constitution taking effect, because enough states had ratified unconditionally. Instead, the only path to amendments was that described in Article V, and that required that New York first join the union under the Constitution. Gilbert Livingston and Zephaniah Platt, fellow Dutchess County Anti-Federalists, followed Smith and echoed his sentiments. There was nothing the remaining opposition leadership could say; Clinton rose merely to say that he would vote according to the wishes of his constituents and support conditional ratification. Kaminski interprets this as a signal to the other Anti-Federalists that it was okay to break ranks: "If their constituents now supported unconditional ratification, Antifederalist delegates ought to support Jones's amendment. With this statement, the governor virtually assured that enough Antifederalists would alter their votes so that the Constitution would be adopted with recommendatory amendments." The vote was taken rather quickly; everything had already been said. Smith and Jones, along with Livingston and Platt, led a dozen Anti-Federalist defectors to the affirmative, accepting unconditional ratification by a razor-thin margin of two. Had even one of them voted against the motion, it would have failed.[38]

After this point, the new Federalist coalition wrapped up its work. The further conditions were made into polite requests. Lansing made one more effort, moving that the following text be added to the form of ratification: "Reserving to this State a right to recede and withdraw itself, as one of the members of the said government at any time after the expiration of ____ years, unless the said amendments shall before that time have been submitted to a Convention in the mode prescribed in the fifth article of the said Constitution." This was the last reasonable suggestion the Anti-Federalists could make with any hope of swaying the moderates. Surely Congress would not reject such an idea, he insisted, if there were such a strong national sentiment for amendments. Jay and Hamilton rather disingenuously lamented that the convention could not be more united on the ratification. Livingston was more to the point, observing that it would be legally difficult for New York to extract itself from the union after several years. It would be better to stay out than to give a temporary approval. Hamilton had written to Madison to ask him how Congress might react to such an idea, and Madison's response, read by Hamilton in convention, was, from the perspective of Congress, that such a scheme "is a *conditional* ratification, that it does not make N. York a member of the New Union, and consequently that she could not be received on that plan. Compacts must be reciprocal," he explained, "this principle would not in such a case be preserved. The Constitution requires an adoption *in toto*, and *for ever*."[39] Madison's speculation was probably just a bluff; the United States needed New York, if only to connect New England to the middle states, and Congress had no incentive apart from spite to reject what was, at least temporarily, a complete ratification. This probably did not convince most of the Anti-Federalists, but it solidified the support of moderates for unconditional ratification. On Friday, July 25, the convention rejected Lansing's motion by a vote of 31–28, and approved the form of ratification by the same margin.

The final and official vote was 30–27 in favor of ratification. Thereupon George Clinton took the important step, as in other states, of signaling the opposition's willingness to acquiesce peacefully. He said that "the probability was, that the body of the people who are opposed to the constitution, would not be satisfied—he would however, as far as his power and influence

would extend, endeavour to keep up peace and good order among them."
The convention unanimously approved a circular letter to the other states,
in which the Anti-Federalists won a small rhetorical victory. "Several Articles in [the Constitution] appear so exceptionable to a Majority of us," it
read, "that nothing but the fullest confidence, of obtaining a Revision of
them, by a General Convention, and an invincible reluctance to separating
from our Sister States, could have prevailed upon a sufficient Number to
ratify it, without stipulating for previous Amendments." The letter insisted
that an immediate convention needed to be called, and New York called
upon the other state legislatures to recommend such a convention. The idea
was already circulating in several other states, and it looked entirely plausible that this was the course of action that would be taken.[40]

This Federalist victory was the most impressive in any state, despite the
extensive concessions; after all, nowhere else did the proponents of ratification overcome such seemingly insurmountable odds. There were a number
of reasons the Anti-Federalist coalition fell apart. Cecil Eubanks offers a
concise summary of the major reasons:

> To begin with, Federalists and Antifederalists in New York were never
> very far apart. Both desired a political community that could provide
> some consistency in trade and money matters along with uniform pro-
> tection of the rights and property of the people and mutual recognition
> of the laws of the individual states. . . . The issue facing both parties
> was, not whether reform was needed, but how much reform was re-
> quired. . . . Thus, New York Antifederalists were not unalterably op-
> posed, as the debates may have suggested. They feared national power,
> to be sure, but many of them favored ratification, with appropriate
> amendments and perhaps a second convention.[41]

There were a number of delegates who, while opposed to the Constitution
as written, were not as strong in their opposition as Clinton and Lansing.
These delegates were open to conviction, so long as they could shape the
form of ratification to best ensure amendments to make the Constitution
safe.

Foremost among these was Melancton Smith, who led the ideological
fight for the opposition before switching sides and seeking conciliation. Because of his prominent role early in the convention, he became the primary
scapegoat for the Anti-Federalist loss. George Clinton would henceforth
inhibit, rather than advance and sponsor, Smith's political career. Gordon Wood sums up Melancton Smith's defection succinctly. "His fear of

disunion," Gordon Wood contends, perhaps too glibly, "eventually over-
came his fear of the Constitution."[42] Theophilus Parsons offers a more interesting and useful analysis of Smith's motives for his defection. Rejecting
the typical interpretation that he was trying to secure his future political
career in Federalist New York City, Parsons suggests that the conversion,
like that of Randolph in Virginia, was principled: "Basically Smith made
his proposals because he felt the Poughkeepsie Convention was serving to
muddy the political principles of the Antifederalists." The fight had become
personal and nasty, and by this point was moot in terms of whether the
Constitution would take effect, so Smith saw more value in changing the
venue of the debate from the state convention to a second national convention. This was not a defection at all, then: "Smith felt his voting for unconditional adoption of the Constitution was consistent with his ideology; indeed
he felt it was the only way that Antifederalist doctrine could be brought to
the public's attention." What Smith wanted was "a fuller and clearer enun-
ciation of the Antifederalist position before a national audience."[43]

Smith was not alone in taking the blame, though. Matthew Lyon of Vermont laid the blame at the feet of Smith's Dutchess colleague Zephaniah
Platt. Platt insisted that he voted for unconditional ratification "not from a
conviction that the Constitution was a good one or that the Liberties of men
were well Secured no—I voted for it as a Choice of evils in our present Situation." Samuel Jones of Queens County played a crucial role in initiating
the conciliatory efforts, even before Smith. On July 14, in the midst of the
debates on the form of ratification, Jones was absent from the convention.
"Mr. Jones is very much terrified," wrote David Bogart to Samuel Blachley
Webb, "this day he was absent on account of Sickness, his Son told me,
though I conjecture political sickness." It is not clear whether he feared re-
prisals or simply did not want to take a public position. Abraham Lansing
wrote on July 20 that Jones "is so much Intimidated by the Threats of the
Federalists that he does not any more take an active part" in the debates.
"If he had the Courage," Federalist Philip Schuyler had written five days
earlier, "he would speak his sentiments which are doub[t]less that the ratification as proposed by Lansingh, could not be construed an adoption."
Avoiding votes was apparently a popular strategy; on July 25, the day that
the convention voted on the report of the committee of the whole, no fewer
than ten delegates failed to show up for the vote. According to Daniel St.
Clair, this was "because their constituents instructed them to vote against
the measure." There were sixty-five delegates, and only fifty-five voted on
this measure, with only fifty-seven voting on the final ratification. Of the
eight not present, seven had at one time opposed ratification; with a margin

of victory of three votes, seven absent Anti-Federalists was a very large number. Still, those seven were fewer than the twelve members of the opposition who actually supported the ratification. These delegates decided to bow to changing political realities, and submit gracefully rather than fighting. The Anti-Federalists were not prepared to give up the fight, but they would pursue it in legal and peaceful channels.[44]

The aftermath of the convention was not all peaceful though; it turned ugly in New York City. On the evening of July 26, the day the convention adjourned, some Federalists went around the city cheering at the houses of Federalists and jeering at those of the Anti-Federalists, occasionally indulging in petty vandalism. Thomas Greenleaf, the printer of the Anti-Federalist *New York Journal*, saw the mob break into his house and office and destroy his printing presses. He fired on the crowd, though he did not kill anyone in part because one of his pistols misfired.[45] Other Anti-Federalists got off easier. John Lamb's house was also a target, but Lamb, "[w]ith the vigilance of an old campaigner," prepared a substantial stockpile of weapons and waited to use them if necessary. Eleazer Oswald of Philadelphia was with him, along with several other friends, and Charles Tillinghast would have been as well had Lamb not insisted he go home. Lamb sent his wife and daughter away for the evening and waited for the mob. When they arrived, Lamb refused to reply to their shouts and threats, and the mob apparently decided that the house would be "vigorously defended," so they "very prudently abandoned the enterprise."[46] Governor Clinton was not yet home, nor was any of his family present except for one of his daughters. Nonetheless, the crowd decided to make a stop at the Governor's house. The *Independent Gazetteer* gleefully related the story:

> At length they arrive before his house—a general hiss prevails, tired of this, huzza! a halter for the governor! At this the little girl throws up the sash, makes them a low courtsey—"I thank you gentlemen, for the compliment you pay my father, he has always had the censure of disorderly people, and I have heard him say, that nothing gratified him more highly than it, except the approbation of good men." Our heroes not being armed for a war of this kind, where good sense was necessary, raise the siege and march off to make use of the arms which GOD accoutred them with in common with the rest of the animal creation.[47]

According to the *Gazetteer*, this encounter was just before the mob attacked Greenleaf's house, and may have contributed to its anger. This story is probably apocryphal, but it fit the Anti-Federalist narrative (particularly in Pennsylvania, home of the *Gazetteer*) that the Federalists were supported by unthinking and dangerous mobs. The opposition, meanwhile, had lost the fight just as they were starting to coalesce in a coherent idea of what it was they wanted.

15

Reconciliation and Resistance

IN MASSACHUSETTS, THE POLITICAL healing may have already been beginning by the early summer in 1788. "An Antifederalist," writing in the *Massachusetts Centinel* in the middle of June, suggested that the contending parties in the ratification debate are not really so far apart in their political principles after all. "Let us now examine the mighty difference between what is vulgarly called a federalist and an antifederalist," he suggests:

> Is it like the difference between a whig and a tory—the one striving to establish British, and the other a republican government? Certainly not. I take it we are all aiming at one and the same thing; and the only difference seems to be this, the one was for swallowing down the new Constitution as it was: The other was for trying at least, to make it a little better; and the difference in opinion with respect to the expediency or inexpediency of making the attempt, seems to constitute the essential difference between them. What a mighty bubble—sufficient to split the nation into parties, fill the world full of yeas and nays, and form prejudices which will be the work of an age to remove.[1]

He suggests that it is important for the nation to come together to give the constitutional experiment a fair test. He also deprecates the earlier disrespect for those who would exercise their freedom of speech and press to point out the defects of the Constitution. The continuing acrimony between the two sides, though, was evident as quickly as the editors' note immediately following the short piece, which suggested that "An *antifederalist* is an enemy to federal government," but acknowledged that there are those who have doubts and concerns who ought to be embraced by those who supported the Constitution. Apparently some of the opposition could not be reconciled, in the view of the *Centinel.*

Nathan Dane, though certainly no enemy to federal government, was among those not yet convinced on the issue. "My fears and apprehensions," he wrote to Samuel Adams, do not arise altogether from a consideration of the faults in the new Constitution; but, in a considerable measure, from a full persuasion that we have many men, and able ones too, in this Country who have a disposition to make a bad use of any government; and who, if not well checked and restrained by the forms of the Government, will, so far as they can have influence produce a wicked and corrupt adminis-tration—and you may, Sir, be assured that the Zealous advocates for the adoption of this Constitution, and who are pretty numerous, artful and active, do not intend that any amendments shall be adopted, even after the Constitution shall be put into operation, if they can any way prevent it.[2]

Coming from Philadelphiensis or Centinel such accusations would have been expected, but Dane was among the more moderate opponents of the Constitution in Massachusetts. Perhaps the reconciliation was not so far along after all.

In Pennsylvania, Tench Coxe saw the opposition winding down after Maryland's ratification, and virtually ceasing upon the news from South Carolina. "Our people seem disposed to be kind & unmindful of all that has past, for which I am happy in giving them a considerable Degree of Credit, as indeed the mode of opposing here was very unbecoming." The satirists of the opposition still had more to say, though; in May the *Independent Gazetteer* printed "The Federalist's Political Creed," which took the pro-ponents of ratification to task for their strong-arm tactics and aristocratic leanings. He wrote that "there never was on earth a set of more firm and sincere *believers*; nor any who were willing to run greater risques in defence of their political dogmas." The attack is an effective statement of the typical Democratic Anti-Federalist view on the entire ratification proceedings. The fourteen points of the "Creed" include the infallibility of the Framers, praise for tyrannical government, and a statement that bills of rights "are musty old things" that are unnecessary and even dangerous. Despite the assurances of Pennsylvania Federalists, at least some of the radical opposition was not prepared to give up the fight.[3]

With the ratification of eleven states, though, the Federalists were able to breathe a collective sigh of relief even if there were pockets of resistance; many of them saw the battle as over. The more astute Federalists, among them Madison and Washington, began discussing amendments, sensing that another battle was on the horizon. Meanwhile, those pockets of resistance remained, especially in western Pennsylvania, in parts of Kentucky, and in the two remaining states whose ratifying conventions had not yet met. The

Anti-Federalists in North Carolina had been watching their colleagues, not just in Virginia to the north but throughout the United States. The opposition here, firmly in control throughout the ratification process, was calmly developing a plan to resist the momentum of ratification, to push for changes to be made, and to reenter the union on their own terms. The opposition here, as elsewhere in the southern states, was predominantly Rights Anti-Federalism, but as in Virginia, the North Carolina Convention mixed concerns about powers with its demands for a bill of rights. In fact, the convention would largely borrow Virginia's amendments, in a show of solidarity to compel others to seriously consider the changes the Constitution needed.

THE DEBATE IN NORTH CAROLINA

Earlier reports of North Carolina's general approval of the Constitution were either completely uninformed or intentionally misleading. All of the leading men in the state knew that the Constitution would not pass, but the Federalists intended to do their best to win converts to the proposed document, especially with enough states ratifying to ensure its implementation. The effort would not be an easy one; not only were the people of North Carolina unconvinced that it was in their interest to ratify, but they were deeply suspicious of just about every state north of them. The Federalists were easily satirized as seekers after glory. "Can there be an American so sordid," writes one "Thomas Tinsel" sardonically, "as to hesitate at sacrificing his dirty cash to glory, especially for glory so certain as this?"[4] The average North Carolinian had little need for national greatness; that was the dream of the northern merchant, or perhaps the Virginian would-be aristocrat. The people of this state were simpler in their desires, content with liberty and making a living. The general split in North Carolina was much the same as elsewhere: coastal areas, and especially commercial interests, favored ratification, and inland rural areas opposed. In this state, though, there was at least one major difference: the vast majority of the state's residents were inland and rural.

Despite the disparity in numbers, there was a vigorous debate in the state. "At the sessions of the courts, at county militia musters, in the taverns, wherever men gathered," writes Louise Trenholme, "the main topics of conversation were the Constitution and its framers."[5] The general objections raised in North Carolina were similar to those discussed elsewhere, but the Rights Anti-Federalist position was predominant. This position was exemplified by a writer in the *North Carolina Gazette* in December 1787. He laments the dangers of federal appellate courts, especially in civil cases. The author is unusual among Anti-Federalists in that he explicitly invokes the specific grievances listed in the Declaration of Independence, noting that Congress objected to the fact that citizens might be subject to standing trial far from home. This is no vague reference to the "spirit of '76." He also notes the objection to standing armies in that document. "It consequently seems extraordinary," he opines, "that, in so short space of time as a period of eleven years, a proposition should be made to the people of America to renounce a right they have shewn themselves so jealous of." Beyond the standing army and appellate courts, the idea of a federal district under the control of Congress is frightening. "It may be made a nursery out of which legions may be dragged to submit us to unlimited slavery, like ancient Rome." He even suggests that Congress should be denied "an exclusive jurisdiction in the forts, arsenals, magazines, dock-yards, they may establish in different parts of the continent." This is certainly radical, and partakes of the Democratic Anti-Federalist position, but his overall argument is still firmly rooted in protecting the rights of the people. He closes with a colorful, though typical, argument for guaranteeing the freedom of the press, "a compliment the American printers had a right to expect." Even if such a clause is, strictly speaking, unnecessary, it is valuable to repeat it, as it is appropriate to compliment a lady on her beauty even if it is obvious. For "whenever a lady ceases to be told that she is a fine woman, the time is pretty near when she will no more be looked upon such," and when the press ceases to be declared as free, one may expect that it will not long remain so.[6] "Common Sense" echoed these concerns over rights, suggesting that the oath taken by North Carolina legislators to uphold the state's constitution requires them to reject the proposed federal Constitution because it would threaten the rights guaranteed to the state's citizens. He warned

> that the chief power will be in the Congress, and that what is to be left of our government, will be a mere shadow is plain, because a citizen may be deprived of the privilege of keeping arms for his own defence, he may have his property taken without a trial by jury, he may be ordered to march with the rest of the militia to New Hampshire, or anywhere else, he may be forced to go to the new seat of government 500 miles off, to oppose an oppressive appeal in spite of our assembly, governor, and judges: These things are entirely contrary to our constitution, and the possibility of them by no means to be admitted.[7]

The danger was tyranny; the rights of the people were threatened.

These were objections that could certainly be handled through amendments. The desire for amendments dominated North Carolina's resistance. "Honestus" expresses hope that the state convention's "acceding to the plan proposed, will be with such amendments as will prevent any encroachment on, but have our present established government for the foundation, to the future allowances, which expressly forbids to keep a standing army." He suggests that the power to raise an army and navy, coupled with the power to mint money, is the "greatest and most powerful objects which will enforce obedience against all resistance," and as such these powers should be carefully limited or preserved to the states. The next week, meanwhile, the *Centinel* published a piece arguing convincingly against amendments previous to ratification. These were the terms of the debate, effectively dictated by the Massachusetts result. Common Sense, however, writing again in June, suggests that some amendments might be easily made and agreed upon; "some of the most essential rights, which the people ought at every hazard, to secure," he contends, "may be established without any difficulty, by inserting proper provisoes." His "provisoes" consist essentially of a bill of rights; Common Sense is doing nothing more than echoing the earlier idea presented by Pennsylvania's M. C. and others.[8]

As the convention approached, news reached North Carolina that New Hampshire and Virginia had ratified, putting ten states in the federal column; this did nothing to deter the opposition leaders. The convention elections themselves were somewhat unusual, because of an addition to the responsibilities of the convention. After determining the particulars of time, place, and manner, the state legislature, as an apparent afterthought, decided to charge the convention with selecting a permanent seat for the state capital. This virtually guaranteed that the Constitution would not be ratified. "The ratification question became entangled in the web of regional interests," Norman Risjord explains. "A number of electoral contests that spring hinged on the capital fight rather than on the Constitution." Perhaps as a result of this second convention responsibility, North Carolina had an unusually distinguished list of failed candidates for the state convention. This list included a Revolutionary War general, a signer of the Declaration of Independence, and two delegates to Philadelphia; all of these individuals were probable supporters of ratification.[9] Nonetheless, the members of convention were distinguished, with a significant number of important state politicians, and an even greater number who were very influential in local politics. This is not surprising given the local question of situating the capital. Still, the Federalists were ably led in the state and in the convention, particularly by Hugh Williamson, William Davie, and James Iredell, but they were easily outnumbered. The Federalists did have the advantage of a largely friendly press, but it did not get them very far. The written efforts in defense of the Constitution in the state were impressive, though, and measured favorably against those of other states. Compared to the Federalists, the opposition in the state apparently made "no such formidable literary effort," though there were several opposition essays that were effective and intelligent. Given the numbers, they had no need for anything more.[10]

The Anti-Federalists were led by Willie Jones of Halifax County, who, because so few of his papers survive, has become something of a mysterious figure. He was democratic in his politics, though with an aristocratic bent in his personal tastes. He was no debater or orator; he was an organizer. In the words of Griffith McRee, biographer of James Iredell, Jones "seldom shared in the discussions. His time of action was, chiefly, during the hours of adjournment: then it was that he stimulated the passions, aroused the suspicions, or moderated the ardor of his followers; then it was that, smoking his pipe, and chatting of crops, ploughs, stock, dogs, &c., he stole his way into the hearts of honest farmers, and erected there thrones for himself."[11] Jones had been selected to attend the convention in Philadelphia, but he had declined without giving a reason, saying only that "it will not be in my power to attend there at the Time appointed."[12] Now, in the debate over ratification, he reemerged from retirement to lead the opposition. He merely needed to marshal his forces and keep them in line to control the outcome in the state, and he had ample help. "From Halifax he personally directed the campaign [against the Constitution] in the eastern and northeastern sections of the state," writes Blackwell Pierce Robinson, "while his henchmen, Timothy Bloodworth, Joseph Caldwell, Judge Samuel Spencer, and Major Joseph McDowell, superintended it elsewhere." He was a persistent campaigner against the Constitution, and he was the acknowledged leader in the convention, though he said little, per his usual approach.[13]

THE FIRST NORTH CAROLINA CONVENTION

As the convention opened, the delegates unanimously elected Federalist Samuel Johnston, the present governor of the state, as the president of the convention. The Anti-Federalist majority saw no reason to contest the decision, as their numbers were sufficient to overturn any unfriendly decisions, and Johnston was the most logical choice anyway. On the third day, after resolving the disputed election in Dobbs County (refusing to seat either delegation) and setting rules of debate, the convention proceeded to read, before the proposed Constitution they had gathered to debate, the state constitution, the Articles of Confederation, and all relevant documents calling for and identifying the purposes of the Philadelphia Convention. Federalists elsewhere resisted this, as the authority of the Convention to propose a new constitution was a potential weakness of their position; here they really had no choice. This would be the first topic of debate, as several delegates questioned the first three words of the Preamble. Johnston also introduced the ratifications from Massachusetts and South Carolina; the published debates offered no explanation for this, despite the fact that only two of the ten state ratifications were introduced. Johnston was undoubtedly presenting these as his preferred models for North Carolina's decision. The two documents were passed by without comment.

Before the substantive discussion even began, Willie Jones demonstrated for the Federalists that the opposition need not debate at all. James Galloway, who would vote against the Constitution but seemed inclined to help the Federalists receive a fair hearing throughout the convention, moved to discuss the Constitution clause by clause. Immediately following this motion, and before any debate, Willie Jones rose to offer an alternative.

> Mr. WILLIE JONES moved that the question upon the Constitution should be immediately put. He said that the Constitution had so long been the subject of deliberation of every man in this country, and that the members of the Convention had had such ample opportunity to consider it, that he believed every one of them was prepared to give his vote then upon the question; that the situation of the public funds would not admit of lavishing the public money, but required the utmost economy and frugality; that, as there was a large representation from this state, an immediate decision would save the country a considerable sum of money. He thought it, therefore, prudent to put the question immediately.[14]

It is highly probable that Jones could have mustered a majority of the convention to support his motion for an immediate vote. This was a move to clearly signal that he was in charge, even as several other prominent Anti-Federalists favored a careful discussion. James Iredell immediately jumped to his feet, bristling at the suggestion that the convention would not deliberate. For one of the few times in the convention he seems to have lost control of himself, suggesting that if the convention was inclined to follow Jones's plan, the state may as well have held a referendum. He did not mention Rhode Island, but the connection must have occurred to the other delegates. Iredell went on to suggest that his opponents were afraid to discuss the Constitution on its merits. This was clearly the reaction Willie Jones wanted to see; he blandly replied that the delegates were in convention because the legislature had called a convention. After quickly retracting his statement, Iredell was faced with Galloway chastising him for suggesting that Jones was afraid to debate. Again Iredell backpedaled; this was not the way the Federalists wanted to start the discussion. He looked irritable and defensive, while Jones was able to appear magnanimous as he withdrew his motion.

The next day, Galloway resumed his suggestion that the convention consider the Constitution by clause, and that it discuss as a committee of the whole. There was some disagreement among Anti-Federalists on this point, but a substantial majority supported the idea. If nothing else, it was an opportunity to put an Anti-Federalist, Elisha Battle of Edgecomb County, in the chair. The majority then set about undermining the Federalist cause. To the argument that North Carolina ought to ratify because ten states had already done so, Griffith Rutherford argued that "we ought to decide it as if no state had adopted it. Are we to be thus intimidated into a measure of which we may disapprove?" When the Federalists defended the legitimacy of the Philadelphia Convention opening with "We the People," the Anti-Federalists turned it into a question of consolidation, just as Patrick Henry had done to the north. "Had it said, *We, the states*," Joseph Taylor asserted, "there would have been a federal intention in it. But, sir, it is clear that a consolidation is intended."[15]

This notion of consolidation was of course one of the pillars of the opposition argument. Most of the objections raised by the Anti-Federalists in the North Carolina Convention, though, were not so central to the position against the Constitution. It is clear that they were toying with the Federalist minority. The chief objection to the first section of the first article was that the Vice President's tiebreaking vote meant that the legislative power was not wholly vested in Congress. William Goudy objected to being represented and taxed for three-fifths of slaves, while Galloway almost immediately suggested that North Carolina was given too few representatives in the initial allocation. Whether the size of the House was too small, or whether it was truly representative, did not come up. Timothy Bloodworth objected to the clauses on impeachment, suggesting that they extended to impeaching minor officials all the way down to tax collectors, and perhaps to impeachment of state officers in the federal Senate. Joseph Taylor added that any citizen who disagreed with a tax collector would have to take him to Congress to see him impeached and tried. Since the tax collectors would undoubtedly be close friends of members of Congress (how else would they get their jobs?), they would be dangerous to oppose. This argument was too much for Archibald Maclaine, who said that anyone who carefully read the clause with even the most casual knowledge of government could not arrive at such a construction. The opponents of ratification were clearly either willfully misinterpreting or merely stupid; such an objection reflected "the most horrid ignorance." "It shows what wretched shifts gentlemen are driven to," he said. "I never heard, in my life, of such a silly objection. A poor, insignificant, petty officer amenable to impeachment!" Maclaine, justified or not, must have been an unconvincing and unsympathetic figure to any undecided or wavering delegates who may have been present.[16] Making matters worse, he accused the Anti-Federalists of being hostile to union, and implied that they were little better than anarchists. Maclaine was not alone in his attacks. Even William Davie was condescending, though not outright hostile. "Every man has not been bred a politician, nor studied the science of government," he said to the largely uneducated men of modest means that made up much of the opposition; "yet, when a subject is explained, if the mind is unwarped by prejudice, and not in the leading-strings of other people, gentlemen will do what is right."[17] Which is, of course, support the Constitution. Davie accused the opposition of absurdity and groundless declamation, like Maclaine undoubtedly winning few friends to their cause. Iredell was much more convincing, maintaining his cool in the face of obvious attempts to antagonize.

The frustrated Federalists, in the absence of a real critique of the Constitution, began to answer objections that had been made elsewhere. Maclaine raised the issue of biennial elections, drawing a comment from a fellow Federalist that it was not the place of delegates to answer objections that have not been made in the convention. This irked Maclaine, who insisted that "if objections are made here, I will answer them to the best of my ability. If I see gentlemen pass by in silence such parts as they vehemently decry out of doors, or such parts as have been loudly complained of in the country, I shall answer them also."[18] Willie Jones, obviously amused by the discomfiture of the Federalists, helpfully suggested that one Federalist delegate might raise objections for another to answer. The next day, on July 25, Stephen Cabarrus, who favored the Constitution, tried just this, asking about the length of Senate terms. No one, it seems, was convinced by the performance, but the Federalists were not deterred from using this tactic periodically.

The Anti-Federalists were not entirely unified in their silence. James Galloway seems to have been committed to keeping the discussion moving, on several occasions effectively shutting off debate on particular clauses, but he actually encouraged his fellow delegates to raise objections. Samuel Spencer objected to the clause allowing Congress to regulate congressional elections, to the relief of the Federalists who were anxious to defend this embattled clause. But Governor Johnston, instead of offering a defense, confessed that he too "cannot comprehend the reason of this part." It was a minor objection, he explained, but it was a flaw in the Constitution. For Spencer, it was a major problem, a "reprehensible clause," because it is an unwarranted attack on the autonomy of the state legislatures. Those legislatures were to be "swallowed up by the great mass of powers given to Congress." Such a consolidated nation can only be governed by military force. Goudy asked why, if the clause was intended to allow for continued function of the government in times of invasion as the Federalists suggested, it was not written to apply only to this specific case. Timothy Bloodworth suggested that Congress might have been given the power to regulate elections only if the states failed to do so, or were unable. Joseph McDowell saw sinister intentions; he believed that "it points forward to the time when there will be no state legislatures—to the consolidation of all the states. The states will be kept up as boards of elections."[19]

Taxes, too, generated real debate. The states would lose all power to tax if Congress were given authority to collect any kind of tax, they insisted, and the states could not survive without revenue. Congress would need revenue too, of course, but the objects of taxation should be allocated between the two levels of government, not shared. Here as elsewhere Anti-Federalists suggested that requisitions ought to be the first step in direct taxes, and that Congress might decide how to collect should the states fail to do so. In an emergency Congress might borrow money while it waited for the revenues to come in. The reason for this plan was simple: only the true representatives of the people ought to levy taxes. "The most certain criterion of happiness that any people can have," said Spencer, "is to be taxed by their own immediate representatives,—by those representatives who intermix with them, and know their circumstances,—not by those who cannot know their situation. Our federal representatives cannot sufficiently know our situation and circumstances." The local situation in North Carolina was particularly problematic, because there was very little hard money in the state. The state legislature could instead collect taxes in the form of farm produce, for example, to be sold for hard money to pay the state's taxes. By requiring requisitions, the people may be taxed by their own representatives in the states. The opposition here firmly believed that there would be need for high taxes. They expected that "the amount of the imposts will be trifling" while "the expenses of this government will be very great; consequently the taxes will be very high."[20]

Slavery became an issue for the Anti-Federalists here as well. Galloway objected to the continuation of the slave trade, and expressed concern that the clause permitting Congress to tax imported slaves would be used to tax immigrants as well. He also feared that the Framers intended Congress to have the power of manumission. If the slaves are freed, Galloway declared, they must be sent somewhere else, for they cannot productively remain within North Carolina.[21]

Despite these issues, on the whole the debate was sparse, because the Anti-Federalists would not cooperate. Davie became animated on this point after the debate on Article I concluded, with few major objections raised, and the reading of Article II, Section 1, was greeted with silence. "Mr. Chairman," he began,

> I must express my astonishment at the precipitancy with which we go through this business. Is it not highly improper to pass over in silence any part of this Constitution which has been loudly objected to? We go into a committee to have a freer discussion. I am sorry to see gentlemen hurrying us through, and suppressing their objections, in order to bring them forward at an unseasonable hour. We are assembled here to deliberate for our own common welfare, and to decide upon a question of infinite importance to our country. What is the cause of this silence and gloomy jealousy in gentlemen of the opposition? This department has been universally objected to by them. The most virulent invectives, the most opprobrious epithets, and the most indecent scurrility, have been used and applied against this part of the Constitution. It has been represented as incompatible with any degree of freedom. Why, therefore, do not gentlemen offer their objections now, that we may examine their force, if they have any?[22]

Iredell too lamented the silence of the opposition on the shape of the presidency. The powers granted to the President would bring several Anti-Federalists from their seats, however. Robert Miller began with concerns about the President's control of the military, suggesting that Congress ought to direct military actions. William Porter followed by insisting that the power to make treaties was a legislative power, not executive, and the House of Representatives ought to have a say over foreign relations.

It was Spencer, though, who really took up the cause against the proposed presidency, with a speech that was rather long for a member of the opposition. The Senate, he insisted, held the balance of executive power; the President would need to ally with that body in order to be effective even in the performance of his executive responsibilities. A council to advise the President, and to concur in executive appointments, would have been safer than placing executive powers in a branch of the legislature. The danger extends to impeachment as well; the Senate will never vote to convict a President unless to cover up its own iniquities. If the President and Senate should combine, they cannot be stopped. Davie attempted to answer these objections, suggesting among other things that Senators were unlikely to be reelected *because* they would be long away from their constituents, but Spencer was unmoved. "He has not removed my objections," Spencer says of Davie. "It is totally out of [the Federalists'] power to show any degree of responsibility. The executive is tried by his advisers."[23] The Senate would become a dangerous aristocracy:

> It appears to me that the powers are too extensive, and not sufficiently guarded. I do not wish that an aristocracy should be instituted. An aristocracy may arise out of this government, though the members be not hereditary. I would therefore wish that every guard should be placed, in order to prevent it. I wish gentlemen would reflect that the powers of the Senate are so great in their legislative and judicial capacities, that, when added to their executive powers, particularly their interference in the appointment of all officers in the continent, they will render their power so enormous as to enable them to destroy our rights and privileges. This, sir, ought to be strictly guarded against.[24]

Spencer, merely by raising objections, was helping the Federalists to have the debate they wanted.

He would continue his opposition efforts in discussing the judiciary. The jurisdiction was too extensive, covering a range of policy "almost infinite" in its scope. Once again, Spencer recurred to the question of rights:

> Our rights are not guarded. There is no declaration of rights, to secure to every member of the society those unalienable rights which ought not to be given up to any government. Such a bill of rights would be a check upon men in power. Instead of such a bill of rights, this Constitution has a clause which may warrant encroachments on the power of the respective state legislatures. I know it is said that what is not given up to the United States will be retained by the individual states. I

know it ought to be so, and should be so understood; but, sir, it is not
declared to be so.[25]

On this point the North Carolina Anti-Federalists were in agreement with
their brethren to the north. A bill of rights, though, was not enough. In a
legislature proper representation protects liberty, and in courts juries serve
a similar purpose. The Constitution guaranteed a jury trial only in criminal
cases, and even then such a jury need only be from the state in which the
crime was committed. The opposition here vehemently insisted on the importance of a jury from the vicinage, and was not prepared to trust Congress
to guarantee it. Trusting to Congress is foolish, the Anti-Federalists argued.
Without such guarantees of rights, the judicial power might by degrees remove the rights of the people just as surely as the executive and legislative.
The state legislatures and the state courts are safer guardians of liberty.
Spencer summed it up nicely for the opposition: "I do not deny the propriety
of having federal courts; but they should be confined to federal business,
and ought not to interfere in those cases where the state courts are fully
competent to decide. The state courts can do their business without federal
assistance."[26]

The final four articles of the Constitution generated less debate than
the first three, though perhaps more significant Anti-Federalist objections.
Bloodworth predicted that the Supremacy Clause would be "a total repeal
of every act and constitution of the states." He also saw danger in the clause
preventing states from issuing bills of credit; North Carolina's paper money,
he insisted, would become worthless, and the people would be forced to
pay their debts in specie, which they simply did not have. On this point the
Federalists did not help their cause; when McDowell asked whether federal
taxes might be paid in paper Maclaine retorted that "taxes must be paid in
gold or silver coin, and not in imaginary money." Such a statement was well
calculated to repel most of the delegates, and must have irked the other Federalist leaders who really hoped to win over at least a few votes, for a small
moral victory against overwhelming odds. The prohibition of religious tests
for office also generated objections. Henry Abbot suggested that all manner
of pagans might be elected to federal office. Caldwell added that the Constitution invited "Jews and heathens" to emigrate and seek political office; he
for one did not want to see such people populating America. Another delegate later added that he wished that "Popish priests" had been specifically
excluded. It was even suggested that the President and Senate might make
a treaty with Rome (without consulting the House of Representatives, of
course) establishing Catholicism as the official religion.[27]

The general theme of the opposition, though, when they bothered to participate at all, was clearly Rights Anti-Federalism. Joseph Taylor contended that "when mankind are about to part with rights, they ought only to part with those rights which they can with convenience relinquish, and not such as must involve them in distress." Unfortunately, in the words of Bloodworth, "This Constitution, if adopted in its present mode, must end in the subversion of our liberties." Goudy added his fear that the Constitution was "a combination against our liberties. I ask, when we give them the purse in one hand, and the sword in another, what power have we left? It will lead to an aristocratical government, and establish tyranny over us. We are freemen, and we ought to have the privileges of such." In the end, it was a bill of rights, or at least a clear statement to the effect that Congress may not exercise any powers not explicitly given, that was necessary to reconcile the North Carolina Anti-Federalists to the Constitution. The Federalists insisted that all powers not expressly given by the Constitution to the national government would be retained by the states, but this was not good enough. "I know that it ought to be so," said Spencer, "it is the general doctrine, but it is necessary that it should be expressly declared in the Constitution, and not left to mere construction and opinion." To secure the liberties of the people, Spencer explained, requires an "express negative," a "fence against their being trampled upon." In the proposed frame of government, Congress "might exceed the proper boundary without being taken notice of." With some written guarantee, the people will have cause to take notice, and recourse to the foundational law. For the opposition here, this was nothing more than common sense. Matthew Locke spoke for many when he said, "I trust this country is too sensible of the value of liberty, and her citizens have bought it too dearly, to give it up hastily."[28]

Upon completing their discussion of the Constitution by clause on July 30, Governor Johnston was the first to act. He introduced a motion for unconditional ratification with recommendatory amendments, as had been done in several other states. Suddenly the Anti-Federalists had a lot to say. It began with a lengthy speech by William Lenoir, who suggested that the Constitution would establish "the most dangerous aristocracy that ever was thought of—an aristocracy established on a constitutional bottom!" He explained that "this is so dangerous, that I should like as well to have no constitution at all." Lenoir was not to be won over by recommended amendments. He complained of the complexity and ambiguity of the document, suggesting that "[a] constitution ought to be understood by every one. The most humble and trifling characters in the country have a right to know what foundation they stand upon."[29] The powers granted were too extensive, the representation was inadequate, the long terms of the Senators and President allowed for corruption, the President's power to pardon facilitated this corruption, and there was no protection for rights. There was no danger in insisting on amendments before accepting the Constitution.

Richard Spaight rose to answer these objections, especially some aspersions on the legality and legitimacy of the Philadelphia Convention, of which he had been a member. McDowell then stepped in with a plea for amendments to the Constitution, insisting that "a great proportion of the people in the adopting states [are] averse to it as it stands." William Lancaster added that such amendments ought to be made conditions of North Carolina's ratification, because the state cannot trust the new government to actually make the requested changes. At this point Willie Jones again rose, and again changed the direction of the convention by calling for a vote on unconditional ratification, after which he could make a proposal concerning amendments. The vote would be advisory, not binding, because it would be taken in the committee of the whole. Everyone knew he had the votes, but the Federalists were not willing to allow for an outright rejection of the Constitution without a fight. The Federalists went on the attack, again noting that objections made outside of the convention had not made their way inside, and insisting that the Anti-Federalists had not given the Constitution a fair hearing. The opposition had heard enough, and loudly demanded that the question be called. Iredell again entered the fray with a final plea. "Mr. Chairman," he said amid the noise, "I desire to be heard, notwithstanding the cry of 'The question! the question!' Gentlemen have no right to prevent any member from speaking to it, if he thinks it." He explained that in trying to avoid tyranny a country might move too far in the other direction, into anarchy. He then proceeded into an ill-advised discussion of the dangers of the British on America's borders, during which he was interrupted with accusations that he was implying that his opponents were sympathizers with Britain. Iredell denied the allegation and "warmly resented the interruption," but it was clear that he was losing ground. He tried one last approach before the vote was taken, suggesting that North Carolina could take no part in the amendment process if it was not part of the union. This plea fell on deaf ears, and the Anti-Federalist majority won the day by a vote of 183–84. The Constitution would not be ratified unconditionally, at least not on this day.[30]

The next day, the thirty-first of July, belonged to the Anti-Federalists; the proponents of the Constitution were entirely on the defensive. Johnston suggested that if the state wanted to suggest amendments without ratifying, they would have to be sent via North Carolina's "ambassadors to the United States of America." The Anti-Federalists did not fear the consequences of rejection; they were confident that they could accept the Constitution after appropriate changes were made. Willie Jones was clear and unequivocal: "It is objected we shall be out of the Union. So I wish to be. We are left at liberty to come in at any time." The Federalists insisted that rejecting the Constitution would give up a state's right to reenter the union when it pleases, and that a conditional ratification was tantamount to a rejection. The Anti-Federalists, more calm than their opponents, respectfully disagreed. The Federalists insisted that North Carolina would lose out on necessary revenue that was to flow into the state from the federal treasury, newly filled with money from impost duties. Locke countered that "all the money raised that way, and more, would be swept away by courtly parade," that the state could dodge the developing aristocracy and all its expenses. At any rate, regarding the impost, Jones had another proposal up his sleeve. He offered a resolution for the convention calling for the North Carolina state legislature to impose an impost identical to whatever the new national government might levy, and to forward all revenues to the national treasury. This would be an act of good faith, to signal that North Carolina still desired union, but did not agree to the terms.[31]

Jones was firmly in control, and he drove the Federalists to anger. Iredell biographer Griffith McRee captures the rage of the Federalists in his description of Jones's leadership of the Anti-Federalists: "Jones's forces were too numerous and too well disciplined to be beaten. With them, his nod was approval of the highest authority; his sneer the refutation of the most perfect logic; the scrape of his foot the signal for attack; his uplifted finger the token of caution or silence." When Johnston attacked Jones for insinuating that he was merely a seeker after federal office, Jones coolly replied that "in every publication one might see ill motives assigned to the opposers of the Constitution," especially that they feared losing lucrative and influential state positions. Jones believed that "it was fair its opposers should be permitted to retort, and assign a reason equally selfish for the conduct of its friends." What must have been most infuriating to the Federalists was that Jones had a fair point, and he presented it without rancor or incivility. He also brought up Thomas Jefferson's expressed desire that nine states should ratify, and then four reject in order to secure amendments, which must have further irked the Constitution's proponents.[32]

Ultimately, the convention, still in committee of the whole, was ready to vote on Jones's proposal to recommend amendments without formally deciding on the Constitution. Iredell described this as "a very awful moment"; he knew that such a decision could not possibly go his way. The convention passed the resolution with a large majority in favor. The next day it would formalize the decision in a regular session. On August 1, Iredell tried to bring the decision to a halt by insisting that the minority have their objection entered in the journals of the convention in the form of a defeated motion for ratification. The Anti-Federalist leaders suggested that the proper time for this would be after the resolution to propose amendments without ratification was formally entered, so Iredell agreed to wait. When he tried again, there was stiff opposition from the majority to even acknowledging the proposal. This prompted Federalist Whitmill Hill to declare that "if the majority persevered in their tyrannical attempt, the minority should secede." This was a fitting end to the ratifying conventions of 1787 and 1788, for in the very first one to meet, in Pennsylvania, the minority insisted that its proposals for amendments should be entered into the journals, but they were effectively shouted down by the large majority. In North Carolina the tables were turned, and the Federalist minority threatened to do exactly what the Pennsylvania Anti-Federalists did.[33]

It was Willie Jones, of course, who smoothed everything over. The Federalists would not have their own resolution in the journals, but they would be on record as proposing an amendment to the resolution of the Anti-Federalists. By a vote of 84 in favor and 184 against, the Federalist motion was defeated, but the statement was made. The Anti-Federalists in this state were (slightly) more magnanimous than the Federalist majority in Pennsylvania. The resolution presented by Willie Jones passed with an identical split, 184–84. It was all over; the Federalists had fought hard, but they did not have nearly enough votes. "It is useless to contend longer against a majority that is irresistible," Iredell had said in introducing his proposal that the Federalists have a motion in the journals. "We submit, with the deference that becomes us, to the decision of a majority."[34] The parallels to Pennsylvania are striking, but both sides behaved with greater decorum here.

In terms of amendments, North Carolina echoed Virginia. The convention adopted a twenty-point bill of rights functionally identical to that proposed by its northern neighbor, as well as twenty-six amendments. These included all twenty of Virginia's proposals, plus six amendments unique to North Carolina. None of the latter were critical changes. They included a requirement for a two-thirds vote to declare a state in rebellion or introduce foreign soldiers to America, a prohibition of monopolies and of treaties that contradict the Constitution, a minor change to the clause concerning interstate shipping, and an explicit prohibition of federal interference with existing state-issued paper money.[35] The Federalists were not pleased with this list, but they were even further from defeating these proposals than were their counterparts in Virginia. Instead they offered a counterproposal that included unconditional ratification and six of the twenty-six amendments. They were willing to concede a clause retaining to the states powers not enumerated as well as one granting the states extensive powers over the militia, the modifications to representation and interstate shipping, the change concerning congressional pay, and the prohibition on congressional interference in election laws. Thus far would they concede, and no further. This in itself is instructive; of the twenty-six amendments proposed by the Anti-Federalists, only three made it into the amendments formally proposed by Congress. All three of these were among the six offered by the Federalists.

Willie Jones followed up the resolution requesting amendments with two more concerning the state of North Carolina. The first urged the legislature to take actions to remain on good terms with the new Congress, specifically to levy an impost identical to whatever impost the new Congress under the Constitution might levy. The second recommended that the legislature get the state's finances in order in anticipation of joining the union in the future, specifically to redeem all remaining paper money as expeditiously as possible. Thus the state might accept and even contribute to the general impost, to remain closely connected to, if not formally a part of, the union, and in the meantime it could redeem its paper money before accepting a Constitution that would make it illegal.

The decision of the convention was undoubtedly popular in the state, but there was still hope for reconciliation. The Federalists complained of "struggling against a torrent of popular phrenzy," but insisted that "a considerable part of her most respectable citizens are still attached to a federal system, from persuasion, that from it alone they can expect exemption from domestic insurrection, defence from foreign invasion, and continuance of the blessings of peace and prosperity."[36] In this they were clearly right; North Carolina had demands to make, but was not prepared to remain outside the union indefinitely. The convention consciously chose neither to ratify nor to reject; its only official decision was to recommend amendments. There was, in fact, broad agreement that the state should join the union, but it should first do what it could to secure amendments.

After the convention, Thomas Person wrote a letter to John Lamb that made explicit the strategy of the Anti-Federalists, built on the hope for amendments. Person noted that the opposition had a clear majority in the convention; "if the total rejection had been proposed, even in terms of Reprobation," he explained, "the motion would have succeeded, but we conceived it more decent & moderate" to recommend amendments and decline to outright reject the document. The reason for this is simple; the Anti-Federalists were out of other options.

There is so little Security left now for obtaining Amendments, especially if your State is adoptive, that it may probably be wise in those
States, or the Minorities in them, to oppose all representation until
Amendments are obtain'd or to send into the New Congress only such
men of unequivocal Characters as will oppose every operation of the
System untill it is render'd consistant with the preservation of our Liberties too precious to be Sacrificed to *Authority, name, ambition,* or
design.[37]

North Carolina would take the first option, declining to ratify, while New
York, which ratified the Constitution before Person's letter was written,
would take the latter, and send legislators determined to make changes to
the Constitution. The North Carolina Anti-Federalists recognized the importance of union, but were determined to join on their terms or not at all.

THE HARRISBURG CONVENTION

North Carolina was not the only place resisting ratification. In Pennsylvania, there were still at least a few who still believed the Constitution could
be stopped. In early 1788, the state legislature received petitions containing
over six thousand signatures asking it to invalidate the state convention's
ratification. The legislature took no action on the petitions, and adjourned
until September. This prompted the state's Anti-Federalists to seek an alternative venue for expressing their disagreement and displeasure. In the early
summer, a circular letter was prepared for distribution throughout the state,
calling for delegates to meet at a convention in Harrisburg in September.
The effort originated in Cumberland County, and was probably largely the
work of Robert Whitehill, who had so ably attacked the Constitution in
convention, and introduced a motion for amendments.[38] The letter was sent
in early July, after the arrival of the news that both New Hampshire and
Virginia had ratified. The stated goal was "to combine the friends to amendments in some place in which they may confidently draw together and exert
their power in unison."[39] One of the primary means for this would be to
nominate a slate of candidates for the first Congress. With ten states approving the Constitution, these elections were no doubt imminent, and the
opposition would be well served to be prepared, since the Federalists were
clearly ready.

    After the news from New York arrived, the tone shifted somewhat. In one
letter in response to the initial circular, the writer suggests that "it would

be the height of madness and folly, and in fact a crime of very detrimental consequence to our country, to refuse to acquiesce in a measure received in form by so great a majority of our country." It would merely be an invitation, he continues, "to shackle us with those manacles that we fear may be formed under the color of the law, and we be led to know it is constitutional, when it is too late to extricate ourselves and posterity from a lasting bondage." For the Anti-Federalists of western Pennsylvania, this language is actually rather conciliatory. This was an area not to be easily mollified. Not all of the delegates to Harrisburg were so conciliatory, though. Ford argues that some, including future Secretary of the Treasury Albert Gallatin, were contemplating secession. Western Pennsylvania could unite with Kentucky and Tennessee to form a new western confederacy. Gallatin had prepared a resolution that stated that "altho the Constitution proposed for the United States is likely to obviate most of the inconveniencies we labored under, yet several parts of it appear so exceptionable to us that nothing but the fullest confidence of obtaining a revision of them by a general convention and our reluctance to enter into any *dangerous*[40] measures could prevail on us to acquiesce in its organization in this state." Thus Gallatin suggested a national convention of "the friends to amendments" in order to discuss how best to obtain amendments.[41]

The Harrisburg Convention was to be the last gasp of the Democratic Anti-Federalists, who had been increasingly marginalized throughout the ratification process. Only in New Hampshire, Massachusetts, and South Carolina had they had much voice at all in the conventions, and only in the western newspapers and in Philadelphia had they received much of a hearing in the public debate. The delegates took a more moderate stance than Gallatin, essentially endorsing the New York plan for a second general convention, and dropping the mention of "dangerous measures." The delegates prepared a modest petition to the state legislature imploring the representatives to vote for calling a national convention. The convention claimed to "possess sentiments completely federal," and requested that the legislature "take such measures as you in your wisdom shall deem most effectual and proper to obtain a revision and amendment of the Constitution of the United States, . . . and that such revision be by a general convention of representatives from the several states in the Union."[42] The petition includes twelve specific amendments. The first is a familiar insistence that Congress exercise only enumerated powers, and not govern by implication. There are several on representation, including the recall of Senators and an increase in the size of the House, as well as a prohibition on Congress altering state regulations on elections. The convention called for a requisition system before direct taxes, and a supermajority for a standing army. There are amendments protecting state prerogatives, including militias, shipping, and courts. In sum, the amendments are neither original nor unusual, but they do represent the kernel of the opposition position in late 1788. Interestingly, there was no bill of rights proposed, suggesting that the Harrisburg gathering partook more of the radical Democratic Anti-Federalism of the western part of the state than the Rights Anti-Federalist position advocated in the ratifying convention a year before.

Many Pennsylvania Federalists were apparently frightened by the meeting.[43] The resolutions were not even inflammatory, though, especially not in light of most of the prior opposition in the state, so there was little here to fear. It is not clear whether the petition was ever formally presented to the legislature, but there is no evidence that the legislature ever considered it. The convention did nominate a slate of candidates for Congress, but the Anti-Federalists failed to get any of them elected, as the Federalist slate was chosen in statewide at-large elections for the eight seats.

William Petrikin, among the most virulent Anti-Federalists in the western part of the state, later expressed disappointment with the moderation at Harrisburg:

> I am Clearly of opinion our Harrisburgh conference did more injury to our cause than all the stratagems of our advarsaries. Our friends throughout the state expected something decisive from us and we spent our whole time Canvassing for places in Congress (a body we had so often reprobated according to its present constitution). I expected the intention of our meeting was to unite the opposition in the different parts of the state that they might act in concert—to form committees and associations and open a Chanel of communication through-out the united states if posible. Had this been done which I think was very practicable the opposition would have appeared so formidable to the Federalists that they durst not have refused us our demands. Had they been so imprudent as still to continue obstonate we could have compeled them to a compliance but the avidity with which some of our leaders courted preferment has defeated every salutary measure and we will perhaps never find the people in the same spirit again.[44]

On the last point Petrikin was certainly prescient; the Anti-Federalists would have no more opportunities. He may have been correct in his entire assessment as well; a more dramatic (though not illegal) act might have rallied the latent opposition still present in the state and increased turnout for the elections. Petrikin spoke of armed resistance, and even bragged about acts of violence against Federalists, but he seemed resigned to the fact that neither he nor his comrades-in-arms against the Constitution could effect any real change at this point.[45]

16

Elections and Amendments

"ONCE THE RATIFICATION game was over," writes Pauline Maier, "the score was tallied, and the crowds went home, a surprising quiet set over the land. After Congress declared the Constitution ratified and called the first federal elections, the country rallied behind the new Constitution."[1] This was not true everywhere, of course, as there were still substantial pockets of resistance, but in many states the conflict died down with shocking speed. This was due in part to a broad consensus that amendments to the Constitution were not only necessary but likely. Although hundreds of amendments had been suggested during the course of the debate, by this point it was clear what the opposition wanted to see: a bill of rights, including a guarantee of trial by jury; less national interference in state affairs, especially in elections; reduced national powers over taxation and the military; and a general clarification limiting Congress to enumerated powers, reserving all other powers to the states. The first was the basis of Rights Anti-Federalism, while the other three were the central arguments of the Power Anti-Federalists. Even the subject of representation had been largely pushed aside; those Anti-Federalists clamoring for government closer to the people had quieted down or had been relegated to the fringes of the debate.

THE PUSH FOR
A SECOND CONVENTION

The preferred Anti-Federalist approach to amendments was a second convention, and in late 1788 it looked entirely possible. The New York Convention had unanimously endorsed the idea, after all, and it had prominent proponents in Virginia. James Madison suggested to Washington that New York's circular letter "has a most pestilent tendency. If an Early General Convention cannot be parried," he insisted, "it is seriously to be feared that the system which has resisted so many direct attacks may be at last successfully undermined by its enemies." Washington responded that he found the letter's unanimous approval by the New York Convention "surprizing," and believed it would "be attended with pernicious consequences." It was, he suggested, even worse than North Carolina's refusal to ratify. Many Federalists resisted the idea of a second convention even more publicly, often suggesting that any changes should wait a few years until there had been time to observe whether it even needed changes. On this point Melancton Smith doubted the good faith of the Federalists: "The fair promises and pretensions of most of the leading men who were in favour of the new System are mere illusions—They intend to urge the execution of the plan in its present form—No reliance can be placed in any of them." Smith may have been having regrets about his efforts to secure a ratification compromise. Still, the votes of the Federalist delegates endorsing the circular letter opened up the possibility of pressure by public shaming. "I hope," wrote "A Federalist who is for Amendments" in the *Daily Advertiser* in November, "none of those who made such professions will be guilty of such duplicity of conduct as to oppose the calling a convention to propose amendments."[2]

In Virginia, Governor Randolph had advocated a second convention since the closing days of the first, and he endorsed the proposal. He made his position clear in his correspondence with Madison in August and September. A second convention, he wrote, "will give contentment to many, who are now dissatisfied." He saw some danger in the amendments that might be made, "but if such be the will of America, who can withstand it?" Madison was alarmed by this position, writing back that a convention quickly assembled "will evidently be the offspring of party and passion, and will probably for that reason alone be the parent of error and public injury." He insisted to Randolph that a majority of Americans "are in favor of the Constitution as it stands, or at least are not dissatisfied with it in that form." Any changes made by a convention would not reflect the popular will, "but will be obtained by management, or extorted by menaces." One wonders if Madison recognized the irony of his words; surely the process of securing ratification was "obtained by management," and the Federalists raised their share of "menaces." At any rate, Randolph was unmoved by Madison's pleas. If such factious characters should try to manage the convention, they would be unable to achieve a consensus, or unable to secure the support of enough states. If there was broad agreement, then such a change ought to be made. If the convention "should be in unison as to even one amendment, it will satisfy, and bear down all malcontents." Randolph himself was to become the primary champion in Virginia of calling for a second convention; he had, after all, been its earliest proponent.[3]

Despite three state legislatures (Virginia, New York, and North Carolina) formally calling for a second convention, the movement failed due to the general inaction of the other ten states. Three states (Massachusetts, Delaware, and New Hampshire) either postponed the issue or sent it to die in committee; Connecticut simply ignored the letter when the governor laid it before the legislature.[4] The Pennsylvania legislature voted against formally considering and debating it, by a relatively close vote of 38–24. Maryland instead considered (but did not vote on) a resolution calling for Congress to propose amendments. Rhode Island, as per its general tendency, referred the question to the towns of the state, which approved the idea of a second convention nine towns to five, with others issuing no instructions on the matter; the predominantly Federalist towns were divided over how to treat the issue. Even with this general support, the state legislature took no further action despite an earlier resolution approving of such a convention in concept. South Carolina did not even look at the issue until just after it voted to ratify the twelve amendments proposed by Congress, and the last two states (New Jersey and Georgia) apparently did not take any action (or even formal inaction) at all.[5] These decisions doomed any chance at calling a second convention; the Constitution stipulated that two-thirds of the states, nine, must call for a convention in order to formally propose amendments. The effort fell six states short. This meant that the contest for amending the Constitution would take place on the floor of Congress, and much would depend on the elections to the first Congress under the Constitution.

As the elections approached, both sides prepared for a fight. Washington wrote in late August that "there are suggestions that attempts will be made to procure the election of a number of Antifederal characters to the first Congress, in order to embarrass the wheels of government and produce premature alterations in the Constitution." He was seemingly quite alarmed by the prospect that the opponents of the Constitution would actually seek elected office. It could not be that these "characters" had real concerns about the document or the imminent new government; such electoral efforts must involve "secret machinations" to overthrow the system before it could even get started.[6] The Federalist paranoia was running high, and had affected even the General. The actual goal of most of the Anti-Federalists was not subversion of the new government, but amendment of the Constitution.

Fortunately for the worried Federalists, the elections did not go well for the opposition. North Carolina and Rhode Island, the two Anti-Federalist holdout states, could not elect representatives or presidential electors. New York and Virginia each had strong opposition to the Constitution, but the Federalists did better than expected in both, winning four out of six House seats in the former and seven out of ten in the latter.[7] Massachusetts and South Carolina also sent split delegations, with South Carolina being the only state to send a majority Anti-Federalist delegation, three out of five seats. The other seven states sent all-Federalist delegations, though some of these Federalists did favor amending the Constitution. The Senate turned out even worse for the opposition. Because the New York legislature could not agree on a process, the state did not elect any Senators in time for the first Congress to meet, and the only state to send Anti-Federalists to the Senate was Virginia.

The election did bring out a curious Anti-Federalist piece in Delaware, which up until this point had not produced a single public opposition argument. Although the writer did not level specific arguments against the Constitution, he did tear into the Federalists and their tactics. "You have been flattered by the advocates of this Federal Constitution," he wrote to the people of the state.

> You have been promised an abundance of cash, an immense price for your produce, happiness and plenty, mountains of gold, and almost a little heaven in the northern part of this western hemisphere. They have told you that the constitution will effect all of itself, and that you will have nothing to do but quietly enjoy the happiness which it will produce. . . . Beware! beware, my fellow-citizens, of the deception! Never suffer yourselves to be the dupes of selfish and designing men! Never submit to the tyranny and despotic rule of crafty politicians! And never nourish and produce a successful enemy within your own bosom, who, under the pretence of patriotism, will lead you to the block and immediately strike the decisive blow, to the confusion of the astonished world! But if you must fall—if death must be your doom— fall nobly!—Fall in the midst of your slaughtered enemies, and leave them a dear-bought victory![8]

It is difficult to decide what to make of this essay. It is definitely Anti-Federalist, suggesting that the people "not trust too much to this new constitution," in a state that did not seem to contain any Anti-Federalists at all prior to this point, nearly a year after the state's ratification. It does not appear to be a satire. One can imagine a lonely Anti-Federalist who had held his tongue, but could not stay silent a moment longer. If more such voices emerged, the elections could have gone very differently.

David Thomas of Virginia, in a letter on March 3, 1789, to Griffith Evans of Philadelphia, perhaps best summed up the frustration that the

Anti-Federalists felt with the whole election process, especially in those states in which they had been shut out by pro-Federalist election rules and a hostile press:

> How does Fedralism go on in your State? does the people know the meaning of the word Fedralism, it is a very pretty word, it has a beautiful Sound, it Charms all the learned the wise, the polite, the reputable, the Honorable, and virtuous, and all that are not Caught with the alurements of its Melody, as poor ignorant asses, nasty dirty Sons of bitches; reserved for future treatment agreeable to their de-merrit.[9]

There was still some defiance spread throughout the states, perhaps even Delaware, but the vast majority of Anti-Federalists had become merely advocates for amendments. With few of them actually seated in Congress, meaningful changes to the Constitution seemed less likely than ever.

AMENDING THE CONSTITUTION

Thomas Jefferson, though still in Paris, undoubtedly captured the mood of many Americans in writing to Madison in late July. "I sincerely rejoice at the acceptance of our new constitution by nine states," he wrote. "It is a good canvas, on which some strokes only want retouching. What these are, I think are sufficiently manifested by the general voice from North to South, which calls for a bill of rights." Jefferson no doubt reflected the opinion of a significant number of Virginians, and Americans more generally, in this view. He suggested no major changes in the structure or powers of the government, though he did suggest that the President ought to be ineligible for reelection. A bill of rights just might be enough to finish the process of constitution-making. Richard Bland Lee reported to Leven Powell from Congress his expectation that "all the amendments tending to the greater security of civil Liberty will be obtained," while "those tending to sap the foundations of United government will be discarded."[10] In doing this, the Federalists could win over the Rights Anti-Federalists, and perhaps a few of the Power Anti-Federalists, without conceding major changes to the Constitution or a second convention. Adding a statement of rights might split the Anti-Federalists just enough to diminish the remaining opposition to a small disgruntled minority. Seen in this light, the Bill of Rights was not so much a set of concessions as it was a political move to consolidate the Federalist victory.

Even the potential political gains of some amendments did not spur Congress to action. James Madison pushed for his colleagues to take up the question, and he received further support from President Washington, who devoted a paragraph of his Inaugural Address to recommending that Congress take action on amendments,[11] but the other pressing business resulted in the question being continually delayed. Madison would not be put off indefinitely, though, and in early June he finally convinced enough congressmen to take the time to consider what changes ought to be made. Still he faced opposition from Federalists; James Jackson of Georgia spoke for many, comparing the Constitution to "a vessel just launched, and lying at the wharf," and recommended a trial voyage to see how seaworthy it really was. Others, too, fought against consideration. Madison, though, was insistent; he explained that a serious effort at amendments "will inspire a reasonable hope in the advocates for amendments, that full justice will be done to the important subject." To set aside the subject indefinitely would undermine the prestige and credibility of Congress.[12]

In a letter to Richard Peters in August, Madison offers a more complete argument for adding amendments. He suggests seven reasons. First, such a statement is not improper or dangerous, even though it may be unnecessary. In many states, including Virginia, he continued, the Constitution would have been rejected had promises of amendments not been made. Similarly, the House candidates in Virginia had won based on similar promises. Fourth, Madison's efforts were a preemptive strike, to forestall much stronger changes proposed by the minority. The next two reasons were connected: to add a bill of rights would defuse the opposition, while failing to act would inflame it. Finally, North Carolina was only going to join the union if certain guarantees of rights were added.[13] This was a reasonable list that suggested that Madison was well in touch with the political reality in Congress, but Peters was not convinced. He wrote that "a Firmness in adhering to our Constitution 'till at least it had a longer Trial would have silenced Antifederalists sooner than magnifying their Importance by Acknowledgements on our Part & of ourselves holding up a Banner for them to rally to." He suggested that as long as the Anti-Federalists have any unaddressed complaints they will remain clamorous for more changes.[14] If nothing else, they would continue to push for further limits on the tax power.

Madison's proposals met with a mixed reception. For the Anti-Federalists, of course, they did not go far enough. Few Federalists were enthusiastic, but most probably agreed with George Clymer's fitting metaphor: "Like a sensible physician he has given his malades imaginaires bread pills powder of paste & neutral mixtures." Madison was administering a placebo to the Anti-Federalists to help them overcome their imagined terrors of the new government. Not all of the Federalists were pleased with Madison's placebo amendments, though; some believed that he was conceding too much, too fast. Theodore Sedgwick, for example, wrote in July that Madison "is constantly haunted with the gohst [sic] of Patrick Henry," and upon reading Madison's speeches and writings it is easy to agree with this assessment.[15]

The first battle was over how to discuss the amendments, with Fisher Ames persuading his colleagues to refer Madison's proposals to a committee rather than bring them to the floor. The Anti-Federalists, led by Elbridge Gerry, put up an impressive fight on this point, to underscore that they would not let the majority run roughshod over them; the proposals by the ratifying conventions would be heard one way or the other. Even so, Madison was hopeful that the resistance could be pacified with reasonable amendments. In April, James Sullivan wrote to Elbridge Gerry that the opposition would wait quietly to see if the new government would take some oppressive measure that they had predicted. The demand for amendments had become latent, a potential firestorm that might be avoided by some nominal efforts. From North Carolina, Madison heard from William Davie that the people there were not really demanding the "farago of Amendments borrowed from Virginia" by the state's convention; what the people really wanted were a few small changes to place reasonable limits on congressional power. Even in Virginia Madison's efforts at adding protection for rights were winning over opponents. "Madison is becoming popular with the Antis," wrote Edward Carrington in early August, "who say they believe he is to be the most depended upon for procuring amendments." A month later he wrote to Madison that the people in Virginia who wanted to see changes made "consider you as the patron of amendments."[16]

Much of the debate in Congress over amendments, in fact, would be procedural. The House debated whether to incorporate amendments into the text of the Constitution or add them to the end, as well as what could be proposed, when, and by whom. Concerning the actual content, Madison's proposals dominated the debate, and the Federalists did not let their opponents make any significant changes. This generated a great deal of resentment on the part of the Anti-Federalists. Aedanus Burke found the proposals "little better than whip-syllabub, frothy and full of wind, formed only to please the palate, or they are like a tub thrown out to a whale, to secure the freight of the ship and its peaceable voyage." The simile is an allusion to Jonathan Swift's *Tale of a Tub*, and it was borrowed by the Federalists as well; Richard Peters suggested in a letter to Madison that no one ought to "throw out Tubs but those who were afraid of the Whale." To Madison, though, the Anti-Federalist whale must have been frightening indeed.[17]

Burke put up quite a fight, backed in particular by fellow South Carolina Representative Thomas Tudor Tucker as well as Elbridge Gerry. They forced debate on amendments to the military power, congressional authority over elections, and various other issues. The Federalists were largely willing to concede additional protection for rights, so the opposition went after the changes they wanted made to the powers of Congress. On each point they failed; there simply were not enough of them. Finally, on August 22, the last day the House was to discuss amendments, Tucker brought up what everyone had been avoiding: taxes. He proposed that Congress be prevented from levying direct taxes unless revenue from the impost should prove insufficient, and that requisitions should be the next option. Everyone knew this was coming, and no one wanted to discuss it. The issue actually split both sides. Samuel Livermore, a Federalist from New Hampshire, came out in favor, noting that without a serious check on the power of Congress, his constituents "would not value [the proposed amendments] more than a pinch of snuff, they went to secure rights never in danger." John Page replied disingenuously that "the warmest friends to amendments differed in opinion on this subject; many of them have ceased urging it, while others have become strenuous advocates for the reverse."[18] If there were such Anti-Federalists, they have proven elusive to history, as there is no extant record of any significant opposition figure reversing his opinion on this issue. However, the Anti-Federalists were split as well, with Gerry voting against this amendment; he wanted to see separate sources of revenue for state and national government, as he had argued since the beginning of the ratification debates. The proposal failed.

When the dust settled, the House of Representatives had passed seventeen articles of amendment, most of which essentially constituted a bill of rights. The opposition was not happy with the result, and many Federalists believed that they had conceded too much. The opposition had fought hard against long odds, and won some concessions. "I shall however console myself," wrote Gerry after the fight, "with the reflection, that should the consequences be injurious or ruinous, nothing has been wanting on my part in Convention or Congress to prevent them."[19] Still, self-consolation aside, there was still a gulf between the two sides concerning the Constitution.

The reaction of George Mason to the amendments proposed by the House
is reflective of how far apart the Federalists and Anti-Federalists still were:

> I have received much Satisfaction from the Amendments to the federal
> Constitution, which have lately passed the House of Representatives; I
> hope they will also pass the Senate. With two or three further Amend-
> ments such as confining the federal Judiciary to Admiralty & Mar-
> itime Jurisdiction, and to Subjects merely federal—fixing the Mode
> of Elections either in the Constitution itself (which I think would
> be preferable) or securing the Regulation of them to the respective
> States—Requiring more than a bare Majority to make Navigation &
> Commercial Laws, and appointing a constitutional amenable Council
> to the President, & lodging with them most of the Executive Powers
> now vested in the Senate—I cou'd chearfully put my Hand & Heart to
> the new Government.[20]

In short, if he could just rewrite the election clause and make a major
change to congressional powers in Article I, add an entirely new executive
body in Article II, which would require a complete rearranging of powers
between the branches of government, and substantially change the judicial jurisdiction in Article III, he could be happy with the Constitution.
These are not minor changes; they require massive alterations to all three
branches of the government. The suggested amendments went far toward
alleviating Mason's concerns about individual rights, to be sure, but the
structure of government was largely unchanged, a major problem for the
opposition. The amendments that were eventually ratified fell far short of
Mason's preferences, and it would seem that he was never fully reconciled
to the Constitution, though he did not seem to hold a grudge against its
advocates.[21]

The House, of course, was not to have the final word; the proposed
amendments had to run the gauntlet of the Senate, in which only two members were clearly in favor of amendments at all. After the House action,
though, the Senate did not dare reject the proposals outright, but they did
substantially modify and weaken the House amendments. The Senate version also omitted Madison's favorite amendment, protecting individual
rights against state encroachment. Grayson wrote that the rights protected
by the House amendments, when they reached the Senate, were "so mutilated & gutted that in fact they are good for nothing, & I believe as many
others do, that they will do more harm than benefit." Lee used similar language in a candid explanation to his brother Francis Lightfoot Lee that the

amendments were "much mutilated and enfeebled." He went a step further to express his concerns for the future of the government: "What with design in some, and fear of Anarchy in others, it is very clear, I think, that a government very different from a free one will take place eer [*sic*] many years are passed." Even Madison was displeased with the Senate changes, "which strike in my opinion at the most salutary articles." Paine Wingate wrote to John Langdon that "Madison says he had rather have none than those agreed by the Senate."[22]

PUBLIC RECEPTION OF THE PROPOSED AMENDMENTS

The two houses ultimately agreed on twelve articles of amendment, ten of which would become the Bill of Rights. The rights incorporated in these changes alleviated many of the Rights Anti-Federalist objections, though not all, and they did virtually nothing for the Power or Democratic objections. Only the Tenth Amendment would speak at all to these positions, and only in vague and undefinable terms. Still, the tub had been tossed, and most of the Anti-Federalists were sufficiently distracted to allow the Federalist ship of state to sail on unmolested.[23] Most of the fight had gone out of the Anti-Federalists, and many of them undoubtedly lamented the result. Patrick Henry expressed his frustration with his customary eloquence. "Right without her Power & Might is but a Shadow," he wrote to Richard Henry Lee. Senator Lee wrote back in similar fashion: "Yet small as it is, how wonderfully scrupulous have they been in stating Rights? The english language has been carefully culled to find words feeble in their Nature or doubtful in their meaning!" He also told Henry about the letter from the assembly of Rhode Island explaining their reasons for remaining out of the union until the Constitution had been appropriately amended. "We ought in common prudence to have done the same," he concluded.[24]

The Federalists were generally pleased. They had made changes addressing many of the complaints without substantially altering the essential powers of the Constitution. The report on the amendments by the *State Gazette of North Carolina*, aiming in part to finally secure ratification in that state, was typical of the Federalist response: "The amendments to the constitution of the United States, proposed by congress will undoubtedly satisfy the minds of *all* its enemies.—Not a door is left open for complaint, should the amendments be ratified by three fourths of the legislatures of the several states."[25] This was a clear exaggeration; many Anti-Federalists remained disappointed and disillusioned with the process. Richard Henry Lee, in one of his letters to Henry, wrote what might well be considered the epitaph of the Anti-Federalist movement:

> As [the proposed amendments] came from the H[ouse] of R[epresentatives] they were very far short of the wishes of our Convention, but as they are returned by the Senate they are certainly much weakened. You may be assured that nothing on my part was left undone to prevent this, and every possible effort was used to give success to all the Amendments proposed by our Country—We might as well have attempted to move Mount Atlas upon our shoulders—In fact, the idea of subsequent Amendments was delusion altogether, and so intended by the greater part of those who arrogated to themselves the name of Federalists. I am grieved to see that too many look at the Rights of the people as a Miser examines a Security to find a flaw in it! The great points of free election, Jury trial in criminal cases much loosened, the unlimited right of Taxation, and Standing Armies in peace, remain as they were. Some valuable Rights are indeed *declared*, but the powers that remain are very sufficient to render them nugatory at pleasure.[26]

Lee indeed put in a monumental effort early in the ratifying process, and in the Senate during the amendment debates, but the opposition largely failed to accomplish its primary goal of establishing a safe, republican federal government.

The twelve amendments proposed by Congress, and the ten ratified by the states, did little to alleviate the concerns of the Anti-Federalists. The Rights Anti-Federalists were partially appeased, with some rights explicitly protected against congressional interference. The Power Anti-Federalists saw one small concession in the Tenth Amendment, which reserved to the states all powers not explicitly granted to the national government, which the Federalists had been vehemently insisting was the case anyway in the Constitution as written. The Democratic Anti-Federalists got nothing more than a token nod toward slightly greater representation in a proposed amendment that did not receive the necessary three-quarters of states to be ratified. None of the twelve amendments proposed by Congress, and certainly none of the ten Amendments ratified, made any real changes in either the structure or the powers of government. "Federalists passed amendments that secured rights, but without incorporating any of the Antifederalists' suggested structural changes in national institutions," writes Siemers. "Although some in both camps disliked this compromise, in the main, the Bill of Rights served to bolster the nascent constitutional consensus." That consensus involved giving the Constitution a fair trial, and undermined any continued efforts at resistance. This was, in some respects, an even more crushing defeat than the ratification struggle.[27] The Anti-Federalists, despite the appearance of concessions to their arguments, clearly lost the fight.

17

The Last Resistance and the Completion of the Union

THE INAUGURAL ISSUE of the *Gazette of the United States*[1] in 1789 included brief descriptions of each of the then eleven states in the union, and the two "foreign states" of Rhode Island and North Carolina. Its description of North Carolina reflects the general view held by the Federalist leaders in the new Congress. "A depreciated paper medium, and a deficiency of political knowledge, are considered as the causes of the anti-national spirit of this State. Her extensive frontier, and being obliged to export the greater part of her productions through Virginia, it is expected will ere long evince the necessity of her acceding to the confederation. This indeed appears already to be the predominant idea of her citizens, by some recent transactions." The charge of "deficiency of political knowledge" is neither true nor fair, but the general characterization of the state's mood was essentially correct. This description contrasts with that given to Rhode Island: "This state again has refused to accede to a union with her sister states, and is now wholly estranged from them and from appearances, will long continue so, unless the measure of the iniquity of her "KNOW YE" gentry should be speedily filled up—or the delusion which has so long infatuated a majority of her citizens should be removed."[2] The difference is striking. Both states had refused to ratify, yet one was treated practically as a state while the other was a rebel. The distinction also appeared in a satirical advertisement in the *New Hampshire Gazette* in late July 1788, just before the state heard the news of New York's ratification.

WANTED,

By the Federalists—*the ratification of North Carolina and New-York*.

By the antis—*eye sight*.

By the R. I. majority—*anarchy.*
By the minority—*a separation.*
And by America in general—*the speedy operation of the new government.*[3]

North Carolina was little more an outcast than New York; in fact Washington believed that the former state's refusal to ratify was less harmful than the latter's circular letter calling for a second national convention. Rhode Island, though, had few defenders or advocates. Nonetheless, with the accession of the other eleven states, along with the amendments proposed by Congress, both outlying states would join the federal fold by the middle of 1790.

By the time Congress sent twelve proposed amendments to the states for ratification, the debate was essentially over in the other eleven states. Even in North Carolina there was little (and declining) opposition. There was some talk of another round of amendments, but it had little support. The Anti-Federalists were a dying breed, and the subject of a satirical advertisement in the *Pennsylvania Mercury*:

> TO BE SEEN, near the Jersey Market, price Two Coppers, a strange sort of an ANIMAL, half Man, half Quadruped, has the properties of a Snapping Tortoise, spitefully snapping and growling at his best friends and benefactors, whenever he hears the words, Federalist, New Government, &c. &c. &c. mentioned, but happily his bite is not venomous, as his teeth are now worn out; he roves about from place to place, and is thought will soon run mad. The public are cautioned to be aware of him. Tis supposed he will endeavour shortly to make his escape to Carlisle, as tis said, at that place, there is a Nursery of a few more Animals of the same Species.[4]

Carlisle was the last bastion of violent Anti-Federalism in Pennsylvania. One newspaper in March reported that "the spirit of political enmity . . . has begun another persecution. While national and private peace pervade the other parts of Pennsylvania, that town is in a state of civil war. Every man's hand is raised against his neighbor. Bludgeons are walking-sticks, and bricks are finger-stones." William Petrikin was unapologetic in his opposition, bragging about the size and training of the Anti-Federalist militia as well as its exploits in violent skirmishes with Federalists. Elsewhere, though, this resistance was rapidly declining.[5]

NORTH CAROLINA'S
RELUCTANT RATIFICATION

The Federalists in North Carolina were irked by their association with Rhode Island as an outlier, and they worked hard to defend the state's reputation. Hugh Williamson, writing as "A Republican" in the *New York Daily Advertiser*, defended North Carolina against the "criticism and censure" that had begun as a result of the state's convention refusing to ratify the proposed Constitution. The state was responsible and patriotic during the Revolution, and had been diligent about paying its debts. North Carolina's concern for amendments to the Constitution, he argued, was now essentially a universal position, and the state's refusal to ratify does more to ensure that appropriate changes are made than its joining and participating would. In the end, Williamson insists, North Carolina will join the union, but some of the state's proposed changes ought to be made in the meantime.[6] This behavior was not that of a rogue state bent on disunion; North Carolina was not Rhode Island.

The problem for the Federalists in the state, though, was that "nine tenth of the people of this State are opposed to the adoption of the New System, without very Considerable Amendments," as Thomas Person put it in a letter to John Lamb. (His estimate was trustworthy because "no man is better Acquainted with the publick mind" than himself, or so he claimed.) In reality, the majority was almost certainly smaller; Timothy Bloodworth's simple assertion to Lamb of "a decided Majority" against the Constitution was more reasonable. It appears, however, that the majority was shrinking. Immediately following the convention, state legislative elections were held, and the Federalists made substantial gains. Willie Jones, still the unquestioned leader of the Anti-Federalists, was returned to the Assembly, where he proposed a second convention to meet late in 1789, half a year after the new government was set to commence business. His colleagues pushed the date back for several more weeks, to November. The legislature also passed a resolution appointing delegates to a national convention to consider amendments, should one occur; the all-Anti-Federalist delegation was headed by Person and Bloodworth.[7]

The Federalists turned to the press to make their case. James Iredell played a major role in the Federalist propaganda campaign; he was a tireless essayist and pamphleteer. Writing as "A Citizen of North-Carolina," he tried to reassure the people that the Constitution was safe for liberty, and that the consequences of defying the other states by refusing the Constitution would be grave. "The majority of the Convention seem not to have considered what they did as a rejection. But it may undoubtedly be considered so by the other states. After not accepting when the opportunity was allowed us, we have no right to chuse our own time at any period hereafter."[8] This was a direct refutation of an argument made by Jones in the convention, and it proved to be entirely wrong. Even at the time there was no reason to believe that Congress would not welcome North Carolina back into the union, but the argument was nonetheless an effective tactic.

Not all of the Federalist material was moderate and well reasoned, though. Much of the campaign involved attacking the Anti-Federalists; Willie Jones and Thomas Person were particularly targeted as the individuals most responsible for the refusal to ratify the Constitution. A pamphlet signed "A Citizen and Soldier" included a particularly virulent attack on the Anti-Federalists, and especially Willie Jones, "the superintendant and principal chevalier of the antifederal junto." He portrayed Jones as a political boss whose word was law for his mindless followers. Worse, he accused Jones of acting on base and self-aggrandizing motives. The Citizen and Soldier even objected to the nature of the decision, which was "not an honest rejection in plain terms, but an artful fraudulent evasion." He claimed that Jones "abuse[d] the deputies of this state to the federal Convention at Philadelphia for a pack of scoundrels, and [said] that they all deserved to be hanged," and he attacked Jones's behavior during the convention:

> [W]ith all these grievances under which an infant people with impotent struggle laboured, he will damn the saviours of our country the Federal Convention, for a pack of scoundrels, go to the Convention at Hillsborough full of damns and G-d damns, blow up an idle fandango about bills of rights and amendments, and what is still more infamous, throw us altogether out of the union. Was this a time to smoak a pipe and suck the paw like a surly bear, when your house was on fire? Was this a time like a Jew broker to bargain about fractions, without a single ship in your harbour or a *dollar* in your treasury? Shall this man be allowed to brand the inimitable Washington with the appellation of scoundrel, when he is unworthy to clean his shoes? Shall he be allowed to condemn to the gallows my brother soldier Col. D[avie], for acting honourably and faithfully? Away with him; he is unworthy of further faith—a second Judas: I tell you he is base, infamous and unprincipled.[9]

These charges were a bit too much for Willie Jones. He briefly responded in the *State Gazette of North Carolina* to deny that he had ever called

Washington, Davie, or the members of the Philadelphia Convention more
generally "scoundrels." Jones did not, of course, answer the other charges,
which were mere hostile rhetoric. "An Honest Man" fired back a week later
in the same paper, writing that Jones's short letter was "but a poor evasion."
Though he acknowledged that the pamphlet was "a clumsy performance,"
he nonetheless urged Jones to "stand forward, answer it, give reputation to
your 182 who negative the learned labour of the choicest worthies of our
Empire.—Produce to public view your thoughts, your wisdom, your objections to the code handed us from the Federal Convention; or like the grave
digger in Hamlet, confess your self; Or in a manly, honest manner, make the
best apology in your power."[10] There is no evidence that Jones did any of
these things, or responded at all. He must have felt his original letter was
enough. Thomas Person, on the other hand, who was himself a general of
the Revolution, "denounced Washington as 'a damned rascal and traitor
to his country for putting his hand to such an infamous paper as the new
Constitution,'" and there is no evidence that he either denied or retracted
this sentiment.[11]

   Though the Federalists were more prolific, the Anti-Federalists were not
silent. On September 21, "Another True Federalist" wrote with effusive
praise of "A True Federalist" (whose original essays are unfortunately no
longer extant) who, the author claimed, thoroughly converted him to the
cause of Anti-Federalism. The original essays, according to this admirer,
had "in the most unanswerable manner, blown away those visionary evils
with which the good people of this state have been persecuted, as the certain
consequence of our non-acceptance thereof." The Constitution, the True
Federalist contended, "was the result of a coalition between the Nationalists
and the Aristocrates, two parties in the grand convention." Another True
Federalist saw this as truly alarming; "is it possible," he asks, "that regal
and aristocratical principles, however blended, could bring forth a constitution calculated for the meridian of a free and enlightened people?" The
people of North Carolina ought not to fall victim to "the boasted, choleric,
and decisive reasoning" of the Federalists. No harm will come to North
Carolina for remaining outside of the union; to the contrary, the people of
the other states, oppressed by excess taxes, will flee to the state and increase
its population and wealth.[12] This prediction was as incorrect as Iredell's
claim that the other states would not readily accept North Carolina's accession, but it must have been convincing to some.

   The Federalist campaign was working to convert the people of North Carolina, but the amendments proposed by Congress probably accomplished
far more toward that end. Upon hearing that Madison had introduced

amendment proposals, Davie wrote to Iredell that "nothing ever gave me so much pleasure." This effort "confounded the Anties exceedingly," because they had been insisting that Congress would never seriously consider making immediate changes. Even before this, though, there were signs of a change of opinion. In December 1788, Willie Jones again retired from the legislature, and largely remained out of public life thereafter, effectively abandoning the fight against the Constitution. In the back country, according to an anonymous correspondent in the *State Gazette*, the people "from rank *anti*'s are now become perfect *fed*'s; so fully are they convinced of the ill policy of separating themselves from the union and of the excellency of our constitution." Willie Jones, the writer went on to explain, had also had a change of heart; when he "had scrutinized the characters of those who were against the constitution, he blushed to think he was seconded by such a vile herd of infamous fellows." Other writers suggested that Jones now believed that he had made a mistake in opposing the Constitution. Most Federalists were undoubtedly skeptical of the change, though. "I hear that even Wiley Jones has Apostatized from Anti-Federalism," one Federalist wrote in January, "another St. Paul's Conversion, if it is really so, tho' I confess I have as little faith as St. Peter had." It is more likely that Jones simply saw the writing on the wall, and decided not to fight the issue anymore.[13]

The Federalists were optimistic as the second convention approached. The decision by Jones not to seek a seat further fueled that optimism. "I am persuaded we might have carried our point last year," wrote Archibald Maclaine to Iredell two months before the convention, "but for Wilie Jones." Though Maclaine did not know at the time whether Jones would be a delegate, he expected in the second convention "a great number of well-meaning members who, ashamed of being led by the nose last year, will prove very restive. Upon the whole, I think we shall succeed." He added in another letter that he expected that many delegates from the first convention who were also chosen for the second "will vote differently than what they did, when they had the honor to be Willie Jones's puppets." In addition to the absence of Jones, the presence of William Blount and Hugh Williamson, both signers of the Constitution in Philadelphia, added considerable weight to the Federalist side.[14]

On November 16, 1789, the second convention of the state of North Carolina met at Fayetteville. Governor Samuel Johnston was elected president of this convention as well, and the delegates began with the usual details of rules and delegate credentials. The next day, Hugh Williamson made a motion to ratify the Constitution, which was referred to the committee of the whole. For three days the Constitution was discussed, along with the twelve amendments proposed by Congress, though the debates were not recorded. On Saturday, November 21, the convention, in regular session, took up the report of the committee of the whole, to ratify the Constitution.

The Anti-Federalists were not quite done, though; James Galloway moved to amend the ratification to be conditional upon the inclusion of several additional amendments. The twelve amendments proposed by Congress, Galloway's resolution explained, "embrace in some measure . . . the object that this State had in view by a Bill of Rights, and many of the amendments proposed by the last Convention," but "some of the great and most exceptional parts of the said proposed Constitution have not undergone the alterations which were thought necessary by the last Convention."[15] He included five proposals. The first two were at the heart of Anti-Federalism nationally, while the final three reflected concerns more specific to North Carolina:

> That Congress shall not alter, modify or interfere in the times, places or manner of elections for Senators and Representatives, or either of them, except when the Legislature of any State shall neglect, refuse or be disabled by invasion or rebellion to prescribe the same.
>
> When Congress shall lay direct taxes or excises, they shall immediately inform the Executive power of each State of the quota of such State according to the Census herein directed, which is proposed to be thereby raised; and if the Legislature of any State shall pass a law, which shall be effectual for raising such quota at the time required by Congress the taxes and excises laid by Congress shall not be collected in such State.
>
> That Congress shall not directly either by themselves or through the Judiciary, interfere with any one of the States in the redemption of paper money already emitted and now in circulation, or in liquidating and discharging the public securities of any one of the States, but each and every State shall have the exclusive right of making such laws and regulations for the above purposes as they shall think proper.
>
> That Congress shall not introduce foreign troops into the United States without the consent of two-thirds of the members present of both Houses.
>
> That no treaties which shall be directly opposed to the existing laws of the United States in Congress assembled, shall be valid, until such laws shall be repealed or made conformable to such treaty; nor shall any treaty be valid which is contradictory to the Constitution of the United States.[16]

Interestingly, the third proposal if adopted probably would have prevented the national government from assuming the debts of the states. All of these amendments suggest a powerful distrust of centralized power, and a belief that Congress would not only interfere with local policies but do so in a decidedly oppressive way.

The Federalists, with the Constitution already approved by eleven states and in operation for half a year, were not about to accept conditional ratification; the motion was defeated in a show of Federalist strength, eighty-two to 187. Davie immediately moved for the original resolution, to ratify the Constitution, and it passed by an even larger margin of 194 to seventy-seven. At this point Galloway tried again, moving his same five amendments as recommendations to accompany the ratification. The convention sent them to a committee (consisting of four Federalists led by Davie as well as Galloway, Bloodworth, and Spencer) and adjourned until Monday.

The committee made substantial changes. Congress was to retain the ability to alter election regulations "when the provision made by the State is so imperfect as that no consequent election is had."[17] Interference with paper money was still to be outlawed, but the clause concerning taxes was removed, along with the last two. In their place were six new amendments:

III. That the members of the Senate and House of Representatives shall be ineligible to and incapable of holding any civil office under the authority of the United States during the time for which they shall respectively be elected.

IV. That the journals of the proceedings of the Senate and House of Representatives shall be published at least once in every year, except such parts thereof relating to treaties, alliances, or military operations, as in their judgment require secrecy.

V. That a regular statement and account of all the receipts and expenditures of all public monies shall be published at least once in every year.

VI. That no navigation law, or law regulating commerce, shall be passed, without the consent of two-thirds of the members present in both Houses.

VII: That no soldier shall be enlisted for any longer term than four years, except in time of war, and then for no longer term than the continuance of the war.

VIII: That some tribunal, other than the Senate, be provided for trying impeachments of Senators.[18]

This resolution passed the convention, and thus Anti-Federalism essentially died with a whimper in the state. Some of these are significant changes, to be sure, but without the provision concerning taxes there was little force to the changes. Nonetheless, this was consistent with the general tone of the opposition in the state; it was not powers but rights that were at the heart of the North Carolina opposition.

The Federalists were pleased with the outcome, of course, but they were especially glad to see that the Anti-Federalists were apparently ready to concede the debate. After the vote, William Dawson wrote a letter to Iredell explaining the result of the convention:

> The business has been conducted throughout with great moderation. Some of the gentlemen of the opposition, to be sure, have been unreasonably tedious, trifling, and, I might add, absurd in their objections, which was all submitted to by the majority with a degree of patience that astonished every body. On taking the question for its adoption, there appeared Yeas 193—Nays 75. The minority seem to be perfectly satisfied since the decision, not because their doubts and fears have been fully removed, but because they have determined to acquiesce cheerfully in every measure which meets the approbation of a majority of their countrymen."[19]

Governor Johnston wrote on the twenty-third of November that "The Anties behave with great good humor on the Occasion" of the vote for ratification.[20]

In the end, North Carolina's ratification was driven more by necessity than conversion. The people still opposed the Constitution in principle, and saw the potential for oppression and tyranny, but they acquiesced because even the danger was preferable to remaining forever out of the union. Within a month after the convention voted to ratify the Constitution, the state legislature approved all twelve of the proposed amendments; it was only the third state to take action on them. With the added protections for individual rights, enough North Carolinians were prepared to accept the Constitution and give the new government a fair chance.

As the state began electing what would be a mixed congressional delegation (two Federalist Senators, three Federalist and two Anti-Federalist Representatives), Alexander Martin, the new governor selected to replace now-Senator Johnston, sent a formal letter to the legislature. In that letter, he praised the new Constitution and warned against the dangers of continuing partisan strife over it. "Let us remember we embarked with our sister states in one bottom, making one common cause," he wrote. It was up to the legislators, as the leaders of the state, "to reconcile those jarring sentiments" aroused by the ratification debate. He warned that "invidious distinctions have arisen. . . . Let hereafter the federal and antifederal name be no more heard as a reproach."[21] It was an impressive and conciliatory letter, and its message, once heeded, effectively closed the book on a contentious ratification struggle in North Carolina.

A LONG-DELAYED CONVENTION

"Rhode Island will reject the proposed Constitution," Henry Channing predicted early in the debate over ratification, "for the D[evi]l hath great wrath knowing that his time is short. They are a truly wretched people and have no prospect of speedy relief, unless there be a union of the other states. In this case I should hope to see them *governed*." By 1789, it seems that most of the rest of the people of the United States agreed. In the aftermath of the state's referendum on the Constitution, Federalist clergyman Enos Hitchcock complained about "the logger-headed assembly of this State," whose members "do not chuse to act like other people, & if they should it would excite just astonishment—nothing can exceed their madness." It was not until January 1790 that the "logger-headed" legislature finally called for a convention.[22]

A lot had changed in the state since its referendum in March 1788. First, and perhaps most important, by late 1789 the entire state debt had been paid in paper money, or forfeited under the state's strict laws.[23] Second, not only had sufficient states ratified the Constitution to put it into effect, but every state other than Rhode Island had come into the union. When Rhode Island had company, it was easier to be defiant. The leading Anti-Federalists, like their counterparts elsewhere, believed that New York would reject the Constitution. Even North Carolina offered some consolation, because that state was deemed important to the union, and was considered more respectable than little Rhode Island. Now, though, the state stood alone outside the union. The Federalists in the state tried to emphasize this political isolation. In early August, a Federalist writing in the *Providence Gazette* pleaded that the state could not survive independent of the union. Rhode Island would be a "Spectacle of Reproach and Derision—a By-Word among the Nations!" if it did not accede to the union.

Can we long exist as a commercial People, after being denied Entrance into the Ports of the Union? Does our Soil produce the Bread we consume? Are the Inhabitants of this small State the only Lovers of Liberty? Can it be supposed that here, and here only, Wisdom, Virtue and Patriotism, have taken up their favourite abode? Let us rather confess that the State is shamefully rent by Party and Faction, and that too many of us are fondly attached to a depreciating, destructive *Paper-Money Bubble*![24]

None of these arguments did much to influence the opinions of the country party leaders. A writer in the Philadelphia *Federal Gazette* in January 1789 observed of the legislature's just-finished session, "They have done nothing respecting the new government, but remain as they were, independent of God, man, and the devil. Happy people!"[25] No inside or outside pressure was going to sway the Anti-Federalists until they were prepared to take action.

Nonetheless, the politics in the state were changing. The country party leaders were quietly preparing to accept the Constitution, but doing so carefully so as not to threaten their political ascendency within the state. In May, the legislature voted to consult the towns on whether to call for a ratifying convention. The message was clear: the people were still opposed. In June, therefore, the country legislators were silent in the face of another effort to call a convention, prepared to vote it down without a word. This enraged the Federalists, who accused the majority of being "either 'ashamed or too ignorant' to make their arguments public." Jonathan Hazard fired back, breaking the country silence, to explain to the angry minority that patience was the proper approach, and that the state could rejoin the union at any time. Though the country party carried the vote, its margin of victory was a little smaller, giving the Federalists some hope.[26]

By September 1789, with the public debts liquidated with paper money, the state legislature in a special session voted to suspend the more onerous regulations on the state's paper money. With the paper money issue behind them, the country leaders wanted ratification, but they again asked the towns and were again informed that the people of Rhode Island wanted no part of the Constitution, and the motion to call a convention failed once more. During this same session, the legislature also approved a letter to Congress concerning Rhode Island's intentions. The delegates invoked the Revolution and their state's role in it, emphasizing their allegiance to the Articles of Confederation. Concerning the Constitution, they acknowledged being outliers on the issue, and ask for patience and understanding.

Our not having acceded to or adopted the new system of government, formed and adopted by most of our Sister States, we doubt not has given Uneasiness to them;—that we have not seen our Way clear to do it, consistent with our Idea of the Principles upon which we all embarked together, has also given Pain to us;—we have not doubted but we might thereby avoid present Difficulties, but we have apprehended future Mischiefs.[27]

The letter suggests that the Constitution looks too much like a first step toward a British-style system of national government. "Can it be thought strange then," the delegates ask their readers in Congress, "that with these Impressions, they should wait to see the proposed System organized and in Operation—to see what further Checks and Securities would be agreed to and established by Way of Amendments, before they could adopt it as a Constitution of Government for themselves and their Posterity?" The delegates even acknowledge "the Extremes to which democratical Government is sometimes liable—something of which we have lately experienced, but we esteem them temporary and partial Evils, compared with the Loss of Liberty and the Rights of a free People." It seems unlikely that many members of Congress found this convincing. The letter closes with the hope that the people of the state "shall not be altogether considered as Foreigners," and the promise that the state will try to fulfill its federal obligations.[28]

The goal of the moderates in the state (and there were some, even in Rhode Island) was to obtain amendments to make the Constitution safe for the state. Few writers thought the Constitution was good as it stood; many found it better than the alternative, but virtually all wrote of amendments. The difficult question was how to obtain such amendments; with eleven states accepting the Constitution, it was clear that the document would have to be altered according to its own procedures, which meant Rhode Island's influence would be far stronger with votes to exercise on behalf of amendments. There were some, though, who were unconvinced whether the Constitution was the proper framework for government, or starting point for reform. "Solon, Junior" advised caution, noting that not all of the evils of the situation of the states could be attributed to the defects in the Articles of Confederation. These evils "are the natural result of the depravity of manners and idleness let in upon us by the late war," so they cannot be checked by any change in government. "I am not yet convinced," he concludes, "that any government can save us without reformation of manners." The writer's solution was a renewed emphasis on education and civic virtue; to expect the Constitution to have a substantial impact was naive. "Whatever the New Federal Constitution is in itself, *its administration* is all that can ever affect the people." He concluded by expressing hope that through the amendment process the Constitution might "soon be made such as the good sense and virtue of the people choose to have it." Solon, Junior, suggested in a later essay that Rhode Island ought to ratify the Constitution in order to have an influence over the amendment process in Congress. "A Friend to Union" made much the same argument, praising the New York Convention for its recognition that it was more likely to secure amendments from within Congress than outside the union.[29]

In January 1790, the Rhode Island legislature again took up the question of a ratifying convention; this was the seventh such attempt by the Federalists of the state. There was talk of sending the Constitution back to the towns for another referendum, but it did not have the votes. On Friday, January 14, a motion to call a ratifying convention, after a long debate, passed by a vote of thirty-four to twenty-nine in the House of Deputies. The jubilation of the Federalists was short-lived, though, as the next day the upper house voted, by a five to four margin, to reject the idea; still, it adjourned only until the next day, Sunday. William Staples suggests that it was probably the first legislative meeting on a Sunday in the state's history, and the galleries were crowded. "Piety gave place to patriotism," he writes.[30] On that day, the lower house again approved a ratifying convention, this time by a vote of thirty-two to eleven. In the upper house, meanwhile, Anti-Federalist John Williams was absent, allegedly attending church services at the time; this resulted in a four-to-four deadlock, and left the fate of the state's ratifying convention in the hands of Governor John Collins, who was authorized to break the tie.[31] Collins, who had been a proponent of ratification all along, approved the measure. On the same day the legislature passed a resolution asking Congress to grant Rhode Island an extension on its existing exemption from restrictive federal trade regulations and tariffs.

The Anti-Federalists were not prepared to simply concede to the Federalists, however. They still had a clear majority in the state, and even if the Constitution were adopted the country party leaders had every intention of retaining their political ascendancy. Thus, "instead of surrendering wholesale to the rising star of Federalism," explains Irwin Polishook, the country party "was indefatigable in securing the election of its delegates to the convention." The ongoing public debate had been changed by the proposed amendments passed by Congress, which emboldened the Federalists, and even many moderates. "A Freeholder" defiantly insisted on ratification, explaining that "The imperfections that the most critical [opponents] could point out, are so trifling as not to be placed in competition with its merits; but however important they are, the amendments proposed by Congress, and already ratified by several States, will remedy those defects." Solon,

Junior, was also satisfied with the proposed amendments and the proceedings of the first federal Congress. He found jury trials well protected under the Judiciary Act and other rights secured in the amendments, and he was willing to trust to elected representatives to remedy remaining defects. He recommended ratification, because the alternative would be far worse. [32]

Not everyone was sold on the Constitution, though. "Greenwichiensis" was outright hostile. "Let the Constitution be immediately rejected," he wrote in the first of a four-part series, "we have dallied with it too long for our interest." Rhode Island, he insisted, can prosper as a free and independent state. The threat of dismemberment by the union was overstated: "Is not this state a free, distinct sovereignty, absolutely independent of the rightful control of any and all the States and kingdoms of the Earth?—and, this being palpably the case, what right have the United States to interfere with US?—What right have they to annihilate, and dismember this State?—What right have they to exercise dominion over us?" He expected foreign nations to come to the aid of Rhode Island should it be attacked. The fears that the state was in danger were "mere scare-crows" designed to intimidate the people into submission. [33]

The elections resulted in an Anti-Federalist victory, but not a dominating one. "The Election of Delegates for the Convention has gone unfavorably," Federalist Henry Marchant wrote in February. "The Anties are about ten Majority—I have Hopes however They will not totally reject the Constitution, but I think They may adjourn it over the Gen[era]l Election." [34] The delegates selected were an impressive gathering for the state. In the words of William Staples,

> It was a Convention of talented men, men of experience in legislative proceedings, men well informed on most subjects, but especially well informed as to the feelings and views of their constituents, who had acknowledged them as their leaders in their party strifes. For years the special subject that they had met to consider, had been a subject of public and private discussion in the State and out of it. [35]

Some of the delegates arrived with explicit instructions concerning how to vote, and even more carried implicit instructions, being selected based on their known views on the subject. The instructions of Richmond no doubt reflect the preference of much of the state. The town told its delegates to

> use their Indevors that the said Constitution be not adopted at said Convention that the Constitutions be duly Considered and that every

amendment That is necessary be proposed if any shall be Required and that said Convention adjourn to a futer Day so as to see the opperation of the General Government that the Citizens of this State May be Convincd of the propriety or impropriety of adopting said Constitution.[36]

This idea of an adjournment was what the country leaders in convention intended, with an eye toward the state legislative elections in April.

On the first of March in 1790, more than a year and a half after the Constitution was officially ratified by the ninth state, and nearly a year after the advent of the new government, the ratifying convention for the state of Rhode Island finally convened. Daniel Owen, the Deputy Governor of the state, was elected the president.[37] The first fight was over rules of order; after a committee to establish rules reported six of them, Job Comstock insisted that a new clause be added ensuring that motions to recommend amendments or to adjourn should take precedence over a vote on ratification. This occasioned rather intense debate, which took up the entire morning of the second, culminating in a vote of thirty-nine to twenty-seven in favor of the change. This was a test vote of sorts, making it clear that the Anti-Federalists were in charge, though not by an overwhelming number. The leadership was effective at holding the coalition together, in part because of the party's "nocturnal conventions," informal party caucus meetings held in the evenings to coordinate convention strategies. After the rules debate, John Sayles moved for a committee to be appointed to draw up amendments, and for the convention to adjourn to a future day. Federalist Benjamin Bourne quickly pointed out that the Constitution had not yet been read. Unfortunately, the rules demanded that a motion to adjourn must take precedence over everything else, so the Constitution could not be read until Sayles's motion was resolved. "The Anties perceived the inconsistency of their Procedure," reported the *Newport Herald*, "to recommend amendments to the people, and adjourn for further consideration of a Constitution that they had not given a reading, would appear the highest of absurdities."[38] Apparently, the party's delegates had not worked this out in their private meetings. The convention therefore adjourned until the afternoon, at which point they tabled the earlier motion and proceeded to read the Constitution, and a discussion of it followed.

Immediately the clause concerning apportionment of representatives and taxes came under fire. Taxes in particular faced scrutiny, with several Anti-Federalists expressing a preference for taxation attached to wealth rather than numbers. The Federalists insisted that the plan by population favored the state, and that estimating the value of property was inconsistent and unreliable, but the opposition was unconvinced. The Anti-Federalists here as elsewhere objected to the power of Congress to interfere in elections, and the vagueness of Congress publishing its journals "from time to time." On this latter point, though, Anti-Federalist leader Jonathan Hazard was curiously dismissive; "There is no Danger," he said in response to the critique, suggesting that this has not been a problem under the Articles of Confederation. "Let us make no objections but such as are necessary."[39] This unexpected defense of a clause that had raised concerns elsewhere presaged the country party's growing willingness to accept ratification.

Strangely, Article I, Section 8, concerning the powers of Congress, seems to have generated no debate. Perhaps the Anti-Federalists were merely saving their energy for the next clause, which concerned the slave trade. Bourne insisted that this clause was a good one, because it implied that Congress might end the slave trade after twenty years, which was more than the old Congress could do. Comstock fired back that if the practice were condoned for a period of time, "there will never be an end of it." William Barton waxed poetic, insisting that "we are all embarked on board one ship the ship of Liberty"; he was "sorry to countenance a Trade to enslave our fellow Creatures." Hazard again stepped in defending the Constitution, arguing that to accept this clause was in no way condoning slavery. "The southern states must answer for themselves," he said. "They must Conduce their own Legislation as they please—They can regulate their Trade as they please—We are not interested [on] one Hand nor answerable in our Consciences on the other—They must answer for [their] own Crimes." To try to remove this clause would undermine any chance of a union under this Constitution, because to attack slavery in the Constitution would be "Stabbing to the Vitals [of] the S[outhern] States." Joseph Stanton was unconvinced and unapologetic, essentially advocating abolition as well as an end to the slave trade. He praised the language of liberty in the Preamble, and then asked, "Why in the Name of Common [Sense] should not this Liberty be extended to the Africans?" Barton too was willing to go this far, invoking the New Testament and the Golden Rule as a justification for ending slavery. "Will the gentleman be willing," he asks, "that his tender Grand Children should be taken and carried away as he sees Africans?" Nathan Miller fired back by quoting Leviticus in defense of slavery. William Bradford tried to put a stop to this debate, pointing out that "It is not before us whether slavery was allowed in the Days of Christ." Nonetheless, the Anti-Federalists came out on top on the issue, claiming the moral high ground against the pragmatism embodied in the Constitution's compromises on this subject.[40]

It is curious that Section 10 did not engender much of a debate; the first clause seemed ready-made for Rhode Island's opposition. This clause states, in part, that "No State shall . . . emit Bills of Credit; make any Thing but gold and silver Coin a Tender in Payment of Debts; [or] pass any . . . Law impairing the Obligation of Contracts." Here we have, in brief, a fine repudiation of Rhode Island's paper money system. Yet neither side had much reason to say anything. The country party had managed to redeem the paper money and pay the state's debts, so it would no longer be in violation of this clause. As for the Federalists, Bishop offers a concise and plausible explanation: "In the Convention," he writes, "the Federalists used all their tact and diplomacy to win over to their side sufficient votes to gain a majority, and hence may have considered it expedient to avoid mention of this explosive subject." Thus the clause passed without objection.[41]

On Thursday, March 4, Stephen Steere moved to form a committee to consider and draft proposed amendments. After some discussion, the delegates decided to finish reading the Constitution before creating such a committee. It seems they intended little more than reading, though; Articles II and III were read without comment, as was Article IV. Barton jumped in to praise Article V, suggesting that it "ought to be written in Letters of Gold," because it was the finest part of the document. Hazard did not share his enthusiasm. "We want a Constitution not to be altered," he said. "The Rich and powerful States will be uneasy till they alter it for their Benefit." Rather than letters of gold, Hazard was "sorry it was ever written in Letters with Ink."[42]

The remainder of the Constitution was read without debate, and the convention turned to the amendments that had been proposed by Congress. James Sheldon immediately arose and, taking a position consistent with Rhode Island's very reason for existence, complained that the amendments did not prohibit states from establishing religion or interfering with the rights of conscience. No decision was immediately made about these proposals, though; they were read for informational purposes, along with the proposed amendments from the conventions of New York, North Carolina, Massachusetts, and Virginia, in that rather peculiar order. Bradford then renewed the question of creating a committee to draft amendments. George Champlin, a strong Federalist, suggested that the committee should consist entirely of those who oppose ratification. This was an unusual twist; Champlin left no clue as to his motives. Robert Cotner offers a plausible theory, that since the Anti-Federalists had the advantage of numbers, "Champlin probably hoped that, by getting all the objections in writing, the Federalists could force a vote to adopt the Constitution with the suggested Amendments."[43]

When the convention reconvened to hear the committee's report, excitement ran high. Foster allowed himself a poetic moment on the historical nature of the proceedings: "And the Business now begins—a Time of Expectation and the House very much crowded—Generals, Colonels, Delegates, &c. being obliged to Stand—The House now calling—Thus Life Passes and carries along the Tide of Time to land us in Eternity of what consequence will then be all this Parade." Before even considering the amendments and bill of rights recommended by the committee, the delegates proceeded to discuss what to do with these recommendations. Comstock wanted to see them sent to the people of the state, in their town meetings. Marchant and Champlin chided Comstock for rushing to this idea before even a discussion on the amendments: "How will Mr Comstock appear," Champlin asked, "when he goes home and the People ask him how he likes the Bill of Rights and he shall say that it was not considered[?]" This prompted the Anti-Federalists to set aside the question of what to do with the amendments, and turn to a discussion of the committee's report.[44]

The amendments were addressed first, and these generated a clear consensus. The first, against which no objections were raised, stated simply that "The United States shall guarantee to each State its sovereignty, freedom and independence, and every power, jurisdiction and right, which is not by this Constitution expressly delegated to the United States."[45] This is the crux of the opposition argument, of course, yet the Federalists had little reason to object because they insisted that in a government of enumerated powers this would be true even without stating it. The second proposal, which faced resistance and was eventually removed from the list, would have removed all representation for slaves. The committee proposed various restrictions on the federal courts and defenses for the state courts, which aroused some Federalist opposition. The convention also wanted to see a requirement that eleven of the original thirteen states must approve any future amendments to the Constitution, as a protection against the future proliferation of western states, as well as wanting to prohibit Congress from interfering in elections, prevent compulsory military service except in cases of invasion, and require that Congress requisition the states and refrain from direct (and especially capitation) taxes.[46] The committee also proposed, and the convention approved, that the journals and receipts of Congress be published at least once a year, that standing armies not be kept in peacetime, that war may not be declared or money borrowed without two-thirds support in Congress, and that Congress act to end the slave trade "as soon as may be." The slave trade once again created controversy, with Federalists insisting that the state ought not attack the southern states in its accession to the union. The Anti-Federalists countered that they were acting on principle: "we ought to bear Testimony against such a Trade," said Stanton. "If we do not we shall participate." Bourne fired back that "We are not a Society of Friends to publish our Testimonials to this," but the antislavery delegates would not budge.[47]

The proposed bill of rights began with several broad statements of principle, including the idea that the people could reclaim political power from the government at any time. This appeared alarming to the Federalists, but Hazard insisted, expressing a sentiment that could have applied to all of the amendments proposed by conventions here and elsewhere, that these statements "will quiet the Mind of the People at large—if there was no other Reason this would be Sufficient—A Government established with the Consent and Confidence of the People will be more firm."[48] This was clearly Hazard's goal, and the reason that he defended the Constitution despite his early and vocal opposition in the state legislature. The other principles espoused in the proposed bill of rights were fairly typical, with substantial similarities to those adopted by the Virginia Convention; and like New York, Rhode Island would place its bill of rights as a preamble of sorts to its ratification. The committee also recommended that the state approve the proposed amendments from Congress, except for the one concerning pay raises for Congress. This was treated with the proposed amendments; the convention apparently did not see these changes as a bill of rights, as later generations would so name them.

On the afternoon of March 6, Elisha Brown moved "That the 'Bill of Rights' and 'Amendments' proposed to the Federal Constitution, be referred to the freemen of the several towns, . . . for their consideration," and the final debate of the session began. Marchant contended that "it belongs to the Convention to finish the Business," and that the convention did not have the power to adjourn, but he was fighting a losing battle. Hazard argued that "We derive our Power from the People. They have a Right to be consulted—They expect the Amendments will be made and sent to them." Both of these men certainly knew that the adjournment was merely a ploy to delay a vote on ratification until after the state legislative elections in April, but the country party delegates had the votes. The Federalists made a desperate appeal for the delegates to consider the merchants of the states, who would be facing stiff tariffs and trade regulations as of the first of April if Rhode Island did not enter the union by then. "We are trifling we [are] sporting with the Privileges of the Means by which the People live," pleaded Marchant, to deaf ears. When the motion to submit the proposals to the towns passed by a vote of forty-one to twenty-eight, the Federalists tried to have the convention meet again in late March, but the country members would not hear of it. There were elections to be considered, after all, so any sooner than the end of April was unacceptable. The motion for the last Monday in March failed, thirty-one to thirty-eight. By a vote of thirty-six to thirty-two, the convention instead approved May 24 as the date to reconvene, and they chose Newport as the place, over East Greenwich, by one vote, thirty-five to thirty-four. The Federalists would have to "suffer another Jigg to be danced" in Newport, though there were reasons to be optimistic. Between the two votes on dates, Anti-Federalist John Williams pointed out that at the time of the convention elections the people of the state clearly opposed the Constitution, and it would take time "to bring the whole People to an Agreement to the Constitution." If the country party delegates were going to try to convince the people to support ratification, then the Constitution had a chance of success in the next dance.[49]

THIRTEEN PILLARS, BY TWO VOTES

The adjournment was entirely political. The Anti-Federalists could have rejected the Constitution, or ratified it, as they wanted, but what they wanted most was victory in the April elections. The constitutional amendments and bill of rights provided suitable cover. Even so, the Constitution did not become a major issue in the election, mostly because the Federalists had incentive not to mention it. "The Federalists were in a nearly hopeless situation," Polishook explains. "If they made ratification of the Constitution a major issue in the election, they might force the country party to assume an inflexibly Antifederalist position. On the other hand, if the Federalists failed to contest the elections, the country party was bound to remain in control of the state. Neither alternative was comforting." In this situation, the Federalists proposed a state unity ticket, with offices split between the two parties. The country party, of course, had no reason to agree to this. Instead, they portrayed themselves as the servants of the people, ever willing to reflect popular sentiment. They were careful not to mention any support for the Constitution, which was still unpopular, and they removed John Collins from the top of the ticket because he had voted for a ratifying convention (though almost certainly with the tacit approval of the other country leaders). At first the country party intended to nominate Daniel Owen, the Deputy Governor, but he soon afterward decided not to run. The nomination fell to Arthur Fenner, a merchant from Providence who had nonetheless been a supporter of the state's paper money system. The Federalists decided that, in the interest of their unity ticket, they too would nominate Fenner. A committee in Providence, formed to carry out this strategy, wrote an open letter to Fenner offering him their endorsement and asking him to support a bipartisan ticket. In the letter, they insist that a coalition "should be earnestly attempted" for the purpose of "the peace and lasting prosperity of the State." The *United States Chronicle* reprinted the letter to Fenner, along with his response. "No man more deeply regrets the unhappy Divisions which have been so long prevalent in the State, or more anxiously wishes that mutual Confidence may be restored," Fenner wrote (undoubtedly with assistance and approval from the country leaders). However, he insisted that the choice of a governor rested with the freemen of the state, and that it would be unseemly for him to accept such a nomination or meet with them to discuss the election. Such actions would "indicate a very extraordinary Fondness of an Office and appear like Presumption and Arrogance." The country party was not biting; all efforts at conciliation would be rejected. In the end, the country party won a resounding victory.[50]

Meanwhile, even as the country leaders were preparing to accept the Constitution, some Anti-Federalists in the state remained adamant against it. When his seriousness was questioned by "Agricola," Greenwichiensis wrote in deadly earnest defending his call for rejecting the Constitution. The idea that the United States would seek vengeance for Rhode Island's secession from the union is wrong, he explained. "We secede from *them*? you mistake the matter, *they* have seceded from us." This was the perspective from which much of the opposition approached the question, and it was a valid point for anyone who took the Articles of Confederation, as an agreement of perpetual union, seriously. Another writer in the same paper also came to the defense of Greenwichiensis, against the attack of Agricola. This writer took a more moderate position, but still stood against ratification: "history shews us that delegated power seldom progresses in favor of the people, and therefore that it ought to be guarded by the strongest barriers; those barriers consist in a well defined constitution; the Federal Compact is not well defined, and consequently ought to be rejected, or subjected to amendments." "It is certain the Constitution has been defective," the author wrote in his second number, "because the collected wisdom of the Union has mended it: It is still obvious to us that some defects remain." The amendments proposed by Congress did not go far enough, but those suggested by the Rhode Island Convention in its first meeting would remedy the remaining defects.[51]

On May 25, the convention again met, this time in Newport. After several days of discussion,[52] Job Comstock, perhaps sensing that the votes were there for ratification, moved for an adjournment. After some debate, the motion failed by six votes. On the other hand, Comstock may have been reacting to the confusion that emerged out of the myriad of positions taken by the towns between the two sessions. Richmond, for example, expressed approval of the Constitution, along with the amendments and bill of rights, but suggested four further amendments. Middletown and North Kingstown each added only that the states set congressional pay and have the power to recall Senators, but insisted that the Constitution be amended prior to ratification by the state. Charlestown took the same position, even agreeing to these specific changes, but added two additional (and very vague) amendments. Portsmouth, not surprisingly, backed ratification, and instructed its delegates to oppose any further attempt at adjournment.[53] Unconditional ratification with suggested amendments was going to be difficult, because there was still substantial resistance to the unamended Constitution in the state. On the other hand, the town of Providence made clear the stakes of a rejection of the Constitution. That town's instructions insisted that

> on the Rejection of the said Constitution, or further Delay of a Decision thereon, the respective Towns of the State have a Right to make Application to the Congress of the United States for the same Privileges, and Protection which are afforded to the Towns under their Jurisdiction: And in such Case the Delegates from this Town be and they are hereby fully authorized and empowered to meet with the Delegates from the Town of Newport and the Delegates from such other Towns as may think proper to join them, for the purpose of consulting and devising such Mode of Application as they in their Wisdom may think proper and to carry the Result of their Deliberations, into immediate Effect and that they make Report of their Doings to the next Town Meeting.[54]

This was nothing short of a call for secession, and essentially treason against the independent state of Rhode Island. Nonetheless, the delegates seem not to have taken any action on it, or reacted much at all. This may be the best evidence that the Anti-Federalist leadership was fully prepared to acquiesce in the ratification.

As the second session unfolded, the delegates continued the discussion of amendments. They voted to add to their amendments the power of states to recall their Senators, as suggested by several of the towns. After another committee to consider amendments was appointed and met, the convention added three more amendments. Two were fairly minor: just two members could demand a roll-call vote in either house of Congress, and Congress may create no monopolies. The other amendment was more unusual: "That Congress have Power to Establish a uniform Rule of Inhabitancy or settl[e]-m[en]t, of the Poor of the United States throughout the United States." The committee also recommended, and the convention approved, that rather than approving of the twelve amendments proposed by Congress, the state convention ought to pass a resolution urging the state legislature, the proper venue for ratifying amendments, to approve of eleven of the twelve. At this point, with four new amendments, a delegate from Portsmouth moved for a brief adjournment, just a day, so he might return home and meet with his constituents one more time. The Federalists carried this motion, with the Anti-Federalists splitting their votes. After the brief break, the delegates from Portsmouth, as well as those from Middletown, returned with new instructions. The change from Portsmouth does not seem to have made much of a difference, as the town was already in favor of the Constitution, but Middletown reversed its position to approve of an unconditional ratification with recommended amendments. This must have been unacceptable to Anti-Federalist William Peckham, who had represented the town up to this point; rather than follow the town's instructions and vote for the Constitution he resigned his seat, and the town sent Elisha Barker in his stead. Barker would vote for the Constitution, as instructed.[55]

At this point, nothing was left but the vote, and it was a close one. Everyone knew it had to be close, because most of the delegates had been instructed one way or the other. According to Polishook's count, thirty delegates, representing eleven towns, were pledged to favor ratification, while in another sixteen towns the thirty-four delegates were instructed to vote against ratification. In the final vote, thirty-four delegates, including Elisha Barker of Middletown, favored ratification, while thirty-two opposed. Three Anti-Federalists were absent. Had Peckham retained his seat and voted against the Constitution, the thirty-three-to-thirty-three tie would have been broken by Deputy Governor (and convention president) Daniel Owen, who had been among the most consistent Anti-Federalists throughout the entire struggle. Owen presumably would have voted against the Constitution. It is not clear why three members of the opposition were absent, or why several others switched sides, but it is probable that enough Anti-Federalists recognized the need to rejoin the union, and turned the final vote into an opportunity for them to save face and avoid changing their officially avowed position. In the words of Theodore Foster, unofficial chronicler of the first meeting of the state convention, "Many of the Antifederalists wish the Business done but do not love to do it themselves." Even so, two delegates voted for ratification in violation of their instructions, and one delegates voted against ratification despite instructions. If Peckham had remained, then, perhaps another member of the opposition would have been unaccountably absent.[56]

The form of ratification mirrored that of New York, with the bill of rights serving as a preamble and statement of principle, and the amendments following the official approval of the Constitution. It was defiant in tone, asserting Rhode Island's right to exist as well as the existence of its people's rights. Nonetheless, the ratification was to usher in an era of greater political harmony in the state. The Federalists even won the first congressional election in the state, as well as one of the two Senate seats.

Bishop's conclusion to his analysis of Rhode Island's resistance perhaps best sums up the reason that Rhode Island held out for so long, on principle more than self-interest: "The Rhode Island Anti-Federalists were strong because they spoke for those fundamental principles of liberty and democracy which the Revolution had popularized and spread throughout the Union. The opponents of the Constitution were strong because they spoke for the vision of a free society—America's greatest contribution to the world."[57] As in most of the states, the Anti-Federalists here saw themselves as defending the Revolution against sinister attacks on individual liberty. The difference here is that the people unequivocally backed them in their opposition to the Constitution.

RATIFICATION'S EPILOGUE: VERMONT MAKES FOURTEEN

The opposition to the Constitution did not quite end with Rhode Island's acquiescence. In 1790, the government of Vermont worked out an agreement with New York to provide for its independence and pave the way to its statehood. Not everyone in Vermont favored such a course of action, however. Levi Allen convincingly argued that Vermont would gain more from independence than joining the United States; the latter course would place Vermont in the position of being "a remote backwater of an expanding empire, of no consequence to the controlling powers of the new nation in New York, and subject to national tariffs."[58] Surely this reasoning must have resonated with many of his fellow Vermonters.

Vermont proceeded to call a ratifying convention for January 1791; at this gathering occurred the final debate of the ratification period. Only four delegates voted against ratification out of 109 who voted, but the opposition put up an impressive verbal fight, even if, in the words of one historian, "[t]here hardly seemed any issues worthy of debate at the convention." The Federalists here clearly wanted to focus on "whether it would be expedient or inexpedient for Vermont to enter the federal union."[59] The Anti-Federalists, though, few as they were, would not be rushed. Benjamin Emmons and Beriah Loomis, neither of whom objected outright, raised practical concerns about how Vermont would be received and how disputes over land ownership, resulting from earlier claims by New York and New Hampshire, would be adjudicated. Daniel Buck, of Norwich, took a philosophical approach, discussing the origin of government, suggesting that it developed from necessity. Was it necessary, he asked, for Vermont to join the union? Or would the state better remain independent? He described the state as relatively homogenous; it

> had an uniformity of interest; that there was no mercantile and landed interests found clashing here, and that of the lord and the tenant was not known; the laws, therefore, were simple and suited to the whole. . . . But if Vermont came into the union, the sacrifice she made must be great—her interest must then bend to the interest of the union—where those clashing interests before mentioned were to be found.[60]

This would disrupt the prosperity and harmony of the state. Such a national government he expected to "destroy that equality among the people, which was necessary to keep one part of mankind from oppressing the other." Instead, by joining the union, "the stimulous to improvement in knowledge . . . would operate on a few only, it would serve but to place them as tyrants over an ignorant multitude." He openly advocated continued independence for Vermont. Buck's argument was quickly dismissed by the proponents of union, because it suggested that the state ought never to join its sister states, and many of his points militated "against government in general."[61]

As the convention debates wound down, Benjamin Emmons became increasingly worried about whether the property rights of Vermonters would be adequately protected in the union; he suggested that the decision on ratifying the Constitution "may not perhaps be unaptly applied to the act of Adam in eating the forbidden fruit." He moved for an adjournment until October; certainly a little more deliberation could not hurt. Beriah Loomis backed this idea, to give the people of Vermont the "opportunity to become better acquainted with the constitution, and obtain satisfaction with respect to the real security of their landed property." The issue involved the question of the legality of New York's act relinquishing its claim on Vermont's lands. It was Levi Allen's brother Ira who addressed this concern, by suggesting that the ratification be conditional on Congress recognizing the title of Vermonters to their own land, rather than competing out-of-state claims. With the opposition thus appeased, the adjournment failed convincingly, and the Federalists, who had the votes all along, ratified the Constitution, and Vermont bit the apple.[62] The last gasp of resistance to ratification had come and gone, and the opposition would turn to the prospects of trying to shape rather than resist the new government.

18

An Anti-Federalist Constitution

By the neglect of the *objectors*, to offer *their system*, it is presumed, that either they have none, or it is such as they know will not be acceptable to the people,—or their design is to prevent any form of Federal Government.—Until the *objectors* explain themselves, by offering their own plan, to dispute with them is wasting time, and throwing arguments to the wind.

—"An American," *Independent Chronicle* (MA), December 12, 1787

[A]ll who object to the plan proposed ought to point out the defects objected to, and to propose those amendments with which they can accept it, or to propose some other system of government, that the public mind may be known, and that we may be brought to agree in some system of government, to strengthen and execute the present, or to provide a substitute.

—"Federal Farmer," November 8, 1787

THE ANTI-FEDERALISTS NEVER really made their case.[1] The Federalists had theirs, in the form of the Constitution. The opposition was on the defensive during the entire debate. To find the Anti-Federalist position, one needs to sort through the arguments made, with an eye toward the sequence of events and the counterarguments raised by the Federalists. The Rights Anti-Federalists were fairly consistent, from George Mason and Richard Henry Lee in 1787 right through Lee's bruising battle in the Senate to secure protections for individual liberties; only late in the debate, especially in the Virginia and North Carolina ratifying conventions, did they seriously consider the extent to which adjusting the distribution of power in the Constitution might effectively strengthen the parchment barrier of a bill of rights. The Power Anti-Federalists, focused on the national and state governments, only later started to really emphasize how much a bill of rights might enable to people to resist governmental overreach. These two strands of opposition thought were just far enough apart through the first six months of the debate for the Federalists to credibly claim that the opposition had no coherent position at all. This claim was further strengthened by the shrill rhetoric of Centinel and the Democratic Anti-Federalists, who never quite adopted the Power and Rights positions, though they did sprinkle the arguments of those two strands of opposition into their own diatribes against the Constitution. Only when the Power and Rights positions converged, and proponents of both arguments began to ignore or disavow their more radical Democratic brethren, did a clear opposition position begin to emerge, much too late in the debate to have much impact.

But what if the Anti-Federalists had been able to articulate such an alternative? What if they had been able to hold a convention of their own, to suggest amendments to the proposed Constitution that had the weight of the entire opposition behind them, and that could be considered nationally alongside the Constitution itself? An ideal Constitution would provide for stability through law, expressed by the representatives of the people in a properly structured federal system. It would allow for state autonomy and cooperation, while preserving the liberty and promoting the prosperity of the people. Several Anti-Federalists certainly could have proposed a concrete alternative. Brutus and Federal Farmer both offered specific suggestions for how the Constitution might be made better, and at times offered specific text to be inserted. The minority opinions from the Pennsylvania and Maryland conventions outlined objections that could easily be incorporated into such a document. Seven state conventions formally proposed lists of amendments. One particularly intrepid group in western Pennsylvania, calling themselves "The Society of Western Gentlemen," went so far as to propose and publish an amended version of the Constitution, though it received little attention.[2] A convention consisting of prominent Anti-Federalists might have produced something more impressive and harder to ignore. Jack Rakove speculates that in such a convention, the Anti-Federalists "might well have been able to unite on a number of points that they generally shared."[3] Such a Constitution would have, first and foremost, been based on a bill of rights. Rakove goes on to identify several broad areas on which the Anti-Federalists generally agreed. Given the speed with which the Federalists moved to ratify, there was no time for an Anti-Federalist convention, but there was much discussion about what should be done by opponents of the proposed Constitution. They could accept the Federalist idea to ratify the Constitution and then make changes through the amendment process; to most Anti-Federalists this seemed incredibly dangerous because of the uncertainty of that process and the likelihood that no such changes

would be made. They could attempt to defeat the Constitution and maintain the status quo; this was even less appealing to most, since even most
Anti-Federalists "felt the feebleness of the ties by which these United-States
are held together."[4] They could attempt to amend the document in ratifying
conventions, which would have been a mess if thirteen (or even, say, three)
different constitutions emerged from the process. Finally, they could push
for a new convention, to start with the Federalist document and incorporate
the ideas raised during the initial ratification debate. This last option was,
to many Anti-Federalists, the best course of action, and many followed just
this route. Whether such a second convention would have produced anything better is certainly in doubt, but it never happened. Instead, the Anti-
Federalists ultimately lost in all thirteen states.

Still, it is interesting and instructive to speculate what the Anti-Federalists
might have done with the Constitution, had they had the opportunity to
amend it to their liking. A document that would have won the acquiescence
of most of the prominent Anti-Federalists would tell us much about the
Anti-Federalist position. This chapter presents and defends such a document. It is based on the original Constitution, heavily altered. It is littered
with footnotes in defense of each change I have made. Some changes would
no doubt have been rejected by certain Anti-Federalists, and I have noted
such objections in the notes, but the overall product would be agreeable to
most, if not all, of the writers opposed to the Constitution. It is the result
of hypothetical compromises, and does not require the assumption of unanimity or even close agreement among the opponents of the Constitution;
it assumes merely enough common ground to find a concrete alternative
to the unacceptable document proposed by the Philadelphia Convention.
It may be argued that this is necessarily a fruitless endeavor, as the Anti-
Federalists would not even attempt to modify the proposed Constitution,
or use it as a starting point. Cecilia Kenyon argues that the Anti-Federalists
did not attempt to modify the proposed governmental framework because
they did not believe such a government could actually carry a national
mandate.[5] If a republican government is impossible over such a large territory, then it follows that one should not attempt to construct such a national republican government. On this point, however, Kenyon is misled
by the negative character of the opposition. As Herbert Storing explains,
the Anti-Federalists (or at least the most reasonable of them) recognized
the importance of a union that was more than a league of friendship. The
Constitution may not have been their starting point for establishing such
a union, but it provides us a convenient basic structure for articulating
Anti-Federalist thought and comparing it to the Federalist position. Finally,

many, if not most, of the Anti-Federalists did not outright oppose the Constitution; there were numerous delegates prepared to accept the document with prior amendments, or to conditionally ratify, reserving the right to withdraw their states from the union if such amendments were not made. Only a few of the Anti-Federalists vehemently opposed the Constitution; the rest were willing to work with it to make it safe for proper republican government.

AMENDING THE CONSTITUTION

A small but significant number of Anti-Federalists suggested that there was nothing wrong with the Articles of Confederation, or at least nothing a couple of amendments could not fix. Rawlins Lowndes presented perhaps the strongest defense of the Articles:

> We are now governed by a most excellent constitution—one which had stood the test of time, and carried us through difficulties supposed to be insurmountable—one that had raised us high in the eyes of all men, and given to us the enviable blessings of liberty & independence—a constitution sent like a blessing from heaven, yet were we impatient to trample it under foot; and for what? why, to make way for another that give power for a small number of men to pull down the fabric which we have spent our blood to raise. Charters are sacred things.[6]

Few Anti-Federalists went so far as to describe the Articles as "excellent,"[7] but many suggested that they were good enough to need only manageable revisions, or at least not bad enough to entirely discard.[8] As Pauline Maier puts it, "In retrospect, it is surprising how readily contestants accepted the Constitution as the basis of reform. Only a minority of the Constitution's critics, including Maryland's Luther Martin, literally opposed the Constitution." "If it was the ragged old coat which had made us like a blackguard throughout all Europe," argued John Bowman in the South Carolina Convention, "let us try to make it better."[9] For "A Countryman," the Articles were not a coat, but a house:

> I should think it a very unwise thing to pull down an old house, in which I lived very comfortably for many years, and which had sheltered me and my family, and move into a new house, just to gratify the

pride and vanity of the children, because it was larger and appeared
fine, on the outside, when I knew at the same time, that it was not well
finished within, that the foundation was bad, the chimnies smoky, the
roof leaky, and many of the posts rotten, so as to make it dangerous to
go in it, and that it would cost me more than I was worth in the world
to furnish and keep it in repair, and I am apt to believe if I got ruined
by it, I should meet with few to pity me.[10]

Nonetheless, here I have used the proposed Constitution as a starting point,
for three reasons. First, there were many Anti-Federalists who argued that
the Articles were fatally flawed, and needed to be replaced. "I know our
situation is critical, and it behoves us to make the best of it," wrote the
Federal Farmer. "A federal government of some sort is necessary. We have
suffered the present to languish; and whether the confederation was capable or not originally of answering any valuable purposes, it is now but of
little importance." Brutus agreed: "We have felt the feebleness of the ties by
which these United-States are held together, and the want of sufficient energy in our present confederation, to manage, in some instances, our general
concerns."[11] Ultimately, most Anti-Federalists would have backed a revised
version of the Constitution over the original Articles.[12] Second, it is difficult to describe amendments to the Articles on which the Anti-Federalists
would have agreed, or what they would have found sufficient, because they
were generally not writing about the Articles. Since they were critiquing
the Constitution, we can incorporate the changes they have suggested into
the original document. Certainly many Anti-Federalists suggested changes
to the Articles that should have been proposed instead of the Constitution,
but it is difficult to find any degree of consensus without ignoring the many
writers who just addressed the Constitution, or making a lot of assumptions
that are difficult to defend. Finally, using the Constitution rather than the
Articles as our starting point better fits our counterfactual story. The Anti-
Federalists did not exist as a group, in fact could not exist as a group, until
the Constitution was proposed. As such, to create a document on which
the Anti-Federalists would have agreed, we must create a document that
comes after the Constitution. If the Anti-Federalists wanted to offer an alternative, it would have made sense politically to offer an amended version
of the Federalist plan, and stake out some middle ground between the consolidation they feared and the status quo. The fact that virtually all Anti-
Federalists suggested amendments, and a significant number suggested that
with amendments they could support the Constitution, leads us to a revision

of the Constitution, not the Articles. The text of the revised constitution is below, broken into sections. Text from the original Constitution that has been removed appears with a strike through it, and text that has been added appears in italics. Each section is described and annotated, to explain and support the changes made.

AN ANTI-FEDERALIST CONSTITUTION

Preamble

"A Real Federalist" in New York, purportedly reporting a speech from the state's ratifying convention, laid out his case against the Constitution:

> In this constitution, sir, we have departed widely from the principles and political faith of 76, when the spirit of liberty ran high, and danger put a curb on ambition. Here we find no security for the rights of individuals; no security for the existence of our state governments: here is no bill of rights, no proper restrictions of power: our lives, our property and our consciences are left wholly at the mercy of the legislature, and the powers of the judicial may be extended to any degree short of almighty. Sir, in this Constitution we have not only neglected, we have done worse; we have openly violated our faith, that is, our public faith.[13]

This is a statement of principles to which the Anti-Federalists would have subscribed, almost to a man. The objections to the Constitution began with the words "We the People," and addressed the theory and understanding of government implicitly found in the Preamble. The beginning of the document was the place for a statement of principles of government, as in several of the state constitutions.

> We the People of ~~the United~~ *these sovereign* States, ~~in Order to form a more perfect Union, establish Justice, insure domestic Tranquility, provide for the common defence, promote the general Welfare, and secure the Blessings of Liberty to ourselves and our Posterity~~ *in forming a Confederation and Perpetual Union*, do ordain and establish this Constitution for the United States of America *on the following Principles of Government:*

1. All power is originally vested in the people, to be exercised either immediately by themselves, or mediately by their representatives;[14]

2. Elections of representatives ought to be free and frequent; and all men having common interest with, and attachment to, the community, ought to have the right of suffrage;[15]

3. There are certain natural rights of which men, when they form a social compact, cannot deprive or divest their posterity,—among which are the enjoyment of life and liberty, with the means of acquiring, possessing, and protecting property, and pursuing and obtaining happiness and safety;[16]

4. The design of civil government is to protect the rights and promote the happiness of the people[17]*; and*

5. The common good is the end of civil government, and common consent, the foundation on which it is established.[18]

There are many potential versions of the opening phrase of the Preamble that would have been more appealing to the Anti-Federalists than the original. The Pennsylvania Minority explained that the original "We the People of the United States" suggested "a compact between individuals entering into a state of society, and not that of a confederation of states." This suggested consolidation, not federalism, and it was a common argument.[19] One might easily suggest, as Findley did in the Pennsylvania Ratifying Convention, some variant of "We the States" without any mention of the people. I have left the people in (while recognizing the sovereignty of the states) because of the Anti-Federalist emphasis on popular sovereignty. Most of the Anti-Federalists were not democrats, but they did emphasize the importance of the voice of the people, and would have still wanted popular endorsement, by state. Brutus described the people as "the fountain of all power, to whom alone it of right belongs to make or unmake constitutions."[20]

It seems fitting that the Anti-Federalists would open their constitution with a statement of principles rather than the Framers' purposes of government. For most of the Anti-Federalists, the problem with the proposed Constitution rested with its perceived abandonment of the principles of the Revolution. Thus this statement of principles, designed to ground all law and government on what they perceived as basic truths of society, echoes the Declaration of Independence. It emphasizes the people, not the states, since the states exist only because they provide the best government for the people; the states are adequately protected through legal safeguards below rather than principles above.

Bill of Rights

The omission of a bill of rights was one of the most frequently repeated arguments made against the proposed Constitution; the importance of its inclusion in this Anti-Federalist Constitution needs no defense.[21] Patrick Henry offered perhaps the most pointed Anti-Federalist response to its absence: "A Bill of Rights may be summed up in a few words. What do they tell us?—That our rights are reserved.—Why not say so? Is it because it will consume too much paper?" There are two difficult questions associated with the bill of rights, though. First, what should be included? The general sentiment was that just about everything conceivable should be there; proposals ran the gamut from freedom of the press to fishing rights. I take up this question below. Second, and in many ways more interesting, where should it go? The Bill of Rights affixed to the actual Constitution was added on to the end; to put such guarantees at the end of the document would have been seen as minimizing their importance. A Georgian suggested a section be added to Article IV: "The freedom of the press, and trial by jury, shall be held sacred and inviolate throughout the United States forever." This is not a complete bill of rights, but it does include the two most frequently cited rights to be guaranteed. Some Anti-Federalists suggested that Article I, Section 9, contained a partial listing of rights, but the end of the article on Congress seems too much buried to satisfy most Anti-Federalists.[22] All things considered, though, most Anti-Federalists wanted to see a bill of rights added to the beginning, an idea eloquently defended by A Delegate Who Has Catched Cold in Virginia:

> Those rights characterise the man, essentially the true republican, the citizen of this continent; their enumeration, in the head of the new constitution, can inspire and conserve the affection for their native country, they will be the first lesson of the young citizens becoming men, to sustain the dignity of their being; in fine the publication of those prerogatives has drawn us the envy and the admiration of all Europe, and being the preamble of our federal constitution, they may be the means of a considerable emigration to this continent.[23]

Since the rights of individuals come before the powers of government, it seemed fitting to put these rights here, before the major articles of government, as Article I. The only object that thus appears before the Bill of Rights is a statement of political principles in the Preamble.

Article I

Section 1: *There shall be no national Religion established by Law; and all Persons shall be equally entitled to protection in their religious liberty and in matters of conscience.*[24]

Section 2: *As the People have a Right to Freedom of Speech, and of writing and publishing their Sentiments; the Freedom of the Press shall not to be violated.*[25]

Section 3: *The Right of the People peaceably to assemble together to consult for the Common Good, or to instruct their Representatives, and the right to petition or apply to the Legislature for redress of grievances, shall not be violated.*[26]

Section 4: *Every Freeman has a right to be secure from all unreasonable searches and seizures of his person, his papers, and property: no warrants to search suspected places, or seize any Freeman, his papers or property, shall issue without information upon Oath or affirmation of legal and sufficient cause, specially naming or describing the places to be searched, or persons or things to be seized.*[27]

Section 5: *The People have a right to keep and bear Arms; Congress shall never disarm any Citizen unless such as are or have been in actual Rebellion.*[28]

Section 6: *The people have a right to hold and enjoy their property according to known standing laws, and such property shall not be taken from them without their consent, or the consent of their representatives; and whenever taken in the pressing urgencies of government, they are to receive a reasonable compensation for it.*[29]

Section 7: *Every Freeman shall find a certain remedy, by recourse to the Laws, for all injuries and wrongs he may receive in his person, property, or character.*[30]

Section 8: *The Privilege of the Writ of Habeas Corpus shall not be suspended, unless when in Cases of Rebellion or Invasion the public Safety may require it.*[31]

Section 9: *The enumeration in the Constitution, of certain Rights, shall not be construed to deny or disparage others retained by the People.*[32]

Section 10: *All Powers not explicitly granted to the United States government in the articles below are reserved to the Legislatures of the several States. Each State shall retain authority over its Militia,*[33] *and shall be sovereign within its own borders. The government shall not interfere in the internal matters of any State, except upon the request of that State, or as otherwise provided in this Constitution.*[34]

There was some disagreement over what rights should be contained in a constitution, but the general outline was consistent across all of the states and most of the opponents of the Constitution. This listing of rights covers the common ground, and, when coupled with the procedural judicial guarantees listed below in Article IV, Section 3, covers virtually everything discussed in relation to individual rights. Freedom of the press was particularly precious to the opposition, who saw efforts made by Federalists throughout the country to silence them. A free press, for them, was a "faithful guardian," in the words of Senex in Virginia, "bringing to light the silent advances of ambition. . . . The present crisis confirms it beyond the reach of scepticism." In the words of a North Carolina Anti-Federalist, even if a clause guaranteeing freedom of the press were not strictly necessary, "It was a compliment the American printers had a right to expect."[35]

For many Anti-Federalists, the most troubling omission in the original Constitution was a clause reserving to the states all powers not granted to Congress. Samuel Spencer expressed most clearly this common sentiment: "I know it is said that what is not given up to the United States will be retained by the individual states. I know it ought to be so, and should be so understood; but, sir, it is not *declared* to be so." Several writers pointed out that such a clause appears in the Articles of Confederation. Centinel suggested that the absence of this clause "manifests the design of reducing the several States to shadows." He argued that if such a clause was necessary in the Articles, it is certainly necessary here. Therefore, this clause has been added, and it contains details not included in the version from the Articles, because this national government is stronger than the previous one.[36]

Representation

Representation was a major issue for the Anti-Federalists, and it led to considerable disappointment with the House of Representatives. Richard Henry Lee, reflecting the prevailing opinion among opponents of the Constitution, found the House to be "a mere shread or rag of representation: It being obvious to the least examination that smallness of number and great comparative disparity of power, renders that house of little effect to promote good, or restrain bad government." The two main issues with the House, then, are the number of representatives and the absence of power. The House can do virtually nothing without the Senate, and many Anti-Federalists suggested that the Senate would control the House, making the democratic branch of the legislature merely "an Assistant Aristocratical Branch." As Montezuma explained, satirically, "In fine, this *plebian house* will have little power, and that little be rightly shaped by our house of *gentlemen*, who will have a very extensive influence, from their being chosen out of the *genteeler class*, and their appointment being almost a life." The Senate, for many, defied the very concept of representation by establishing equality among the states. Brutus of Virginia asked, "why Delaware, that pays but a sixty-seventh part of the general expences, should vote on a money bill in the senate equally with Virginia that pays a sixth part of the same expences?" Such calls were not unusual, but they did not represent mainstream Anti-Federalist thought, nor did they represent the kind of compromising attitude necessary for writing a constitution.[37] Brutus suggested a standard for representation that was widely advocated: "The very term, representative, implies, that the person or body chosen for this purpose, should resemble those who appoint them—a representation of the people of America, if it be a true one, must be like the people."[38]

Article II
Section 1. All legislative Powers herein granted shall be vested in a Congress of the United States, which shall consist of a Senate and House of Representatives.

Section 2. The House of Representatives shall be composed of Members chosen every second Year by the People of the several States, and the Electors in each State shall have the Qualifications requisite for Electors of the most numerous Branch of the State Legislature.

No Person shall be a Representative who shall not have attained to the age of twenty five Years, and been seven Years a Citizen of the United States, and who shall not, when elected, be an Inhabitant of that State *and of the district* in which he shall be chosen.[39] *No Person shall be elected a Representative who has served in that position for more than three of the four years previous to the election.*

Representatives ~~and direct Taxes~~[40] shall be apportioned among the several States which may be included within this Union, according to ~~their respective Numbers, which shall be determined by adding to~~ the whole Number of free Persons *therein,* ~~including those bound to Service for a Term of Years, and~~ excluding Indians not taxed~~, three fifths of all other Persons~~. The actual Enumeration shall be made within three Years after the first Meeting of the Congress of the United States, and within every subsequent Term of ten Years, in such Manner as they shall by Law direct. The Number of Representatives shall ~~not exceed~~ *be* one for every ~~thirty~~ *twenty* Thousand, *until the Number* of *Representatives exceeds three Hundred, at which time Congress may by Law determine the proper Ratio,* but each State shall have at Least one Representative; and until such enumeration shall be made, the State of New Hampshire shall be entitled to chuse ~~three~~ *six*, Massachusetts ~~eight~~ *sixteen*, Rhode-Island and Providence Plantations ~~one~~ *two*, Connecticut ~~five~~ *ten*, New-York ~~six~~ *twelve*, New Jersey ~~four~~ *eight*, Pennsylvania ~~eight~~ *sixteen*, Delaware ~~one~~ *two*, Maryland ~~six~~ *twelve*, Virginia ~~ten~~ *twenty*, North Carolina ~~five~~ *ten*, South Carolina ~~five~~ *ten*, and Georgia ~~three~~ *six*.

When vacancies happen in the Representation from any State, the Executive Authority thereof shall issue Writs of Election to fill such Vacancies.

The House of Representatives shall chuse their Speaker and other Officers; and shall have the sole Power of Impeachment.

Section 3. The Senate of the United States shall be composed of two Senators from each State,[41] chosen by the Legislature thereof, for ~~six~~ *four* Years, *subject to recall by the Legislature and ineligible to return to the Senate for at least three years upon the expiration of his term or his resignation, or upon being recalled*; and each Senator shall have one Vote.

Immediately after they shall be assembled in Consequence of the first Election, ~~they shall be divided as equally as may be~~ Into ~~three~~ *two* Classes, *with one Senator from each State in each of the two Classes.* The Seats of the Senators of the first Class shall be vacated at the Expiration of the second Year, *and* of the second Class at the Expiration of the fourth Year, ~~and the third Class at the Expiration of the sixth Year,~~ so that one ~~third~~ *half* may be chosen every second Year;[42] and if Vacancies happen by Resignation, or otherwise, during the Recess of the Legislature of any State, the Executive thereof may make temporary Appointments until the next Meeting of the Legislature, which shall then fill such Vacancies.

No Person shall be a Senator who shall not have attained to the Age of thirty Years, and been nine Years a Citizen of the United States and who shall not, when elected, be an Inhabitant of that State for which he shall be chosen.[43]

~~The Vice-President of the United States shall be President of the Senate, but shall have no Vote, unless they be equally divided.~~

The Senate shall chuse their *Speaker and* other Officers,[44] ~~and also a President pro tempore, in the Absence of the Vice-President, or when he shall exercise the Office of President of the United States.~~

The Senate shall have the sole Power to try all Impeachments.[45] When sitting for that Purpose, they shall be on Oath or Affirmation. When the President of the United States is tried, the Chief Justice shall preside: And no Person shall be convicted without the Concurrence of two thirds of the Members present.

Judgment in Cases of Impeachment shall not extend further than to removal from Office, and disqualification to hold and enjoy any Office of Honor, Trust or Profit under the United States: but the Party convicted shall nevertheless be liable and subject to Indictment, Trial, Judgment and Punishment, according to Law.

Section 4. The Times, Places and Manner of holding Elections for Senators and Representatives, shall be prescribed in each State by the Legislature thereof; *each State Legislature shall divide the State into a number of Districts equal to the total number of Representatives to which it is entitled, and each District shall elect a representative by a majority of Votes, the Vote of each eligible Person counted equally.*[46] ~~but the Congress may at any time by Law make or alter such Regulations, except as to the Places of chusing Senators.~~

The Congress may by Law establish a Time for the Election of Representatives in all States, but otherwise shall not alter such Regulations as may be established by the States unless a State shall fail to establish such Regulations.

The Congress shall assemble at least once in every Year, and such Meeting shall be on the first Monday in December, unless they shall by Law appoint a different Day.

In the states during the late 1780s, most elective offices were elected annually, so naturally many Anti-Federalists wanted to see annual elections to Congress. Centinel contended that "the term for which they are to be chosen, [is] too long to preserve a due dependence and accountability to their constituents." Some Anti-Federalists wanted not only annual elections, but also the right to recall representatives. Neither position has been adopted here. The two-year term for the House enables members to become more acquainted with their responsibilities, which is of course the Federalist argument. Concerns that representatives will not adequately represent the people are instead answered through provisions for a rotation in office, another common Anti-Federalist theme. Aedanus Burke, in South Carolina, articulated this theme: "The only security the people had for their liberties lay in their officers of government being rotationary; history abounded with instances of tyranny and corruption in officers continued for an unlimited time." The Federal Farmer suggested that after serving four years in the House, a member ought to be ineligible for two; this is the restriction that is adopted here.[47]

The number of representatives was another major point of contention, with general agreement that the initial sixty-five was not enough. Doubling the initial representation seems to have been the general consensus of many Anti-Federalists, but setting the initial number high enough is not sufficient. The Constitution as written allowed Congress to remain very small, or even become smaller. Many Anti-Federalists also objected to the stipulation that each representative represent at least thirty thousand constituents, generally because they cannot possibly represent all of the various classes of citizens. To fix these problems, Melancton Smith suggested giving one representative per twenty-thousand people until the House reaches three hundred members, and then leaving it up to the House.[48] He said that "the number of representatives should be so large, as that while it embraces men of the first class, it should admit those of the middling class of life." This principle leads to the changes made here; the initial representation has been doubled, and Congress is instructed to give one representative per twenty thousand people until the number reaches three hundred, and then that the size of the House will never drop below three hundred members. The original Constitution allowed states to decide how House members would be elected, leading to statewide at large elections in several states in the first elections. This possibility led several Anti-Federalists to recommend that the states be divided into districts, each of which shall elect one representative. Representatives must now reside in the district they represent, not just the state.[49]

The Senate, of course, carried its own issues. "Six years is a long period for a man to be absent from his home," wrote Brutus; "it would have a tendency to wean him from his constituents." Gilbert Livingston offered a more extreme assessment: "In this Eden, will they reside, with their families, distant from the observation of the people. In such a situation, men are apt to forget their dependence—lose their sympathy, and contract selfish habits." The moderate Anti-Federalists generally converged on three- or four-year terms rather than six-year ones.[50] Calls were made for more Senators and even direct election, but these were not strongly supported. Here again the ideas of rotation in office and recall appear, and more strongly than for the House. The idea of recall was especially important because, as "A Farmer" argues in Pennsylvania, it would give states an element of "sovereignty" in the system rather than just "ministerial agency." Luther Martin added that states would not truly be represented unless they could instruct their Senators, and recall them when they fail to represent state interests.

"The senators will represent sovereignties, which generally have, and always ought to retain, the power of recalling their agents," explained the Federal Farmer; "the principle of responsibility is strongly felt in men who are liable to be recalled and censured for their misconduct; and, if we may judge from experience, the latter will not abuse the power of recalling their members; to possess it, will, at least be a valuable check." The idea of recall generally went along with a rotation in office; the specific terms of rotation here have been taken from Brutus, preventing Senators from returning to office for three years after completing a term, resigning, or being recalled.[51]

Section 4, which allowed Congress to set the dates and places of its own election, was seen by many Anti-Federalists as an open invitation to manipulate the electoral process. Many Anti-Federalists opposed this power, and none accepted it without substantial conditions attached.[52] For most, the only condition under which regulations concerning elections might legitimately be altered was if a state failed to establish such regulations; this policy, variations of which were proposed by five states,[53] has been established here. Congress has been given the power to establish a national election day for the House, but cannot otherwise interfere.

Perhaps the most controversial part of this part of the Constitution, and maybe of the entire Constitution, was the disposition of slavery. A series of compromises in the Constitutional Convention led to the Three-Fifths Clause, a fugitive slave law, and a prohibition against ending the slave trade for twenty years, as well as a simple majority vote for acts of legislation concerning commerce. In this Anti-Federalist constitution, much of that compromise has been reversed, because a more limited national government can do less to interfere with slavery, and because there was an overriding objection to even the mention of slavery among northern Anti-Federalists. Concerning the representation of slaves established in the Three-Fifths Clause, "A Republican Federalist" made a persuasive argument:

> If the *slaves* have a *right* to be represented, they are *on a footing* with *freemen, three* of *whom* can then have no more than an equal right of representation with *three slaves*, and these when qualified by property, may elect or be elected representatives, *which is not the case*: But if they have not a right to be represented, their masters can have no right derived from their *slaves*, for *these* cannot transfer to others what they have not themselves.[54]

A concern for proper representation drove the opponents of the Constitution more strongly than the supporters, so the three-fifths clause has been removed in favor of a representation based on free persons. This is obviously a significant blow to the southern states, but the inclusion below of a two-thirds requirement for commercial legislation, which of course applies to the slave trade, protects the institution of slavery. Furthermore, Congress has no enumerated power to interfere, except with the sale of slaves across state lines, and there are ample protections against implied powers. Finally, taxation is now apportioned on the value of property, not just land or population, which shifts more of the fiscal burden to the north.

Legislative Procedures and Member Compensation

Sitting between the structure of the House and Senate on one side, and the powers of Congress on the other, this part of the Constitution did not receive much attention in the ratifying conventions or elsewhere. Still, several issues, including salaries and the congressional journal, did generate some spirited debate.

Section 5. Each House shall be the Judge of the Elections, Returns and Qualifications of its own Members,[55] and ~~a Majority~~ two-thirds of each shall constitute a Quorum to do Business; but a smaller Number may adjourn from day to day, and may be authorized to compel the Attendance of absent Members, in such Manner, and under such Penalties as each House may provide.

Each House may determine the Rules of its Proceedings, punish its Members for disorderly Behaviour, and, with the Concurrence of two thirds, expel a Member.[56]

Each House shall keep a Journal of its Proceedings, and ~~from time to time~~ publish the same *not less than once each year*, excepting such Parts *relating to treaties, alliances, or military operations*, as may in their Judgment require Secrecy; and the Yeas and Nays of the Members of either House on any question shall, at the Desire of one fifth of those Present,[57] be entered on the Journal.

Neither House, during the Session of Congress, shall, without the Consent of the other, adjourn for more than three days, nor to any other Place than that in which the two Houses shall be sitting.

Section 6. The Senators and Representatives shall receive a Compensation for their Services, to be ascertained by Law, and paid out of the Treasury of the United States, *provided that no law, varying the Compensation for the Services of the Senators and Representatives,* *excepting the first such Law, shall take effect, until an Election of Representatives shall have intervened.* They shall in all Cases, except Treason, Felony and Breach of the Peace, be privileged from Arrest during their Attendance at the Session of their respective Houses, and in going to and returning from the same; and for any Speech or Debate in either House, they shall not be questioned in any other Place, *except when they shall be called upon for that purpose by their constituents.*[58]

No Senator or Representative shall, during the Time for which he was elected, be appointed to any civil Office under the Authority of the United States, ~~which shall have been created, or the Emoluments whereof shall have been encreased during such time~~: and no Person holding any Office under the United States, shall be a Member of either House during his Continuance in Office.[59]

Section 7. All Bills for raising Revenue shall originate in the House of Representatives; but the Senate may propose or concur with Amendments as on other Bills.[60]

Every Bill which shall have passed the House of Representatives and the Senate, shall, before it become a Law, be presented to the President of the United States; if he approve he shall sign it, but if not he shall return it, with his Objections to that House in which it shall have originated, who shall enter the Objections at large on their Journal, and proceed to reconsider it. If after such Reconsideration two thirds of that House shall agree to pass the Bill, it shall be sent, together with the Objections, to the other House, by which it shall likewise be reconsidered, and if approved by two thirds of that House, it shall become a Law.[61] But in all such Cases the Votes of both Houses shall be determined by Yeas and Nays, and the Names of the Persons voting for and against the Bill shall be entered on the Journal of each House respectively. If any Bill shall not be returned by the President within ten Days (Sundays excepted) after it shall have been presented to him, the Same shall be a Law, in like Manner as if he had signed it, unless the Congress by their Adjournment prevent its Return, in which Case it shall not be a Law.

Every Order, Resolution, or Vote to which the Concurrence of the Senate and House of Representatives may be necessary (except on a question of Adjournment) shall be presented to the President of the United States; and before the Same shall take Effect, shall be approved by him, or being disapproved by him, shall be repassed by two thirds of the Senate and House of Representatives, according to the Rules and Limitations prescribed in the Case of a Bill.

All Bills regulating Commerce shall require the concurrence of two-thirds of Members present in both Houses before becoming a law with the approval of the President, and three-quarters of Members present without his approval.

A few relatively minor changes have been made to the legislative process. The Federal Farmer recommended that a quorum in either house be larger than a simple majority, either two-thirds or three-quarters.[62] Although no other significant Anti-Federalist directly advocated this, many opponents of the Constitution used the quorum rule to argue that the House and Senate were too small. A quorum of sixty-five is thirty-three, the argument went, and a majority of that is seventeen. In the Senate, the numbers are twenty-six, fourteen, and eight. Thus, the Anti-Federalists liked to conclude, twenty-six men (seventeen representatives, eight Senators, and a President) can pass any law. This assumes, of course, massive absenteeism, but the new quorum of two-thirds partially alleviates this argument, and the expanded House and reduced powers of the Senate should remove virtually all of these concerns.

The clause requiring Congress to publish its journals "from time to time," and allowing it discretion to maintain secrecy, drew nearly as many attacks as any other clause in the Constitution. Three state conventions formally objected to this clause.[63] Patrick Henry claimed that such a clause would allow for Congress to duck responsibility: "Such transactions as relate to military operations, or affairs of great consequence, the immediate promulgation of which might defeat the interests of the community, I would not wish to be published, till the end which required their secrecy should have been effected. But to cover with the veil of secrecy, the common ro[u]tine of business, is an abomination in the eyes of every intelligent man, and every friend to his country." Melancton Smith added that "*from time to time* might mean, from century to century, or—in any period of twenty or thirty years."[64] George Mason called for a clause more akin to that found in the Articles, requiring monthly reports and allowing secrecy only in certain cases. Under the Articles, Congress had some difficulty publishing the journals monthly, so annually seems more reasonable here.

Salaries for representatives raised some concerns among the Anti-Federalists, many of whom objected to a legislature with the power to set its own pay. Specific suggestions for who ought to set congressional pay, however, were rare. Federal Farmer suggested that the pay for congressmen be fixed, and Congress given the power to alter it with the consent of a majority of the state legislatures, but this seems a bit impractical. More practical is the suggestion by the Virginia Convention, echoed by North Carolina, that any pay raises not take effect until after the next election. This idea eventually became the Twenty-Seventh Amendment, after it was proposed by the first Congress. This change has been made. The source of the income of representatives was also in dispute, with several Anti-Federalists wanting to see the Representatives, Senators, or both paid out of the states' treasuries. Nonetheless, with added safeguards for representation, the salary question becomes less troubling.[65]

The issue of veto power was not a major issue in the ratification debates, though a few Anti-Federalists did oppose it.[66] Most Anti-Federalists, though, were willing to give some form of veto power to the President, so it has been preserved.

One major change appears in this section, related to the compromise over slavery. Many southern Anti-Federalists demanded that all laws concerning commerce should require two-thirds of votes to pass, and the conventions of Virginia and North Carolina formally proposed the change.[67] This has been inserted for the southern states in exchange for the relative loss of representation in the House of Representatives.

Powers of Congress

Discussion about the powers of Congress, and those of the national government more generally, dominated the ratifying conventions. In particular, Anti-Federalists worried about the wisdom (or folly, as they would have it) of lodging the powers of the purse and the sword in the same institution. William Goudy, in the North Carolina Ratifying Convention, sounded a common Anti-Federalist theme: "I ask, when we give them the purse in one hand, and the sword in another, what power have we left? It will lead to an aristocratical government, and establish tyranny over us." The Anti-Federalists were not entirely opposed to giving Congress some power over money and soldiers, however. James Monroe "would consent to give the General Government every power contained in [the Constitution], except that of taxation." This obviously includes powers over the military. In New York, John Lansing suggested that the problems with the Articles might be fixed "if Congress could be vested with a power to raise men and money." The purse and the sword must, then, be lodged in Congress, but they must be limited and carefully controlled. The issue, as Charles Turner puts it, is that "Relinquishing an *hair's breadth* in a constitution is a great deal; for by small degrees has liberty in all nations, been wrested from the hands of the people. I know great powers are necessary to be given to Congress, but I wish they may be well guarded."[68] This brings us to the question of which powers should specifically be vested in Congress.

Two general strategies emerged for defining and limiting the powers of Congress. "William Penn" suggested that the appropriate powers for the national government include "all powers which cannot be exercised by one state, without endangering the other states."[69] This includes foreign relations and regulation of commerce, among other things. These require, for example, congressional power to levy imposts and raise armies. The other strategy involves a distinction between external and internal objects of government; the Federal Farmer explained this clearly:

> Those [powers] respecting external objects, as all foreign concerns, commerce, imposts, all causes arising on the seas, peace and war, and Indian affairs, can be lodged no where else, with any propriety, but in this government. Many powers that respect internal objects ought clearly to be lodged in it; as those to regulate trade between the states, weights and measures, the coin or current monies, post-offices, naturalization, etc. These powers may be exercised without essentially effecting the internal police of the respective states: But powers to lay and collect internal taxes, to form the militia, to make bankrupt laws, and to decide on appeals, questions arising on the internal laws of the respective states, are of a very serious nature, and carry with them almost all other powers. These taken in connection with the others, and powers to raise armies and build navies, proposed to be lodged in this government, appear to me to comprehend all the essential powers in the community, and those which will be left to the states will be of no great importance.[70]

This distinction is not always sharp; naturalization, for example, which the Federal Farmer included among those internal concerns belonging to the national government, might be left with the states instead, as Agrippa suggests.[71] Still, this internal/external distinction takes us a long way toward finding the proper line between federal and state power.

Brutus summed up quite succinctly the reason so many changes have been made to this section: "one of the most capital errors in the system, is that of extending the powers of the foederal government to objects to which it is not adequate, which it cannot exercise without endangering public liberty, and which it is not necessary they should possess, in order to preserve the union and manage our national concerns."[72] The idea that the national government should preserve the union and handle "national concerns," presumably leaving local and regional concerns to the states, runs through much of the Anti-Federalist literature. As the Constitution stands, the national government has great latitude to encroach on the states. The changes to this section reflect the priority of giving to national government the power to handle national concerns, and no more.

Section 8. The Congress shall have Power To lay and collect ~~Taxes, Duties, Imposts and Excises~~ *Duties and Imposts*, to pay the Debts ~~and provide for the common Defence and general Welfare~~ of the United States *and fulfill the enumerated responsibilities of the government thereof;*[73] but all ~~Duties, Imposts and Excises~~ *Duties and Imposts* shall be uniform throughout the United States, *and shall be collected by residents of the respective States acting on behalf of Congress;*[74]

To request from the States, when the revenues raised from the above sources shall be insufficient, such taxes as shall be deemed necessary by the Congress, with the concurrence of two-thirds of members in both houses, apportioned according to the value of all land and personal property within each State, estimated according to such mode as the United States in Congress assembled, shall from time to time direct and appoint;[75]

To lay direct taxes upon any State, or the people thereof, whenever such State shall fail to supply the requisition of Congress;

To borrow Money on the credit of the United States, *with the consent of two-thirds of members present in both houses of Congress;*[76]

To regulate Commerce with foreign Nations, and ~~among~~ *between*[77] the several States, and with the Indian Tribes,[78] *upon the approval of two-thirds of members present in both Houses;*

To establish an uniform Rule of Naturalization,[79] and uniform Laws on the subject of Bankruptcies throughout the United States;[80]

To coin Money, regulate the Value thereof, and of foreign Coin, and fix the Standard of Weights and Measures;

To provide for the Punishment of counterfeiting the Securities and current Coin of the United States;

To establish Post Offices and post Roads, *provided that such Roads shall not be established, altered, and repaired without the consent of the State;*[81]

To promote the Progress of Science and useful Arts, by securing for limited Times to Authors and Inventors the exclusive Right to their respective Writings and Discoveries;

To constitute Tribunals inferior to the supreme Court;

To define and punish Piracies and Felonies committed on the high Seas, and Offences against the Law of Nations;

To declare War, *provided two-thirds of members in both houses concur,*[82] grant Letters of Marque and Reprisal, and make Rules concerning Captures on Land and Water;

To raise and support Armies, but no Appropriation of Money to that Use shall be for a longer Term than ~~two~~ one Years,[83] *and no standing Army shall be maintained during times of peace without the concurrence of two-thirds of members present in both houses of Congress, and no soldier shall be enlisted for any longer term than four years, except in time of war, and then for no longer term than the continuance of the war;*[84]

To provide and maintain a Navy;[85]

To make Rules for the Government and Regulation of the land and naval Forces;

To provide for calling forth the Militia to ~~execute the Laws of the Union,~~ suppress Insurrections and repel Invasions, *but Congress shall not call or march any of the militia out of their own state, without the consent of such state, and for such length of time only as such state shall agree;*

To provide for organizing, ~~arming,~~ and disciplining, the Militia, and for governing such Part of them as may be employed in the Service of the United States *during times of war, invasion, or rebellion*, reserving to the States respectively, *the provision of Arms*, the Appointment of the Officers, and the Authority of training the Militia according to the discipline prescribed by Congress, *or according to such discipline as the State prescribes in the absence of direction by Congress;—And*

To exercise exclusive Legislation ~~in all Cases whatsoever, over~~ *establishing government and maintaining order in* such District (not exceeding ~~ten~~ *five* Miles square)[86] as may, by Cession of particular States, and the Acceptance of Congress, become the Seat of the Government of the United States,[87] and to exercise like Authority over all Places purchased by the Consent of the Legislature of the State in which the Same shall be, for the Erection of Forts, Magazines, Arsenals, dockYards, and other needful Buildings;~~—And.~~

~~To make all Laws which shall be necessary and proper for carrying into Execution the foregoing Powers, and all other Powers vested by this Constitution in the Government of the United States, or in any Department or Officer thereof.~~

The power to tax, described in the first clause of this section, was perhaps the most discussed part of the Constitution during the ratification contest. The concern over tax powers was tied up in the fear of consolidation. George Mason drew this link: "The assumption of this power of laying direct taxes, does of itself, entirely change the confederation of the States into one consolidated Government. This power being at discretion, unconfined, and without any kind of controul, must carry every thing before it." In addition to concerns about national taxes, there is also a distinct antitax sentiment, even concerning state taxes; one writer predicted a fierce competition between national and state governments for tax revenue; this sharing "will induce them to vie in the race of taxation to snatch the prize, the spoils of the citizen, that is to glut the vanity of their respective consequence!" Joseph McDowell is even more dramatic and direct: "If the tax-gatherers come upon us, they will, like the locusts of old, destroy us." Not all Anti-Federalists went to this extreme, however. Caleb Wallace, for example, saw danger here, but conceded that he could accept it as "a necessary evil"; still, "if it can in any way be restrained or guarded from abuse, nothing can be more advisable." Most Anti-Federalists wanted to see a national government able to raise revenue. There is some disagreement as to how Congress should be able to raise that revenue, but there is a general consensus that some, and probably most, revenue must be left to the states.[88]

A distinction between internal and external taxes was fairly common, with internal taxes left to the states and external taxes given to Congress. Because of this distinction, the majority of Anti-Federalists believed that it was proper to allow Congress to levy imposts and duties. Excises, on the other hand, were the subject of a number of specific objections. Even the word "taxes" in this section was the source of objections, in large part because it was interpreted to mean direct taxes.[89]

The revenue from the impost and customs duties, however, may not be enough.[90] Congress must have another method for raising additional revenue. The convention of Rhode Island was willing to allow direct taxation with the approval of three-fourths of the states, but this would not have been practical. John Hancock and Samuel Adams suggested that direct taxes should be allowed during times of war, but this exception was not echoed by others. Instead, a consensus formed around the plan included in this constitution. This plan gives to Congress the power to levy imposts and duties, but removes the unconditional power to lay taxes. Instead, it allows Congress to requisition money from the states, according to both land and personal property, and to tax directly only in such states as might fail to provide the revenue requested. A plan along these lines was suggested by no fewer than five state conventions and many individuals.[91] This method provides Congress with the necessary revenue as effectively as direct taxation, because the requisitions are backed by force in the form of direct taxation. As Samuel Spencer puts it, "The right of Congress to lay taxes ultimately, in case of non-compliance with requisitions, would operate as a penalty, and would stimulate the states to discharge their quotas faithfully." As for the states, this method enables them to decide what method of taxation will be the most appropriate to their particular circumstances. Because this method preserves taxation discretion for the states, yet secures for Congress needed revenue, George Mason described this change as an "indispensable amendment." The Federal Farmer wanted to add an additional check by requiring a majority of state legislatures to concur in assessing direct taxes, but in addition to being impractical it does not give Congress an effective means to force states to pay their quotas, especially if many states fall short.[92]

In addition to concerns about taxes, the Anti-Federalists demanded some substantial changes to the military powers of Congress, starting with the militia. The use of the militia "to execute the Laws of the Union" raised a great deal of alarm, as some saw this as an invitation to a tyrannical police state. The removal of the clause leaves law enforcement up to civilian officers. Similarly, keeping the militia in their own states prevents the national government from using the people of one state against another. The Pennsylvania Minority insisted on this restriction, and it was suggested in New York and Maryland as well. The minority in Pennsylvania also argued that organizing, arming, and disciplining the militia should belong to the states, but the prohibition of a standing army makes a nationally organized militia important for defense. Patrick Henry and "John DeWitt" both emphasized the importance of the states arming the militia, because that would enable some defense for the people against a tyrannical central government, should it become necessary.[93] Thus the states are given the power to arm the militia, and retain the appointment of officers, while Congress can organize and provide for the discipline of a potential national defense force. The states are also given the authority to train the militia even if Congress does not provide guidelines, as suggested by Virginia and North Carolina.

The dangers of a standing army were a popular topic among opponents of the Constitution. Brutus wrote that standing armies "have always proved the destruction of liberty, and abhorrent to the spirit of a free republic." Because of this, a two-thirds vote for Congress to maintain a standing army would be seen by many Anti-Federalists as an insufficient limitation, but Brutus's suggestion that only such soldiers as "shall be deemed absolutely necessary" for basic protection leaves too much discretion with Congress. The two-thirds plan was proposed in Virginia, New York, and North Carolina, plus the Maryland minority, while Massachusetts and New Hampshire suggested three-fourths. The state of Rhode Island suggested that Congress not be allowed to keep any army in times of peace, and several Anti-Federalists agreed. Benjamin Gale spoke the mind of many Anti-Federalists when he said, "A mild government, gentlemen, wants no military force to support it, and an arbitrary and oppressive government doth not deserve it."[94] In the end, though, more moderate Anti-Federalists would likely carry the day by pointing out that if two-thirds of representatives in both houses are willing to vote in favor of tyrannical measures, then a constitutional prohibition is unlikely to carry much weight anyway. In addition to restrictions on a standing army in peacetime, several other enumerated powers have the added requirement of a supermajority in Congress to exercise. This was seen by many as an adequate defense against dangerous abuses.

The question of a federal city was a controversial one, but few Anti-Federalists outright opposed the idea. The Federal Farmer suggested that such a district is antirepublican, and George Mason believed that such a place would become a haven for criminals who cannot be touched by the states once they enter its jurisdiction. Caleb Wallace went further, writing that the federal district "will be the most successful nursery of slaves that ever was devised by man," "a market where liberty may be sold for a valuable consideration." It is an idea "dictated by vanity and not by necessity." The inclusion of a bill of rights here provides some relief, and further restriction on the powers of Congress over the federal city provides more.[95]

The Necessary and Proper Clause, or, as one Anti-Federalist called it, "the *omnipotent* clause," has been removed entirely. There was plenty of opposition to this open-ended grant of power, and no notable Anti-Federalist supported it.[96]

Restrictions on Congress and the States

Sections 9 and 10 of Article I place prohibitions on Congress, including a limited bill of rights, as well as limits on the states. The limits on the states are fairly benign, certainly compared to the broad expanse of congressional powers. The Anti-Federalists suggested more limits on Congress, and some of the guaranteed rights have been moved up to the new Article I.

Section 9.[97] ~~The Migration or Importation of such Persons as any of the States now existing shall think proper to admit, shall not be prohibited by the Congress prior to the Year one thousand eight hundred and eight, but a Tax or duty may be imposed on such Importation, not exceeding ten dollars for each Person.~~

~~The Privilege of the Writ of Habeas Corpus shall not be suspended, unless when in Cases of Rebellion or Invasion the public Safety may require it.~~[98]

No Bill of Attainder or ex post facto *criminal* Law shall be passed.[99]

Congress shall not introduce foreign Soldiers into the United States without the consent of two thirds of the Members present of both Houses.[100]

No Soldier shall, in time of peace, be quartered in any house without the consent of the Owner, and in time of war in such manner only as the law directs.[101]

~~No Capitation, or other direct, Tax shall be laid, unless in Proportion to the Census or Enumeration herein before directed to be taken.~~[102]

No Tax or Duty shall be laid on Articles exported from any State *to any other State.*[103]

No Law shall be passed to restrain the Legislatures of the several States from enacting Laws for imposing Taxes, except Imposts and Duties on goods imported or exported.[104]

No Law shall be passed to alter the Laws of Descents and Distribution of the Effects of deceased Persons, the Titles of Lands or Goods, or the Regulation of Contracts in the individual States.[105]

Congress shall not, directly or indirectly; either by themselves or through the Judiciary, interfere with any one of the States in the redemption of paper money already emitted and now in circulation, or in liquidating and discharging the public securities of any one of the States; but each and every State shall have the exclusive right of making such Laws and Regulations, for the above purposes, as they shall think proper.[106]

No Preference shall be given by any Regulation of Commerce or Revenue to the Ports of one State over those of another: nor shall Vessels bound to~~, or from, one State, be obliged to enter, clear or pay Duties in another~~ *a particular state be obliged to enter or pay duties in any other; nor, when bound from any one of the states, be obliged to clear in another.*[107]

Congress shall erect no company of merchants with exclusive advantages of commerce.[108]

No Money shall be drawn from the Treasury, but in Consequence of Appropriations made by Law; and a regular Statement and Account of Receipts and Expenditures of all public Money shall be published ~~from time to time~~ *not less than once each Year.*[109]

No Title of Nobility shall be granted by the United States: And no Person holding any Office of Profit or Trust under them, shall~~, without the Consent of the Congress,~~ accept of any present, Emolument, Office, or Title, of any kind whatever, from any King, Prince, or foreign State.[110]

Section 10. No State shall enter into any Treaty, Alliance, or Confederation; grant Letters of Marque and Reprisal; coin Money; emit Bills of Credit *without the consent of Congress*;[111] make any Thing but gold and silver Coin a Tender in Payment of Debts; pass any Bill of Attainder, ex post facto Law, or Law impairing the Obligation of Contracts, or grant any Title of Nobility.

No State shall, without the Consent of the Congress, lay any Imposts or Duties on Imports or Exports, except what may be absolutely necessary for executing it's inspection Laws[112]~~: and the net Produce of all Duties and Imposts, laid by any State on Imports or Exports, shall be for the Use of the Treasury of the United States;~~[113] and all such Laws shall be subject to the Revision and Controul of the Congress.

No State shall, without the Consent of Congress, lay any Duty of Tonnage, keep Troops, or Ships of War in time of Peace, enter into any Agreement or Compact with ~~another State,~~[114] ~~or with~~ a foreign Power, or engage in War, unless actually invaded, *experiencing insurrection*,[115] or in such imminent Danger as will not admit of delay.

Almost any restriction on Congress seriously proposed would be acceptable to most Anti-Federalists; many clauses have been added to Section 9. Congress has been further restricted in its potential encroachments within the states. It can no longer interfere with state taxes or with contracts. It cannot interfere with paper money already in place. Congress cannot create monopolies. Additional safeguards can be found in the new Articles I and VII. The changes to Section 10 are designed to strengthen states, even if the changes are relatively minor.

As for the first clause in Section 9, the subject of the slave trade raised some lively debate. In North Carolina, James Galloway expressed a "wish to see this abominable trade put an end to," and he was not alone in the convention. In Virginia, George Mason objected as well: "As much as I value an union of all the States, I would not admit the Southern States into the Union, unless they agreed to the discontinuance of this disgraceful trade, because it would bring weakness and not strength to the Union." There were defenders of the slave trade and of slavery in the southern states, but they were generally not as enthusiastic as might be expected. These defenders of the institution tended to rest their arguments on interests, not morals. The opponents of the slave trade in the North were numerous. Centinel called the tacit approval of slavery by the Constitution "especially scandalous and inconsistent in a people, who have asserted their own liberty by the sword." Republicus offered an especially scathing critique: "An excellent clause this, in an Algerian constitution: but not so well calculated (I hope) for the latitude of America." He described this clause as a "shocking absurdity," inappropriate for a constitution based on liberty. Oddly enough, the most practical statement on the topic came from Rhode Island, hardly a proslavery state. When the clause was discussed, the general consensus was that allowing the slave trade was wrong, but outlawing it was impractical because it would undermine the union. As Jonathan Hazard put it, "If we totally ab[o]lish Slavery it will Ruin many persons." Ultimately, the Anti-Federalist position on slavery, in the north and the south, was perhaps best summed up by a rather obscure Anti-Federalist from Connecticut, Benjamin Gale: "It might have been sufficient, one would have thought, not to have said anything about it." Thus the clause concerning the slave trade has been removed entirely, leaving Congress the potential to regulate or even end it, but since it is a question of commerce, only by two-thirds vote in both houses.[116]

The Presidency

The presidency was in many ways less controversial during the debate over ratification than it was in the Constitutional Convention. There was virtually no opposition to having a single chief executive, though there were frequent demands for a council of some sort to advise him. There was little complaint about the Electoral College, except that there were too few electors;[117] only a few writers advocated direct democratic elections.[118] For all the discussion of congressional and even judicial salaries, there was hardly any mention of presidential salary, and his qualifications were little questioned. The oath of office was also little discussed. The main issue with the presidency, apart from his powers (discussed below), was his term of office and eligibility for reelection.

Article III

Section 1. The executive Power shall be vested in a President of the United States of America. *Every four Years,*[119] *he shall* ~~He shall hold his Office during the Term of four Years, and, together with the Vice President, chosen for the same Term,~~ be elected, as follows:

Each State shall appoint, in such Manner as the Legislature thereof may direct, a Number of Electors, equal to the whole Number of Senators and Representatives to which the State may be entitled in the Congress: but no Senator or Representative, or Person holding an Office of Trust or Profit under the United States, shall be appointed an Elector.

The Electors shall meet in their respective States, and vote by Ballot for two Persons, of whom one at least shall not be an Inhabitant of the same State with themselves. And they shall make a List of all the Persons voted for, and of the Number of Votes for each; which List they shall sign and certify, and transmit sealed to the Seat of the Government of the United States, directed to the *Speaker* ~~President~~ of the Senate. The *Speaker* ~~President~~ of the Senate shall, in the Presence of the Senate and House of Representatives, open all the Certificates, and the Votes shall then be counted. The Person having the greatest Number of Votes shall be the President, if such Number be a Majority of the whole Number of Electors appointed; and if there be more than one who have such Majority, and have an equal Number of Votes, then the House of Representatives shall immediately chuse by Ballot one of them for President; and if no Person have a Majority, then from the ~~five~~ *three*[120] highest on the List the said House shall in like Manner chuse the President. But in chusing the President, the Votes shall be taken by States, the Representation from each State having one Vote; A quorum for this Purpose shall consist of a Member or Members from two thirds of the States, and a Majority of all the States shall be necessary to a Choice. ~~In every Case, after the Choice of the President, the Person having the greatest Number of Votes of the Electors shall be the Vice President. But if there should remain two or more who have equal Votes, the Senate shall chuse from them by Ballot the Vice President.~~

The Congress may determine the Time of chusing the Electors, and the Day on which they shall give their Votes; which Day shall be the same throughout the United States.

No Person except a natural born Citizen, or a Citizen of the United States, at the time of the Adoption of this Constitution, shall be eligible to the Office of President; neither shall any Person be eligible to that Office who shall not have attained to the Age of thirty five Years, and been fourteen Years a Resident within the United States.

No Person having been twice elected to the office of President shall be elected, unless at least eight Years have passed since his previous Term as President.

In Case of the Removal of the President from Office, or of his Death, Resignation, or Inability to discharge the Powers and Duties of the said Office, the Same shall devolve on the Vice President, ~~and the Congress may by Law provide for the Case of Removal, Death, Resignation or Inability, both of the President and Vice President, declaring what Officer shall then act as President, and such Officer shall act accordingly,~~ until the Disability be removed, or a President shall be elected.[121]

The President shall, at stated Times, receive for his Services, a Compensation, which shall neither be encreased nor diminished during the Period for which he shall have been elected,[122] and he shall not receive within that Period any other Emolument from the United States, or any of them.

Before he enter on the Execution of his Office, he shall take the following Oath or Affirmation:—"I do solemnly swear (or affirm) that I will faithfully execute the Office of President of the United States, and will to the best of my Ability, preserve, protect and defend the Constitution of the United States."

The House of Representatives each year shall elect a Council to advise the President; there shall be seven members of this Council, with not more than one chosen from any given state, and each meeting the qualifications of a Senator as listed above. Members of this Council may not at the same time hold any other office in any government. The Council shall select a Vice President from among its members to serve as its chairman.

There may not be another part of the Constitution that drew so many varied suggestions for change as the term and reelection of the President. Several Anti-Federalists argued that a hereditary king would be better than the President as he was described. Cato suggested that the President's term should be shorter than four years; Agrippa advocated annual elections.[123] Several writers suggested that the President be ineligible after a single four-year term in office, while the Federal Farmer proposed that the age of eligibility should be raised to forty or forty-five along with this one-term limit.

A Georgian suggested four years out of every eight, while George Mason suggested eight out of every twelve. Edmund Randolph, apparently unable to decide precisely what to do, merely suggested ineligibility "after a given number of years." Two specific proposals came from the ratifying conventions: Virginia and North Carolina proposed a limit of eight out of every fifteen years, while New York suggested a single term of seven years. Although the opponents of the Constitution did not agree on the details, they generally agreed that a President always eligible for reelection represented a danger of monarchy, and hence tyranny. A Farmer and Planter predicted that "a four-years President will be, in time, a King for life."[124] Clearly some limit is necessary for the Anti-Federalists, so this constitution takes a moderate route and prohibits more than eight years in office at a time, requiring eight years out of office before becoming eligible to return.

The method of election proposed in the original Constitution may have been a novel one, but it seems to be one that was acceptable to most Anti-Federalists, based on the relative absence of complaints. Cato noted that "It is a maxim in republics, that the representative of the people should be of their immediate choice," yet he observes that the president will be their choice "at the fourth or fifth hand." Like most of his colleagues, however, even those who shared his concern on this point, he did not explicitly endorse direct election of a President, nor did he endorse some other method.[125] Thus the Electoral College has remained in this constitution, with only minor modifications.

A constitutional council has been added. Several Anti-Federalists, most prominently George Mason, called for some sort of council to advise the President and participate in the appointment of officers; without one, Mason argued, the President "will therefore be unsupported by proper Information and Advice; and will generally be directed by Minions and Favourites—or He will become a Tool to the Senate."[126] There was no clear consensus on the shape this council should take, but for its advisory role it should be small; Samuel Spencer's suggestion in the North Carolina Convention that there be one member per state probably makes it too large. The idea that different states should be represented is important, though, and seven different states will always be represented under this plan. Mason suggested six members, while the Federal Farmer wanted seven or nine. Richard Henry Lee proposed eleven. Seven seems large enough to represent different interests and resist corruption, but not too large to provide effective advice. Mason suggested election by the House, and this serves three purposes that fit well with general Anti-Federalist sentiment. First, it removes some power from the Senate. Second, it allows the power to try impeachments to be lodged in the Senate without fear of collusion, since the Senate does not now participate in appointments. Third, it gives a little more power to the democratic House, and gives both houses an executive role to play and a meaningful check on the President. The Vice President, whose primary responsibility now consists of chairing this council, is now elected by the members of it; this was suggested by Richard Henry Lee in his amendments presented in Congress.[127] There is no special reason for the council to serve one-year terms beyond the general preference for annual elections, but this allows for such advisers to serve for a short period of time while they do not hold another office. It also permits each Congress to select two sets of members, allowing for a policy shift between congressional elections.

Presidential Powers

Patrick Henry, it seems, was rather concerned about the presidency. He found much to critique in the Constitution, but he saved his strongest ire for Article II. "Among other deformities," he said in the Virginia Convention, "it has an awful squinting; it squints towards monarchy." He was not the only one of this opinion; Philadelphiensis agreed emphatically: "Who can deny but the *president general* will be a *king* to all intents and purposes, and one of the most dangerous kind too; a king elected to command a standing army?" This elective king was perhaps the greatest danger, for, as Cato of South Carolina declared, "if ever America be enslaved by any fault in her constitution, it will be by the ambition of a President."[128]

Most Anti-Federalists did not complain that the President was too powerful as described, but rather that his power was not sufficiently detailed. Many of them took issue with the imprecision of having the President faithfully execute the laws of the United States. One asked, "was ever a commission so *brief*, so *general*, as this of our President? Can we exactly say how far a faithful execution of the laws may extend? or what may be called or comprehended in a faithful execution?"[129] Unfortunately, as many opponents of the presidency acknowledged, it was difficult to define his powers any more precisely. The solution was additional limitations, qualifications, and restrictions on his power.

Section 2. The President shall be Commander in Chief of the Army and Navy of the United States,[130] and of the Militia of the several States, when called into the actual Service of the United States; he may require the Opinion, in writing, of the principal Officer in each of the executive Departments, upon any Subject relating to the Duties of their respective Offices, *or of any or all members of his Council,* and he shall have Power to grant Reprieves and Pardons, *upon conviction,*[131] for Offences against the United States, except in Cases of Impeachment *or Treason.*[132]

He shall have Power, by and with the Advice and Consent of the Senate, to make Treaties, provided two thirds of ~~the~~ *all* Senators ~~present~~ concur, *and provided such Treaties not conflict with the laws of the United States, or the Constitutions of the several States;* and he shall nominate, and by and with the Advice and Consent of the ~~Senate~~ *Council,*[133] shall appoint Ambassadors, other public Ministers and Consuls, Judges of the supreme Court, and all other Officers of the United States, whose Appointments are not herein otherwise provided for, and which shall be established by Law: but the Congress may by Law vest the Appointment of such inferior Officers, as they think proper, in the President alone, in the Courts of Law, or in the Heads of Departments.[134]

~~The President shall have Power to fill up all Vacancies that may happen during the Recess of the Senate, by granting Commissions which shall expire at the End of their next Session.~~[135]

Section 3. He shall from time to time give to the Congress Information of the State of the Union, and recommend to their Consideration such Measures as he shall judge necessary and expedient; he may, on extraordinary Occasions, convene both Houses, or either of them,[136] and in Case of Disagreement between them, with Respect to the Time of Adjournment, he may adjourn them to such Time, *proposed by either House,*[137] as he shall think proper; he shall receive Ambassadors and other public Ministers; he shall take Care that the Laws be faithfully executed, and shall Commission all the Officers of the United States, *by and with the advice of the Council.*[138]

Section 4. The President, Vice President and all ~~civil~~ *executive* Officers of the United States, shall be removed from Office on Impeachment for, and Conviction of, Treason, Bribery, or other high Crimes and Misdemeanors.[139]

Among the powers of the President, none garnered more attention from Anti-Federalists than the power to make treaties. The idea that the President, with two-thirds of Senators present, could make binding, supreme law was seen as at least unwise, and probably dangerous. William Lenoir objected that this was a legislative power, and ought not to belong to the

President. The President, he said, "with the Senate, is to make treaties, which are to be the supreme law of the land. This is a legislative power given to the President, and implies a contradiction to that part which says that all legislative power is vested in the two houses." This is a fair observation, and it led many Anti-Federalists to argue that the House should be involved in making treaties. "Sentiments of Many" likely reflected his pseudonym when he argued that "We have hitherto been taught that all laws binding on the community, ought to be made with the consent of the people, or by that of their representatives, in their legislative capacity." At the most extreme, William Grayson proposed that treaties require a three-quarters vote in both houses of Congress.[140] The principle of representation could also be satisfied by requiring ratification of treaties by states. This latter option was probably too unwieldy, and there was some resistance to the former as well. The Federal Farmer, as usual, articulated a moderate position worth considering:

> I am not perfectly satisfied, that the senate, a branch of the legislature, and court for trying impeachments, ought to have a controuling power in making all treaties; yet, I confess, I do not discern how a restraint upon the president in this important business, can be better or more safely lodged: a power to make and conclude all treaties is too important to be vested in him alone, or in him and an executive council, only sufficiently numerous for other purpose[s], and the house of representatives is too numerous to be concerned in treaties of peace and of alliance. This power is now lodged in congress, to be exercised by the consent of nine states. The federal senate, like the delegations in the present congress, will represent the states, and the consent of two-thirds of that senate will bear some similitude to the consent of nine states.[141]

He suggested that commercial treaties will require additional laws to implement, so the House will have a role in those anyway. Still, even writers like the Federal Farmer who supported the power of making treaties as it stood were not entirely comfortable, because of the possibility for collusion by the President and Senate. Along with sharing in appointments, especially judges, treaties would be a tool by which the President and Senate could establish a permanent aristocracy.

Rather than significantly change the process of making treaties, this constitution puts additional limitations on them. When it comes to actual amendments, most Anti-Federalists would have likely come around to the

Federal Farmer's position, so long as the treaty power itself could be weakened. This is why, in this constitution, treaties must accord with the laws of the United States, which prevents the President and Senate from overruling the House. This preserves an indirect role for the House in this, since the Senate and President cannot ignore existing laws. Treaties also may not conflict with the state constitutions, and this gives the states a little extra protection against federal encroachment. State laws may be superseded, but these changes, recommended by the Pennsylvania Minority and the New York Convention,[142] retain for the states some defense. The requirement for two-thirds of all Senators rather than those present is simply an extra safeguard to satisfy those who envisioned a faction within the Senate controlling the government.[143]

Of course, this change to the treaty power, along with the more minor changes and presence of an advisory council, would be unlikely to win over all of the Anti-Federalists. The President still has ample power and prestige to appear kingly, if not become a king. "Away with your President," Patrick Henry would retort, "we shall have a King: The army will salute him Monarch; your militia will leave you and assist in making him King, and fight against you: And what have you to oppose this force? What will then become of you and your rights? Will not absolute despotism ensue?"[144] This is a fundamental dilemma faced by the Anti-Federalists, the question of whether to include an executive and risk monarchy, or to enfeeble the government through the lack of a proper executive branch. The moderate Anti-Federalists here overrule Henry's concerns.

The Judicial Branch

Brutus provided the most comprehensive Anti-Federalist account and critique of the constitutional provisions for a federal judiciary, but he was certainly not alone in his critique. This branch of government, deemed the least dangerous by the Federalists, was clearly the least defined, prompting opponents of the Constitution to see danger in every possibility. Issues over the jurisdiction, location, and even existence of the lower courts were significant, but jury trials and procedural guarantees were paramount in the debate.

Since Brutus offered the best critique of the courts, the changes below lean heavily on his suggestions. When read carefully, though, he called for surprisingly few changes to the judicial branch. His objections centered on the idea that the courts will consolidate power in the national government because the language of the Constitution invites them to do so. Changing that language makes the courts far less dangerous, and in the end Brutus endorsed an independent judiciary to settle constitutional disputes: "The proper province of the judicial power, in any government, is, as I conceive, to declare what is the law of the land. To explain and enforce those laws, which the supreme power or legislature may pass; but not to declare what the powers of the legislature are."[145] Such a branch of government is still necessary, as most Anti-Federalists allow, so it has been preserved in modified form.

Article IV
Section 1. The judicial Power of the United States, shall be vested in one supreme Court, and in such inferior *appellate* Courts as the Congress may from time to time ordain and establish. The Judges, both of the supreme and inferior Courts, shall hold their Offices during good Behaviour,[146] and shall, at stated Times, receive for their Services, a Compensation, which shall not be diminished during their Continuance in Office.[147] *Judges shall be removed from Office on Impeachment for, and Conviction of, Treason, Bribery, or other high Crimes and Misdemeanors, or for negligence to properly perform the duties assigned.*[148] *Judges shall not hold any other office of profit, or receive the profits of any other office under the United States, or any of them, during the time they hold their commission.*[149]

Section 2. The judicial Power shall extend to all Cases, in Law and Equity,[150] arising under this Constitution, the Laws of the United States, and Treaties made, or which shall be made, under their Authority;—to all Cases affecting Ambassadors, other public Ministers and Consuls;—to all Cases of admiralty and maritime Jurisdiction;—to Controversies to which the United States shall be a Party;—to Controversies between two or more States;—between a State and Citizens of another State;—between Citizens of different States;—*and* between Citizens of the same State claiming Lands under Grants of different States, and between a State, or the Citizens thereof, and foreign States, Citizens or Subjects.

In all Cases affecting Ambassadors, other public Ministers and Consuls, and those in which a State shall be Party, the supreme Court shall have original Jurisdiction, *with such Exceptions, and under such Regulations as the Congress shall make.*[151] In all the other Cases before mentioned, *the Courts of each State shall have original jurisdiction over all cases that shall originate within the borders of that State, and* the ~~supreme Court~~ *Courts established by Congress* shall have appellate Jurisdiction, ~~both~~ as to Law ~~and Fact~~, with such Exceptions, and under such Regulations as the Congress shall make. *The executive authority of each State shall prosecute violations of the Laws of the United States, and the Laws of the State.*[152]

The judicial power shall extend to no case where the cause of action shall have originated before the ratification of this Constitution, except in suits for debts due to the United States, disputes between states about their territory, and disputes between persons claiming lands under grants of different states.[153]

Section 3. The Trial of all Crimes, except in Cases of Impeachment, *and of all controversies respecting Property and suits between Citizens,* shall be by Jury; and such Trial shall be held in the ~~State~~ *vicinage* where the said Crimes shall have been committed; but when not committed within any State, the Trial shall be at such Place or Places as the Congress may by Law have directed.

No person shall be tried for any crime, by which he may incur an infamous punishment, or loss of life, until he be first indicted by a grand jury, except in such cases as may arise in the government and regulation of the land and naval forces.[154]

In all criminal and capital prosecutions, a man hath a right to demand the cause and nature of his accusation, to be confronted with the accusers and witnesses, to call for evidence, and be allowed counsel in his favor, and to a fair and speedy trial by an impartial jury of his vicinage, without whose unanimous consent he cannot be found guilty (except in the government of the land and naval forces); nor can he be compelled to give evidence against himself.[155]

No freeman ought to be taken, imprisoned, or disseized of his freehold, liberties, privileges, or franchises, or outlawed, or exiled, or in any manner destroyed, or deprived of his life, liberty, or property, but by the law of the land.[156]

Excessive bail shall not be required, nor excessive fines imposed, nor cruel nor unusual punishments inflicted.[157]

Section 4. Treason against the United States, shall consist only in levying War against them, or in adhering to their Enemies, giving them Aid and Comfort, *provided that no acts by Persons or States pursuant to the authority of the Government of any State shall be considered Treason or punished as such.*[158] No Person shall be convicted of Treason unless on the Testimony of two Witnesses to the same overt Act, or on Confession in open Court.

The Congress shall have Power to declare the Punishment of Treason, but no Attainder of Treason shall work Corruption of Blood, or Forfeiture except during the Life of the Person attainted.

The number of courts to be established was a key point of contention. The Constitution required at least fourteen, since trials must be held in the state in which the crime was committed, and there must be a Supreme Court. Congress, though, could establish any number of courts. If the courts were few, then an individual would have to travel far for the administration of justice, even further on appeal, and only the rich would truly be able to have a fair trial. If the courts were many, they would necessarily be unacceptably expensive and encroach on the jurisdiction and prestige of the state courts.[159] Luther Martin offered the means to get out of this dilemma, a proposal that surprisingly did not find many advocates (or opponents) later in the ratification contest:

That the different *State judiciaries* in the respective States would be *competent to*, and *sufficient for*, the cognizance in the *first instance* of all cases that should arise under the laws of the general government, which being by this system made the supreme law of the States, would be binding on the different State judiciaries—That by giving an *appeal* to the *supreme court* of the United States, the *general government* would have a *sufficient* check over their decisions, and security for the enforcing of their laws.[160]

Thus the expense for courts would be only slightly greater than under the Articles and the state constitutions, and there would still be an appeal to federal courts. The states would retain authority, and would actually hold some power to interpret national laws, but the appellate jurisdiction of the national courts would prevent the states from undoing congressional laws. Perhaps most importantly, the state courts retain a significant role. In New Hampshire, Abiel Parker argued "that the cognizance of all the cases therein enumerated was confined to the federal courts." This interpretation, coupled with the common interpretation that the jurisdictions given to the federal courts are so extensive as to encompass everything, leads to the conclusion that the state courts would become irrelevant and ultimately cease to exist. Under this new construction, there is no danger of the obsolescence of the state judiciaries.[161]

There was substantial debate over the jurisdiction of the federal courts as well. Candidus spoke for many Anti-Federalists when he suggested that the judicial power should extend only to national matters, such as treaties. Cases involving federal laws, federal officers, and the Constitution clearly fell to the federal courts, as did maritime law cases and suits against the national government. Cases between two states really had nowhere else to go but the federal courts. On the other hand, cases involving citizens suing another state, or another state's citizens, along with foreign citizens suing states, were unacceptable to the Anti-Federalists. The idea that states could not defend themselves in their own court was seen as an unjust appropriation of power from the states. As Brutus wrote, "It is improper, because it subjects a state to answer in a court of law, to the suit of an individual. This is humiliating and degrading to a government, and, what I believe, the supreme authority of no state ever submitted to." The idea that citizens of one state could not sue those of another in state courts was seen by Centinel as "a very invidious jurisdiction, implying an improper distrust of the impartiality and justice of the tribunals of the states."[162] Under this revised constitution, these problems are less significant because all of these cases would start in state courts, but the Anti-Federalists would have liked to see them end in state courts as well. The issue of land grants, however, was generally considered to be a reasonable area of jurisdiction, since multiple states might claim the same land. Thus the only remaining jurisdictions involving states are cases directly between two states and those involving disputed land claims.

The appellate jurisdiction of the federal courts has been limited to questions of law, and not of fact; the Anti-Federalists were unified and insistent on this. Centinel observed that "It would be a novelty in jurisprudence, as well as evidently improper to allow an appeal from the verdict of a jury, on the matter of fact." Facts are for a jury to decide, and the idea of using a jury on appeal runs counter to the common emphasis on a local jury. This is not just an issue for the individual involved; it would undermine the judicial system. The Impartial Examiner asked, "what is an appeal to enquire into facts after a solemn adjudication in any court below, but a trial *de novo*? And do not such trials clearly imply an incompetency in the inferior courts to exercise any kind of judicial authority with rectitude? Hence, will not this eventually annihilate their whole jurisdiction?" Trials held in state courts, with appeal to national courts on questions of law, and only over national concerns, answer most of the Anti-Federalist objections to the federal judiciary, as well as many concerns about consolidation.[163]

Many Anti-Federalists demanded that jury trials be preserved in civil as well as criminal cases. "A Planter" asserted that "a jury in civil cases is, without any manner of doubt, the only sure palladium of the rights, liberties, and the property of society." As essential as the right to a jury is, it must be a fair and impartial jury of one's peers. The Anti-Federalists in the North Carolina Convention, led on this point by Samuel Spencer, insisted that a trial held in the same state was not sufficient, that the trial must be by a jury of the vicinage in order to find jurors that were truly peers of the accused. This was not provided by the Constitution. Such a guarantee has been made here, along with other procedural rights of the accused.[164]

The States in the Federal System

The original Article IV discusses the states in the federal system. It was not an area of controversy as significant as the previous three articles, but several issues came up in the ratification debates, especially concerning the relationship between states and national government. The Federalists pointed to this article as part of the evidence that the system was a federal one, and not one of consolidation, and the changes below reflect a desire on the part of the opponents of the Constitution to make this more explicit.

Article V
Section 1. Full Faith and Credit shall be given in each State to the public Acts, Records, and judicial Proceedings of every other State. And the Congress may by general Laws prescribe the Manner in which such Acts, Records, and Proceedings shall be proved, and the Effect thereof.

Section 2. The Citizens of each State shall be entitled to all Privileges and Immunities of Citizens in the several States.[165]

A Person charged in any State with Treason, Felony, or other Crime, who shall flee from Justice, and be found in another State, *or in any Territory governed by the United States,*[166] shall on Demand of the executive Authority of the State *or Territory* from which he fled, be delivered up, to be removed to the State having Jurisdiction of the Crime.

No Person held to Service or Labour in one State, under the Laws thereof, escaping into another, shall, in Consequence of any Law or Regulation therein, be discharged from such Service or Labour, but shall be delivered up on Claim of the Party to whom such Service or Labour may be due.[167]

Section 3. New States may be admitted by the Congress into this Union, *with the consent of the Legislatures of two-thirds of the States;*

but no new States shall be formed or erected within the Jurisdiction of any other State; nor any State be formed by the Junction of two or more States, or Parts of States, without the Consent of the Legislatures of the States concerned as well as of the Congress.[168]

The Congress shall have Power to dispose of and make all needful Rules and Regulations respecting the Territory or other Property belonging to the United States; and nothing in this Constitution shall be so construed as to Prejudice any Claims of the United States, or of any particular State.[169]

Section 4. The United States shall guarantee to every State in this Union a Republican ~~Form~~ *Constitution* of Government, and shall protect each of them against Invasion; and on Application of the Legislature, or of the Executive (when the Legislature cannot be convened) against domestic Violence. *Neither Congress nor any part of the United States Government shall attempt to alter or interfere with the Government of any State unless that State shall fail to provide for a Republican Constitution, as determined by two-thirds of members present in both Houses of Congress.*

The first two sections of this article address the interactions between states, and all of the guarantees included here are generally endorsed (or at least not opposed) by most Anti-Federalists. The third section discusses the admission of new states. Several Anti-Federalists professed a preference for the method from the Articles of Confederation, where nine of thirteen states needed to approve.[170] This two-thirds requirement, expressed through the state legislatures, was reinstated here, and Congress must also approve.

There was some discussion about the clause in Section 4 guaranteeing republican government in the states. Agrippa pointed out that there are aristocratic as well as democratic republics, so this guarantee was unclear. The Impartial Examiner was skeptical about the clause, because it does "not guarantee to the different states their present forms of government, or the bill of rights thereto annexed, or any of them; and the expressions are too vague, too indefinite to create such a compact by implication." Such a guarantee, though, would have made it difficult for the states to change their own constitutions. Instead, the vague guarantee that is included "meddles too much with the independence of the several States, so also it answers no valuable end to any or to the whole." A Watchman argued that this clause "deprives the people in the several states of the liberty of making their own constitution, and vests it in the hands of Congress." Ultimately, two changes were made in this guarantee. The first is simple, suggested by Sidney: the word "form" was changed to "constitution." This is more specific. Second, Congress is forbidden from meddling unless two-thirds of members deem the state in question to have failed to provide for republican government. This restriction would allay Anti-Federalist fears of national encroachment on state prerogatives regarding self-government. Of course, it is not nearly as important for that purpose as the guarantee embodied in the new Article I.[171]

Amending the Constitution

During the ratification contest, the amendment process became inextricably tied to the question of whether amendments ought to be made before ratification. Thus most of the Anti-Federalist complaints dealt with the probability of obtaining subsequent amendments, and the prognosis did not appear good to them.[172] It is difficult to determine how much this was a strategic argument designed to force prior amendments, and how much a genuine concern that amending the Constitution would be too difficult. An Old Whig offers us some insight into this question, and I believe his position was typical among Anti-Federalists. He opened his first letter with a critique of the amendment process: "This appears to me to be only a cunning way of saying that no alteration shall ever be made; so that whether it is a good constitution or a bad constitution, it will remain forever unamended." He later admitted, however, that the difficulty of amendments would be salutary if the initial constitution was good. This suggests that it was not a problem with Article V but a list of problems with the Constitution that inspired the complaints about the process of amendments. Hampden, unusual among Anti-Federalists, actually endorsed the amendment process as it stood. "The exceeding *slow*, *precarious*, and *expensive* method for amendments, proposed in this Constitution, will prevent those frequent attempts which otherwise might create parties, to the great injury of the general government." He endorsed prior amendments, but he found this a suitable process for future changes.[173]

Article VI
The Congress, whenever two thirds of both Houses shall deem it necessary, shall propose Amendments to this Constitution, or, on the Application of the Legislatures of two thirds of the several States, shall call a Convention for proposing Amendments, which, in either Case,

shall be valid to all Intents and Purposes, as Part of this Constitution, when ratified by the Legislatures of three fourths of the several States, or by Conventions in three fourths thereof, as the one or the other Mode of Ratification may be proposed by the Congress; Provided that no Amendment which may be made prior to the Year One thousand eight hundred and eight shall in any Manner affect the first and fourth Clauses in the Ninth Section of the first Article; and that no State, without its Consent, shall be deprived of its equal Suffrage in the Senate.

There are no changes in this article, but at least two were specifically proposed that were not related to the goal of obtaining prior amendments. In the Rhode Island Ratifying Convention, Jonathan Hazard suggested that amendments should be not easier, but impossible: "We want a Constitut[io]n not to be altered. The Rich and powerful States will be uneasy till they alter it for their Benefit." Obviously, this is not a practicable solution, but it is one that might have surprising support among Anti-Federalists. A more practical version, requiring eleven states out of thirteen rather than nine, was officially proposed by the Rhode Island Convention. Another suggestion came from the people of the town of Preston in their instructions to their delegate to the Connecticut Convention. They objected to the fact that amendments were not to be presented to the people for ratification: "We ever supposed legislative bodies chosen for the purpose of making laws and not for the purpose of altering the original compact of the people." This is an interesting suggestion, and one that might generate some support, but because it comes from such an obscure place in the Anti-Federalist literature and did not make it into any mainstream debate over the Constitution, this change has not been made.[174]

Supremacy and the Oath of Office

The oath of office sparked some debate, but the Supremacy Clause was the key issue in Article VI. The case for the consolidating tendencies of the Constitution rested primarily on this claim of supremacy for all national laws over all state laws. This, to the Anti-Federalists, meant nothing less than that Congress could overrule the state legislatures, in virtually all cases. This does not necessarily mean that national laws should not be supreme, though. "I should make no objection to this clause were the powers granted by the Constitution sufficiently defined," said James Galloway; "for I am clearly of opinion that it is absolutely necessary for every government, and especially for a general government, that its laws should be the supreme law of the land."[175] A national government with carefully limited and checked powers could still be supreme, but the Constitution required some careful revision before that became the case.

Article VII
All Debts contracted and Engagements entered into, before the Adoption of this Constitution, shall be as valid against the United States under this Constitution, as under the Confederation.[176]

This Constitution, ~~and the Laws of the United States which shall be made in Pursuance thereof,~~ and all Treaties made, or which shall be made, under the Authority of the United States, shall be the supreme Law of the Land; and the Judges in every State shall be bound thereby, any Thing in the Constitution or Laws of any State to the Contrary notwithstanding. *The Laws of the United States which shall be made in Pursuance of this Constitution shall not be enforced in violation of the Constitution of any State.*

The Senators and Representatives before mentioned, and the Members of the several State Legislatures, and all executive and judicial Officers, both of the United States and of the several States, shall be bound by Oath or Affirmation, to support this Constitution, *the Constitutions of the several States, and the People of the United States*; ~~but no religious Test shall ever be required as a Qualification to any Office or public Trust under the United States~~ *but no religious denomination shall ever have preference to another in matters of state, and all religious societies shall have equal liberty and protection.*[177]

The oath of office was seen by some as just another indication of the consolidation promised by the Constitution. Otherwise, why make all *state* officers pledge to support the national Constitution, but not require a similar pledge of support for the state constitutions? Taking separate oaths to support the state and national constitutions might force state officeholders to break one oath to keep the other, should the two conflict. Why not pledge an oath to support the United States, or the people? A clearer Supremacy Clause makes supporting both state and national constitutions more consistent, and adding the people echoes the basic principle that the people are sovereign, so this modified oath covers state, nation, and people.[178]

The issue of religious tests for office came up in several state conventions. Two major objections were raised. First, the clause potentially allows "for the Jews, Turks, and Heathen to enter into publick office," or even "a Papist, a Mohomatan, a Deist, yea an Atheist at the helm of Government." Second, it raises the question of "how and by whom they are to swear, since no religious tests are required—whether they are to swear by Jupiter, Juno, Minerva, Proserpine, or Pluto." On the other side of the issue, Samuel Spencer admonished his fellow Anti-Federalists in North Carolina, arguing "that no one particular religion should be established. Religious tests . . . have been the foundation of persecutions in all countries." Although the gulf between these two positions seems wide, there was a consensus position here. Freedom of religion was important, but the presence of religion in public life was important as well. The issue of pagans and atheists elected to office was not a significant one, as long as there was popular suffrage and the majority of the nation was Christian, but the idea that officeholders should be Christian or at least profess a belief in God appeared frequently. Many even saw the process of taking an oath as itself a sort of religious test. "Samuel" saw in this clause an entire rejection of religion, which he found unwise. Ultimately, Reverend Francis Cummins of South Carolina proposed the language that has been adopted here, to ensure equal liberty without undermining the potential religious undertones of the oath of office. Most Anti-Federalists would line up behind this language in place of the other.[179]

The objections to the Supremacy Clause have been answered here by establishing a clear hierarchy of laws. The Constitution is supreme, followed by treaties, which must be made consistent with the Constitution. The more reasonable Anti-Federalists acknowledged the importance of supremacy in these clear national cases. State constitutions come next; they cannot override treaties or the national Constitution, but they can override laws. In this way, a state bill of rights may not be violated by a simple act of Congress; this answers a key Anti-Federalist objection.[180] National laws can overrule ordinary state laws, however. This gives the national government its proper place of supremacy on national issues, but permits states, through constitutional amendment, to override laws they see as particularly egregious. It is an open question how well such a concept would have worked in practice, but the Anti-Federalists would have approved such a hierarchy.

Ratification

The process of ratification was attacked on several grounds. Federal-minded Anti-Federalists were inclined to insist that the states were the constituents of a federal government, and thus the states must approve the Constitution, not the people; Luther Martin and Patrick Henry were in this camp. More democratic-minded Anti-Federalists, like Centinel, objected that the Framers "have not even condescended to submit the plan of the new government to the consideration of the people, the true source of authority." The Constitution, Centinel argued, should be subjected to a referendum. Still other Anti-Federalists, defending the Articles of Confederation, insisted that Congress and the legislatures of all thirteen states must approve a new plan of government, as per Article XIII of the old system.[181]

Article VIII
The Ratification of the Conventions of nine States, shall be sufficient for the Establishment of this Constitution between the States so ratifying the Same.

In the end, the mode of ratification proposed by the Framers bridges this gap between the Anti-Federalists; this constitution is presented to the delegates of the people, elected for that purpose, but the people meet as states rather than one nation. Most of the Anti-Federalists wrote or spoke to discourage ratification; it was a relatively small minority that tried to halt the process altogether as illegitimate. At any rate, to deny the voice of the people in favor of the legislature runs counter to basic tenets of Anti-Federalist thought, so the ratification method was preserved.

THE ANTI-FEDERALISTS AND
THE CONSTITUTION

The Anti-Federalists did have a set of principles of government on which they generally agreed. They believed in federalism, that the states were sovereign and the national government had no authority to undermine that sovereignty. They believed in representation, that the people had the right to control and even overrule their rulers. They had a sense of political equality that took different forms in different situations, but always pointed to a basic sense of fairness. Because of these beliefs, they saw the Constitution as dangerous, and saw it as their patriotic duty to alter it, or defeat it.

This revision of the Constitution is not the only imaginable version; this is why it is titled "an Anti-Federalist constitution," rather than "the." It is, however, a plausible version that would have achieved widespread support among the Anti-Federalists in virtually every state. We might say of this

Constitution, as Brutus did of the original, that "There are many objections, of small moment, of which I shall take no notice—perfection is not to be expected in any thing that is the production of man."[182] This document, though, Brutus would find far more agreeable, creating a "more perfect union" on more explicitly federal terms.

19

The Prospects of an
Anti-Federalist Constitution

MORTON BORDEN'S CONTENTION that "it is entirely conceivable that an Antifederalist government, if possible, might have resulted in as much progress,
prosperity and democracy as has been achieved under the Constitution"
stretches credulity. With the benefit of hindsight, it seems that the Anti-
Federalist conception of government, if strictly adhered to and not adjusted
to circumstances, would not have lasted; if nothing else, a violent resolution
to the issue of slavery, which was probably inevitable, would have torn the
union asunder, and a weak central government would have been powerless to hold it together. Even if it had not, many of the significant national
accomplishments of the last two centuries would not have been possible.
"Adhering strictly to the Antifederalist vision of government," writes David
Siemers, "would have prevented some of the greatest accomplishments of
the past century, including the broader application of civil rights, the introduction of pure food and pure drug legislation, and the protection of the
environment to name a few."[1] One might add virtually any national social
welfare program and most of America's foreign policy commitments. Even
so, with an Anti-Federalist government outlined in the preceding chapter,
it will be valuable here to speculate on the prospects of such a system, and
the prognosis is not as bad as it first appears. Such speculation, based on
a hypothetical counterfactual document, is necessarily tenuous at best, but
there are some historical parallels that offer some insight into how such an
experiment would have turned out.

THE FLAWS OF AN
ANTI-FEDERALIST CONSTITUTION

A brief examination of the document makes it clear why we might expect this Anti-Federalist Constitution to fail, at least without substantial

amendments. It has several clear weaknesses. First, the emphasis on state power maintains the fiscal weaknesses found under the Articles of Confederation. Notwithstanding the frequent arguments that the new tax clause effectively grants the national government the power to levy direct taxes when really necessary, the Congress under this Constitution would once again be placed in the position of supplicant vis-à-vis the states. Should Congress place requisitions, and should a state be defiant and refuse to pay its quota, Congress would have no recourse but to send military force to collect the taxes. If the people were willing to pay, then their representatives in the state legislatures would have collected without difficulty; thus we can assume in such a situation that the people are hostile to parting with their money. We cannot assume that the state power would assist in the collection of federal direct taxes if the state government failed to raise revenue to pay its requisition. Congress would of course be reluctant to turn military force on its own people; even if they were willing, this would be an expensive undertaking, and a Congress levying quotas on the states is obviously short of money and cannot afford to collect taxes from unwilling citizens. Congress could, of course, try to borrow the money to pay the cost of collections, but even this would be unlikely with a two-thirds vote requirement for borrowing. Thus these changes render nugatory the taxing power, except for customs duties. Should these prove inadequate, and virtually everyone agreed that they would eventually fall short of expenses, the national government would have needed to beg the states to contribute.

Second, the military power is structured in such a way as to rely on citizen militias for national defense. Congress cannot be expected to raise any kind of an army to stand ready for war; during the first several decades under the actual Constitution, majorities in favor of an army were very rare, and a two-thirds vote for it would have been impossible. The militias have some value, certainly, but they are very limited in that states could keep them within their own borders. Raising a continental army during the Revolution had been exceedingly difficult, and the provisions of this revised Constitution, especially concerning revenue, would have made that task even more difficult. The United States under this Constitution would have been quite susceptible to invasion.

Third, the strongest point of this Constitution, that it truly creates a government of enumerated powers, is also its weakest point. This Anti-Federalist Constitution has no flexibility outside of the amendment clause, and the amendment process is slow and difficult. Crises that call for unusual measures could not be answered, because there are no loopholes on which to rely for a temporary expansion of power. This does not mean that

Congress might not simply seize additional powers; it only means that they would have no justification on which to fall back other than necessity, a highly risky proposition for any magistrate hoping to retain the confidence of the people. By the time Congress came around to approving emergency powers, it might well be too late to react to a crisis. To borrow a Hamiltonian concept, this government, without elastic clauses, lacks energy. The clauses that remain could be read broadly, but to do so clearly violates the spirit of this document.

All of these point to the truly fatal flaw, that this Constitution establishes a confederation disguised as a federal government.[2] The Articles of Confederation granted substantial powers to Congress, and on paper created a strong national government. State sovereignty, though, kept Congress toothless; it had no enforcement mechanism for any of its powers. In this Constitution there are some enforcement mechanisms built in (after all, the Anti-Federalists were not oblivious to the failures of the Articles), but they are ultimately ineffective ones. Congress has only limited access to the purse, as the states can effectively pull the strings at any time, and Congress may not effectively wield the sword without at least tacit permission from the states to draw it from its scabbard. Congress is even prevented from any kind of creative measures to get around these stumbling blocks, because its powers are carefully enumerated, and implication is outlawed. There are advantages to a mere confederation, of course, and many Anti-Federalists preferred just this. A confederation made to look like a national government, though, creates a situation in which foreign policy is impossible because foreign nations have no way of knowing with whom they should actually negotiate, and in which the states can pass the buck to the national government on unpopular issues even as the members of Congress are lamenting the do-nothing obstructionist states. In prosperous peacetime without crisis this is not a problem, but once things begin to go wrong it is a recipe for disaster.

All of these flaws, we must remember, are *intentional* in this Anti-Federalist Constitution. In a certain respect Cecilia Kenyon is right to call the Anti-Federalists "men of little faith"; they had no faith in the ability of a national government to govern effectively a large nation without reverting to tyranny and oppression. The flaws here are the result of an ideological position, which means that we can expect changes to address these shortcomings to be painfully slow, not because the amendment process itself is slow, but because such changes would require a shift in political attitudes toward national government, and political culture changes very slowly. An Anti-Federalist victory would have shaped American political culture much as the Federalist victory did: the majority of people were willing in 1789 to try a more consolidated national political system rather than a confederation, but had this Constitution passed they would have not been so willing.

It is impossible to say how American history would have played out differently under this Anti-Federalist Constitution; it would have led to a different set of policies and a different set of problems, but it is hard to say exactly how they would differ. Such questions venture far afield and I have no intention to pursue them here. Instead, in closing, a few words about the legacy of the Anti-Federalists in actual American history are appropriate.

THE LEGACY OF THE ANTI-FEDERALISTS

Pauline Maier writes that "the Constitution's critics did not simply 'lose.' They got almost everything they wanted, though not always in the form they expected or within their lifetimes."[3] The first part is undoubtedly true; if the opponents of ratification were entirely unhappy with the result, they would not have been so quickly reconciled to the Constitution. On the second point, though, I respectfully disagree with Maier. She points to a number of policies that followed Anti-Federalist preferences in the early (or later) republic as evidence that the Anti-Federalists, in the long run, got what they wanted. She includes the rapid expansion of the House of Representatives, the Judiciary Act of 1789, and the taxes actually levied as examples; in each of these cases, though, the erstwhile opponents of the Constitution saw their preferred policy enacted, though not guaranteed. The House was made larger, but population growth eventually made any notion of real representation, as the Anti-Federalists saw it, effectively impossible. Growing from three million people to three hundred million was going to cause this in any case, of course, so it is hard to see any way they could have won this point in the long run, except by *retaining more power in the more representative state governments*. The states retained a great deal of power for a time, but the national power overtook them eventually, and state resistance to national encroachment is relatively feeble in our present system. Trials by jury were of course guaranteed in the Bill of Rights, and the federal jurisdiction was scaled back by the Eleventh Amendment, but the courts still routinely become more involved in policy questions than the Anti-Federalists would have liked, and they do generally rule in favor of stronger national power at the expense of the states, just as Brutus predicted, a few devolution decisions notwithstanding. As for taxes, the national government in the long run did come to rely on direct taxes, and did expand its spending as it raised more revenue, creating new programs that would have appalled most Federalists as much as their opponents. Even before the income tax became a regular source of revenue, the government did institute excise taxes almost immediately, and occasionally levied direct taxes, albeit temporarily. Maier also noted later developments, including presidential term limits and the incorporation of the Bill of Rights to apply to the states to suggest that the Anti-Federalist ideas continued to resonate in the twentieth century; never mind that on taxes, federalism, and representation, three areas in which the opposition did well early, events had turned convincingly against the Anti-Federalists by then. Actually, the idea of incorporation, which according to Maier created "a federal Bill of Rights worth having,"[4] was something the Anti-Federalists did not even want. James Madison, in the first Congress, had suggested amendment language preventing states from encroaching on rights, but the handful of Anti-Federalists in the House at the time did not like that particular proposal; the states had bills of rights and did not need the national government imposing them on the safer states. Experience, of course, has proven the states just as dangerous to rights, if not more so, but that does not make this an Anti-Federalist victory; it was something they resisted including in a federal constitution. Had the states retained primary political power, the state bills of rights may well have had more of an impact anyway, though the protected rights might vary considerably from state to state without a strong national government to impose uniformity.

Although these changes in the political system do not represent Anti-Federalist victories, they certainly do reflect Anti-Federalist influence over American political development. "The American regime is a hybrid," explains David Siemers. "Neither the Federalists nor the Antifederalists controlled the outcome of the ratification process, but both groups affected it mightily. Their legacy can still be felt, even after more than two hundred years."[5] This is clearly the case, as the Anti-Federalist influence continues to be felt in recent efforts to restore state powers, and especially in efforts to restore the national government to strictly prescribed constitutional limits. After all, if the Anti-Federalists could have been assured that the national government would stick to enumerated powers and responsibilities, the ratification debates would have been far less contentious. The most powerful opposition argument of all was that the Constitution was too vague, and would enable the national government to interpret its own powers ever more broadly, until there was a consolidated national government ruling over subordinate states and oppressed people.

Unfortunately for the Anti-Federalists' legacy, history is generally written by the winners, and it has not been kind to those who opposed the

Constitution. The Anti-Federalists undoubtedly considered how the Federalists might portray them in their version of the history of the struggle over
the Constitution; it was not likely to be any more positive than the rude and
misleading name "Anti-Federalist" that the Constitution's supporters had
already assigned to their opponents. At least three Anti-Federalists planned
to write histories of their own. Aedanus Burke of South Carolina aimed at
regional balance in his account; for this purpose he wrote to Samuel Bryan
of Pennsylvania and Elbridge Gerry of Massachusetts. He sent a list of questions to each of them, and received a detailed response from Bryan. Though
Bryan's comments shed considerable light on how the Pennsylvania Anti-
Federalists viewed the ratification, Burke seems never to have begun writing
his history.[6] In New York, Abraham Yates did write a draft of his historical
project, but he did not publish it. Where Bryan, in his answers to Burke,
had declined to charge the Federalists with conspiracy, Yates's version of
events framed the debate in exactly those terms. The account "anticipates
remarkably the Beard-Jensen version of the decade 1778–88," telling "a tale
of sinister conspiracy springing from a lust for power."[7] This history, though
more complete than the answers from Bryan prompted by Burke, sheds considerably less light on these events.

The only Anti-Federalist to publish a history from an Anti-Federalist perspective was Mercy Otis Warren, and hers took the form of general comments at the end of her history of the American Revolution. "Many of the
intelligent yeomanry and of the great bulk of independent landholders, who
had tasted the sweets of mediocrity, equality, and liberty," she wrote, "read
every unconditional ratification of the new system in silent anguish, folded
the solemn page with a sigh, and wept over the manes of the native sons of
America, who had sold their lives to leave the legacy of freedom to their children." She praised the opposition, describing the Anti-Federalists as "men
of the first abilities in every state" who "were solicitous that every thing
should be clearly defined," and believed "that every article that admitted of
doubtful construction, should be amended, before it became the supreme
law of the land." By the time her history was published in 1805, though, the
Constitution was apparently acceptable to Warren; she wrote of it in glowing terms, asserting that "the young republic of America exhibits the happi-
est prospects." Nonetheless, she warned that the government would only be
safe for as long as America chooses good men to govern. So long as America
stands by her republican principles, she will endure and flourish under this
Constitution. Nonetheless, her account is tinged with sadness and regret, as
if America had lost some part of herself in accepting the government written
by the Philadelphia delegates in the summer of 1787.[8]

For the Anti-Federalists, something truly had been lost, but it is not clear they could have done anything to prevent it. The decline in the American spirit and mores, as a number of opposition writers pointed out, was the result of lavish consumption and changes in lifestyle, and this had little enough to do with questions of government. A different form of government might have slowed the change, or reignited some of the republican spirit, but it is hard to imagine that very many people were much more sanguine than Mercy Otis Warren on this score. Preserving the republican spirit of the people may not have been possible, so the Anti-Federalists set out to preserve the freedom of the people instead. If they could not keep the republic, at least perhaps they could avoid tyranny and live their lives in peace. In this effort, the Anti-Federalists succeeded more admirably than perhaps even they thought; the Anti-Federalist spirit moderated the implementation of the new Constitution and prevented the consolidation of too much power too fast. It seems unlikely that any alternative they might have offered could have done any more.

NOTES

In citing works in the notes, short titles have generally been used. Works frequently cited have been identified by the following abbreviations.

ABBREVIATIONS

CAF   *The Complete Anti-Federalist*, edited by Herbert Storing

CBR   *Creating the Bill of Rights*, edited by Helen E. Veit, Kenneth R. Bowling, and Charlene Bangs Bickford

Debates   *The Debates in the Several State Conventions on the Adoption of the Federal Constitution*, edited by Jonathan Elliot

DHCUSA   *Documentary History of the Constitution of the United States of America*

DHFFE   *Documentary History of the First Federal Elections*, edited by Merrill Jensen and Robert A. Becker

DHRC   *Documentary History of the Ratification of the Constitution*, edited by Merrill Jensen et al.

MSA   "Notes of Arguments in Convention," taken by William Tilghman, Maryland State Archives, Special Collections

Records   *The Records of the Federal Convention of 1787*, edited by Max Farrand

RIC   *Foster's Minutes of the Rhode Island Convention*, edited by Robert C. Cotner

RICC   *Rhode Island in the Continental Congress, with the Journal of the Convention That Adopted the Constitution, 1765–1790*, edited by William R. Staples

SRNC   *The State Records of North Carolina*, edited by Walter Clark

CHAPTER 1: THE ANTI-FEDERALISTS AND THE DEVELOPMENT OF DISSENT

1. Jack N. Rakove, *Original Meanings: Politics and Ideas in the Making of the Constitution* (New York: Alfred A. Knopf, 1996), 132.

2. Robert Rutland divides credit for the Bill of Rights between Anti-Federalists who demanded such amendments and conciliatory Federalists who recognized that the desire for them was widespread. His portrayal of the amendments offered by Madison, as well as the version of them that finally passed through Congress, as conciliatory, attempting to reconcile all parties, does not ring true; it is clear from the documentary record, and especially from the reactions of many prominent

Anti-Federalists, that the major opposition concerns were not met, and that the Anti-Federalists believed that the Federalists were trying to limit the changes to those which represented no real change at all. Murray Dry compiled the eighteen most important amendments introduced in the various ratifying conventions, of which James Madison included only three in his initial draft of amendments; only two were actually adopted in the amendments proposed to the states, and one of those included a substantial alteration that weakened its effect. I discuss this at length in chapter 16. Robert A. Rutland, *The Birth of the Bill of Rights, 1776–1791* (Chapel Hill: University of North Carolina Press, 1955); Murray Dry, "The Antifederalists and the Constitution," in *Antifederalism: The Legacy of George Mason*, ed. Josephine F. Pacheco (Fairfax, VA: George Mason University Press, 1992), 39–40.

3. For example, see Robert W. T. Martin's account of Anti-Federalism as a part of a broader tradition of dissent in the early republic. Robert W. T. Martin, *Government by Dissent: Protest, Resistance, & Radical Democratic Thought in the Early American Republic* (New York: New York University Press, 2013), 55–81.

4. DHRC 4:399.

5. DHRC 8:408–417.

6. DHRC 9:769–779.

7. DHRC 4:293–294.

8. John Fiske, *The Critical Period of American History, 1783–1789* (New York: Houghton Mifflin, 1888), 329.

9. For example, in a study on the Harrisburg Convention of 1788, published between his two collections of ratification writings, Ford was remarkably uncharitable toward the Anti-Federalists in Pennsylvania, contending that those who opposed ratification did so for three reasons: first, the Constitutional Party in the state controlled the patronage apparatus, and were concerned about losing the political power attached to that; second, the farmers in the west feared higher taxes, as well as higher commodity prices due to a congressional preference for merchants; and third, Congress would bargain away rights to the navigation of the Mississippi River for commercial advantages, and take away western property that formerly belonged to loyalists. These real reasons for opposition, of course, were "too mercenary to publicly appeal to the people on," so they used the typical arguments raised elsewhere. These arguments, he suggests, "were the phantasies with which the 'Antis' sought to raise the people against" the Constitution. Ford's contention here is dubious at best; he himself points out that "[e]xcept for the question of taxation, they are not even mentioned in the lengthy discussions in the legislature and the convention, nor in the newspaper arguments with which the press teemed for nearly a twelvemonth." As evidence of these ulterior motives, Ford points only to a meeting led by George Bryan to coordinate opposition to the Constitution. Ford admits that the Federalists effectively strong-armed the opposition to win a quick ratification, but he seems to find such tactics justified. Paul Leicester Ford, *The Origin, Purpose and Result of the Harrisburg Convention of 1788* (Brooklyn, 1890), 4–7.

10. E. Wilder Spaulding, *His Excellency George Clinton: Critic of the Constitution* (New York: MacMillan, 1938), 166–167. Spaulding is far from alone in this sentiment among biographers of Anti-Federalists. Even the titles of such biographies (other than Spaulding's) tend to describe their subjects as "forgotten," or emphasize their contributions during the Revolution rather than their roles as Anti-Federalists.

For example, see Jeff Broadwater, *George Mason: Forgotten Founder* (Chapel Hill: University of North Carolina Press, 2006); Bill Kauffman, *Forgotten Founder, Drunken Prophet: The Life of Luther Martin* (Wilmington: ISI Books, 2008); J. Kent McGaughy, *Richard Henry Lee of Virginia: A Portrait of an American Revolutionary* (Lanham, MD: Rowman & Littlefield, 2004); Mark Puls, *Samuel Adams: Father of the American Revolution* (New York: Palgrave Macmillan, 2006); Harlow Giles Unger, *Lion of Liberty: Patrick Henry and the Call to a New Nation* (Cambridge, MA: DaCapo, 2010).

11. In this he was following fellow historian J. Allen Smith, who had already described the Constitution as an aristocratic document, but it was Beard who took on the individuals involved. J. Allen Smith, *The Spirit of American Government: A Study of the Constitution: Its Origin, Influence and Relation to Democracy* (New York: MacMillan, 1907).

12. Charles A. Beard, *An Economic Interpretation of the Constitution of the United States* (New York: Macmillan, 1921), 234.

13. Philip A. Crowl, "Anti-Federalism in Maryland, 1787–1788," *William and Mary Quarterly* 4, no. 4 (October 1947): 447.

14. Robert E. Brown, *Charles Beard and the Constitution: A Critical Analysis of "An Economic Interpretation of the Constitution"* (Princeton: Princeton University Press, 1956).

15. Forrest McDonald, *We the People: The Economic Origins of the Constitution* (Chicago: University of Chicago Press, 1958), 415.

16. Staughton Lynd, *Anti-Federalism in Dutchess County, New York* (Chicago: Loyola University Press, 1962), 5.

17. Beard, *Economic Interpretation of the Constitution,* 292.

18. Charles W. Roll, Jr., "We, Some of the People: Apportionment in the Thirteen State Conventions Ratifying the Constitution," *Journal of American History* 56, no. 1 (June 1969): 26.

19. Cecilia M. Kenyon, "Men of Little Faith: The Anti-Federalists on the Nature of Representative Government," *William and Mary Quarterly* 12, no. 1 (January 1955): 37–38.

20. Robert A. Rutland, *The Ordeal of the Constitution: The Antifederalists and the Ratification Struggle of 1878–1788* (Norman: University of Oklahoma Press, 1966), 313.

21. Stanley Elkins and Eric McKitrick, "The Founding Fathers: Young Men of the Revolution," *Political Science Quarterly* 76, no. 2 (June 1961): 181–216. A similar point was made three decades earlier, though not elaborated, by Charles Warren. Charles Warren, "Elbridge Gerry, James Warren, Mercy Warren and the Ratification of the Federal Constitution in Massachusetts," *Proceedings of the Massachusetts Historical Society*, Third Series, 64 (March 1932): 145–146.

22. Jackson Turner Main, *The Antifederalists: Critics of the Constitution, 1781–1788* (Chapel Hill: University of North Carolina Press, 1961), 259.

23. Main, *Antifederalists,* 249. The six states with Anti-Federalist majorities, according to Main, were Rhode Island, both Carolinas, New York, Massachusetts, and Virginia. The possible seventh is New Hampshire. Based on election results for ratifying conventions, North Carolina, Rhode Island, New York, and New Hampshire almost certainly had majorities against the Constitution, and Massachusetts

probably did; each of these conventions began with a majority opposed to the Constitution, or at least skeptical of it. South Carolina had a majority of Federalists in convention, but only because of malapportionment; by one estimate the Anti-Federalists there, about a third of the delegates, represented a majority of the people, and this does not include Anti-Federalist delegates who switched sides to support ratification in the final vote. Virginia is questionable, in part because there seems to have been an unusually high number of people there who liked the Constitution in principle, but strongly favored amendments; Main offers a brief appendix justifying his claim of an Anti-Federalist majority in that state, but his argument is less than convincing. Owen Ireland convincingly argues that Pennsylvania, despite the assertions of its Anti-Federalists, probably had a majority in favor of ratification. Delaware, New Jersey, Georgia, and Connecticut almost certainly had such a majority. Maryland is difficult to determine, because the Anti-Federalists did a remarkably poor job contesting elections for the state convention, but the opposition's performance in the first federal elections in 1789 suggests that the Federalists had a majority in the state, albeit a small one. The most comprehensive analysis of public opinion on the Constitution, though, is Orin Grant Libby's work, in which he argues that the voting in the ratifying conventions largely reflected public sentiment, suggesting a Federalist majority overall. Roll, "We, Some of the People"; Main, *Antifederalists*, 285–286; Owen S. Ireland, "The People's Triumph: The Federalist Majority in Pennsylvania, 1787–1788," *Pennsylvania History* 56, no. 2 (April 1989): 93–113; Orin Grant Libby, "The Geographical Distribution of the Vote of the Thirteen States on the Federal Constitution, 1787–8," *Bulletin of the University of Wisconsin: Economics, Political Science, and History Series* 1, no. 1 (1894): 1–116.

24. Main, *Antifederalists*, 1, 266–278, 280.

25. Main, xi.

26. Main, 173. It is worth mentioning here that there were prominent exceptions. For example, Main identifies the "Cincinnatus" series as among the most democratic writings against the Constitution; these essays were almost certainly written by Arthur Lee, a member of one of the most prominent families in Virginia. Main, 174.

27. Gordon S. Wood, *The Creation of the American Republic, 1776–1787* (New York: W. W. Norton, 1969), 485, 516.

28. Gordon S. Wood, "Interests and Disinterestedness in the Making of the Constitution," in *Beyond Confederation: Origins of the Constitution and American National Identity*, ed. Richard Beeman, Stephen Botein, and Edward C. Carter, II (Chapel Hill: University of North Carolina Press, 1987), 109.

29. James H. Hutson, "Country, Court, and Constitution: Antifederalism and the Historians," *William and Mary Quarterly* 38, no. 3 (July 1981): 337–368.

30. J. Thomas Wren, "The Ideology of Court and Country in the Virginia Ratifying Convention of 1788," *Virginia Magazine of History and Biography* 93, no. 4 (October 1985): 389–408. Ivan Jankovic also critiques the use of country ideology to understand these debates, suggesting that the supposed "country" Anti-Federalists embraced positions that made that label misleading, if not outright wrong. Ivan Jankovic, "Men of Little Faith: The Country Party Ideology in Britain and America," *American Political Thought* 5, no. 2 (Spring 2016): 183–218.

31. Steven R. Boyd, *The Politics of Opposition: Antifederalists and the Acceptance of the Constitution* (Millwood, NY: KTO Press, 1979), xii.

32. Boyd, 168.

33. Herbert J. Storing, *What the Anti-Federalists Were For* (Chicago: University of Chicago Press, 1981), 3.

34. Storing, 4, 7, 71.

35. The legacy of the Anti-Federalists has elicited several valuable works. Saul Cornell examines how the Anti-Federalists helped shape the Democratic-Republican Party in the early republic. David Siemers looks at how each side continued to attack the other in the late eighteenth and early nineteenth centuries, and how the writings on ratification became partisan weapons, sometimes for the other side. Both authors find for the Anti-Federalists a significant ongoing role in American political thought, as have others. Saul Cornell, *The Other Founders: Anti-Federalism and the Dissenting Tradition in America, 1788–1828* (Chapel Hill: University of North Carolina Press, 1999); David J. Siemers, *Ratifying the Republic: Antifederalists and Federalists in Constitutional Time* (Stanford: Stanford University Press, 2002). See also Morton J. Frisch, "The Persistence of Antifederalism between the Ratification of the Constitution and the Nullification Crisis," in Pacheco, *Antifederalism*, 79–90; Jennifer Roback, "The Antifederalist Tradition in the Nineteenth Century Democratic Party," in Pacheco, *Antifederalism*, 91–109; Paul Peterson, "Antifederalist Thought in Contemporary American Politics," in Pacheco, *Antifederalism*, 111–132.

36. W. B. Allen and Gordon Lloyd, eds., *The Essential Antifederalist* (Lanham, MD: University Press of America, 1985), xiii–xiv.

37. Storing, *What the Anti-Federalists Were For*, 65.

38. This is not to say that few have written about the Anti-Federalists at all; there is a lot of material on the topic. Most of it, unfortunately, makes little attempt to seriously examine the ideological position of those who opposed the Constitution. Some go so far as to insist that there was no opposition position; Pauline Maier refuses even to consider the Anti-Federalists as a coherent group united by anything beyond their opposition to the Constitution. Maier, *Ratification: The People Debate the Constitution, 1787–1788* (New York: Simon & Schuster, 2010).

39. Michael Lienesch, "In Defence of the Antifederalists," *History of Political Thought* 4, no. 1 (Spring 1983): 65–87. Kupersmith also discusses the influence of Montesquieu on the Anti-Federalists. Abraham Kupersmith, "Montesquieu and the Ideological Strain in Antifederalist Thought," in *The Federalists, the Antifederalists, and the American Political Tradition*, ed. Wilson Carey McWilliams and Michael T. Gibbons (New York: Greenwood, 1992), 47–75.

40. Cornell, *Other Founders*, 30–31.

41. Rakove, *Original Meanings*, 147.

42. Cornell, *Other Founders*, 12.

43. David J. Siemers, *The Antifederalists: Men of Great Faith and Forbearance* (Lanham, MD: Rowman & Littlefield, 2003).

44. Michael Klarman draws a similar division, contending that the Anti-Federalist objections to the Constitution fall into two main groups, the absence of a bill of rights and the structure and power of the federal government. He does not note that some radical Anti-Federalists made a much more democratic argument, as I discuss below. Michael J. Klarman, *The Framers' Coup: The Making of the United States Constitution* (New York: Oxford University Press, 2016), 317.

45. An abridged collection of essays, titled *The Anti-Federalist*, was published as well, but in displaying the variety of Anti-Federalist writings it fell decidedly short of Kenyon. A few years later, *The Essential Antifederalist*, edited by W. B. Allen and Gordon Lloyd, was published as another alternative. Probably the best short collection of essays available is David Siemers's much newer *The Antifederalists: Men of Great Faith and Forbearance*. The title takes a rather unnecessary shot at Kenyon, but the introductory content and selection of materials are exemplary.

46. John P. Kaminski, "Antifederalism and the Perils of Homogenized History: A Review Essay," *Rhode Island History* 42 (February 1983): 35. Kaminski's review notwithstanding, the collection was generally well received by scholars. For a more positive review, see, for example, Walter Nicgorski, "The Anti-Federalists: Collected and Interpreted," *Review of Politics* 46, no. 1 (January 1984): 113–125.

47. Kaminski, "Antifederalism and the Perils," 34.

48. M. E. Bradford, *Original Intentions: On the Making and Ratification of the United States Constitution* (Athens: University of Georgia Press, 1993).

49. Elkins and McKitrick, "Founding Fathers," 215.

50. Rutland, *Ordeal of the Constitution*; Boyd, *Politics of Opposition*; Maier, *Ratification*.

CHAPTER 2: THREE STRANDS OF ANTI-FEDERALISM

1. *Records* 2:631.

2. Randolph actually suggested the idea on the tenth of September, but this was in direct response to a discussion of the method of ratification, not the Constitution as a whole. *Records* l2:560–561.

3. One can question whether Randolph can even be considered an Anti-Federalist. In the Virginia Ratifying Convention, he supported ratification, and in fact argued effectively for that end. Even at the end of the Philadelphia Convention, he suggested that he may not oppose it. He makes this more explicit in a letter on September 18: "Altho' the names of Colo. Mason and myself are not subscribed [to the Constitution], it is not, therefore, to be concluded that we are opposed to its adoption." His implication that Mason might support the Constitution was wrong, but Randolph himself reversed course. He explained that reversal, and his refusal to sign, in the Virginia Convention. Ultimately, he explains his motives in defending his final vote in favor of the Constitution: "The suffrage which I shall give in favor of the Constitution will be ascribed, by malice, to motives unknown to my breast. But, although for every other act of my life I shall seek refuge in the mercy of God, for this I request his *justice* only. Lest, however, some future annalist should, in the spirit of party vengeance, deign to mention my name, let him recite these truths—*that I went to the federal Convention* with the strongest affection for the Union; that I acted them in full conformity with this affection; *that I refused to subscribe, because I had, as I still have, objections to the Constitution*, and wished a free inquiry into its merits; and that the accession of eight states reduced our deliberations to the single question of *Union or no Union*." Still, since he played a significant early role in the opposition to the Constitution, his objections must be understood in the context of the Anti-Federalist position. *Records* 3:83; DHRC 9:931–936; 10:1537.

4. *Records* 2:631, 646.

5. CAF 2:97.

6. *Records* 2:632.

7. *Records* 2:632–633.

8. *Records* 2:633. In a letter to John Adams at the close of the Convention, Gerry writes that the Constitution, "with a check on standing armies in time of peace, & on an arbitrary administration of the powers vested in the Legislature, would have met with my approbation." This emphasis, dropping trial by jury and failing to mention a bill of rights, suggests that Gerry is very much concerned with the question of power over that of rights. DHRC 4:16.

9. Although Madison does not mention it, Rufus King's notes of the convention suggest that Gerry also objected to the absence of a bill of rights. According to King, Gerry argued that "Freemen giving up certain rights should be secured in others." He does later advocate such a change. Still, rights seem a secondary concern to Gerry in his opposition to the Constitution. *Records* 2:635.

10. CAF 2:6–7.

11. These objections were originally listed on Mason's copy of a draft of the Constitution, and they were later published in slightly altered form in newspapers and as a broadside. *Records* 2:637–640; CAF 2:9–14.

12. *Records* 2:640.

13. DHRC 15:393.

14. Samuel Adams and Melancton Smith were among the most prominent individuals to share this position with Randolph. I discuss this idea in more depth elsewhere. Michael J. Faber, "The Federal Union Paradigm of 1788: Three Anti-Federalists Who Changed Their Minds," *American Political Thought* 4, no. 4 (Fall 2015).

15. CAF 2:139, 142.

16. CAF 2:178–179, 175, 177, 137–138.

17. CAF 2:160, 157.

18. CAF 2:179.

19. CAF 2:186.

20. CAF 2:372.

21. CAF 2:365, 368.

22. CAF 2:381, 384.

23. CAF 2:395, 400.

24. CAF 2:402, 405, 406.

25. CAF 2:407–408, 414.

26. Washington's stirring speech against the Newburgh conspirators on the ides of March in 1783 probably did not win over so many of the army's officers as his statement upon donning reading glasses to read aloud from a letter at the end of that speech. "Gentlemen," he said. "You will permit me to put on my spectacles, for I have not only grown grey but almost blind in the service of my country." Several officers openly wept at his words and actions, and that was the end of the conspiracy. In his discussion of the Newburgh Conspiracy, Brutus states that "It remains a secret, yet to be revealed, whether this measure was not suggested, or at least countenanced, by some, who have had great influence in producing the present system." This somewhat cryptic comment may well be an allusion to Alexander Hamilton,

who wrote to Washington on March 25, 1783, discussing the dangers of an angry army and a Congress that seemed unable to find any way to pay its soldiers. Confessing that "I often feel a mortification . . . that sets my passions at variance with my reason," he disavowed violence and military coups, yet concluded with the curious statement that "I confess could force avail I should almost wish to see it employed. I have an indifferent opinion of the honesty of this country, and ill-forebodings as to its future system." Washington responded, noting that he read Hamilton's letter "with pain, & contemplated the picture it had drawn with astonishment and horror." "The idea of redress by force," he chastised Hamilton, "is too chimerical to have had a place in the imagination of any serious mind in this Army," and, by implication, it is at best impolitic for a sitting member of Congress to even hint at such a thing. The army, after all, "is a dangerous instrument to play with." It is not clear whether Brutus knew about these letters, was speculating about Hamilton's position on Newburgh, or was merely using innuendo to cast aspersion on the Federalists for an alleged willingness to achieve political consolidation by military force if necessary. Thomas Fleming, *The Perils of Peace: America's Struggle for Survival after Yorktown* (New York: HarperCollins, 2007), 271; CAF 2:414; Harold C. Syrett et al., eds., *The Papers of Alexander Hamilton* (New York: Columbia University Press, 1961), 3:306, 315, 316.

27. CAF 2:410, 416.

28. CAF 2:419.

29. CAF 2:419, 441, 420, 428, 424, 425.

30. CAF 2:432, 433, 434, 435.

31. CAF 2:438.

32. CAF 2:442–443.

33. CAF 2:444, 446.

34. The *Massachusetts Gazette*, on the first of January, referred to it as "the CREAM OF ANTI-FEDERALISM." The same newspaper also described it as "nearly *equal* to the celebrated *Aggripanian harrangues* in the Mass. Gazette," so the paper's judgment can be considered flawed, or at least biased. The *American Herald* described the pamphlet in the following words in an advertisement for its sale: "*Although the above Pamphlet is not bulky, nor yet over 'wordy,' it breathes the pure, uncontaminated air of Republicanism, as well as the celebrated spirit of the year 1775. It is written coolly and dispassionately, taking Reason for its guide, and solid argument for its basis.—It gives 'a sea' of sentiment in '40 pages of octavo.'—But it is needless to speak its praises in an advertisement*—Purchase, *and read for yourselves, ye Patriots of* Columbia!" DHRC 5:546, 548.

35. CAF 2:132, 248.

36. CAF 2:232, 240–241.

37. CAF 2:240.

38. CAF 2:251.

39. Paul Leicester Ford described the second series as "largely repetitions of the first," and thus declined to include them in his important collection *Pamphlets on the Constitution*. Forrest McDonald, in compiling a more recent collection of the Federal Farmer essays, determined that only four of the essays in the second series (6, 7, 14, and 17) were worth reprinting, and agreed with Ford about the rest. I believe that both editors have missed some elements of importance in the second series, and

I have addressed the second series here as well as the first. Paul Leicester Ford, ed., *Pamphlets on the Constitution of the United States, Published during Its Discussion by the People, 1787–1788* (Brooklyn, 1888), 277; Forrest McDonald, ed., *Empire and Nation* (Indianapolis: Liberty Fund, 1999), xvi.

40. CAF 2:69, 281.
41. CAF 2:196.
42. CAF 2:196, 190, 217.
43. CAF 2: 287.
44. CAF 2: 291.
45. CAF 2:348.
46. CAF 2:344, 282.
47. CAF 2:302.
48. CAF 2: 331, 335–336, 334. The Farmer offers an alternative explanation for the problems faced by America in the late 1780s: "It was the war that disturbed the course of commerce, introduced floods of paper money, the stagnation of credit, and threw many valuable men out of steady business. From these sources our greatest evils arise; men of knowledge and reflection must perceive it." This is certainly partially true, but to attribute all evils to the war is really no more plausible than attributing all evils to the Articles of Confederation. CAF 2:334.

CHAPTER 3: FIRST IMPRESSIONS
AND INITIAL OBJECTIONS

1. DHRC 1:345.
2. DHRC 1:348, 326.
3. DHRC 1:328, 336.
4. DHRC 1:337–338.
5. DHRC 1:345.
6. DHRC 1:346.
7. DHRC 2:71, 72.
8. John Bach McMaster and Frederick D. Stone, eds., *Pennsylvania and the Federal Constitution, 1787–1788* (Lancaster: Historical Society of Pennsylvania, 1888), 4. Samuel Bryan's later description was equally colorful. In his words, McCalmont and Miley "were made prisoners insulted & dragged back, by the Sergeant at Arms & a Mob of Assistants." Saul Cornell, "Reflections on 'The Late Remarkable Revolution in Government': Aedanus Burke and Samuel Bryan's Unpublished History of the Ratification of the Federal Constitution," *Pennsylvania Magazine of History and Biography* 112, no. 1 (January 1988): 130.
9. The other members of the legislature decided instead to attack and abuse him and his request. "Well, sir," Hugh Brackenridge said mockingly, "I conceive the question is, what is to be done now he is here, for how he came here can form no part of our inquiry, whether his friends brought him (and I should think they could not be his enemies, who would compel him to do his duty and avoid wrong), I say, sir, whether his friends brought him, or by the influence of good advice persuaded him to come, and he did come; or whether to ease his difficulty in walking to this room, they brought him in a sedan chair, or by whatever ways or means he introduced

himself among us. All we are to know is that he is here, and it only remains for us to decide, whether he shall have leave of absence." Such language was unnecessary, but it underscores the hostility that was already building in Pennsylvania. DHRC 2:105.

10. DHRC 2:109.

11. DHRC 2:113.

12. "You have a right, and we have no doubt you will consider whether or not you are in a situation to support the expense of such a government as is now offered to you, as well as the expense of your state government or whether a legislature consisting of three branches, neither of them chosen annually, and that the Senate, the most powerful, the members of which are for six years, are likely to lessen your burthens or increase your taxes or whether in case your state government should be annihilated, which will probably be the case, or dwindle into a mere corporation, the continental government will be competent to attend to your local concerns? You can also best determine whether the power of levying and imposing internal taxes at pleasure will be of real use to you or not or whether a continental collector assisted by a few faithful soldiers will be more eligible than your present collectors of taxes? You will also, in your deliberations on this important business, judge whether the liberty of the press may be considered as a blessing or a curse in a free government, and whether a declaration for the preservation of it is necessary or whether in a plan of government any declaration of rights should be prefixed or inserted? You will be able likewise to determine, whether in a free government there ought or ought not to be any provision against a standing army in time of peace or whether the trial by jury in civil causes is become dangerous and ought to be abolished and whether the judiciary of the United States is not so constructed as to absorb and destroy the judiciaries of the several states? You will also be able to judge whether such inconveniences have been experienced by the present mode of trial between citizen and citizen of different states as to render a continental court necessary for that purpose or whether there can be any real use in the appellate jurisdiction with respect to fact as well as law?" DHRC 2:116.

13. DHRC 2:116.

14. DHRC 2:146.

15. DHRC 2:149–150, 152, 154. "This redoubted hero," Tullius wrote of the first response, "who wallows in scurrility and nonsense, quotes from me a passage I never used, and, without even *attempting* to refute a single argument, struts and frets his minute on the stage—and then goes off (with *peculiar* propriety) in a coat of TAR and FEATHERS." Nestor was treated more carefully, as Tullius found more to answer in the critique of that "futile reasoner" and "profound quibbler," who is nonetheless treated to a healthy dose of sarcasm and attack. *Freeman's Journal*, October 10, 1787.

16. DHRC 2:178–179; McMaster and Stone, *Pennsylvania and the Federal Constitution*, 87; DHRC 13:303, 362; 2:136–137, 155–156, 201–203, 182–185, 293, 689.

17. CAF 2:137–138.

18. CAF 3:89–90. "Montezuma" makes much the same point, satirically. CAF 3:53–57; Jackson Turner Main, *The Antifederalists: Critics of the Constitution, 1781–1788* (Chapel Hill: University of North Carolina Press, 1961), 173.

19. DHRC 2:203–204.

20. CAF 2:105.

21. CAF 2:137. See chapter 2 for a full discussion of Centinel.

22. CAF 4:7–8.

23. CAF 4:5–6; 5:119–124.

24. The letters from the Federal Farmer are discussed in chapter 2.

25. CAF 5:113, 114.

26. See chapter 2 for a full discussion of Brutus's essays.

27. It was not lost on some Pennsylvanians at the time that Brutus, Jr., fit better with Pennsylvania's democratic ideology than New York's political tendencies; the *Independent Gazetteer* was urged by some subscribers to reprint the essay, because "it seems to be better calculated for the meridian of Pennsylvania, than the one it was written for" (November 14, 1787).

28. CAF 6:7–17, 36, 38, 39.

29. CAF 4:24, 21, 25.

30. CAF 4:28, 31.

31. CAF 4:29.

32. CAF 4:48, 49; DHRC 4:192.

33. CAF 4:45.

34. CAF 4:41.

35. For a rare example of Rights Anti-Federalism in Massachusetts, see "Portius," whose two objections were the absence of a bill of rights and the violation of the unanimity requirement to change the Articles of Confederation. In New York, "Timoleon" suggested that the Constitution threatens the right of conscience and freedom of the press, as well as trial by jury. Such objections were of course raised by others in the northeast, but rarely was the question of rights the central objection in any given essay. DHRC 4:216–219; 19:166–170.

36. DHRC 4:251, 138, 123, 226.

37. CAF 6:44; 4:57, 60, 62.

38. Robert M. Weir, "South Carolinians and the Adoption of the United States Constitution," *South Carolina Historical Magazine* 89, no. 2 (April 1988): 74.

39. DHRC 8:150–151.

40. DHRC 8:156, 38, 51.

41. DHRC 8:220.

42. See the discussion of M. C. above.

CHAPTER 4: OPPOSITION IN PENNSYLVANIA

1. Attempts to refute Wilson directly were made by "A Democratic Federalist," "Cincinnatus," "A Republican," an anonymous correspondent in Virginia, and "An Old Whig" and Centinel, discussed below. Thomas Wait commented in a letter that "some of [Wilson's] observations were very good—and some, in my opinion, were very good for nothing." One writer perhaps best summed up its influence in saying that "Mr. Wilson's speech is read with much approbation here [in New York], *by one party*; the other party see nothing but nonsense and contradictions in it." The importance of Wilson's speech has more to do with the volume of Anti-Federalist attacks directed at it than with its content. Even a fellow federalist described it as "an

extemporaneous harangue, to a few particular friends, intended more as a sample of oratory than of logic" rather than "a logical, written defence and recommendation of the new Constitution." CAF 3:58–64; 6:5–33; DHRC 19:130–133; 8:138–139; 4:295; *Columbian Herald*, November 26, 1787; DHRC 19:264.

2. CAF 3:25, 35.

3. George Washington still takes a shot here: "Is it derogating from the character of the *illustrious and highly revered* WASHINGTON, to suppose him fallible on a subject that must be in a great measure novel to him?" At least this time Centinel discusses him by name, and follows up with some praise to soften the attack: "As a patriotic hero, he stands unequalled in the annals of time." CAF 2:144.

4. CAF 2:146, 154.

5. CAF 3:37.

6. CAF 3:102.

7. CAF 3:112.

8. CAF 3:108.

9. CAF 3:110, 109.

10. CAF 3:110.

11. CAF 3:112.

12. CAF 3:45.

13. DHRC 2:308.

14. CAF 3:74.

15. CAF 3:85, 76.

16. DHRC 2:309–311.

17. CAF 3:97.

18. The extant records of the debates present some problems for scholars. A shorthand writer, Thomas Lloyd, was hired to take notes of the debate and later publish a volume of speeches, but some Federalists, in an effort to suppress opposition arguments, apparently bought him off. Lloyd delayed publishing anything at all, and then eventually released a volume of speeches by Thomas McKean and James Wilson, with but a single Anti-Federalist comment in there (an interjected question by Smilie during a James Wilson speech). Alexander Dallas, who worked for the *Pennsylvania Herald*, attended the sessions and took what must have been substantial notes; he began publishing newspaper accounts that were balanced until he was abruptly fired as a result of Federalist pressure on the newspaper's editor. His records cover only a few days, beyond which the only records of Anti-Federalist speeches are scanty newspaper summaries and notes taken by several Federalists, most notably James Wilson.

19. DHRC 2:384–385, 439.

20. Michael J. Faber, "Democratic Anti-Federalism: Rights, Democracy, and the Minority in the Pennsylvania Ratifying Convention," *Pennsylvania Magazine of History and Biography* 138, no. 2 (April 2014): 150.

21. DHRC 2:336, 503.

22. DHRC 2:385, 392, 441.

23. DHRC 2:425, 453, 592.

24. I discuss this at length elsewhere. Faber, "Democratic Anti-Federalism," 154–159.

25. CAF 3:153–154, 158.

26. DHRC 2:503, 504, 565.

27. CAF 3:162–163.

28. DHRC 2, 459, 465. Several newspaper essays suggested that what the minority truly wanted was a unicameral legislature based on the Pennsylvania constitution, but this seems highly unlikely. Because Centinel explicitly advocated such a legislature in the national government, it seems reasonable to conclude that Samuel Bryan would have liked to see such a proposal in the Dissent. Based on its absence, it is possible that Bryan could not convince (or perhaps did not try to convince) the dissenting delegates to include such a proposal. It was no secret that the delegates advocated amending the Articles of Confederation, with its unicameral legislature (a diplomatic rather than legislative body, as Smilie observed), but the suggestion that they wanted a national government that looked like Pennsylvania's runs counter to available evidence. DHRC 2:650, 653–654.

29. Faber, "Democratic Anti-Federalism," 157–158.

30. DHRC 2:649, 652, 657.

31. CAF 2:171.

32. CAF 2:172, 176, 172–173.

33. CAF 2:175.

34. CAF 3:142–143.

35. CAF 3:116.

36. CAF 3:120, 121; 2:202.

CHAPTER 5: FEDERALIST MOMENTUM

1. DHRC 3:105; Robert A. Rutland, *The Ordeal of the Constitution: The Antifederalists and the Ratification Struggle of 1878–1788* (Norman: University of Oklahoma Press, 1966), 60.

2. The *New Jersey Journal* reported that, "notwithstanding the dispatch of the Convention, many supposed exceptions were agitated; but that the Honorable Judge Brearly, with a perspicuity of argument and persuasive eloquence which carried conviction with it, bore down all opposition." "Unitas" made the same claim about a week later. There may have even been some sentiment for amendments. "The New-Jersey members did agree to the plan," wrote "Honestus" in North Carolina, "but observed, that some alterations were essentially requisite, viz. That the president should not be elected for four years, but for one year only; nor should he have the power to keep a standing army or navy, neither the sole power to mint money for all the states, nor to establish that high and arbitrary court in law, nor the toleration act, by which every Jew or Infidel could come into an office." DHRC 3:194, 194–195; *Wilmington Centinel*, June 18, 1788.

3. DHRC 3:140; 18: 275.

4. DHRC 3:143; Charles A. Beard, *An Economic Interpretation of the Constitution of the United States* (New York: Macmillan, 1921), 271; Richard P. McCormick, *Experiment in Independence: New Jersey in the Critical Period 1781–1789* (New Brunswick, NJ: Rutgers University Press, 1950), 277–278.

5. CAF 5:129–136; DHRC 3: 254, 259.

6. DHRC 3:259–261.

7. DHRC 27:419.

8. Wilson died in March, at the age of thirty-six, reportedly after "a short ill-ness." It is likely that his injuries from the Carlisle riot were at least in part to blame, which would make him the first casualty of the ratification debates. He would not be the only one. DHRC 2:673.

9. DHRC 2:675, 678, 693.

10. DHRC 2:685, 688, 690.

11. DHRC 2:704.

12. Saul Cornell offers a more extensive discussion of the riot and its aftermath. Saul Cornell, "Aristocracy Assailed: The Ideology of Backcountry Anti-Federalism," *Journal of American History* 76, no. 4 (March 1990): 1148–1172.

13. DHRC 2:664.

14. This was no mere conspiracy theory; the Federalists actually did try to pre-vent publication. This was apparent in Thomas Lloyd's accounts of the convention debates, or rather his volume of some of the Federalist speeches. Lloyd, a well-known shorthand writer at the time, applied to the convention for the place of assistant clerk, but was refused. He promised to publish a full account of the debates anyway. The only volume that ever appeared, however, contained only speeches by James Wilson and Thomas McKean, with nothing more than a single line by the opposition, an interjection by William Findley in one of Wilson's speeches. McMas-ter and Stone offer a concise explanation: "The reason is not far to seek. He was bought up by the Federalists, and, in order to satisfy the public, was suffered to pub-lish one volume containing nothing but speeches made by the two federal leaders." There was an active effort by Pennsylvania Federalists to push ratification through as quickly as possible, and even to suppress opposition arguments. A similar effort was already underway in Connecticut. John Bach McMaster and Frederick D. Stone, eds., *Pennsylvania and the Federal Constitution, 1787–1788* (Lancaster: Historical Society of Pennsylvania, 1888), 14–15.

15. CAF 2:181; DHRC 16:546–547, 545.

16. DHRC 16:558, 561. Though most of the attacks on the post office came from the opponents of the Constitution, and the issue was largely partisan, one of the harshest attacks on the post office came from the *New Jersey Journal*, hardly an Anti-Federalist publication. "For some weeks past, we have scarcely received a paper from our numerous correspondents in the different states. The motive for this suppression of intelligence is best known to the post-master general! It has an oblique aspect of sinister views.—It is a disgrace to this enlightened age, and an harbinger of slavery, that when the press, under the most arbitrary governments, is daily growing more and more free, that the post-masters, or their jackalls, should essay to stop all communication between the states at this important crisis, by pro-hibiting that exchange of papers printers have enjoyed since the first establishment of a post-office in this continent. Such a most attrocious attack upon public freedom, demands the attention and resentment of every friend to the rights of his country; for if this mutual exchange cannot be accomplished without being subject to the caprice of a post-rider, besides satisfying his inordinate and unlimmitted demands, there will be few presses, and they will soon become entirely subservient to the influence of government. Instead of being the guardians of the public rights, they will be made the dangerous engines to gloss and colour over the most fatal designs

against the common liberty and happiness.—Rouse, Printers! and oppose the hydra in embrio." There was a principle at stake, as well as substantial self-interest. The printers wanted to ensure both their independence and their livelihood, and the new post office policies threatened both. Fortunately for the Anti-Federalists, statements such as this only strengthened their case that the United States was headed toward despotism. DHRC 16:547.

17. DHRC 16:554–555, 567–568, 569, 596.

18. When it came time to appoint a postmaster, George Washington, as President, chose to replace Hazard rather than reappoint him; Hazard was one of very few Confederation officers not continued in their offices. Washington's position on Hazard is clear in a letter he wrote to John Jay in July 1788. He wrote that "if the Postmaster General (with whose character I am unacquainted & therefore would not be understood to form an unfavorable opinion of his motives) has any candid advisers who conceive that he merits the public employment they ought to counsel him to wipe away the aspersion he has incautiously brought upon a good cause–if he is unworthy of the Office he holds, it would be well that the ground of a complaint, apparently so general, should be enquired into, and, if founded, redressed through the medium of a better appointment." DHRC 16:596.

19. DHRC 3:351; *Maryland Journal*, November 2, 1787; DHRC 3:368, 396, 455.

20. DHRC 3:330, 457–458, 578–579; 19:353.

21. DHRC 3:494–495; 15:258.

22. DHRC 3:421, 588.

23. DHRC 3:439, 441.

24. DHRC 3:406, 501–502.

25. Jeremiah Wadsworth identified his cousin James as "the only man of any real consequence" among the Anti-Federalists. DHRC 3:565. At least three other delegates identified as Anti-Federalist leaders, Erastus Wolcott, Joseph Hopkins, and William Williams, voted for ratification. It is not clear how vocal the Anti-Federalists were in convention, aside from Wadsworth, but it is clear they were outmatched in prestige and ability as well as numbers. As Hugh Ledlie admits to John Lamb, the Federalists "have got almost all the best writers (as well as speakers) on their side, tho we vie with and, I believe, overbalance them in point of honesty and integrity." DHRC 3:577.

26. DHRC 3:547–548.

27. DHRC 3:576.

28. DHRC 3:594, 598, 580.

29. DHRC 20:693.

30. DHRC 20:700.

31. DHRC 20:719, 721, 730–731.

32. DHRC 5:646, 840–841, 715–716.

33. DHRC 7:1538–1539.

34. Gore was likely wrong on the point of authorship. Though we cannot be certain, James Warren seems a more likely author of the Helvidius Priscus essays. DHRC 5:535.

35. DHRC 5:556.

36. DHRC 5:618, 1335.

37. DHRC 5:627.

38. Nathaniel Gorham does note that Adams "opened fully & possitively in op- posisiton" at the dinner, "& declared that he would continue so to do in Conven- tion." Gorham, however, was not at the dinner, and received this information from "one of the company." His informant was probably Christopher Gore, so this does not corroborate anything. DHRC 5:629.

39. DHRC 5:626; 7:1598.

40. The meeting of the mechanics at the Green Dragon, and the resolutions ad- opted thereby, are matters of history, but the story of how Adams was informed of the meeting is almost certainly apocryphal. Still, it underscores the importance of the people for Adams. Ira Stoll, drawing from fellow Adams biographer William Wells, tells it well: "A group of delegates who favored ratification came to see Hancock and found Adams at his bedside. The visitors asked the two revolutionary leaders of Boston what their objections were, and Adams and Hancock listed issues that, if handled with amendments, would win their support for the Constitution. If Adams had any further doubts, they were allayed when Paul Revere hand-delivered a set of resolutions in favor of the Constitution that had been approved by the skilled workingmen of Boston, or mechanics, at the Green Dragon Tavern. Daniel Webster recorded the interaction as follows: 'How many mechanics,' Adams asked, 'were at the Green Dragon when the resolutions were passed?' 'More, sir,' Revere replied, 'than the Green Dragon could hold.' 'And where were the rest, Mr. Revere?' Adams inquired. 'In the streets, sir,' said Revere. 'And how many were in the streets?' Ad- ams asked. Answered Revere: 'More, sir, than there are stars in the sky.'" The Green Dragon resolutions might well have swayed Adams, but it seems likely that they were only one of many factors. Ira Stoll, *Samuel Adams: A Life* (New York: Free Press, 2008), 234.

41. DHRC 5:814.

42. DHRC 5:852–855.

43. "I am much Mortified at the Mixture of Legislative and Executive Powers in the Senate, and wish for Some other Amendments," John Adams wrote to Cotton Tufts in January. "But I am clear for accepting the present Plan as it is and trying the Experiment. at a future Time Amendments may be made. but a new Convention at present, would not be likely to amend it." DHRC 5:778.

CHAPTER 6: THE HEART OF
THE NATIONAL DEBATE

1. DHRC 14:103.

2. CAF 2:118.

3. Lansing and Yates left after the proceedings on July 10. Since this letter was not written until December, it is impossible to say what exactly prompted the two to leave so long after the decision to essentially write a new constitution and thus set aside the instructions to the Convention, yet before some of the major provisions of that emerging document were decided. Neither Yates nor Lansing was particularly active during their last few days at the Convention. Yates, who kept careful notes through July 5, had apparently lost interest in that endeavor, because although he

was present he ceased to document what happened on the next few days before he left. Lansing's notes leave off on the ninth of July. Neither delegate spoke in the Convention about their reasons for departure, and there are no surviving written records of their reasons before the December letter. Yates and Lansing contend that enough of the Constitution had already taken shape: "We were not present at the completion of the new constitution; but before we left the convention, its principles were so well established as to convince us, that no alteration was to be expected to conform it to our ideas of expediency and safety. A persuasion, that our further attendance would be fruitless, rendered us less solicitous to return." In hindsight, of course, this prediction was borne out. At the time, though, it was not nearly so clear how the document would turn out. It is worth questioning at least the sincerity of Yates and Lansing in their professed reasons for their departure. CAF 2:18.

4. CAF 2:17.

5. DHRC 19:295, 302–303, 473–476.

6. CAF 6:58, 51, 56, 61.

7. CAF 6:25–29, 62.

8. CAF 6:77.

9. CAF 6:77.

10. CAF 6:78.

11. CAF 6:81.

12. CAF 6:82.

13. CAF 6:87.

14. DHRC 4:374, 349.

15. Agrippa's argument against giving the national government power over naturalization makes clear his distrust of foreign influence and people. This power given to Congress concerning naturalization, he argues, "ought never to be given them; for though most of the states may be willing for certain reasons to receive foreigners as citizens, yet reasons of equal weight may induce other states, differently circumstanced, to keep their blood pure. Pennsylvania has chosen to receive all that would come there. Let any indifferent person judge whether that state in point of morals, education, energy is equal to any of the eastern states; the small state of Rhode-Island only excepted. Pennsylvania in the course of a century has acquired her present extent and population, at the expense of religion and good morals. The eastern states have, by keeping separate from the foreign mixtures, acquired their present greatness in the course of a century and an half, and have preserved their religion and morals. They have also preserved that manly virtue which is equally fitted for rendering them respectable in war, and industrious in peace." Whether Agrippa's assessment of the morals and virtues of the states is fair or not, this sentiment is certainly a xenophobic one, and suggests the degree to which Agrippa believes that the states ought to remain separate from one another. CAF 4:85–86.

16. CAF 4:81, 71, 84, 82.

17. CAF 4:70, 73, 75, 76, 84.

18. CAF 4:89–90.

19. CAF 4:90.

20. DHRC 5:581; CAF 4:94–95, 100.

21. CAF 4:97, 99, 103, 105.

22. CAF 4:127, 131–132, 129–130.

23. Cornelius declares that the Constitution has received widespread praise, and that "Not the least objection, that I recollect, has publickly appeared against it." Since he is writing in the western region of Massachusetts, it is plausible that he has not seen much public opposition, though by December it seems very unlikely that he has seen none. The *Hampshire Chronicle*, in which the essays of Cornelius were published, carried accounts of the Pennsylvania legislature calling a ratifying convention, but without any of the substantial arguments for or against the Constitution. It also printed, on October 30, the address of the minority of the Pennsylvania legislature. On November 13, the paper printed the objections of Elbridge Gerry. Then, on November 27, the paper printed the twenty-three objections of "An Officer of the Late Continental Army." Perhaps Cornelius was so caught up in reading every installment of "The Shipwreck and Adventures of Monsieur Pierre Viaud," which took up the first page of nearly every issue of the *Chronicle*, that he failed to notice the other pages. CAF 4:139.

24. CAF 4:140, 145.
25. DHRC 4:391–392; 5:561; CAF 4:120–121.
26. CAF 4:152.
27. Brutus makes a similar argument. CAF 2:426–427.
28. DHRC 5:618.
29. CAF 4:164, 169, 165.
30. CAF 4:178.
31. CAF 4:168.
32. DHRC 5:832.
33. CAF 4:193, 195.
34. DHRC 5:718, 716.
35. DHRC 5:872, 873; 8:367.
36. DHRC 5:710.
37. CAF 4:224–225.
38. CAF 4:227, 157, 160, 230.
39. CAF 3:46, 50.
40. DHRC 8:210, 232, 249–252, 275–276, 364–366.
41. DHRC 8:259.
42. DHRC 8:383.
43. DHRC 8:386, 387.
44. DHRC 8:435.
45. CAF 5:145, 146, 147; DHRC 15:486.
46. DHRC 8:353, 354.
47. DHRC 8:342.
48. DHRC 8:343.
49. DHRC 8:398.
50. A desire to preserve the union was a decisive factor for many reluctant supporters of the Constitution. This was especially true of several key figures, including Samuel Adams and Melancton Smith along with Randolph. Michael J. Faber, "The Federal Union Paradigm of 1788: Three Anti-Federalists Who Changed Their Minds," *American Political Thought* 4, no. 4 (Fall 2015).
51. CAF 5:140, 142.
52. CAF 4:207, 208.

53. DHRC 5:758.
54. CAF 3:168, 169, 172.
55. CAF 3:125.
56. CAF 3:127–128, 128, 129.
57. CAF 6:31; DHRC 19:403–406.
58. DHRC 20:673, 615–616.
59. CAF 4:117, 118.
60. CAF 4:39.
61. DHRC 8:283–284, 324.
62. DHRC 8:357, 358.
63. DHRC 8:355, 321, 309, 359.
64. CAF 4:211.
65. DHRC 19:276; CAF 6:46.
66. DHRC 5:704.
67. DHRC 5:786–787.

CHAPTER 7: COMPROMISE
IN MASSACHUSETTS

1. Samuel Bannister Harding, *The Contest over the Ratification of the Federal Constitution in the State of Massachusetts* (New York: Longmans, Green, 1896), 14.
2. Pauline Maier writes that Dana "seemed to steal the show." During one of his speeches the press observers were so captivated that they forgot to take notes. Jeremy Belknap was more evocative, writing that "Judge Dana thunders like Demosthenes." Pauline Maier, *Ratification: The People Debate the Constitution, 1787–1788* (New York: Simon & Schuster, 2010), 184; DHRC 7:1534.
3. Van Beck Hall suggests that the Boston election results "worried the Federalists" because of the election of Adams, Hancock, and Thomas Dawes, the three of whom Hall describes as "ideological Antifederalists considered neutral toward the Constitution." This phrasing is interesting, and possibly the most accurate brief description of the position of Adams at least, and perhaps the other two as well. Van Beck Hall, *Politics without Parties: Massachusetts, 1780–1791* (Pittsburgh: University of Pittsburgh Press, 1972), 276.
4. DHRC 7:1598; 5:642; 6:1244.
5. DHRC 7:1545; Maier, *Ratification*, 127.
6. DHRC 5:648; 7:1572; 5:1102; 7:1602, 1552; 5:624. Fiske praises the Massachusetts Convention for admitting these men as delegates. "It was a wholesome no less than a generous policy," he suggests, "that let these men come in and freely speak their minds. The air was thus the sooner cleared of discontent; the disease was thus the more likely to heal itself." This interpretation gives the leaders of the state far too much credit. If the legislature, or Governor Hancock himself, had tried to stop Shaysites from being elected by the towns in which they were still quite popular, the state would have had another uprising on its hands. The local democratic process in the state inevitably produced a few Shaysite delegates and even more sympathizers with Shays, and the Federalists could do nothing about it but acquiesce. At any rate, they were probably not as dangerous as they were often made out to be

by the Federalists. Bradford suggests that "for all their troublesome noise," Shays's followers really wanted "no more than tax relief, lower legal fees, and a better circulation of money." Nonetheless, Shays's Rebellion had a significant impact in uniting the financial interests of the state behind the Constitution. John Fiske, *The Critical Period of American History, 1783–1789* (New York: Houghton Mifflin, 1888), 340; M. E. Bradford, *Original Intentions: On the Making and Ratification of the United States Constitution* (Athens: University of Georgia Press, 1993), 47; David P. Szatmary, *Shays' Rebellion: The Making of an Agrarian Insurrection* (Amherst: University of Massachusetts Press, 1980), 133–134.

7. Pauline Maier offers an excellent discussion of the debates over delegate elections. Her discussion, much more comprehensive than the one here (and including the towns in Connecticut as well), is incredibly valuable for making sense of this complicated part of the ratification debates. Maier, *Ratification*, 125–153.

8. Maier, *Ratification*, 151, 150; DHRC 5:1003, 967–969.

9. DHRC 5:997.

10. DHRC 5:785, 651, 708.

11. DHRC 5:617.

12. Bradford, *Original Intentions*, 50.

13. DHRC 7:1561.

14. James T. Austin, *The Life of Elbridge Gerry*, vol. 2 (Boston: Wells and Lilly, 1829), 71; George Athan Billias, *Elbridge Gerry: Founding Father and Republican Statesman* (New York: McGraw-Hill, 1976), 213; DHRC 7:1534.

15. DHRC 6:1193.

16. Adams biographer John Miller offers a different interpretation of this exchange, suggesting "Ames answered [Adams's question] with a speech of such cogency and force that Adams dropped the matter as though he had touched a red-hot iron." This account does not ring true. Had Adams been raising an objection as Miller implies, it would have been entirely out of character for the fiery old revolutionary to phrase it as a question, and it is implausible that Adams would have meekly submitted had he not been convinced. John C. Miller, *Sam Adams: Pioneer in Propaganda* (Stanford: Stanford University Press, 1936), 380.

17. Fiske, *Critical Period*, 327. Immediately following Adams's statement, Gilbert Dench stated that "his objections to biennial elections were removed." General William Heath then gave a moderately long speech on the importance of annual elections, only to end by stating that he is now in favor of two-year terms for congressmen. Charles Turner and General Samuel Thompson still raised brief objections, the latter with an allusion to the Bowdoin administration's handling of Shays's Rebellion, which created quite a ruckus in the convention and forced an early adjournment for the day. Following this, the remaining discussion of elections focused less on how long the constitutional terms of office were, and more on the probability that future Congresses might alter or cancel elections to perpetuate themselves in office.

18. DHRC 6:1335.

19. Herbert S. Allan, *John Hancock: Patriot in Purple* (New York: MacMillan, 1948), 328; DHRC 7:1541.

20. DHRC 7:1584; Miller, *Sam Adams*, 378–384; Jürgen Heideking, *The Constitution before the Judgment Seat: The Prehistory and Ratification of the American*

Constitution, 1787–1791, ed. John P. Kaminski and Richard Leffler (Charlottesville: University of Virginia Press, 2012), 292; Maier, *Ratification*, 197; Michael Allen Gillespie, "Massachusetts: Creating Consensus," in *Ratifying the Constitution*, ed. Michael Allen Gillespie and Michael Lienesch (Lawrence: University Press of Kansas, 1989), 138–167.

21. Harlow Giles Unger, *John Hancock: Merchant King and American Patriot* (New York: John Wiley & Sons, 2000), 313; Bradford, *Original Intentions*, 51; DHRC 7:1772, 1796.

22. Gillespie, "Massachusetts," 139, 151–158; Thomas C. Amory, *Life of James Sullivan*, vol. 1 (Boston: Phillips, Sampson, 1859), 224; Allan, *John Hancock*, 327; James Sullivan, *Biographical Sketch of the Life & Character of His Late Excellency Governor Hancock* (Boston, 1793), 14–15; DHRC 7:1566; Thomas H. O'Connor and Alan Rogers, *This Momentous Affair: Massachusetts and the Ratification of the Constitution of the United States* (Boston: Trustees of the Public Library, 1987), 55.

23. This does not preclude the possibility, of course, that Hancock struck some kind of political bargain with the Federalists; in fact it is almost certain that he demanded certain concessions from the Federalists in exchange for his public support of ratification. Rufus King had little incentive to defame Governor Hancock in a private letter to Henry Knox, in which King explained the terms of the deal. "Hancock will hereafter receive the universal support of Bowdoins Friends," he wrote on February 3, "and we tell him that if Virginia does not unite, which is problematical that he is considered as the only fair candidate for President." Hancock may well have favored ratification anyway, perhaps with amendments, but it is clear that he wanted to gain politically from his position if he could. Samuel Adams, on the other hand, apparently extracted no promises; he was either more idealistic or less shrewd politically than the governor, almost certainly the former. Allan offers an excellent discussion of Hancock's motives as perceived by early historians. DHRC 7:1572; Allan, *John Hancock*, 331–332.

24. Gillespie, "Massachusetts," 153.

25. Theophilus Parsons, Jr., in no uncertain terms, claims authorship for his father, but this is doubtful. Parsons was not among the moderates in the convention, nor was he among those who entertained serious doubts about the Constitution. He may well have been involved, or even outlined the ideas, but his son's claim that "my father wrote them, and every word of them" is clearly false. The influence of others, including those I have named, is readily apparent. DHRC 7:1790.

26. DHRC 7:1775–1776.

27. Tristram Dalton wrote to Michael Hodge on January 30 to tell of the governor's appearance in convention and his not-yet-public support of the Constitution. "I will tell you," he adds, "that Mr. S. Adams will come out in favor of the Constitution. This and the Governor on the same side will settle the matter favorably. All this is scarcely known out of our caucus, wherein we work as hard as in convention." DHRC 6:1560.

28. DHRC 7:1585, 1581, 1586–1587; Billias, *Elbridge Gerry*, 206; Gillespie, "Massachusetts," 159.

29. DHRC 6:1469–1470.

30. DHRC 6:1404, 1408; 8:437; 7:1701.

31. DHRC 6:1226, 1353, 1287, 1290, 1309, 1227, 1310, 1365, 1399.

32. DHRC 6:1367, 1450, 1490; Miller, *Sam Adams*, 383; John K. Alexander, *Samuel Adams: The Life of an American Revolutionary* (Lanham, MD: Rowman & Littlefield, 2011), 282.

33. DHRC 6:1450. Barrell ultimately did defect from the opposition, later explaining that his opposition was "folly" that he pursued "till powerful reason flash'd conviction on my mind, and bore down all before it, in spite of the almost invincible resistance of deep rooted prejudice." This was some conversion, as upon his election he had told his constituents that "he would loose his right hand before he would accede to the proposed Constitution," undoubtedly an homage to George Mason's similar statement in the Philadelphia Convention. Upon his return to York, his constituents may well have been in the mood to take him up on it; his Anti-Federalist colleague Samuel Nasson reported that Barrell "was much Abused" upon his homecoming (though Nasson tried to defend his reputation if not his vote). DHRC 7:1589; 5:490; 7:1708.

34. DHRC 7:1690.

35. Harding, *Contest over the Ratification*, 67.

36. At least, the minority was treated well publicly. In private letters, the Federalists often had nasty things to write about their opponents. Jeremy Belknap described the opposition as "very clamorous—petulant tedious & provoking," "whose only force lies in noise & opposition." "The Speakers on that Side," wrote David Sewall, "in general was really Contemptible in every Sense"; he went on to accuse the Anti-Federalists of relying on others outside the convention to write speeches for them. Henry Knox charged the opponents of ratification with anarchism; their opposition, he claimed, was based not on "the merits or demerits" of the Constitution, "but from a deadly principle leveled at the existence of all government whatever—; The principles of insurgency expanded, and deriving fresh strength and life from the impunity with which the rebellion of last year was suffered to escape." Even Nathanial Barrell, a convert from the opposition, referred to his former colleagues as "a set of the most unprincipled of men." The principles of the Federalists could be questioned as well, of course. There was probably private pressure put on wavering delegates; Henry Jackson admits that the Federalists were circulating a rumor that the delegates might only get paid for their services in convention if the Constitution was ratified, and many Anti-Federalist delegates would be hard-pressed to even make the journey home without receiving their pay. Wealthy Federalists hosted lavish dinner parties in an attempt to win over their poorer opponents. Shortly after the convention, John Quincy Adams notes in his diary that Theophilus Parsons "speaks with pleasure of every little trifling intrigue, which served to baffle, the intentions of the *antifederalists*; though many of them to me exhibit a meanness which, I scarcely should expect a man would boast." During the debates, a piece in the *Boston Gazette* claimed that Federalists from Rhode Island were paying off delegates to buy votes for ratification. After the vote, the *Freeman's Journal* in Philadelphia, noting the small majority, claimed that several Maine votes had been bought with a promise of separate statehood. Although these claims generally remain unsubstantiated, in all these debates there was some unseemly (though very practical) political activity behind the scenes, by both sides. DHRC 7:1534–1535, 1593, 1587, 1590, 1571, 1691; 5:760; 7:522.

37. O'Connor and Rogers, *This Momentous Affair*, 17; DHRC 6:1487.

38. Harding, *Contest over the Ratification*, 7, 74.

39. DHRC 8:491.

40. This description of that essay is an especially arrogant one for Samuel Bryan, the author of the Centinel essays, because he also wrote the Reasons for Dissent. His own arguments, of course, he finds "unanswerable." His Centinel essays, he is certain, "have met the approbation of the community." One need not question Bryan's supreme confidence in his own abilities. CAF 2:206.

41. CAF 2:197, 204; 3:132.

42. CAF 5:77.

43. CAF 4:257, 258.

44. DHRC 7:1749; CAF 4:264.

45. DHRC 7:1692, 1696–1697, 1718–1719, 1727, 1725.

46. DHRC 7:1662, 1672, 1678, 1711.

47. DHRC 7:1758, 1759, 1695; Austin, *Life of Elbridge Gerry*, 2:58, 84–86; DHRC 7:1607, 1762, 1726.

48. CAF 4:273–274, 272, 274.

49. CAF 4:276, 277, 279, 281, 280.

50. CAF 4:296.

CHAPTER 8: SETBACKS IN
THE NORTHEAST

1. DHRC 20:809. A few Anti-Federalists had given up the fight, of course. Much of the Massachusetts minority, as well as their brethren in Connecticut, were no longer resisting ratification. Richard Henry Lee, by early March, had reportedly "so far assented" to the Constitution "as to declare that he will not oppose it." DHRC 8:457.

2. CAF 3:130, 131.

3. CAF 3:135–136, 135, 136, 138.

4. DHRC 2:722, 712–713, 713n2, 714.

5. CAF 2:202–203, 203–204.

6. CAF 3:194, 195.

7. CAF 3:200, 202, 204, 206–207, 198, 209.

8. CAF 3:183, 184, 188.

9. CAF 3:192–193.

10. This localism was dominant among farmers in New Hampshire, who were not swayed by Federalist arguments about facilitating commerce or the importance of strong central government. Jere Daniell, *Experiment in Republicanism: New Hampshire Politics and the American Revolution, 1741–1794* (Cambridge, MA: Harvard University Press, 1970), 210–211.

11. CAF 4:238, 240–244.

12. Michael J. Faber and Robi Ragan, "Organized Opposition: The Anti-Federalist Political Network," in *Public Choice Analyses of American Economic History*, vol. 3, ed. Joshua Hall and Marcus Witcher (New York: Springer, 2019).

13. Albert Stillman Batchellor, *A Brief View of the Influences That Moved in the Adoption of the Federal Constitution by the State of New Hampshire* (Concord:

Rumford Press, 1900), 14, 23; Nancy Elaine Briggs Oliver, "Keystone of the Federal Arch: New Hampshire's Ratification of the United States' Constitution" (PhD diss., University of California, Santa Barbara, 1972), 46.

14. Atherton was a controversial figure, and perhaps the most loquacious Anti-Federalist in the nation aside from Luther Martin. The Portsmouth postmaster Jeremiah Libbey was hopeful that Atherton "will destroy what he aims to accomplish by his overmuch talking. There is no paragraph but he objects to, & I think from his over zeal he will eventually serve the cause he means to injure." Nathaniel Joseph Eiseman, "The Ratification of the Federal Constitution by the State of New Hampshire" (MA thesis, Columbia University, 1938), 48.

15. The *Maryland Journal* on March 7 reported that Peabody "had expressed himself in favour of its adoption," which is certainly false. Libbey's statement that Peabody "does more mischief than he could do had he a seat" is undoubtedly more accurate. Peabody was quite active during the convention and its recess, drumming up support for the Anti-Federalist cause. Eiseman, "Ratification of the Federal Constitution," 60.

16. "The Antifederalists, except two or three of their leaders," wrote Libbey, "are as dumb & obstinate as ____. They will not say a word on the subject, even in private conversation, being determined (to) put the issue on the important sign of (li)fting their hands, and I suppose every one of them has capacity to do that." Certainly most of the opposition delegates were silent in convention, deferring to their leaders, but this is true of most of the other conventions as well. Eiseman, "Ratification of the Federal Constitution," 60.

17. *New Hampshire Spy*, February 23, 1788.

18. *New Hampshire Spy*, February 23, 1788.

19. DHRC 16:184. This was correcting a report in the *American Herald* that said: "The Convention of the State of New-Hampshire, on Friday last, brought on the decisive Question respecting the New Constitution—yeas 51—nays 54.—This Question being reconsidered, it was then moved for an Adjournment, and was carried, yeas 53, nays 52, to meet again on the third Tuesday in JUNE next." The erroneous account in the latter paper was reprinted almost as often as the correct description from the *Centinel*. DHRC 16:184.

20. Lawrence Straus offers an excellent discussion of the period between the first and second sessions of the New Hampshire Convention. He discusses both the Federalist reaction and the media campaign to win over sufficient support for ratification. This will be discussed further below. Lawrence Guy Straus, "Reactions of Supporters of the Constitution to the Adjournment of the New Hampshire Ratification Convention—1788," *Historical New Hampshire* 23, no. 3 (Autumn 1968): 37–50.

21. DHRC 16:530, 531, 183–184; Pauline Maier, *Ratification: The People Debate the Constitution, 1787–1788* (New York: Simon & Schuster, 2010), 221.

22. Oliver, "Keystone of the Federal Arch," 74; DHRC 16:478.

23. "Mr. Carter," the author wrote to the newspaper's editor, "You have been obliged to give your customers such a long *lent*, and diet them so *plaguy hard*, with *new Constitution* and *state conventions*, that many of them are not only thoroughly *tired*, but very near *starved*;—therefore I think it high time to contrive a little about *eating and drinking*." This introduction was reprinted in the *Documentary History of the Ratification of the Constitution*, but the article itself was not. DHRC 24:248.

24. The dislike of Rhode Island was not quite universal. In a rare exception, "A Watchman" in Massachusetts, a radical democrat, praised the state for its resistance to centralized power. He sees in Rhode Island a positive example of effective and economical democracy, and suggests that others should follow its example. "Keep the power in your own hands," he exhorts his readers, "and let nothing be established that may deprive you of your liberties and make you unhappy." CAF 4:233.

25. DHRC 13:132; James T. Austin, *The Life of Elbridge Gerry*, vol. 2 (Boston: Wells and Lilly, 1829), 67; DHRC 21:1348.

26. John Kaminski offers an excellent brief discussion of Rhode Island's decision not to send delegates to the Convention, and the reactions to the decision. John P. Kaminski, "'Outcast' Rhode Island—the Absent State," *This Constitution* 15 (Summer 1987): 36–37.

27. DHRC 24:32, 72, 59, 252, 256.

28. DHRC 24:257.

29. DHRC 24:53, 27, 39.

30. DHRC 24:87.

31. DHRC 24:101.

32. DHRC 24:271, 272, 28.

33. DHRC 24:58.

34. DHRC 24:250.

35. DHRC 8:455; 24:60–61.

36. Maier, *Ratification*, 224.

37. Frank Green Bates, *Rhode Island and the Formation of the Union* (New York: Macmillan, 1898), 148; Irwin H. Polishook, *Rhode Island and the Union* (Evanston, IL: Northwestern University Press, 1969), 164, 182.

38. DHRC 24:90. Nonetheless, the delegates in the state's eventual convention were prepared to fight this fight. The Anti-Federalists in the convention would raise this as a major objection, and would include a clause against slavery among the convention's proposed amendments.

39. Polishook, *Rhode Island and the Union*, 191–192; DHRC 24:34, 51, 75.

40. Polishook, *Rhode Island and the Union*, 191.

41. DHRC 24:74, 62.

42. DHRC 24:44. In their next session, the legislature would send Peleg Arnold and Jonathan Hazard to represent the state in Congress.

43. DHRC 24:50; Maier, *Ratification*, 223; DHRC 24:108.

44. Polishook, *Rhode Island and the Union*, 198. "A Friend to Rule and Order" made much the same argument in a more public venue, in the *Providence Gazette* on March 15. DHRC 24:139.

45. DHRC 24:138, 143, 150.

46. Polishook, *Rhode Island and the Union*, 199.

47. There was at least some sentiment that the people of Rhode Island might approve the Constitution in the referendum. In neighboring Massachusetts, the *Massachusetts Centinel* suggested that a referendum was "the mode . . . most likely to insure the ratification of the Constitution" by the state. Either the printer was wildly guessing, or his source was thoroughly misinformed. "A Federalist" chastised the printer a week later for the error. DHRC 24:136, 140–142.

48. This unusual estimate appeared in separate stories a week apart in New York and Maryland; presumably the source was the same. DHRC 24:227.

49. DHRC 24:228, 218.

50. DHRC 24:158, 194, 196, 183, 181.

51. DHRC 24: 230, 235.

CHAPTER 9: SUMMER CONVENTION ELECTIONS

1. DHRC 9:766; 10:1586.

2. CAF 5:174, 186, 187, 181, 182.

3. CAF 5:176, 179, 185, 178.

4. DHRC 8:419, 420.

5. DHRC 8:425; CAF 5:164, 165, 167.

6. CAF 5:168, 169.

7. CAF 5:170.

8. DHRC 9:740; 8:477, 437.

9. DHRC 9:782–784, 882–883.

10. DHRC 8:470, 471.

11. DHRC 8:506–507.

12. CAF 5:201–206; DHRC 8:458–459.

13. DHRC 8:507–509.

14. DHRC 8:478.

15. DHRC 9:588.

16. The Federalist leanings of his constituents were apparently not the only reason that Mason was unpopular in his home county. James Hughes claimed in November that Mason "would hardly get twenty votes in the whole County for, he has made himself odious, by an illiberall abuse of the Commissioners of the Turnpike, & an attempt, to divide the Town, from the County." DHRC 9:582.

17. DHRC 9:585, 607, 584.

18. DHRC 9:614.

19. DHRC 9:698, 583.

20. DHRC 9:606; Pauline Maier, *Ratification: The People Debate the Constitution, 1787–1788* (New York: Simon & Schuster, 2010), 231; DHRC 9:609, 609–610.

21. DHRC 9:615–616.

22. Their objections included that the Senate was too powerful, as was the judiciary; the President should have a council to advise him; the states ought to have complete jurisdiction over matters within their own borders; the people need the protection of a bill of rights; appellate courts should decide only matters of law, not fact; the state courts should keep sole jurisdiction over local matters; civil trials should be by jury; and taxes ought to be raised through requisitions on the states rather than direct taxes whenever possible.

23. DHRC 9:611–612.

24. DHRC 8:436–437, 475; 9:592.

25. Jon Kukla attributes Madison's election to the support of the Orange County Baptists, despite their strong objections to the Constitution because of the absence of

a clause protecting religious liberty. On his way home to campaign Madison stopped to visit John Leland to discuss the Constitution, and Leland's support of Madison was good enough for many Baptist voters. Kukla, "A Spectrum of Sentiments: Virginia's Federalists, Antifederalists, and 'Federalists Who Are for Amendments,' 1787–1788," *Virginia Magazine of History and Biography* 96, no. 3 (July 1988): 282. Undoubtedly the influence of Leland helped Madison, though his own presence and his election day speech were probably still necessary for him to win the seat.

26. DHRC 9:602, 598, 706, 603.

27. Norman K. Risjord, *Chesapeake Politics, 1781–1800* (New York: Columbia University Press, 1978), 304; DHRC 9:620, 825.

28. DHRC 9:765, 766, 786, 879, 880, 765.

29. DHRC 9:622–626.

30. Maier, *Ratification*, 237.

31. Louise Irby Trenholme, *The Ratification of the Federal Constitution in North Carolina* (New York: Columbia University Press, 1932), 109–111.

32. DHCUSA 4:771.

33. Trenholme, *Ratification of the Federal Constitution in North Carolina*, 115.

34. William K. Boyd, ed., "News, Letters and Documents Concerning North Carolina and the Federal Constitution," *Historical Papers Published by the Trinity College Historical Society* series 14 (1922): 75–76.

35. Trenholme, *Ratification of the Federal Constitution in North Carolina*, 11, 113, 114–115.

36. *Maryland Chronicle*, May 28, 1788. This paragraph was reprinted from the *North Carolina Gazette*, but I was unable to locate the original. DHRC 20:1106.

37. Boyd, "News, Letters and Documents," 76–77.

38. Griffith John McRee, *Life and Correspondence of James Iredell* (New York: D. Appleton, 1858), 1:178; *Maryland Journal*, April 29, 1788.

39. John Kaminski offers an in-depth discussion of the elections by county. John P. Kaminski, "New York: The Reluctant Pillar," in *The Reluctant Pillar: New York and the Adoption of the Federal Constitution*, ed. Stephen L. Schechter (Albany: New York State Commission on the Bicentennial of the United States Constitution, 1985), 77–99.

40. DHRC 21:1359, 1366. An Anti-Federalist, signing as J. M., responds to this accusation by W. M. in almost exactly the same terms, complete with the allusion to the witches of *Macbeth*. It is difficult to decide who makes for stranger witches: George Clinton, John Lansing, and Melancton Smith; or Alexander Hamilton, John Jay, and Robert R. Livingston. I am inclined to see the latter as an altogether better coven. DHRC 21:1373.

41. DHRC 21:1554, 1470.

42. Yates was widely criticized by the more aristocratic elements in the state for his writing style, as both the "Rough Hewer" and "Sidney." His efforts to appear well educated "made him an easy target for federalists who mocked the pedantry of his essays." The verbal attacks were sometimes savage, and always rested on the idea that a commoner like Yates ought not dabble in debates best left to the better sort of people. The Brutus essays are of a different style, so it is unlikely that Yates was their author. I believe that Melancton Smith is the most likely attribution. Saul Cornell, "Politics of the Middling Sort: The Bourgeois Radicalism of Abraham Yates,

Melancton Smith, and the New York Antifederalists," in *New York in the Age of the Constitution 1775–1800*, ed. Paul A. Gilje and William Pencak (Madison, NJ: Fairleigh Dickinson University Press, 1992), 154.

43. CAF 6:90, 94.

44. DHRC 20:661, 663, 662, 826, 665, 664. In the original draft of the Expositor written by Hugh Hughes, he actually uses the word "abortion," though his editor apparently decided that the language was inflammatory or inappropriate, and softened it to an allusion rather than an explicit statement. DHRC 20:666.

45. DHRC 20:794.

46. CAF 6:129, 137.

47. CAF 6:140–142.

48. DHRC 20:967, 888.

49. DHRC 20:894–895.

50. DHRC 18:51.

51. DHRC 18:55; Linda Grant DePauw, *The Eleventh Pillar: New York State and the Federal Constitution* (Ithaca, NY: Cornell University Press, 1966), 129.

52. DHRC 20:834–836.

53. CAF 6:122–127; DHRC 21:1388–1401, 1405–1407, 1408.

54. DHRC 20:677, 830–833, 870–871.

55. DHRC 20:1107, 891, 1151; 15:415–416.

56. DHRC 20:914–916.

57. DHRC 21:1539, 1540, 1433–1434, 1573, 1577, 1534, 1420.

58. DHRC 21:1500, 1501, 1518, 1519.

59. DHRC 21:1560–1563, 1446, 1448, 1467.

60. DHRC 21:1413.

61. DHRC 21:1369.

62. In response to rumors that Scotsmen in the city opposed ratification, fifty-five Scotsmen from New York City and fifteen from Albany signed an address, printed as a broadside in April, supporting the Constitution. The Anti-Federalists countered with the claim that those who signed were misled into doing so, in addition to claiming that forty-one Albany Scotsmen in Albany opposed ratification. DHRC 21:1403–1405, 1412.

63. DePauw, *Eleventh Pillar*, 139; DHRC 21:1418.

64. DHRC 21:1580.

CHAPTER 10: MISSED OPPORTUNITIES IN MARYLAND

1. *Maryland Chronicle*, November 7, 1787; DHRC 11:16–17, 17–19. The essay by "Caution" was published on October 12, 1787, while the reply by "A Friend of the Constitution" appeared on the sixteenth. On October 30, another reply, signed "Sky Augusta," offered a less constructive (if somewhat more poetic) answer even than the Friend: "It appears now, that the Devil is got in you or among you.— Exorcise him!—Expel him! Bribe him with the carcass of the Demoniac who writes under the Signature of CAUTION.—The political Devil is possessed of too much *Caution* to receive him alive, lest he should sow the Seeds of Sedition among his less turbulent Subjects." DHRC 11:29.

2. Martin biographer Bill Kauffman is quite insistent in observing that several other delegates had a lot more to say at the Convention. Gouverneur Morris, James Wilson, James Madison, and others made far more speeches than Martin's fifty-three. Nonetheless, "Landholder's" description of Martin's "eternal volubility" and "endless garrulity," along with his claim that Martin "exhausted the politeness of the Convention, which at length prepared to slumber when [he] rose to speak," stuck. At least two other delegates agreed in principle with this characterization of Martin as needlessly verbose. James Madison, in his notes on the debates, wrote of a lengthy two-day speech by Martin that it "was delivered with much diffuseness & considerable vehemence," but Madison apparently felt that a brief summary was sufficient, as he did not record the speech in nearly as much detail as most of the others that he heard in convention. William Pierce of Georgia, who offered brief sketches of each delegate's personality, presents perhaps the best contemporary description: "This Gentleman," he explains, "possesses a good deal of information, but he has a very bad delivery, and so extremely prolix, that he never speaks without tiring the patience of all who hear him." Add to this the length and tedium of the "Genuine Information" and his other writings in the ratification debates, and Pierce's description seems reasonable. Kauffman's indignation on this point is fair to an extent, but Martin's excessive verbosity is adequately documented nonetheless. He may not have spoken most often in the convention, but his major speeches there, as in the courtroom, were tedious two-day affairs. Bill Kauffman, *Forgotten Founder, Drunken Prophet: The Life of Luther Martin* (Wilmington: ISI Books, 2008), 86–87; DHRC 16:267; *Records* 1:445; 3:93.

3. John Thomas Scharf, *History of Maryland from the Earliest Period to the Present Day*, vol. 2 (Baltimore: John B. Piet, 1879), 540; Kauffman, *Forgotten Founder*, 74.

4. CAF 2:26, 28, 51.

5. CAF 2:33, 37–38, 40.

6. CAF 2:41, 44.

7. CAF 2:49.

8. CAF 2:46, 47, 53.

9. CAF 2:52–53.

10. CAF 2:55, 60, 68, 61–62.

11. CAF 2:58, 59–60.

12. CAF 2:32, 78, 79.

13. In addition to Martin's voluminous and passionate defense, Gerry defended himself on two occasions: first, on January 5, to assert that the allegations were false, and again on April 18, in which he presents an answer far more effective than Martin's verbose, though often entertaining, letters. DHRC 15:273; 17:172–177.

14. DHRC 15:415–416.

15. DHRC 15:416; 16:416.

16. CAF 2:193–194. Philadelphiensis perhaps comes closest, noting in the wake of the publication of Martin's speech that "the proceedings of the *dark conclave* have undergone an *ordeal* in Maryland, that exhibits the monarchy-men in convention as a set of the basest conspirators that ever disgraced a free country." This is, of course, more radical attack on the Federalists than it is praise of Martin; but the writer's rhetoric is always sharp. CAF 3:131.

17. CAF 5:14, 13.

18. CAF 5:37, 27, 37, 42, 44.

19. CAF 5:30.

20. Benjamin Lynerd offers an excellent discussion of the Farmer's views on democracy, and in particular his discussion of Switzerland as a potential model for American government. He suggests that the Farmer is writing from a point of view somewhat detached from the ratification debates, which is why the essays seem a little out of place. Benjamin T. Lynerd, "Democratic Opposition to the Constitution: A Swiss Counterproposal from the Maryland Farmer," *American Political Thought* 7, no. 2 (Spring 2018): 243–270.

21. CAF 5:49. This idea is strikingly similar to that proposed by Thomas Jefferson nearly three decades later, in his famous letter to Samuel Kercheval. Jefferson there suggests that each county be divided into wards small enough to allow the people to govern themselves, in person, on local issues. Jefferson did not, however, suggest that these local meetings vote on national policy; his was a more pure federalism, while the Maryland Farmer is suggesting a national democracy through local participation. Paul Leicester Ford, ed., *The Works of Thomas Jefferson* (New York: Knickerbocker Press, 1904–1905), 12:3–15.

22. CAF 5:19, 20, 27, 28, 45.

23. CAF 5:23.

24. DHRC 16:501.

25. DHRC 16:502.

26. DHRC 17:19, 21–22.

27. Philip A. Crowl, "Anti-Federalism in Maryland, 1787–1788," *William and Mary Quarterly* 4, no. 4 (October 1947): 446–469, 469.

28. Edward C. Papenfuse, "An Afterword: With What Dose of Liberty? Maryland's Role in the Movement for a Bill of Rights," *Maryland Historical Magazine* 83, no. 1 (Spring 1988): 62; DHRC 11:183; Bernard C. Steiner, "Maryland's Adoption of the Federal Constitution, Part I," *American Historical Review* 5, no. 1 (December 1899): 37; DHRC 12:444–448.

29. CAF 5:51.

30. More parts were perhaps intended, as the fifth installment ends with "To be continued," but no more essays were published.

31. *Maryland Journal*, January 15, 1788.

32. Gregory A. Stiverson, "Necessity, the Mother of Union: Maryland and the Constitution, 1785–1789," in *The Constitution and the States*, ed. Patrick T. Conley and John P. Kaminski (Madison, WI: Madison House, 1988), 131.

33. Pauline Maier, *Ratification: The People Debate the Constitution, 1787–1788* (New York: Simon & Schuster, 2010), 243.

34. Stiverson, "Necessity, the Mother of Union," 146; Gregory A. Stiverson and Phebe R. Jacobsen, *William Paca: A Biography* (Baltimore: Maryland Historical Society, 1976), 63.

35. DHCUSA 4:641–642.

36. James A. Haw, "Samuel Chase and Maryland Antifederalism: A Study in Disarray," *Maryland Historical Magazine* 83, no. 1 (Spring 1988): 39.

37. CAF 5:74. The Farmer and Planter was evidently not alone in his radical democratic rhetoric; Philip Crowl identifies two other writers who wrote "in a similar

tone": "Betsey Cornstalk" and "An Annapolitan." Both appeared in the *Maryland Gazette*, but I have been unable to locate either. Philip A. Crowl, *Maryland during and after the Revolution: A Political and Economic Study* (Baltimore: Johns Hopkins University Press, 1943), 133.

38. CAF 5:77.

39. It appears that, in this election at least, there was heavy campaigning. Daniel Carroll reported to Washington after the convention that "S Chase went into one part of the County and harangued; Mercer & J Chase did the same in another part." Among other things, they distributed the handbill noted above. DHCUSA 4:636.

40. DHRC 12:548, 594, 570–571, 578–581; Crowl, *Maryland during and after the Revolution*, 135–136; DHRC 12:582–587; Gregory A. Stiverson, "Maryland's Antifederalists and the Perfection of the U.S. Constitution," *Maryland Historical Magazine* 83, no. 1 (Spring 1988): 23; Haw, "Samuel Chase and Maryland Antifederalism," 40.

41. CAF 5:94; DHCUSA 4:581; DHRC 12:675; Stiverson, "Necessity, the Mother of Union," 147.

42. Two sets of notes on Chase's speech can be found in the Maryland Archives, one by Federalist Nicholas Hammond and the other with no name noted. Neither reveals much about the speech that is not apparent in Chase's own notes, except for the fact that Chase apparently did not follow his notes in the order in which they are written. Neither was reprinted in the *Documentary History of the Ratification of the Constitution*. MSA 1592–4, 1592–9.

43. Stiverson, "Maryland's Antifederalists," 26–27.

44. CAF 5:81.

45. CAF 5:89.

46. DHRC 12:674; James Haw, Francis F. Beirne, Rosamond R. Beirne, and R. Samuel Jett, *Stormy Patriot: The Life of Samuel Chase* (Baltimore: Maryland Historical Society, 1980), 154.

47. CAF 5:93. Hanson bristled at this claim, defensively insisting that "The speakers did not all use the same precise form of words. Each man expressed himself in his own way." He does not claim that this effort was not premeditated or coordinated, however. DHRC 12:675.

48. MSA 1592–9, 1592–2. Stiverson offers a good discussion of the debates. Stiverson, "Maryland's Antifederalists," 28–29.

49. DHRC 12:693.

50. A week before the convention Daniel of St. Thomas Jenifer wrote to Washington that he believed that "Mr. Paca will vote for the proposed plann as it stands—& recommend amendments—rather than risque a new Convention." If Jenifer had known about a deal made with Paca, there is no reason to be coy about that knowledge with a leading Federalist like Washington. Stiverson claims that a deal was struck, though he offers no evidence for that claim. DHCUSA 4:580; Stiverson, "Necessity, the Mother of Union," 149; Stiverson, "Maryland's Antifederalists," 30.

51. CAF 5:94. Hanson contends that this is misleading nonsense. "In what light the subject was viewed, and on what footing amendments were considered by the convention, and the committee," he wrote, "may best appear from the proceedings of each. . . . No part of the proceedings of either can demonstrate, that a majority esteemed amendments *necessary to perfect the constitution*. An opinion was indeed

taken up, by some gentlemen, that, altho' they could not, in their conventional capacity, propose amendments to the future congress, in behalf of the people, they might, nevertheless, in their private capacities, to gratify the wishes of some of the minority, make certain propositions to the people themselves." The defensiveness is telling; Hanson does not actually deny that a "general murmur of approbation" occurred, only that it did not reflect the official position of the convention. This suggests that the minority's version of events can be believed in this instance. DHRC 12:676.

52. CAF 5:94; DHRC 12:650, 680–681; Paul Leicester Ford, *The Origin, Purpose and Result of the Harrisburg Convention of 1788* (Brooklyn, 1890), 4.

53. Scharf, *History of Maryland*, 2:545–546. Steiner suggests that it may have been Hanson himself who tried to derail the amendments. Given his words and actions elsewhere, coupled with the fact that he was apparently the only committee member who felt the need to defend the majority in writing against the minority, it is highly likely that Hanson had a great deal to do with the breakdown of the negotiations. Bernard C. Steiner, "Maryland's Adoption of the Federal Constitution, Part II," *American Historical Review* 5, no. 2 (December 1899): 213–214.

54. DHRC 12:732, 681.

55. Stiverson, "Maryland's Antifederalists," 33; MSA 1592–12; Stiverson, "Maryland's Antifederalists," 31–32; Haw, "Samuel Chase and Maryland Antifederalism," 41.

56. CAF 5:94–98.

57. MSA 1592–8.

58. Kauffman, *Forgotten Founder*, 108.

59. CAF 5:99.

60. Hanson sent his draft to James Madison in Virginia, where it might have had a "chance of rendering service in Virginia, either by giving spirits to the friends of the general government, or by discouraging it's enemies, who may look for countenance and support from the people of Maryland" (DHRC 12:671). It is not clear whether Madison circulated it, or used it at all.

61. Norman K. Risjord, *Chesapeake Politics, 1781–1800* (New York: Columbia University Press, 1978), 293.

CHAPTER 11: FUTILITY IN SOUTH CAROLINA

1. DHRC 17:107.

2. DHRC 17:127, 107.

3. DHRC 27:128, 126, 152.

4. DHRC 27:126.

5. DHRC 27:154.

6. DHRC 27:108.

7. Harriott H. Ravenel, *Life and Times of William Lowndes of South Carolina, 1782–1822* (Boston: Houghton, Mifflin, 1901), 26.

8. Robert L. Brunhouse, "David Ramsay on the Ratification of the Constitution in South Carolina," *Journal of Southern History* 9, no. 4 (November 1943): 553; DHRC 27:196, 154.

9. DHRC 27:155–156, 157.

10. DHRC 27:200.

11. DHRC 27:51, 291; Carl J. Vipperman, *The Rise of Rawlins Lowndes, 1721–1800* (Columbia: University of South Carolina Press, 1978), 253.

12. Not all of the Federalist delegates recognized their advantage. John Kean of Beaufort wrote to his wife on May 15 that "what the result will be it is impossible to say," noting that the backcountry delegates were strongly opposed to ratification, but he was optimistic. DHRC 27:351.

13. Jerome J. Nadelhaft, "South Carolina: A Conservative Revolution," in *The Constitution and the States*, ed. Patrick T. Conley and John P. Kaminski (Madison, WI: Madison House, 1988), 175.

14. DHRC 27:336.

15. In the records and accounts of the convention, Charles Pinckney is generally referred to as "Mister" or "Governor," while his cousin Charles Cotesworth Pinckney is invariably referred to as "General." The former served as president of the convention, while the latter was the more heavily involved in the debates carrying the Federalist argument. To prevent confusion, Charles Cotesworth Pinckney will always be referred to here as General Pinckney, or by his full name.

16. DHRC 27:339, 345, 346.

17. Brunhouse, "David Ramsay on the Ratification," 555; DHRC 27:343, 342, 345, 340.

18. DHRC 27:357. This statement by Fayssoux was the subject of controversy in the *City Gazette*. The *Gazette* of May 23 printed two notes from him defending his conduct and insisting that "the paragraph inserted in the Morning Post of Tuesday last, was a false and infamous lye." The next day the paper printed a letter from Fayssoux, including his version of the speech, above its original paragraph, with the note that their version *"will appear to every candid and dispassionate person tantamount to what is published above,"* Fayssoux's version. Given the two versions, it is hard to see Fayssoux's objection, though the paper's version does suggest that any opposition to the Constitution at this point is "criminal," while Fayssoux used the word to describe only such vocal rhetorical opposition as that in which he engaged in convention. DHRC 27:356–358.

19. DHRC 27:366. The delegates clearly saw this as a sort of test vote that would reflect the relative strength of each side. It revealed a rather large Federalist advantage. DHRC 27:371–375.

20. Pauline Maier, *Ratification: The People Debate the Constitution, 1787–1788* (New York: Simon & Schuster, 2010), 251.

21. Elliot places Tweed's speech before Dollard's, with a speech by Charles Pinckney between the two. The *City Gazette*, though, clearly stated that Tweed's comments were "added" to those of Dollard, and printed Dollard's first. The latter is more likely to be correct, and this is the order in which they appear in the DHRC.

22. DHRC 27:378–380, 380–381.

23. DHRC 27:361.

24. DHRC 27:401.

25. DHRC 27:464, 473.

26. DHRC 28:55–56. The acquiescence of the South Carolina Anti-Federalists may be explained by the general nature of their objections to the Constitution.

Jerome Nadelhaft argues that those who opposed ratification here were not in disagreement with broad Federalist goals. They merely had "little faith that representatives could remain honest, committed, and responsible while serving for long periods far from home." If good representatives could be found, the Constitution might even have a positive effect. Anti-Federalists seem to have turned to finding such good representatives; South Carolina was the only state to send a majority Anti-Federalist delegation to the first House of Representatives. Jerome J. Nadelhaft, *The Disorders of War: The Revolution in South Carolina* (Orono: University of Maine at Orono Press, 1981), 190.

CHAPTER 12: THE VIRGINIA CONVENTION

1. Its drama has not gone unappreciated; the convention has even been written into a play. Robert O. Byrd's *Decision at Richmond, June 1788* uses the published accounts of the convention debates to re-create the convention, with narrated editorial commentary. Robert O. Byrd, *Decision at Richmond, June 1788: A Documentary Drama of the Constitutional Ratification Convention in Virginia* (Chicago: World without War, 1986).

2. DHRC 9:763, 795–796.

3. Michael J. Faber, "The Federal Union Paradigm of 1788: Three Anti-Federalists Who Changed Their Minds," *American Political Thought* 4, no. 4 (Fall 2015): 541–546.

4. DHRC 9:699, 706, 738.

5. DHRC 9:748.

6. Jon Kukla offers an excellent discussion of the three groups, though his placement of several Virginians is debatable. Two prominent moderates in particular seem to have shifted groups during the course of the debate: Randolph, by the convention, seems to have become an unapologetic Federalist, while Mason seems to have shifted decidedly in the other direction. Jon Kukla, "A Spectrum of Sentiments: Virginia's Federalists, Antifederalists, and 'Federalists Who Are for Amendments,' 1787–1788," *Virginia Magazine of History and Biography* 96, no. 3 (July 1988): 276–296.

7. DHRC 9:895; 8:226–227.

8. CAF 5:261, 262, 266.

9. CAF 5:268–274.

10. CAF 5:189, 190.

11. Hugh Blair Grigsby, *The History of the Virginia Federal Convention of 1788* (Richmond: Virginia Historical Society, 1890), 31–32; DHRC 10:1617.

12. DHRC 8:522.

13. Grigsby, *History of the Virginia Federal Convention*, 28.

14. DHRC 9:911.

15. This move by Mason, immediately supported by Madison and unanimously approved by the convention, has been seen by some as a tactical error by Mason. According to Hugh Blair Grigsby, "The Federal Constitution, to be opposed successfully, must be discussed on the ground either of its unfitness as a whole to attain the end of its creation, or on the dangerous tendency of its various provisions. To

preclude the debate on the first head, and to narrow the debate on the second to the consideration of a single clause, was almost to resign the benefits of discussion to the friends of the system." Pauline Maier disagrees, pointing out that both sides saw such a discussion as advantageous; Richard Henry Lee had suggested it to Mason to help the opposition sound out the feelings of the delegates and suggest appropriate amendments. The opposition also needed time to win over a few votes, and Patrick Henry was not about to be bound by procedural concerns anyway (and in the committee of the whole he could not be called to order). Madison probably supported this measure to keep the discussion as much as possible on the Constitution, rather than on amendments. Alan Briceland puts the end result succinctly: "Antifederalists would have the time they needed, but the fight was to be on grounds advantageous to Federalists." Grigsby, *History of the Virginia Federal Convention,* 72; Pauline Maier, *Ratification: The People Debate the Constitution, 1787–1788* (New York: Simon & Schuster, 2010), 259; Alan V. Briceland, "Virginia: The Cement of the Union," in *The Constitution and the States,* ed. Patrick T. Conley and John P. Kaminski (Madison, WI: Madison House, 1988), 214.

16. DHRC 10:1620.

17. DHRC 9:917. Briceland suggests that "Henry must have sensed that the power of Pendleton's logic had crushed any doubts he had raised, for he thereupon withdrew the request and took his seat." This is implausible, as Henry further pursued the point unabashed. The more likely explanation is that Henry merely wanted to raise the issue of what the Philadelphia Convention had been called to do; the delegates knew very well what was in those documents without hearing them read. Briceland, "Virginia," 215.

18. DHRC 9:1072.

19. Richard Beeman sees the wide range of Henry's objection as a weakness for the Anti-Federalists. "If Henry had focused his attacks on just a few themes," Beeman writes, "then perhaps his efforts at winning delegates to his side might have been more successful. He failed to do that, however, and instead wasted his oratory, and tried the patience of his audience, on too many indiscriminate, scattershot attacks on nearly every specific provision of the proposed Constitution." I do not find this entirely persuasive, but there is an element of truth to it. Richard R. Beeman, *Patrick Henry: A Biography* (New York: McGraw-Hill, 1974), 159.

20. DHRC 9:936, 939.

21. DHRC 9:963, 964, 952, 959.

22. DHRC 9:952.

23. DHRC 9:965, 954.

24. DHRC 9:1168, 1169.

25. DHRC 9:1036, 1046–1047, 1070, 956; 10:1190.

26. DHRC 9:1066.

27. DHRC 9:1045, 1055, 1170.

28. DHRC 9:1065, 1271.

29. DHRC 10:1277.

30. DHRC 10:1275.

31. DHRC 10:1282, 1284.

32. DHRC 10:1322.

33. DHRC 9:1108–1109.

34. DHRC 9:1111.
35. DHRC 9:1068, 1041.
36. DHRC 9:1062–1063, 1064, 1066–1067.
37. DHRC 9:1112.
38. DHRC 9:1157.
39. DHRC 9:1158.
40. DHRC 9:1155.
41. DHRC 10:1328.
42. DHRC 10:1329.
43. DHRC 10:1345, 1346, 1331, 1347.
44. DHRC 10:1333, 1353.
45. DHRC 9:1072–1073.
46. DHRC 9:932, 933.
47. Faber, "Federal Union Paradigm," 541–546.
48. DHRC 9:1573, 1574, 1618, 1587–1588, 1573.
49. DHRC 9:951, 966, 960, 953.
50. DHRC 9:1058, 1162. Forrest McDonald alleges, by implication, that Randolph was persuaded by unethical means, including bribery and the offer of a position in the new government. He offers nothing but circumstantial evidence, however, and this is not consistent with Randolph's character. Forrest McDonald, *E Pluribus Unum: The Formation of the American Republic, 1776–1790* (Boston: Houghton Mifflin, 1965), 339–340.
51. DHRC 9:1055.
52. DHRC 9:1050.
53. DHRC 9:1081–1082. Grigsby states in no uncertain terms that Randolph was out of line. "Parliamentary decency" does not restrict a delegate from calling out another for inconsistency in political positions, and Henry's attack was not personal. (That it was inconsistent with friendship may well have been true, of course.) Meanwhile Randolph responded with threats that appeared to be much more personal in nature, which was a breach of decorum. Grigsby, *History of the Virginia Federal Convention,* 163–165.
54. DHRC 9:1159. Henry Lee, perhaps born without a sense of humor, criticized Mason for his levity: "He has endeavored to draw our attention from the merits of the question by jocose observations and satirical allusions. He ought to know that ridicule is not the test of truth. Does he imagine that he who can raise the loudest laugh is the soundest reasoner? Sir, the judgments, and not the risibility, of gentlemen, are to be consulted." We may only speculate what he might have thought about Grayson's comments, immediately following his statement. DHRC 9:1163.
55. DHRC 9:1167.
56. Grigsby, *History of the Virginia Federal Convention,* 201–202. Grayson may well have possessed the sharpest wit of the convention, no small feat with the sharp tongues of Henry, Mason, and others. Grigsby offers another example. Grayson was consistently engaged in correcting the generally poor Latin pronunciation of the Federalists. "He was not surprised, he is reported to have said, that men who were, in his opinion, about to vote away the freedom of a living people, should take such liberties with a dead tongue." Grigsby, *History of the Virginia Federal Convention,* 202.

57. DHRC 9:1168.
58. DHRC 9:1057, 1037, 1052, 1053, 1070.
59. DHRC 10:1328.
60. DHRC 10:1353.
61. DHRC 9:1171; 10:1184, 1186, 1185, 1192.
62. DHRC 10:1235, 1253, 1245.
63. DHRC 10:1247.
64. DHRC 10:1622, 1619, 1621, 1636, 1660.
65. DHRC 10:1338, 1341, 1344.
66. DHRC 10:1355, 1356.
67. DHRC 10:1371, 1375.
68. DHRC 10:1381, 1367.
69. DHRC 10:1374, 1394, 1390.
70. DHRC 10:1401, 1419, 1420, 1446.
71. DHRC 10:1424.
72. DHRC 10:1421, 1466, 1469, 1452, 1467.

CHAPTER 13: ANTI-FEDERALISTS OF NEW YORK

1. DHRC 20:1119, 2349.
2. DHRC 21:1202.
3. DHRC 21:1206–1207.
4. DHRC 21:1230.
5. DHRC 22:1798; 23:2357.
6. DHRC 21:1202.
7. DHRC 21:1202, 1264–1265, 1306, 1315, 1278.
8. DHRC 21:1240, 1320, 1339–1340; 20:1095–1096; 23:2371; Theophilus Parsons, "The Old Conviction Versus the New Realities: New York Antifederalist Leaders and the Radical Whig Tradition" (PhD diss., Columbia University, 1974), 464; Linda Grant DePauw, *The Eleventh Pillar: New York State and the Federal Constitution* (Ithaca, NY: Cornell University Press, 1966), 233–236.
9. DHRC 20:972–973, 1115, 1097.
10. DHRC 21:1298, 1224.
11. DHRC 22:1705.
12. DHRC 22:1712, 1737.
13. DHRC 22:1785, 1786, 1793.
14. DHRC 22:1713.
15. DHRC 22:1837, 1748–1755, 1754, 1759.
16. DHRC 22:1810, 1812, 1819, 1821; Saul Cornell, "Politics of the Middling Sort: The Bourgeois Radicalism of Abraham Yates, Melancton Smith, and the New York Antifederalists," in *New York in the Age of the Constitution 1775–1800*, ed. Paul A. Gilje and William Pencak (Madison, NJ: Fairleigh Dickinson University Press, 1992), 166.
17. DHRC 22:1825.
18. DHRC 22:1795; DePauw, *Eleventh Pillar*, 191.

19. DHRC 22:1717, 1910. Smith opened himself to an easy but effective shot by James Duane here. Duane suggested that the people of New York must oppose Smith's proposed requirement that a Representative must be a resident of his district. "Otherwise," he asked, "why go to New York for Members to represent Counties?" Clinton and Smith, both residents of the city of New York, represented Ulster and Dutchess counties, respectively, because they stood little chance of election from New York. DHRC 22:1915.

20. DHRC 22:1841, 1879.

21. DHRC 22:1919, 1922, 1973, 2065.

22. DHRC 22:2075, 2089.

23. DHRC 22:1935, 1936, 2032.

24. DHRC 22:2051.

25. DHRC 22:2103, 2107.

CHAPTER 14: THE CONSTITUTION RATIFIED

1. Lynn Warren Turner, *The Ninth State: New Hampshire's Formative Years* (Chapel Hill: University of North Carolina Press, 1983), 78; Lawrence Guy Straus, "Reactions of Supporters of the Constitution to the Adjournment of the New Hampshire Ratification Convention—1788," *Historical New Hampshire* 23, no. 3 (Autumn 1968): 41.

2. Straus, "Reactions of Supporters," 42.

3. Forrest McDonald, *E Pluribus Unum: The Formation of the American Republic, 1776–1790* (Boston: Houghton Mifflin, 1965), 350. "The enemies of the Constitution have been indefatigable in disseminating their opinions, personally, among the interior inhabitants of this State," wrote Tobias Lear. He claimed that had the Anti-Federalists simply played on the fears of the farmers and insisted that New Hampshire would have been harmed by the document, rather than focusing on more abstract threats to the liberties of the people, they might have obtained a different outcome, but they stood on principle rather than descend to fear. This claim is doubtful, but it portrays the opposition as principled and genuinely concerned about the rights of the people. Coming from Lear, a friend of the Constitution, this was substantial praise. Nancy Elaine Briggs Oliver, "Keystone of the Federal Arch: New Hampshire's Ratification of the United States' Constitution" (PhD diss., University of California, Santa Barbara, 1972), 82.

4. Jere Daniell, "Counting Noses: Delegate Sentiment in New Hampshire's Ratifying Convention," *Historical New Hampshire* 43, no. 2 (Summer 1988): 153. The new delegates included one who actually lived in a town other than that which he allegedly represented, who was never even elected by his supposed constituents. The Federalists were clearly willing to take any measure to carry the Constitution. Pauline Maier, *Ratification: The People Debate the Constitution, 1787–1788* (New York: Simon & Schuster, 2010), 314–315.

5. Albert Stillman Batchellor, *A Brief View of the Influences That Moved in the Adoption of the Federal Constitution by the State of New Hampshire* (Concord: Rumford Press, 1900), 29; Daniell, "Counting Noses," 139.

6. *New Hampshire Spy*, June 21, 1788.

7. Jere Daniell offers an excellent discussion of the breakdown of votes. He explains that the Federalists believed they had a majority of one, but with three supposedly Anti-Federalist delegates supporting ratification, and four more declining to vote either way, the margin became ten. The Federalists had miscounted the number of delegates in the room, so it was fortunate that this unexpected help showed up; they had only fifty-four definite votes out of 108 delegates, not 107 as they believed were present, and so would have fallen one vote short of victory. It is worth noting here that none of the members whose instructions are known to historians voted against the wishes of their constituents, though a few managed to avoid voting on the Constitution altogether. Daniell, "Counting Noses."

8. *New Hampshire Recorder*, June 24, 1788; DHRC 18:52.

9. F. Claiborne Johnston, Jr., "Federalist, Doubtful, and Antifederalist: A Note on the Virginia Convention of 1788," *Virginia Magazine of History and Biography* 96, no. 3 (July 1988): 334; DHRC 10:1670, 1655.

10. DHRC 10:1425.

11. DHRC 10:1537–1538, 1474.

12. DHRC 10:1476–1477.

13. DHRC 10:1478–1479, 1481.

14. DHRC 10:1482, 1623, 1624, 1625, 1628.

15. DHRC 10:1489, 1490, 1491, 1495.

16. DHRC 10:1497, 1498.

17. DHRC 10:1501, 1505.

18. DHRC 10:1506.

19. DHRC 10:1511.

20. Hugh Blair Grigsby, *The History of the Virginia Federal Convention of 1788* (Richmond: Virginia Historical Society, 1890), 317; DHRC 10:1512.

21. Grigsby, *History of the Virginia Federal Convention*, 320; DHRC 10:1516, 1517, 1518.

22. Grigsby, *History of the Virginia Federal Convention*, 336; DHRC 10:1526, 1528.

23. DHRC 10:1536, 1537. George Mason tried to organize a postconvention opposition, and called a meeting of the Anti-Federalist delegates for this purpose. The meeting did not produce either a strategy for opposition or a dissenting document like those published in Pennsylvania and Maryland. According to various accounts, it was either Patrick Henry or Benjamin Harrison who defused the angry delegates and derailed any effort at continued opposition. Mason remained resistant, but he had no intention of continuing a public opposition alone. DHRC 10:1560–1562.

24. DHRC 10:1677, 1699.

25. DHRC 10:1553–1554.

26. DHRC 10:1556.

27. The full text of the bill of rights and amendments can be found in the DHRC and Elliot's *Debates*. DHRC 10:1551–1556; *Debates* 3:657–661.

28. DHRC 10:1677, 1704, 1701, 1691–1693.

29. Johnston gave a substantial and powerful speech in favor of the Constitution on June 25 that might have swayed a few wavering moderates. William Nelson reported to William Short that "Z Johnson surprised every body, altho' every body

knew him to be very sensible & clear-headed. Indeed, I heard a man of judgement declare, that Johnson's speech was the best which was delivered in the convention" (DHRC 10:1702). Given the quality of the debates in the convention, this is both high praise and substantial hyperbole. Nonetheless, it was an effective speech.

30. DHRC 10:1631, 1632, 1652, 1675. Grigsby claims that "at least ten members voted, either in disobedience of the positive instructions of their constituents, or in defiance of their well-known opinions." He adds in a footnote, by way of explanation: "Sympathizing as I do with the views of Henry, Mason, &c., who opposed the Constitution, it might appear invidious to give the names of those who voted as charged in the text." This might have been reversed: "The vote on striking out the first resolution, and inserting the amendment in its stead, was the test vote, and lost by eight votes. A change, therefore, of four of the votes of the majority would have made a tie, and a single additional vote would have settled the fate of the Constitution for that time. Had Moore and McKee obeyed their instructions, and had Stuart, of Augusta, remained at home at the time of the Botetourt election, instead of using his influence effectually on the ground in favor of the Constitution, and of causing the Botetourt candidates to pledge themselves to sustain that system, and had Paul Carrington voted with his colleague, Read, in favor of it, those five votes would have been forthcoming. That some of the delegates voted in opposition to the wishes of their constituents was well known at the time." The Botetourt delegates, who voted in favor of the Constitution, were William Fleming and Martin McFerran. Moore and McKee represented Rockbridge County. Judge Carrington was initially opposed to the Constitution. Adding Edmund Randolph and Zachariah Johnston to these five makes seven of the ten. Three Kentucky delegates, Robert Breckenridge and Rice Bullock of Jefferson County and Humphrey Marshall of Fayette County, supported ratification; these may have been Grigsby's final three. A switch of all ten delegates for the vote on conditional amendments would have given the opposition a decisive 90–78 victory, and any five would have secured the object. Undoubtedly, there were more Federalist delegates with serious reservations as well. Grigsby, *The History of the Virginia Federal Convention*, 41–42, 346–347n265.

31. DHRC 22:1899, 1902, 1903, 1911, 1912.

32. DHRC 21:1261, 22:2024.

33. DHRC 22:1975; 23:2371; 22:2084.

34. DHRC 22:2128.

35. DHRC 22:2143–2144, 2146.

36. DHRC 23:2202.

37. DHRC 23:2212. One interesting exception was an amendment calling for an advisory council for the President, an idea supported by both Melancton Smith and John Lansing, but opposed by forty-six of the fifty-six delegates voting. DHRC 23:2267.

38. DHRC 23:2375, 2283; John P. Kaminski, *George Clinton: Yeoman Politician of the New Republic* (Madison, WI: Madison House, 1993), 164.

39. DHRC 23:2290, 2374.

40. DHRC 23:2324, 2335.

41. Cecil L. Eubanks, "New York: Federalism and the Political Economy of Union," in *Ratifying the Constitution*, ed. Michael Allen Gillespie and Michael Lienesch (Lawrence: University Press of Kansas, 1989), 329.

42. Gordon S. Wood, *The Making of the Constitution* (Waco: Baylor University Press, 1987), 35. I argue elsewhere that Smith, like Edmund Randolph and Samuel Adams before him, saw the choice as between ratification and disunion, and voted to ratify despite his objections. Michael J. Faber, "The Federal Union Paradigm of 1788: Three Anti-Federalists Who Changed Their Minds," *American Political Thought* 4, no. 4 (Fall 2015): 541–546.

43. Theophilus Parsons, "The Old Conviction Versus the New Realities: New York Antifederalist Leaders and the Radical Whig Tradition" (PhD diss., Columbia University, 1974), 371–372, 355, 377.

44. DHRC 23:2455, 2433, 2176; 21:1330; 23:2176, 2445.

45. DHRC 23:2408. Isaac Leake offers an extensive account of the attack on Greenleaf's house and office. Isaac Q. Leake, *Memoir of the Life and Times of General John Lamb* (Albany: Joel Munsell, 1850), 332–334.

46. Leake, *Memoir of the Life*, 334–336.

47. DHRC 23:2411.

CHAPTER 15: RECONCILIATION AND RESISTANCE

1. DHRC 7:1762.

2. DHRC 7:1757.

3. DHRC 10:1596; 18:5–6.

4. *New York Journal*, April 23, 1788. This essay originally appeared in the *Wilmington Centinel*, but that original issue is not extant. It was reprinted in the *New York Journal*, cited here.

5. Louise Irby Trenholme, *The Ratification of the Federal Constitution in North Carolina* (New York: Columbia University Press, 1932), 107. Trenholme offers an excellent discussion of these issues, and North Carolina's particular spin on them, closing with the comment that, here as elsewhere, the chief question was not whether amendments should be made, but whether they should be prior to or after ratification. Trenholme, *Ratification of the Federal Constitution*, 138–145.

6. *North Carolina Gazette*, December 19, 1787.

7. *New York Journal*, April 21, 1788. This essay originally appeared in the *Wilmington Centinel*, but that original issue is not extant. It was reprinted in the *New York Journal*, cited here.

8. *Wilmington Centinel*, June 18, 1788, June 25, 1788, July 16, 1788.

9. Norman K. Risjord, *Chesapeake Politics, 1781–1800* (New York: Columbia University Press, 1978), 318; Trenholme, *Ratification of the Federal Constitution*, 109. The signer of the Declaration, William Hooper, not only lost the election in Orange County, but lost a fight with an Anti-Federalist and ended up with a couple of black eyes. Trenholme, *Ratification of the Federal Constitution*, 102.

10. Trenholme, *Ratification of the Federal Constitution*, 150–152, 129.

11. Griffith John McRee, *Life and Correspondence of James Iredell* (New York: D. Appleton, 1858), 2:232.

12. SRNC 20:611. Blackwell Pierce Robinson notes that Jones did not oppose the Convention or sending delegates, but that he probably declined "because he felt that he could do far more good at home in exerting his influence in the interests of state

sovereignty." He probably thought that Governor Caswell would appoint someone similar in his place. North Carolina's actual delegation to Philadelphia did not reflect Jones's preferred political position at all. As Albert Newsome writes, "not one of the five [delegates from North Carolina] represented in his background, social and economic status, opinions, or interests of the small-farmer majority of the State's population." Robinson suggests that Alexander Martin was closest to Jones's position. Blackwell Pierce Robinson, "Willie Jones of Halifax, Part II," *North Carolina Historical Review* 18, no. 2 (April 1941): 148; Albert Ray Newsome, "North Carolina's Ratification of the Federal Constitution," *North Carolina Historical Review* 17, no. 4 (October 1940): 288.

13. Robinson, "Willie Jones of Halifax," 148. Davie wrote to Iredell in January 1788 that "Mr. Jones continues perfectly anti-federal; and is inducing the people here to doubt, very generally, of [the Constitution's] adoption in the present form." In another letter later that month, he added that "Mr. Jones continues to assail the constitution. . . . You know his opinion has great weight here, and that it is much easier to alarm people than to inform them." McRee, *Life and Correspondence of James Iredell*, 2:215, 217.

14. *Debates* 4:4.

15. *Debates* 4:15, 24.

16. *Debates* 4:43, 37. Taylor responded to Maclaine's rhetoric with biting sarcasm. "If we are not of equal ability with the gentleman," he said, "he ought to possess charity towards us, and not lavish such severe reflections upon us in such a declamatory manner." Timothy Bloodworth was just as amused. "I confess I am obliged to the honorable gentleman for his construction" of the impeachment clauses, he said sardonically. "Were he to go to Congress, he might put that construction on the Constitution." The Anti-Federalists would have some fun at Maclaine's expense, as that delegate was often pushing the limits of decorum. *Debates* 4:46, 50.

17. *Debates* 4:62.

18. *Debates* 4:29–30.

19. *Debates* 4:50, 51, 57.

20. *Debates* 4:80, 87.

21. *Debates* 4:101.

22. *Debates* 4:102–103.

23. *Debates* 4:124.

24. *Debates* 4:131–132.

25. *Debates* 4:137.

26. *Debates* 4:164.

27. *Debates* 4:179, 188, 199, 212.

28. *Debates* 4:36, 55, 56, 152, 168, 170.

29. *Debates* 4:201.

30. *Debates* 4:210, 218, 221.

31. *Debates* 4:223, 225, 239.

32. McRee, *Life and Correspondence of James Iredell*, 2:234; *Debates* 4:227.

33. *Debates* 4:228, 247.

34. *Debates* 4:241.

35. The full text of the bill of rights and proposed amendments can be found in the DHRC and Elliot's *Debates*. DHRC 28:314–320; *Debates* 4:242–247.

36. *Wilmington Centinel*, September 17, 1788.

37. DHRC 18:60.

38. John Bach McMaster and Frederick D. Stone, eds., *Pennsylvania and the Federal Constitution, 1787–1788* (Lancaster: Historical Society of Pennsylvania, 1888), 552.

39. DHFFE 1:240.

40. Gallatin wrote "violent" above the line here, apparently as a potential alternative to "dangerous."

41. DHFFE 1:250; Paul Leicester Ford, *The Origin, Purpose and Result of the Harrisburg Convention of 1788* (Brooklyn, 1890); DHFFE 1:259, 260.

42. DHFFE 1:262.

43. Samuel Miles, writing on behalf of a committee of concerned Federalists, notes that the meeting gave "serious alarm" to the supporters of the Constitution. "A Federal Centinel" suggested that the delegates to the convention, despite the publication of their proceedings, were conspiring against the new government. "A Freeman" echoes this sentiment, and several other essays were published to discredit the Harrisburg Convention as well. A more reasoned response was offered by Richard Peters in a letter to Washington: "In short their convention was a mere election job and no harm is to be expected from it except they get into the government which in the whole cannot be prevented. When they have got warm in their seats they will, as it always happens in such cases, find it in their interest to support a government in which they are sharers." DHFFE 1:270, 267–269, 271, 273, 275.

44. DHFFE 1:406.

45. Steven Boyd suggests that the Anti-Federalists had given up the opportunity for radical action far earlier in the debate, when they implicitly accepted the Federalists' framework for how the debate would take place and how the Constitution would be adopted. This made it difficult for Anti-Federalists of a less extreme type to dispute an outcome that was achieved through a democratic process that they had already accepted as legitimate. Steven R. Boyd, "Antifederalists and the Acceptance of the Constitution: Pennsylvania 1787–1792," *Publius* 9, no. 2 (Spring 1979): 123–137.

CHAPTER 16: ELECTIONS AND AMENDMENTS

1. Pauline Maier, *Ratification: The People Debate the Constitution, 1787–1788* (New York: Simon & Schuster, 2010), 432.

2. DHRC 23:2454, 2456; DHFFE 1:46; CBR 222; DHRC 23:2497, 2510.

3. DHFFE 1:88, 96, 118.

4. James Wadsworth, the most vocal critic of the Constitution in Connecticut, was a member of the legislature, and had several allies with him; yet, according to Jonathan Trumbell, Jr., "no one had hardiness enough to call up the consideration of that Letter, or to mention one word of its subject—Thus passed, in silent review, that formidable communication." DHFFE 2:27.

5. DHRC 23:2508–2509.

6. DHFFE 1:109–110.

7. The election results do not fully capture the political dynamic in Virginia, however. James Madison was elected after running a campaign in which his central

promise was to work toward amendments, and he was not alone in taking such a stance. As Richard Beeman observes, "Madison's shift was part of a trend that affected nearly all Virginia's representatives in the nation's capital. Within the next few years most of Virginia's Federalist congressmen would moderate their positions in an attempt to court powerful political groups within Virginia committed to preserving their tradition of local, decentralized government." This is not to say that the Federalists became Anti-Federalists, only that there was some Anti-Federalist influence beyond the few seats that they won. Richard R. Beeman, *The Old Dominion and the New Nation, 1788–1801* (Lexington: University Press of Kentucky, 1972), 27–28.

8. DHFFE 2:82.

9. DHFFE 4:466.

10. Charles F. Hobson and Robert A. Rutland, eds., *The Papers of James Madison, Congressional Series* (Charlottesville: University Press of Virginia, 1962–1979), 11:212; CBR 225.

11. It should not be a surprise that Washington's Inaugural Address included such a paragraph, as it was Madison who wrote most of the Address. Washington merely approved the inclusion of the sentiment, and thus lent his prestige to the idea. Incidentally, Madison also wrote the House's official response to the Inaugural Address, as well as Washington's reply to that response. Ralph Ketcham, *James Madison: A Biography* (New York: Macmillan, 1971), 283–284.

12. CBR 70, 65, 245, 259, 73.

13. CBR 281–282. Congress seems to have been very sensitive to the requests of North Carolina. "It is supposed," read a letter printed in the *Fayetteville Gazette* in September 1789, "that the critical situation of your state, had much weight with some of the members . . . and the members in general say, that they are heartily willing to remove any fair scruple of North-Carolina, when her sentiments are so moderate and becoming." One is tempted to wonder what inducements might have been offered to Virginia or New York, had either state held out. Rhode Island, on the other hand, apparently received no such consideration. *Fayetteville Gazette*, September 14, 1789.

14. CBR 289.

15. CBR 255, 263.

16. CBR 232, 246, 271, 292.

17. CBR 175, 259.

18. CBR 210.

19. CBR 294.

20. CBR 292.

21. In 1790, upon the death of Senator William Grayson, Governor Beverley Randolph of Virginia offered Mason Grayson's Senate seat. His response was characteristically cantankerous; he declined, citing "my present State of Health (if I had no other Objection) rendering me unable to discharge the Duties of the Office." Undoubtedly, Mason still had other objections, and it seems likely they were based on political principle. Still, he wrote to Jefferson in 1791 that Madison "is one of the few Men . . . I really esteem," but he was worried that the disagreement over the Constitution "had caused a Coolness between us." Jefferson wrote back to assure him that Madison had no hard feelings. Robert A. Rutland, ed., *The Papers of George Mason, 1725–1792* (Chapel Hill: University of North Carolina Press, 1970),

3:1192, 1218, 1224; Robert A. Rutland, "George Mason's 'Objections' and the Bill of Rights." *This Constitution* 18 (Spring/Summer 1988): 13.

22. CBR 300, 294, 296, 297.

23. The debate to ratify the amendments was not much of a debate. "The Antifederal leviathan had submerged," writes Bowling, "and no new, unified opposition had replaced it." In eight states there was little resistance, though in two of these (Connecticut and Georgia) the amendments were not ratified. In Massachusetts an effort to add additional amendments resulted in deadlock that prevented ratification. The New York Anti-Federalists were upset, but they had lost their majorities in both houses of the state legislature so they could do little. North Carolina and Rhode Island both ratified the Constitution after the amendments were proposed, and quickly thereafter ratified most of the amendments. When Vermont joined the union in 1791, it increased the minimum number of states necessary to secure amendments, but the state approved all twelve. Only in Virginia was there a serious and contentious debate; the Anti-Federalists were quite insistent that the tax power of Congress be restricted, but in the end the legislature approved most of the amendments, becoming the eleventh state necessary for ten of the amendments to be added to the Constitution. Kenneth R. Bowling, "'A Tub to the Whale': The Founding Fathers and Adoption of the Federal Bill of Rights," *Journal of the Early Republic* 8, no. 3 (Autumn 1988): 247.

24. CBR 289, 298–299.

25. DHFFE 4:321.

26. CBR 295.

27. David J. Siemers, *Ratifying the Republic: Antifederalists and Federalists in Constitutional Time* (Stanford: Stanford University Press, 2002), 198. Despite the fact that the amendments barely addressed any Anti-Federalist concerns, the opponents of ratification still get lots of credit from scholars. Woody Holton's assertion that we have the Anti-Federalists to thank for securing our rights is typical: the Anti-Federalists, he insists, "were the ones who extracted from the Federalists the strategic concessions we call the Bill of Rights." But it was the Federalists that decided what rights would be protected, and how. William Riker suggests that this was because by emphasizing the importance of a bill of rights, the Anti-Federalists prevented themselves from effectively making the case for structural alterations. Woody Holton, *Unruly Americans and the Origins of the Constitution* (New York: Hill and Wang, 2008), xi; William H. Riker, *The Strategy of Rhetoric: Campaigning for the American Constitution* (New Haven: Yale University Press, 1996), 241–249.

CHAPTER 17: THE LAST RESISTANCE AND THE COMPLETION OF THE UNION

1. The *Gazette* was conceived as a national newspaper, centered on the proceedings of the new federal government. In its first issue, the printer, John Fenno, proclaimed it to be "established upon NATIONAL, INDEPENDENT, and IMPARTIAL PRINCIPLES"; its purpose was to report on Congress and on national issues and events. *Gazette of the United States*, April 15, 1789.

2. *Gazette of the United States*, April 15, 1789.

3. DHFFE 1:774.

4. DHFFE 1:244.

5. DHFFE 1:407, 406.

6. DHFFE 4:315–317.

7. DHRC 18:59; Louise Irby Trenholme, *The Ratification of the Federal Constitution in North Carolina* (New York: Columbia University Press, 1932), 204–205.

8. Hugh T. Lefler, ed., *A Plea for Federal Union: North Carolina, 1788* (Charlottesville: University of Virginia, 1947), 35.

9. Lefler, 46, 68, 47, 51. Judas was not the only, and perhaps not the worst, villain to whom the author compared Jones. Julius Caesar, Cain, Benedict Arnold, and even Satan himself were offered up as apt comparisons. He was also called an "accursed fiend" and a "monster of society," and the author wrote that "his ways are ways of wickedness, and all his paths are iniquity." The writer apparently did not think highly of Willie Jones. Lefler, 47–48, 53, 54, 48.

10. Charles Christopher Crittenden, *North Carolina Newspapers before 1790* (Chapel Hill: University of North Carolina Press, 1928), 68, 69.

11. Trenholme, *Ratification of the Federal Constitution*, 107.

12. *Fayetteville Gazette*, September 21, 1789.

13. Griffith John McRee, *Life and Correspondence of James Iredell* (New York: D. Appleton, 1858), 2:260; DHFFE 4:321; SRNC 21:522.

14. McRee, *Life and Correspondence*, 2:266; DHFFE 4:320.

15. SRNC 22:45.

16. SRNC 22:50. The final resolution is misprinted the first time the resolutions appear in *The State Records of North Carolina*, on pages 45–46. It is printed correctly after the ratification vote, when the resolutions were reintroduced by Galloway.

17. SRNC 22:51.

18. SRNC 22:52.

19. McRee, *Life and Correspondence*, 2:272.

20. DHFFE 4:325.

21. DHFFE 4:350.

22. DHRC 3:353–354; 24:219.

23. The editors of the *Documentary History of the First Federal Elections* estimate that 10 percent of the state debt had been paid with paper currency, and the remaining 90 percent repudiated. DHFFE 4:381.

24. DHRC 25:565.

25. DHFFE 4:387.

26. Irwin H. Polishook, *Rhode Island and the Union* (Evanston, IL: Northwestern University Press, 1969), 204.

27. DHRC 25:605.

28. DHRC 25:605–606.

29. DHRC 25:386–388, 399–400, 413–417.

30. RICC 628.

31. The true explanation for Williams's absence is not entirely clear. Whether he was actually at church cannot be verified. John Kaminski writes that he had simply left for home on Saturday, but this explanation is even more suspicious than the traditional one, since Williams must have known the business would again be raised

on Sunday. There are three plausible explanations. The first is that the Federalists merely took advantage of an absence they knew would occur; this is doubtful because the Anti-Federalists, with their majority, would undoubtedly have seen this coming and adjourned until Monday instead. The second is that Williams had a change of heart, and absented himself in order to allow the convention to be approved without the personal appearance of a reversal. This too seems unlikely, that he changed his mind in the course of a single day, though he may have felt the same on Saturday but had no excuse to miss the vote. The third and most plausible explanation is that the country party members were prepared to let a ratifying convention occur, but wanted to make sure that they did not appear to be changing their position. This is borne out by the party's decision to dump Governor Collins from its ticket in the next election, ostensibly as a consequence of his vote for a ratifying convention. They needed a scapegoat, and Collins was the man for that job. John P. Kaminski, "Rhode Island: Protecting State Interests," in *Ratifying the Constitution*, ed. Michael Allen Gillespie and Michael Lienesch (Lawrence: University Press of Kansas, 1989), 383; Polishook, *Rhode Island and the Union*, 212–213.

32. Polishook, *Rhode Island and the Union*, 213; DHRC 26:727–728, 744–747.

33. DHRC 26:734, 735.

34. DHRC 25:707.

35. RICC 634.

36. DHRC 25:704.

37. Two men sought the office of secretary: Daniel Updike, who won the position, recorded the official minutes and fragmentary notes of the debates, while Theodore Foster, the losing candidate, remained in the galleries to witness the debates and take notes of his own. Though both sets of notes are fragmentary, they agree on the general contours of the debate, and between them give us a fairly clear picture of the broad themes of the discussion.

38. DHRC 26:915.

39. DHRC 26:921.

40. DHRC 26:923, 925, 926, 929.

41. Hillman Metcalf Bishop, *Why Rhode Island Opposed the Federal Constitution* (Providence, RI: Roger Williams Press, 1950), 28.

42. DHRC 26:937, 938.

43. RIC 60n77.

44. DHRC 26:943, 945.

45. DHRC 26:979.

46. The requisition system proposed by Anti-Federalists in many of the states must have especially made sense to even the Federalists in Rhode Island, because the state used a similar system, and taxes had always remained light and reasonable. As Bishop explains, "The Legislature might apportion the taxes among the towns, but the actual assessment and the collection of the taxes were undertaken by the towns." Bishop, *Why Rhode Island Opposed*, 11.

47. DHRC 26:955.

48. DHRC 26:952.

49. RICC 656–657; DHRC 26:959, 961, 962, 965, 967.

50. Polishook, *Rhode Island and the Union*, 223; DHRC 26:772–773, 775.

51. DHRC 26:766, 768, 798.

52. There is no extant record of the debates. Foster apparently did not attend this session, and Updike recorded only an incomplete outline of the proceedings.

53. DHRC 26:830–836.

54. DHRC 26:889–890.

55. DHRC 26:988, 992.

56. Polishook, *Rhode Island and the Union*, 229; DHRC 26:887–888; Polishook, *Rhode Island and the Union*, 230.

57. Bishop, *Why Rhode Island Opposed*, 47.

58. Michael A. Bellesiles, "Anticipating America: Levi Allen and the Case for an Independent Vermont," in *A More Perfect Union: Vermont Becomes a State, 1777–1816*, ed. Michael Sherman (Montpelier: Vermont Historical Society, 1991), 93.

59. Bellesiles, 95; DHRC 29:199.

60. DHRC 29:207.

61. DHRC 29:207–208, 209.

62. DHRC 29:215, 216; Bellesiles, "Anticipating America," 97.

CHAPTER 18: AN ANTI-FEDERALIST CONSTITUTION

1. Murray Dry goes so far as to suggest that this is precisely why they lost the debate, that they failed to offer a convincing plan that was between the failed Articles of Confederation and the proposed Constitution. Murray Dry, "The Constitutional Thought of the Anti-Federalists," *This Constitution* 16 (Fall 1987): 14.

2. DHRC 9:769–779. The Political Club of Danville, Kentucky, made a similar effort, though they apparently only made it as far as Article III before abandoning the enterprise. DHRC 8:408–417.

3. Jack N. Rakove, *Original Meanings: Politics and Ideas in the Making of the Constitution* (New York: Alfred A. Knopf, 1996), 147.

4. CAF 2:363.

5. Cecilia M. Kenyon, ed., *The Antifederalists* (Indianapolis: Bobbs-Merrill, 1966), cxvi.

6. DHRC 27:107.

7. Agrippa does argue that no change is needed. CAF 4:76.

8. For a few examples: CAF 2:163–164; 3:67–68, 141–143, 112; 4:89–91; 5:174–175; DHRC 9:1108–1109; DHRC 27:155.

9. Pauline Maier, *Ratification: The People Debate the Constitution, 1787–1788* (New York: Simon & Schuster, 2010), 430; DHRC 27:346.

10. CAF 6:82.

11. CAF 2:224, 363–364.

12. Of course, there are exceptions. One would expect it to be difficult to win over An Officer of the Late Continental Army, who refers to "that political monster THE PROPOSED CONSTITUTION." On the other hand, William Findley, the most likely author, was reconciled to it, and served for years in the new federal Congress. Lowndes and Agrippa, who saw no danger in the Articles, were unlikely to come on board. The radical Democratic Anti-Federalists in some cases preferred no union at all to a national government of any strength. Centinel would have been a hard sell, as well as Patrick Henry, but both may well have approved it as the best attainable

option. Still, this group is but a small faction of the Anti-Federalists, and even most of the Federalists would likely find this constitution preferable to the Articles of Confederation. CAF 3:95.

13. DHRC 23:2555.

14. Wording from The Impartial Examiner. CAF 5:192.

15. Wording from the Rhode Island Convention.

16. Wording from the Rhode Island Convention.

17. Wording from Brutus. CAF 2:408.

18. Wording from Brutus. CAF 2:373.

19. CAF 3:157. The same argument can be found elsewhere. CAF 2:425; 4:178–179; 5:80; DHRC 2:407–408; DHRC 9:930, 951; *Debates* 4:24.

20. DHRC 2:447; CAF 2:364.

21. Dozens of essays made this claim, which was also made repeatedly in ratifying conventions. CAF 2:248–250, 372–377; 3:34–38, 84–85; 4:102–104, 120–122; 5:116–118, 246–251, 8–16; DHRC 2:203–205; 4:216–219; 8:150–151, 220.

22. DHRC 10:1331; CAF 5:135, 105.

23. CAF 5:273.

24. Wording suggested by the minority in Maryland. Similar provisions were proposed in New Hampshire, Virginia, North Carolina, and Rhode Island. See also CAF 2:262; 5:116; DHRC 26:939.

25. Similar provisions were proposed in Maryland, Virginia, North Carolina, and Rhode Island. See also CAF 2:143, 262; 3:102–106, 111–112; 5:116.

26. Wording taken from the Virginia Convention. Similar provisions were proposed by North Carolina and Rhode Island. See also CAF 2:262; 5:117.

27. This wording is adapted from the Virginia Convention. Similar provisions were proposed in Maryland, North Carolina, and Rhode Island. See also CAF 2:262; 5:117.

28. Wording taken from the New Hampshire Convention. The right to bear arms also appears in the recommendations of the conventions of Virginia, North Carolina, and Rhode Island, and in the recommendations of the Pennsylvania Minority.

29. This wording is adapted from the Federal Farmer. CAF 2:262.

30. Wording taken from the Virginia Convention. North Carolina and Rhode Island propose similar language.

31. This clause has been moved here from the old Article I, Section 9, because it belongs among the rights guaranteed in this article. A Georgian suggests habeas corpus "remain, without any exceptions whatever, inviolate forever." Most Anti-Federalists will allow for some exceptions, so it has been left as it was. CAF 5:133.

32. This wording is taken from the Ninth Amendment. Many Anti-Federalists wanted such a clause in the Bill of Rights, but none suggested adequate wording.

33. This answers Patrick Henry's objections in the Virginia Convention, as well as those of others. DHRC 10:1309–1310; CAF 2:58–60; 3:202–204; 6:62; DHRC 8:435; 22:2088–2089; DHFFE 1:263–264.

34. The Pennsylvania Minority demands a clause like this. CAF 3:151.

35. DHRC 8:506; *North Carolina Gazette*, December 19, 1787.

36. *Debates* 4:137; CAF 3:23; DHRC 10:1326; CAF 2:146–147, 169.

37. CAF 5:114; 4:27; 3:54; 5:205. It is worth noting that there was a group of Anti-Federalists on the other side, insisting on equal representation for states in both

houses. This was based on the presumption that any national government ought to be a confederation, and thus the states would be its constituents. Luther Martin was the most prominent advocate of this position. This position was no more popular than the extreme democratic one, though it did attract more prominent statesmen. CAF 2:35–37.

38. CAF 2:379.

39. Objections to the qualifications of Representatives were relatively rare and quite inconsistent. A Watchman believes that the age should be lower and the residency shorter, while a Republican Federalist objects that foreigners can become Representatives in only seven years. Samuel advocates religious and property requirements for all federal offices. A Bostonian suggests that judges (and perhaps lawyers but he is not entirely clear on this point) should be barred from holding office in Congress. In the end, no changes have been made, because few Anti-Federalists objected, and no consensus emerged among those who did object. CAF 4:232, 184–185, 193, 229–230.

40. The apportionment of direct taxes, when appropriate, is described in a new clause in Article II, Section 8.

41. Several Anti-Federalists argued against equal representation in the Senate. Brutus actually changes his mind, and defends equal representation. CAF 2:97, 118, 379; 4:29–30; 2:444.

42. A Federal Republican asks of the original three-class system how the classes will be determined, fearing that "the jealousy of the states may rouse the animosity of party division to such a pitch as to endanger the springs of government." Four-year Senate terms, divided into two classes of Senators, offer a simple solution to this problem as well. CAF 3:73.

43. The objections to the qualifications of Senators were similar to those for Representatives, and they were also rare.

44. The Vice Presidency has been eliminated in favor of a constitutional council. Richard Henry Lee suggested that the Senate might choose its own speaker to secure better separation of the legislative and executive branches. DHRC 13:239–240.

45. Several Anti-Federalists objected to holding trials for impeached executive officers in the Senate. This has not been changed, however, because the Senate no longer approves executive appointments, making the point moot. CAF 2:238; 6:19–20, 23–24; *City Gazette*, May 21, 1788.

46. Counting each vote equally was simply assumed by most Federalists and Anti-Federalists alike, but the ability given to Congress to alter the methods of elections was alarming to some. Patrick Henry in particular worries that voting may not be equal, but that it may be done by property or wealth. Thus the equality of all votes is made explicit here. DHRC 9:1070.

47. CAF 2:118–119; 3:94; 4:236–237; 6:62; 2:142; 4:140–141, 232; *New Hampshire Spy*, February 15, 1788; CAF 2:290–292; 3:94; *City Gazette*, May 19, 1788, May 20, 1788; CAF 2:291–292.

48. CAF 2:119, 380; 5:117; 6:131; 2:277–278; DHRC 22:1718; 6:1237; CAF 4:182–184; DHRC 9:939, 953; CAF 2:142, 383–385; 3:70–71; 5:89–90, 192–193; DHRC 22:1718. The conventions of Massachusetts, New Hampshire, Virginia, and North Carolina proposed similar plans.

49. DHRC 22:1750; CAF 2:386–387; 5:131–132; DHRC 22:1907.

50. CAF 2:444; DHRC 22:1837; CAF 2:288–289; 5:294; 6:62. A few Anti-Federalists insisted on annual elections even for the Senate, but this was not a mainstream position. CAF 4:140–141, 236–237.

51. CAF 5:86, 294; 3:188; 2:46–47, 289, 444–445; DHRC 10:1292; DHRC 22:1838, 1877–1878.

52. CAF 2:124–125, 140–141, 235–236, 386; 3:73–74, 151–152; 4:42–43, 102–104; 6:31, 137; DHRC 2:308, 448; DHRC 9:740; *Debates* 4:51.

53. The five states were Massachusetts, New Hampshire, Virginia, North Carolina, and Rhode Island. Such an amendment was proposed in Maryland, but did not receive sufficient support. See also CAF 4:199; DHRC 6:1214; DHRC 22:1904–1905; DHRC 24:921.

54. CAF 4:179.

55. Cornelius argues that this amounts to "a negative on elections in general," but there is no other logical place to lodge this power. CAF 4:142.

56. The conventions of Virginia and North Carolina, along with Randolph, suggest that some other venue be declared for the impeachment of Senators, but the power of state legislatures to recall them, coupled with expulsion by two-thirds, makes this unnecessary. CAF 2:97.

57. The Rhode Island Convention wanted this one-fifth requirement to be reduced to two members.

58. A Georgian suggests this idea that Representatives and Senators must answer to their constituents. It fits very well with the Anti-Federalist theory of representation. CAF 5:132.

59. Several Anti-Federalists propose making congressmen ineligible for any office, not just those created, or salary increases, during their time in office. The Federal Farmer suggests ineligibility during time in office and for a period afterward, but that suggestion was not made by anyone else, including the state conventions of Virginia and North Carolina, which formally proposed this change. CAF 2:52; 5:294–295; DHRC 22:1916; CAF 2:303–304.

60. William Grayson opposes any Senate involvement on money bills, or at least he opposes the power of the Senate to amend. The power to amend, he claims, is essentially the same as the power to originate. A Gentleman from Massachusetts points out that the English House of Lords cannot amend a revenue bill passed by the House of Commons. Nonetheless, with the House more accountable to the people and the Senate more accountable to the states, the advantages of having a piece of legislation go through both houses of Congress outweigh the dangers of the Senate's involvement in revenue bills. DHRC 10:1267; CAF 4:10.

61. The Impartial Examiner argues that the presidential veto will generally be final. "For as a law, which has been once disapproved by the president, cannot be repassed without the agreement of *two-thirds* of *both houses*, there can be no doubt, it will frequently happen that this concurrence of *two thirds* cannot be obtained. The law must then fall." This does not necessarily mean that this power needs to be changed, and it has not been. CAF 5:196.

62. CAF 2:338.

63. Virginia, North Carolina, and Rhode Island all suggest that the journals should be published annually and that secrecy should only be allowed for "treaties, alliances, or military operations," as allowed in the Articles.

64. DHRC 9:1067; 22:1952.

65. CAF 2:97; 4:238; 5:86; 2:286, 46; 5:132; DHRC 6:1283–1284; 27:127; 3:494.

66. CAF 3:172–173.

67. CAF 2:12–13; 97; 5:97, 115.

68. *Debates* 4:56; DHRC 9:1111; 22:1705; 6:1226.

69. CAF 3:186.

70. CAF 2:239.

71. Agrippa argued that "though most of the states may be willing for certain reasons to receive foreigners as citizens, yet reasons of equal weight may induce other states, differently circumstanced, to keep their blood pure." This argument is decidedly xenophobic, but it does speak to state powers. Most Anti-Federalists would likely have endorsed the Federal Farmer's position, and given this authority to Congress, as it is given in the section below. CAF 4:85–86.

72. CAF 2:384.

73. Brutus warns that the members of Congress "are the sole judges of what is necessary to provide for the common defence, and they only are to determine what is for the general welfare." He explains that the power to tax, as originally included, "is neither more nor less, than a power to lay and collect taxes, imposts, and excises, at their pleasure." Centinel is more extreme, claiming that "The Congress may construe every purpose for which the state legislatures now lay taxes, to be for the general welfare, and thereby seize upon every object of revenue." As William Symmes puts it, "A more general dedition or surrender of all ye property in the United States to Congress could not perhaps have been framed." Limiting taxes to raising money for enumerated powers, coupled with the removal of the Necessary and Proper Clause later in this section, prevents such abuse. CAF 2:366, 140; 4:57.

74. Cato Uticensis suggests this measure, and it is certainly in the spirit of Anti-Federalist objections to national government reaching directly into states. Luther Martin also expresses a preference for local tax collectors. CAF 5:123; 2:55.

75. This language is taken from the Articles of Confederation, slightly modified to include property other than land and buildings.

76. Brutus is especially concerned about the ability of Congress to accumulate debt: "By this means, they may create a national debt, so large, as to exceed the ability of the country ever to sink. I can scarcely contemplate a greater calamity that could befal this country, than to be loaded with a debt exceeding their ability ever to discharge. If this be a just remark, it is unwise and improvident to vest in the general government a power to borrow at discretion, without any limitation or restriction." Brutus suggests that borrowing should require the approval of two-thirds of states, but a two-thirds vote in Congress, suggested by the conventions of New York and Rhode Island, is more practical when deficit spending becomes necessary in a crisis. CAF 2:405.

77. A particularly prescient anonymous writer in Massachusetts argues that Congress will claim the power to regulate commerce within the states as well. The word "between" is more precise than "among," which might be interpreted to allow for internal regulations as well. CAF 4:6.

78. Sydney objects to Congress being granted this power, insisting that the state of New York always has and ought to continue to negotiate directly. Still, the Federal

Farmer and other more moderate Anti-Federalists see this as properly part of foreign affairs, and thus a national power. CAF 6:110–112.

79. Agrippa objected to this, as discussed above, but this was not common. CAF 4:85–86.

80. Considering the significance of Shays's Rebellion in the calling of the Convention, there is very little said about Congress's power to write bankruptcy laws. The Federal Farmer: "If uniform bankrupt laws can be made without producing real and substantial inconveniences, I wish them to be made by congress." He later changes his mind. Still, the absence of objections in the Anti-Federalist literature suggests that the Anti-Federalists had Shays in mind as well. CAF 2:243, 343–344.

81. This was requested by the convention of New York, and since it reinforces state sovereignty without seriously impairing national power, it would likely be approved by most Anti-Federalists.

82. The two-thirds vote was proposed by the conventions of New York and Rhode Island.

83. Several Anti-Federalists pointed out that in England, annual appropriations are required. This change does not answer the objection of William Symmes that Congress can simply renew allocations indefinitely, but a limit would be impracticable, and unnecessary with proper representation secured. CAF 2:118; 3:75–76; 4:58.

84. The four-year limit was proposed by the ratifying conventions in Maryland, Virginia, and North Carolina.

85. William Grayson contends that the United States needs no navy, but most Anti-Federalists acknowledge the need to build one eventually, if not immediately. The Federal Farmer suggests that the power to raise a navy properly belongs with Congress, because it cannot rest anywhere else. DHRC 10:1314–1316; CAF 2:342.

86. A Georgian suggests five miles square: "a larger extent might be made a nursery out of which legions may be dragged to subject us to unlimited slavery, like antient Rome." The exact size probably makes little difference, but the reduction of the size is symbolic of the general distrust of this clause. This is a small change that would have likely met the approbation of most of the Anti-Federalists. CAF 5:133.

87. Both Virginia and North Carolina requested that the powers of Congress over the capital be limited to police powers and government. New York went further, demanding other specific restrictions, but those demands are largely answered in this change and others throughout this constitution.

88. DHRC 9:936; CAF 5:123; *Debates* 4:88; DHRC 9:783.

89. CAF 2:240, 365–366, 391–393; 3:41, 186–187; 5:75–76, 121–122, 132, 181; 4:199; 5:132; 6:131.

90. DHRC 10:1492.

91. The states were Massachusetts, New Hampshire, Virginia, North Carolina, and Rhode Island; the Maryland Minority also sought such an amendment. In addition, many opposition writers proposed similar plans. Samuel Chase was one of the few Anti-Federalists to oppose resorting to requisitions; he wanted to give Congress the power to directly tax in limited ways. He suggested imposts first, then export duties, plus stamp and post office fees, and then, if necessary, excise taxes. If all of those should fall short on revenue, he suggested a direct tax on land. An Old Whig also opposed this requisition plan, but for different reasons. He suggested

that the government should "try at least how far the customs and back lands would go" before granting direct taxation, if it becomes necessary. After all, "Men do not usually give up their whole purse where they can pay with part." These positions, though, would clearly be overruled by the number of Anti-Federalists who favored requisitions backed by direct taxation. CAF 2:55–56; 5:180–181; DHRC 2:308; 10:1185–1186; 22:1919, 1925; CAF 5:83–84; 3:41.

92. *Debates* 4:81; DHRC 9:940; CAF 2:337.

93. CAF 3:152; DHRC 9:957–958; CAF 4:36–37.

94. CAF 2:370, 406–417, 416, 58, 118; 4:39–40; 5:28, 116; DHRC 3:428.

95. CAF 2:344–348; DHRC 10:1317; 9:782, 783. A few Anti-Federalists clearly opposed Congress having any authority at all over a federal capital. "A territorial legislation over the district where Congress reside ought not to be granted to them," wrote an Anti-Federalist in North Carolina. "If such a sovereignty is given to them, over the smallest extent of territory, they will easily find the mean of removing the boundaries of their dominions." He extended his argument to the erection of forts and other buildings mentioned at the end of the clause as well; he was prepared to give Congress control over no land at all. This is much more extreme than most of his colleagues, which suggests that the compromise here reflects a moderate opposition position. *North Carolina Gazette*, December 12, 1787.

96. CAF 4:187; 2:177, 365–367; 3:24–25, 154–155, 156; 6:86–87; DHRC 8:324.

97. Patrick Henry describes this section as "in the shape of a Bill of Rights," and finds it inadequate and dangerous: "The restraints in this Congressional Bill of Rights, are so feeble and few, that it would have been infinitely better to have said nothing about it. The fair implication is, that they can do every thing they are not forbidden to do." The Federal Farmer agrees: "In fact, the 9th and 10th Sections in Art. I. in the proposed constitution, are no more nor less, than a partial bill of rights; they establish certain principles as part of the compact upon which the federal legislators and officers can never infringe." Since most of the clauses here are direct limitations of congressional power or protections for the states, I have left the section here. Only one guarantee is truly individual, the right of habeas corpus, and that clause has been moved. DHRC 10:1345; CAF 2:248.

98. This guarantee belongs in the bill of rights; as such, it has been moved to Article I.

99. George Mason and Patrick Henry argue that this clause is pernicious if not restricted to criminal laws. It threatens the collection of outstanding state debts. "Neckar" made a similar argument in Maryland. DHRC 10:1354–1363; 12:444–448.

100. The convention of North Carolina proposed this. It seems an unlikely scenario, but one that might be a precursor to tyrannical government.

101. This was proposed by Maryland, New Hampshire, Virginia, North Carolina, and Rhode Island, and it was emphasized by Patrick Henry in the Virginia Convention. DHRC 10:1299.

102. Many Anti-Federalists, and the conventions of New York and Rhode Island, demanded that no capitation taxes be levied at all. The changes made in Section 8 above, while not entirely ruling out such taxes, make this clause obsolete.

103. Mason objected to the prohibition on taxing exports, and this clears up that objection. CAF 2:13.

104. This wording is taken directly from the Pennsylvania Minority. The original proposal included as a second clause "and no Taxes, except Imposts and Duties upon Goods imported and exported, and Postage on Letters shall be levied by the authority of Congress," but that is clearly unnecessary given changes to Section 8 above. The first part is still valuable as a protection of the states' powers to tax. CAF 3:151.

105. This change was requested by the Pennsylvania Minority. These are all things that the Minority believed ought to be left to the states. CAF 3:152.

106. The North Carolina Convention requested that this be added. It is probably redundant with the previous clause, but no Anti-Federalist would likely object to making limitations on Congress more specific.

107. The North Carolina Convention suggested this change to clarify the clause.

108. This clause was proposed by the conventions of Massachusetts, New Hampshire, New York, North Carolina, and Rhode Island.

109. The conventions of Virginia, New York, North Carolina, and Rhode Island call for the publication of annual reports of receipts and expenditures. This goes along with annual reports on proceedings.

110. The conventions of Massachusetts, New Hampshire, New York, and Rhode Island request that no officeholder be allowed to accept any such award or gift, regardless of the consent of Congress.

111. Luther Martin argues for states to be permitted, with congressional consent, to emit bills of credit. In the Convention, he says, this allowance was removed for fear of paper money. William Symmes agrees that states need the power to emit bills of credit, at least in the short term until the United States becomes more prosperous. CAF 2:64; 4:59.

112. Caleb Wallace objects to the requirement that states receive congressional approval for taxing imports and exports, a clause he believed would be "ruinous to those whose local situation makes it necessary to discourage foreign superfluities and to encourage home Manufactures." This is an isolated argument, however, and unlikely to receive enough opposition support to justify a change here. DHRC 9:783.

113. Luther Martin wants this clause removed. Doing so reserves revenue collected by the states for the use of the states. CAF 2:65.

114. William Symmes contends that this restriction is ridiculous. Under a proper federal system individual states should be free to enter compacts with other states, so long as they do not violate national laws. CAF 4:59.

115. Patrick Henry points out that while states can defend against invaders, they are not here authorized to defend against insurrection. In that case, they must defer to Article V, Section 4, and request national intervention. This addition fixes that problem. DHRC 10:1309.

116. *Debates* 4:101; DHRC 10:1338; CAF 2:118, 378–379; 3:94; 4:240–241, 259–262, 269; 5:276; 6:78–79; DHRC 28:208–209; 23:2555–2556; CAF 2:160; 5:169; RIC 47–54, 51; DHRC 3:425.

117. For example, a Georgian suggested this. The issue is partially resolved through the expanded size of the House in the old Article I, now Article II. CAF 5:133.

118. CAF 4:278; 5:87, 167–168; DHRC 10:1373.

119. It was objected by several writers, most notably Cato of New York, that this clause as written did not require a second election ever to be held. Though this objection is absurd on its face, it was easy to rectify. "Was it not as easy to have said the President should be chosen every fourth year," asked "A Customer," "as to have said the Representatives shall be chosen every second year?" It was easy, so it has been done here. CAF 4:203.

120. George Mason suggests the two highest, to give the people a greater voice in the process. Three seems like a reasonable compromise likely to achieve widespread agreement. DHRC 10:1376.

121. Deliberator objects to this, noting that "thus may the great projects of this supreme magistrate of the United States be exercised, *for years together*, by a man who, perhaps, never had one vote of the people for any office of government in his life." The Federal Farmer points out that this seems to leave open the possibility that an election could be put off indefinitely. These concerns are answered by the requirement above that an election be held every four years. CAF 3:178; 2:313–314.

122. Cornelius argues that this compensation must be substantial, because it "must, and ought, to be suited to the dignified station in which that officer is placed, which cannot be considered as far below that of an European Monarch." Thus, he concludes that the President will at least resemble, if not actually become, an elective king. Still, he does not actually object to the provision for the presidential salary. CAF 4:143.

123. CAF 2:114. Agrippa's plan for presidential selection was unique: "The president shall be chosen annually and shall serve but one year, and shall be chosen successively from the different states, changing every year." Such a plan was unlikely to find much support, but it is decidedly (and radically) Anti-Federalist to require that the states rotate in the position of chief executive. CAF 4:112.

124. CAF 2:312–313; 5:140–141, 147, 266; DHRC 8:477; CAF 5:133; DHRC 10:1366; CAF 2:97; 5:76.

125. CAF 2:115. "Republicus" does call for direct election, but this is not a common position in the opposition. CAF 5:168.

126. CAF 2:12. The New York Convention and Maryland Minority also call for a council. See also CAF 2:306; 3:152; 5:117, 97; *Debates* 4:117.

127. DHRC 13:239–240.

128. DHRC 9:963; CAF 3:128; 5:142–143.

129. CAF 4:60.

130. Some Anti-Federalists object to the President commanding the army, especially in person, without leave from Congress (see, for example, CAF 5:266, and the amendments from New York and Maryland), but in the end the limitations on raising armies make this a less troubling power.

131. Samuel Chase objects to the power to pardon before conviction, as does George Mason. This is a small limit on the pardoning power that prevents the President from using his pardoning power to halt investigations into criminal activity. CAF 5:87; DHRC 10:1379.

132. George Mason suggests that a President might conspire with a traitor, and then use the pardon to shield himself. That seems extreme, but limiting the presidential pardon here seems reasonable from an Anti-Federalist perspective. Mason

repeats his objection in the Virginia Convention. Edmund Randolph and Cato raise similar objections. CAF 2:12; DHRC 10:1378–1379; CAF 2:97, 114.

133. Brutus objects to the Senate's participation in the appointment of executive officers, but he does not explain why; he left it to future letters that were never written. The Federal Farmer notes that this check on the President is "badly lodged," but wants to see someone approve presidential appointments. He later suggests a council similar to that describes in Article III, Section 1, above. CAF 2:446, 246.

134. A Georgian suggests this last clause be eliminated, and the Senate approve all appointments. The Federal Farmer disagrees, because Congress can revoke this alternative method of appointment, as experience dictates. The Federal Farmer's position is ultimately more practical. He even suggests that some appointments could be given to the legislature, but it would be difficult to enumerate such offices in the Constitution, and dangerous to let Congress decide which officers they should appoint. CAF 5:134; 2:307, 309.

135. With the constitutional council, this power becomes unnecessary.

136. Cato makes the interesting point that this clause can only apply to the Senate: "No occasion can exist for calling the assembly without the senate; the words *or either of them*, must have been intended to apply only to the senate." This is not entirely true, but it seems unlikely that the President would call the House just to initiate impeachment proceedings, the only notable power belonging just to that house. Cato does not object to the clause, though, so it has been left in place. CAF 2:123.

137. This prevents the President from indefinitely adjourning Congress, an unlikely but dangerous scenario. Instead, he can only choose between the two times in dispute, proposed by each house. CAF 5:141.

138. A Georgian suggests that "by and with the advice of the senate of the United States" be added. The council makes more sense in this version. CAF 5:134.

139. A separate provision has been included for the impeachment and trial of judges. See Article IV, Section 1, below.

140. *Debates* 4:27; CAF 2:12, 122–123; 3:26–27; DHRC 2:309; *Debates* 4:115; CAF 5:276; DHRC 10:1496.

141. CAF 2:293.

142. The Federal Farmer also pointed out that the Constitution does not require treaties to be made "in pursuance of the constitution," but this falls under the definition of laws in this new clause. North Carolina requested that treaties not contradict existing national laws, and the minority in Maryland suggested that they not overrule state constitutions. CAF 2:246.

143. This two-thirds requirement also satisfies proposals by Virginia and North Carolina, although both states demanded two-thirds of all members only for commercial treaties.

144. DHRC 9:964.

145. CAF 2:428.

146. Brutus sees it as unnecessary to appoint judges for life. In England it is necessary to secure their independence from the king, but in America where every office is elected it is not an essential protection for the courts. Still, he does not object to the idea, if judges are properly constrained in power. There was, however, some impulse in the most democratic wing of the Anti-Federalists for elected judges. The people of the town of Preston offer one example; in their instructions to their delegates to

the Connecticut Convention, they call for elected judges: "Their continuance in office pursuant to their appointment ought, in our opinion, to be periodical and new appointments ought to take place as often as the new elections of the representative body of the legislature. Any longer term of holding the judicial powers are inconsistent in a free country." This position is not consistent among the opponents of the Constitution, and it had too few supporters to overcome the probable opposition by more moderate Anti-Federalists. CAF 2:438–439; DHRC 3:440.

147. The Federal Farmer suggests legitimate circumstances under which judicial salaries should be lowered, but this is not a major objection. CAF 2:318–319.

148. Brutus, among others, emphasizes the need for different impeachment standards for judges than for executive officers. "Errors in judgement, or want of capacity to discharge the duties of the office, can never be supposed to be included in these words, *high crimes or misdemeanors*." A clause has been added here to provide for the removal of incompetent judges, as well as those who commit crimes. CAF 2:440.

149. A restriction like this was requested by the minority in Maryland as well as the Rhode Island Convention, and it would have been unlikely to see any opposition.

150. Brutus, in his later letters, objects to allowing the Supreme Court to act as a court of equity, particularly concerning treaties. His fine distinctions, though, did not seem to affect his fellow Anti-Federalists, so this change has not been made. CAF 2:419, 428–429.

151. Brutus explains the need for exceptions. CAF 2:431–432.

152. A Georgian suggests a clause specifically requiring the states to enforce national laws and prosecute transgressions of them. CAF 5:135.

153. George Mason suggests this addition, and it would likely receive wide support. DHRC 10:1409.

154. Wording taken from the Massachusetts Convention. Also proposed by New Hampshire. Hampden also calls for such a guarantee. CAF 4:200.

155. Wording taken from the Virginia Convention. Similar provisions were proposed in North Carolina and Rhode Island. The Federal Farmer also calls for all of these guarantees, as does the Pennsylvania Minority. Richard Henry Lee calls for trial by jury in the vicinage. Abraham Holmes calls for protection from self-incrimination. CAF 2:262; 3:151; 5:116–117; DHRC 6:1367.

156. Wording taken from the Virginia Convention. North Carolina and the Pennsylvania Minority propose similar language.

157. Wording taken from the Pennsylvania Minority. Similar provisions were proposed in Virginia, North Carolina, and Rhode Island. See also CAF 5:117; DHRC 6:1367.

158. Luther Martin suggests such a provision. CAF 2:72.

159. CAF 2:231; 5:134; DHRC 28:211; CAF 4:144.

160. CAF 2:57.

161. DHRC 28:212; CAF 2:140; 3:56–57.

162. CAF 4:129; 2:426–428; 4:199; 5:87; 6:137; DHRC 2:308; CAF 2:429, 148. This change was eventually made in the Eleventh Amendment, but the Anti-Federalists would have made the change before the Constitution was ratified.

163. CAF 2:322, 432–433; 5:95; DHRC 2:308; CAF 2:143; 5:182.

164. CAF 2:70–71, 149, 319–322; 3:151; 4:122; 5:38, 95, 116, 134; 6:12; *Debates* 4:167; DHRC 3:300; *Debates* 4:154; CAF 2:148, 244, 4:200; DHRC 6:1366.

165. Brutus argues that "It will therefore be no fiction, for a citizen of one state to set forth, in a suit, that he is a citizen of another; for he that is entitled to all the privileges and immunities of a country, is a citizen of that country. And in truth, the citizen of one state will, under this construction, be a citizen of every state." Nonetheless, I have left this clause intact. Brutus's argument is raised in the context of lawsuits between individuals from different states, which was discussed above in the jurisdiction of the courts, and it seems almost certainly disingenuous. It does not appear to be a true objection to this clause. CAF 2:427.

166. This ensures that fugitives may not escape by hiding in the capital, or any territory outside the individual states. William Grayson presents this concern. DHRC 10:1319.

167. This is the only slavery clause that has been left in this amended constitution. It is unlikely the southern states would have given it up regardless of any compromise, and it is less objectionable than the representation of slaves or the express (if temporary) approval of the slave trade.

168. Several Anti-Federalists objected to this clause specifically because they wanted to see Vermont join the union as a state, and feared that New York, claiming jurisdiction, would not consent. A similar argument could have been made for Maine, Kentucky, and Tennessee, and for any new states carved out of the western territories. Still, there is no other way to admit new states without invading the sovereignty of existing states, which would be unacceptable to most Anti-Federalists. CAF 4:207, 242.

169. Benjamin Gale calls this an "absolute grant of all our western territory." A Gentleman from Massachusetts exclaims: "so concise, and so ample a conveyance of such an extent of territory, couched in such smooth and easy language I never before read." The second part of this clause, however, suggests that states' claims will be respected. Few Anti-Federalists seemed concerned, so the clause has been left untouched. DHRC 3:428; CAF 4:11.

170. CAF 5:276.

171. CAF 4:102–104; 5:178–179; 4:62, 233; 6:113.

172. Patrick Henry made perhaps the strongest argument that amendments are unlikely, even if a two-thirds vote in Congress can be obtained. "To suppose that so large a number as three-fourths of the States will concur, is to suppose that they will possess genius, intelligence, and integrity, approaching to miraculous. It would indeed be miraculous that they should concur in the same amendments, or, even in such as would bear some likeness to one another. For four of the smallest States, that do not collectively contain one-tenth part of the population of the United States, may obstruct the most salutary and necessary amendments. Nay, in these four states, six tenths of the people may reject these amendments. . . . A trifling minority may reject the most salutary amendments. Is this an easy mode of securing the public liberty? It is, Sir, a most fearful situation, when the most contemptible minority can prevent the alteration of the most oppressive Government; for it may in many respects prove to be such. Is this the spirit of republicanism?" DHRC 9:956; see also CAF 4:20–21, 176–177; DHRC 3:260.

173. CAF 3:19, 50; 4:201.

174. RIC 57; DHRC 3:441.

175. *Debates* 4:190.

176. Centinel points out that "there is no provision that the debts, etc. due *to* the United States, shall be valid or recoverable. This is a striking omission, and must have been designed, as debts of the latter description would naturally occur and claim equal attention with the former. This article implied, cancels all debts due to the United States prior to the establishment of the new constitution." This clause, Centinel argues, combined with the prohibition of ex post facto laws, will prevent the recovery of prior debts. Since that change has been made, this one is not necessary, as Congress will have the authority to collect those debts. CAF 2:198.

177. This language is suggested by Francis Cummins in South Carolina. DHRC 27:361.

178. CAF 2:348; DHRC 2:448; CAF 4:51–53; 6:83–84; 4:195.

179. CAF 4:232, 242; *Debates* 4:192, 200; CAF 4:247–248; DHRC 6:1376–1377; 28:214; CAF 4:195–196; DHRC 27:361.

180. CAF 6:13; DHRC 9:1158.

181. CAF 2:77–78; DHRC 9:958; CAF 2:157; 4:99, 280.

182. CAF 2:372.

CHAPTER 19: THE PROSPECTS OF AN ANTI-FEDERALIST CONSTITUTION

1. Morton Borden, ed., *The Antifederalist Papers* (East Lansing: Michigan State University Press, 1965), viii; David J. Siemers, *The Antifederalists: Men of Great Faith and Forbearance* (Lanham, MD: Rowman & Littlefield, 2003), 33.

2. To be sure, the Constitution as it was approved may well have established a consolidated national government disguised as a federal one, which is a different issue entirely. I discuss this elsewhere. Michael J. Faber, *Our Federalist Constitution: The Founders' Expectations and Contemporary Government* (El Paso: LFB Scholarly Publishing, 2011), 183–230.

3. Pauline Maier, *Ratification: The People Debate the Constitution, 1787–1788* (New York: Simon & Schuster, 2010), 464.

4. Maier, 466.

5. Siemers, *The Antifederalists*, 28.

6. Saul Cornell, "Reflections on 'The Late Remarkable Revolution in Government': Aedanus Burke and Samuel Bryan's Unpublished History of the Ratification of the Federal Constitution," *Pennsylvania Magazine of History and Biography* 112, no. 1 (January 1988): 103–130. Gerry's copy of Burke's questions was inside a trunk that was stolen from him before he could answer. Cornell, "Reflections," 104n2.

7. Staughton Lynd, "Abraham Yates's History of the Movement for the United States Constitution," *William and Mary Quarterly* 20, no. 2 (April 1963): 228.

8. CAF 6:211, 209, 247.

BIBLIOGRAPHY

Alexander, John K. *Samuel Adams: The Life of an American Revolutionary.* Lanham, MD: Rowman & Littlefield, 2011.

Allan, Herbert S. *John Hancock: Patriot in Purple.* New York: MacMillan, 1948.

Allen, W. B., and Gordon Lloyd, eds. *The Essential Antifederalist.* Lanham, MD: University Press of America, 1985.

Amory, Thomas C. *Life of James Sullivan.* Vol. 1. Boston: Phillips, Sampson, 1859.

Austin, James T. *The Life of Elbridge Gerry.* Vol. 2. Boston: Wells and Lilly, 1829.

Batchellor, Albert Stillman. *A Brief View of the Influences That Moved in the Adoption of the Federal Constitution by the State of New Hampshire.* Concord: Rumford Press, 1900.

Bates, Frank Green. *Rhode Island and the Formation of the Union.* New York: Macmillan, 1898.

Beard, Charles A. *An Economic Interpretation of the Constitution of the United States.* New York: Macmillan, 1921.

Beeman, Richard R. *The Old Dominion and the New Nation, 1788–1801.* Lexington: University Press of Kentucky, 1972.

———. *Patrick Henry: A Biography.* New York: McGraw-Hill Book, 1974.

Bellesiles, Michael A. "Anticipating America: Levi Allen and the Case for an Independent Vermont." In *A More Perfect Union: Vermont Becomes a State, 1777–1816,* edited by Michael Sherman, 79–111. Montpelier: Vermont Historical Society, 1991.

Billias, George Athan. *Elbridge Gerry: Founding Father and Republican Statesman.* New York: McGraw-Hill, 1976.

Bishop, Hillman Metcalf. *Why Rhode Island Opposed the Federal Constitution.* Providence: Roger Williams Press, 1950.

Borden, Morton, ed. *The Antifederalist Papers.* East Lansing: Michigan State University Press, 1965.

Bowling, Kenneth R. "'A Tub to the Whale': The Founding Fathers and Adoption of the Federal Bill of Rights." *Journal of the Early Republic* 8, no. 3 (Autumn 1988): 223–251.

Boyd, Steven R. "Antifederalists and the Acceptance of the Constitution: Pennsylvania, 1787–1792." *Publius* 9, no. 2 (Spring 1979): 123–137.

———. *The Politics of Opposition: Antifederalists and the Acceptance of the Constitution.* Millwood, NY: KTO Press, 1979.

Boyd, William K., ed. "News, Letters and Documents Concerning North Carolina and the Federal Constitution." *Historical Papers Published by the Trinity College Historical Society* series 14 (1922): 75–95.

Bradford, M. E. *Original Intentions: On the Making and Ratification of the United States Constitution.* Athens: University of Georgia Press, 1993.

Briceland, Alan V. "Virginia: The Cement of the Union." In *The Constitution and the States,* edited by Patrick T. Conley and John P. Kaminski, 201–223. Madison, WI: Madison House, 1988.

Broadwater, Jeff. *George Mason: Forgotten Founder.* Chapel Hill: University of North Carolina Press, 2006.

Brown, Robert E. *Charles Beard and the Constitution: A Critical Analysis of "An Economic Interpretation of the Constitution."* Princeton: Princeton University Press, 1956.

Brunhouse, Robert L. "David Ramsay on the Ratification of the Constitution in South Carolina." *Journal of Southern History* 9, no. 4 (November 1943): 549–555.

Byrd, Robert O. *Decision at Richmond, June 1788: A Documentary Drama of the Constitutional Ratification Convention in Virginia.* Chicago: World Without War, 1986.

Clark, Walter, ed. *The State Records of North Carolina.* 30 vols. Raleigh, NC: P. M. Hale, 1886–1914.

Conley, Patrick T., and John P. Kaminski, eds. *The Constitution and the States: The Role of the Original Thirteen in the Framing and Adoption of the Federal Constitution.* Madison, WI: Madison House, 1988.

Cornell, Saul. "Aristocracy Assailed: The Ideology of Backcountry Anti-Federalism." *Journal of American History* 76, no. 4 (March 1990): 1148–1172.

———. *The Other Founders: Anti-Federalism and the Dissenting Tradition in America, 1788–1828.* Chapel Hill: University of North Carolina Press, 1999.

———. "Politics of the Middling Sort: The Bourgeois Radicalism of Abraham Yates, Melancton Smith, and the New York Antifederalists." In *New York in the Age of the Constitution 1775–1800,* edited by Paul A. Gilje and William Pencak, 151–175. Madison, NJ: Fairleigh Dickinson University Press, 1992.

———. "Reflections on 'The Late Remarkable Revolution in Government': Aedanus Burke and Samuel Bryan's Unpublished History of the Ratification of the Federal Constitution." *Pennsylvania Magazine of History and Biography* 112, no. 1 (January 1988): 103–130.

Cotner, Robert C., ed. *Theodore Foster's Minutes of the Convention Held at South Kingstown, Rhode Island, in March, 1790, Which Failed to Adopt the Constitution of the United States.* Providence: Rhode Island Historical Society, 1929.

Crittenden, Charles Christopher. *North Carolina Newspapers before 1790.* Chapel Hill: University of North Carolina Press, 1928.

Crowl, Philip A. "Anti-Federalism in Maryland, 1787–1788." *William and Mary Quarterly* 4, no. 4 (October 1947): 446–469.

———. *Maryland during and after the Revolution: A Political and Economic Study.* Baltimore: Johns Hopkins Press, 1943.

Daniell, Jere. "Counting Noses: Delegate Sentiment in New Hampshire's Ratifying Convention." *Historical New Hampshire* 43, no. 2 (Summer 1988): 136–155.

———. *Experiment in Republicanism: New Hampshire Politics and the American Revolution, 1741–1794.* Cambridge, MA: Harvard University Press, 1970.

DePauw, Linda Grant. *The Eleventh Pillar: New York State and the Federal Constitution.* Ithaca, NY: Cornell University Press, 1966.

Documentary History of the Constitution of the United States of America 1786–1870. 5 vols. Washington, DC: Department of State, 1905.

Dry, Murray. "The Antifederalists and the Constitution." In *Antifederalism: The Legacy of George Mason,* edited by Josephine F. Pacheco, 25–41. Fairfax, VA: George Mason University Press, 1992.

———. "The Constitutional Thought of the Anti-Federalists." *This Constitution* 16 (Fall 1987): 10–14.

Eiseman, Nathaniel Joseph. "The Ratification of the Federal Constitution by the State of New Hampshire." MA thesis, Washington, DC, Columbia University, 1938.

Elkins, Stanley, and Eric McKitrick. "The Founding Fathers: Young Men of the Revolution." *Political Science Quarterly* 76, no. 2 (June 1961): 181–216.

Elliot, Jonathan, ed. *The Debates in the Several State Conventions on the Adoption of the Federal Constitution.* 2nd ed. 5 vols. 1836; Philadelphia: J. B. Lippincott, 1901.

Eubanks, Cecil L. "New York: Federalism and the Political Economy of Union." In *Ratifying the Constitution,* edited by Michael Allen Gillespie and Michael Lienesch, 300–340. Lawrence: University Press of Kansas, 1989.

Faber, Michael J. "Democratic Anti-Federalism: Rights, Democracy, and the Minority in the Pennsylvania Ratifying Convention." *Pennsylvania Magazine of History and Biography* 138, no. 2 (April 2014): 135–162.

———. "The Federal Union Paradigm of 1788: Three Anti-Federalists Who Changed Their Minds." *American Political Thought* 4, no. 4 (Fall 2015).

———. *Our Federalist Constitution: The Founders' Expectations and Contemporary Government.* El Paso: LFB Scholarly Publishing, 2011.

Faber, Michael J., and Robi Ragan. "Organized Opposition: The Anti-Federalist Political Network." In *Public Choice Analyses of American Economic History,* vol. 3, edited by Joshua Hall and Marcus Witcher, 53–73. New York: Springer, 2019.

Farrand, Max, ed. *The Records of the Federal Convention of 1787.* Rev. ed. 4 vols. New Haven, CT: Yale University Press, 1966.

Fiske, John. *The Critical Period of American History, 1783–1789.* New York: Houghton Mifflin, 1888.

Fleming, Thomas. *The Perils of Peace: America's Struggle for Survival after Yorktown.* New York: HarperCollins, 2007.

Ford, Paul Leicester, ed. *Essays on the Constitution of the United States, Published during Its Discussion by the People 1787–1788.* Brooklyn: Historical Printing Club, 1892.

———. *The Origin, Purpose and Result of the Harrisburg Convention of 1788.* Brooklyn, 1890.

————, ed. *Pamphlets on the Constitution of the United States, Published during Its Discussion by the People 1787–1788.* Brooklyn, 1888.

————, ed. *The Works of Thomas Jefferson.* 12 vols. New York: Knickerbocker Press, 1904–1905.

Frisch, Morton J. "The Persistence of Antifederalism between the Ratification of the Constitution and the Nullification Crisis." In *Antifederalism: The Legacy of George Mason,* edited by Josephine F. Pacheco, 79–90. Fairfax, VA: George Mason University Press, 1992.

Gillespie, Michael Allen. "Massachusetts: Creating Consensus." In *Ratifying the Constitution,* edited by Michael Allen Gillespie and Michael Lienesch, 138–167. Lawrence: University Press of Kansas, 1989.

Gillespie, Michael Allen, and Michael Lienesch, eds. *Ratifying the Constitution.* Lawrence: University Press of Kansas, 1989.

Grigsby, Hugh Blair. *The History of the Virginia Federal Convention of 1788.* Richmond: Virginia Historical Society, 1890.

Hall, Van Beck. *Politics without Parties: Massachusetts, 1780–1791.* Pittsburgh: University of Pittsburgh Press, 1972.

Harding, Samuel Bannister. *The Contest over the Ratification of the Federal Constitution in the State of Massachusetts.* New York: Longmans, Green, 1896.

Haw, James A. "Samuel Chase and Maryland Antifederalism: A Study in Disarray." *Maryland Historical Magazine* 83, no. 1 (Spring 1988): 36–49.

Haw, James, Francis F. Beirne, Rosamond R. Beirne, and R. Samuel Jett. *Stormy Patriot: The Life of Samuel Chase.* Baltimore: Maryland Historical Society, 1980.

Heideking, Jürgen. *The Constitution before the Judgment Seat: The Prehistory and Ratification of the American Constitution, 1787–1791.* Edited by John P. Kaminski and Richard Leffler. Charlottesville: University of Virginia Press, 2012.

Hobson, Charles F., and Robert A. Rutland, eds. *The Papers of James Madison, Congressional Series.* 17 vols. Charlottesville: University Press of Virginia, 1962–1979.

Holton, Woody. *Unruly Americans and the Origins of the Constitution.* New York: Hill and Wang, 2008.

Hutson, James H. "Country, Court, and Constitution: Antifederalism and the Historians." *William and Mary Quarterly* 38, no. 3 (July 1981): 337–368.

Ireland, Owen S. "The People's Triumph: The Federalist Majority in Pennsylvania, 1787–1788." *Pennsylvania History* 56, no. 2 (April 1989): 93–113.

Jankovic, Ivan. "Men of Little Faith: The Country Party Ideology in Britain and America." *American Political Thought* 5, no. 2 (Spring 2016): 183–218.

Jensen, Merrill, and Robert A. Becker. *The Documentary History of the First Federal Elections 1788–1790.* 4 vols. Madison: University of Wisconsin Press, 1976–1989.

Jensen, Merrill, John Kaminski, et al., eds. *The Documentary History of the Ratification of the Constitution.* 27 vols. so far. Madison: State Historical Society of Wisconsin, 1976– .

Johnston, F. Claiborne, Jr. "Federalist, Doubtful, and Antifederalist: A Note on the Virginia Convention of 1788." *Virginia Magazine of History and Biography* 96, no. 3 (July 1988): 333–344.

Kaminski, John P. "Antifederalism and the Perils of Homogenized History: A Review Essay." *Rhode Island History* 42 (February 1983): 30–37.

———. *George Clinton: Yeoman Politician of the New Republic.* Madison, WI: Madison House, 1993.

———. "New York: The Reluctant Pillar." In *The Reluctant Pillar: New York and the Adoption of the Federal Constitution,* edited by Stephen L. Schechter, 48–117. Albany: New York State Commission on the Bicentennial of the United States Constitution, 1985.

———. "'Outcast' Rhode Island—the Absent State." *This Constitution* 15 (Summer 1987): 36–37.

———. "Rhode Island: Protecting State Interests." In *Ratifying the Constitution,* edited by Michael Allen Gillespie and Michael Lienesch, 368–390. Lawrence: University Press of Kansas, 1989.

Kauffman, Bill. *Forgotten Founder, Drunken Prophet: The Life of Luther Martin.* Wilmington: ISI Books, 2008.

Kenyon, Cecilia M., ed. *The Antifederalists.* Indianapolis: Bobbs-Merrill, 1966.

———. "Men of Little Faith: The Anti-Federalists on the Nature of Representative Government." *William and Mary Quarterly* 12, no. 1 (January 1955): 3–43.

Ketcham, Ralph. *James Madison: A Biography.* New York: Macmillan, 1971.

Klarman, Michael J. *The Framers' Coup: The Making of the United States Constitution.* New York: Oxford University Press, 2016.

Kukla, Jon. "A Spectrum of Sentiments: Virginia's Federalists, Antifederalists, and 'Federalists Who Are for Amendments,' 1787–1788." *Virginia Magazine of History and Biography* 96, no. 3 (July 1988): 276–296.

Kupersmith, Abraham. "Montesquieu and the Ideological Strain in Antifederalist Thought." In *The Federalists, the Antifederalists, and the American Political Tradition,* edited by Wilson Carey McWilliams and Michael T. Gibbons, 47–75. New York: Greenwood, 1992.

Leake, Isaac Q. *Memoir of the Life and Times of General John Lamb.* Albany: Joel Munsell, 1850.

Lefler, Hugh T., ed. *A Plea for Federal Union: North Carolina, 1788.* Charlottesville: University of Virginia, 1947.

Libby, Orin Grant. "The Geographical Distribution of the Vote of the Thirteen States on the Federal Constitution, 1787–8." *Bulletin of the University of Wisconsin: Economics, Political Science, and History Series* 1, no. 1 (1894): 1–116.

Lienesch, Michael. "In Defence of the Antifederalists." *History of Political Thought* 4, no. 1 (Spring 1983): 65–87.

Lynd, Staughton. "Abraham Yates's History of the Movement for the United States Constitution." *William and Mary Quarterly* 20, no. 2 (April 1963): 223–245.

———. *Anti-Federalism in Dutchess County, New York*. Chicago: Loyola University Press, 1962.

Lynerd, Benjamin T. "Democratic Opposition to the Constitution: A Swiss Counterproposal from the Maryland Farmer." *American Political Thought* 7, no. 2 (Spring 2018): 243–270.

Maier, Pauline. *Ratification: The People Debate the Constitution, 1787–1788*. New York: Simon & Schuster, 2010.

Main, Jackson Turner. *The Antifederalists: Critics of the Constitution 1781–1788*. Chapel Hill: University of North Carolina Press, 1961.

Martin, Robert W. T. *Government by Dissent: Protest, Resistance, & Radical Democratic Thought in the Early American Republic*. New York: New York University Press, 2013.

McCormick, Richard P. *Experiment in Independence: New Jersey in the Critical Period 1781–1789*. New Brunswick, NJ: Rutgers University Press, 1950.

McDonald, Forrest, ed. *Empire and Nation*. Indianapolis: Liberty Fund, 1999.

———. *E Pluribus Unum: The Formation of the American Republic, 1776–1790*. Boston: Houghton Mifflin, 1965.

———. *We the People: The Economic Origins of the Constitution*. Chicago: University of Chicago Press, 1958.

McGaughy, J. Kent. *Richard Henry Lee of Virginia: A Portrait of an American Revolutionary*. Lanham, MD: Rowman & Littlefield, 2004.

McMaster, John Bach, and Frederick D. Stone, eds. *Pennsylvania and the Federal Constitution 1787–1788*. Lancaster: Historical Society of Pennsylvania, 1888.

McRee, Griffith John. *Life and Correspondence of James Iredell*. 2 vols. New York: D. Appleton, 1858.

Miller, John C. *Sam Adams: Pioneer in Propaganda*. Stanford: Stanford University Press, 1936.

Nadelhaft, Jerome J. *The Disorders of War: The Revolution in South Carolina*. Orono: University of Maine at Orono Press, 1981.

———. "South Carolina: A Conservative Revolution." In *The Constitution and the States*, edited by Patrick T. Conley and John P. Kaminski, 153–179. Madison, WI: Madison House, 1988.

Newsome, Albert Ray. "North Carolina's Ratification of the Federal Constitution." *North Carolina Historical Review* 17, no. 4 (October 1940): 287–301.

Nicgorski, Walter. "The Anti-Federalists: Collected and Interpreted." *Review of Politics* 46, no. 1 (January 1984): 113–125.

O'Connor, Thomas H., and Alan Rogers. *This Momentous Affair: Massachusetts and the Ratification of the Constitution of the United States*. Boston: Trustees of the Public Library, 1987.

Oliver, Nancy Elaine Briggs. "Keystone of the Federal Arch: New Hampshire's Ratification of the United States' Constitution." PhD diss., University of California, Santa Barbara, 1972.

Pacheco, Josephine F., ed. *Antifederalism: The Legacy of George Mason*. Fairfax, VA: George Mason University Press, 1992.

Papenfuse, Edward C. "An Afterword: With What Dose of Liberty? Maryland's Role in the Movement for a Bill of Rights." *Maryland Historical Magazine* 83, no. 1 (Spring 1988): 58–68.

Parsons, Theophilus. "The Old Conviction Versus the New Realities: New York Antifederalist Leaders and the Radical Whig Tradition." PhD diss., Columbia University, 1974.

Peterson, Paul. "Antifederalist Thought in Contemporary American Politics." In *Antifederalism: The Legacy of George Mason*, edited by Josephine F. Pacheco, 111–132. Fairfax, VA: George Mason University Press, 1992.

Polishook, Irwin H. *Rhode Island and the Union*. Evanston, IL: Northwestern University Press, 1969.

Puls, Mark. *Samuel Adams: Father of the American Revolution*. New York: Palgrave Macmillan, 2006.

Rakove, Jack N. *Original Meanings: Politics and Ideas in the Making of the Constitution*. New York: Alfred A. Knopf, 1996.

Ravenel, Harriott H. *Life and Times of William Lowndes of South Carolina, 1782–1822*. Boston: Houghton, Mifflin, 1901.

Riker, William H. *The Strategy of Rhetoric: Campaigning for the American Constitution*. New Haven, CT: Yale University Press, 1996.

Risjord, Norman K. *Chesapeake Politics, 1781–1800*. New York: Columbia University Press, 1978.

Roback, Jennifer. "The Antifederalist Tradition in the Nineteenth Century Democratic Party." In *Antifederalism: The Legacy of George Mason*, edited by Josephine F. Pacheco, 91–109. Fairfax, VA: George Mason University Press, 1992.

Robinson, Blackwell Pierce. "Willie Jones of Halifax, Part II." *North Carolina Historical Review* 18, no. 2 (April 1941): 133–170.

Roll, Charles W., Jr. "We, Some of the People: Apportionment in the Thirteen State Conventions Ratifying the Constitution." *Journal of American History* 56, no. 1 (June 1969): 21–40.

Rutland, Robert A. *The Birth of the Bill of Rights, 1776–1791*. Chapel Hill: University of North Carolina Press, 1955.

———. "George Mason's 'Objections' and the Bill of Rights." *This Constitution* 18 (Spring/Summer 1988): 11–13.

———. *The Ordeal of the Constitution: The Antifederalists and the Ratification Struggle of 1878–1788*. Norman: University of Oklahoma Press, 1966.

———, ed. *The Papers of George Mason, 1725–1792*. 3 vols. Chapel Hill: University of North Carolina Press, 1970.

Scharf, John Thomas. *History of Maryland from the Earliest Period to the Present Day*. Vol. 2. Baltimore: John B. Piet, 1879.

Sherman, Michael, ed. *A More Perfect Union: Vermont Becomes a State, 1777–1816*. Montpelier: Vermont Historical Society, 1991.

Siemers, David J. *The Antifederalists: Men of Great Faith and Forbearance*. Lanham, MD: Rowman & Littlefield, 2003.

————. *Ratifying the Republic: Antifederalists and Federalists in Constitutional Time.* Stanford: Stanford University Press, 2002.

Smith, J. Allen. *The Spirit of American Government: A Study of the Constitution: Its Origin, Influence and Relation to Democracy.* New York: MacMillan, 1907.

Spaulding, E. Wilder. *His Excellency George Clinton: Critic of the Constitution.* New York: MacMillan, 1938.

Staples, William R. *Rhode Island in the Continental Congress, with the Journal of the Convention That Adopted the Constitution, 1765–1790.* Providence: Providence Press, 1870.

Steiner, Bernard C. "Maryland's Adoption of the Federal Constitution, Part I." *American Historical Review* 5, no. 1 (October 1899): 22–44.

————. "Maryland's Adoption of the Federal Constitution, Part II." *American Historical Review* 5, no. 2 (December 1899): 207–224.

Stiverson, Gregory A. "Maryland's Antifederalists and the Perfection of the U.S. Constitution." *Maryland Historical Magazine* 83, no. 1 (Spring 1988): 18–35.

————. "Necessity, the Mother of Union: Maryland and the Constitution, 1785–1789." In *The Constitution and the States,* edited by Patrick T. Conley and John P. Kaminski, 131–152. Madison, WI: Madison House, 1988.

Stiverson, Gregory A., and Phebe R. Jacobsen. *William Paca: A Biography.* Baltimore: Maryland Historical Society, 1976.

Stoll, Ira. *Samuel Adams: A Life.* New York: Free Press, 2008.

Storing, Herbert J., ed. *The Complete Anti-Federalist.* 7 vols. Chicago: University of Chicago Press, 1981.

————. *What the Anti-Federalists Were For.* Chicago: University of Chicago Press, 1981.

Storing, Herbert, and Murray Dry, eds. *The Anti-Federalist.* Chicago: University of Chicago Press, 1985.

Straus, Lawrence Guy. "Reactions of Supporters of the Constitution to the Adjournment of the New Hampshire Ratification Convention—1788." *Historical New Hampshire* 23, no. 3 (Autumn 1968): 37–50.

Sullivan, James. *Biographical Sketch of the Life & Character of His Late Excellency Governor Hancock.* Boston, 1793.

Syrett, Harold C., et al., eds. *The Papers of Alexander Hamilton.* 27 vols. New York: Columbia University Press, 1961.

Szatmary, David P. *Shays' Rebellion: The Making of an Agrarian Insurrection.* Amherst: University of Massachusetts Press, 1980.

Tilghman, William. "Notes of Arguments in Convention." Maryland State Archives, Special Collections, 1788, MSA SC 1592.

Trenholme, Louise Irby. *The Ratification of the Federal Constitution in North Carolina.* New York: Columbia University Press, 1932.

Turner, Lynn Warren. *The Ninth State: New Hampshire's Formative Years.* Chapel Hill: University of North Carolina Press, 1983.

Unger, Harlow Giles. *John Hancock: Merchant King and American Patriot*. New York: John Wiley & Sons, 2000.

———. *Lion of Liberty: Patrick Henry and the Call to a New Nation*. Cambridge, MA: DaCapo, 2010.

Veit, Helen E., Kenneth R. Bowling, and Charlene Bangs Bickford, eds. *Creating the Bill of Rights: The Documentary Record from the First Federal Congress*. Baltimore: Johns Hopkins University Press, 1991.

Vipperman, Carl J. *The Rise of Rawlins Lowndes, 1721–1800*. Columbia: University of South Carolina Press, 1978.

Warren, Charles. "Elbridge Gerry, James Warren, Mercy Warren and the Ratification of the Federal Constitution in Massachusetts." *Proceedings of the Massachusetts Historical Society*, third series, vol. 64 (March 1932): 143–164.

Weir, Robert M. "South Carolinians and the Adoption of the United States Constitution." *South Carolina Historical Magazine* 89, no. 2 (April 1988): 73–89.

Wood, Gordon S. *The Creation of the American Republic, 1776–1787*. New York: W. W. Norton, 1969.

———. "Interests and Disinterestedness in the Making of the Constitution." In *Beyond Confederation: Origins of the Constitution and American National Identity*, edited by Richard Beeman, Stephen Botein, and Edward C. Carter, II, 69–109. Chapel Hill: University of North Carolina Press, 1987.

———. *The Making of the Constitution*. Waco: Baylor University Press, 1987.

Wren, J. Thomas. "The Ideology of Court and Country in the Virginia Ratifying Convention of 1788." *Virginia Magazine of History and Biography* 93, no. 4 (October 1985): 389–408.

INDEX